D0961458

Ned Rorem

Ezra Pound

Elisabeth Bishop

Jean Cocteau
* 1963

Knowing When to Stop

A MEMOIR

NED ROREM

SIMON & SCHUSTER
New York London Toronto Sydney Tokyo Singapore

SIMON & SCHUSTER
Rockefeller Center
1230 Avenue of the Americas
New York, New York 10020

Copyright © 1994 by Ned Rorem

All rights reserved,
including the right of reproduction
in whole or in part in any form whatsoever.

SIMON & SCHUSTER and colophon are registered trademarks
of Simon & Schuster Inc.

Designed by Levavi & Levavi
Picture research: Natalie Goldstein
Manufactured in the United States of America

10   9   8   7   6   5   4   3   2   1

Library of Congress Cataloging-in-Publication Data
Rorem, Ned.
    Knowing when to stop : a memoir / by Ned Rorem.
        p.   cm.
    1. Rorem, Ned.   2. Composers—United States—Biography.
I. Title.
ML410.R693A3   1994
780′.92—dc20
[B]   94-19899
                                                         CIP
                                                          MN

ISBN: 0-671-72872-5

The letters of Marc Blitzstein, previously published in *The Yale Review,* Vol.
81, #3, July 1993, are published here with the permission of the estate of
Marc Blitzstein.
An excerpt from *Answered Prayers: The Unfinished Novel* by Truman Capote,
Copyright © 1976 by Truman Capote, is reprinted by permission of Random
House, Inc.
"Freud" by Paul Goodman, from *Collected Poems,* is used by permission of
Sally Goodman.
The lines of verse on p. 306, from *Collected Poems* by Paul Goodman, are
used by permission of Sally Goodman.
"Near Closing Time" by Paul Goodman is used by permission of Sally Good-
man.

To Marie Arana-Ward and Georges Borchardt,
whose idea it was.

To Michael Korda and Chuck Adams
for their faith.

To Barbara Harkins and Bruce Macomber
for their painstaking diligence in typing and copy editing.

Last and most,
to my dearest friend, Jim Holmes,
for his eleventh-hour deletions and suggestions,
and for his decades of patience.

Contents

Part Two   205

Part Three   389

Part One

In a dim corner of my room
> For longer than my fancy thinks
> A beautiful and silent sphinx
Has watched me through the shifting gloom.
> —Oscar Wilde

Prologue:
Last Things First

At death, you break up:
   the bits that were you
start speeding away
   from each other for ever
with no one to see . . .
                    —Philip Larkin

I was working at the piano when the Cadbury doctor phoned to say that Gladys Rorem had "expired" at the dinner table an hour earlier. It was 6:20, a warm Sunday, and from the kitchen floated the aroma of those two yams I'd just put in the oven. Going into JH's room I burst into tears. The moment seems already far away, as this paragraph will soon seem far away, yet indelible as a pistol shot.

By coincidence Rosemary was here in New York for the weekend visiting her son Paul. No point making the two-hour trek to Jersey tonight. Father would be asleep (he was not to be told about Mother until we arrived), the nursing home might be closed, and anyway the body was even now being transferred to the funeral parlor in Merchantville. So Rosemary, with Paul and his infant daughter, came over and spent the night in their sleeping bags on our living room floor, and next morning, 11 April 1988, we all drove down in a rented car.

How many scores of times have we made this trip since Mother and Father withdrew to their Quaker-founded retirement home on Route 38 near Cherry Hill! How many times—with JH always at the wheel—have I silently played the pointless compulsive game of reading road signs backward: Park Exit becomes Tixe Krap, Merge becomes Egrem, and (my favorite) Speed Limit becomes Timil Deeps, like some sacred Hindu tarn. That first visit six years ago seemed like this morning (at Cadbury time does not pass), Father stoic, Mother resistant. The director, a Mr. Yarnell, only twenty-nine, likable and colorless in tortoise-shell glasses and immaculate chinos, had showed me and JH the premises—potted ferns throughout the vast halls and stairways, communal dining room seating 150, a pretty good library, bourgeois one-room apartments with wall-to-wall rugs—and confided, when I remarked on his youth, that "the board feels the personnel should be young. It gives the guests [he meant the inmates, who pay a fortune] a sense of still belonging to a vital world." Within eighteen months Yarnell himself was dead. (When the platform collapsed beneath the multitude of spectators at the beheading of Beatrice Cenci, those spectators perished ahead of the woman they had come to see die.) Meanwhile the "guests," blurry or keen—and I got to know dozens by sight, sometimes by greeting—in their nonagenarian glory, persisted in treading this tragic and silly planet. There's no right time for death, at least not for survivors, and the longer death's delayed the less seemly. (Sharp Turns becomes Snrut Prahs, McDonald's becomes s'dlanoDcM.) Already I missed Mother as though she were my child, yet who could claim as unjust her vanishing into the scheme of things? She was ninety-one.

Convening at Cadbury where niece Charity, having come over from Philly, joined us, we picked up Father, had lunch, then drove, the seven of us, plus JH's white bichon Sonny, to Brown's Funeral Home in nearby Merchantville, Father speaking with difficulty because of his recent little stroke, but not otherwise confused, not yet: "Don't worry too much about my morale. Mother died for me three years ago." The establishment was cheery, shady, familial, even luxurious. Mr. Brown had a style of rehearsed congeniality as we discussed costs, cremation details, obit notices. Soon we removed en masse to an adjacent room to "view" the deceased.

There on a bier lies mother, spouse, granny, great-grandmother, the strangest hour of my life. Gazing down at the so-familiar features, "arranged" by the *croque-mort,* Mother is a house no longer inhabited; she is there, with Father and me and Rosemary, but not there.

Vanished from the universe. Pathetic creature, wee, marbleized, still, icy—is this the body from which my sinful hulk emerged sixty-four years ago? Is there in fact a body? The winding-sheet's taut and without contour. Has the undertaker either not troubled (why should he?) to adjust limbs and torso, or simply severed the head and placed it calmly at the top of the sheet? (This doesn't occur to me until later, like a remembrance of the heads in *Réflexions sur la guillotine,* which Camus insisted can actually *think* for more than a minute after the jugular is sliced.) Through the window on this golden afternoon sparrows chirp their birdy messages while building their first nests of the season, unconcerned about our peopleish things. Down the street the tinkle of an ice cream wagon, also the first of the season, identical to the ones fifty-five years earlier that we heard, sitting with our erections, in Miss John's algebra class, which I twice flunked.

I cry. Charity cries. Father cries and utters, "She's had a rough few years." Thank heaven for Mrs. Peacock, we all think tacitly. Mrs. Peacock, a mere eighty-four, is the wise and cultured lady Father befriended at Cadbury a couple years ago when Mother's state turned vegetal. Where there's life there's hope. Father enunciates hesitantly now, loses track, but won't dissolve, at least not because of Mother.

Suddenly I'm another person. Through it all I am able to stand aside. I feel guilty about this, but not very, and watch me being sorrowful. Is there even a thrilling twinge of respectable glamour at being finally an orphan, or anyhow a half-orphan, like everyone else?

In all my years scarcely a day has passed when I've not thought of Mother, wherever in the world I was. For the next week I thought of her still more, of course, mostly with wistfulness, sometimes with giddiness. Funny how one can know a person so long yet suddenly discover that some essential knowledge is missing. For instance, did she believe in God? She did believe in poetry, and maybe that's the same thing. So at the memorial the following Saturday, at Friends Monthly Meeting in Philadelphia, I read aloud these verses which Mother knew by heart and often quoted:

> Good-bye my fancy—I had a word to say,
> But 'tis not quite the time—The best of any man's word or say,
> Is when its proper place arrives—and for its meaning,
> I keep mine till the last.

As it happens, I had been setting this to music when the phone so fatally rang, and Whitman's words became the start of an oratorio performed two years hence in Chicago. Others present: the six Marshall kids, some older Quakers unknown to me, business colleagues of Father's and Father himself, patriarchal in a wheelchair. Everyone spoke and got choked up, except Rosemary and Paul. Young nephew Per Marshall's guitar song and move-with-the-flow spiel seemed more about himself than Mother, whose very existence was consecrated to what Father called her "militant pacifism." The best way to eliminate wars is not to wage them, said she, cutting the Gordian knot. JH spoke about "Mrs. Rorem" as one who was a fighter in all ways except physical, and who with independence and originality moved *against* the flow in her notions and comportment; the world paid no heed, so she willed herself to die, unfulfilled and alone. He added that she was the sole person to comprehend him in his time of crisis, years ago. Mary read the Twenty-third Psalm (in a trite translation), and Bob Sigmond spoke of "Gladys's wit" and her love of walking. Cookies served. After an hour, Father, needing to go to the bathroom, wheeled himself off, like Lear, and the meeting ended.

Her mind was like a window shade slowly lowered against the world. Hair combed straight back, like Garbo's in *Mata Hari,* eyes big as eagle eggs, tobacco colored, wistful, uncomprehending, strapped in bed.

I never heard them quarrel, or even disagree, yet each was strong-minded. There *was* a rift, at least once, when Rosemary was . . . But I'll come to that. . . .

She hated the flag for what it had done to her kid brother, killed in the Great War. But it was her flag, too—she had a right to hate it, like patriotism, or anything *not* one world.

She was only the second dead person I'd ever seen.

JH's first exposure to Mother, circa 1967, when she said to her friend Marion, who admitted to finding solace in prayer: "Oh Marion, you don't!"

She never clearly explained to me, as a child, why I couldn't marry her when I grew up.

My sister's swains found Mother sexy.

Mourning should last four seasons, plus maybe a fifth season of grace, but no more. If time could flow backward and we could revive the dead, would we . . . be bored?

In a dream I was told that there is a bridge to death—that even in the most hideous executions, during that nonmoment between being and not being, we soar over a limitless field of silver daisies in a yellow light so dazzling it is no longer light.

She bore Father's weight.

Etcetera.

The foregoing paragraphs are from notes made at the time of the memorial, on 16 April 1988.

Five months later, on 19 September, Father died.

To be in the subway for the tenth time this week or in a taxi whirling you through Central Park on the first gentle day of spring; to be sitting with a parent who is lonely and sad or at a party laughing with someone you've just met but aren't listening to; to be loitering in the bakery or chatting with your life's mate; and suddenly to feel a shiver down your spine, for you realize yet again that you're absolutely alone in the world.

In Nantucket the whole summer, I didn't visit Father. From my diary:

1 July 1988. Regular calls to & from Rosemary in Philadelphia who makes a daily schlepp to Father at Cadbury. He's worse, incontinent, wears diapers, slurred speech, doesn't always make sense or recognize her, cries a lot. What's worse is that the aides are rude, scold him when he falls, imperiously treat him like an ornery burden (Father: the innovative and rational economist!). The catch is that although they don't have time to dress Father at a fixed hour each morning so that Mrs. Peacock can wheel him about, *we* are not allowed to hire someone to dress him because that infringes on the nurses' code. Meanwhile, those nurses are rude too to Mrs. Peacock, considering her an interferer. Mrs. Peacock has singlehandedly organized all musical activity in the institution, with her octogenarian choir and her piano playing at religious functions. She's apparently the sole female at Cadbury less interested in blue hair dye and Bingo than in classical music. But beyond adoring Father, she has her own problems. Her daughter, struck with a virulent cancer, has nonetheless just completed a book on women in music.

4 July. Father whimpers a lot, although I never saw him do so in the old days. Does he mourn his wife, about whom he never talks, or simply the weight of years—the unretrievable past? Mrs. Peacock and Rosemary decipher references to *his* father. It seems logical (unbroken chain, etcetera) how clearly I can recall Grandfather Rorem in all his accented gruffness on the Iowa farm in the late twenties.

8 July. Christopher Marshall phones from Philly. He's returning to Maine and wants to strew Mother's ashes in the Hudson en route. I said no. Both of Rosemary's eldest are getting intimations of mortality, and all six had been deeply close to Granny, as they call her. But JH feels we should wait, mingle Mother's ashes with Father's, have a larger community ceremony, perhaps at Cadbury. Then RR calls, wondering what I'd told Christopher. She also says that various Quakers had been impressed by JH's remarks at the memorial on 16 April— that everyone else (like me, all teary) had talked about how unhappy we were, while JH spoke of Mother's qualities. But he did so, he himself claims, to counteract young Per's formulaic bromides.

19 July. Father still gets invitations to offer paid advice here & there. Out of the question. He cannot locomote, his speech is undecipherable, and he sobs too much. Rosemary says: Let him simply be a legend from now on.

Re Father's sobbing: JH says he's always been shocked at how we four Rorems are obsessed with ourselves. Such introspection was unseemly in his Kansas childhood. (He's just clipped back the indoor hanging ivy in what he calls the Gertrude Stein cut, to make it sprout more evenly. JH is, I may as well explain now, James Holmes, my more-than-friend, with whom I have lived since 1967.)

On the second Monday of September, as I've done each year since 1980, I resumed teaching at Curtis in Philadelphia. Arrived there from New York in the morning, and in late afternoon Rosemary picked me up at school and we drove to Jersey. My first visit since May, though Rosemary has been every day. When Father saw me his face lit up like a sunrise. "You're a pacifist, aren't you?" he whispered. Then he stopped trying to speak, his sad features forcing a smile from time to time, looking like his own father, Ole Jon. How does he survive without eating? He only vomits. Rosemary brushes his lips with lemon water, and he whispers "good." When we leave he once more whispers: "I love you both so much."

20 September. Again at Curtis. Emergency call from Rosemary, the head nurse had phoned her. Again we drive to Cadbury, spend six hours there, a windless late afternoon in the gardens with acorns falling on our heads. We wait. A stroll to the E wing where Mother had lived and died. Familiar faces of some of the crazies. R says: "Yesterday he managed to say, 'I thought I was dead.'" And we wait some more. Only last Thursday he received a medal, but did he know it? Mrs.

Peacock's fruit juice, etc. Her pastel gowns and rosewater. Mother left us five months ago. Their sexual relations continued into their eighties, Father once told me. His sorry little emaciated body now like a Dachau inmate.

The gasping; the unseeing eyes. The breathing, quieter and quieter. The nurses, friendly now and efficient. The dark falling outside. Rachel & Mike & Sara & Mary bring lasagna. They leave, Mary stays, also Charity. My mind wanders. I read *The New Republic*. I'm supposed to fly back to Nantucket tomorrow morning. What if we flung Father onto a flaming pyre? Would he awaken with a screech?

I still don't realize what Rosemary realizes—that *it is happening*. We touch him a great deal. Rosemary believes in the laying on of hands. Respiration still calmer. Slower. No odor. Thank God I stayed. Father's eyes roll up into his head, just the whites show.

With inevitable certainty, we all mysteriously know that there are just twenty more intakes of breath left in his lungs, then nineteen, then twelve, then six. Twitching of the mouth (like our cat Wallace's rictus when he died), twice at the end, a minute apart. Was he already gone? A breeze at the window.

"I think that's it," I say.

Rosemary (to Father): "Well, you finally made it."

Tears all around.

Charity: "Let's pray." Mary reads from Corinthians (again in a frightful translation, as at Mother's memorial).

Mr. Cornelius (Father's ancient roommate who has been out of sight behind a screen all evening): "Who's crying there?"

The nurse confirmed that Father died at 8:50 p.m., was cordial, phoned Brown's Funeral Home. They would be there within the hour for "the remains."

In the hall at nine the quiet bustle of evening continues as though nothing had changed. (Metaphor: a crashed car whose occupants are dead but whose dashboard radio continues to blare *Petrushka*.) We go for tea to Mrs. Peacock's pleasant room and chat without morbidity. All the corny sentiment (I even believe in God for three seconds) seems necessary.

Drive back into Philadelphia where I'll spend the night at Rosemary's, for tomorrow there's a return visit to Brown's. Phone JH in Nantucket to change my reservation to tomorrow night.

So it's over. Is that all there is? To exist for a few moments, rising from a void, then back to a void. The span is perhaps wondrous, but is it wondrous enough?

• • •

Do I physically resemble him more and more? Father, with his rimless glasses and thick hair which, like mine, grayed only after sixty, was facially regular-featured, like me, though bodily much shorter. But what he and I perceived from our twin sets of eyes was so different. He was neither a narcissist nor, he claimed, the least bit gay; indeed, homosexuality was incomprehensible to him, like being musically expressive beyond the mere notes on the staff, though he loved to sing, even as Mother loved to play, so badly, the piano. (She, meanwhile, once admitted to having certain "longings" for other women from time to time.) In many ways I was what he wanted to be; rather than stifling he encouraged me always, even when, like any American parent, he was unclear about the status of an "artist" in the family. If my work was a mystery to him, in its subjective dealing with the emotions of others, Father's work was a mystery to me, with its objectivity, its order, its businesslike practicality.

Next evening, from the ten-seat plane descending into Nantucket I see down there the ever-welcome presence of JH growing larger and larger, with his white shadow, Sonny.

The New York Times, Wednesday, September 21, 1988:

C. ROREM, 93, ECONOMIST;
HIS IDEAS LED TO BLUE CROSS PLANS

C. Rufus Rorem, an early proponent of prepaid health care whose studies led to the creation of Blue Cross and Blue Shield, died of heart failure Monday at the Cadbury retirement community in Cherry Hill, N.J., where he lived. He was 93 years old.

In the early years, working as an economist for the Julius Rosenwald Fund in Chicago, Mr. Rorem was the principal author of a report on the costs of medical care that advocated group medical practice and prepayment of hospital bills.

At the time the concepts were radical, but in 1937 he became the head of the American Hospital Association's committee on hospital services, which fostered the first prepaid hospitalization plans in New York and other cities, followed in the 1940's by doctors' group practice.

Earlier this year Mr. Rorem was one of the first people named to the Health Care Hall of Fame, which was inaugurated by Modern Healthcare magazine. He was a fellow of the American Public Health Association and the American Institute of Accountants.

A native of Radcliffe, Iowa, he was a graduate of Oberlin College and received his master's and doctoral degrees in economics from the University of Chicago. In World War I he served in the United States Army, rising to second lieutenant from private.

After the war Mr. Rorem taught economics and accounting at Earlham College and at the University of Chicago until 1929, when he joined the

staff of the federally sponsored Committee on the Costs of Medical Care
and began his career in the health field.

After World War II he was named a consultant to the commission that
shaped the medical plans that later became the Blue Cross and Blue Shield
Association. He served for 13 years as director of the Hospital Council of
Philadelphia and, after retirement in the mid-1970s, he became a consultant to a number of local, state, and national health care organizations.

Mr. Rorem's wife, Gladys Miller Rorem, died earlier this year. He is
survived by a son, Ned Rorem, the composer, a daughter, Rosemary Marshall of Philadelphia, six grandchildren, and seven great-grandchildren.

It pleases me to think that, as with Mann's Aschenbach, a shocked
and respectful world received the news of his decease. Obituaries and
condolences flowed in from all over the country. Virgil Thomson,
Father's precise contemporary, sent these words, handwritten and un-
wavering:

21 September 1988

Dear dear Ned

Your father, according to the N.Y. Times, was a great man, and I'm glad
they gave him a fine obit. For you I am sorry and full of sympathy, knowing
as I do how you were attached to him. Ninety-four is a good age to live to,
but you'll be missing him all the same. And now you are a chef de famille,
you will be a good one. Do come to see me when you can, and tell me all,
and I will hold your hand, which I am sure Jim is doing right now.

Everything ever
Virgil

David Diamond, the senior colleague to whom, despite decades of
hot and cold, I remain most devoted, wrote:

It is with much sadness that I read of your father's death. Certainly this
handsome and gallant man leaves you full of memories that will often
haunt you as well as taunt you in *your* final days, and so the sadness and
loss you feel now will slowly relinquish its hold on you and become part
of eternity....

And a day or two later:

I find it strange that I can write about death and dying but find it
difficult to talk about. Your words, "so now they're both gone," tell me so
much of what you have passed through. But what extraordinary human
beings they were! I truly feel I respected them more than anyone else,
more than my parents, more than Dimitri [Mitropoulos]. Their strong
quietness, their constant interest, their fairness and equanimity—no wonder they have left this world with Love floating all about them....

The following year my diary contains these entries:

4 February, New York. Long talk with Rosemary. As usual the question comes up of what to do with our parents' remains. R's kids, who doted on their grandparents, are in turn less keen on my placing the ashes in the Nantucket plot than in having some communal ritual in Philadelphia, or chez Christopher in Maine. R feels, meanwhile, that since Mother left no testament, and never really had a say in major decisions (despite Father's seeming magnanimity, he ran the show), she nevertheless did write down, on two occasions, crosswise in shaky script in her address book, that she wished to be cremated and flung to the Hudson River. Well, Jesus, I concur. Rosemary wants us all to gather in Battery Park, maybe board the ferry, and sing "The Lordly Hudson" while performing the funerary act. As to how simple, or indeed how legal, the act might be (the mortal dust, laced with weighty bone fragments, might blow back into our cold faces, not to mention blinding other passengers) is anyone's guess. I do feel less strongly about their remains—and my own—than I felt a year ago.

21 February. Proust was hardly the first to stress that our yesterdays, once lived, vanish forever—that the past exists only inside the head (even the holocaust?), and that attempts to retrieve it are *current* impulses which distort, of necessity, since we know now more than we knew then; so the past is by definition embellished—just as we can't hear Haydn as he heard himself, because Ravel, whom he never knew, blocks the way. But last night I saw *Jezebel* for the first time in nearly fifty years and recalled each frame, each strain of music, even the sense of silliness I'd felt at sixteen, as though they'd just occurred.

There rests no filmed history of Mother & Father. If one day I compose a memoir, will my recall be such that their snapshots will peel off the album page and return to life, at least in my mind if not on the typewriter?

30 March. Rosemary has come by morning train to New York with the ashes (not ashes, really, more like hunks of dry cartilage and mineral and sharp metal slivers in gray dirt) of Mother and Father stored in two boxes of five pounds each. We mix them in an urn of biodegradable pottery fired by R herself in the kilns of Pendle Hill. We conjoin our parents (holding a bit aside which I put into two small spice jars), then tie them in an old towel. Cousin Sara joins us with her car.

Cold, raw, gusty, rain. We get lost repeatedly, seeking possible accesses to the river between the illegal cliffs of Jersey opposite the Cloisters. But over there—isn't that a blocked entry to the Palisades? We remove the chain, drive a descending half-mile, spot a police van. Sara, who is not afraid of people, gets out to speak with a sort of mounty, who nods, and we proceed. No one in sight for acres and acres of bleak freezing space.

At the river's edge we throw forth the—the what—the debris?— using as tiny shovels the sides of the now-broken urn. It takes a while. Through our tears we can scarcely read the Twenty-third Psalm, asked for by Mary, or her own brief typewritten statement sent from California:

> Your granddaughter Mary offers prayers to God that your journey may be peaceful and full of joy and that she meet up with you again in some form, at sometime, somewhere in the universe.

(Well, as far as I'm concerned the universe wouldn't exist if we hadn't imagined it. Why have we made it so unfathomably pointless?) Rosemary too had written a "dear folks" letter, chatty, wistful.

We stroll a mile upstream through the drizzle and are met by a pair of Canada geese, later by a flock of mallards, for whom we have no crumbs.

It is soon over. These distinguished long-lived citizens have disappeared forever in the choppy waves, and nobody knows about it but us.

Sara had to get home, but swung down by Seventieth Street and let us out without coming up to the apartment. Rosemary and I ate cold quiche and a can of Del Monte peaches. Having accomplished what she came for, R took a cab to Penn Station, hoping to get back to Philly before dark.

1. Baby Pictures

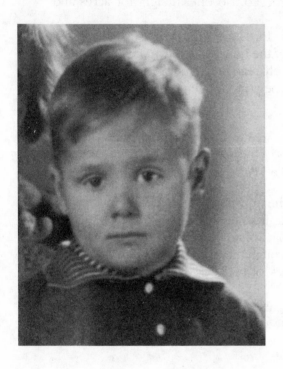

I very early understood that the universe is divided between two esthetics: French and German. *Everything* is either French or German. Blue is French, red is German. No is French, yes is German. Cats are French, dogs are German. Night is French, day is German. Women are French, men are German. Cold is French, hot is German. Japanese are French, Chinese are German (although Chinese become French when compared, say, to Negroes, who are German). Gay is French, straight is German (unless it's the other way around). Schubert is French, Berlioz is German. Generalities are French, specifics are German.

If all this is true—and it *is* (you disagree? you're German)—then I fall roundly into the French category. How do I draw these distinctions?

The difference between French and German is the difference between superficiality and profundity. To say that the French are deeply shallow is to allow that superficiality is the cloth of life. One's daily routine is mostly casual, fragmented, perishable, mundane, but the years flow by, and through such give and take our little lives are rounded. Even with close friends, how often do we sit and ponder the meaning of the cosmos? Such meaning is reserved for work.

French is superficial in the highest sense of the word, skimming surfaces to invent Impressionism, the sight of an apple-cheeked child caught for a millisecond before the fading sun shifts ever so slightly through the sycamores, the never-to-recur Debussyan glint on an unseen ocean wave at the stroke of noon. The French are not long-winded, but like cheetahs they cover distance fast. French is economy.

German meanwhile is superficially profound, driving one spike as deep as it will go, like Beethoven's motive of da-da-da-DUM hammered 572 times into his Fifth Symphony, devitalizing any subject by overanalyzing it, even humor. (A German joke is no laughing matter.) German is extravagance.

The famous quip of Jean Cocteau's (which in my presence he once generously claimed to have "borrowed" from Péguy), "One must know how far to go too far," might be expanded: A true artist can go too far and still come back. Satie does this, Bruckner doesn't. The secret lies in knowing when to stop.

Cocteau in 1920 contrived the scenario for Darius Milhaud's ballet *Le boeuf sur le toit*. Gide, Colette, and Proust respectively published *Si le grain ne meurt, Chéri,* and *Le côté des Guermantes.* George Santayana, already settled in Rome, issued this assessment of the period: "Civilization is perhaps approaching one of those long winters that overtake it from time to time. Romantic Christendom—picturesque, passionate, unhappy, episodic—may be coming to an end." Meanwhile, in New York that year Edith Wharton's *The Age of Innocence* had just appeared, so had *This Side of Paradise* by Scott Fitzgerald, while farther west, in Yankton, South Dakota, my mother met my father at a picnic in the early spring.

The intermediary was Father's former college roommate at Oberlin, Art Borough, now already married to Marie, Mother's best girlfriend. (The Boroughs were Catholics, an exciting, strange, even wicked condition when I became aware of them in Chicago. Marie had kissed the Blarney Stone. That fact plus her long hair formed a magical combination. I used to plead with Mother to let me visit Marie on Stoney Island Avenue, so that I could comb her dark Rapunzelian tresses, her *Catholic* tresses. Mother did not acquiesce, any more than she acquiesced when I wanted to play the role of Jo in a school production of *Little Women*.) On 10 August, Clarence Rufus Rorem and Gladys Winifred Miller were married.

Clarence, as his siblings always called him, or Rufe, as all outsiders including Mother called him, was the youngest among five offspring —and the only one with a university education—of Ole Jon Rorem who had emigrated in the 1880s to become a well-off Iowan farmer until the crash of '29. Ole Jon, born in 1854 (why, he was eleven years older than Rasputin!) in the valley of Rørhjem—meaning "mixed home," and shortened to Rorem at Ellis Island—on the Isle of Ømbe in the harbor of Stavanger on Norway's southern coast. (I'm still not sure how to pronounce our name. Father said Ror-em, Mother said Ro-rem.) Ole Jon married Sine Tendenes, a fellow Norwegian, only after reaching America. Sine never made it into the twentieth century. My father's sole recollection of his mother was as a corpse, when he was four, with family members moaning. When he felt moved to moan, too, the infant Clarence was shushed by the grown-ups; his shock at this mean reaction was a lifelong trauma. Grandfather Rorem, whose singsong "squarehead" accent was hard to understand, remains a remote presence, as does his second spouse, whom I never cared for, Elizabeth, an American in the style of the viragos forever taunted by the Marx Brothers.

As a boy Father had a formidable power of concentration. He was literary but not, as the saying goes, creative; about those who were, he felt wistful rather than jealous, and spoke admiringly of Thorton Wilder, a mere freshman at Oberlin when Father was a senior, who wrote sonnets in Latin. Father himself knew French, had even seen Bernhardt's *La dame aux camélias* in Mason City, Iowa, circa 1915; but if he never mastered the language orally, he read it fluently and regularly throughout his life, especially Anatole France and the bathetic love lyrics of Paul Géraldy, *Toi et moi,* which he translated and offered as a gift to young Gladys.

After Oberlin, a dignified stint in the army during the Great War, and a trip abroad, post-armistice but still in uniform with his father and my uncle Silas, he became a salesman for Goodyear. It was as a traveling salesman that he happened to be in Yankton. Though we used to kid him about it, and though they did speak of a miscarriage during their first year, I doubt if Mother was pregnant at the wedding. Except for a mournful period after their first decade their fidelity was (I believe) continual.

Gladys, as her family called her, or Glad, as all outsiders including Father called her, was fourth of the five offspring of a dirt-poor itinerant Congregational minister, the Reverend A. C. Miller, of Dutch-German descent, and of Margery Beattie, who had been born in Newcastle, England. The esprit de corps was contagious among the Millers (my middle name is Miller) and a sense of jollity in the face of adversity as they traveled from town to middle-western town. The jollity was curtailed when the youngest son, Robert, underage and patriotic, was killed at Belleau Wood in 1918. Gladys never recovered from the news, spent a full year in seclusion, while the remaining years of her life were a roller coaster from lowish heights to darkest depths, with always a revulsion for war and any civil injustice. Judging from early photographs, however, the melancholy only added to her beauty. The silken mahogany hair, the gigantic deepset eyes, the overample bust, the firm waist and erotic hips (her legs were a sore point, but their unesthetic thickness did keep her close to the good earth and lent stamina to the long and hearty daily walks) and general stance of flirtatious vulnerability were surely traits that so quickly drew Rufus to her. Grandaddy Miller married them in a garden ceremony, after which they spent (so far as I can deduce) a year on the road, eventually taking a small apartment in Sioux Falls, South Dakota, in 1922.

That was the year of *The Waste Land* and *The Enormous Room,* of the Sitwell-Walton *Façade* and Willa Cather's *One of Ours.* It was also the year of *Ulysses,* of the death of Proust, and of the birth of my sister, Rosemary. Father, who was permitted to assist as spectator at the births of both my sister and me, says that Rosemary, although the result of a long labor, emerged as daintily as a rose unfolding, and was pretty, if grave, from the very start.

She and they removed then to Richmond, Indiana (for the record, to an apartment on National Road in West Richmond, on the second floor of a private house owned by people named Leslie), where Father taught accounting at the Quaker college of Earlham. They also renounced their former religions (Father had been raised Methodist) to become permanent members of the Society of Friends. The decision was philosophical rather than godly. Mother, especially, sought to ally herself with a group actively devoted to promoting a concept of peace in time of peace as well as in time of war.

The year of their conversion, 1923, was the year of Huxley's *Antic Hay,* of Ronald Firbank's *The Flower Beneath the Foot,* which the author described as "vulgar, cynical and horrid, but of course beautiful here and there for those who can see...," of Willa Cather's *A Lost Lady,* Djuna Barnes's *A Book,* and Wallace Stevens's *Harmonium.* Nineteen twenty-three also saw the appearance of Millay's *The Harp Weaver and Other Poems;* Stravinsky's greatest ballet, *Les noces;* Falla's

El retablo; and Honegger's *Pacific 231;* plus Chaplin's movie *A Woman of Paris* and George Grosz's picture *Ecce Homo.* Hitler led his "Beer Hall Putsch" in the Bügerbrautskeller outside Munich. Katherine Mansfield died at thirty-four, as did Radiguet, age nineteen (the same age that Rimbaud "retired"), likewise Sarah Bernhardt, who in 1844 had been born, as was Franz Liszt, on my birthday, 23 October.

Mother said I "slipped out like an eel," easier and happier than Rosemary. I was also longer, twenty-one inches, and would grow to be the tallest of the whole clan, including first cousins on both sides. Apparently I beamed continually, despite being circumcised on the second day, like most middle-class gentiles of the period. Unlike Rosemary, who was breast-fed for a year (which left Mother's "bosoms"— as she called them—pendulous and sacklike), I took to the bottle at six weeks, and announced each meal's end by hurling the bottle from the cradle with a crash. Also unlike Rosemary, I was what's known as a birthright Quaker. Again, unlike Rosemary who grew gregarious only as her years unfolded, I began by sitting on the laps of anyone who'd permit it and demanding "Rock me," while as *my* years unfolded I built a glass wall around me and, grimly shy, frowned on the extroverts outside.

The red is genetically in the green tomato, it's only a question of waiting. Were my so-called talent, sexual bent, love of candy and alcohol, latently in me as I lay there smiling? Was the oratorio, *Good-bye My Fancy,* which I would be composing when the phone rang sixty-four years later to say that Mother was dead—was it already in the blood?

Life has no meaning. We've concocted the universe as we've concocted God. (Anna de Noailles: "If God existed, I'd be the first to know.") Our sense of the past and our sense of encroaching death are aberrations unshared by the more perfect "lower" animals. On some level everyone concurs—pedants, poets, politicians, and priests. The days of wine and roses are not long, but neither are they short; they simply aren't. Hardly a new notion, but with me the meaninglessness was clear from the start. Our family stressed neither God nor the devil, so the indoctrination of meaning was no more crammed down our craws than was, say, the *idée reçue* that Beethoven had genius. When I first saw photos of the Gazelle Boy, raised by wild creatures and captured too late for the grace of civilization to take effect, I was enthralled to apprehend that if one is not conditioned to "learning" during the first three years, one will never read or even speak. Similarly the Roman church knows that a true Catholic cannot be sculpted from an unbeliever after age seven. (In *Catherine Was Great* Mae West, as the lusty empress, requests that the handsome man who has lived in the dungeon since birth and never seen a woman, be brought before her. We are not shown the outcome.)

To contend that life has no meaning is not to say that life is not worth living. For if life is not worth living, is it then worth dying? Calderón said life's a dream. Isn't it rather a game? The charade of self-expression, so urgent in childhood, and the rat race not only of moneymakers but of Great Artists, is a not-so-complex competition to kill time before time kills us.

Yes, the red waits in the green tomato; but no, the artistic tendency is not there from the start, it's socially induced, in Debussy as in Palestrina—Debussy inhabiting an era like ours where art is socially superfluous, and Palestrina in an era where art was an unquestioned angle of routine. What *is* there from the start is the gene of *quality.* I've often claimed that I can teach anyone to compose a perfect song, according to the laws of prosody, melodic arch, and so forth. But I cannot guarantee that the song (even my own song) will bleed and breathe, that it will be true music, worth heeding. Only God can guarantee that—the God I don't believe in.

What do I believe? For years I believed (still do, sort of) that you, them, it, all of us, exist only in my fancy. All will stop when I stop. Then do I still ache for a more decent world? Sure. But at the age to which I've come, seeing new men in high places still stumbling into the old cruelties, there seems no hope until we evolve, or perhaps dissolve, from *Homo sapiens* into another species.

How I came to such belief will not be a basis for this book of memories, except insofar as such belief, being pure sense, is the basis of all culture. My life—my *meaningless* life—has, after all, been not unfair. Everything connects.

No one is more different from oneself than oneself at another time. Standing back to focus on other Neds at various heights and shapes cavorting, I will surely experience more than a twist of envy, of as- tonishment, of embarrassment, of ho-hum. If the vantage were from tomorrow or yesterday the recipe would surely vary, with anecdotes added or removed. But today is the day I've planned—since a year ago—to begin the trial, and I'm an organized creature. Organization keeps me from suicide.

Otherwise stated: If indeed the universe is divided into French and German, then Mother was German and Father was French, or mad and sane; and if indeed I'm a combination of the two of them, my whole existence—though I am seldom conscious of it—has been passed in crawling from the wild contrasts of folly into the dreary safety of routine without which work is implausible, then falling back, then crawling forth again, continually.

2. Looking Forward to the Past (1924–29)

In June 1924, aged eight months, I moved to Chicago, taking with me my sister and Mother, and of course Father, now a professor of economics at the university. For a year we lived at 5464 Woodlawn, then until May of 1927 at 5537 Kimbark, neither of which I remember. In 1928 the very young Robert Maynard Hutchins would impose his enlightened presidency on the university ("No faculty member can ever be fired except for rape or murder committed in broad daylight before three witnesses"), but the so-called Lab School, still active today, already functioned as a continuing flow of experimental curriculum, from nursery through graduate college. Progressive education, it was called. I was enrolled immediately in the nursery, Rosemary, too, and a cluster of other faculty brats, including three who would become "best friends": Jean, child of Davis Edwards of the speech department; Bruce, child of surgeon Dallas Phemister; Hatti, whose father, Frank Heiner, who had been born blind, was a sometime lover of Emma Goldman's.

Experiments began. At two I was isolated for a fortnight with a group of male peers, our sole diet: canned apricots. Coming home, none the worse for wear, my first request was for canned apricots. Moral: Familiarity does not breed contempt, it just breeds more familiarity, a truism I sometimes stress when lecturing on what is still called "modern music." If familiarity bred contempt, people would long always for less food or less sex after a good meal or a good screw.

Chicago is the root, the home stable, the site of all first times, the losing of so many virginities. To think back is to be dominated by the smell of Lake Michigan. Everything—classrooms, bed sheets, Rush Street pubs, furtive matings in Jackson Park—remains awash in the permanent freshwater fragrance unique to the Windy City, just as the Mediterranean and the Atlantic would influence whatever I did or thought during my twenties and thirties in Morocco and Provence with their stifling salty scent. Even those huge seas were substitutes; still today, in whatever new environment, the initial instinct is to turn east where some protective lake should be. More even than music, odor excites nostalgia.

Earliest memories.

Strangling a baby duck on Grandfather Rorem's farm in Iowa. Why this, I who then knew naught of death, just of toys? Was it what others told me later?

Wondering why, when Grandfather Rorem "gave" me a 500-pound Guernsey heifer, we couldn't bring it back to our Chicago apartment.

Sitting on the kitchen radiator and asking Mother, "When will I be four?"

A face appearing at the screen door, a hobo wanting food, Mother turning him away, then having second thoughts. Grabbing me by the hand she rushed after the man striding south on Kimbark. Mother unsmiling, dramatic, hair in the wind. We brought him back, sat him on the back porch, gave him dishes of this and that which he devoured. I stared unembarrassed. How was anyone so hungry? What had changed Mother's mind? Why did she not allow the tramp into the kitchen? (Three decades later that scene revived when a female beggar came to my door in Rome, requesting "qualcosa da mangiare." I gave her two croissants and two oranges, then, hiding behind the window, I followed her with my gaze as she retreated, retching as she stuffed the food into her mouth. I felt . . . complacent. A good deed.)

Yelling Nigra or Niggero in the presence of blacks, to see if they'd react. We'd been taught always to say Negro.

Making ice cream in the wooden churn with a metal cartridge, surrounded by smoking dry ice and rock salt, and containing eggs, sugar, vanilla beans, and heavy country cream, plus a quart of fresh peaches, whole. We children, one at a time, sat on the lid, giggling while Father turned the crank. Delirium of licking the dasher.

Treating Rosemary's gashed knee with perfume (because there was no iodine) which she'd rammed on a spike in her race to see, from the upstairs window, the approach of Uncle Al, Aunt Mildred, and Cousin John.

Had Mother once been an actress, we longed to know? She was so good at directing plays. Were we adopted, we hoped to learn? Cousin Jan, Silas's daughter, was adopted. And where did our parents dig up our names? "There's Rosemary, that's for remembrance," sang the fair Ophelia, "—pray you, love, remember. And there is pansies, that's for thoughts." The name Ned, too, is Shakespearean, the contraction of Mine Edward. But if with the years we came to resemble our given titles as people resemble their dogs, we did play with alternatives. Rosemary wanted the same initials as Father, C. R. R., so for a while she decided that her given name was Catherine. I wanted the same initials as Mother, G. M. R., so decided that my given name was Geraint. But the birth certificate says Ned—not even Edward.

Since childhood I've had a recurring nightmare. All is normal: in the sunlit parlor Mother is doing what she always does, Father is doing what he always does, Rosemary and the collie, Simba, are doing what they always do, while the vase, the oriental rug, the oak table are pristinely where they always are. Yet nothing is normal: Mother and Father and Rosemary and Simba are . . . not dead, exactly, but inanimate, robotic, prefilmed, while the vase, the oriental rug, the oak table harbor propensities of malice, of suffocation. Now the parlor grows huge as the heavens, its contents proportionately huge (yet how can I know, since, with no point of comparison, a two-foot-high vase and a quadrillion-foot-high vase are the same?). But I am not dreaming the dream, nor even aware of being there to experience the dream. On awakening in a sweat I see that all is normal: Mother is doing what she always does, Father . . .

The game Rosemary played with Father is identical to the game I played with him, only she named it Happerso and I named it Dimpy. Father lay on his back and we jumped over him, back and forth. That's all. Except that in so doing we shrieked with joy. Were I to read these words in somebody's autobiography would I yawn? Yet the scene— the rusty blue of that Chicago carpet, the parent's long male taboo body, Rosemary's silky hair, the clang outside of garbage cans—remains more etched in the mind than "more important" things. What's more important: the first tintinnabulation of a Griffes keyboard poem or the texture of Mother's powder puff in its tortoiseshell étui? What's living? Is the resurrection of ancient scenes the end of living? Experience does not mean to have, but to have had. Except for food, music, sex, and waiting for the subway, nothing *is:* everything *was,* or *will be.* To live in the present is impossible.

Tolstoy got it wrong. Unhappy families are all unhappy in the same way, while happy families are happy in different ways. Unhappiness renders virtually anyone undifferentiated and flat, and is the norm. Happiness is rare, and should be; to be happy is to be unaware, a negative target in an unjust world. Happiness is blindness. Paradoxically most people are blind, yet most people are miserable. I say people, not families, since even in America families are made up of divergent, unmelded parts.

Our family was educationally upper class, financially lower middle, bohemian in the safe style of university denizens, and engagée out of earned conviction (pacifism was a golden rule—there is no alternative to peace) rather than out of chic. In those days a social stance may have evolved from political belief, but the left wing was seldom monied. So of course we were unhappy, and of course we were happy, in our unselfconscious solidarity.

As a family of four we went naked, literally. As a Wasp enclave we were not tactile like Jews and Italians—seldom kissing, seldom hugging—but we nonetheless paraded nude among ourselves. The manner was utterly unsensual, even businesslike, hardly worth mentioning were it not for the shock in learning that other families did not so behave, that indeed they in turn were shocked by "the Rorems' suspect behavior." Mother, Father, and Rosemary continued this shameful practice forever, while at adolescence I desisted when the serpent beguiled me to eat of the fruit. Thus the female body was never a mystery; the female body pleases but does not divert. I savored the fragrance of starched skirts, pencil shavings, carnation soap, sugar and spice and all that is nice exuding from schoolgirls, but prepubescent eroticism lay in the tang of fishing tackle, lank hair, clean sweat, the very words "man," "male," "masculine." From the beginning such fancies welled within one part of the brain, growing guiltlessly as physicality grew, while another part of the brain, like Wilde's beautiful sphinx, watched me without comment from a dim corner of the room.

. . .

The last two years of the decade were lived at 5519 University Avenue, whose long-dead sumac shrubs begin to quiver again and whose brick walls and dingy fire escape acquire a dim but true form as I type this sentence. Images still tend to be isolated, non-narrational, the mundane juxtaposed indiscriminately upon the grotesque, with no chronology.

More memories:

Mother crying at the kitchen table. "Why are you crying, Mother?" "I don't know. That's just how I am."

Lost at the beach, age four (the same beach I'd be cruising ten years hence), when a strange woman picked me up, held me high, until Mother, frantic, came to the rescue.

Older female relatives declaring, "Look at those big brown eyes. He'll be a real heartbreaker when he grows up." Could physical attributes or the fact of Love be used painfully? Apprehending the power of sexuality, I later wrote: If I can cause one heart to break I shall not have loved in vain. (This, well before reading of Forster's longing to be able to *hurt* an innocent manly man.)

Rosemary's ear being accidentally nicked by the scissors of a country barber who, when she shrieked, gave her a Baby Ruth, free. He didn't nick my ear, so no Baby Ruth.

Benign rivalry twixt she, who loved Father, and me, who loved Mother. She liked wholewheat bread with butter, so I liked plain white bread, preferably Bond's, with holes through which grape jelly leaked. She and Father liked Beatrix Potter, Mother and I favored A. A. Milne. In the 1930s as we edged into more "sophisticated" prose, she pushed Wilder's *The Woman of Andros* and Sigrid Undset's *Kristin Lavransdatter,* which I never read but nonetheless pooh-poohed in favor of Pierre Louÿs's *Aphrodite,* which mesmerized me for years, as did the Ibsen plays. She was a populist, I an aristocrat, yet our love-hate spats contained no hate. I cannot forget how once, in early adolescence, she announced to a room full of people, "I like to look at Ned, because then I realize how beautiful I am."

Beautiful she was, with flawless (by Hollywood standards) traits beneath a helmet of gold curls. But beautiful I was not, at least as a child in his smug baby fat. Meanwhile we were both raised on Mother Goose, of course, and later *Cranford,* Mother's favorite novel, which I never caught the hang of. The above-mentioned Scandinavian masterpiece, of course, was Father's influence; ever proud of his Norwegian forebears, in the last years he planted and cultivated a family tree branching back to the fifteenth century. I have kept a colored picture book of Norse mythology which I used to pore over: Syf, goddess of beauty (who resembled my sister), shielding her golden apples from

Thor; Loki and his mischief-making with laurel-crowned Balder, the pure; Freya, Odin, and the mystical others whose names Richard Wagner purloined and teutonized.

We had no hymns on Sunday. Indeed, no music. Quakers have no music.

"Look, Grace, look. See the little bird, Grace? See the little bird?" These sappy phrases learned by rote and seared onto the brain by dint of a thousand repetitions, appeared on page 1 of a primer from which, to impress listeners, I pretended to read. One day I turned the page and, magically, continued reading beyond the memorized portions. Dizzy, I couldn't stop. Next day I began another book, and the practice grew into a compulsive salubrious illness from which I've never recovered.

Today it seems clear that repetition and association, rather than sentimentality, jog memory even beyond Alzheimerian borders. Consider: Oliver Sachs, the Dershowitz of psychiatry, is a publicity-doting specialist who gets things skewered. Last night PBS showed him benignly lording it over a clutch of patients who have lost their memories. Now the Power of Music, claims Sachs, has helped some of them, at least for a time, to regain the past. The Music turns out to be archfamiliar pop tunes badly played. Still, it was clearly not the power of this art, as Sachs would sanctimoniously have it, that revitalized the memory, but one thing leading to another. The smell of patchouli or of a roasting capon might turn the same trick as the playing of Our Song. The mad Nijinsky, more intrinsically musical than these filmed inmates, was nonreactive when confronted with the sound of masterpieces he had once danced to. But the elderly Aaron Copland, who drew blanks from one five-minute period to the next, was nonetheless able to conduct his half-hour *Appalachian Spring* from start to finish —though on leaving the stage he could not recall what he had just performed; he had been wafted by the rote, by the inertia, by the programmed kinetics of his own creation. We do not forget our language. But Force of Art, alas, cannot save lives. (It's said that Garbo used to watch her own films while talking of herself in the third person: "Now she's going to do this, she's going to do that." But of course she was *not* talking of herself but of the role, implicitly declaring: "Now Anna will do this, Marguerite will do that.")

Was my vocabulary formed in the kitchen, that word associations remain almost strictly culinary? Associations of musical keys are not for me, as they were for Scriabin and Messiaen, symbolized in color combinations. But to this day I recall the geographical circumstances of every word, among thousands, I ever learned.

How did I pronounce these words? People used to point out my lisp (they don't anymore), though in fact my problem with esses is the contrary of a lisp: I have no sibilant. I do still speak from the side of my mouth, judging from the few TV playbacks I've seen, and dislike.

For our delectation Father wrote (in longhand) a book called *Two City Children*. Even as an infant I had the tact not to admit the boredom I felt as chapter succeeded chapter. Was the university section of Chicago, known as Hyde Park, truly our city? Still today the neighborhood, unchanged in so many ways, looks suburban, even rural with its vacant lots, wide alleyways, and yellow three-story granite apartment buildings with their uniquely Chicagoan back porches of gray-painted wood.

We did go to the real country, however, during summers between 1924 and 1929, stopping first at the maternal relatives in South Dakota, then to Grandfather's Rorem's in Clear Lake, Iowa.

At 916 Pine Street, kitty-corner from Yankton's college campus, Grandaddy and Mama Miller owned half a brick house which contained themselves; their oldest daughter, Pearl (my mother's sister); and Pearl's six children by her ex-husband, Nash: Margery, Robert, Lois, Kathryn, and the twins, Ralph and Richard. The spontaneous tonality of this warm tribe was all that Mother loved and missed and, in her dotage, languished for, mixing it in her dreams with her own laughter and casual upbringing before World War I. She worshiped her father with wistful resentment; shouldn't the long hours spent on the souls of his congregation have been better passed with his wife and children? But when he *was* home, he had lavished his time on the prettiest garden in town.

> I am in love with him to whom the hyacinth is dearer
> Than I shall ever be dear.

Mother used to quote Millay's verses with a frisson:

> On nights when the field-mice are abroad he cannot sleep:
> He hears their narrow teeth at the bulbs of his hyacinths.
> But the gnawing at my heart he does not hear.

Gladys never allowed cut flowers in our home, and attributed to her father's garden her hay fever, which I so violently inherited.

Grandaddy, venerable now, was adorable and kind, every inch a retiree from the ministry, a twinkling eye, a Van Dyke goatee, and a continuing fondness for plant life. He honored culture without being cultured, and was proud of having heard, more than once, the singing in recital of Adelina Patti. He also knit, and taught us all to do likewise. Booties were a specialty, azure and pink, but sweaters and scarves too. I learned to cast on, but not to cast off, so that the mufflers I devised in winter grew to thirty feet and had to wait till summer for Grandaddy to give them the coup de grâce.

Mama Miller: feeble, smiling, long-suffering, tresses coiffed high in Victorian style. Pearl and her brood were earthier, less problematic, than we Rorems. The twins ribbed Grandaddy ("When was Lincoln shot?" "Why, in 1865." "Wrong. Nine months before he was born." Hoots of laughter. I didn't get it), and they would ride me, the urban sissy, by grabbing my neck and forcing my face into their pungent armpits. Robert, graver and older, nevertheless cracked jokes and cut capers in imitation of Jack Oakie. He would marry early and propagate, leaving more of his flesh to the world when killed by the new war than did his uncle and namesake when killed in the old war. The girls talked about boys while making peanut-butter fudge, pitcher after pitcher of Kool-Aid, and deep trays of Jell-O embellished with apples and cherries to soothe us from the parching heat which relentlessly, almost visibly, rolled east from the Badlands undiluted by a Great Lake. Ruby-throated hummingbirds throbbed motionless in midair before darting into the bloody hollyhock.

Because of the heat I was allowed to spend nights on the lawn with the twins. We lay on our backs to watch the shooting stars of August while chomping on raw potatoes, neatly peeled and flavored with salt which turned their white flesh blue. The twins, five years older than me, emitted a rustic masculinity which I found disturbing without knowing why. Toward dawn cool breezes rose; but with the first sun ray the insulting warmth returned. Drugged in the grass and sweating with insomnia we would stare at the now-ugly cinnabar sky seeping mercurial pus between clusters of steaming clouds like old ladies wringing their hands, then stagger back toward the house in slow motion, turn on the fans, and go to bed.

Once on the slow train to Yankton out of Sioux City, we saw a girl, about ten, screaming. She screamed and screamed, distracting the whole car, then ceased and bit her fingernails. Then began to gyrate and yell, "I'm going to dancing school, that's where I'm going." Her sole companion was an older man who seemed embarrassed. Father told us they were probably headed for Redfield, where the state asylum for children was. He explained that the girl was insane. I'd never heard the word, and thought about it a lot.

On Clear Lake little returns to mind beyond the bitter privet leaves that we would chew into a pulp, slate sidewalks on which to play hopscotch, and the unshaded whine of midwestern female relatives sounding sad even at their happiest, like certain lesbians whose vocal drone resolutely shuns the giveaway nuance they deem too feminine.

Does a diarist recall an occasion more radiantly through what he later wrote about it than through how it now rattles the memory without benefit of interim editing? In April 1974 I returned for several days to South Dakota and Iowa for the double premiere in those states of a big oratorio called *Little Prayers.* This evening I remember nothing of how Yankton looked that April, although I mentioned the occasion at length in a published diary. But the Yankton of forty years earlier still throbs like the hummingbirds undimmed.

I think, therefore I am. Well yes, of course I think. But am I?

Somewhere along the line Rosemary had her tonsils out. Oh, the sight of her sitting there, on the counter in the entrance of Chicago Memorial Hospital, bright tam-o'-shanter atop her frightened face, little legs in half-hose dangling as Father filled out forms or something.

She grows smaller. Do people leave daughters alone in hospitals? That picture too is fading. . . .

In Paris during the summer of 1953 I composed, with no special aim, a setting for chorus and organ (the first of many works for that useful combination) of the un-Parisian thirteenth chapter from Corinthians. Rereading the text, I wonder if I believed it then, as I disbelieve it now, especially these phrases:

> When I was a child, I understood as a child, I thought as a child:
> but when I became a man I put away childish things.
> For now we see through a glass darkly; but then face to face:
> now I know in part; but then shall I know even as also I am known.

Had I, have I, become a man? To understand as a child—isn't that the mysteriously lucid mode of an artist's mind? Isn't the putting away of childish things the abandonment of scope and fancy, acquiescing to the safety of grown-up reasoning? Is it not adults who see through glasses darkly, children who see face to face? Yes, I still know only "in part," but shall never aspire to "know even as also I am known." (Gide: "Do not be too quick to understand me.") And though age is more precious than youth—anyone can make a child, while long survival takes channeled energy (or is it merely blindness that allows us to prevail on this sorry planet?)—still, youth is the madness of ego.

Anyway, I never put away childish things to a point of forgetting the manic idiocies of the under-ten. That aimlessly complex game, for instance, of leaping over Father as he lay on the parlor floor. Yes, Rosemary had dolls, Patsy-Ann dolls, which didn't interest me, but neither did baseball. We both had bedtime companions, slices of old sheets or of Mother's cast-off pink silk slips, which Rosemary called Whoffy and I called Foffy, and which we would cuddle as we fell asleep.

Pink cheeked and wide eyed, children have undifferentiated notions of justice; their knack for cruelty turns even rawer than that of big folk whose power they seek to emulate. (The Sioux, exhausting their program of tortures, turned captives over to the children.)

Am I interested in children? Not especially. I identify with them, am jealous of them, can admire the more gifted of them, but on the whole they bore me. I resent their breathing of my air, and their being, finally, stronger than I in their guilty naïveté and dumb, smooth bodies.

Power of children. The last time Father took me over his knee I burst out laughing. Spankings were ended forever.

Was there any crime on earth for which I did not feel responsible? About homosexuality I had no guilt at all; I tried to, but could not.

How I loved Mother, her lemony hair which I brushed, her lap which I jumped into, her aromatic clothes closet which left me intoxicated, her ability to bend her double-jointed elbows like Sargent's portrait of Madame X. But I tested her by kicking tantrums without (I can still think of no) reason.

Do mothers experience the same pleasure nursing a female infant as a male? Do fathers experience the same satisfaction teaching a male child as a female to steer a car, with that child sitting in his groin?

Summer of 1929, for the first time, we spent in Oberlin, site of Father's alma mater, and current home, on Woodland, of his eldest sister, Agnes Thompson, and her five good-looking offspring, all much older than us: Olga, the blond eccentric; Phyllis, who married a Catholic; the two boys, Maxford and Junior, who were house painters with their father, Emmett; and Kathleen, the youngest, who was learning the viola, later to join the Toledo Symphony, marry flutist Ted Harbaugh, and have a son, Ross, currently cellist with the New World Quartet.

Of Oberlin I retain the picture of a long Giverny garden of zinnias —coppery, russet, fire, crimson. And kohlrabi, a staple on the Thompsons' table. The menu otherwise resembled that of Yankton or, indeed, that of ourselves in Chicago: overcooked vegetables, scalloped potatoes, overcooked pork chops and steak, no seafood ever except salmon loaf, popovers, salads of apple and walnut melded with Kraft mayonnaise, or of cottage cheese and pineapple and marshmallows, desserts with a gelatin base, or of chocolate wafers slapped together with home-whipped cream. (It would take another decade before I tasted garlic, or even heard about corned beef, pasta, gefilte fish.) No one in the Middle West "ate dinner"; one "had supper," and preparations for this, especially in large families like our country relatives, required an afternoon. During years of dining at the better tables of France I never encountered the . . . the *final* satisfaction of American cuisine (including canned apricots), and loathed rare beef.

Scene: Playing King of the Mountain with plump Mrs. Wigton and her two sons, Teddy and Billy, who lived next door. We'd try to climb on the bed while Mrs. Wigton pushed us off with her feet. The back of my head was ripped open against the radiator, and to this day I have a scar where no hair grows.

Aunt Agnes played piano and gave us lessons in sight-reading. (Or was this a few summers later?)

Where indeed was music during the formative years? Yes, our parents were "cultured," immersed as they were in the intelligentsia of the University of Chicago's young marrieds, but our exposure to the finer things of life came mostly through books and pictures (every painting in the Art Institute of the 1920s is as branded on my brain as Cleopatra's "burnished throne burned on the water," and so are the two brass lions welcoming visitors to Michigan Avenue). Music would surge only in the 1930s.

I do remember one event, a Passion perhaps it was—but where did it take place? in a church?—with massive clanging, wild-eyed women rushing up and down aisles with shawls on their heads, singing, and I shook with incomprehension and fear. Mother said I shook because of Art. And don't I remember a choral event in Orchestra Hall where the singers issued onto the bleachers endlessly—"like a nosebleed," was my simile—followed by harps and tubas and such, which were as much fun to watch as to hear? But it didn't stick.

If this was Art, I hadn't yet grasped that its appreciation required the shifting of a perception from one plane to another, that music was the translation of an experience into a separate form. Much less did I grasp that the shifting, the perception, were controlled by the artist. Or that the artist is like everyone else, only more so. Like everyone else, but no one else is like him.

I was thus even further from learning that an artist is not his work, that I could feel cheated and lonely because, say, Wilde the man died before I was born, we never shared this world. Does he live still in his book? No, the book is not him; it doesn't know us, we know it. What about tenth-rate artists who are nevertheless "sensitive"? What of themselves lies in their (derivative) oeuvre? Stravinsky claimed he was merely the vessel through which *The Rite of Spring* flowed. He was an idiot savant. Geniuses are all village idiots.

"**D**on't look back," said Cocteau, who spent his life looking back, "or you risk turning into a pillar of salt—that is, a pillar of tears." I have just looked back over these first pages and have not turned into a pillar of tears, though I do weep at their inexpert and fragmentary form, and realize in my flailing soul that what counts has already been used up, is unrevivable.

In autobiography, as in any crafted work, technique lies in omitting. Not omitting through tact, but through a sense of shape. Actual life repeats and repeats and repeats itself.

When I tell people I'm writing a memoir they say, "Isn't that what you've been doing for ages?," referring to the published diaries covering the years 1951 through 1985. A memoir is not a diary. Diaries are written in the heat of battle, memoirs in the repose of retrospect. A journal entry, even when honed before printing, is made from reaction to a recent occurrence, or to a current state of mind or heart. A diary has no responsible literary outline, is forever ongoing. A memoir melts the jellied past into a new consistency. It does have an outline, but the outline must be discovered, chiseled from an already existing shape which, paradoxically, is not already existing.

One of Ray Bradbury's sci-fi heroes takes a day trip back through Time to the jungles of prehistory. There he finds a transparent floating path winding without contact among the lianas and coelophysis. The understanding is that the hero will look but not touch, for if the least ant is crushed the future will be altered. Nevertheless he plucks a leaf. When he returns across eighty million years to the present, he is able to read but not to comprehend the world he left only yesterday. Each word and thing is slightly askew.

Would my memory of Bradbury's story prove incomprehensible to Bradbury? Would these recollections from the trove of childhood prove incomprehensible to the child himself, were he to return and coexist with me, which in fact he has?

3. Preadolescence (1930–36)

In 1929 my father's knowledge of accounting, business, and statistics earned him an appointment to work on studies that already had been started by the Committee on the Cost of Medical Care. In the next two years he completed and saw the publication of two such studies: *The Public Investment in Hospitals* in 1930 and *Private Group Clinics* in 1931. This work took Father to Washington, D.C., for eighteen months. We lived in Chevy Chase—first at 18 Hesketh, later on Rosemary Street (the name was a thrilling fortuity for my sister)—the only period in my familial cohabitation centered elsewhere than Chicago, and the only period when we lived in houses, not apartments.

Closing my eyes tight I squeeze out images as from a painter's tube and smear them pell-mell upon the page. Here is our bungalow on Hesketh, Mother handsome as a model flapper, likewise cousin Olga, who is staying with us; there is the new puppy, Simba, half collie, half shepherd. (Father and sister are not in the picture.) Behind the house glimmers what seems a forest but is probably no more than an overgrown suburban acre, uninhabited. The lungs of the forest exhale green rot and a rusty growth of moss, tortoises, ferns, oaks, and crickets, all to my ecstatic joy, for I want to be a biologist someday, and move to Africa and live with Tarzan.

Tarzan gave me an erection. The twins in Yankton said Jean Harlow gave *them* an erection—a hard-on, they called it—and couldn't understand why Tarzan, or indeed the entire unquiet universe of Edgar Rice Burroughs, should affect me so. The phenomenon accounts for the first of three episodes I recall from Hesketh Street:

Discovering that a mere thought could visibly affect my anatomy in a trice, it seemed proper to share the game. A prepubescent erection may be a pathetic twig of hairless ivory, yet an erection it remains. One morning, faking a fever, I stayed home from school. Amid the bedclothes I built a farm, using pillows, little boxes, and other paraphernalia about the room. Then I concentrated on Tarzan, got the erection, called Mother. "This is the farmyard," I said. "Here is the barn, here is the pigsty, and here"—I displayed myself—"is the silo." She was shocked. I must never do that again, she would tell Father.

Second episode. What grade was I in in Maryland? (I remember first grade in Blaine Hall at the University of Chicago because a soprano came to the holiday party and sang a quick ditty, rolling her Rs, "Merry Merry Christmas," which caused giggles; and second grade with Miss Parker; and third grade with Miss Richardson. Were Rosemary and I here at some intermediary class?) The school building itself remains indelible, across a vacant lot, walking distance from home. One day there appeared in the vacant lot a deep hole with a dead horse, eviscerated. We were drawn to it, stunned; the glassy eyes, the clotted mane, the cramped pose, the wound from which flowed yards of multicolored intestines, the brown blood, the suffocating feculent stench. For weeks afterward, in confusion and terror, we played Dead Horse, twisting bedsheets into the shape of rainbow ejecta, laying the ghost.

Third episode. Early morning. Our parents tell us to go look out the back window, there's something new. That automobile, we assume, is the neighbors', so "something new" must be the wheelbarrow. But no, the car is ours, an Essex, secondhand, odd colored, like khaki or a fat tick or baby vomit. Immediately we took a ride through Rock Creek Park. Father was a pretty good driver, if overfast and absent-minded. Mother had country talents: she could rend an apple neatly in twain with a twist of her bare hands; could peel the rind from an orange in one long golden belt. But her driving was ponderous, dutiful.

The Essex served us for many seasons. When we traded it for a blue Buick, I kept a metal doorknob. If gold could be melted, so too could pewter or nickel or whatever the doorknob was made of. For an hour I fried it in a skillet. Nothing happened.

The house on Rosemary Street also abutted a wood, conifers rather than oaks; the smell comes through more acutely than the sight. Indeed, although we were in the house later than the one on Hesketh, memories seem more blurred. A few tableaux persist, the first one painful.

Mother's mother, Mama Miller, visits us. How frail and ancient she's become, still with that wistful trusting smile. She is taking a bath. I chat with her, watching those sacklike breasts in the soapy steam, and she is laughing. Without warning I draw forth the pitcher of ice water hidden behind me, and throw it on her. Her false teeth fall out from the shock. I flee. From downstairs I hear Mama Miller crying and choking. When Mother comes home, Mama Miller tells her all. I deny it.

In Chicago we'd had a maid. Everyone had a maid, usually Negro, in those days, even lower-middles, and so did we, except during Mother's spells of melancholia when Olga, who had been a nurse, would come to stay with us as friend, cook, and therapist. Olga was gone now, and we seem to have hired a man, black. He didn't know how to mix bread with milk for breakfast. Once, when he drove me to town, he stopped off somewhere leaving me to wait in the car for what seemed hours. He came back smelling of what turned out to be alcohol. Why would anyone drink? It seemed a pursuit without a goal.

If Mother told Father about the farm scene on Hesketh Street he never mentioned it. Did we yet know where babies come from? Our parents answered questions as they came, thoroughly and frankly, but didn't answer what wasn't asked. First things first, one thing will lead to another. Sex was not (yet) an obsession, but animals were, and would become more so. *Skippy,* a movie about a lost dog, came out that year, so did *The Champ,* both with Jackie Cooper, whom I loved, and both so terribly sad.

Father when he kissed us good night had a stubble which we liked and didn't like. I wore corduroy knickers and was sloppy.

We always had a baby-grand piano, a Stark. Father maintains that when I was four I stood at the keyboard one fine day and to everyone's surprise played, lentissimo but without missing a beat, "My Country, 'Tis of Thee" in C. Obviously I was imitating some grown-up. Since then—I realize this now—most of what I've learned about piano playing has come from emulating peers. The same goes for composition: I've gleaned less from formal lessons than from piracy. (Chaplin, on being complimented for his tenor voice, replied: "But I don't really sing at all. That was my imitation of Caruso.") Formal lessons, though as yet nonexistent, were just around the corner.

If they were financially middle class, our parents were culturally faintly highbrow. If they were not specifically musical, they did eventually aim to expose us kids to the best of everything as they understood "best." Mother was a fair sight-reader of hymns and carols. She could thump out *Pomp and Circumstance,* "The Wedding of the Painted Doll," Chopin's Prelude in A Major (the "easy" one), solos of Ethelbert Nevin, and dozens of songs popular in her girlhood. She had neither technique nor feeling, and performed always at the same dynamic level, loud and hard. Father had a good light baritone and loved to use it. His renditions of "Danny Boy," "Old Folks at Home," and Dvořák's lilting "Songs My Mother Taught Me" made me cry. So did "Old Man River," "Sylvia's Hair Is Like the Night," and especially "From the Land of the Sky Blue Water" (which Mildred Bailey recorded a swing version of, end of the decade). When they could afford it they would go to the theater, or to concerts with a repertory classier than the one they professed at home.

One late evening when they returned from a Paderewski recital in Constitution Hall, we were awakened by Mother at the piano improvising extravagantly inaccurate arpeggios. Coming downstairs we found her, still in her blue sealskin coat, seated at the keys in a swoon of exaltation at what she'd earlier experienced.

Next day Rosemary and I began piano lessons. She was eight, I was seven.

All piano teachers are women, and all are called Mrs., the noun—or is it an adjective?—of the safely mated or widowed. There exists no such breed as the male music instructor for beginners, men having more solemn concerns.

Such misconceptions are no less prevalent today than in 1930, when we began to "take" from the first of seven women who would represent Art in my early life. (Rosemary eventually dropped out. As older female sibling with less facility, rivalry developed, and she settled the score by switching to theater.) This was Mrs. Davis, an amateur musician who had a way with beginners. She taught me to read notes. Just as the nearly imperceptible span between being unable to decipher words ("Look, Grace, look. See the little bird?") and seeing a page as an unfolding flower, so it was with staves and clefs and rests and flags. The *sight* of sound became an adventure and, for the future composer, a challenge. But of repertory I remember nothing, and thus the bewitchment of music was not yet there for me.

In June of 1931 we moved back to Chicago for good. Our apartment, in the eight-story structure at 5617 Dorchester Avenue, was on the second floor above the north archway leading to the garages. This was my realest and firmest home, the only one I think of when dwelling upon my Chicago youth, my growing up, the site of all First Times, deflowerings, anxieties, and wicked joys. (For the record, our phone number was Midway 7231.) Much of this zone of Chicago's South Side called Hyde Park, more specifically the university area, is unrecognizable today, but our block, between Fifty-sixth and Fifty-seventh streets, is unchanged. When I returned sixty years later, the wire fence between our garage area and the Edwards's backyard still sagged from where I had vaulted it a thousand times, and in the pavement remained the initials N.R., incised when the cement was wet. Nothing today seems larger or smaller, nothing seems dreamlike or haunted, the neighborhood has simply frozen, reinforcing the happy truth that I will never grow up. From where do we draw our sustenance? From the evanescent past which is nonetheless always here? Or from the unstable present which shifts mercurially each millisecond even as we talk? Not, certainly, from the future which by definition can never exist.

On nearby Kenwood Avenue stands the bank of buildings where Mrs. Pickens, the second piano teacher, professed her craft. She wore purple and served tea brewed from senna leaves after each lesson. With her guidance I quickly mastered "Cherry Blossoms," all on the black keys, and another more complicated number called "Mealtime at the Zoo" in which I crossed hands. Soon I graduated to Mrs. Hendry, befriended by my parents at Friends Meeting. At her students' recital on Blackstone I played, badly, the Brahms A-flat Waltz, after which I felt undeserving of the hot chocolate and oatmeal cookies served to the assembled families. To this day I'm queasy about eating if I've not worked well, and still nurse a vague guilt—increasingly vague, thank God—about taking money for the exhaustingly agreeable task of composing music.

I was (so was Rosemary) back in the University Lab School now, to remain for the decade.

In second grade occurred a Parents Evening at which each pupil demonstrated, as at a fair, that section of a medieval castle he had constructed. Edith Harris's elaborate portcullis was the best. The worst was my keep, or larder, for which I'd prepared a dreary little speech starting, "This is the keep." When Edith's mother paused to inspect my work, I began, "This is the keep . . . ," but she moved quickly on.

When the Sino-Japanese War resumed I only half understood, even as today I only half understand, any plans for armed force. (While I write this, 11 January 1991, it is no secret that 80,000 body bags are being flown, along with living troops, to Saudi Arabia in preparation for the insane conflict that is due to begin next Tuesday night.) In third grade with Miss Richardson, War was a storybook noun. Now I picture myself perusing the "funnies" in the Sunday *Chicago Tribune* as Mother and

Father explain that a real war is erupting in the East. Was that a first indication that I am not the center of the universe? Here on the sun-swept dining room floor the colored paper is spread out, while across the globe seven-year-olds like me are screaming.

Another trauma of the period was Roosevelt's repeal of Prohibition, legalizing first beer and wine, then strong spirits. I was afraid to walk to school alone; the movie of *Huckleberry Finn* proved that any boy could fall prey to drunk monsters running loose. Nor was the recent kidnapping of the Lindbergh baby very comforting. I was bemused that my own parents should welcome repeal—that, indeed, Quak-erism notwithstanding, our larders should be stocked with wine.

But they were Quakers philosophically, not religiously. If pacifism as a mode was implanted at birth, God was never shoved down our throats. Sunday was a special day but not a holy day. (Mother says I always said I'd know Sunday in a cave. Anyone growing up in Chicago is imbued, if only through osmosis, with Seurat's *Grande jatte,* which hangs in the Art Institute but splays its Sundayness throughout the city.) We went regularly to Sunday school, while the elders went to Meeting, always followed by a midday Sunday dinner across the street at the Quadrangle Club, or at home, prepared by the maid. Roast chicken, candied sweet potatoes, braised celery, lettuce and tomato salad without dressing, and a dessert of Bavarian cream or, if there were guests, hot raspberry tarts. Sunday school consisted of reading plays and poems and sometimes preparing skits. Meeting was a silent and intimidating ritual, inspiring uncontrolled laughter when we chil-dren attended. The maid, depending on the year, was Mary or Minnie or Adele or Helen; Mother, for reasons of equality, always addressed each by her family name. The guests would be left-wing, well-read Quakers, or colleagues from the university, or business associates of Father's.

The business associates, some of them close friends known as the Committee on the Cost of Medical Care, set up shop in New England for four summers. In 1930 the center was Burlington, Vermont, where we rented a cabin with Olga.

In 1931 and 1932 we settled in Wolfeboro on Rust Pond, where Father taught us to swim. There were my water wings and bathing suit (males didn't yet wear trunks) and Father's broad hand supporting my belly in the waves, a hand he gradually withdrew, along with the water wings, leaving me afloat without realizing it. Like reading words or reading notes, a kinetic knowledge, absent in the morning, is present at noon and forever thereafter.

We all got conjunctivitis in the pond and bumped blindly about the kitchen, eyes sealed shut by pink glue.

Blueberries by the billions, the size of cherries, were picked, as well as tiny wild strawberries on the slopes of Copplecrown and Tumbledown Dick. Hawthorne was evoked in the murky caverns near the Old Man of the Mountain, and kerosene wicks were clipped weekly in our unelectrified cottages as Mother spoke of her girlhood in the inflammable haylofts which passed for inns when she was a PK. Always in the background was Father's secretary, a Miss Ring—she had no first name—dowdy, businesslike, a pince-nez, resembling pictures of Emma Goldman, and using a cane, cordial but aloof from Mother and me and Rosemary.

One of these summers Father wasn't around much. Mother with us kids, plus Simba, went on a fortnight's car trip through New England and lower Canada, aimless, languorous, searching for something that didn't exist. Mother often took a room to herself where we occasionally heard her sobbing. In Maine we shared *à trois* the unforgettable oceanic sunsets smearing the horizon with conch-shell pink and nectarine and sorrow. The sadness of nature seemed suddenly so much vaster, more important, than the sadness of man.

We had a meal in a woodsy retreat off the highway, very Vermont, candlelit tables, cranberry muffins. (Years later I would realize that the French, as public gatherers, prefer fish-bowls; Americans collect in caves.) At a nearby table were a man and two women. Were the women beautiful? They wore hats with wide brims tilted at a rakish angle. They wore rouge, lipstick, earrings, and sported cigarette holders. We stared. Mother said maybe they were from New York. Maybe actresses.

Somewhere in New Hampshire we stopped at a tourist home with a white out-of-tune upright upon which I banged out little motives. Also a rambling garden, like Grandaddy's, with flocks of those rubicund sparrows one never sees in the city, row upon blood-red row of snapdragons into which we put our fingers and pretended they'd been bitten, and boulders big and little placed about with Japanese randomness. I darted among the rocks, insouciant. The lady who ran the inn told Mother that my childlike energy reminded her of her dead son. Next day I darted again, no longer insouciant, aware of being watched, and taking cruel joy in this.

Another guest at the inn was a woman alone. She would converse with Mother. Didn't Mother think *The Well of Loneliness* was a beautiful book? Mother stiffened. No, she didn't especially think so. Early next morning we left.

I asked Mother about *The Well of Loneliness*. Well, it's about "thesbians," people drawn to their own sex. "I think I'm a thesbian," I said.

I am gazing at a snapshot in the family album, taken by Father. I am scowling, unkempt, holding at my hip a pan such as prospectors use. Near me is a neighbor boy, nameless, a foot taller than me, brown curly hair, ruddy cheeks, what Mother would call a handsome lad. He too holds a pan. Am I eight? Is he ten? When Father's not there this "lad" pushes me around, torments me, and his skin smells troublingly of sunlit masculinity. The pans contain botanical specimens, moss and algae, maybe some beetles, even thrush eggs. These too I inhale anew with pleasure. Nearby, on a fetid pond, the purple dragonflies, in chains of three, four, even five, perform their iridescent gangbangs. This boy chopped off the legs of live frogs, saying that they were eatable. The frogs' bodies flopped about for a while, then grew still.

Annual motor trips East stretch into four days, stopping at attractions like the Finger Lakes, and in Oberlin to see paternal relations. Likewise the trek back West where, after the virulent healthiness of three months in the great outdoors, the vaguely ominous Burma Shave ads strewn along the route, and the grimy oxygen as we skirt Gary, the eventual smallness and startling familiarity of Hyde Park contain a definite glamour. School days are again imminent; but here suddenly we've returned too soon—nothing's in the refrigerator, dust everywhere, and the fall leaves aren't yet falling. Excitement of eating out, maybe at the Quadrangle Club, more likely at some dump on Fifty-fifth Street in the urban dusk, while Olga, always on a diet yet always overweight, unpacks back at the apartment, gives Simba his dogfood, makes our beds.

Back to school. One night I paint my toenails with a banana-smelling polish called Scarlet Tanager from my sister's makeup kit. (Rosemary was going to be an actress, and makeup was very important.) Next morning, a Friday, is swimming day in gym class. While I and another boy are propelled through the pool on the shoulders of Mr. Prosser, the gym teacher, I glance down at my naked feet, see the forgotten red nails, leap humiliated into the waves, half drowning the other boy and Mr. Prosser.

When Miss Richardson assigned an oral report on A Recent Interesting Experience there was no question but that I should review Mary Wigman's solo dance recital. Wigman, the expressionist, the "dark, heavy, earthbound" (her words) choreographer from Germany, precursor of Martha Graham, had performed the week before in Orchestra Hall and left me intoxicated. One dance involved nothing but herself for seven minutes twirling, twirling, silver lamé skirt fanning out to defy gravity, right arm crooked at the elbow and raised, palm out, like a Navajo saluting, left arm crooked at the elbow and lowered, palm back, like an Egyptian profile, arms together thus forming a swastika as they continually traded positions. Another dance, called *Lament* (that was my first brush with the evocative word), was accompanied solely by a gong—a square gong.

Other boys in the class reported on the talents of Babe Ruth. That my presentation on Mary Wigman should be met with glazed stares by one and all, teacher included, was more curious than wounding. Hawthorne wrote: "It is a good lesson, though it may often be a hard one, for a man who has dreamed of literary fame, and of making for himself a rank among the world's dignitaries by such means, to step outside the narrow circle in which his claims are recognized, and to find how utterly devoid of significance, beyond that circle, is all he achieves, all he aims at." Substitute "musical creation" for literary fame" and that sentence describes the lifelong frustration of myself and each one of my colleagues.

Like every child I hated scales. When I was able to get around the keys I became more intrigued by improvisation than by practice. Obsessed with the notion of inventing sounds, I would quit the dinner table, unexcused, and rush to the piano. Or leave the bathroom, pants still around my ankles, and rush to the piano. I spent whole days pounding our Stark, making up pieces but not writing them down. (Except for titles: "Tragic Bubbles on the Ruby Lagoon," "Corpse in the Meadow," "A Streamlined Carol.") Most parents do not have a preadolescent who prefers Scriabin to softball. Nor does every son assume that his classmates rush home after school, as he does, to write music.

.   .   .

Wilhelm Pauck, of the theological seminary at the university, and his wife, like other academic Germans who could afford it, Gentile as well as Jew, had fled the homeland for America as Hitler's rumblings augmented. It was they, as friends of my parents, who invited us to Mary Wigman's dance concert and who took us backstage. (I had never been backstage, much less seen a theatrical personality at close range, or heard a foreign language, and the chattering of German was as euphorically strange as the choreography.) It was they who introduced my parents to Paul Tillich.

Father was frequently out of town in the line of duty, visiting hospitals and the nuns therein, and Mother sometimes saw friends on her own. One of these was Tillich, with whom she had a date. Tillich was already on his way to becoming the world's most famous theological philosopher, and Mother may have been flattered by his attentions. Anyway, when they came back to the apartment my sister and I, who shared a room, were long since abed in our double-decker. Rosemary's whisper awakened me. She bade me accompany her to the kitchen. Through a crack in the swinging door we saw Mother and Tillich embracing dramatically, in the style of Hollywood stars, he leaning over her like Valentino, she with her head bent back and laughing. Rosemary and I, with our dear, trusting voices, called quietly: "Mother, Mother." Immediately Tillich came to his senses, apologized, vanished. It happens that my report card had arrived that morning, and as usual it was distressing. I said to Mother: "I won't tell Father about Mr. Tillich if you don't tell him about my low grades."

Tyranny of innocence! What did I learn from this blackmail? Not, certainly, how to manipulate people through bargaining, since Mother did tell Father about Tillich and about the grades. I learned, but only in retrospect, that a Great Thinker, who preaches that God is the object of the human search for truth and purpose manifested in Christ, can be as fired by a lowly *élan vital* as you and me, and that a Great Artist is usually, in his flesh, merely another *homme moyen sensuel*. In less than five years this truth struck still closer to home, when younger members of the philosophy department said within earshot, "Ned is okay for screwing, but spare us his literary opinions." I had thought that philosophy, not to mention raw intelligence, were tools for making what is known as a kinder world.

Arnold Schoenberg was another teutonic refugee who passed through the university. The elder Rorems, the Paucks, the Tillichs, and also Cecil Smith of the music department and an appendage of the young marrieds, all attended a lecture by the Master. With a blackboard and a yardstick, Schoenberg explicated his twelve-tone system in an English incomprehensible to both Germans and Americans. During the speech Father composed this limerick:

Here's to our Austrian cousin
Who handles his notes by the dozen,
Some of us wept
And some of us slept,
But none of us understood nozzen.

Frenchness arrived, oddly enough, in the guise of yet another German. The pianism of Walter Gieseking in the repertory of Debussy and Ravel (also Liszt and Mozart, who are French, too, of course) was more persuasive than the same repertory under the fingers of any Frenchman, including the ubiquitous Casadesus family. The French, at least in the first half of our century, love their own music too intensely to know how to play it. They overindulge it, caress it with nuanced sighs and romantic smiles. Ravel's piano music at its most ornate has never a note too many, and, by being tailored, spare, crystalline as Dom Pérignon and resistant to interpretation, is strictly twentieth century. Ravel's own performance of this music was strictly nineteenth century (Germanic nineteenth century at that), with left hand anticipating right when the two hands are scored together, and with otherwise "meaningful" phraseology. Debussy too, judging by early piano rolls, missed the point of his own music. His mind was in the present, his fingers were in the past. Gieseking had the virtuosity to play what was on the paper and no more; shading for French music lies on the page, not in the interpretive imagination.

Among other pianists we were taken to hear, usually in Orchestra Hall but occasionally in the civic Opera House on Wacker Drive, I recall the hoary sight of that archetypical genius, Paderewski, furrowing his brow 'neath a snowy mane and curving an elegant digitus o'er his own Minuet in G, not to mention attacking with his whole torso the annunciatory octaves of Grieg's Concerto. I recall the giant specter of Rachmaninoff, salt-and-pepper crew-cut set off by a military tux, hovering above his inevitable Prelude in C-sharp Minor, which he deigned to offer as a *bis*. (I wasn't yet aware of Rachmaninoff as final embodiment of the nineteenth-century virtuoso wherein performer and composer were one, the composer being not only his own best interpreter but a finished executor of other men's music. Nor was I aware of the Russian's self-destructive youth, by which I would later justify the poignancy of my own.) I recall the businesslike stance of Josef Hofmann, acolyte of the legendary Anton Rubinstein, seated at the forty-five-inch Steinway keyboard specially built to accommodate his little hands. Hofmann, too, was a composer (pseudonym: Michel Dvorksy) and a sometime carouser who in 1926 became for twelve years the director of the Curtis Institute, among whose students I would eventually be listed and among whose faculty I currently preach.

All was not piano and dance in the extra-academic culture of our childhood. My sister and I were entranced by the husky diction and stagy action of the Russian actress Alla Nazimova, who brought her Ibsen repertory regularly to the Loop. We were taken to *Hedda Gabler* (which I later memorized, to Father's nationalistic pleasure, and which introduced the allure of suicide), and twice to *Ghosts,* which disturbed us mightily, without our having an inkling about syphilis. During intermission at the latter play my sister and I, feeling grown up, remained seated with our parents. A dowager behind us murmured to her companion, "Imagine bringing children to a play like this," whereupon Rosemary turned around: "It's people like you that make plays like this necessary."

I bit my fingernails to the bloody quick, everybody did. (Rosemary could bite her toenails too, as could our cousin Kathryn, but I was never that limber, boys aren't.) Mrs. Allee, our Sunday-school teacher, offered a dollar to the first person who allowed his nails to grow to "normal" length. After a restrained fortnight, I won. Immediately I began to gnaw my nails again. Mother was taking a psychology course offered free to faculty wives. She learned that people who bite their nails are short on Mother Love. That's when she asked: "Did you ever think you'd like to marry your poor old mother?" I wanted to, and never understood years later why I couldn't—after all, she'd asked me. (Later still, with equal discipline used to stop biting my nails, I would "control" drinking for set periods, only to replunge worse than ever.)

I earned another dollar shortly thereafter. Father, convinced I must learn the value of money, not to mention how to interact with strangers, launched me on my magazine route. How I loathed it, pretending to care about money, pretending to enjoy competition which here as in sports was an end in itself, pretending to be alert as I slogged along my beat through Hyde Park, knocking on doors with the pitch, "You don't want to buy a *Saturday Evening Post,* do you?" Unbeknown to me, Father followed at a distance, his heart breaking as I became a man. Well, I did sell a requisite number of subscriptions (was it my parents who bought them?) and received the coveted one-dollar bonus offered by Curtis Publishing to enterprising scouts.

What did I spend the dollar on? At the butcher shop on Fifty-fifth and Kenwood, Jean Edwards and I purchased a goose for exactly one dollar, a live goose, which we brought home as a pet. None of our parents would permit the fowl in residence. We had to return it. The butcher claimed the goose had lost a pound and gave us back only ninety cents. I learned the value of money.

Jean Edwards was my staunchest pal for years. I don't recollect her from kindergarten, when our respective parents became intimate, but we played daily after 1931 when the Edwardses moved to 5623 Dorchester, the building next to ours.

A rebellious tomboy, Jean had an open face, dark eyes, straight hair with bangs of chestnut silk which she never combed. Against what was she rebelling? Her family, I guess. Jean's father, Davis Edwards, plain and walleyed like Sartre, but suave and provocative, was a professor in the speech department from whence, in mellifluous tones, he broadcast playlets over the university station about matters cultural. (Us kids—*we* kids?—once took roles, one line each, in a spelling bee led by lexicographer Samuel Johnson.) Jean's mother, Jill Edwards, beautiful and suave, was a radio actress. She and her friend Judy had a weekly fifteen-minute slot on WGN called "Jill and Judy" consisting of giddy chatter on serious subjects. Later, as Mary Morgan, Jill hosted a variety show starring Don Ameche (for weeks I thought Donna Meechie was a woman), then published a book called *Personality Pointers* which Father described as "lessons in how to paint diamonds." Jean's older sister, Carolyn, was svelte and stuck-up; her kid brother, Clark, played jacks and scraped his knees. The elder Edwardses stood for "appearances," but the privacy of their apartment was squalid. Against this stagy propriety, then, Jean reacted, with me as foil, sometimes as subsidizer (I got twenty-five cents a week allowance, she only ten).

I am not a leader, I'm an aggressive follower, but I follow only what interests me and quit the path when it grows too straight. I have no ideas, I exploit those of friends, but I choose friends according to inborn taste and revise their notions into—I like to think—a personal lexicon. For about four years Jean was my leader toward occasional virtues and frequent follies. We brought out the worst in each other.

Our follies, all instigated by Jean but abetted by me, were standard: We stole from Kresge's, small coin purses mostly, and were caught by the manager, who called our parents, but a week later we stole again and were caught again. From the balcony of the United Artists movie house we shook pepper down onto the audience, which sneezed paroxysmally, and were caught by the management, who called our parents. We hung by our knees upside down from the fire escape eight floors above the concrete pavement; from that same vantage we aimed water bombs and rotten eggs at passersby. We tormented a waitress at Steinway's drugstore by saying, with a bratty snap of our bubble gum, that her engagement ring was cheap. At the school gymnasium, during noon recess when the building was vacant, we swung wildly from the rings, pissing and shitting onto the polished cedar floor; next day we did the same and were caught, our parents alerted.

Because our families would not let us convert to Catholicism, we took revenge on the church itself. Weekdays after school we snuck into the empty Saint Thomas's, stole rosaries from a statue of the Virgin, prayer books from the pew, spangled cloth from the altar, then hollered "fuck," spit in the font of holy water, and fled. After weeks of celebrating a black mass in Jean's messy bedroom we grew weary of the rite, packed up the relics, and sent them anonymously to Jean's girlfriend, Ruth Bonfield, a Catholic. Ruth told us of her family's horror, but we never confessed.

We also spit in the sugary fudge we confected and tried to sell from a stand on the street, along with puny bouquets of lilac stolen from Gale Smith's backyard; whoever refused to buy was tripped by a rope we'd stretched across the sidewalk. We put clay in the keyholes of classrooms in Blaine Hall. We corraled the entire fourth grade and urged them to jump from a second-floor window as we ourselves had learned to jump by ricocheting from a nearby tree, were caught, and forced by the fearful Miss Burris to sit with our heads lowered onto our desks during geography. We quickly but studiously soaped the windows of some stranger's Pontiac, after rifling keys and driver's license lying loose in the seat, and throwing these into a trash can.

I never heard my parents raise their voices, or even disagree, except with the mutual respect of affectionate peers. Jean's parents were therefore impressive with their theatrical bickering, or their periods of refusal to speak to each other. Eventually they divorced. Jean's mother, Jill, moved with a new husband to the suburb of Homewood, last stop on the southbound IC—or Illinois Central—into a house three miles from the small township. One weekend when the elders were away, I went to visit. The cook was there to supervise, and a caretaker, Jake, who was not right in the head. Friday evening Jean and I strolled into town for a movie. The midnight walk back to the house was spooky. Seeing headlights approach from afar, we flung ourselves in the roadside ditch and played dead. The car slowed down, idled a moment, then sped off. We resumed walking. Minutes later a cop appeared, explained that a killer seemed to be loose and insisted on driving us home.

We picked on poor Jake, calling him crazy, he grabbed a crowbar and chased us into the house. We locked ourselves in a tower room. Jake, unable to pry open the door, barred it. Then, screaming threats, he began circling the tower with his crowbar and a ladder that was too short. For what seemed hours we cowered. (This was only the second insane person I'd seen, after that girl on the train in South Dakota.) The cook meantime phoned Jean's father, Davis Edwards, who drove down from Chicago, pacified Jake, delivered us from maiming, and scolded us.

Our occasional virtues were these: We learned to tap dance. How, I don't know—perhaps from Ruby Keeler movies, or from the spectacular matinee of Thurston the Magician who sawed his blonde daughter in half, after which she came back to life and tapped her way into our hearts. In any case we perfected a "routine" to a recording of "Anything Goes," and presented the result at a school show, wearing identical outfits of black velvet pants and white satin shirts. I can still duplicate the steps. Less proficient was our ice skating. In winter everyone goes to the Midway, that twelve-foot-deep mile-long stretch of Jackson Park bordering the university between Harper and Cottage Grove and stopping at Laredo Taft's block-wide sculpture which we used to crawl around in. The entire expanse is flooded to form a rink. One afternoon, after struggling for an hour on the ice, ankles splayed outward, home-knit mufflers of scarlet wool flowing dramatically (so I imagined) as in a Brueghel tableau while a loudspeaker blasted "The Music Goes Round and Round," we vainly sought our shoes, which had been left on the bank. To this day my left Achilles heel is warped from walking home on the skate blades. We also mastered acrobatics, since we hoped to join the circus when we grew up. I can still stand on my head, walk on my hands.

Nineteen thirty-three saw the Chicago world's fair, promoted as A Century of Progress, and launching the term *streamlined*. Cars were streamlined, skyscrapers too, and so were all aspects of the fair. Jean and I daily that summer boarded the IC for downtown and spent the day in the various "streets." "Streets of Olde England" featured the Globe Theater in streamlined versions of Shakespeare. We sat through *The Taming of the Shrew* (thirty minutes) eight times for love of the rugged Petruchio. *Romeo and Juliet* was shrunk to the Balcony and Entombment scenes, but remained indelible. "Streets of Paris" was risqué because it starred Sally Rand and her fan dance. Although the city's consensus pronounced it vulgar, Miss Todd, our art teacher, assured the class that this dance was beautiful—that the female form was nothing shameful. Parents took sides. The brouhaha provided a chance to abuse the fan dancer's younger half-brother, Eugene, in the class behind ours, with chants of "Sally Rand, she lost her fan."

(A not unsimilar issue, on which parents took sides, occurred contemporaneously. President Hutchins's wife, Maude Phelps, was a sculptor, author, liberal, and an "eccentric." Maude made a realistic line drawing of their daughter Franya, a classmate who, like the rest of us, was on the threshold of puberty. The drawing was a frontal nude from tip to toe with budding breasts, hairless pudendum, and a pouty face in exquisitely unmistakable likeness framed by girlish braids. The picture was reproduced a thousand times on 8- by 10-inch Christmas cards and mailed to the entire faculty. Franya was taken out of school for a semester.)

Grant Chave was the smartest boy in class, yet carnal with his intellect. During math he would delight those sitting parallel with him in the back row when he placed an eraser on his fly and bounced it around with the aid of his (newly found) erection. Like learning to ride a bike no-handsies. Interrupted by Miss John's, "Grant, give us the square root of ninety-seven," he'd reply:

"Could you repeat the question?"

"I was speaking loud and clear."

"Please repeat the question."

"The square root of ninety-seven?"

And Grant, furrowing his brow for a moment, answered correctly. I could not have answered, yet I did not bounce erasers off my fly. I am not a leader.

John Dillinger was gunned down as he emerged from the Biograph Theater after seeing a Myrna Loy movie. But that was in another part of town. Still, merely to be a Chicagoan was cause for comment, especially in France, for years afterward (though now not). Was I a gangster? the French elite inquired. Marie-Laure maintained that, yes, I was.

The duet with Jean Edwards as enfants terribles dwindled naturally, not because the government of family and school felt we should be separated but because our interests were fundamentally different. Jean was in no way musical. For all her naughtiness she was unread and sexually naïve. After sixth grade she went to Hyde Park High, a public school, while I stayed on. She blossomed into a stunning creature, unselfconscious always; and though she remained in the neighborhood and had brief flings with various friends, she faded gradually into the distance. Her story contains something of Dorothy Parker's rhymed saga of two girls, one bad and one good, who both end up marrying well and leading identically conventional lives. In 1980, when I passed through Chicago for a lecture-recital in Thorne Hall, Jean showed up backstage with one of her eight children. She seemed subdued, intimidated, and not about to recall the bad old days.

Mischief perpetuated in Saint Thomas's Church was no gratuitous tantrum like so much of the other mischief. It was a bid to be noticed, no matter how abjectly, by some power—a person, a philosophy— inherently unattainable. Raised a Quaker, meaning in silence, I was drawn to the taboo glamour of the sonorous Roman mass. (Had I not been a Quaker might I not have been a composer?) Our Sunday school took field trips into "alternate" sites of worship. We sampled other Protestant sects including Baptists white and black; the long beards and orange tapers of the Greek Orthodox service on Halstead Street; the various layers—reform, conservative, orthodox—of Jewish sabbaths where we chanced upon chums from grammar school (David Levy one Monday whispered in my ear, as though it were somehow unspeakable, "Are you Jewish?"); and the regular services of the Episcopal Church of the Redeemer, just around the corner on Blackstone, where Rosemary and I were for a time choir children. But when we began constructing crucifixes from the family silver, Mother and Father grew leery. They grew leerier still at my pleading to become a Catholic. The removal from Quaker austerity, the galactic exploitation of the five senses in a mass that is tasted, sniffed, touched, heard, and watched, the brass and incense ornamenting the simple saints' lives, all this returns to me whenever in the world I enter the church. Catholicism is as powerful and ubiquitous to me as the odor of Lake Michigan. Yet I am appalled by its bloody history and the fetters it has imposed on so many of my friends, alive and dead.

During soccer, when Bruce Phemister and I were goalies, we'd discuss Nijinsky or Mae West until the enemy ball came our way; with a desultory kick we'd send it off, resuming the discussion. In the locker room where the pubic hair of upperclassmen was a thing of awe for all, I was treated like a sissy by the class jocks. Once at the entrance to the gym I was briefly surrounded by menacing bullies, who quickly lost interest. I quivered as much from embarrassment as from fear; I also watched myself quivering. I examined the world in a grain of sand, the civilizations in the furrows of that porous brick an inch from the eye, and wept at the limitless melancholy latent in this new perspective. From the brick's rusty rivulet flowed dangerous tribes from *She*. Or did Marlene Dietrich emerge, as an ally against the opposing team, murmuring phrases from *The Garden of Allah*? Why did these boys care so much that I was not like them? That they were not like me was sexy.

Later that day I and two others tormented Theodore until he dissolved into tears, tripping him from behind and telling him he resembled a baboon. What elation! But when I went home to supper, nervousness set in. The knack of hurting as one has been hurt is a heady dose. Give an iota of unearned power to a weakling and he joins the Gestapo. Did I apologize to Theodore? I was afraid to apologize.

Bruce Phemister became my new leader. Since nursery school he was more organized and a harder studier than I, getting always straight A's to my C average. But he was never much of an influence until after Jean Edwards left. Bruce's parents were more straitlaced than Jean's, and better off. His father was Chicago's most eminent surgeon and an aloof presence; his mother an ample matron in the style of Lucille Watson. They lived on the top floor at 5620 Dorchester, just across the street.

I have known Bruce virtually all my life, from age six months to the present day, but we only became "best friends" (and remained so through high school) in the fifth grade when we sat next to each other in the classes of Mrs. DePencier, with whom we both fell in love.

At the start our antics were as dumb as the ones with Jean. In our unchanged voices, imitating upper-crust ladies, we ordered elaborate menus by phone with expensive restaurants where we—the "ladies" —planned to throw a party. From a local florist, also by phone, we ordered an orchid ship to be sent to young Billy Balaban, a brat we scorned. We listened to music in the booths of Lyon & Healy's, then shattered the records with the excuse that we were emotionally upset. In the margins of our notebooks we drew inexpert pictures of Claudette Colbert naked with spit curls, as she looked in the role of Poppea, and mutely displayed them to Mrs. DePencier. We appeared in the French Christmas play together in which I, as a shepherd, memorized my first *réplique* in a foreign tongue: "Certainment il y aura une messe de minuit. Il faudra chercher un autre agneau, c'est tout." We spent a weekend at The Dunes in Indiana with Jimmy Sutherland. When, during an outing, Jimmy had to do "number two" in the wilds, I inadvertently gave him poison ivy leaves to wipe himself with.

We also saw our first dead person together. We were at Jay Wimple's at the Windemere apartments on Saturday afternoon with Jimmy Sutherland and other boys playing Monopoly, when someone came in and said, "A man fell out of a window at the Saranac. He's just lying there." We rushed over to the stone court at the neighboring building and there beheld—surrounded by cops and the curious—"The man who jumped off the Saranac," as we came to call him ever afterward. What did he look like? Well, he looked like a man, not a woman. His wrists were cut. He'd leapt from the seventh floor (the cops said) and landed in a pose almost coyly mangled. His eyes were open. Open! Bruce and I were traumatized, we wanted to leave. Jay and the others forced us to return to the Monopoly game. They even told jokes. (Irvin Cobb, overhearing someone say about his belly, "If that were on a woman I'd say she was pregnant," answered: "It was and she is.") We didn't get home until after dark, in a state of morbid excitement which didn't abate for days.

These are souvenirs off the top of my head. Some years later, when the Phemisters had moved to the spacious house on University Avenue, Bruce and I hosted a party together. We asked the entire class (a departure—only girls gave parties) and everyone came, except maybe the most popular kids. "Informal," read the formal invitation. Hors d'oeuvres, cakes, soft drinks, dancing to Raymond Scott records. Mrs. Phemister and Mrs. Rorem were chaperones. Was it a success? We played Josephine Baker songs in French, and nobody reacted. It was all rather stiff. But Mother, who had always found Mrs. Phemister forbidding, later told me she was moved when Mrs. Phemister confided that Bruce had once said, "Why can't we do interesting things like the Rorems do?" Bruce was referring to the fact that we often had Negro guests, and that I was by then taking piano with black Margaret Bonds.

Meanwhile I had another piano teacher. None of the previous instructresses had provided much sense of need; I may have been learning piano but I was not learning music. Now, Nuta Rothschild was the Russian spouse of art historian Edward Rothschild, and like many a sensitive university wife she had time on her hands. Bruce and I went to see her together. That first meeting opened a wild door. This was no lesson but a recital. She played Debussy's *L'île joyeuse* and *Golliwog's Cake Walk* and during those minutes I realized for the first time that here was what music was supposed to be. I *didn't* realize that this "modern stuff" repelled your average Music Lover, for it was an awakening sound which immediately, as we Quakers say, spoke to my condition, a condition nurtured by Mrs. Rothschild, who began to immerse me in Impressionism. If Bruce showed less knack than I for the keyboard, I showed less knack than Perry O'Neil, our grammar school's official genius (he had a scholarship and was elsewhere a student of Rudolph Ganz's). The three of us would go Saturdays to the booths of Lyon & Healy's, where our credibility was reinstated, and listen and listen and listen. Debussy led us forward to Ravel and Stravinsky, not backward to Brahms and Verdi, and I was unquestioningly at home with the garish roulades of *Scarbo* and the so-called percussion pianos of *Les noces* before I'd ever heard a Chopin nocturne.

Bruce, who did not aspire to a musical career, still had a more investigative nose (ear) than I. Eventually he would introduce me to, on the one hand, discs of the Australian Marjorie Lawrence singing Richard Strauss in French and, on the other hand, to the German Greta Keller singing Dietrich's repertory in English—so vocally superior to Marlene, so charismatically inferior. (The *point* of the one-of-a-kind Dietrich is that she sang off pitch in her gasping baritone, while we sighed with satisfaction. She was the tragic Florence Foster Jenkins.)

Such scores and discs as we could not afford with our allowances, we stole. I devoured Romola Nijinsky's dubious portrait of her husband, and Lockspeiser's biography of Debussy, which remains, alas, with its mean, inexpert biases, astonishingly the only extant book on the subject. I had half learned all of Debussy's piano repertory when the dilettantish Mrs. Rothschild, upon the death of her young husband, left Chicago forever.

"**H**ow do you plan to make a living?" asked Father, on learning that I wanted to be a composer when I grew up. Apparently I replied, "What difference does it make, if I can't be a composer?" That answer was so un-American as to impress Father, who, although a breadwinner, took seriously his not-so-sublimated baritone. To his eternal credit he agreed then and there to be supportive of the family freak. He has never been a Stage Mother, but Father nonetheless believed in work. It was time for a real teacher.

The former Julius Rosenwald mansion, located on Ellis and Fifty-first, was now the site of the Julius Rosenwald Fund. It had a richly antique ambiance, with its arched entrance for automobiles and a garden with more arches in granite and brick. I remember seeing, maybe even meeting, old man Rosenwald once or twice: he seemed mummified, like John D. Rockefeller, rather than handsome and easygoing like rich people in the movies. The Fund was not only the backbone of the Committee on the Cost of Medical Care, of which Father was coordinator, but sponsor for Negro fellowships in the Arts & Sciences. The comparative radicalism of this, coupled with our pacifist leanings, lent the Rorems a reputation for being benignly odd. We were no threat when we invited Negro guests to dine. Such guests invariably arrived late, or so it seemed, earning them the slogan CPT, or Colored People's Time. The lateness, Father explained, stemmed not from rudeness but from insecurity about the rare practice of inter-racial socializing. Among beneficiaries of the fellowships were Katherine Dunham, Marian Anderson, Howard Swanson, and Margaret Bonds.

The last-named at twenty-one was already a middle-western "personality," having played John Alden Carpenter's Concertino with the Chicago Symphony under the composer's direction, and being herself a composer of mainly spiritual arrangements and of original songs in collaboration with Langston Hughes. It was Margaret Bonds—*Miss* Bonds—who was to be my next piano teacher. Every Saturday morning I boarded the streetcar for her house in the ghetto of South Wabash. At our first lesson she played me some ear-openers: *The White Peacock* by Griffes, and Carpenter's *An American Tango*. Had I ever heard American music before, beyond "To a Wild Rose," which Mother used to thump out? Fired by my enthusiasm, she assigned these pieces on the spot, with no talk of scale-and-trill practice. In this day or any other it's scarcely revolutionary for a male pupil to have a woman tutor. But for a white child to have a black teacher was not standard practice in Chicago during the 1930s, and is there a reason not to be proud of it?

Margaret, ten years older than I, played with the authority of a professional, an authority I'd never heard in a living room, an authority stemming from the fact that she too was a composer and thus approached all music from the inside, an authority that was contagious. She dusted off the notion that music was solely for home use. She also showed me how to notate my ramblings—"Just look at how other composers put it down"—hoisting the ephemeral into the concrete: once his piece is on paper a composer is responsible for it, for it can now be reinterpreted by others, elating or shaming its maker.

Rosemary was piqued at what she thought to be my preferential treatment. Mother responded to this pique till the end of her life; she was proud of my accomplishments (horrified at my "defective" behavior) but may have felt sentimentally nearer to my sister as a fellow childbearer. Why should an artist be more pampered than other people? Wasn't Rosemary just as talented as Ned? Rosemary nevertheless, as elder sibling, remained wistful long after she married and had six children. Father identified with me and tolerated, albeit uneasily, my spoiled-brat stance. In a subtle shift, my role as Mother's boy was switched to Father, Rosemary's role as Father's girl switched to Mother.

4. Mother's Diary

After Mother died I came across—in her very small cache of intimate keepsakes—two journals, one from 1934, the other from our European trip in 1936, both written in her bold, byzantine script alternating between lead pencil and green ink. The first notebook is half filled, with fourteen entries between 10 October and 10 December, and covering twenty ruled pages. After this she must have lost interest.

Chicago, October 10, 1934

Our neighbors to the right (or is it to the left)—depends upon the way one is standing—have a lovely little flower garden. It is a nosegay in the heart of the city. Every day I glance at it as I sweep our back veranda. I do not know the names of our neighbors. They are a pleasant appearing man and woman. Not young in years—not old either—just people who love flowers. Some day I mean to speak to them and tell them what a joy they have created for the sixteen families living in our apartment building. Some days I contemplate the garden even when not sweeping the veranda. In the late afternoon I sometimes relax in an easy chair with a collection of Great Poems of the English Language. I like combining the poems with the flowers. Then again I go to attend to the two Zebra finches and the two canaries (which belong to my son and which he should be attending) as they make their residence on the porch. There is also a gold fish there but poor fellow he doesn't count. We try to give him away, now since Ned has the birds, but nobody wants him. Why is it people almost never want gold fish? It seems that their home is either too hot or too cold for fish, or they have a pet cat and you know what pet cats do to gold fish. (They tell you.) Then often there is a baby who would be sure to put his fingers in the bowl and would probably pick out the fish and swallow it raw. Then there are people who have owned gold fish who have actually had days ruined because of a guilty feeling which will not leave them, when they neglect the fish by not feeding them and changing their water. So you see! We continue to keep the gold fish but it offers me the chance to view our neighbors garden when I go out to feed it its holy wafer.

These words belie her contention—or my recollection—of her negative attitude about flowers. Still, I don't remember cut flowers, bouquets, chez nous.

October 11. Every evening I plan to put down some thoughts before retiring. I am writing in bed. (I like to read in bed too.) Rufus (my husband, good and kind) just turned out the electric lamp on the high boy beside me and replaced it with a candle. He thought the muses would adapt themselves better to candle light. Autumn is here and tonight I can hear the wind playing with the falling leaves. The vines on our neighbors' windows to the rear of us, have turned red. These neighbors live across the court and I do not know their names either. They appear youngish through the windows. I should say they are a newly married couple. This evening I read two chapters of "Water Babies" aloud to Rosemary (my daughter—12 and Ned my son—10). Rufe sat in my room with us. He was trying to read a French book to himself. He listened some to us. We all like Tom, the Water Baby. Rufe and I are reading "Seven Gothic Tales" by Isak Dinesen aloud to each other. They are fantastic and sort of Arabian Nightish. Margery my niece, who is spending the winter with us, made grape jelly today. She comes from South Dakota and is 19.

October 12. Ned and I went bicycle riding after school. We stopped in at Laredo Taft's studio where we gazed at some lovely objects. I was glad to be taken for Ned's sister by one of the artists (woman) who lives there in the colony—sort of a joy in one's maturity. The sewing machine man took us for a ride in his ratty Ford to see a little old woman who had a canary to sell. When we arrived the dame had flown with the canary. I am sorry to keep birds in cages yet children are more important to me than birds and Ned loves pets so much and birds seem to be the best mannered creatures to keep in apartments. Tomorrow evening I must write a theme and not ramble as I have done for two writings.

Earlier that year—was it at a Friends Meeting?—I met a young ornithology professor from the biology department named Ralph H. Mazure who introduced me to his living collection of multicolored finches, kept in a glass aviary filled with ferns. A rainbow explosion! Vitality glittering in a chirpy tongue which I immediately understood. I persuaded the family to let me order a pair of zebra finches from a farm called Bird Haven in California. Awaiting their arrival, Mazure helped me put together my own glass cage, which I furnished with miniature branches imbedded in plasticene plinths made in Miss Todd's art class. The arrival of the birds, in their tiny wooden cage, "express collect" (a phrase I grew to cherish), was a thrill. Rosemary named them Cosette and Marius. The male zebra finch, half the size of a canary, is garbed in speckled gray-black feathers, tight and neat, with a zebrine face dominated by a beak of Chinese red. The female wears a uniform gray with the same bright beak. Their continual song is a monochrome fluty cheep switching in spurts between two pitches a minor third apart. I can still imitate the effect by flipping my tongue against the palette. We placed their transparent home on the platform window in our living room. Their diet was a commercial mix of millet, hemp, and rape seed. Days on end I spent transfixed by their darting avian play when not reading about related breeds, all from Australia, in *Aviculture* magazine. Once, while I was cleaning the cage, they escaped and flew behind a bust of Shakespeare atop the six-foot book-shelf. From then on we allowed them the freedom of the house, leaving open the door of the cage, where they returned for meals. Soon they were carrying bits of lint or string from the rug up to their Shakespearean aerie—building a nest. We gave them swatches of old linen and cotton, and they wove a cozy home. Cosette lay one egg which she incubated for weeks, but it never hatched. I kept it like a pearl in a little box hidden in the grandfather clock. In April, Cosette and Marius were moved to the screened-in back porch where they built another nest. Cosette died in childbirth—she was "egg-bound," according to *Aviculture*. Marius grieved. We bought him a new mate, Esmeralda, but they fought viciously and killed each other.

The brush with death was a tearful occasion which I dramatized out of proportion, as I had dramatized the death of Mama Miller the previous summer. (We had taken a cabin for a month at a resort in Lake Geneva, Wisconsin. I picture Mother still, removing her wet bath-ing suit, when the telegram from Grandaddy arrived. She began to cry, and out of sympathy so did I, though I felt no special sorrow for Mama Miller, only anxiety that Mother seemed far away. She bade me shut up—I was usurping her voluptuous emptiness, the letting go in the face of loss.) During the next months other shipments from Bird Haven arrived. First a pair of strawberry finches, smaller even than the zebras—indeed, like giant strawberries—named Zeus and Hera. Then a pair of society finches, rather larger, clad in terse squares of brown and white. A pair of expensive (ten dollars) Lady Gould finches, of which the male's plumage, in its neatly delineated radiance, mirrored Fra Angelico's *Angel Musicians*. This creature, the size of a sparrow, is of stained glass tinted by beverages or fruits: a lemonade head, burgundy wings, pomegranate breast, thick orange rump. Then there were the Java ricebirds, who needed a cage to themselves (they bite off the legs of other species), and the three pair of parakeets—cobalt, emerald, and azure. All were given free reign of the apartment by day, returning to their covered cages by night. In the morning before school I would remove the covers, like opening a jewel box. To pals after school, or Mother's friends, there was always the risk that a feathered friend would swoop past to let loose a dropping in their teacup.

I brought the birds to Doctor Frank's biology class and gave a speech on their care and feeding. Could I explain their attraction then, since I can't comprehend it now, beyond the sense of ownership, of responsibility for so many autonomous lives, of pride in a novel hobby? Yes, one of the parakeets, named Ichabod, was tamed to perch on finger and shoulder and would kiss my ear and pluck seeds from my lips. But an anthropomorphic exchange, much less affection, was absent. Yet I wept at every death, and since their life spans were brief, I wept a lot. (Ralph H. Mazure, who was also a taxidermist, taught me to eviscerate and embalm my dead pets. I did it once, against my nature, like stuffing one's own baby.) I had no success in breeding them. But I did launch a mode—many school friends took to collecting birds, mostly canaries because of their song, and we talked about birds as much as we talked about poetry. The craze lasted for several years.

October 13, 1934. Rufe went to a smoker for a Negro who is here as a guest from out of town. It seams that this colored man was an officer in the army during the late world war. When the war was over he returned in uniform to his native city in one of the southern states. While there he was treated courteously by every one but when he left town and he was a few miles out, the train was stopped and a delegation of white men got on and took his uniform off of him. He swore then never to put on a uniform of the United States of America again or defend it in any way. Good for him! The hysteria that the average southern white person has about the Negro is a disgrace to our country. And there are some northern white people who also have that mental disease.

Could this "colored man" have been W. E. B. Du Bois? No, he was too old for World War I. But I do remember him in our parlor, good natured about the fauna, and Father driving him downtown to Union Station where, since sleepers were not available to Negroes, Father bought a ticket in his own name for Du Bois's night trip back south. And I remember Ethel Waters, during her tour of *Mamba's Daughters,* in our motley armchair by the fireplace, one arm thrown back, as guest of honor at Mother's black and white tea party, and our maid Helen (Mrs. Coleman, to Mother) all agog, peeking through the same kitchen door Rosemary had peeked through at Professor Tillich, and Ethel shouting, "Hello, sister!"

Mother involved herself with every right-thinking left-veering organization she could. The Urban League and the NAACP for works of Negro betterment, the Society of Friends, then much later the War Resisters League for works of pacifism. During and after the Second War she acted as professional advisor to would-be conscientious objectors, who could not (as Quakers could) claim legal exemption and be classified as 4-E. Even in the last years of her life, until her mind gave way, she worked with women's groups, prochoice groups, and even marched, I am proud to state, in a Parents of Gays parade. At eighty she stood in the rain on Eighth Street and Sixth Avenue in an equal rights demonstration. In all of this she was somewhat unfocused, instinctive, the reverse of her hyperlogical spouse, especially when working with such organized persons as Grace Paley, who found her dithering. She was a pioneer, unsung but indefatigable. Her diary skims the surface of these concerns. Then on 21 October she writes:

I have skipped a few days. Too occupied. Last evening we had eight guests for dinner at the Quadrangle club. Afterward we danced. Rather fun. I prefer simple pleasures but one must participate in some of the artificial activities if one belongs in modern society. Life is complex for me. If I had my choice I would be domestic by day—care for my family and be nice and good, then at night I would go out and get drunk and swear—maybe worse! Confessions of a Minister's daughter above. . . .

I built a fire in the grate today. I love that. Rosemary and Ned are at Sunday School. Rufe took his father to the fair. The latter is here for a couple of days. He is a dear—so serene in his old age. . . . It is lovely to be alone. I feel like Hamlet and like it.

October 23. Today is Ned's eleventh natal day. He is having a company of boys for dinner also Jean Edwards and his sister are to be present. . . . On Saturday or Sunday evenings there is a company of us who read plays together. It is so much fun. Last week we read O'Neill's "Marco Millions." This week I chose "King Lear." . . . Indian summer lingers on. The sadness of autumn is not yet in the air. I long for a day in the country.

And the sadness of her own interior is not in these entries—though who am I to know? Was it this year or earlier—it *was* during my period of fear of repeal—that the parents went out on the town, Mother in her blue taffeta formal, a hundred glass buttons down the front. When they returned Mother's groans lasted until dawn, she couldn't stop vomiting, and we visualized the chore of Father disrobing her. (Cocteau in *Le grand écart* quotes the suicide note of an Englishman: "Trop de boutons à boutonner et à déboutonner. Moi je me tue.") But she was not alcoholic. Over the course of her long life her norm was two drinks a day—not one, not three—just two, usually whisky with water, or maybe beer, a relaxing draft. Her depressions came and went. When they came, Olga would do all to keep her up and swimming, even into November. One saw the two women on autumn evenings walking east on Fifty-seventh Street toward the lake in their slippers, bathing suits, long robes trailing. Mother was being led then. At her lowest, she once said, everything, even the lampshade, even the bathroom, is a menace.

October 25. I observe that some days pass and I do not put down any thoughts. Today I visited a musical assembly that Rosemary helped to "put on." She and Miriam Carey sang a duet together by Hopkinson, "My Days Have Been So Wondrous Free," an early American song. They were in Colonial costume. Perry O'Neill accompanied them. He is a young genius. The girls sang sweetly too. I attended an anti-munitions gathering. Gee, there is much to do there to enlighten the public. I feel that I must do something for that cause and am going to. . . . I was asked to direct a group of seniors in High School today in dramatics. I love that and I am hoping we can put on a play for Yule. . . .

November 1. On Monday evening we had two colored couples for dinner and one white, eight of us. Dr. and Mrs. Bousfield and Mr. and Mrs. Scott were the Negroes and Michael and Janet Davis along with us were the nordics. We *repaired* to "Run Little Chillun" afterward. This is an all-Negro cast play now on in Chicago. This was the first night and so a little at loose ends but fun. Dr. Bousfield and Michael Davis are with Rufe in the Rosenwald Fund and Mr. Scott is an artist. Mrs. B. is a Principal of a colored school, Mrs. S. a social worker. Janet Davis manages a home as I try to do.

We have one of Mr. Scott's pictures which he painted in Haiti and it is very interesting as he is. The others were interesting too. We find it fun having these "mixed" parties.

The hamper in our linen closet was sandalwood flavored. I would curl up in the hamper for hours, for no particular reason. Once I hid there all day. Nobody knew where I was. They called the police. Did other children gauge their value financially? When I'd been bad, the sound of my own voice to Mother returns: "Am I still worth a million dollars to you?"

I wrote short stories by the drove, including one about a boy who lives in a hamper. I followed Mother around, reading her my stories and poems. The poems were spin-offs of Amy Lowell, the stories of Galsworthy. Once I read to her from Galsworthy's *The Apple Tree* and burst into tears. She was cleaning the good silver, called Etruscan, a wedding present, because it was "tarnished," and Adele, our maid then, was cleaning the Quimper dishware, the family's pride. Mother understood the tears, which she always credited to Art, which left one on the edge.

I longed for a corner of my own. But the apartment was small, and cousin Margery had the little guest room.

November 6. Saturday evening after a church supper we had a "wild" party—another incongruous combination Rufe and I have. We took Margery and our children to the supper and had a good time. We lean toward the Friends or Quakers. The wild party consisted of Dale and Paul Cooper, Dale's brother Stan, and some of their radio, champagne selling, car parts selling and mail order selling friends. I liked them all. We drank some, danced, played checkers, craps, and Rufe and Doris Keane sang beautifully to my accompaniment. Jill and Davis Edwards came too. They are fun. Jill talks on the radio and teaches my daughter dramatics in H.S. Davis teaches Public Speaking in the U. of C. . . . . Last evening while Rufe was out making a speech I finished "Seven Gothic Tales." Great book! It was wonderful having a peaceful book-reading evening by myself. . . . One of our guests at the Saturday wild party has religion and after a long talk with him I nearly became a Universalist especially after both of us had had several drinks of egg nog.

I remember the church suppers with pleasure because of the obligatory meat loaf with overdone scalloped potatoes. I also remember Dale Cooper, who taught us how to pedicure our toes. She was rather cheap—looked like Nancy Carroll in *Women Accused*—and turned out not to be legally married to Paul, who, when he left her, caused great sorrow. (Mother hoped this would teach us a lesson about the sanctity, not to mention security, of marriage.) How "wild" those postchurch parties got, I do not know. I do recall the "filthy" jokes that were told *en famille* by the Edwardses and the Coopers and the Rorems, and seemed no tamer than those told in the locker room. Example: "My Lord, there is a lady without." "Without what?" "Without food or raiment." "Well, give her food and bring her in." Shrieks of delight.... Louder shrieks as, with the years, we graduated into dirty words with such puzzles as: "Do infants have as much fun in infancy as adults do in adultery?" Or: "What goes in hard and comes out juicy?" Answer: "A stick of Spearmint—if you think it's something else you have a low mind."... Later still: "Did what made Oscar Wilde make Thornton Wilder?" Language was all, blending into literature.

I worked on my handwriting so that it would have *personality,* using Mother's as a model. (Father's was Spencerian, predictable.) For a while I dotted my *i*'s with wee circles, the way Edith Harris did, because Edith got the highest grades in class, while I got the lowest. (Also, her father had thrown himself from a window of the Palmer House, which made Edith a celebrity for a while.) Then I wrote in backhand. My calligraphy eventually righted itself to become what it is today. With one stopover. In 1951 Henri Fourtine said the N in Ned looked like an M. I changed it *sciemment.* Should my signature have been reregistered at the bank and on my passport?

November 21. We celebrated Rufe's fortieth natal day November 17. He doesn't look and doesn't seem that age. He is a dear. The other evening we attended a dinner at the Quadrangle Club—a mixed white and colored group. I was so glad to have such a group in such a club. The Club is an exclusive club at the U. of C. and not many Negroes go there I am sorry to say. We thence repaired to Mandel Hall to hear Zora Neale Hurston, a negro writer and anthropologist, give a speech. She was the guest of honor at the dinner. Quite a colorful person (both literally and figuratively speaking). I read her "Jonah's Gourd Vine." Rufe's father and Elizabeth (step-mother) spent a few days with us as they were bound for Florida. Fortunately we had a tolerable time. I never can express myself perfectly with either of them. I think Dad Rorem is a dear and so kind but he retains some of the old political and social ideas that leave me cold. Eliz is hopeless in that respect. I just must say this some place. What is a journal for but that. She is stultified! [The last sentence is penciled out] I pray that I may be open-minded and tolerant as I grow older so that young people and others too will feel free to express themselves to me and that I will not be shocked. This will sound as a family prejudice but my own father is the most tolerant of individuals in my opinion (Rufe is a close second). I could tell Dad anything, vulgar or beautiful, and he "gets it."...

Ned and I are reading "The Three Musketeers" together aloud. Rosemary and her father are studying French together in the evening....

I remember deaf old Grandfather Rorem with his Acousticon, and the redoubtable Elizabeth with her grainy whine. And Father's embarrassing us when he imitated *his* father, Ole Jon, in the singsong Scandinavian accent, "Vell, I tank I go to bed now," and we'd groan and roll our eyes. We, of course, were Rosemary and myself. We looked like twins, but she said vanilla so I said vanella.

November 28. The day before Thanksgiving "and all through the house et cetera." We are going to La Petit Gourmant [Le Petit Gourmet], a French restaurant, with our offspring for that occasion. They are studying French in school and it will give them an opportunity to show what they know. We vetoed a big party this year.... I am busy as anything directing two plays for Yule. We will put on "Six Who Pass While the Lentils Boil" ... and some scenes from "Alice in Wonderland." ... Then the Friends are working up a nativity play for Meeting. The adults are more difficult to handle than the children. Some person always wishes to tell the director how to do it. There is one in every home. I'll have my troubles but it gives me a smile too. Anyway working with plays is fun.... Am reading John Locke on Education. He is quite sound after 200 years—amusing too. We saw Reinhardt's "Midsummer Night's Dream" with Helen and Karl Klein and it was exquisitely done. Want Rosemary and Ned to see it. Puck was played by a twelve year old boy and most convincing. He can show my players just how good a child can do on the stage. My two children and eight others are in the juvenile group which I organized and dubbed The Mimes.

Other than *Six Who Pass* and *Alice* (in which I played both the Mad Hatter and the Dormouse), she directed *A Christmas Carol* (I played the cruel Scrooge) and a version of Oscar Wilde's *Birthday of the Infanta* (Rosemary played the cruel Infanta). Of the eight others I remember Jean Goodman, Miriam Carey, Robert Kincheloe from the fifth floor (he was the dwarf in the Wilde play), David Fox from the fourth floor, and of course Jean Edwards.

December 10. We had an interesting experience the other night when we dined with Flora and Walter Hendricks (two young poets). As their other guests were two other young people, also poets, one a man and one a woman. The young man, Elder Olson by name and an excellent writer of lyrics, is very temperamental but sweet. We chatted for some time before dinner and then when we sat down to consume the food he suddenly jumped up (after one bite of radish) and dashed upstairs. I thought that perhaps he had a stomach ache but he did not come down for some time so Flora went up and he was having nervous indigestion. He braced up and returned to the table, took another bite (this time of celery) and once more repaired to higher regions. I sat beside him at table and thought mayhap I was offensive in some manner. But anon he appeared again.

This time he snatched his coat, hat and scarf and dashed out wildly into the night. After the young woman poetess had departed Flora, Walter, Rufe and I tried to unravel his condition. . . . Gertrude Stein was speaking that night to a select few and he and the girl each had a ticket (the rest of us did not). We concluded he did not wish to make an appearance at her speech with this young girl because he feared what his friends and acquaintances might say or think, not being especially interested in the girl and being in love with a married woman in Evanston. It was a real mad tea party!

The Hendrickses and the Rorems were cofounding members of the Fifty-seventh Street Meeting of Friends, which hived in John Wollman Hall, along with the Unitarian Church, between Woodlawn and University. Walter was a Leslie Howard type with blond hair and a handsome worried look; Flora a Pre-Raphaelite beauty with raven tresses done up in a bun. Two daughters, Hilda Marie and Cynthia, inherited their parents' gentle sober beauty. We saw the Hendrickses often, especially during summers in Vermont, where they bought a house with a good tract of land near Marlboro. The girls were younger than us, mere charming scamps. But the parents interested me, not least because they gave me pointers on my own poems, and because in the thick mock orange about their home were robins' nests from which I could filch blue eggs, which looked like Father's eyes, for my collection. One winter in Chicago, Cynthia died. Her doctor was also our doctor, Dr. Carey. Rosemary and I didn't learn about the death until the next morning, but all night long there was a coming-and-going, with Walter staying on our living room sofa. A decade later Walter founded Marlboro College, from which, after five years, he was, in 1951, summarily fired. The house in which they lived all those summers is today the central bureau of Rudolf Serkin's Marlboro Festival. How many months after Cynthia's death did Dr. Carey commit suicide? His daughter, Miriam, a Ginger Rogers type, was Rosemary's best friend. She was "fast," she necked, and at sixteen lost her virginity with young Sam Norwood, intern. Sam lived in the Carey's house on nearby Kenwood Avenue. There was a shed behind it. After Cynthia's death, Dr. Carey grew increasingly depressed and, according to Sam Norwood, gave himself a hypodermic, then took a butcher knife to the shed where he stabbed himself. Miriam married Sam, moved to Atlanta, raised a family. She too killed herself. She had a lovely voice and emulated Jeanette MacDonald.

. . . A few nights later we heard Gertrude Stein speak (as members of the Renaissance Society). She isn't bad. We sat at a table with some North Shore socialites. Awful bores! The most fun of that occasion was afterward when we went to Fred and Francis Beisels (young artists) and heard two of our young colored friends sing and play. John Greene and Margaret Bonds.

Very engrossed directing my two plays, working in school's Christmas Shop, attending music recitals of the children, going for walks with friends, going to a party now and then and doing a little reading. I just finished James Stephens' "Crock of Gold" and like it. . . . Esther Johnson (my coloratura soprano) asked me to accompany her in practice. I should love to but must wait until after the holidays. She is the only woman friend I have at present with whom I can giggle. I do appreciate that.

The day was full of domestic activity. I cleaned closets, cedar chest, etcetera. Cleaning the cedar chest consists of reading old letters and burning half of them. The difficult task is to decide which half to burn—which would make the best memoirs.

In that cedar chest, now at my sister's in Philadelphia, I found Mother's little diary. Have I quoted overlong? Overlong means self-indulgently. But I'm indulging Mother. True, nothing is said in three hours that can't be said more clearly in two. Any Mahler symphony is prolix to a francophile. Even Proust, had he survived another year, would have tailored that book of his, I am convinced. The recent TV five-day documentary on the Civil War—I am writing in the summer of 1991—by being granted maximum time, grew repetitious where it should have been concise. (This paragraph needs pruning.)

Yet Mother means all to me, and she never published her Letter to the World. Without her few frail pages here her voice is as hushed as a Sumerian slave's. Of course, nothing lasts, everything fades: our children, our parents, our statues, our pyramids, our dinosaurs, the sun itself. I cling to her words. Printed here they grow perhaps less perishable, stalling the dust. Like a work of art, like a life preserver for the dead.

5. Interlude

Room after room,
I hunt the house through
We inhabit together.
Heart, fear nothing, for, heart, thou shalt find her,
Next time, herself! not the trouble behind her....
— "Love in a Life": Robert Browning

Rooms. They contain our lives. Wards, cradles, nurseries, parlors, boudoir and bathtub, kitchen and sacristy, even the halls of open fields bordered by leafy wall and blue-gold ceiling. Even the coffin. Throughout life and death we cannot escape our rooms. We are the fingers within their glove, corridors of either velvet or iron: the hand inside moves according.

According to our environment we choose our environment—our glove, our room. As hands we react tactilely. But as persons attached to those hands we react with heart and mind, and with the five senses which interact with heart and mind and sometimes with themselves, especially in artists who say they can see sound, sniff green, hear marble, taste terror, and fondle F major. Still, the arts are specialized and are all, without exception, visual or auditory. Yet they have been said to derive from that most painful of pleasures, which is nostalgia.

Paradoxically, nostalgia arises through those two senses with which no art primarily deals: taste and smell. They can't be channeled, intellectualized, communicated, as can sight and sound and sometimes touch. Tongue and nose single-mindedly burrow through diamond-hard culture barriers to instinct.

. . .

That effusion stems from finally being given my own room, the tiny one down the hall, formerly the "maid's room," with its own bath. It became an empire.

In newfound privacy I created my own rules, confounding the senses in the best Rimbaudian style. Amid stolen incense I played at full volume on the old phonograph Milhaud's *La création du monde* (which ended on a tonic seventh chord, as did Ravel's *Jeux d'eau,* which Margaret Bonds was to play so gleamingly, Duke Ellington's "Mood Indigo," plus everything of mine), and Stravinsky's *Les noces* in the composer's English-language recording with its coarse close, when four pianos crash together in the straightforward mystery of fucking—the fucking of adolescents, what's more. (The first music to represent the thrust of a screw as distinct from a standard Wagnerian swoon.) This is the room where I eventually learned to masturbate, while reading the scene of seduction by Lyceaneum of Daphnis, in the Longus pastoral. Where, as the weeks flowed by, I discovered I couldn't see clearly for more than two yards—that I harbored a galloping myopia, the symptom of one who seeks to shut out the world.

In this room after midnight I consumed leftover meringues while strutting about in Mother's high heels and declaiming Ibsen to get rid of a speech defect. My sweet tooth—worse, my vicious *compulsion* toward sugar, retained to this day—was the alcoholic's quick fix before the fact. Mother's clothes were more disguise than drag—I have never wanted to be a woman, though I have wanted "female privileges." The speech defect was—is—an inability to say ess.

I did not differentiate then as now I do between high and low art. The movie of *Madame Butterfly* starring Sylvia Sidney, which I saw time after time, may have led my parents to take me to my first opera, *Madama Butterfly,* as well as to *The Mikado,* but it also led me to see many another Sylvia Sidney movie over the years. *Queen Christina* was an opera in itself, so was *Christopher Strong,* and these led me to lie on my back and eat grapes like Garbo, garbed in gold lamé like Hepburn. When Bruce took me down the block to hear *Daphnis et Chloé* (that "leafy study," he dubbed it) on the Robertstons' Capeheart, we came home and with the same set of ears listened to Mildred Baily moaning "More Than You Know." If Bruce induced me to read *Nightwood,* he also pushed me to ask the university's football (or was it baseball) champion, Jay Berwanger, for his autograph, and to buy the records of Josephine Baker. Movies were more cogent than plays, simply because there were more of them. The "fine" films from Europe, like *Les misérables* or *M,* were shown at International House, while the trashy movies (as Mother called them), like *Of Human Bondage* or *Forty-second Street,* came mainly to the Frolic or the Piccadilly. Since I saw two films a week, and sat through them each a half-dozen times, how did I get my schoolwork done, much less my piano practicing? I didn't. Father feigned sarcastic surprise at my C-minus average when I should be receiving straight Fs. The piano was a means to an end (repertory) rather than an end in itself (virtuosity). It also, when the lid was up, resembled a winged horse, and the Pegasus myth was a favorite mystery.

During the summer of 1934 in Yellowstone Park we ran into the Carey family and rode horseback with them among the geysers. There I discovered, after skinning my shin on a stirrup, a violent allergy to horses. I bled, swelled like a fat hen, sneezed unstoppably. This made me love horses more, not only for their eldritch beauty but for their power, and later—after reading Swift's *Voyage to the Houyhnhnms*—for their rationalism. I still carry in my wallet a warning against horse serum, which, in case of accident, might be fatal.

I remember nothing learned in school that fall, but I did see *Naughty Marietta* and *Klondike Annie*. In the former Jeanette MacDonald, a rich French princess in the eighteenth century, before running off to the American wilderness, "liberates" the domesticated parakeets in her huge aviary into the wintry streets of Paris, where of course they will perish in a day. (She also wears a wristwatch.) In the latter Mae West kills her Chinese lover-jailor (stabbing him during a kiss in a graphic close-up permanently excised by censors the following year) and flees to Nome. During recent reruns of both films I am bemused at how accurately I recall each frame, the pacing, the songs, the food, the single hair out of place, as though I were again a preteenager. Everything is indelibly the same except the essential—the plots are full of holes and the naughtiness is puerile. The genius and horror of the VCR is that, by making forgotten films available again, we can, like Emily and her poignant excruciation in *Our Town,* literally reexperience our youth down to the last dumb mistake.

The summer of 1935 we visited Yankton again, stopping in Minneapolis to see the Millers: Mother's brother, the jovial Uncle Al; his wife, Aunt Mildred; and their one son, John, who is today a cellist and composer. With John we dressed up in fur hats and overshoes during the worst heat wave of the century and went to see *Baby Take a Bow,* our first exposure to Shirley Temple, whose rise in the world I followed with awe, and who now seems an empty, self-important little snot.

We also returned to Vermont, this time with a fellow traveler, one of Rosemary's swains, Eddie, a good-looking athletic redhead who rode with us as far as Brattleboro, then hitch-hiked on to Maine, where his parents were. Was he thirteen? Fourteen? In the stopover tourist cabin Eddie and I shared a bed. In the early hours he approached me from behind, put an arm around me, and remained in this posture for an hour during which I held my uncomprehending breath. Then he rolled away with a snore. Next morning I spoke of this, in front of Eddie and Rosemary, to unresponsive parents who changed the subject. En route, in Amherst, we bought another dog, a rusty cocker spaniel puppy named Geoffrey. I don't remember what became of Simba. And we saw *Flying Down to Rio,* or was that a few summers earlier? Chronology fumbles. I do know that this Astaire/Rogers movie was the first seen by me in New England, and that I purchased the sheet music of "The Carioca," which Jean Edwards and I then choreographed.

We visited the Hendrickses again, in Marlboro. They had an old-fashioned harmonium, my first contact with a "sustaining" instrument, one which, unlike the piano, can hold a chord without the sound decaying. Pumping away at the wheezy pedal I improvised on *The Afternoon of a Faun.*

Flashbacks:

—I was raised not to say "I." Or to begin a sentence with "I."

—Billy Stickney died of mononucleosis caught in the school pool. Bruce and I went to the funeral, though we really hadn't known him that well. Interlopers in melancholy. Funerals are for grown-ups. Grown-up audience, grown-up corpse.

—What befalls those fluffy day-old chicks acquired at Easter by city kids who live in small apartments? Mostly they die of neglect and are thrown out with the garbage. One of ours grew into a rooster that crowed. We had to give it to James, the janitor, and ask him not to tell us its fate. Another, while still a baby with blameless black eyes, became a screeching cripple when I accidentally dropped a rock on it. Father then killed it with a whack of his tennis racket. As for an Easter bunny named Harriett, who never died but who gnawed at the piano legs, leaving sawdust on the oriental rug, she too was entrusted to James. I then wrote a story about a rabbit that cried real tears.

—Father on one of his trips East was to appear on a lecture platform with Eleanor Roosevelt. I gave him my little green plush autograph book, hoping he'd ask her then and there for her signature. He didn't.

—Along with Mozart's *Turkish March,* Debussy's *La fille aux chev-eux de lin* (which Virgil Thomson always called *The Girl with the Linen Hair*), and Carpenter's *An American Tango,* I learned to play, from the sheet music, "Dizzy Fingers" by Zez Confrey, and "Walkin' My Baby Back Home." I also improvised a piece called *The Fountain and the Stars,* recorded it for a dollar at Lyon & Healy's, and sent the disc to John Alden Carpenter, Chicago's chief musical glory who lived on Lake Shore Drive. Margaret Bonds was abashed when Carpenter, gently, advised me to learn how to put my ideas on paper. It was then that Margaret, from my dictation at the piano, notated *The Glass Cloud,* influenced by her other star pupil, Gerald Cook, a year or two older than I, and taught me from that to notate. I have a dozen notebooks from that period brimming with Impressionist studies.

—Hatti Heiner, who with the advent of first grade went off to a public school, would come back into my life in the late 1930s. Meanwhile her blind father, Frank, estranged from her mother but still married, radical left-winger, was a charming raconteur and good acquaintance of my parents'. Mother told Frank Heiner about her childhood friend, Glenys Rivola, an overripe unmarried blond who lived with her mother, Flora, in Yankton, a few houses down from Granddaddy on Pine Street. (Flora, an English teacher, had encouraged my poetry writing.) Frank began a correspondence with Glenys, which ended when he boarded a train with his beautiful female German shepherd guide dog, arrived in Yankton 600 miles later, brought Glenys back to Chicago, divorced his wife, and got rid of the dog. "One bitch in the family is plenty," said Glenys, who married him. Hatti, sensing I was at the bottom of her parents' divorce, never forgave me.

—Do you remember Sarnat's drugstore, dear Hatti, on Blackstone and Fifty-seventh, where for a nickel you got a cone of orange ice double-dipped in chocolate sprinklings? It was across from the Christian Science Church which we used to stare at. Our rabbit, Harriett, was named after you.

—Margaret Bonds wore open-toe high heels. I'd never seen such things. Was it because she couldn't afford whole shoes?

—The thirteen-year scope, like a ridged fan, or like the hills and dales of a landscape which when flown over can be topographically grasped at a glance but which when traversed on foot become comprehensible only with time, was dominated by the benevolent despot, Franklin Roosevelt, a Big Brother, a fixture, taken for granted by my generation. Hoover was within memory, but Truman would arrive only after our basic training (thrills of music, first love and other sorrows, menstruation and change of voice) had stamped us forever.

But during what Auden termed this "low dishonest decade" (what decade isn't?), from one season to the next, the rich and poor alike were uncertain. Roosevelt, the ruler, did good things (the WPA Arts Project) and bad (getting us into the war), but I couldn't see it because I was seeing it: nothing except eating and sex can be perceived *in medias res.* Today I remain as dumb about politics, the *details* of government, as I then was. I realize only that merely to want to be president means you're already corrupt—the role is by definition capitulative.

So what I would be I already was, a practicing musician. The professionality (ability to notate) was there, though I'd never heard a note of mine played by someone else. The *sense* of music, of course, was absent, since music, as distinct from painting and poetry, has no sense. Despite my garrulous innocence, I inhabited an inviolable niche: my world versus *the* world—the physical drama of Then and Now. Despite future pleasures and wistful perils of sex and love and friendship, of travel and art and whisky, life and the universe seemed already veiled in a perpetual sadness without meaning.

6. Ned's Diary (I)

In 1936 we went to Europe. It was a grand tour, eleven weeks, including two on the water. After a fortnight in London we went to Stratford and saw Shakespeare. Then Newcastle to search in vain for Mother's forebears, and from where we sailed to Stavanger. In Stavanger we found Father's forebears, and proceeded up the fjord to Oslo, then Copenhagen, then Geneva, finally Paris.

A dark cloud had already settled over Europe, but there is no hint of my awareness in the 140-page journal scrawled during the trip. The Ned reflected therein is an unneurotic overweight Little Brother playing the role of Little Brother (as I always would with Rosemary's beaux), and a relentless optimist. He expresses reactions, but no judgments, and often refers to this or that as indescribable. Of course, any writer who called something indescribable is not a writer.

8 July 1936: Coburg Court Hotel. I won't tell much about the boat except that Rose made a very good friend while she was on the boat whom she likes even better than Miriam Carey. Her name is Doris Garner and she lives in Canada. I, myself, didn't find anyone whom I should wish to know personally. We were seasick the first few days. We also saw *four* movies while on board.

The reason I'm so brief about everything so far is that I'm catching up on what has happened in the past month, but soon I'll come to what has happened in the past week and then I shall write daily.

...We landed in Southampton on the 5th of July. I must say our first sight of land for eight days was certainly wonderful. It really looked beautiful and green although I don't think it's any nicer than America. ...

[Mother had another slant:

On Tour with the Family June 27 to September 15, 1936
Rufus had to go to Europe on business so he asked the children and me
to join him and combine business with pleasure. We were not sure which
was business and which was pleasure by the time the tour was finished.

The children are Rosemary who is fourteen and Ned who is twelve. I
am Gladys their mother. Rufus is their father.

The children and I had never before been on a great liner and the
excitement at leaving was intense.

Being very much a part of land and provincial and peaceful in my
disposition the voyage over was rather an ordeal for me. I thought the
boat would sink any minute. Even now it seems amazing that we arrived
at Southampton without disaster at sea.

Not long after gazing at the Statue of Liberty as it faded from view we
sought our cabins. Down many flights of stairs we went brushing by other
American tourists who also seemed in confused states. Rufus and Ned had
a stateroom together and it seemed very far away indeed from the one
occupied by Rosemary and me.

Many times my thoughts turned to my mother who crossed the ocean
when she was an infant with her young parents. Her mother bravely left
with her father, much against the wishes of her parents and was thereby
disinherited. I thought also of my father and two brothers who crossed
over during the world war, one of them never to return. He was my
younger brother whose grave I would visit in France.

Tho I became accustomed to the sea in a way, still, I felt on landing that
I would have to seek a new home in England or Europe so that I would
not have to cross back again to the states.]

8 July. Tuesday we went to see Charlie Chaplin in *Modern Times*. It
was very funny. Mother just laughed and laughed. I like to see Mother
laugh because she so seldom has a real good laugh. . . .

9 July: 9:55 a.m. Last night we went to *Pride and Prejudice*. It was just
swell. The English actors are *very* good. We saw it at the St. James
theatre. . . .

12 July: Sherington Hotel, Stratford-on-Avon, Rather Street, England.
This is a very nice hotel. . . . Tonight we saw *Romeo and Juliet*. It was
swell. It was so sad I nearly cried. The acting was *very* good. . . . (*13
July*) We have just come home from *Troilus and Cressida*. It was *very*
sad. The same girl that played Juliet last night played the lead in this
tonight. . . . This morning we went bisycling to Ann Hathaway's cottage.
We didn't go in as we had no money and we probably wouldn't have
anyway. . . .

24 July: Hotel Victoria, Stavanger, Norge. The reason I didn't write about *yesterday,* last night, was because I was terribly seasick for 28 hours on the North Sea from Newcastle to Norway.... *(25 July)* ... Then the whole family went to *Peter Ibbetson* with Gary Cooper and Ann Harding. It's the most *beautiful* movie I've ever seen. The acting was just *wonderful* and they played "Debussy music" all through it. ... *(29 July)* We were invited to Mr. Bryne's "private" island today. We took Ragner Husebo (3rd cousin) and "Grandfather" Tendines with us. I like Ragner very much although he can't speak any English. While we were on the island we went around together picking blueberries, climbing steep hills, swimming, rowing, etc. We had a nice meal. Then came home.

5 August: Grand Hotel, Oslo; 11:00 p.m. This is the most wonderful hotel I've ever been in. Oslo isn't what I thought it'd be like at all. It reminds me of America. I miss America like everything. Well anyway —instead of having a bus when we left the hotel this morning we had a private car all to ourselves for three hours. We drove on the edge and down in the valleys of the steepest "cliffiest" mountains. Mother and Father said they were even more magnificent than the Grand Canyon.... Father said we'd never see anything like it again so that we should look at it all as much as we could.... *(6 August)* ... Tonight the whole family went to *Show Boat*. Pa and Ma thought it was swell. I sure love Helen Morgan. I'm going to write her a fan letter....

10 August: Grand Hotel, Copenhagen; 10:45 p.m. Yesterday I bought a mistery by Edgar Wallace called *The Green Archer*. I am already halfway through it as I've been doing nothing else all morning but reading it.... Went to the Tivoli, the amusement park we visited yesterday. We went on the same roller-coaster 11 times....

15 August: Hôtel de Famille, Geneva, Switzerland.... The Alps are rather disappointing.... *(24 August)* ... Tonight Father and I took a walk in what is called the Old Town. We went down the spookiest, most interesting and old narrow side streets, that it is very hard to explain it.... *(25 August)* ... This morning Father and I went bike riding and I bought a real beautiful big cross (crucifix) made of wood. In case the reader doesn't know it, I am a very ardent collector of such things.... Tonight we went to the orchestra but when we got there we found that they weren't playing tonight, we had peaches and ice cream instead. Tommorow morning we are leaving for Paris on the 9:42.

26 August: Hôtel Perey, Paris, France; 11:03 p.m. We have been on a hot, sticky, stuffy train, all day for nine hours, and I never was so tired and uncomfortable in all my life. Well finally we came to Paris and *were we glad!* There are more bird stores and markets in this town. We counted 20 bird shops on one street on the way to our hotel.

28 August: 37 rue Cambon, Hôtel de Castille; 9:30 p.m. We are now in a much nicer hotel than the other one and nearer the American Express and the center of town. . . . Tommorow I am going on a bus tour by myself of the left bank of Paris, where all the artists (etc.) live. . . .

30 August: Hôtel de Castille; 10:33½ p.m. This morning Mother and I got up early, and went to the services in Notre Dame, but the organ playing was over when we got there. So while Mother sat in the tower behind the church I paid a france (6¢ [at present]) to climb 567 steps to the two towers on the top of the church. I never had more strenuous excersise than going up those dark, winding stairs. People were fainting all over the place and most of them didn't actually come up as far as I did. Then Mother and I discovered a huge bird market right there on the island, but we won't buy any for 8 days though. . . . (*2 September*) . . . Tonight Father and I went on the subway to the outer walls of Paris. (There was a drunk man on the train that had a horrible gash on his forehead and was so sleepy he was always falling on the floor. He was terribly dirty and red eyed and spooky looking and I know I'm going to dream about him tonight.) Father and I then went to the hill that St. Denis walked up with his head . . . just wonderful, "Paris by night." . . . (*4 September*) . . . We have made two very good friends at this hotel. One is a real pretty jewish woman Mrs. Shearer and the other is an interesting Catholic woman Mrs. Pope who buys cloth by the bolt from Schiaparelli. We have very long talks with them about religion & various other subjects. Mrs. Pope thinks its funny that when I get married I want to have fat blond baby girl twins. . . .

6 September: Hôtel de Castille, 10:11 p.m. Well, this morning, while Mother, Rose and the quaker were at Versailles, Father and I went to the bird market and got 16 birds.

9 September: On board RMS *Aquitania.*

10 September: 11:00 p.m. This morning the firefinch I bought for Jimmie died. We had an elaborate funeral at sea with flowers and other stuff.

—THE END—

. . .

While reading those pages by the preadolescent Ned, I am tempted to belittle him, to put him down, to show impatience at that other Ned's inability to see, like any logician, two sides of the same coin (or, like any artist, three sides). Tempted to sneer at how, for him, history seemed less alluring than a need to wash his hair at every stop; at his obsession with movies which he nevertheless reviewed as simply "interesting" or "swell"; at his inability to impart his feeling for "modern music" other than by saying he *had* a feeling; at his concern with dieting or aviculture in the light of the ever-shifting continental masterpiece. I am tempted to explain, to edit, to forgive that young Ned's shallow outlook. But I shall not—lest another say that my present guile is more pernicious, less winsome, and just as dull as the 1936 Diary.

Still, that young Ned *is* me. I can evoke this very morning what would never have occurred to me to notate twenty thousand mornings ago: How Rosemary and I yelled *Heil Hitler!* in the Hamburg street, just to be quaint, and were shushed by our elders; how the bearded mouth of the lithe metro conductor might feel caressing my own red mouth; indeed, how an incipient but quite unacknowledged carnality lurked beneath every quotidian political banality—how good and evil are sister and brother.

I couldn't know then (though such crisscrossed paths are common food for thought), as I "gazed" onto Kensington Gardens, that sooner or later I'd be cruising those gardens without family surveillance; or rambling through Copenhagen's Tivoli Gardens with more on my mind than roller-coasters; or that three blocks from those Champs-Elysées cinemas loomed Marie-Laure de Noailles's mansion, which one day I would call home; or that a poet named Cocteau inhabited the Hôtel de Castille when we did, and was evicted for smoking opium —Cocteau, whom a more Rastignacian Ned would befriend fourteen years and one World War later.

Our apartment at 5617 Dorchester, lodging as it did four souls— sometimes five, when cousins were in town—was not huge. A living room, a dining room, kitchen, two bedrooms with one bath, a smaller bedroom with a smaller bath, back porch, railroad hallway with a door to the service stairway, and another door to the front elevator entrance. In this entrance was a grandfather clock, an heirloom which, without its ever driving me crazy, chimed each quarter hour to the tune of Big Ben in C major (though every sixty minutes when the hours struck, the strokes were in A-flat—that is, a C which to my ears sounded not like a tonic but a third). Within this clock, before leaving for Europe, I cached my collection of finch eggs. These were sky blue, the size of jellybeans, wrapped individually in cotton and stored in one of Mother's black-and-orange Coty face-powder boxes. My first act on returning from Europe, even before checking on the live birds, was to rush toward the clock and check on the eggs.

The live birds, meanwhile, had been tended by Minnie, our one white maid in a succession of "colored" maids, who was elderly, fat, not pretty, bossy, and semiliterate. (Mother's diary lists "Minnie's sayings": shrubbery = scrubery, aluminum = alumitum, crêpe de chine = crepe machine, waiter = waitress—"He was a waitress.") She also had a mustache, and armpits with warts used for mashing potatoes, or so I supposed. Minnie told us that the two canaries, Archibald and Miriam, had produced one egg; it hatched a cripple which they proceeded to peck to death.

As for that clanging clock, I wonder. With the dawn of puberty I fell prey to the madness of insomnia, which has never ceased. Anything awakens me—a faucet dripping miles away, a spider sighing, a neighbor's sweaty dreams—and once awake I circle the possibility of sleep for hour after hour, like the astronaut seeking that invisible slit through which he will reenter the "envelope" of atmosphere. It would be nice to say that these periods are fruitful; in truth all half-waking thought becomes banality, just as the inspiration of dreams turns to trash in the morning. Today any noise not my own is terror, like the threat not of a tinkling piano in the next apartment but of a rock band on a subway neighbor's earphones. Because my profession deals with my choice of sound, all other sound is painful.

In two hundred months I've scarcely had one so-called good night's rest. Even drunk, when too often I'd pass out or black out, awakening came soon. Through a splitting head thoughts raced and never stopped, while from behind closed eyes, from malodorous bedsheets, I'd watch day turn into night again, then arise and go out drinking anew. These three sentences were scratched onto a notepad beside my bed at five this morning, after hours of wakefulness. They could as easily have been scratched yesterday at the same time, or the day before, or a year, or twelve years, ago.

> While Sherwood was still in Paris, John the son was an awkward shy boy. The day after Sherwood left John showed up, sat easily on the arm of the sofa and was beautiful to look upon and he knew it. Nothing to the outward eye had changed but he had changed and he knew it.
>
> —*The Autobiography of Alice B. Toklas*

(If I do not further name the author of the above remarks—she who once remarked that "remarks are not literature"—it is that Toklas *is* the author. Gertrude Stein, according to Maurice Grosser, who knew, just signed her name for publicity purposes. Maurice it also was who took the loose paragraphs of *Four Saints in Three Acts* and shuffled them into a usable libretto for the opera.)

In that autumn of 1936, almost from the moment we stepped off the boat, everything to the outward eye had changed in me while nothing changed inside, but did I know that?

If, on returning to France in 1949 I had for a decade been aware of my body and of its effect on others, using that knowledge for good and bad, to a point where historian Philippe Erlanger, himself majestically ugly, proclaimed that I was everything a mother would *not* want her son to grow up to be, in early 1936 I was still unaware of myself-as-object, being overweight, on the verge, yet still ignorant, of impending adolescence, and something only a mother could love. Now the larval narcissism through which I saw the world evolved overnight to another kind of narcissism: how did the world see me? Body and voice changed, height soared, I was no longer a subject perceiving but an object receiving. Sex was everywhere, not just in locker room and jungle book but in doorknobs and sausages and clouds. That the sex was exclusively male-oriented, as it had been chez moi since the age of reason (about three years old), disturbed me not at all. It may have occurred to me wistfully that I would "outgrow" these leanings, but I did not suffer. I have never suffered from being queer, from not being a regular guy. My friends and I felt superior to the regulars (more *subtle* was the word), we felt they were missing something in not reading Knut Hamsun and Pierre Louÿs, in not basking in Ravel and Varèse, in not going to the ballet as we regularly did. A rationalization, maybe. Most minorities (Jews, artists, German tourists in Italy) defensively cast themselves as superior to the norm about them. Some, however, are at a loss, traumatized at the thought of "coming out," and long to be part of the mob. Today, when the fact of homosexuality is so prevalent in the bourgeois air, all around one hears confessions of men born since World War II, how they hid their penchants from everyone, themselves included, remaining closet virgins until twenty-five, in an effort to be accepted by the gang, the gang being not just neighborhood roughs but intellectual undergraduates at Yale. No, my rejections have come far less from being involuntarily gay than from choosing to be a serious composer in our philistine world.

Priorities shifted.

Crushes were still on female teachers as they had been on Miss

Richardson in third grade (though not the dreaded Miss Burris in fourth grade, with her wide rump and rimless specs, the only one I ever hated), and on Mrs. DePencier in fifth, with her lovely clothes and graphic descriptions of Hannibal crossing the Alps. (Is it risky to say that widows more than spinsters make caring instructors? Yes, in the light of Nadia Boulanger, *l'éternelle mademoiselle,* our century's greatest pedagogue.) I was bewitched by Mrs. DePencier, who, at the present writing, is still, in her late nineties, active and always present when every few years I am in Chicago for concerts. But she was already a past presence when school began again after our summer in Europe.

The scholastic year 1936–37 brought Miss Lemon—*young* Miss Lemon, blond with jazzy checkered suits—who goaded me to memorize dozens of Edna Millay's sonnets and to read, and read again, *Quo Vadis.* I was a freshman now in the University of Chicago High School, U-High to us, Jew-High to the denizens of nearby Hyde Park High, the much larger public school. That someone of my sweet age could be entering high school was not due to precocity—except for English and music my grades continued lousy, even in French, and remained so until graduation in 1940—but to Hutchins's merging of seventh and eighth grades into what he called subfreshmen.

Simultaneous with Rosemary's first menstruation came my myopia. Like Bruce, I now wore glasses, rarer then than now, and hated them. Nearsightedness meant that one could be seen without seeing; glasses meant that one could be masked while seeing. Emotionally I wished only to be seen. Rationally I longed to see without limit.

And to hear without limit.

That winter Stravinsky conducted his *Rite of Spring* with the New York Philharmonic, broadcast live across the country. Hearing it, I grew sick. And never recovered. This, finally, was what music's all about! Its controlled insanity, straightforward barbarism, disturbingly simple tunes (disturbing, because they were Russian, not Kentuckian), continually irregular rhythms which did and did not seem sexual (sex always comes with a steady beat), and progressively mounting ecstasy culminating not in heaven but on earth! Surely every other thirteen-year-old across the country was equally bowled over? The subtitles included a *Dance of the Adolescents,* which reeked of smegma. Was the word *adolescence* allowed in polite society? Igor Markevich, the late Franco-Russian conductor, born in 1912, the year of *The Rite*'s premiere, claimed to have made that work popular throughout the globe but lamented never having heard it in the old days. He quotes composer Georges Auric, born in 1899, as telling him with melancholy: "Tu connais tout du Sacre sauf ce qu'il eut d'ahurissant la première fois." ("You know everything about *The Rite* except what was so stunning the first time.") (Was Auric, at age thirteen, at the premiere?) Markevich then comments: "Les oeuvres ont leur virginité que les conservatoires ignorent." ("Musical works have their own virginity which the academy can't know"—echoing Pascal's "The heart has its reason which Reason ignores.")

To know everything but the essential! Stravinsky's broadcast was on a Sunday afternoon, and the essential was imparted to me, if for no other reason than that I had no previous experience with which to compare it. On Monday I put all my birds into one large wicker cage —finches, waxbills, parakeets, and canaries—took them on the IC to Vaughan's Seed Store on Randolph Street, and sold the lot for seventeen dollars. From Randolph I walked to Lyon & Healy's on Van Buren, and with the money from the sale bought the score and disc of *The Rite of Spring*. For the next forty years I paid no further attention to birds, nor indeed to nature, and grew more and more nearsighted.

Then, in the summer of 1973, my friend James Holmes brought home a large middle-aged Russian Blue cat named Wallace, and I reverted. This was the start of menopause, my eyes increasingly improved, and whether or not I practice what I preach, the rights of all animals, even roaches, seem sacred.

Meanwhile, back in 1937, with all my comparative suavity in matters artistic, I had not yet had an orgasm, nor even knew the word.

7. Dance of the Adolescents

Jackson Park in the thirties—maybe long before, maybe still today —was an irregular verdant expanse free of commerce, extending south from Fifty-sixth Street to around Sixty-seventh Street, bounded on the west by Stoney Island and on the east by Lake Michigan. Like an indelible squish of Prussian violet from Manet's tube, Chicago's noble lake has governed all mundane actions inviolably for centuries. The university's sages, the floating corpses, are all as one to the water, the water. At the top of the park looms the Museum of Science and Industry erected in 1929 by Julius Rosenwald. Memory hints that the structure is two storied, the top half held up by giant caryatids of granite, themselves four yards above ground level on a ledge a foot deep. Upon this ledge Jean Edwards and I, for no other reason than that it was there, once walked sideways for the entire mile-long circumference. Into the museum proper, a year or two later, I ventured with Norris Embry, who headed straight toward a phonographic display which allowed you to hear your own voice. Into a hand-held microphone Norris intoned:

Margaret, are you grieving
Over Goldengrove unleaving?
Leaves, like the things of man, you
With your fresh thoughts care for, can you?

with such simple eloquence that even before he pressed the playback button, Hopkins's rhythm, new to me, was incised on my psyche and would become the source of my first true song. Behind the museum began the lagoon, wending its shallow path, wide and narrow, the length of the park and emptying into the Great Lake. A quarter mile from home, this area with its thousand crannies and thickets had been familiar since perambulator days. It was there that I, age eleven, had directed my steps in order to commit suicide, like Hedda Gabler, when Father refused to let me buy a pair of cinnamon canaries from the pet department of Marshall Field's ("We have enough birds in the house"), and where Father secretly trailed me in the new blue Buick.

By night Jackson Park is a cruising ground. Same trees, same by-ways, same oak and forsythia which in the afternoon seem real, even banal, change meaning as shadows take over. The city's mouth exhales over the vanished hubbub, emitting an incense of lust; children's cries melt into silence, the ever-present odor of the lake intensifies with menacing promise, a new provisional neighborhood vibrates on the old soil; and the lovers' lanes, so lately quaint and precise, become a blur of lewd possibility. In *The Grand Piano* Paul Goodman speaks of the hours that grow into years while "looking for love where it can't be found, waiting for love where it will not come," a refrain more familiar to gay than to straight citizens, if only because promiscuity is —was—a mode imposed from without. Might one argue that hetero-sexual males, given the opportunity for unpunished promiscuity, would jump at the chance? By extension they too might argue that sex with one person doesn't necessarily "get better"; on the contrary, the first time can be so great as to brook no repetition: anonymity releases inhibitions (idiocy being the goal of good sex), and man-as-animal shows his true nature. Gide even suggests (or makes his character Olivier suggest in *Les faux-monnayeurs*) that death is a lyrical reaction to the perfect screw—"He understood killing oneself, but only after having reached such heights of joy that anything afterward must be a descent." In any case, cruising in search of the chance encounter—an encounter more evaded than welcomed, since just around the corner something better, etcetera—is excellent exercise and geographically educational.

Such clever ruminations were far from my mind when Géorg Red-lich, knowing my limited sexual intercourse had hitherto been prac-ticed only among equally limited peers, led me into the park like a mother bear with her stupid cub, proposing to teach me the feints and ruses of the chase. I am not an aggressor (though I like to get my way), and my style, such as it was, would have to emerge solely through trial and error. So long as Géorg, or any other "peer" bent on mutual mischief, was with me in the park, I never did a thing.

One unseasonably mild March evening, when I was fourteen, I went alone into Jackson Park, veering now from the usual paths toward what was called The Wooded Island, a picturesque but remote area in the central lagoon, approached by bridges at either end that were closed off at midnight. Sporting a too-warm maroon crewneck sweater which I felt made an apt pedestal to offset my young head, and car-rying Anatole France's *Le lys rouge,* partly because it was bound in matching maroon leather and partly for conversational purposes (yet who would converse?), I was perspiring at the gorgeous horror of the unknown. I had almost reached the second bridge without passing a soul and was about to turn back and call it a night when a form materialized from the gloom and planted itself before me. This was a man—that is, not a boy but a grown-up, a mystery, aged nineteen or maybe thirty, a novel category. He was bigger than I, virile and wiry, with black curly hair and a two-day stubble, smelling dimly but sexually of gasoline and whisky. He could have been a garage mechanic, a trigonometry major, or a shoe salesman. He sized me up with a charcoal gaze, then without a word steered me under the bridge where he pushed me, calmly but firmly, onto a heap of dry ferns which seemed to be there for just this purpose. I was tense, confused, thrilled, passive, not as a woman but as a little boy, as he bestrode me like a sheet of hot snow from lips to ankles. For several moments he lay thus, not moving; then quickly opened his pants, and mine, and for perhaps five minutes ground down on me interfemorally until he spewed a liquid paste across my thighs and belly. No word was spoken. Again he lay still until his panting subsided. Rising up he buttoned his clothes, and with a "So long, kid," disappeared forever through the dark elms.

At home in bed his sweat remained with me, the eternal fragrance of Lake Michigan was wafted through the window infusing the little room as it had infused the park an hour ago, and I felt dizzy with unreleased violence. Next night I looked for him in vain, finding only *Le lys rouge* forgotten among the leaves. The next week too I looked, and for the next few months.

If I describe this adventure so "finely" it's because I had fallen in love. The heart, when first taken out of its antiseptic box and exposed to air, aches more poignantly than it ever will again. I blush to note it here, but soon after this episode I sketched music for the famous verses: "By night on my bed I sought him whom my soul loveth: I sought him, but I found him not. I will rise now, and go about the city in the streets, and in the broad ways I will seek him whom my soul loveth." (Knowledge of this poetry came not from any Bible class but from my first Dietrich movie, *Song of Songs.*) In fact, I sought the man with the stubble more than "in the broad ways": I sought him in the gardens of Monet, the novels of Genet, the preludes of Ravel, the statues of Easter Island, the biographies of Jack the Ripper, and in a thousand beds and bars of Europe and the East. The *not finding* is, in a sense, art. Though art isn't, conversely, not finding. (Picasso: "Je trouve d'abord, je cherche après.") (Imagine being rich as Croesus and able to trace the past. Imagine being led to "his" hospital room today in, say, Urbana or Wichita, or rather, to his grave. The joke of it!) Those musical sketches for "Song of Songs" I showed to Leo Sowerby, but didn't tell him what had impelled me toward the text. I never told anyone.

The park became a habit. I would sit on a bench or not sit, wait or not wait, talk or not talk to strangers. Mostly I was a prick-tease, not knowing quite what was expected of me, or too shy to initiate, even to acknowledge, what I might ache to perform. Would I go home to cry or masturbate? Not always. Sometimes I'd go to "their place" and not put out. Most often what was done was done in the grass. Risks in retrospect appear ghastly—weren't there muggings in the old days? Or was I too naive to sense danger in either anticipation or disappointment, and thus protected from evil? There is no god except for drunks, say the French.

Six conclusions:

1. Was he a child molester? (A mole-ster, as I used to misread the word, the way I misread goatherd as goath-erd.) The only trauma was a broken heart. I have never been molested by an adult, though as a minor I molested adults, in the sense of posing as inflammatory. The sense of myself as an erotic object, as it does with all children, came early. But I was never arrested for adult abuse.

2. The fact of being passive was something I took to like a duck to water, literally. That scene with the unshaven adult mirrors the imprinting of ducks which, hatched in a laboratory, think of humans as their mothers. Homosexuality is not a choice, but homosexual *roles* might be. The geography, the choreography, of our first gay experience, if we take to it (but we will take to it only if we're already queer), affects all ensuing experiences. Do I believe this? Or did my "role" already come naturally? (The business of role-playing may seem anathema to gays of the 1990s for whom turnabout seems always fair play.) My alcoholism, innate but revealed only years later, was at first an excuse to be passive without guilt. Yet to be passive—successfully so —is to be loved. Anyone can love, but to *be* loved requires qualities that are neither taught nor bought. *N'est pas aimé qui veut.*

3. Is the physically weaker person—the woman—always the subservient one? In choral music the basses are the bottoms, the sopranos the tops. But for every top there must be a bottom? Not so. An unaccompanied soprano can be convincing. Yes, but a single line always has an implied harmony supporting it from below. (To the ancient Greeks high and low in music meant the reverse of what they mean to us. Or so I once was told.)

4. Man is a preorganizer of his senses. That one sensual occasion, in all its solitudinous melancholy, did not make me what I was; I was

what I was and thus sought and recognized that one sensual occasion, an occasion replicated ten thousand times, in fantasy and fact, with ten thousand stubble-chinned males. By the same token I later came to sigh with exasperation—won't they ever learn!—when reading yet again some biographical phrase like: "Rorem's long years in France were crucial in determining his musical style." My musical style was determined at birth, and was fully realized before I moved to France. (What are "long years" as distinct from "short" ones?)

5. Homosexuality in itself is not interesting, any more than hetero-sexuality. Only as a political issue—which it nearly always is today—does it become worth talking about. Except, of course, in autobiographies. So there's my dirty little secret. Not so dirty, really, and hardly a secret. Little? No, big as a cyclone enveloping my every behavioral viewpoint since infancy.

6. I don't much care for the "me" herein portrayed. But then, I am not my type.

The Wooded Island by day was something else, a suite of small formal gardens shaded by large Japanese pavilions, relics from the 1893 world's fair. The two pavilions, one a tearoom-giftshop, the other a residence, were caretaken by Shoji and Frances Osato, a Japanese-American couple, very cultured. Mother and Father had chatted with them and, learning that their daughter Sono was a member of the Ballets Russes de Monte Carlo, told us about them—"us" being me and Perry O'Neil.

Perry remained the premier pianist in U-High, but we were hardly rivals—were in fact intimate despite his being an upperclassman. Dangerously intimate, Mother felt, playing all that "sentimental" music (her word for both Serge Koussevitzky and Artie Shaw) on the bedroom phonograph. In public Perry loved Rosemary, in private, me. We bought gallery tickets to every performance of the Ballets Russes, which arrived for a fortnight each Christmas at the Auditorium Theater. We apotheosized the stars who, by virtue of being tangible dozens of times each winter, became "friends," mute and glowing: stylish Riabouchinsky, craning her neck and flapping huge yellow wings before the curtain at the start of Rimsky's *Coq d'or;* pretty Baranova disguised as a frump in Nabokov's *Union Pacific;* exotic Toumanova in the blue-lit magic of Chopin's *Sylphides.* These girls were mere teenagers, like us, yet not that far from the great Diaghilev whom we had read about, over and over and over, in Romola Nijinsky's scandalous biography. The mature females were Danilova, wistful as she waved good-bye at the end of *Gaîtés parisiennes* and Tchernicheva, who as the sultana in *Scheherazade* seemed even then old-fashioned, like Pola Negri. The *danseurs nobles* were more enchanted still: Youskevitch, Frederick Franklin (with whom I would work in Washington a quarter century later), the volatile Massine with his already legendary *Tricorne,* and *Le rouge et le noir* based on Shostakovich's First Symphony, a masterpiece from the musician's nineteenth year. (No other nineteen-year-old in our century has written as flawless a work of that scope—not even in the France of Rimbaud, or in America, land of the young.) Sometimes these glimmering presences would come into the lounge during intermission, or into the auditorium drugstore where we had sodas after the show. They spoke French, Russian, seemed short and theatrical yet timid, like us, when we asked for autographs.

At home in our living room Perry and I (blush!) re-created *L'après-midi d'un faune,* using a mess of incense, scarves from Mother's cedar chest, and the tastelessly tasteful Stokowski record which gave new meaning to the concept of rubato by stretching solo lines of flute and oboe into an irresistible excruciation of silver taffy. Ah well, as the ever-wise Montaigne decreed: "It needs at least as much perfection to develop an empty theme as to sustain a weighty one." So Perry and I, like every adolescent in history (except maybe Rimbaud), confusing enthusiasm with self-expression, and self-expression with art, developed to perfection our empty theme.

To this spectacle—so oft rehearsed, so amateur—we invited the Osatos. Frances came with her younger Nisei daughter Teru, who, after my sister, Rosemary, was the most beautiful girl I'd ever seen, all ivory and jet and peach, with a smile inscrutably American. For them we danced our duet. Perry, I'm afraid, played the nymph, short hair and hirsute thighs, whisking out of sight at crucial moments to turn over the Red Seal disc. I "danced" the faun, inviolable and icy, ruminating on David Lichine's slow-motion antics, while audibly sniffing mucus as I sounded an invisible reed.

Frances in turn invited us to a matinee featuring, like a sparkler on the Fourth of July, Sono as chief odalisque in *Scheherazade.* And we went backstage. What a wonderland compared to Mary Wigman's backstage! The unchoreographed agitation of the corps rushing this way and that! The undisguised safety pins in Sono's pink costume ("No one sees them from the audience," she explained)! Her layers of makeup, and her indifference to me and Perry! Even so, Sono would become a friend in later years when the rest of the Osato clan had vanished.

Very young I had somehow learned that mixed marriages, being the opposite of incest, made for a balanced longevity. Looking now through the sheaf of melancholy letters, I am reminded of how Frances remained staunch. During the war she stayed with her husband in an internment camp (while her elder daughter, to keep hold on the ballet, became Sono Fitzpatrick), then divorced him, moved to New York where Sono became a semi-icon as the first ballerina to defect to Broadway in *One Touch of Venus*, while Frances herself became a high-class seamstress. We met often, went to the theater, and practiced songs at home together. Frances was handsome and elegant, continental out of Nebraska, and with a soprano voice which, though grainy and faint, sent thrills up the spine when she intoned Debussy's "Je tremble en voyant ton visage" and Basque folk tunes learned on the knee of her beloved French tutor, Bertelin. Proud of her son Tim's West Point career, Frances was chagrined that I allowed myself to be rated 4-F at my third and final induction examination, even after the war. Still, as a woman she felt ill-placed to lecture a man on patriotism since his very life was at stake. Today, feminists who feel that men get all the breaks, must bear in mind that millions of male teenagers, against their will, even against their awareness, are conscripted, indeed *jailed,* by their country to serve as cannon fodder. Again today, as a Quaker and pacifist, I could wish that women and gay men would spend less time petitioning for equal rights in the military and more time getting *rid* of the military.

I have a long letter from Frances, in her scrawl which could be Mother's, detailing her deterioration by cancer in 1952. Teru had died of the same at twenty-five. Now Tim, in 1954, wrote me of his mother's death, sending along a box of her precious songs. Tim himself, beset with an increasingly physical neurasthenia, killed himself a generation later. Sono, a treasured acquaintance, survives. Once while drunk in 1962 I took a bed rail and banged my left shin until it cracked and bled, for no other reason than to show my lover I was alive. My life was saved, over the years, by the tenets of AA, while that of Sono Osato is held together by other necessities.

Perry, meanwhile, and I understandably went "all the way" with our sentimental revels. Not just *The Afternoon of a Faun,* but *Daphnis and Chloë, The Rite of Spring,* and tens of other Stokowski interpretations whose sensuous exaggeration goaded us down the primrose path. We "had sex," lost our cherries—if that loss can be defined through nonejaculatory friction. (For a decade, after I'd slept with hundreds of men, the concept of virginity still seemed represented as something one lost only to the opposite sex. Though virginity's where you find it; mine had been lost, all alone, to Igor Stravinsky. Could current times define grown-up sex as anything that might cause AIDS?) Ejaculatory friction came months later with D., more male than Perry, with gnarled biceps and ruddy cheeks. D. had gained cachet on the block not only by being a super athlete with super grades, and by playing the risky game of pressing our neck arteries so as to produce in us a popperlike swoon, but of teaching other boys to cum. When in the intimacy of his gray sheets he brought me to orgasm I thought something terribly wrong had exploded in my urethra. Yet for a week I masturbated three times a day, winnowing that down to twice, then once a day for months. Those wads of Kleenex, those mucky socks. D. was straight, merely horny. He became an eminent professional still in Chicago's South Side. Perry, after premiering Ravel's *Left-hand Concerto* rippingly with the WPA's new Illinois Symphony under Madame Antonia Brico in 1941, premiering my own Second Sonata in WQXR in its first version ten years later, and recording the four MacDowell sonatas on a small label, suddenly quit. He was a terrific pianist, far better than I, with an infallible metronomic instinct, mercurial fingers in Rachmaninoff as in Scarlatti, a neat, ruby tone, and a dependable, caring style in chamber music. But as prodigy confronting the real world he found the rat race unremunerative, threw in the sponge, and became a librarian. Today he lives quietly on Jane Street with his friend Tom and never listens to Stokowski. (I just phoned him. He said: Sure, write anything you want.)

Like everyone of my generation I was weaned on Leopold Stokowski. From *Saint Matthew* to *Sacre* "his" classics give off an opulence so contagious that we were all immured in the viewpoint—or earpoint —whether or not we approved. Being idolized by the idle rich and the vast unwashed, as well as by specific eccentrics (i.e., poor composers), Stokowski became, with the Garbo-*Fantasia*-Vanderbilt era, a legend. Legends, emerging as they do from myths, can never by definition be touched personally; and indeed, I never truly knew the man. But we did have a certain personal rapport which I now recall with mixed feelings. To peek ahead for a minute:

During the early 1950s we were introduced a couple of times in Paris. His cool social loftiness, in contrast to his conductorial fire, intimidated. I had no idea that he remembered these meetings (maybe he didn't), much less that he knew my music, when a decade later he included my *Eagles* on his debut (!) concert with the Boston Symphony. I was impressed that he had not contacted me, that he had not (unlike most performers who deign to play American music) insisted on a first performance; rather, that he simply programmed this already published music as though it were a natural repertory item. His broad-cast of *Eagles* (10 March 1964) was the most scintillating interpreta-tion I ever heard. I admired Stokowski, as all composers must, for the attitude that the newness of new music is irrelevant to its worth: our music is music, not "modern music." . . . When I told him this a year later (at another of those strained backstage encounters), he greeted the praise with a glazed stare and didn't seem to know who I was.

Nevertheless, in 1972, he performed me again. In my diary for 2 March I noted: "With a mild sense of guilt I went alone last night to *A Clockwork Orange* at precisely the moment when Leopold Stokowski, in Town Hall, was conducting my *Pilgrims for Strings.* Now Stokowski is a great man, an idol of my childhood, . . . but I don't like *Pilgrims* anymore. My contention: the worse a piece is the worse it will sound the better it's played, like a wart in a well-focused photo. Apparently the maestro gestured for me to rise, but I was invisible, so he shrugged and went on to the next work. (I know about this from the newspaper. No one invited me either to a rehearsal or to the program.)"

A month later I sent to Leopold Stokowski a ninetieth-birthday hom-age in the guise of a heartfelt and handwrought salute. He never acknowledged it.

Back in the 1930s I was less *désinvolte.* On Fifty-fifth next to the Frolic where we had seen *Madame Butterfly* and the scarifying *Before Dawn* with Warner Oland (I longed to flee but was restrained by braver cohorts) was a shop where you could buy sheet music, not just the latest hits from *Flying Down to Rio* or *Going Hollywood,* but classical scores. I still have the iron-blue copy of *Rhapsody in Blue* with my childish fingerings noted, and Gershwin's own recording, neurotic and true. And I still have the aria (what was an aria?) for which I composed the text that starts: "Poor Boris lives in an attic, We love him though he lives in an attic," to the rifled tune from *Carmen*'s duet which Father used to sing all by himself: "Tout cela, n'est-ce pas, mignonne, de ma part, tu le lui diras."

(An aria—if not by definition, at least by tradition—is designed for applause and is a part of a larger issue. A song, by its nature of minia-ture, is . . .)

Earlier in these pages I hinted that as a child I felt the cosmos to be my own invention, and that I still to some extent believe this. I did not magnanimously add, Don't we all?, because the "we" was also, by definition, my fabrication. Do I then feel alone in the universe? Yes, except that the universe does not exist except in my conditioned imagination. (Conditioned by whom?) Life is merely one minor possible result of the Big Bang. Reality's dreary, art's dreary. Those quadrillion lifeless galaxies out there are surely as curious, as *potential,* as Earth, which we perceive with only our five miserable senses. Yet I alone created and imagine it. Did I too create my own limited perceptions, an inability to grasp the nuances of philosophy, government systems, mathematical formulas? Did I create them so as *not* to understand them?

Maybe that's all guff, but it's me, my paragraph. Still the paragraph can't explain, since I myself can't, a lingering remoteness from other people and their concerns. It *does* explain my ease at aping Mallarmé's faun, French par excellence. But if France means cool, or at least objective, why can I, who am distant, be so moved by that country's art, while finding the universe—be it God's or mine—so second rate? Am I the author of my own auto-da-fé, should it arrive? Or of the various expensive and painful physical woes that beset me this past winter? Is it odd that Thomas Mann a century ago invented a German protagonist, in his *Disillusionment,* with whom I feel the most . . . not empathy exactly, but identity? ("Yes, death is awful and love is wonderful, but not *that* wonderful and awful"—the source, Jerry Leiber once told me, of his lyric for Peggy Lee, "Is That All There Is?")

Yes, I am an atheist. There is no God, nor will I be cajoled by smarmy shots at metaphor—"Oh, Mr. Rorem, your music is so beautiful! Surely music is your God"—unless they make me, myself, God— a God I can't believe in. No, I don't believe in Him, but I do believe in Belief, and in the sincerity of such Belief, which has long inspired both great and wretched works of art. Some of these works have been sources for my musical impulses. Among my earliest real songs were Psalm settings. It was not my belief in God but my belief in King David's belief in God that caused these settings to be. My musical catalogue is vast (although listed on paper it looks vaster than it lasts since hundreds of titles are simply two-minute songs). Half of that large oeuvre is choral, and half of *that* in turn is what the trade calls "sacred"—a musicalizing of texts suitable for church. Why do I set these texts? Because I am commissioned. (Brahms, to a fan who asks why his slow movements are so beautiful: "Because the publishers order them that way.") If such sacred choral works are my sideline— my pornography, as Gore Vidal once termed his pseudonymous novels—they may nonetheless be seen (heard) by posterity, if there is such a thing (but of course there is, since I alone proclaim it), as my best works. A poet's personal convictions have nothing to do with his quality; and what, anyway, is a sideline: I have not composed an uncommissioned piece in decades.

Does one stop living in order to write about having lived? Is autobiography different in kind from symphonic composition? Symphonies do not demonstrably deal with facts of the past, nor even facts as they are currently perceived.

Autobiography meanwhile is not, as GBS would have it, the ultimate lie. We are who we pretend to be. We are our own invention, which distinguishes us from animals. (Doesn't it?)

Recurring dream: I sit at a Steinway in front of seven judges. They say: Sight-read, up to tempo, this twenty-minute *Etude in Sevenths* by Schoenberg. If you succeed you will be given the kingdom of heaven; if you miss one note your hands will be chopped off.

People I meet in foreign towns today are generally concert managers, conductors, and affable hostesses to whom I send thank-you notes and never see again. When I revisit Hyde Park, as a side excursion during infrequent visits in the line of duty to Chicago, not one old friend remains in the city that was once my world. (Virgil Thomson in later life: "When I go to Rome now, I don't know a soul except the American ambassador and the pope.") The weird thing is how little has changed; a new cast of actors in the same old décor. Or almost the same. Nothing, nothing is left of the brief block of one-story artist studios just east of the IC tracks on Fifty-seventh Street. That was once our neighborhood's Bâteau-Lavoir. Roff Beman, Géorg Redlich, Gertrude Abercrombie, how many vanished painters, brought to the fore by the WPA and its local director, Norman MacLeish (Archibald's brother), were toiling and giggling and drinking and dying within a bohemia that casually bisected the university milieu of my parents! Musicians too. There were the young George Perle and Laura Slobe with their fierce intelligence and bodies like Lembrecht sculptures, and John Cage passing through with his crew cut and idiosyncratic gamelans. Charlie Biesel was the crosspoint, elderly with rheumy eyes and a conventional easel style. At one of his parties somewhere in 1937 Mother and Father met and liked Belle Tannenbaum, who became my next piano teacher.

Belle was a big-time local virtuoso and free-lance professor, bitter competitor of Molly Margolies's, who was Ganz's tenured assistant and scapegoat. Belle immediately tried to straighten my Impressionist bent by pushing the more "honorable" repertoire of Haydn. She was maybe fifty, four feet eleven, plump, with spindly calves, platinum hair, a huge bosom and tight black dresses, a coarsely amicable social

style, and the keyboard technique of Horowitz. I adored her. Pianisti-
cally she was capable of anything. Her fingers glittered like—as she
herself put it—greased lightning, in such bonbons as Ernst Toch's
Juggler or the delicious bagatelles of the young Tcherepnin. But she
played lentissimo too. Any Chopin nocturne was as satisfying as it will
ever need to be, with its proper waits and weights.

Thanks to Belle we cashed in the old Stark and invested in a newish
Steinway B. I can still see us that afternoon in Lyon & Healy's wide
storeroom crowded with the winged horses, Belle testing the mahogany lids with her tiny fists, kicking at the brittle wooden legs which
she likened to her own "piano legs" (though aren't true piano legs
those foot-thick cylinders found on earlier models?), sitting now at this
keyboard, now at that, each time easily playing—as though opening a
faucet of nectar—the infinitely ruminative Prelude in G by Rachmaninoff. She sculpted my life as a pianist.

My life as a composer remained unsupervised. Was there formal training for teenage composers in Chicago? Is there indeed such a beast
today, other than through imitation? I continued writing pieces "in the
style of," not knowing then, as I still don't know, that Art must be
Original, though I'd already heard Rimbaud's much misused dictum,
and thought it snazzy: "Il faut être absolument moderne."

Without ever having met another composer, something already told
me that Originality is at best a minor virtue. Anyone can build a better
mousetrap, but it still snares the same old mice. Poulenc, Britten,
never set down an underivative measure, yet their every measure is
stamped with their personality, involuntarily. In the thirties aesthetes
shrieked their awe at Stravinsky's newness, while I, in my inadvertently
proper education (that of learning my own century first and foremost),
took Stravinsky as a *donnée,* not knowing, as I would years later, that
all his devices were stolen goods.

Minor artists borrow, great ones steal. All art is clever theft. Conscious that he is stealing, the artist seeks to cover his traces. In so
doing he expresses himself despite himself. The act of covering one's
traces is the act of creation.

Art is a misquotation of something already heard. Thus, it becomes
a quotation of something never heard.

When I noted that all happy families are happy in their own way, I
meant that there is a banality to sorrow, while communal respect
seems rare. Not that happiness should be life's goal; can one be happy

when half the world's burning as the other half fiddles? But happiness that is a wise pooling of resources, a healthy eccentricity sparked by the conjoining of disparate gifts, was a part of the Rorem family's unconscious pact.

Oh, we did have misunderstandings, even violent quarrels despite Quakerism. Concerning their early apprehension of my homosexuality, for example, my parents, who simply didn't know about such things (maybe just vaguely through Bourdet's *The Captive,* that radioactive coal on the shelf) felt it was "wrong." At least Mother did. Father tried, but just couldn't fathom the male torso as an erotic reference. They both, I think, considered gayety a phase, a touch of glamour to garb my passing artiness. Still, they trundled me off to a psychoanalyst, female. I just sat there. Refused to speak. Unlike most analysts, who themselves are mute, inciting patients to jabber madly, this woman prodded me. Silence. She told my parents they had "nothing to worry about," that I was assuredly normal. And so I was: normally queer. That was the law, set down then and there, no further discussion. Rosemary and Mother and Father and I were maybe a bit uneasy, but we were "happy" with it.

Not that they weren't aware of The Other. Even snide at times, to my insincere surprise, for I too was snide, and cruelty comes natural to children. True, they'd joined the Society of Friends as counteraction to the human trait of collective hate. Yet Father was capable of saying at the theater, "If I leave my seat during intermission, I might come back and find it occupied by a Jewess." And he liked the rabbi's quip about the synagogue defecting to Quakerism: "Some of my best Jews are Friends." If they were easier on Negroes, was it that Negroes were more vulnerable in those prewar years? In later years Mother, always suspicious of foreign languages, could refer to the influx of skinny Puerto Rican females as "jabbering birds." She believed in equality for all, but shunned physical inconvenience (as I do) more than did Father, maybe because she was raised poor. Like Marc Blitzstein, who forever championed the working class but avoided rubbing elbows with them unless they were rough trade (which wasn't quite elbows). Were the poor, when you got to know them, more worthy, more interesting, than the well off?

Quakerism did explain my fascination for Catholicism, my eventual alcoholism, my preemptively edgy conversation, the need to be dominant in the parlor and submissive in the bedroom, and grossly shy, like Baudelaire's self-tormenter.

Je suis la plaie et le couteau!
Je suis le soufflet et la joue!

Je suis les membres et la roue
Et la victime et le bourreau.

Trying to revive the origins of these conclusions I think back. But everything fades. The smells, the bodies, the woods at night, all music, all anxiety. Nothing remains. The wind remains.

8. U-High—Part I

Chicago 1940—Clockwise from front: Hatti Heiner (with bottle), *cousin Lois Nash, Mother, Father, Rosemary, with NR in center.*

Summer of 1937 I went to Camp Highlands in upstate Wisconsin, while Rosemary went to Camp Osoha, allowing our parents, for the first time ever, a month to themselves. Mother afterward felt guilty. Camp wasn't going to toughen me, and why should one be toughened anyway; group living proved nothing except that it wasn't for me. I was less lonely than bored: songfests, ball games, competition, blurring of singularity into common fun seemed aimless. Perry had been there for a month before me and was the life of the party. During recreation he played the piano in the dining room—early Debussy, Mompou's *Scènes d'enfants,* as well as Mozart and Scarlatti—and managed with his panache to hold the attention in a manner inconceivable with such an age group today.

We were less close now—he, reveling in popularity, I, a lone wolf

—but we did manage to swipe together a mass of provisions from shop (brushes, chisels, canvases; why I don't know) and to hide them beneath our beds in separate dorms. When the loot was found during a general search, I pleaded innocent—it had been "planted." (I continued to steal longer than most kids. Not only discs from Lyon & Healy's but in college, a score of Delius's *Summer Night on the River* and of Ravel's *Trois chansons* from the Northwestern library—I have them still and they've served me well. I always denied everything, smiling inscrutably when confronted, wondering why nobody saw through me.)

News of George Gershwin's early death that July reached even Camp Highlands, and I was shocked. I remember wandering off alone to the algae-covered frog pond that glowed in sad shafts of fragrant green sunshine, and jerking off (jacking off, as they say in the Middle West) into the water. I remember at 3 a.m. lifting the blanket of the boy in the bunk next to mine, to shine my flashlight on his extremely circumcised erection. And I remember a counselor, who ran the shop class, being investigated for having had some pupil jack *him* off. It somehow seemed so unimportant.

I also took a couple of bassoon lessons supervised by fat Mr. Vail, the chorus master, who was also the music instructor back at U-High. Back at U-High that fall Mr. Vail, along with teaching everyone to sing college songs in unison, presented an "appreciation" course that included *La mer* and *Boléro*. Invited by my parents, Mr. Vail came chez nous to hear me play, so that I could gain special dispensation from gym in order to practice. Besides a Mozart rondo, I showed off with Cyril Scott's *Autumn Idyll,* a seductive wisp of treacle (is that a proper metaphor?) which he thought the loveliest thing he'd ever heard.

After Vail's class, in that big room on the ground floor of Belfield Hall, Bruce and I used to play our own new records, notably Edgard Varèse's dumbfounding *Ionization* for thirteen percussion instruments. This rasping etude with its moaning sirens and jangly drums, as conducted by Slonimsky, enraptured us. It was original, risky, kinetic, cultish, the true way. To a few stray students who had hung around, we explained that this was Bach. *Late* Bach.

Autres temps, autres moeurs. How tame it sounds today! A new CD of Boulez conducting Varèse shows the breathtaking derivativeness of a big work like *Amériques.* It could be from a notebook of rejects for *The Rite of Spring* in its tantrumlike tunes, rhythms, harmonies. Indeed, all of Varèse's music is warmed-over Stravinsky, shapeless, charmless, irritating. *Ionization* itself, once so necessary, now comes off as merely decorative. Is there any Western music in which nonpitched battery behaves as more than maquill-age?

Most of us kids had grown up together from nursery school. Now the autumn brought new faces.

Maggy Magerstadt. Impossible to underestimate her urgency in my life, all the more singular in that she wasn't interested in music, that is, classical music. Apple-cheeked, blond as an apricot, quite good figure, brash. The brashness, in the shape of wisecracks backed by intelligence, blew fresh air into uptight U-High. She had the larynx of a man, and perfected a cruel imitation of Tom Nell, our class's prize baritone, singing "The Road to Mandalay." Her grades were even worse than mine; like many with low grades she grew up and is today more cultivated literarily and geographically than most of her grade-A money-making classmates. Maggy was an actress with brains, if that is not an oxymoron, more popular with girls than with boys, and the boys she knew were likely to be out of school and older. Except for me. She was, I believe, protective of if impatient with me, appreciating my less-than-callow (which in memory seems pure corn) contrast to the local mob. I was drawn to her extroversion, her catholicity. We dated, yes we did, for four years going to the school dances. There they stood, the girls in their peach taffeta formals with azure velvet trim; the boys, eyes to the ceiling, in their white summer tuxes, chic and silly. Me and Maggy, willfully contrary, in saddle shoes and day-time wardrobe, chewing gum. Never did I feel a part of anything, accepted, still don't. Suppose I were? The confinement! But only now is that apparent. Then it was the frustration of youth, unable to explain itself to itself. . . . After the dances we'd go downtown to gay bars: Waldman's in Michigan Avenue where the jukebox blared Ella Fitzger-ald's "Cootchie Coo" and where members of the all-male clientele would send glasses of champagne to our table, amused that these dewy juveniles couldn't get otherwise served; the Rush Street bars, and two hangouts in far west borderline neighborhoods, one called Ganna Walska's and another simply The Club Gay, whose plump owner, Babe, played piano. We were good jitterbuggers and could cut the Big Apple fine.

Frazier Rippy, overweight with his cardigan sweater and coy curls, looked like the child singer Bobby Breen and got good grades. He was mannered, even precious, but could, when called upon, become persuasively imperious: he played Creon to Maggy's Antigone in the Playfesters' production, and they both meant business. When I gradua-ted to Northwestern in 1940, he and Maggy stayed on at the University of Chicago. After we had all migrated to New York, he was the first to move on to Europe, choosing Rome over Paris, dubbing Italian movies for a living, even acting a little: in Fellini's *8½* he played the cardinal's secretary. In the late 1970s he committed suicide, perhaps for reasons of the heart.

Hatti Heiner reappeared now at ballet intermissions, ripe, purse-lipped, hay-colored, opinionated, and we became close again—one could only be near or far with Hatti. Though she had "taken" dance, as I took piano, with local modern-dance luminaries like Kurt & Grace Graff and Bertha Ochsner, she now turned up her nose at "self-expression," preferring the colder Russian mode of style-before-content.

Other balletomanes not connected with U-High were Don Dalton and Dick Jacob, two years older than us, roommates on Ellis Avenue. They already had jobs in the Loop, and were pals of David Fox upstairs. Dick was effete, smart, a touch nasty, with a shock of bright hair and too full lips. Don was more direct, clever but less smart. A first remembrance of them was on coming home late with Maggy, when the parents were still out, and finding our parlor rearranged: the naked statuette of the Venus de Milo turned to the wall, the firescreen upsidedown, books neatly refiled. Dick and Don, not finding David in, had knocked on our door and cousin Olga, enchanted, had let them in. Dick aspired to dramaturgy, and for a while was a BMOC at the university as author of a wildly popular review called *Those Who Are Fools*. As with Perry O'Neil, he eventually surveyed his artistic past without bitterness but with disinterest. As for Don, what would he have become, had not the war killed him in 1944?

Géorg Redlich we—Rosemary and I—met as follows. One of our parents' hard-drinking Bâteau-Lavoir chums, Roff Beman, felt that his pair of beautiful daughters should mingle a bit in a genteel ambiance. They came to dine, all dressed up, they smoked, dabbed at their plates, conversation faltered, until we asked them to introduce us to their bohemia. Géorg, who spelled his name German style but with the *accent aigu* and pronounced it Gay-org, was the nicest person in my life. Short, plain, a limp from polio, Jewish, with ulotrichous hair, a smile that lit the sky and a gift for listening as well as for imparting, he was a painter—Modigliani merged with Van Gogh, not bad. Very poor, as were his parents and siblings, all living at the Century Hotel on Fifty-fifth, supported by the WPA. Géorg was twenty-three, the officially sanctioned "fairy" in the militant left wing of our local artist colony. That colony did and did not approve of nonpolitical "capitalists" like the Rorems. We were doubtless more borderline between the haves and the have-nots than other university families. Everyone loved Géorg. His studio was a meeting place, a ground of truce when not of amicability, with our host setting the tone and sitting on the floor.

He declared himself in love with me. But what did I know of love, especially with one so physically uninviting? He settled for instructing me, like the madam of a whorehouse, in what he felt were the ruses of seduction, and preened when drones approached, in bars or parties or parks, not admitting that the approach was not toward an experienced geisha but toward an available boy. Géorg was the first to instill in me a notion of myself as more than a baby brother. His life would be short, but during what remained of it he was a unique friend, good without being wishy-washy.

David Sachs, maverick from a normal North Side fatherless Jewish family, phoned me after Rosemary, who'd met him at a party, said she had a brother "who wrote poetry." In fact I had even written a book. It was titled (gulp!) *The Door to Sorrow's Chamber,* combining the styles of Oscar Wilde, Radclyffe Hall, and James T. Farrell in a loose tale of Chicago behavior among the very young and bright and drunk. But I had never encountered a scholarly intellectual of my generation. David Sachs, impudent, of roan pigmentation, and resembling already at sixteen the famous bust of Socrates, was so far beyond me in literary repertory and organized thought that while praising my body he belittled my taste (except in music, which, like most intellectuals, he knew nothing about), giving me the inferiority complex which to some extent is retained still. David was self-assured, bad-mannered, disavowing of his sires, terribly likable, and, like Géorg, something of a pet of my parents, who dubbed him "the redheaded poet." Though not joined to the university as either student or teacher, he had connections there and took me to weekly gatherings of a poetry club, which convened in the Harriet Monroe Library. In the shadow of McKeon's protégés—Paul Goodman, Tom Stauffer, Edouard Roditi, Bill Earls, glib philosophers already in their late twenties—I learned to keep mum about my crush on Amy Lowell ("Christ! What are patterns for?" said the weary seamstress) when Ezra Pound was talked about. Paul Goodman, years afterward when he had become the poet to whom, as a composer, I most often petitioned for usable texts, recalled his most Proustian souvenir. In 1934, scarcely knowing me, he and Roditi had stopped by our Dorchester Avenue apartment as a lark, to pay an impromptu visit. Mother said, "Sit down, young men, Ned will be right out." To prepare an entrance, I washed my hair. By the time I emerged they had left.

Was there nothing David did not expound upon in his incongruous upper-class voice and above-it-all stance ("Don't be dismayed, dear Ned, just because my vocabulary consists of a few hundred more words than yours")? He would even be granted a cameo, as Miss Flora Sachs, in Goodman's first novel, *The Grand Piano*. But David did not develop as an inventor, nor, after a few years, did he persist. He went to Saint John's College in Annapolis, then to England for a while, then became a star in the philosophy department at Johns Hopkins. His habitual loftiness merging with teacherliness when we were kids was occasionally shattered by susceptibility. Look at this note—the only one I ever had from him—penned in red ink, with its echoing, mannered tone and final twist of Conrad Aiken so in vogue back then. It is honest, hence touching. And isn't the reference to art as "that formal sigh" as apt this evening as it was when David Sachs slipped these words under my door fifty-five years ago?

> Ned—This is the only water to write with in the house. Now, after this time, let me say this: I think your self, or what is you, is beautiful. That your person can still image as uncorrupt a landscape as any. That within you there is possible that formal sigh given to a handful. I doubt that I have it. . . .
> Believe me your physical presence has little for me. It is that which is not stuff of touch. Which is always wanting to bathe in pure waters. To wash what has been, and what is. Be alone, you will learn yourself. For those waters in your eye, are more than your eye.
> David

Another friend appearing extracurricularly in the late thirties was the Evanston painter Norris Embry. What was one to make of that body, so Christ-like and proto-Giacomettian, that troubled and lovely face resembling the young Cocteau's, the breathless speech, part world weary and part juvenile, which never uttered banalities, the sadness, the craziness? He went to a different school, never quite fit in, but hung around, knowing everyone and everything but remaining forever an anchorite. He too went on to Saint John's College, site of neurotic male Wasp geniuses, was expelled from there, then from other schools, for being, so far as I can judge in retrospect, not so much drunk as overly fanciful. He would fall out of windows, break bones, get beat up by rough trade, send poems and poseys to impossible recipients (movie stars, prizefighters), and end up for long stays in loony bins. During one such stay, exasperated and done in by the academic specialists' Freudian prying, he finally, out of sheer boredom, rushed to the door, pointed down the hall, and screamed: *"RABBITS! Here they come!"* For that he was given an A.

Norris set up house eventually in Mykonos, where the locals found him apparently no weirder than most Americans, and where he could dispense his meager but regular allowance (the family paid him to stay away) on wine, men, and song. For all of us over the years, wherever and whenever Norris appeared, he was as welcome for his adaptability (he could just curl up over there in the corner) as for his huge talent. For he worked as hard as he played. He never sent a letter (and he sent thousands) without enclosing an inked comic strip à la Dubuffet of what he was up to. During none of these "appearances" was he without a suggestion for a poem I might set to music. This poem he would immediately write out from memory on the back of a menu, and yes, I *would* set it to music. My dearest songs are those that would not have existed but for Norris. (I have no taste in poetry, but infallible taste in those who do.) I saw him last in Baltimore in 1979, with David Sachs, at his filthy flat. He was an outpatient at Johns Hopkins. I bought three powerful paintings. They hang in my front hall. He died two years later, aged fifty-nine.

Then there were Rosemary's beaux, in whose presence I for too long played precocious kid brother. Chief among these for a time was Donald—known as Didi (he was born in China)—Robertson, who lived down toward International House on Dorchester, with two brothers and parents, cultured to the gills. (It was on their Capeheart that we had first heard *Daphnis* melting out onto the pavement, though Robertson père thought it would be healthier for us to heed Mozart.) Didi was bright and infantile, cute, straight, big crush on my sister, a devotee of Aristotle as well as the then-in-vogue Saroyan, and a terrific pop pianist. He grew up to marry a pop singer, and to play in jazz bands, and to take very seriously Elvis Presley. His effervescence lacked mystery.

This dramatis personae was not a gang. It included from time to time our cousins, Kathryn and Lois Nash, who came from Yankton for protracted stays, and who fit neatly into the rounds of bars. Many of the cast scarcely knew, or cared for, the others; the common bond was me. Nearly everyone had dallied with at least one other member. Did anyone say "I love you"?

Love? Well, at least it shows you you're alive. Can anything else positive be claimed for the asinine folly? (I speak here about being in love, not about loving *tout court*.) Unrequited, nothing productive comes from the anguish. Requited, it's *égoisme à deux*. Either way there's little to show for it, except scars without a battle. Being in love doesn't take you out of yourself, the way, say, that "good works" or art are said to do; it takes you into yourself. Sex and love are mutually exclusive, and sex as an exercise is probably the healthier of the two.

That said (I could not have thought so back then), did we pause to consider it? Love was a phenomenon in the air more than now, a "commitment." But how could I so soon consider Love, in the light of Edouard Roditi at the poetry club intoning in his continental accent, Kay Boyle's oh-so-sophisticated *Defense of Homosexuality* ("I speak of it as a thing with a future/As yet badly done by amateurs/Neglecting the opportunity to be discriminating. . . . a vocation as engrossing as bee raising/And as monotonous to the outsider")?

We all smoked a lot, as did our parents. In my case it was nontipped Chesterfields, even after king-sized filters arrived. A pack a day from 1937 to 1972, about a million and a half cigarettes.

We all drank a lot, mostly draft beer, sometimes Tom Collinses when on a date, later dry martinis at any time of day or night. In retrospect, except for me and Norris, I don't recognize it as a developing problem for anyone.

We all drove around a lot in our families' cars—those whose families had cars. This did not include Géorg or Dick Jacob or the Young Communist Leaguers, by definition poor. It was Rosemary who taught me to drive, one morning in an empty parking lot near Jackson Park, and Don Dalton, a week later, who threw me into the maelstrom of the Loop, where no one was allowed to sink. I was a skilled driver, drunk or sober, denting the fender no more than three or four times. I chalked up 100,000 miles before leaving the Midwest for good, end of 1942. I never drove again, though in 1961 when I tried for a license renewal in Provence, I failed. God no longer wanted me to drive.

No sooner did I learn than Miriam Carey, who was "fast," urged me to take her to that same empty parking lot and "neck."

Maggy Magerstadt was hardly so aggressive. Because we were in classes together daily and "went out" in the evenings, we were all inseparable. Indeed, when Maggy flunked algebra in Miss John's junior class, I flunked too, on purpose, so as to stay with her the following year. We loved each other but without carnality. Here is the moment to say that, despite the until recently dispelled *idée reçue,* I am no descendant of Oedipus. I adore my father. And I adore women. I like to dance with them, comb their hair, listen to their logic, which, when educated, seems tighter than male logic. I like to read their books, see them act, feel their clothes. I like everything about women except sexual contact. That instantaneous Yes or No with which we silently size up everyone we meet, for me was never Yes with women. Even with men, I'm indifferent to perhaps 99 percent. Of course, the remaining 1 percent takes up a great deal of room.

The sense of removal I spoke of springs consciously from this period, although possibly the sense was there from birth. We choose, after all, which specific moments to be influenced by; and if I have no moral instinct, at least I select the "right" people to emulate in a moral climax. An incident lingers. Autumn of 1937 we went en masse to Capra's *Lost Horizon*. Its premise was strange and alluring, as was the scenery. But even then I saw through the sexist smarm, and the unexplained contradiction in the murder by the Shangri-la contingent of a Chinese pilot so as to kidnap the Caucasian passengers into a finer world. When the movie was over, Didi Robertson, moved to the quick, sat, head in hands, long after the lights came up and other filmgoers had filed out. I waited unenthralled like the Black Fairy, until we could escort Didi in tears from the theater. It struck me as vulgar that one might so publicly show one's emotions, and as obscene that these emotions should spring from such a specious load of crap. Spontaneity, like overreaction, embarrassed me.

Liquor would become a great leveler, a mode for, among other virtues, indulging silliness like Didi's with a clear conscience. I drank intensely and often, though not yet to the point of losing consciousness and suffering blackouts. I worked intensely and often, already to the point of finding oblivion in a concentration that ignored the rights of others, or even the fact of others. A universal but unspoken conundrum had begun to swell like a boil inside me, continuing with the years but never bursting: How can an artist attain the discipline to create lasting beauty without simultaneously being seduced, even dissipated, by that beauty? (Beauty, of course, doesn't mean just roses: a Greco crucifixion is as "beautiful" as a Boucher nude. Not content, but form: artists don't primarily deal in subject matter—despite what Didi and other layfolk prate about "inspiration"—so much as in shape; *The Rite of Spring* in all its complexity is perfect, i.e., inevitable; you need only change one note to introduce a rotten apple.) I resolved the paradox, unlike Mann's Aschenbach, by slicing the Gordian knot, having my cake and eating (drinking) it. Those who say, "If only Ned hadn't been so self-indulgent, etcetera, what he could have produced!" aren't talking of Ned but of some romantic hero who thinks Good Thoughts. Artists don't think Good Thoughts, though they sometimes describe them. Only saints are good. *Et encore!*

Arthur Danto, *The Nation*'s long-winded art critic, recently asked himself why he was never convinced by the paintings of Francis Bacon. Then he came upon an interview wherein Bacon claimed that the *Screaming Pope* series was not a trauma about, or a commentary on, life today, merely studies of a screaming pope. Danto, decreeing what should or should not preoccupy creators as they create, concluded that Bacon was superficial. I can't read Danto anymore without giggling. (Kafka, according to Max Brod, who told Manuel Rosenthal, who told me, thought of his stories as studies: *The Penal Colony* to him was a great joke.) The artist is simply a conduit twixt the Great Unknown and the concertgoer, and need have no fixed notions of his own. He is god without a message. We consumers will make the message.

As I type this paragraph there is a drizzle over Nantucket the late morning of 27 July 1992. The sky is dark and cold, crows and gulls squawk out there, the lamp is on in here, while downstairs ensues a lulling, undecipherable conversation between Veronica and Danny, teenagers from the Dominican Republic whom, along with two others, JH has brought out for the week. Danny is ironing. In faraway Yugoslavia women and children and animals, men and churches and museums, are inanely slaughtered. Masses of bismuth-hued roses in the backyard (I perceive them over the top of my glasses as I write) are fading. The drizzle has stopped, at least momentarily. Who beyond myself is aware of this congruence of "messages"? What's important and what's not? By afternoon I, too, will have forgotten, or at least rejuggled the priorities of, these discrepancies. How much more imprecise are the distant episodes in a memoir, my viewpoint shifting day by day according to mood and sharpness of recall. All is mercury. There simply is no past. But neither is there a present.

Rosemary was having an affair with an older boy. She had begun to frequent a branch of the YCL, or Young Communist League, which convened, at least on social occasions, in the minuscule one-story shack of a Morry Wessel, on Fifty-seventh across from Steinway's drugstore. It was there we heard for the first time records of Milhaud's gigantic *Choéphores* (did I already know his *Création du monde?*), Carillo's *Preludio al Cristóbal Colón* (eerier even than *Ionization*), and, almost incongruously, "The Red Army Song," while drinking wine from gallon jugs. And it was there that Rosemary met a Japanese-American named Bob Chino, known to all simply as Chino. He was sinewy, cocky, handsome (a male counterpart of Teru Osato), caramel colored, defensive, very political. Politics, then as now, was low on my list; to me the YCL crowd was appealing—unlike their later one-track-minded humorlessness—for their rowdy, liberated artiness and magnanimity rather than for their concern with world injustice. But the stinking winds of Nazism were blowing over our chaste Midwest. One afternoon in Scammons Gardens I overheard some kids improvising lyrics to the then-popular ditty "You, Too, Can Be the Life of the Party":

> You, Jew, can be the life of the party,
> You, Jew, can be the hit of the show.
> You can learn to stamp
> In a concentration camp,
> Leading by a nose and a toe.

I supposed it was witty but didn't know what a concentration camp was.

Chino knew. Indeed, there was a question of his family's being interned right here in the USA. And Rosemary took the aims of the YCL, and of Chino, to heart for years. She marched with them—with *him*. In front of the Piccadilly, where the film *Blockade* was showing, they held high their placards shouting WHERE IS THE CONSCIENCE OF THE WORLD. These were the final lines of the movie about the Spanish Civil War, a war in which Géorg had served, volunteering with other American Loyalists. Despite this valor, Chino never took Géorg seriously, homosexuality being frowned upon even by the highbrow Communists.

I meanwhile was having an affair with Thomas Stauffer, a university graduate in philosophy, proud of having hosted Bertrand Russell and fixing him up with a very blond matron. Athletic, Stauffer was tall, with a brush cut, superciliously sadistic with me, physically exciting, but a boor and musically reactionary. (Ravel, who had died at Christmas in 1937, leaving me brokenhearted, was, according to Stauffer, a zero compared to Mozart. Mozart remains the undisputably safe idol for musical know-nothings.) Whether Rosemary went farther with Chino than I with Stauffer, I cannot guess. I would go to his room in the family house on Kimbark after midnight. We kissed a lot, then I would sleep. How can I forget his observation that "anyone who's as pretty asleep as awake is inherently stupid"? Should not philosophy teach people to be nice to each other? Yet he wrote me a note about the lingering taste of tobacco on his lips (he didn't smoke, I did) and how that distracted him from his work. Mother read the note, then asked me about the hickey on my neck (how did she know the word? I didn't). I protested weakly that it must have been Marilyn Joselit who gave it to me. Marilyn was president of the Blue Mirror, U-High's poetry group.

It was then that Mother sat me and my sister down for a talk. We were at a perilous crossroads, she said, but she had once been our age. She was profoundly anxious that Rosemary might get pregnant, profoundly anxious that I might be cruel. Miriam Carey had already at sixteen become pregnant. To her credit she married the culprit, and, as Mrs. Sam Norwood, lived happily ever after in Atlanta until her suicide forty years later. "I won't mind what you do," Mother told me, "as long as you don't make others unhappy. Try to be happy yourself. It may not be easy."

And it was then that she told us that she and Father had had their ups and downs. Could we think back to when she used to cry so much? When Father was gone so much? Well, he was having an affair with Miss Ring, his secretary. And Mother herself was having an affair with Davis Edwards, Jean's father.

I was stunned. Not because I couldn't imagine my parents in such a posture: Father, after all, though not an *homme moyen sensuel,* was certainly an *homme exceptionnel sensuel,* while Mother loved perfumed soap and Carl Sandburg and highballs. It's that Miss Ring and Mr. Edwards were . . . such bizarre choices: she a cripple, he walleyed. Never, so far as I know, were there other infidelities, and these had caused more anguish than joy.

Did Rosemary and I learn more from this lesson than that our parents were just like us? Well, she eventually had six children in wedlock, and I may have made somebody unhappy. But it wasn't our fault.

Let me catch my breath.

Have I been heading uphill or down? Have I practiced what I preach about knowing when to stop? Are many people really interested in other people's Sensitive Childhood? Don't readers prefer, even from Einstein, gossip? Is gossip ever interesting—or even applicable—before there is adult interaction with others?

Now, interaction with others precludes, for an artist, getting his work done, yet it is because of his work that he qualifies as a memoirist, even if he can't write. Even if he *can* write, an artist doesn't know the secret of his art, much less how to impart the secret except through the art itself. If he could define the secret, he could bottle it and make a killing. So when all he has to mull over is his Sensitive Childhood, it's hard to know what to leave out.

I've been cohering these pages from hundreds of scattered notes, which Father used to claim is the wrong way to go about anything. Make notes, yes, then throw them out and plow on chronologically. Shall I speed things up for the next few years?

9. U-High—Part II

Rosemary at seventeen, Ned at fifteen, in Twig, Minnesota, summer 1939.

Summer of 1938 in Canada is recalled mainly through our photo album: no peaks, no shallows, no rifts, no movies, no music, and certainly no sex.

Movies from the previous winters had mainly been seen at the Art Cinema on Michigan Avenue: *Club des femmes,* in which pretty Josette Day, after being defiled by a rich American, showers with a huge sponge (could I find a huge sponge in Chicago?); *Princess Tam-Tam,* in which beloved Josephine Baker danced savagely in sequins before the Parisian *gratin* (might I find sequins?); *La grande illusion,* in which Von Stroheim is bemused to hear of prisoners escaping dressed as women (men dressed as women?). But American movies too. Today, with memory jogged by TV reruns, I seem to have seen every film ever made. Not just grade-A vehicles of our sacred monsters—

Mae West, Dietrich, Garbo, Crawford, swathed in the pelts and plumes of slain ermines and egrets, with their short bodies, strong shoulders, and large heads (Bill Flanagan used to call them the Rat Ladies, while Parker Tyler named them "impersonators of female impersonators") —but all the middle-class comedies and dramas of Gail Patrick, Fay Ray, Joan Blondell, Dorothy Jordan. Do I mention only actresses? Actors were appendages.

Music consisted of heavy doses of the Chicago Symphony under Frederick Stock, plus season tickets to a piano series sponsored by the Adult Education Council. How many times did we hear Artur Schnabel and his definitive renditions of the Austrian giants. Born in 1882, a mere fifty-five years after the death of Beethoven, Schnabel seemed the current embodiment of that composer with his authoritative free-dom, sloppy accuracy, unfrightened rinforzati, and trancelike color-ations, not to mention the audible snorts that accompanied every phrase, making us unsure of what to listen for through this static, beclouding a presumed authenticity.

Then there were heavy doses of the so-called popular: Benny Good-man and Artie Shaw, the mother and father of a generation, with their Gershwin and Porter songs equal in vocal arch and harmonic ingenu-ity to the songs of Monteverdi and Schumann. And the rarefied divas. Bruce showed up with still another album of Dietrich singing "Ja so bin Ich," "Allein in einer grossen Stadt," and "Wo ist der Mann" with a baritone growl never heard before on land or sea, pitched only vaguely, but licentious and involved, permitting one who didn't under-stand German to understand German. (Does that define good lieder singing?) Norris showed up with an album of Mae West, "Easy Rider," "Frankie and Johnny," and "A Guy What Takes His Time." At the start of the last named we hear a thrice-uttered "Oh," the lewdest lone syllable ever recorded. Mother thought Mae West was cheap (well I guess so) and irresistible.

Stirring this recipe of films into the good and bad plays we regularly saw (Helen Menken in *The Old Maid,* Eugenie Leontavich in *Ro-mance*), stirring the Ballets Russes and modern dance recitals (Ted Shawn, for instance, and Ruth Page, who was a local star) into the touching antics of Rogers and Astaire, stirring the programs of grand opera (which I couldn't take to, except for *Madama Butterfly*) and Gilbert and Sullivan into the indiscriminate fare of pre-Broadway try-outs like *You Never Know* with the shocking Libby Holman, or WPA shows like *Meet the People,* I realize now that without batting an eye we mixed high and low art, giving them always equal billing.

· · ·

On the return from Canada that fall of '38 it was thought I should seek supplemental formal training. As a university man, Father took a dim view of conservatories like the Chicago Musical College, where Perry had his weekly lessons with Ganz. But after conferring with Belle, who knew a thing or two about the local scene, my parents allowed me to enroll in a harmony course at the rival school, called the American Conservatory, on Wabash Avenue.

Leo Sowerby was, with John Alden Carpenter, the most distinguished composer of the Middle West. It was he, somewhat to my surprise, who would teach the humble class to which I repaired each Wednesday after school for the next two years. Of my parents' generation, a bachelor, reddish complexioned like David Sachs and milky skinned, chain smoker of Fatima cigarettes, unglamorous and nonmysterious, likable with a perpetual worried frown, overweight, and wearing rimless glasses, earthy, practical, interested in others even when they were talentless, a stickler for basic training. Sowerby was the first composer I ever knew, and the last thing a composer was supposed to resemble. He was a friendly pedagogue.

There were five in the class which was "noncreative": we harmonized in the abstract, using given soprano lines or figured basses, we did not harmonize in the concrete, nor did we analyze preexisting works. We weren't composers: all was theory, rigorous, nonevolving. Sowerby could absorb at a glance any veering in our exercises from the narrow paths of each eight-measure period we "realized." In those twenty-four months, how many thousands of eight-measure periods did I grind out? What had this to do with inspiration? Would it in some way steer me to becoming an expressive artist? I didn't think so, though I did feel that in industry as in romance it is better to act and have remorse than not to act and have regret. If I had a regret it's that I did not take a simultaneous course in counterpoint (the word rang with the fright of adulthood), but how could I have known? I do believe now that those studies bore a direct relation to the canny voice-leading on my every page today, to my conviction that every note must be accounted for in rapport with every note preceding, and that in music as in life one thing leads to another.

From this cool dryness how did I, a teenager, become so socially warm with Leo Sowerby, aged forty-four? Did he, who lived in a third-floor apartment a few blocks north of us ever visit us on Dorchester as I visited him on Blackstone? In the family we all referred to him as Leo, but did they ever see him? If one thing leads to another in life as in music, who took the initiative? At any rate, on various occasions I was Leo's weekend guest at Palisades Park in his native Michigan. His summer house there, modest to a fault, was really a screened-in cabin, one of dozens on a steep, gloomy hill overlooking the lake. Leo always had another guest, a colleague perhaps, or a former pupil. Meals, preceded by martinis, were cooked (without my help; what did I know? I was supposed to be scribbling harmony in the next room) on a kerosene stove, like those we once used in Vermont, served with quarts of red wine, and consumed in the glow of oil lamps. I will not forget the episode (even now I shudder) of growing rapidly tipsy one evening, rising from table and, with what I may have thought of as a Brontëan sweep, rushing pell-mell out of the house and down toward the beach, unaware of a thick wire en route, breast-high in the underbrush, that could snap a body in two. Leo yelled through the darkness while his other guest (Dick Cornelius, a graduate student) rushed after and tackled me. That night Leo put me to bed shakily, bending over to kiss me full on the lips, tears in his eyes. What was I to think? It hadn't occurred to me that mature men from the world of thought could harbor affectionate, much less sensual, feelings for someone as insignificant as myself.

It was at this time I showed Leo my notes for "Song of Songs" (again I shudder), feeling a surge of pride as he showed the opening bars to Delamarter. "Look at the curve of that alto line. Isn't it beautiful?" But Leo was not a composition professor. He looked kindly at my unshaped assays but didn't make suggestions. Nor was he an intellect—what we called sophisticated—despite his quick intelligence and specialized prolificity. I advised him to read Pierre Louÿs and Knut Hamsun, of which he found *Aphrodite* "precious," but *Growth of the Soil* "the real thing." (Would these favored novels ring true today, or pall, on the one hand with rehearsed decadence and on the other with proto-Nazism?)

As to Leo's own music, I was shy of it. That he served as organist and choirmaster at Saint James's Church on Rush Street (between two gay bars, though he wouldn't have known), and excelled in sacred music, was stuffy and off-putting. Not until 1943, when I heard Paul Callaway in Washington play the haunting and sinuous *Arioso* for organ solo, and a few years later heard Hugh Ross in New York conduct the premiere of the cantata on texts of Saint Francis, did I realize there was more to Sowerby than academic facility.

Paul Callaway was another passing guest in Palisades. A wiry pixie with a constant smile, fourteen years my senior, he was a charmer with a major job—music director of Washington Cathedral. He asked me to phone him in a week, at the Palmer House, when he'd be back in Chicago. Leo later, in private, said that I should.

I had not before associated drinking with eating. Getting drunk with peers on Saturday nights was postprandial behavior (the prandial behavior itself having been with our families), though we might at 3 a.m. have a hamburger at some White Tower. The ceremony, robust as it was, of including wine with meals chez Leo Sowerby was an odd though easy pleasure. Surely it loosened my tongue—enough to repeat the now-tired joke, "Who are the three Bs of music? Answer: Bach, Beethoven, and Sowerby." Leo proffered a lame smile. To atone I composed for him an *Ave Maria*. He also prodded me into writing an (unfinished) organ sonata.

I did phone Paul Callaway and accepted his dinner invitation, telling my parents the truth—that he was an important middle-aged associate of Leo's. "Why is he so interested in you?" they wondered. At the Palmer House we dined on room service, downing split after split of sparkling burgundy, the ultimate luxury. Then we went out to some dreary bars in the Loop. We returned to the hotel and had more burgundy, which tasted now less thrilling. When Paul kissed me in the ear my first response was: "What would Leo say?" "He would approve, I assure you." One thing led to another, which was a luxury too. I told Hatti about it next day, and she was thrilled—sex with a bona fide grown-up!

I have kept the radiant letters Paul Callaway mailed over the next months. I dwell on him now because he would become one of the crucial figures in my professional life, and the first of My Three Pauls. (The others were Goodman and Bowles.)

Word associations:

Billie = white bread in stewed tomatoes

Holiday = Waldorf salad (apples, nuts, celery, mayonnaise)

But the two words together evoke a near-morbid enchantment, wrenching the spirit from the body and letting it rise to heaven, which turns out to be hell.

Somewhere in 1938 Dick Jacob—or was it Don Dalton?—brought over the new Commodore record of Billie Holiday's "Strange Fruit," paving the way by playing the reverse side first, "Fine and Mellow" ("so you can get used to her strange style"). The process was slower than with *The Rite of Spring,* but the effect of her performance would be as singular on my notion of what music was all about. "Fine and Mellow," with Holiday whining her own iambic pentameter ("My man doesn't love me, treats me all so mean/He's the lowest man that I've ever seen") was an ideal curtain-raiser to "Strange Fruit," the portrait of a lynching. Had anything remotely like it been heard before ("Miss Otis Regrets" and "Suppertime" were mere teases)? Billie's oxymoronic qualities—the studied freedom; the sorrowful pleasure; the tinny, velvet timbre—defined the music, even as they answered Yeats's question: "How can we know the dancer from the dance?" Other than these two one-of-a-kind songs, we soon discovered that her repertory was largely mediocre Tin Pan Alley rejects. It wasn't the tune but her way with the tune. She did sing classics of Gershwin and Porter, and lesser but solid ditties like "More Than You Know" or "My Man." But these somehow were wrenched from their composers and, despite herself, appropriated by Billie Holiday. One definition of jazz as distinct from classical: a music wherein composer and performer are one, and where that "one" is different at each presentation. (A Schnabel may evoke, even become, Beethoven, but he doesn't rewrite Beethoven.) In bending a phrase, stretching a melody, delaying the beat so as to "come in wrong" just right, she forever influenced my own approach to song writing.

Billie Holiday appeared that winter at the Sherman Hotel's Panther Room. We all went—as did, seemingly, every white liberal collegian in Illinois. We downed our Tom Collinses, then ordered more. And waited. (Drinking age in Chicago then was twenty-one; how did we get served, much less get drunk, as regularly as we did?) When finally she materialized, without fanfare but in purple, she sang something called "Jim," a spin-off of Kern's "Bill," which hypnotized us despite the stunning banality of the lyrics ("Jim doesn't ever bring me pretty flowers, Jim doesn't try to fill my lonely hours"). We had no previous concept of how she'd look. Now there she stood, handsome and straight, magnetic and still, except for a slight circular motion of the left arm, snapping her fingers imperceptibly. Unlike the overwrought delivery of so many female pop singers who *interpret,* explaining the words with their bodies and who between stanzas play with their hair, but like her grand international peers, Piaf and Lenya, Holiday scarcely moved, saving until the climax the moment for closing her eyes, tilting back her head, as mountains crumbled. When the room darkened, except for a blue spotlight on her head, and she began "Strange Fruit," a unison "Ah!" sounded from the assembly, a sound I have always loathed, but of course I uttered it too.

We didn't try to speak with her. I do remember jitterbugging on the parquet, appropriately enough to " 'Taint what you do, it's the way how you do it," falling flat on my face, trying to drag Hatti down with me, and gazing up at the indifferent, well-off, left-wing dancers as I rubbed my sprained ankle.

Interesting, isn't it, how Billie Holiday, who is said to have spoken for her people more than any other black singer, spoke through white music? It lay in tone of voice. Not for years would she be a jukebox fixture, like the bright and younger Ella Fitzgerald, of whom Billie was the dark side. But if Ella had optimistic groupies, the tragedian Billie already had her cult, mostly of the Caucasian intelligentsia, though she didn't quite know what to do with them.

Did she have charm? She, the woman, had charm, but her singing, while touching you at the shuddering core, oddly lacked charm. Billie's singing had—has—no dynamic nuance: it is all an unshaded mezzo forte within a tessitura of one deep octave. Given this, the variety makes a prismatic paradox.

David Sachs loaned me Gide's 1925 *The Counterfeiters,* and also *Les enfants terribles,* which was the unchanged title of the translation of Cocteau's 1930 novel. (Paul Goodman contended—wrongly—it should have been Englished as *The Holy Terrors.*) Cocteau's book is strongly influenced by Gide's, wherein Cocteau himself is nonetheless caricatured as the Comte de Passavant, a licentious poetaster. Each book deals with alienated youth, but otherwise the claustrophobic power of *Les enfants* couldn't be more distant from the open-aired *Counterfeiters.* I was intensely drawn to both works. Indeed, as happens in love—be it with a person, a pet, an artifact—I wished in some way to *be* these works. But just as I was not aware of the increasing mass of individuals across America who felt they had a unique claim on the dazzling victim, Billie Holiday (as they would feel a generation later about Marilyn), neither did I realize that across the ocean at that moment scores of young people were claiming to have been the models for the faintly incestuous brother and sister, and their small coterie, who were the enfants terribles.

Random recall:

—Leo Sowerby said to look at people when they talked to me, not stare around the room like a child.

The morning after that kiss, he explained quietly that he was bisexual. I'm still inclined to believe whatever I'm told, at least at first blush. Bisexual, however, since it by definition required at least two other people, implied unfaithfulness to one of them. Was this Christian, even for a person less involved than Leo with the church? (Is a person who makes love to himself by definition homosexual?)

—Christian history already struck me as contradictory, blood soaked, and infinitely sad because it used for its identity the form of Christ on a cross. And "The Second Coming" already struck me as the perfect poem in every way except its basic premise: Was the "rough beast, its hour come round at last," really so much more horrific than that other slouching toward Bethlehem twenty centuries ago?

—We were faithful weekend clients of the Cabin Inn on South State Street. This vast barn featured Miss Valda Gray and her Beauties. The Beauties included Miss Carole Lee, Miss Alice Faye, and the number-one draw, Miss Jo-Ann Crawford, all of them six-foot black males in inexpensive semidrag. Accompanied by a terrific jazz quintet, they would sing ("Honeysuckle Rose," "A Tisket, a Tasket," "A Good Man Is Hard to Find") and dance with a tricky step that involved swirling their floor-length trains with tiny kicks in one direction while revolving in the other direction. Hatti mastered the step. I almost did.

John Barrymore was in Chicago costarring in a piece of fluff with his then wife, Elaine Barrie. Their drunken spats were publicized: 'twas even rumored he spanked her on stage. One midnight Barrymore showed up at the Cabin with an entourage. Jo-Ann Crawford was in heaven. "Work it, Miss Crawford, work it, girl!" screamed the other Beauties as she crooned "Honeysuckle" straight at the star who feigned embarrassment. They left the club together at 4 a.m. Miss Crawford was never again the same.

During final exams Maggy and I, during lunch hour in the blaze of noon, decided to peek into the Cabin Inn. The cigarette butts, the shafts of sunshine italicizing the cheap checkered tablecloths which last night looked sumptuous, the stale smell of beer, the silence, except for the clean-up women and their buckets—all this had a certain panache of its own. I went up onto the empty stage and played Debussy's brassy Prélude from the *Suite pour le piano*. The cleaning women put down their buckets. "Will you listen to that! Just like Paderooskee!" Do cleaning women make such observations still?

—*The Chicago Daily News* spoke of soldiers in Europe throwing babies in the air, like balloons, and catching them on their bayonets.

—Maggy and I, accompanied by Marian Weinberg, our class's jazz piano player, danced the "Blue Tango" for a school function. To prime ourselves we drank straight bourbon, then mugged during the performance. Nobody clapped much. We then drove to the Cabin Inn where, unbeknown to us, my parents were seated with four friends. They'd come to see what this was all about. It wasn't so bad, they said.

—The same percentage of people seem to be left-handed as queer. Me, I was right-handed in all ways except (this was clear from the start) in opening combination locks and in turning handsprings. Then as now I couldn't enter a grocery store without pondering the percentage of items which, within a year, would be ingested and excreted.

—Church and state were never a cause at U-High with its large Jewish population, but state and school were. With anxiety increasing abroad, conspicuous patriotism increased at home. "The Star-Spangled Banner" was everywhere. Rather than remain seated while it was intoned, Rosemary and I would leave the public hall or schoolroom. Mother and Father stood by us (sat by us?) despite the shock of their friends and the contempt of our classmates.

—"Why, you're really a nice person," says someone after meeting me for the first time, implying they'd thought I wouldn't be a nice person, and they have the gall to say it. I point this out, which makes me less of a nice person, thank God.

—Did you ever meet Greta Garbo?
   I don't recall.

—Later adolescence, redolent of gin fizzes, menstrual ooze and semen, banana splits, Woody Herman and broken dates, and the jitters of an already-raging war that would, at the very least, revamp America's notion of art (for maybe too brief a time) and of totalitarianism. Whereupon Dick Jacob said: "There's a man named Alfred, who lives just around your corner, on Fifty-seventh, who will do to you what you've never had done." So I called Alfred (since he was not a human but a function, one could phone the stranger without embarrassment) and we made a date for tonight. Beforehand, I rode the bike to the Piccadilly and saw *The Goldwyn Follies,* starring Zorina. Later at Alfred's, he did do something to me that I'd never had done, and there went another virginity! In the words of Felix Krull, "I need not go into details—the episode [with the family nursemaid] had the usual features, too well known to be of interest to a cultured audience." Alfred, however, turned out to be something of a pianist. On his Baldwin baby grand he played Cyril Scott's *Lento* and *Lotus Land,* during which two figures who inhabited the shadows of his apartment wandered into the front room. One of these was James Purdy, whom I revisualize as being wraithlike and drastically blond with a troubled expression that would infiltrate his marvelous crazy prose in years to come.

The sound of Cyril Scott inevitably revives this incident, even as the sight of the granite corner on Fifty-seventh evokes a touch of evil. Both Purdy and Zorina (the latter known to all as Brigitta), when I later

knew them, professed a mild appreciation of having indirectly participated in this deflowering.

Children's very innocence renders them cruel.

—In Québec at the shrine of Sainte Anne de Beaupré, still intoxicated
with forbidden Catholicism, I persuaded Father to buy me an expensive gold and pearl rosary which I kept always in my pocket as the
Greeks keep worry beads. Now, months later, standing with Bruce on
the bridge of the Wooded Island, I ostentatiously drew the rosary forth
and with flare flung it into the air, where it caught the sunlight for a
moment, then vanished into the murk below. No one paid attention,
Bruce was disgusted. Father at the end of the day despaired that I still
hadn't learned the value of money.

—Often during high school, then during the fifties in France, I dyed
my hair. Rosemary too. Sometimes we were redheads. Sometimes
blonds.

—Why am I writing this book?

To revive a tottering conviction, long ago banished to a dim corner
of my room, that if we could Only Connect the world would have
meaning. But what's the meaning of connect? And isn't the sense of
life just as full or empty when alone? Nothing can penetrate the sumptuous solitude of Everyman, yet I have a frantic urge (many people I
know do not, including composers and writers) to *leave* something.

—On 2 April 1939 James Holmes is born in Pittsburg, Kansas. Unknown to each other, our lives will flow parallel and distant for twenty-
eight years, when we will meet and remain together for the rest of
our time on earth, with an understanding that is far more than love,
and without which life would be mere existence.

10. U-High—Part III

The Rorem family.

New York hadn't changed in the three years since I'd been there, but I had. As one's voice lowers, perspective widens to include the city's echoing avenues at four in the morning. What was I doing there, aged fifteen (going on sixteen), during the summer of 1939?

In Chicago, that spring—perhaps at the moment JH was being born —Géorg and I were cruising the empty Hyde Park. Round about midnight, over by that lilac bush we perceived a standing man, arms crossed, legs planted firmly. Nearer, we saw the smiling Irish mug and curly hair of a nineteen-year-old collegiate type. Minutes later, beneath the streetlamp on Stoney Island, we marveled at his very green eyes. Do people actually *see* out of green eyes? Are they useful as well as beautiful? His name was Wally. Géorg went home with him, and told me about it next day. We got acquainted. He was what we then dubbed "an ordinary person," with all that the label infers in earthiness—none of the brainy repartee that stands in the way of sex. Learning that Wally planned to go to the world's fair, I wanted to go to. Surprisingly, they said okay, my parents.

Of the train, coach class, I recall nothing beyond the endlessness and, I suppose, a certain eagerness. The fair itself was less a lure than the intoxication of being on my own, for the first time ever. Once arrived, the New Yorker Hotel on Eighth Avenue was the only familiar landmark, so there I registered. Now what? I phoned Wally, the sole person I knew, at the Sloane House, not realizing the Sloane House was just across the street on Thirty-fourth. After a day or two he persuaded me to move there.

Of the fair, somewhere out in Queens, I recall little beyond a feigned dutiful interest; I had seen all this back home in 1933. We went there several times (I think), but I longed to get back to Manhattan in time for the purposeful night.

The purposefulness centered on Fifty-second Street between Fifth and Sixth avenues, a block of seemingly nothing but nightclubs. I was drawn immediately to Kelly's Stables to hear Billie Holiday, arriving at around nine to a near-empty room. But there she stood in a green and yellow evening gown, with another woman at the near end of the bar. I had a drink, maybe two or three (in New York the legal age was eighteen, and draft cards were not yet demanded for proof), smoked a Chesterfield, maybe two or three, blowing smoke rings, for which I had a talent, plus a talent for disposing of the butt with a blasé flick of the middle finger. Then I approached Miss Holiday uncertainly to ask if she might sing "Under a Blue Jungle Moon." She sized me up, said she *had* made a record of it but couldn't remember the words, and the piano player didn't know it. She was civil, sober, not encouraging. I had no notion of how to develop a conversation, so that was that, except for the "set," which she performed with her pianist a few minutes later, and then another some time after, both ending with "Strange Fruit." Then I crossed the street to the Dizzy Club.

The Dizzy Club was a basement joint with two straight bartenders, a gay clientele, and an entertainer named Daisy, whose thing was to rush about disheveled in a child's dress shrieking Eva Tanguay's "I Don't Care." On his night off, one bartender would return to the place, drunk, as a customer; likewise the other bartender on his free night. Who else should show up as a customer, when the joint down the street had closed, but Billie Holiday herself, as warm here as she'd been cold there, so attractive in her street clothes and hat, so New York, so charismatically perfumed (though this was well before the signature gardenias in her pomaded hair), so campy, as she kept up a running commentary on "Old Rocking Chair" being crooned by the pianist in the corner. *My dear old Aunt Harriett*—"Yeah, she was queer too!"

Suddenly there was a hush. Billie had begun to sing, and a sense of awe filled the room. The song was "Night and Day." How could she shift, in the space of a breath, from giddy banter into high tragedy?— because "Night and Day" *was* tragedy from her lips, anything was; she couldn't not be sad with even the happiest song.

The answer: We are what we speak. My English is not the same as yours, or his, or the Queen of England's or even my sister's, by virtue of the day I was born and the street I live on. Of the 116 million Japanese, each one speaks his version of that language, though to us who don't understand that language in any version, the whole of Japan behaves according to the language, inflected in every way. A Frenchman, even if you're married to him, differs from you by being raised more thriftily: having fewer words, he combines them more ingenuously. Conversely, we speak what we are. Mae West or Tallulah Bankhead inadvertently lent to their mildest declaration—"I like cof-fee"—a blush-making innuendo. Sarah Vaughan, who by academic standards had a better voice than Billie's, was but a shallow ornamentalist in the identical repertory. Thus Billie's background, and her reaction—conscious or not—to that background, colored her speech and her musicalization of that speech.

I could never go on this way about any musical executant other than Billie Holiday, not Schnabel or Callas or Belle Tannenbaum, for what have they given to great music that was not in the music already? Even with composers I'm shy of rhetoric, though despite the ken of our increasingly philistine intelligentsia, one Olivier Messiaen is, by the nature of things, worth a hundred Itzhak Perlmans. Since in jazz (as I wrote earlier) performer and composer are one, or become one, definitions swerve. Billie could make a masterpiece out of a lousy tune. And she entered my life early enough to become—like a mother duck to a lost baby chick—imprinted on my uninhibited consciousness. So I grant her all.

Out in the dawn of Fifth Avenue, after the Dizzy Club, if Wally wasn't around to lead me back to Thirty-fourth with his green eyes, I'd go home with whoever asked (and someone always did)—it seemed simpler than saying no. One hitch lay in my being so often drunk. I didn't drink because people bored me (that would come) or because I bored myself, but because I needed to become uninhibited enough for sex. Not that sex, as such, inhibited me, but the craving to be passive shamed me as much as it excited me. Was this craving due to a stringent Quaker background that gears one to turn, so to speak, the other cheek? What then of aggressive Quakers? More likely it was pure narcissism.

There's a Cheever story with the line: "You just talked yourself out of a good fuck." Well, I drank myself out of many a good fuck, passing out more often than putting out. As on a silver screen showing an old movie I see Ned, with the resilience of youth, disentangling himself from another New York bed that looks like a battleground, tiptoeing away from a sleeper who is already a forgotten lover. I clearly remember my final night on the East Coast, being in a man's car on the West Side Highway. He was trying to grope me while driving. At around 180th Street, when I wouldn't come across, he reached over me and opened the door, saying calmly, "Get out!," which I did, and lived to tell the tale. Next day I took the train back to Chicago earlier than I'd planned.

Each week brought news of Hitler's advance through eastern Europe. I could not grasp then, and cannot now, why any one could want to subjugate another person, let alone an entire civilization, to the point of obliteration. Why not make the point by composing a symphony?

Back in the Windy City I became a prodigal son, impressing the family with what I portrayed as the conquest of Billie Holiday. At the piano I worked out the chord changes of "Night and Day" in Billie's key of A-flat, in case I were ever called upon impromptu to accompany her. (I never was.)

Later that summer we removed for a month *en famille* to a log cabin on a lake in Twig, Minnesota, a dozen miles out of Duluth, taking along our cousin (Mother's niece) Kathryn Nash. Kathy was between me and Rosemary in age, with long thick hair—red-gold, like the gilt-edge pages of a Bible—framing her ruddy features. She had spent the winter with us, which included a fling with D., and now would round out the year in Twig. The log cabin having no toilet, we used an old WC twelve yards away. Which means that in my fastidiousness I shat no more than five times that month. Day after day went by when, despite prunes and processions to the hut with Kathy carrying an enema with rubber attachments, I would just sit there, moody and clenched, on the wooden hole six feet above a pile of rotten leaves and human dung and buzzing flies. My constipation was such that, although I'm more or less "regular," as the Ex-Lax ads used to say, even today, twenty thousand bowel movements later, I'm still queasy each time I go.

Excitement consisted in going by day to a Duluth drugstore and gorging on cherry pie à la mode followed by devil's-food cake, and by night to a country club where we danced to Glenn Miller's "Sunrise Serenade" and to Ella Fitzgerald singing "Don't Worry 'bout Me," the first five notes of which, in rhythm and pitch, were identical to the first five in "You Go to My Head" (an octave pickup to a quarter-note triplet finishing on a half note). Every evening at sunset Mother and I each drank two cans of beer—not one, not three, but two. And I wrote stories in the telegraphic style of Dos Passos.

Father and I left Twig for Chicago before the others, so as to attend a Rorem reunion in Clear Lake, Iowa. There I persuaded Father to let me go on to the city a day ahead of him. On the train I read with ecstasy *The Grapes of Wrath,* arriving back home around dusk. Just as I can never hear Delius or sniff the taboo incense of a Catholic church anywhere in the world without floating back to the Dorchester Avenue bedroom, so the September return from the healthy country into any city's dusty allure contains, for an hour or two, a power more persuasive than art—Debussy (or Steinbeck, if you will) is mere embellishment. I scrambled some eggs, not knowing that butter's a prerequisite, and stank up the house. Then went to Géorg's at the Century Hotel. We both picked up Hatti and the three of us made the rounds of Fifty-fifth Street bars—the Old Bear, The Wharf, the University Tavern, Hanley's. Do you recall those long-razed haunts? In the middle of the night (bars shut at four in Chicago, three on Saturdays) I invited them, plus a stranger culled en route, back to the apartment, only to find that Father had arrived in the early evening. All my life Father has had the at once touching and exasperating habit of turning up unannounced on my doorstep anywhere in the world, a reverse of the classical scenario.

In his little tale, *La farce du château,* Cocteau portrays a group of children who concoct an elaborate surprise for their beloved mother. Dressed in masks and robes they crawl up to her balcony and into her room, only to find her in bed with a strange man.

> ... nothing is as unfortunate for the people as reigns which last too long. I hear that God is eternal—which says it all.
>
> —Chamfort

That week Hitler entered Poland, and a world war became irreversible. Man seemed not to have evolved with the millennia, not shown himself essentially "good," nor even better than he should be; nor will he again achieve the disinterested level of other vegetables until he has hatched from out of ugly *Homo sapiens* confines, into the unflawed air of Bach and Giotto. Then again, Giotto and Bach depict crucifixions, while in the ideal world there would be no need of art. Or so I concluded. If the human race were evil by nature, that would have to include Roosevelt. Just to want to *be* president seemed corrupt inherently, concessions being obligatory from the word go. (I think I've used this sentence earlier. But I'm writing in an election year, forgive me.)

In the strain of resurrecting geographies and histories and liaisons of yore, the core gets lost. What was I *thinking* while in Twig, or Yellowstone, or at the world's fair? What was I thinking in the arms of those strangers—or at the announcement of German encroachments —beyond how to protect my own skin? Most of the time I was thinking about music, or writing it, or reading and dreaming about it. The issue of that thinking was, ten years, forty years after, more thinking and reading and writing, while the world proper grew increasingly invisible to me, and I to it. That is the pith of an artist's life. So his biography contains everything but the essential.

With the autumn I became sixteen and a senior in high school even as Rosemary began her freshman year at Beloit. I don't remember how the ensuing scholastic season seemed in an atmosphere with Rosemary gone. I do remember learning, though scarcely mastering, all thirty-two Beethoven sonatas, all twenty-four Debussy preludes, and dozens of bonbons by Poulenc and Palmgren, though I'd never heard of Copland. This music, digested overnight, still remains in my hands but remains wrong, impatiently fingered, sloppily vanquished in my haste to devour it, like the drugstore pies I couldn't enjoy for thinking of the cakes to follow. Then I played in public for the first time. In that little recital hall of the Lyon & Healy building, the hall where Edward Steuermann had given his incomprehensible all-Schoenberg program, and we didn't know if he could really play until the encore, which was Ravel's *Ondine,* and we all expired at the accurate glitter; the hall where we listened to George Perle's new Trio, wherein the flute, viola, and piano blend in a braid of wine, silk, and quartz. With Belle as orchestra at the second piano, I performed the great Mozart D-minor Concerto, schmaltzy cadenza by Reinecke. This was in, I think, November.

The following June I played with an orchestra for the first time—

which, as it happened, was also the last time—when Belle arranged for the American Concert Orchestra—a subsidiary of the WPA's Illinois Symphony—to accompany me in the first movement of Grieg's Concerto. (A moldy scrapbook tells me that this occurred on 21 June 1940, with one William Fantozzi conducting in the Illinois Music Hall at 632 North Dearborn. A very mixed program also featuring two solo singers.) I carefully told everyone, especially Perry, the morning of the concert, that I hadn't yet memorized the piece. This was not true but seemed somehow theatrical, as did my bows, during which as I bent my waist I raised my eyes to take in the audience at a sweep.

Later that night, natty in my white suit and maroon tie—the required outfit for graduation from high school the previous week at Rockefeller Chapel—I drove with Maggy back to the South Side, specifically to the lagoon's edge behind the Museum of Science and Industry. With us was Loren Smith, a dashing married man, perhaps thirty, on whom we both had a crush. Maggy and Loren necked. I just sat there, left out. I include this mainly because Loren was a good, simple, handsome friend to us all; so when the draft began gobbling males during the next two years, Loren was our first war casualty. In the navy, he seems to have been slammed in the head by an iron chain, on a dock in San Francisco, and killed outright.

Between these two concerto performances flowed the final semesters at U-High. Was I popular? Heavens, no! Too effete to be a jock, too pretty to be a nerd, too indifferent to be a prize student, too lazy to pretend to be straight, and preferring music to sports, I hardly fit in the narrow standards of the Beautiful People, although I admired, without envy, the throbbing physicality of Chuck Cahn and Elise Leiberman, of Tom Mullins and Dorothy (Bitsy) Goes, royalty all.

Father continued to be bemused by my dreary grades. He had been a Phi Beta Kappa, an organized, indefatigable worker excelling in virtually anything that can be learned, like geometry, cattle breeding, carpentry, accounting (which for years was his bread and butter), even practical English grammar, which he wrote a handbook about, predating—and terser than—Stumph's; thus he was distressed at my profligacy. On the other hand, though he didn't begrudge my hours passed in record listening, he felt I should channel them more systematically; since he could master that which can be learned, he envied those who could master that which can't be learned, i.e., the arts, and felt I was going about it wrong.

Cynically staring back upon the University of Chicago's Lab School, I learn that I learned nothing—nothing, that is, that was provided in exchange for the hefty tuition—and this was not my fault. Classes were pointless interludes between extracurricular activities. Subjects were not imparted with any sense of purpose, of delight, of goal, but as abstractions: algebra for its own sake, biology too, even French. French had begun back in third grade, under the pristine Miss Spink (very feminine, with tresses rolled into a bun encased in a blue lace snood, sharing a house on Kenwood at Fifty-seventh with Miss Millis, very masculine, with neckties neat on a stiff white shirt tucked into a wool skirt), who on the first day taught us to say: "Je prends le livre, et je le pose sur la table." Thereafter, from Miss Spink through Monsieur Bovée, with the redoubtable wart on his forefinger, to Madame Greene, with her mean smile gleaming through the conjugations, I retain nothing. Because nothing was more than itself. Where was Madame Bovary when I needed her? During most of the 1950s French would be my sole language, no thanks to that early training, which didn't even inform us of the second person singular, since the *tutoiement* had no equivalent in English. How did I master the language? Through the poetry in Poulenc's songs—Apollinaire and Eluard and Aragon. Admittedly, this wasn't much help with Parisian cabdrivers at first, but one thing leads to another.

Good teaching means leading a horse to water and making him drink, not solely through knowledge and nouns but through enthusiasm. Yes, one thing leads to another: the horse, the rein, the water. Nor had I found cause and effect with Leo Sowerby; what had four-part harmony to do with the music I loved? Nor did one thing lead to another at Northwestern University, where the next two and a half years would be spent.

How did I end up in Evanston? Father, dismayed at my rejected application to his alma mater, Oberlin, because of low grades, and armed with a dozen of my composition notebooks, undertook a visit in person to Dean Beattie of the Northwestern Music School. The following week I auditioned there in person ("Can you play for us 'Way Down Upon the Swanee River' in D major?") and was accepted.

On 14 June the Germans entered Paris without resistance and hung their banner on the Eiffel Tower. We wept; it was our France too. Special urgent value was given each free day before the start of a frightening new school next September.

Random recall:
—New Year's Eve 1939, stricken with a strep throat, I could not go out on the town with the others, so went to bed with *The Magic Mountain,* which had just come out in English and which Rosemary

had bought at Marshall Field's as my Christmas present. Reading until dawn (as I would with *The Idiot* six years later), I finished the first third and learned more French in the Walpurgisnacht conversation between Claudia Chauchat and Hans Castorp than in all those years in class.

—Strep throats became such a recurring theme that sometime during the next year—or was it in 1941 or '42—my tonsils were ripped from my adult body at Chicago Memorial Hospital, where Rosemary's had been ripped years ago. The night before, I was in the front seat of a car, parked in the shadow of International House on Blackstone, with a man who forced me—but it didn't take much force—to go down on him. Well, I thought, as I nuzzled his velour thighs, I might as well be killed for a goat as a lamb—or whatever the saying is! Next morning the operation was traumatic. Anesthetic didn't function, the doctor explicated each bloody rent to a pair of anxious interns, then dangled the severed tonsils in his forceps before my eyes. I cried profusely for hours. Next morning they gave me pear juice, sent me home, couldn't swallow for days, but sulpha coated my throat in ermine. A week later, out drinking, a hemorrhage let loose. Convalescence for a month. I never saw the man in the car again, but would have liked to. I still get strep throats.

—To be in your parents' car taking you to church, and to drive by the place—a bar, a bench—where last night you fell in love.

To be in a police car taking you to jail, and to drive by your own house where Mother is expecting you home from school.

—Sunday afternoon outing with the whole family where they're showing *Kitty Foyle*. Across the lobby is Frank with a group of friends. I'm currently having an affair with him, but my family certainly doesn't know. We nod imperceptibly to one another.

—Did I mention that, with Mann and Cocteau and Dos Passos, Hugh Walpole was my favorite writer, and that I planned to make an opera from *The Inquisitor*? Did I mention that I hate the jangle of ice cubes? Or that when we sang the college songs in Mr. Vail's music class, I heard them as the French hear what they call olorimes: "Wave the flag for Old Chicago, without a peer she stands" evoking a stalwart female, somehow headless (on our library shelf stood a miniature reproduction of the Nike of Samothrace), walking on water? ("Lead me not into temptation" became Lead me not into Penn Station, and Inquire became ink wire.) Did I mention that Laurence Olivier and Vivien

Leigh, already a mythological pair in early 1940, performed *Romeo and Juliet* in the drafty Auditorium Theater, after the Ballets Russes had left, but no one could hear a word. (Twenty-five years later, when Olivier had his face-lift, he told John Houseman who told Virgil who told me: "I looked so good I wanted to go down on myself.") Did I mention that Ella Fitzgerald's way with words was a way culled from the twenties and stretching outmodedly into the sixties: she put a mordant—a sort of tilde à la Falla—on unimportant words like "the" as well as on important ones like "love"? Or like Debussy's self-conscious setting of the word "nu," with a little trill, in *Placet futile*. Or like Genet's comparing Nijinsky's dancing to his name: the dotted j twixt the two dotted i's sinks and rises in jerky slow motion. (Mae Swenson once in a poem drew our attention to the same iji, hoping, I suppose, that we wouldn't have seen it already chez Genet.)

—Can there be a shape to a memoir other than through the straight line toward death by natural causes (which includes accident, suicide, and murder)? We always die alone, yes, but we live alone too. Since Man has no soul (though certain animals have), shape is moot, does not exist in nature, and the memoir will sink and rise in jerky slow motion, arbitrarily, like some negligible detail out of the Big Bang or, more likely, the Big Whimper.

11. Northwestern 1940–41

While revisiting Northwestern in 1977 to get an honorary doctorate and to give the commencement address for the music department, I passed a free hour alone in the strange, familiar patterns of the campus, stretching for a mile along the lake which gave off the identical taut, sad smell of muscle and wind as thirty-seven years earlier when I had arrived, sixteen and anxious, with my sister and her swain from Beloit, Bill Harrison, who would deposit me at the dorm, have a hamburger, then leave me to my fate away from home. Was I lonely or was it indifference? For the next two years I would not feel a part of the scene, retreating to Hyde Park on frequent weekends (against the better judgment of the parents who so carefully hoped to wean me) or to the Near North Side to see old pals and otherwise get into mischief.

There was no question of pledging any fraternities with their Neanderthal elite, but I did bunk for the first year in a men's residence, Lindgren House, nestled in fraternity row and peopled with one-dimensional Phi-Delt hopefuls (no females allowed, which was okay, since I had frequent male overnight guests, being more able then than now to sleep in a single bed *à deux*), and was obliged to wear the green cap of the frosh. The cap seemed out of sync with my extracurricularity. For example: Part-time lover, Frank (how I met him I don't recall, a blond white-collar worker, around twenty-one), who sometimes shuttled the fifty miles from his room in Hyde Park to my room at Lindgren House, was, oddly enough, a protégé of Lucius Beebe's, gossip columnist on *The New York Herald-Tribune*. Beebe, a professional snob in his late thirties, was a horny class-conscious lush who traveled in a private railway car, and whom I'd heard of, if only because his likeness had just adorned the cover of *Life*. When he passed through Chicago one weekend that fall Frank arranged a gangbang in

Beebe's suite at the Ambassador East, which included me, another librarian boyfriend of mine named Joe Stein, Don Dalton, and a shop-keeper sidekick of Frank's. Room service sent up magnum after magnum of Dom Pérignon (the word magnum seemed sophisticated, as did the champagne—which Beebe called simply wine) and there was lots of self-conscious orgifying lolling around, passing out, pairing off, downing raw eggs in orange juice so as—according to our host, who was pleased to *épater* us midwestern hicks—to replenish the sex ducts, sniffing the bottle of Russian Leather cologne on the dresser, plus one sortie to a dyke bar called Billie Leroy's to eat rare steak. Twenty-four hours of such glamorous tedium was too much for my sixteen-going-on-seventeen years. I asked Don into the marble bath-room so as not to be alone when I evacuated; we then snuck off, took a bus home to Dorchester (setting a portable alarm to ring when we reached Fifty-seventh), and I sobered up for another twenty-four hours by the family fire. Back to the campus on Monday, I redonned the green cap of innocence.

One mile south of the dorm and almost in town loomed the Music Building, a dirty-white Victorian barn quite out of keeping with the vine-covered gentility of the campus proper. The building emitted a continually amicable clank, for in the basement were practice rooms always in use. All music classes were held here: harmony (but hadn't I had enough at the conservatory?), taught by wizened little Albert Nolte, a schoolmate of Richard Strauss's, and rumored to have a beau-tiful wife; keyboard harmony and also counterpoint with wry Earl Bigelow, who also taught piano; modern music with Felix Borowski, who was lucid and caring about Scriabin's *Prometheus*, which swept us all away, but I recall no other pieces; chorus with Robert Howerton, glib and wisecracking, who that year would inaugurate the new Lutkin Hall with the American premiere of Ravel's unaccompanied *Trois chansons* (the middle one, "Trois beaux oiseaux du paradis," is not only the most movingly perfect short piece ever composed but the best model since Monteverdi's madrigals for a cappella writing); and private piano lessons—piano was my major—with Harold Van Horne, a bespectacled forty-year-old technician whom I liked immensely, and who committed suicide in the 1950s, I don't know why. In the Gym occurred Phys Ed (for boys only, the draft was imminent), and in the Journalism Building occurred English lit., taught by Moody Pryor, sarcastic and well-informed, who whistled with contempt at my book report on Kay Boyle's *Gentlemen, I Address You Privately*. (This was in freshman year. As a sophomore, after having been to Mexico, I took Spanish with Señor Carter.) We could smoke in class. And teachers no longer called us by our first names.

My friends? I didn't have any that measured up to those I'd been raised with—toward whom my heart ever yearned. Besides, I felt that Northwestern as a center of musical instruction was pedantic and off center. (The center should have been, of course, contemporary music. Let us concentrate, as every century but our own has always concentrated, on our own music and let the dreary classics shift for themselves.) The people I did hang out with were all Jews, and they welcomed me with an instantaneous warmth that the sniffier goyim withheld. In my reticence I felt at once beholden and indolent. I felt guilty too, as a Nordic erotically drawn to Semites.

Does prejudice come in layers? In the end of Spike Lee's film, when the pizza-parlor owner—exhausted from harassment during a heat wave—finally yells "Nigger," does that imply that when the chips are down his true feelings will out? Do Mencken's swipes at Jews in his *Diary* equate him with the Ku Klux Klan, despite his public statements in support of minorities? Do cruel words during a lovers' quarrel express repressed truths, or are they merely the quickest path to the jugular? To wound a friend is to attack what he cannot deny (a big nose, a small cock, old age, or, indeed, negritude or Jewishness). *Veritas* lies not in momentary *vino* but in years of fermentation. I am not race prejudiced, but I make prejudiced-sounding remarks to certain people under certain conditions. Admittedly, I resent antigay remarks under all conditions, except from gays to other gays.

Anyway, since high school, where'er in the world I roam forlorn, it is the Jews, thank God, who act as a welcoming committee. Thus for two years my "crowd" contained mostly those I met that first week. Yet, except for violinist Ellen Greenberg, who briefly turned up later in New York, I never saw any of them again after I quit Northwestern. Slowly but surely I was absorbed, with all my shyness, into a heterosexual Jewish ambiance. But if somehow that didn't count (since Jews are notoriously friendly, and I as a Wasp was automatically desirable, where's the challenge?), neither did it count with women. Not until I was forty did I allow that the other sex was not inferior; those extraordinary females in my life were the grand exceptions—monsters with male attributes, like brains.

I do remember Anna Louise de Ramus, black piano student of Pauline Manchester's, whom Gerald Cook had told me to look up, and who was also adopted by the Jewish contingent. And Ralph Meeker, a good-looking product of the School of Speech, who, like so many actors, came to our side of campus for voice lessons, and who was

affable, very. I do not remember any soloists, and certainly no composers, who went on to greater fields.

Because the university offered degrees, and because Father believed in degrees, I remained at NU while envying my friends at the
Chicago Musical College downtown, which seemed more purposeful.
Classes seemed déjà vu except for my major. As a pianist I became
something of a star (which only proved what a dreary lot they were
here, for to myself I was middling). Under Van Horne's tutelage I grew
intimate with virtually all of Chopin as well as with the Ravel Concerto
in G—the one for two hands recorded by Marguerite Long and published by Durand in a lavish red and silver edition.

Sometimes the new friends took me to football games, where I
pretended to be engrossed, while inwardly frowning as ten thousand
anonymous robots rose in concert and roared while something incomprehensibly minute transpired down there in the field; the
Quaker in me rebelled at the players' competitiveness, and at the
spectators' willing renunciation of their separate identities. Sometimes, if I had the family Buick, which was rare, we'd drive down to
Howard Street for a drink or three, Evanston being dry, and Howard
Street defining the city limits of Chicago. Sometimes, too, I'd attend
campus events of real singularity. For example, when the Bartóks gave
a two-piano recital, Robert Trotter and I were chosen, what an honor!,
to serve as page-turners. I turned for mad Dita. Bartók's eyes, like
Picasso's, were rays that pierced to your unworthy soul, but whereas
Picasso's were hot and humorous, Bartók's were like black ice. Their
program featured both Debussy's magical and disturbing *Lindaraja*
(which I never heard again, but which lingers indelibly), and his *En
blanc et noir* which in retrospect is the one mistake from he-who-can-
do-no-wrong (everything's right about it except *it*). Another time I
attended a lecture by Thomas Mann, sitting noticeably in the front
row, a dissolute Tadzio, so as to distract the master, who gave an anti-
German speech in a gruff accent, and who didn't once glance my way.

Mostly, however, the nonscholastic hours were spent on home
ground. I felt more comfortable in Mandel Hall's coffee shop at the
University of Chicago with Maggy than at any Evanston hangout, or
seeing French movies at International House—called Int-house—up
on the Midway with Hatti. Maggy had now left home and was living
with Hatti in an empty flat on Harper and Fifty-seventh. Hatti, meanwhile, finding herself pregnant, married the "evildoer," a fetching
French cellist named Andrew Martin. (The apartment was called Mag-
Mar, though I don't recall Andrew living there.) Down the street was
the Art Center, where Mother volunteered and where tea was served
in the late afternoon, when she would don a bandanna and read

palms, a craft learned from her sister, Aunt Midgie. Still further down were the university hangouts like Woodworth's bookstore, then the university itself with the blond poetasters and stocky hockey players, an alluring milieu into which I blended—and yet didn't—with Maggy, who was the unique friend to still call me by the baby name of Nedo. Here too, in this ocean of Gentiles, I felt guilty, since I should legally be in Evanston where tuition was being paid. I felt guilty at being innocent—at *playing* innocent (the besotted Tadzio)—just as I felt guilty at liking sweets. The mere word *cake* embarrassed me: what tastes good must be bad. Like sugar, like Debussy, like wine, like passivity, and yes, like Jews. And now like Gentiles, when they became taboo.

Everyone's life is an act. We play ourselves.

Did we break each other's hearts? Looking back, did we have the time? Promiscuity reigned. We kept lists of those we slept with. My own list grew so extensive, finally so nameless (the boy from The Wharf, the man from the beach), that it bored even me. Was there safety in numbers? Was love—that cinematic category—ever in question? What about Rosemary's virginity? I thought it mature to persuade her to lose it, like the all-knowing siblings in *The Blood of the Walsungs,* ah Mann!

I drove up to Beloit to visit Rosemary one weekend. With me was Don Hopkins, a fraternity man who was trying unsuccessfully to pledge me. (He was the only carnal encounter I ever had at Northwestern, nor had I any local gay confidant during all that time there.) We took Rosemary the sensational new twelve-inch two-sided Gene Krupa version of "Sing, Sing, Sing," a rhapsody in percussion improv. Rosemary was one of a trio, Andrews-sisters style, that performed at school dances ("If You Ever Change Your Mind" a specialty), the three with their cropped yellow curls looking fresh as peaches or baby foxes. Rosemary was otherwise, thanks to Chino, an apologist for the Soviet Union, though it remains uncertain how focused her ideas were.

With a diary each day blots out the previous one unless snared and glued to the page. With an autobiography the years themselves grow chronologically confused. The pressure of a diary is necessarily unavailable to a memoir, even as a diary is by definition antinostalgic.

I read *The Girl with the Golden Eyes, Swann's Way* (which Maggy said "makes gayety so chic"), and reveled in movies made from the early Maigret novels.

Proust is close to Balzac. Simenon is close to Balzac. But Simenon is not close to Proust.

Géorg went to Mexico and returned excited. The excitement was contagious to all, not least to a certain dancer, Josephine Ubry, svelte, coyly tough, good looking, conniving but not unlikable, who had choreographed Copland's rambunctious *El Salón México* to the recent Koussevitzky recording, and who longed to visit Mexico. Géorg in turn longed for the security which he felt, as so many gay men did, was located uniquely with a woman. He married Jo. They honeymooned for several months in Mexico, came back with Jo pregnant. Géorg used to sit close to her on the sofa, his crippled leg tucked beneath him, and while the stained and stubby fingers of his left hand nursed the ubiquitous cigarette (an Avalon, thirteen cents a pack versus fifteen cents for Camels), with his right hand he caressed her preposterously huge belly, or put his ear to her navel, and smiled: *he* was the source of this life; he was a *man!* A daughter, Carla, was accordingly born. Then things fell apart.

It had been with Géorg that I swallowed my first real drink, a straight shot of whisky from my parents' cupboard. I took to it like a duck to . . . to water? That shot was revelatory, instant protection, freedom of a sort. Freedom from people? Everyone seemed to drink. Just as it never occurred to me that classmates were mostly not planning to become composers, so it never occurred to me that everyone didn't drink to excess. Excess has no meaning except to other people. A transparent wall builds itself gradually but inexorably around the incipient alcoholic; a liquid wall so nurturing that he'll sell his own mother to stay inside.

Water, pure water. If you've never been on a three-day bender you can't know the ecstasy in a glass of water, pure water, even when you can't keep it down. Oasis of dehydration . . . mucous-colored drizzle in a cheap hotel room. Is it 9 a.m.? 5 p.m.? Outside the rumble of a real world. Inside a rational voice—me there versus me here—asks if an arm is broken, a wallet swiped, as I smell my own gassy breath. No one else. Go back to sleep before taking stock.

This will recur on a weekly average throughout the world for the next thirty years. At the moment, the resilience of youth was phenomenal; I've always worked as concentratedly as I play. Drinking has often interfered with my social and sexual lives, rarely with my professional life. Being a periodic binger, as distinct from a continual loner, I early learned to stagger (pardon the expression) the binges so as not to conflict with professional work. Cause and effect were indistinguishable: a binge was the macabre reward for violent work, while musical composition was the guilt-edged punishment for the violent binge. But I learned this the hard way.

Example: So dazzlingly did I master the Ravel Concerto that Harold Van Horne recommended me as the chief feature for next Tuesday's solo class at 10 a.m. We performed it at two pianos; I was instantly the toast of the school and invited by Dean Beattie to repeat the feat next month. Next month, the night before the performance, I went out on the town with David Thompson (a philosophy graduate of the University of Chicago and a beau of Maggy's, but that's another story), ending up at the Orrington Hotel with two bottles of champagne, and at 4 a.m. leaving a call for nine. I had thought one day bore no relation to the next. I played like a pig in a fog. When the student audience nevertheless went wild, Van Horne with sarcasm said, "It must be your red hair." An indelible souvenir for two reasons: first, it demonstrated what has later been confirmed only too often—that even specialized audiences don't know good from bad; second, it must indeed have been my red hair. Van Horne's remark, because he was a gentle soul usually, was wounding. Never again have I played in public without allowing at least a week to pass between a binge and the performance, just as conversely I would never swallow an Antabuse before swallowing a martini. (John Cheever: One glass of sherry shows on the page you're writing.)

In our separate ways Rosemary and I now led such gaudy lives that the parents thought maybe, during the summer break in 1941, it would be wholesome for the girls (Mother and Rosemary) and the boys (me and Father) to split for a month or two. Blackening clouds preempted European tourism. Since Géorg—a family favorite, especially now that he was "normal"—was constantly plugging Mexico, it was decided that Father and I together would take a trip south of the border.

12. Mexico 1941

Was Mexico "wholesome"? Well, wholesome's a matter of age as well as of vantage, and the strength of a vice—of a virtue, too—alters with clocks and the weather. (Lapps drink differently than Libyans.) Also, in time of war a moral relaxation pervades a society, even when that society is not itself at war. The fact that "they" are dying over there justifies the *carpe diem* over here. Add to this the very tonality of Mexico, an augmented-fourth skip away from Illinois, and you'll find that wholesome is as wholesome does. The Europe of our experience four summers previous was the Europe of Protestant snow—Newcastle, the North Sea, Oslo, and Hamburg. Chartres was as close as we came to Catholic Rome. Now, the two thousand miles south toward Acapulco was psychologically farther than the five thousand west across the ocean. Even Father, who prided himself that in the line of duty he had visited all forty-eight states, and during World War I went all through France and England, had never visited Italy or Spain, much less seen an Aztec Catholic. He too, as we "boys" headed south, was, like me, invaded bit by bit with a laissez-faire indolence while the sun soared closer to the zenith and farther from the girls.

How many days between Chicago and Mexico City? Three? Four? Father is very much at ease chatting with common strangers. When I ask why he always talks to middle-aged people he replies: "Do you want me to talk to a flapper and be bored?" We're at ease with each other too. Did we share a compartment on the train? What about meals? I do remember changing in Saint Louis, and in Laredo de-training to sup in some squalid café where we were serenaded by green-gowned girls who were actually *putas*—or so we were assured by a knowing male passenger. And I remember that a glass-domed observation car was attached at the frontier, and that the night between Laredo and Monterrey was so thick with shooting stars they seemed a trillion barrels of sapphires aimed at our heads. Then that changed to rain. With the dawn a tropical rainbow, of colors more primary than our Anglo-Saxon rainbows, covered the whole sky, softening the flat scenery that remained along the Sierra Madre before Mexico City. The first glimpse of the city itself was *something else,* like the entry to Fez that I would come to know so well, with the steep fall from the heights into that meaningful valley of ten million souls (including Dolores Del Rio's) all speaking Spanish.

Our plan was to stay there for a week before continuing to Taxco, so that Father, as he always did everywhere, could consult with hospital supervisors. The brutal grandeur of Xochimilco Park still comes back in dreams, as do the meringue pies at Sanborne's. We looked up an artist friend of Géorg's, one Jose Paredes, who showed us his studio from where I bought an extraordinary mask, carved in cork, of a distorted weeping face, crimson and tan, twice life size and ponderous but weighing a mere six ounces. (I have lived with this mask for fifty years, am looking at it now as I type.) I was embarrassed to tell Paredes that we were lodged at the pretentious Hotel Reforma, he seemed so plain and serious, so poor. We invited him to the Bellas Artes to hear, among other things, Debussy's *El mar* (the sea is masculine for the Spanish), conducted by Chávez, whose own *Sinfonia de Antígona* and *Sinfonia India,* so stark and spare and diatonic, were close to my heart. Indeed, just as New Orleans today summons up the plays of Tennessee Williams more powerfully than it imposes its proper identity, so the music of Chávez yesterday evoked Mexico more than Mexico evoked itself. Nature imitates art; now there he was, swarthy and fierce, in person on the stage of his homeland. I had observed Chávez once before, the previous winter, from the highest gallery of Orchestra Hall, when he conducted his Concerto for Four Horns. (The Chicago Symphony for the 1941–42 season had commissioned composers throughout the world to celebrate its semicentennial. The centennial in 1991 would feature my own oratorio, *Good-bye My Fancy.*)

After the concert Paredes at our request guided us to El Salón México. "A Harlem type night-club for the peepul," said the guidebook. "Three halls: one for peepul dressed in your way, one for peepul dressed in overalls but shod, and one for the barefoot." Each hall featured a Cuban or mariachi band, all playing simultaneously; one could appreciate the tempting challenge to Copland of merging this Ivesian din into a cohesive, succinct, danceable medley. Yet I didn't care for the place. It lacked what I thought of as glamour, and it certainly lacked sex. Here again was nature imitating (badly) art. Copland's terse evocation of the dance hall was more inspiring than the dance hall's unknowing evocation of Copland. And so, since during this first week, giddy at the altitude and queasy at the prospect of Montezuma's revenge, drinking was taboo, we left the premises early. But not before Paredes introduced us to a handsome Hispanic with charcoal eyes and a sky-blue necktie. Carlos, too, was a friend of Géorg's, or rather, of both Géorg and "Josefina" Redlich. In fact, I'm not sure why, he drew forth a letter he had received that morning from Jo. The letter, in Spanish which I could not decipher, was signed *Te amo*, which of course I could decipher. I pointed to these words and asked, "What does that mean?"

We went to Taxco by bus, stopping for lunch in Cuernavaca, and arrived midafternoon. Taxco, so lewdly quaint, was nearer to a fairy tale than to America's Midwest, and there was an instant familial glow even before we stepped from the bus. Not "family" in a sense of mutual love but in a sense of everyone knowing everyone—the Spanish, the Mayans, and the loco Yankees who, were it not for the war, would be in Capri or Cannes, converged to make Taxco an operetta town, Latin division. Certainly there was suspicion, even hate, amongst the social and racial groups, but not inhibition. Géorg had forewarned: everyone's available as long as you don't take them for granted; one tourist's head was cut off for having seduced a native, not because the native resented the act but because he resented being taken for queer. Standard rough-trade reaction, Géorg had said, about which I was more naïve than not. Anyway, Father knew still less of such things.

We stayed at the Tasqueño Hotel on the edge of a cliff on the edge of the town. Two dashing waiters in white coats served meals; I loved them both and wondered what they thought of me. Dogs barked nearby and all through the valley continually, especially at night. Father said nothing could be done about it.

The chemical makeup of whisky is close to that of sugar, which is why recovering alcoholics crave sweets. That may explain, since Father and I to avoid dysentery were still taking Enterovioform, why the sight of that American cake after a week's diet of rice and beans seemed so mouthwatering. The rich yellow batter in three layers, topped by fudge frosting identical to the kind I regularly baked in the States, was displayed on the tea cart of Magda and Gilberte, a pair of handsome forty-year-old European ladies sitting out the war in Taxco, and whom Géorg had told us to look up. I begged Father to let me visit them alone; a parent, especially a male parent, appeared de trop if I was to mingle with the Mexican elite. Twenty years later, to my shame, this notion still held water. While professing at Buffalo University in 1960 I invited Mother up to hear Josef Krips's crisp performance of my Third Symphony. But I asked Father not to come, explaining, "Composers don't have fathers." Father often quoted that to friends when the occasion arose and smiled, no doubt to clothe his hurt.

Gilberte and Magda announced that we would be joined by the composer Paul Bowles and his wife. The name rang a bell. Dick Jacob the previous winter had seen the touring company of Helen Hayes's *Twelfth Night*, which he found dreary except for the music, which he raved about, by someone named Paul Bowles. Except for Sowerby, I had never met a recognized composer, nor anyone whose reputation preceded him. But since I didn't know his music I was not intimidated. Bowles did not, any more than Sowerby, look like a composer, i.e., a somber, thoughtful, bearded nineteenth-century German. His direct Americanness, the blond thirty-year-old good looks, and informality despite the necktie in July, made him seem accessible in the extreme, at least on that day in that climate. An ivory cigarette holder was his sole exotic accoutrement. With passing years I would discover that Paul was accessible to no one; whether involuntary or by design his oxymoronic stance was one of aloof friendliness, beckoning unapproachability, the artist as voyeur, more concerned with the hopeless sensuality of all men than with the eager sexuality of one man. Here, however, he seemed to want to give the impression (I've observed this often in married homosexuals) that he wasn't all that "involved" with Jane. "Such intimacy!" quoth he, to my astonishment, as Jane, seated next to him on the Indian leather love seat, gigglingly ran her fingers down his spine. That their identities, separately or together, were other than heterosexual never occurred to me. Jane was neither hot nor cold *à mon égard,* but I found her immensely beguiling with that ski-jump nose and frowsy hair, like a boy in a skirt, sexless but vital. Three languages were in session (for Magda was a Spanish marquesa, Gilberte a French countess), and this impressed me enough to want to go home and study, especially when Paul described a giant scorpion in his bathtub, and the countess cried, "Quelle horreur!" which sounded so much stronger than "How horrible!" Paul invited me to his studio next afternoon, as one musician to another.

For one so worldly—been everywhere, known everyone—Paul coveted aloneness, still does. The studio, if I recall, was off in the wilds and contained a serape-covered mattress, upright piano, phonograph, records, and a thousand books. I had dutifully brought along a manuscript: a set of piano variations on the French noel "Il n'y avait ni chandelle ni feu," puerile, overly ornate, with a penultimate movement grandly titled Cadenza. Paul glanced at it. "I'll bet you can play the cadenza," said he, rather patronizingly as though to a kid. He put on a recording of Copland's *Music for the Theater* which bowled me over. The zany opening trumpet resolving into the stern, sweet strings! The nervy, brash Scherzo! The lean but telling language of a land I knew well but had never heard spoken! American music! Paul then played a piece of his own, the score for a documentary film, I think, and I tactfully said, "It sounds like *Music for the Theater.*" He drew forth *Modern Music* magazine and quoted an essay apropos of himself and Copland: "The master has been more influenced by the student than vice versa."

Did Paul Bowles run his fingers down my spine? I don't remember seeing him again that trip, though Jane was ever in view, coming and going through the byways, usually in the station wagon of an odd-looking "older woman" named Helvetia Perkins, and at Paco's.

Paco's was *the* café, a tiny restaurant with a balcony overlooking the central *xocalo* where everyone hung out during the afternoon and early evening before going to parties. It was there one languorous Sunday that two young male Americans—as people from the States are called—approached Father and me and invited us to a gathering later at the Major's. The Major turned out to be a middle-aged retiree; his gathering featured effete tequila-laden lads of various backgrounds and a few sociable dowagers to whom Father talked. I talked to Robert Faulkner, known to the world as Bu, a sometime employee at *The New Yorker*, with somnolent eyes, a blobby mouth, and the reputation, despite drunken incoherence half the time, for being hysterically funny. Within five minutes he uttered this cosmopolitan limerick:

There was a young lady from Spain
who had a peculiar pain.
She opened her cunt
and found Alfred Lunt,
Noël Coward, and Lynn Fontanne.

It was rumored that Bu was paid by his family (as Norris Embry was paid by his) to stay away. During the following decades I ran into his always pleasant but idle company wherever in the globe I wandered —Florence, Paris, Tangier—except Keene, New Hampshire, his hometown, where I passed two summers at the MacDowell Colony. While Bu rattled on I eyed a short, swarthy American with intelligent eyes who was soberly holding up an inebriated Indian called Aldo. The American eyed me back.

Next afternoon while Father was taking his nap I sat in the *xocalo*. (Father's naps from time immemorial were sacred in the family, they kept him young, and the rest of us were admonished to silence during the ritual. At Cadbury, the retirement home, the nap times had expanded. "I take a nap before each meal," said Father, "including before breakfast.") The swarthy American with the intelligent eyes walked by, spotted me, and sat down on the bench. This was Maurice R., about thirty, an instructor of romance languages in California. Within an hour we had decided to visit Acapulco together, if I could persuade my father to let me go. Which I did, but without saying that I was taking the trip with another person.

I have never gone back to Taxco. But early in 1968 I did see Acapulco again and found it unrecognizable. The town had become a city with stucco hotels, terraced lawns, menacing somehow, with its brothels and discos and money. La Playa Caleta is a country club today. In 1941 it was a wild near-empty beach of incandescent splendor miles from the center. It was here that Maurice and I settled after a five-hour bus ride, dangerous and affectionate, in a French pension on the south end, fifty yards up the hill. On another hill at the north end a mile away was a similar pension, and in between on the expanse of snowy sand that sloped into the emerald Pacific was a large *cabaña* with several tables and a jukebox that continually played the two sultry hits of that summer, "Esta noche" and "Amor," plus the standard frisky airs named for local cities, "Guadalajara" and "Tampico."

By day we swam and drank *cerveza* and made love in a hammock on the private deck, and by night we made love and swam and drank *cerveza* against a sonic blend of wind and chirping insects and the jukebox far down on the beach. The "making love" was not complex. I may have been promiscuous but was certainly no callous roué nor even very adventurous; it was almost sufficient to know I was desired: the knowledge replaced the act. Then, too, Maurice may have not wanted to damage the goods, knowing they would eventually be delivered back to Father. He would speak about Ravel's String Quartet, about his teaching curriculum, and then about my body "gleaming with a golden adolescent fuzz like the marble dust on a just-finished statue" (does one forget such words?), which gave me a feeling of power, as did my Gentile versus his Jewish aura. Once he said, "You know, in Taxco nobody believes your father is your father." I was surprised and offended.

When I told Father, he was not amused. He meanwhile had remained in Taxco, befriending Bu and a dozen others sitting around at Paco's, including Magda and Gilberte. They said to him, on hearing he was from Chicago, "A young composer from Chicago recently came to tea, but he didn't want to bring his father, imagine!" During this fortnight separation I don't remember how, or if, we kept in touch. I do know that when Maurice and I left the Pacific we hired a third-rate automobile with two chauffeurs and went straight to Mexico City, stopping in Taxco only for a quick tequila while the drivers refueled. So it must have been somehow understood that Father and I would rejoin each other in the capital. When night fell and an icy breeze wheezed through the car windows, Maurice and I covered ourselves in the back seat and made love unbeknown to the drivers, or so we thought.

Of the second stopover in Mexico City I remember only that Father and I returned to El Salón México, this time with Maurice R., whom Father was meeting for the first time and liked (I explained that we had met in Acapulco), and that Jose Paredes and Carlos were also there. I got drunk on *cerveza,* said nothing but lowered my head on my arms, face to the table, and listened to the drone of chatter and to the irritating mariachis. Father had never before seen me under the influence. We were staying now at the Hotel Montejo—more intimate and presentable than the Reforma to our new friends—where I passed out, to his dismay. And I don't remember bidding good-bye to Maurice after this, my first honeymoon, nor how I felt then about it. A year or so later he passed through Chicago. I met his train (many hours late) at Union Station, and we sat in his berth and kissed. Then in 1944 he visited me briefly in New York chez Morris Golde. In anticipation of this visit I made a piano arrangement of the Ravel quartet to play for him. We never saw each other again. But in 1991 he wrote me care of my music publisher. Did I remember those tropical weeks a half century ago? he wanted to know.

Father and I returned to Chicago gradually by way of Louisiana, where again he had consultations with hospital supervisors, and where again I left the hotel to cruise the Vieux Carré, and again got tight. What was I after—there, or in the thousand bars during the thousand years to come? Father was always an attractive combination of optimism and cynicism. The world could be a better place, yes, especially if it followed his advice about group medical insurance. He also believed that, yes, rich people are evil, but so is everyone else. (He liked to say that someone was born "of poor but dishonest parents.") He was naïve, too, and certainly not lubricious.

Five years after that Mexican summer Paul Bowles wrote a story called "Pages from Cold Point." It presents a widowed American father and his sixteen-year-old son, Racky, who take an extended vacation on a Caribbean island. Racky gets into serious trouble, which the father at first refuses to recognize, by seducing every male native in the area, threatening their exposure (he is a minor) if they don't put out. The father ultimately forbids the son's sorties, has an incestuous affair with him, then sends him off to Havana, where Racky will continue his free style. The tale, in the first-person voice of the father, flows with such smooth grace and fierce heat—the double face of goodness—that one wonders whence sprang the polished technique in so short a time. In 1941 no one thought of Bowles as a writer.

Back in Chicago my first actions were to buy the record of Copland's *Music for the Theater,* and to begin composing another piano suite, *La playa Caleta.* To Maggy and Hatti I gave cruciform earrings from Bill Spratling's silver shop in Taxco, and to Rosemary and Mother, silver brooches and silver eggcups to contrast with the brass-and-wooden ones from Stavanger. For Géorg and Jo Redlich, to tickle their nostalgia, went discs of "Amor" and "Esta noche." These were received quietly.

One Saturday night Maggy and Géorg and I went to a small all-boy party where Géorg, in his cups, wept out his woes. Jo, he said, disliked him, had married him only to go to Mexico, laughed at him, while delivering the final zinger—their daughter, Carla, was sired by Carlos. I drove Maggy home, leaving Géorg in the arms of a brown-haired stranger. Next morning Mother, annoyed by my indolent liquid sleep habits, forced me to go with the family to Sunday Meeting. When we returned shaky in the sunlight, the phone rang. It was Jo, saying cheerfully that Géorg was in the morgue, and could Father go down and identify him? There'd been a car wreck, the brown-haired stranger had been lacerated (both ears sliced off), and Géorg killed outright. Father said Géorg's head had swollen to twice its normal size.

This was my first death, from which I have yet to recover. It had no meaning, art was no substitute, death was for grandparents, not for peers, and life, at least for survivors, goes on forever, shifting. *Ars brevis, vita longa.* Music's no good in time of sorrow. Music accentuates the emotions it seeks to appease. Unless, of course, it gets the listener's mind off the emotion, or the composer's mind away from the mundane.

But does music, for its composer, mirror his feelings of the moment? Probably not in the way that a poet's feelings are mirrored. A composer writes tragic music out of what he knows about tragedy, from experience or hearsay, but not during the heat of the tragedy. Tears in the eyes drip down and smudge the ink, where clarity should be all that matters.

13. Northwestern 1941–42

That fall I moved off campus to a timely address, 1942 Orrington, the house of a Mrs. Klingen who lived on the ground floor. I had a front room on the second floor, sharing a bath with two journalism majors with whom I was on a nodding acquaintance. The top floor was a quaint garret occupied by a Speech School graduate who resembled a shaggy Wasp version of Maurice R. and who played classical records. One evening I sat on the stairs in his garret, pretending to listen to the music, hoping he'd invite me up. This was Milton Lomask, mature, attentive without sentimentality, a protégé of actor Whitford Kane's, a star in character roles on the English-speaking stage. We had a fiery friendship until Milton was called into the army, at which point I moved to the garret and rejoiced for once in privacy. On weekends, I went out with old friends from the South Side—these now included my cousin Lois Nash, Kathryn's older sister, who was staying with the Rorems while attending nursing school—who would inevitably drive me back on Sunday nights, and we'd have drinking parties in the little attic room. By mid-autumn the closet floor was so strewn with empty bottles that Mrs. Klingen threatened eviction unless I got rid of them. A weak threat, to be sure; tension was rife, and with it a special tolerance, particularly of draft-age men.

After the hallucinatory attack of 7 December the war turned real. Sooner rather than later the Germans would descend upon New York, the Japanese upon Los Angeles, but was the Midwest safe for a while? When I'd come home to Dorchester Avenue on Fridays the Foxes' radio upstairs hummed newscasts all day and all night. Was this indeed a Just War? The concept that all war was bad, that there is no alternative to peace, was implanted in the family psyche. The conflict now felt not so much endless as routine, bringing with it the gloomily urgent excitation of living on the verge. Art, the quintessential positive force on our planet, provokes at its best a collective erection, and so does war, the quintessential negative force.

Business as usual meanwhile on the Northwestern campus. I was now a part-time music critic on the school daily, which also printed my poems and stories. The bromidic criticism concerned local events like the Wa Mu show or the Sibelius Violin Concerto intoned by our students. The poems were sonnets about sailors in the style of Keats. The stories were self-conscious vignettes about misfits who strangle their pets.

More important, my piano repertory was fast expanding. I undertook to fathom the entire *Wohltemperierte Klavier*, all ninety-six pieces. One morning, while playing for Mr. Van Horne the B-flat-minor fugue from Book I, I paused. "Why do these six measures make my eyes well up?" I asked. "Why do Bach's cross-relations break my heart?" He regarded me with pleasure, as though no student had ever made a similar reflection. Why, I wondered, and still wonder, do these lush acidic resolutions so satisfy, exactly as Debussy satisfies? The music hardly needs to be played, just pondered. (For the record, the measures are 56–61.) I invited Bob Trotter, the favorite pianist in school, to perform Milhaud's two-piano suite *Scaramouche* with me and practiced like a fiend in anticipation. The night before our first reading I couldn't sleep, intoxicated at the thought of working—playing—in tandem. I learned Ravel's *Tombeau de Couperin* while simultaneously studying Couperin's *Leçons de ténèbres* (for Holy Wednesday), whose ecstatic first pages "open up the heavens and bring down the house," as Virgil Thomson wrote of Messiaen. I mastered Beethoven's Thirty-two Variations in C Minor and offered them to whoever would listen, mainly in the practice-hall corridors. Why this semisudden spurt of serious gymnastics? Because, like every other pianist at school, I was auditing the semifinals and finals of tryouts for the Adult Education Course series in Orchestra Hall. The winner would be given a recital on that same annual series, which included Schnabel et alia. Hearing these contestants, some of whom would eventually become friends, I discovered what small potatoes were my own pianistic pretensions—that talent meant nothing without systematic labor, that content was nil without style, and that style is one-tenth flair and nine-tenths push-ups. (The winner that first year was Alice Martz, with Jacobeth Kerr and Perry O'Neil as runners-up, all pupils of Ganz's.) It would take a couple of years before I realized that the public virtuoso's life, even at its most flamboyant, was intellectually not for me. "Intellectually" is stressed advisedly. What could be drearier than petrifying into the same endlessly repeated masterpieces, with nary a minute and seldom an urge to investigate new works. Casals's pronouncement that no day goes by without his culling something new from Bach's cello sonatas seems so somehow hopeless: no one work is inexhaustible to the exclusion of other works, especially those of today. Where does the living composer fit in?

More important still, my compositional output was also fast expanding. My first songs date from then, and perusing them now I am not ashamed. People often ask (at least they *used* to ask, before that fragile phenomenon called American Art Song and that staple of elegant concertizing called the Song Recital both got swept away by Big Management twenty years ago) whether I am a singer, since I so obviously love the human voice, as evidenced in my treatment of it. Well no, I'm not a singer, and neither are any of the hundreds of composers I've known (with the possible exception of Blitzstein and Barber), although, since song is the primal musical utterance of every society, it could be argued that inside every composer lurks a singer longing to get out. So yes, I am a singer, for all music is a sung expression, even a piano toccata or a timpani etude. I hope my music sings, but my own physical voice raised in song is nothing you want to hear. Do I love the human voice? Not especially. My first songs were composed (perhaps all my songs) not from love of the voice but from love of poetry, and from a need to conjoin my two loves, music and words, into a third entity of a greater, or at least a different, magnitude than its separate parts. Since we are what we speak, and since song precedes speech (the inflection and accent of any country's language derive from the music—even the nonvocal music—of that country), we are what we sing. Music is not a universal tongue.

Anyway, since I was steeped in E. E. Cummings, it seemed logical to *acquire* Cummings—to make him mine—by setting him to music. One day I wrote two songs: "All in Green Went My Love Riding" and "in just spring," then made legible copies. Next day, overhearing an incantation issuing from a practice room and, peering through the little pane, realizing that the charm came from a girl rehearsing one of Ravel's *Trois chansons,* I entered without knocking and asked her to read through my new songs. Singers are a breed apart, even in music schools. I had never met one before but sensed that here was a kindred soul, if not a mind, who by the nature of her profession was outward and giving, stagy and physical. A singer's instrument is in her body—she is born with it—not in her hands, so she doesn't (necessarily) have to practice to thrill us. Singers used to have a reputation for being dumb; the reputation still holds somewhat, at least among soloists (choristers must be able to sight-read or they'll lose their jobs). For my part, I look upon the entire interpretive world as upon talking dogs. From this remark I don't expect to make any friends among performers. But since in the current professional music world performers *are* that world (in the ken of even an enlightened public) while composers are not even pariahs (to despise something, it first needs to exist, and composers are invisible), they can act huffy all the way to the bank. A singer may earn in one evening what I may be paid to write an opera which would take a year. Composers are to singers as nectar to humming birds. The parasite is more famous than the flower, but crucial to the dissemination, from town to town, which the creator hasn't time to . . . etcetera.

Frances Maraldo, a stream of black hair falling around her face as she leaned to squint at the manuscript on the piano rack, now deciphered quite creditably with her very red lips the settings of Cummings verses as I, tense and patient, accompanied her. Hers was the very first voice ever to sing my songs! After an hour of polishing, we sought the public. Upstairs we ran across Earl Bigelow in the hallway. Would he listen? He would. So here was the very first audience ever to hear my songs! At seventeen I was none too young.

I wrote more songs, on my own words, on those of Bruce Phemister, on the sonnets of Millay and Blake of course, and even an *Ave Maria* as homage to Leo Sowerby. (Leo found my calligraphy and spelling pretentious. I had, for example, in notating for a soprano in the lowest register, used the bass clef. My clef signs looked spidery. And I thought it stylish to use double—even triple—sharps.) Frances and I performed them for parental friends at a tea on Dorchester Avenue. Did we perform them at school too? I can't recall. But during the next decade I completed a hundred songs, sung by America's best, with major reviews as to how I was unsurpassed in comprehending the artifice of the human voice. Yet I didn't know terminology, couldn't define a mezzo as distinct from a spinto, a baryton martin as opposed to just a plain tenor. I'm not entirely ashamed of this. I still feel that singers are too quick to limit themselves according to high notes, to restrict themselves according to what their teachers tell them is good for their range rather than according to what, emotionally, they are longing to wrap their tongues around. I wrote music, not *vocal* music; the singer within me, not the bass or the soprano within me, silently transcribed the impulse to paper. If I wrote what singers call "grateful" songs—an arching line that follows the text—it was not from love of the lyrical but from respect for the lyric. Respect is alive. Who was I, after all, to take a preexisting shred of literature and proceed to wrench it from its contextual shape and crucify it on a clef? I had no knowledge, let alone theory, on how this should be done properly. Only later, when I created for specific singers, and when I beheld the carnage wrought by fellow composers on their fellow poets, did I convert my practice into theory. Only then did I learn what the larynx was, technically; only then did I put into essays the ABCs of how to write a song. But my new songs were no better for all this. In fact, I finally sought to emulate the Ned of yore when he didn't know any better.

Frances Maraldo did not, so far as I know, become "someone" in the cruel and rewarding spheres of opera and song. After Northwestern I lost track of her for around forty years. Then out of the blue she too wrote me a letter.

I have been married eleven times but never divorced.

If marriage means a two-person rapport that contains more than sex and that lasts at least a year (my most recent "marriage" has lasted twenty-seven years), then eleven it is for me—with perhaps another eleven semimarriages, a score of uncommitted honeymoons, and unlimited anonymous one-night stands.

Was it during intermission in that marble room on Orchestra Hall's second floor that George Garratt and I first stared at each other, each from the confines of his own entourage? He was a rangy, horsey, hard-drinking and heavy-smoking twenty-three-year-old maverick from a well-off Pittsburgh family. Now he was a postgraduate double-major, the pet both of Ganz and of Max Wald, who was the composition professor at the Chicago Musical College where George played the role of mad genius. He was a pianist of thunderous agility, excelling in Rachmaninoff and Scriabin, and a composer of breathtaking accessibility, resembling Scriabin and Rachmaninoff. Like so many of the students at the college, he exuded instant know-how (a cachet lacking at Northwestern), which stemmed from being active in the real world of professional music. Because of George I began hanging out with that crowd, pianists Alice Martz and Jacobeth Kerr particularly, and composer Hall Overton, in the confines of the Loop and of the Near North Side, while continuing classes and residence in Evanston where George contributed his share of empty gin bottles to the closet floor.

George himself had a flat in a brownstone on Bellevue, heavily carpeted and agreeably gloomy, where we holed up for days emulating the two gentlemen in *Murders of the Rue Morgue* and read aloud to each other while drinking straight bourbon. I recall an issue of *Hound & Horn* featuring *The Burning Cactus,* with its problematical protagonist named Tyl. So then I stopped being a Poe character and became a Stephen Spender character. Not that George was a thinker (his favorite book was *Jean Christophe*); his keyboard alacrity came less from staunch practice than from canny aping of knuckle-busters like Horowitz and Arrau; his own compositions, exclusively for piano, though well formed, were instinctive, emotional, aspiring toward grand melody without being impelled by a true gift of tune. I was not uninfluenced by George's musicianship, based on bluff and mindless inspiration, because it "spoke," because it was out there being played, not back in the classroom, and because he had an extroverted panache which I had not. And I was influenced because he was that much older than me, and by his glass-in-hand stance, plus his authoritative style, though he never said anything very memorable. He also lied. Since I, although in other ways monstrous, am not a liar, the trait seems anathema and otherwise tedious. George's lies, like all good-hearted liars' lies, were based partly on what he thought we wanted to hear and partly on the resulting inability to state a plain fact without amendment. On the one hand, for example, he claimed to know people he didn't know. On the other hand, he would say, "There are three apples on this table," when in fact there were four. But he was good to have around in those days and was hugely likable.

Father liked him too. During the summer of 1942 he worked as an errand boy in Father's Blue Cross offices on Division Street, his first "responsible" job, which he held for a season despite neurotic flare-ups. And Mother liked him. Many a sober afternoon was passed on Dorchester Avenue, making fudge, investigating phonographic repertory, or picnicking nearby off the rocky barricades in Lake Michigan across from the Palm Grove Inn where Dorothy Donegan used to play. Given his intuitive (as distinct from brainy) artistry, I shouldn't have been surprised at George's deficient sight-reading, yet was uneasy when we played four-hands on the new Steinway—his reflexes were stagnant. When we banged away at Ravel's La valse, Mother burst out laughing. "It's like moving mattresses," said she.

Hatti meanwhile was now attending Moholy Nagy's School of Design. She had moved downtown to a dreary apartment on Wabash, just off Chicago Avenue and right above Tin Pan Alley, a claustrophobic tavern hosting such jazz artists as pianist Lil Armstrong and drummer Baby Dodds, whose throbbing echoed till dawn throughout the building. I don't remember her infant, David, but Hatti seemed already estranged from her legal spouse (the fetching Andrew Martin) and was going with Davis Pratt. None of which slowed down our patronage of the Rush Street bars or of our own parties. In different corners of Hatti's room, four or six or eight of us would neck all night long (but only with our mates) while Bessie Smith wailed from the phonograph, "Black Mountain Blues" ("Going back to Black Mountain—with my razor and gun,/Gonna shoot him if he stand still, gonna cut him if he run"), "Baby Doll" ("I want to be somebody's baby doll, so I can get my loving all the time") and "Young Woman's Blues" ("See that long lonesome road, Don't you know it's got an end,/But I'm a young woman and I can get plenty men"), drowning out the ruckus from the dive downstairs.

George moved to a high rise on East Delaware where I see myself poised shakily in the window thirty floors above the abyss and shrieking "I've had enough of life" while George played Rachmaninoff's Third. Stagy behavior was par for the course; how I made it to morning classes, much less how I practiced with the sturdy regularity needed merely to acquaint oneself with the wide repertory, I cannot imagine. Except to say: youth has time for what it needs, and youth needs all. I have never comprehended those who declare, "Gee, I'd love to read more but just haven't the time."

Do not forget Frank Etherton, for he will weave in and out of the next fifteen years. Frank Etherton was what the French call an invention—and which we call a protégé—of Maggy's, although he had a firm identity before she took him up. Maggy, by now a philosophy major at the U of Chicago, was also, along with Dick Jacob, red-hot in the theater department. So was Frank Etherton. It's uncertain whether Frank ever actually enrolled at the university, but he indisputably had the female lead in that winter's Blackfriars show. As such he was so convincing as to take away the parodistic enjoyment: he *was* a woman. In real life he was a woman, too, or rather, the fairy mascot of fraternity row. Like Truman Capote's, Frank Etherton's effeminacy had less to do with homosexuality than with chutzpah; he would be safe in the roughest locker room for the simple reason that no one could quite believe it. Indeed, it was the duty of one hapless pledge to escort Frank, in drag, to a fraternity dance. After the dance they went, just the two of them, to Riccardo's famous restaurant. Riccardo himself served them the ravioli and champagne, intrigued by this weird lady. At closing time Frank sent the pledge home and went off with Riccardo. For days afterward he abstained from bathing, so as to retain the victorious smell of his conquest.

Frank Etherton was bright, aggressive, weak-chinned, with high-pitched, breathless speech and insane eyes framed by tortoiseshell glasses, and was good company for about thirty minutes, if you too were drinking or, more seriously, smoking pot. But it was hard to talk about, say, Rilke with him (he would yawn at your pretension), or to imagine him with a breaking heart. He had a thousand confidants, but did he have friends? Or lovers, given his sole predilection for doing rough trade? In 1947 Paul Goodman and I wrote musical skits for him to perform with John Myers in Greenwich Village. Ten years after that he killed himself in Cuba, swallowing thirty-four Nembutals, one for each year of his life, but leaving no identification beyond an unsigned note. His image was flashed across the TV screens of Havana and recognized finally.

Somewhere in 1942 I was summoned by the draft to report for a physical. When in 1949 I saw Franju's brutally compassionate film *Le sang des bêtes,* about Parisian slaughterhouses wherein condemned beasts are dealt with anthropomorphically (mass hysteria, tears in their eyes), I thought back to this dehumanizing trauma. It took place in some great bare arsenal. A thousand naked boys, joking and scared shitless, were lined up and prodded by their experienced superiors as though this were already their first day in boot camp. I felt both empathy and scorn for my fraternal cannon fodder, sick that they should suffer this indignity, yet aware that never would I be able to share their *fausse bonhomie* and would decay alone.

Mother hoped my classification would be 4-E, conscientious objector, which as a certified Quaker I could register as. This merely meant that I wouldn't go to jail, but *would* go, unpaid, to a CO camp for the duration and work in reforesting or as a hospital orderly. Father, though proud to have been honored in World War I, felt pragmatically that since war was unrelated to morality, why be moral about methods for avoiding it. I was an artist before I was a war resister. "Tell them anything," said Father, "so long as you stay out, but we'll stand behind you whatever." Meaning, I suppose, that I should tell the army doctor about my love life and be branded 4-F.

But the army doctor was uncaring, and I didn't have the nerve to tell him "anything" (as I would during identical examinations in 1943 and again in 1947). They gave me a deferment because of school— 1-D, I think it was.

Is there no crime for which I don't feel guilty? Paradoxically I feel no guilt for anything I've ever done. (Regrets, sometimes, for what wasn't done, but no remorse for what was.) Yet there I sit, on trial for my life —for having performed some act or believed some tenet that never harmed a soul. If you're a gay pacifist alcoholic atheist Quaker composer, they'll get you coming or going, but for which category depends on the year. As Quakers are legal COs, so they are legally excused from swearing "to tell the whole truth, so help me God," on the grounds that they don't swear, that they don't lie (but that if they do, swearing won't keep them from it), and that God is beside the point. And what is the truth—that wavering monolith—as distinct from fact? Cocteau said: "Je suis le mensonge qui dit la vérité"—his definition of art. A tree on a canvas is not a tree, *La mer* at the concert is not the sea.

During the summer of '42 while George worked for Father, Father let me take special courses at the Chicago Musical College. Which meant private lessons with Max Wald and a class called piano technique with Molly Margolies, Ganz's assistant and, some say, mistress.

For Wald I composed pieces, real pieces rather than exercises, for the first time under supervision. Physically Max Wald was a doughy, featureless, middle-aged presence; socially, although of no compositional reputation, he was a self-assured monologuist who could go on about, say, MacDowell's healthy home life as opposed to Stefan Zweig's sad-gay fiction, even to singers who couldn't care less. I retain not a word of what he said about my little Garratt-style impromptus, but at least I was free legitimately to express myself. (Be it said at this point that I've never retained any wisdom from any comp professor. There is no such creature as the teacher of composition. The only composers I've ever learned from are those I've never met.)

Physically Molly Margolies was a brunette Belle Tannenbaum (her chief Chicago rival): a levantine body, squat torso with spindly legs, big head and broad shoulders, five feet tall; socially, although of no continuing public career, she was a dynamo of opinion, half gossip and half common sense on how to play the piano. The perfect performance, said she, was no more and no less than playing the right note with the right tone at the right time. In my private treasure chest, which otherwise contains Mother's letters and a lock of Marie-Laure's hair, lies the rare Breitkopf & Härtel edition of the Chopin *Etudes* with Molly's indispensably useful markings in red and blue pencil.

I did not know, on starting the junior term that fall at Northwestern, that I would remain only through December. George Garratt and I would live together at the halfway mark between his school and mine, in a six-story edifice on Kenmore, around 5600 North. The one-bedroom apartment contained a piano which we fought over when returning, each from his own daily forays elsewhere, in the evening. Or else we fought *tout court*. I still have visions of our chasing one another fiercely through the halls, past the front desk and into the street, for no reason other than drunken games, cruel or coy.

I can't focus on what any of us, male or female, now that we were involved in grown-up love affairs, thought about fidelity, or how we

defined it. Certainly we didn't practice it according to Victorian pre-
cepts. When I discovered I had the ability to hurt people, I hurt people. It gave an illusion—no, a reality—of power, ergo of existence,
and stemmed directly from having been shunned by those butch numbers at U-High (not to mention from too many Bette Davis movies like
In This Our Life which I sat through four, eleven, times at the Harper
Theater).

We were young enough not to bother emulating the great lovers of
literature. Romeo and Juliet didn't endure long enough to apprehend
the horrors of bourgeois fidelity; the classics never portray love as
long-lived. Tristan and Isolde ingested a potion brewed to last three
years, the maximum period that any two persons find each other
bodily stimulating; after that, if the marriage prevails, it's based on
sterner values (but Isolde and Tristan had no chance to learn them).
Zeus and Hera quarreled about who takes more pleasure in love, men
or women. Zeus claimed women, Hera claimed men. To settle the
matter they consulted the hermaphrodite Tiresias, who said: "Women
take more pleasure in love than men." In her fury Hera struck Tiresias
blind. In his compassion (since one god cannot undo the damage of
another) Zeus told Tiresias: "Though you are blind, I will grant you
the gift of foresight."

Am I imposing a morality as I view it now upon a morality as I
thought I viewed it then? In reality, as well as anyone can relive it a
half century later, wasn't every young person with ambition and talent
and brains and looks and energy behaving pretty much as we were,
making their loved ones wince, but making them proud, too, and
behaving thoughtlessly in a thoughtful manner?

I have no doubt been faithful to a type—that unshaven grown-up
in the park—yet fidelity in its most literal sense is a chimera, a potion
like Tristan's.

(To prate in print about sex, as I so mildly do, makes me apprehensive. Might I be derided, jailed, tortured, guillotined? A government
that bans abortion may, in later years, impose abortion.)

The apartment on Kenmore, like the room on Orrington before that,
and before *that* the room in Lindgren House, was almost certainly a
seat of industry and rest nine tenths of the time. Those nine tenths are
forgotten, congealed in their own dimension known as an oeuvre; a
composer, a writer, forgets pretty much what he's said or how it's said
once the saying's in print. It's the other tenth that is recalled, however
askew. (Could this be said to hold for painters too? Looking years later
at their portrait of Madame X, can they not more readily than a com-

poser return to the room where the seances occurred? Is their own life reflected in the features of the sitter? We are whom artists make of us. Six photographers in the same room at the same minute with the same model will portray six models. Even in a photograph of, say, the Washington Monument, the artist's nationality will be betrayed: a Japanese manages for a cherry blossom to peek over the edge of the lens.)

We gave parties. Alice Martz played, over and over, the F-major Ballade. Over and over I played Ravel's *Forlane,* during the second theme of which George would swoon, saying, "That makes my triangle tingle." Such was his wit. Norris Embry and David Sachs, now colleagues at Saint John's College along with a few hundred other enfants terribles, showed up and talked of *Sang d'un poète* by the same Jean Cocteau who had written *Les enfants terribles.* With them was Robert Anderson, no fool, despite being tall, blond, and handsome (and straight), and their description of the movie was graphically so precise as to leave no surprise when I finally saw it myself two years later. Hilda Mary Thomas, an overweight fluffy soprano with chablis-colored hair, materialized regularly to intone "Un bel di," followed by "Blues in the Night" to her own raucous accompaniment.

Then there was Arthur Weinstein, whose cousin Harold, manager of Russack's men's store on Michigan Avenue, was a footballish opportunist known to us all through his generous horniness. When Arthur, a Manhattanite of impeccable manners and angelic features, came for a visit Harold was anxious to launch him. He was a hit: infinitely cultivated, witty, pretty, tactful but sassy, musically versed, well dressed to a fault, he did not lack for adventures. I never knew quite what he did, but like his opposite number, Frank Etherton, he would regularly come strolling around the corners of my life, garbed in a silken shirt.

We went to a roundtable in Thorne Hall (now razed) near Navy Pier. Topic: "Music in our Changing Society." Moderator: Cecil Smith, parents' old pal and colleague from university days, now critic on *The Chicago Tribune.* Panelists: Lehman Engel, composer and conductor, in a sailor suit; Virgil Thomson, critic and composer of *Four Saints in Three Acts*, which we'd heard of but not heard; and some woman, now forgotten. Opening volley: the obligatory struggle to define music. The others were falling back on Shakespeare's "concord of sweet sounds" when Thomson shrieked: "*Boy, was he wrong!* You might as well call painting a juxtaposition of pretty colors, or poems a succession of lovely words. What is music? Why, it's what we musicians do." That settled that. His unsentimental summation was the first professional remark I'd ever heard—music is what musicians do—and could well have marked my semiconscious acceptance of myself as French and not German.

In early December of 1942, Father, who was then twenty-three years younger than I am today, on one of his peregrinations to Philadelphia, stopped by the Curtis Institute of Music and left a sheaf of my manuscripts at the front desk, even as he had at Northwestern nine seasons before. Why did he? Was it because I was treading water at Northwestern? Because the draft status was perilous and a change of venue would delay being called up? Or that a scholarship to so prestigious a school would prove to him that I was the real thing, thus worthy of his further support in a world which largely didn't care for (i.e., pay for) classical music.

I was accordingly accepted, midterm, as a private pupil of Rosario Scalero's and immediately sent eastward. With the knowledge of hindsight this *dépaysement* describes the first of three vital uprootings to occur in my longish life.

14. Philadelphia 1943

No one strolling through Rittenhouse Square in 1943 could have foreseen the transformation of its environs during the coming generations. Two of the four sides were then flanked by dignified brownstones, the high rise which currently straddles the library on the south corner was a one-story bar and grill where after class we swilled Jack Roses (Philadelphia's indigenous libation), and right across from there the Crillon tower rose alone, waving like a concrete feather. But the park proper today remains identical to itself of a half century ago. Indeed, when I report to the Curtis Institute every few weeks (for I am now on the faculty), walking from Thirtieth Street Station even on stormy mornings and enjoying a perhaps false sense of security after the assault of Manhattan, the clock stops. I'm again a student with the queasy thrill of not knowing enough—or maybe knowing too much —to pass the course. The six lanes of Rittenhouse that intersect at the fountain, the bronze goat, the central booth, the petunia-bordered lawns, have not budged; the circle in the square with its many stone benches still plays host to a rotation of students, housewives, and workmen by day, and by night to a lazy flood of systematized cruising until dawn. On Eighteenth Street the Curtis Institute, outside and in, looks the same, although two new buildings have been added down on Locust Street, and the front office is now occupied by Ms. Elaine Katz.

In 1943 it was occupied by Miss Hill—Jane, to some older students —an officiously motherly type with a Continental veneer, like Frances Osato, skilled at welcoming greenhorns. January I was to start here in the midst of the fray, where everyone else knew everyone else. Was my protecting father with me? Would he have explained to Miss Hill that he "happened to be in the East on business," and stayed just long enough to ensconce me in a one-room flat above Gessell's Florist Shop on Twenty-first, fifteen dollars monthly?

At school, organist David Craighead was assigned to show me around. He introduced the composer flock: Wainright Churchill, Rolf Sherer, David Kimball, and Clermont Pepin whose teenaged Canadian sister was married to our common composition professor, Maestro Scalero, aged seventy-three. These colleagues seemed uppity and reactionary. Asked about their tastes, they mentioned Schubert and Reger; asked to show their wares, they stalled like brainwashed foreign agents. At my first lesson with the maestro, things grew clear.

Rosario Scalero, born in Turin in 1870 and retaining an accent thick as minestrone, had studied with Ernesto Sivori (student of Paganinni's) in Genoa, and had actually known and venerated Brahms. In 1919 Scalero immigrated to the USA, where later at Curtis he became the sole mentor of the adolescent Gian Carlo Menotti and Samuel Barber. Nothing if not technically adroit, these two had been guided by Scalero's iron hand through an endless maze of counterpoint and branded by his special conservatism (Respighi was the last European composer he approved of). On them it looked good. But Barber and Menotti were beginners when Scalero found them; I was already nineteen, with years of rigorous academic baggage, a preoccupation with the music of today, and a few notions of my own. When Scalero now explained that we'd be doing counterpoint and nothing but, and that if he caught me writing "original" pieces I'd be fired, I felt less offended than miffed. I gazed into his empty, hazel, always leaky eyes and wanted to puke. These weren't terms to make a budding artist bloom—yet where could I turn? My parents were dazzled and vindicated by the fact of the scholarship. I could hardly retreat to Chicago. Besides, I'd begun to make friends.

The first and most crucial of these was a seventeen-year-old pianist who lived one floor above me at the Gessells'. Eugene Istomin, the only child of white Russian émigrés whose existence revolved around his career, was Rudolf Serkin's prize pet. In a few months he would be debuting with Ormandy (the Chopin F minor), would win the precious Leventritt Award, would perform (the Brahms B-flat) with the New York Philharmonic and become an overnight star. For now he was winding up the scholastic year, practicing all day, dining always at L'Aiglon nearby, where his father was maître d'hôtel, reading heavy stuff (Thomas Mann, Leibniz) and going to movies. Istomin père was good-looking, imperial, aloof. Istomin mère was dark-eyed, emotional, with a "telling" Slavic alto which she used for mournful love songs accompanied with artful campiness by her son. That son was physically a dusky, worried cherub with a social stance that combined warmth and hauteur in equal doses. (When at fifty he finally married it was to the strong and beauteous Martita Casals, a reincarnation of his mother.) He knew his worth at seventeen: a master pianist already, he never improved, and I mean this as a compliment. Great interpreters don't progress—except sometimes negatively, the way a cancer progresses—so much as expand or contract repertorially; they are what they are by midadolescence, because excellence and comprehension don't come with age, they're inborn. Thus for teachers to admonish students, as Serkin did, not to attempt this or that masterpiece until they're "ready" is to pity the students should they die beforehand.

Meanwhile Eugene liked me, but was wary. Curtis was not riven by hierarchies and lowerarchies, but it *was* segmented, and the specialists didn't overlap, especially the composers, who were a breed apart. Eugene, whose role model was an older pianist, the absent (in the army, like so many others) Byron Hardin, a boisterous Don Juan whose glamour was advertised in hushed tones at school, may have found my French biases effete. But I amused him too. When we grew more friendly his childishness rather than his maturity (which was largely a pose anyway) came to the fore. My urbane generalities would reduce him to conniptions of hiccuping laughter, and he greeted my serious affirmations with incredulous appreciation. For instance, in the game of What If the Famous Dead Came Back to Earth, I said I'd be less interested in playing *The Rite of Spring* for Bach than in showing Nero how to use the vacuum cleaner. When he played Chopin a new world opened up for me. Eugene did not believe in cleaning the piano keys—soap renders them chalky, ungiving, while the encrusted grime of labor renders them homey, elastic. On his unhygienic keyboard he would pause occasionally, in a Largo section, to vibrate a digit upon an ivory as upon a violin string—a hopeless action, but a *musical* action nonetheless, and *musical,* a new term for me, was used in Philadelphia to describe a human trait. (In Chicago, we said "musicianship.") Eugene contended that the violinist Jascha Heifetz influenced his piano playing as much as any pianist, and that he sought, through his buttery legato, to extract from a Steinway what nature had bestowed only on a Stradivarius. During that year I heard Eugene practice and perform for hundreds of hours. His nature became my second nature. I myself am hardly a great pianist but I am a good impersonator; when people comment on my pianism, I say: I can't play at all, I'm doing an imitation of Eugene. If more than the singing of any classical musician, the blues of Billie Holiday (not the tunes themselves, but her *way* with the tunes) have colored my way of composing songs, so the artistry of Eugene Istomin has influenced the way I approach all music, even music he despises.

Other pianists? Besides Eugene, Serkin taught five more geniuses.

Of these, in 1943, I remember mainly Teddy Letvin, who was never depressed, and played with the assurance of inexperience. Seymour Lipkin, who was never without his copy of Van Loon's *The Arts,* and played Ravel's *Le tombeau de Couperin* intellectually, meaning with a deemphasis on dazzle, even in the Toccata, and stressing inner voices.

Sharing the piano faculty was Isabelle Vengarova, a bejeweled virago who frightened me from across the lobby. Her students were to Serkin's (in the ken of the cognoscenti) what Baldwin is to Steinway. Eugene's imitation of "the Vengarova method" consisted of an arched hand producing a satiny but weightless gloss. Still, Madame Vengarova's entourage remains clearer in memory than Serkin's. Is little Gary Graffman, whose olden rendition of the A-flat Ballade remains indelible, truly the current director of the Institute for whom, a half century later, I've just completed a *Left-hand Concerto?* There was Eileen Flissler, too, she of the brassy laugh and rosebud lips, who could sight-read anything. After marrying Aaron Rosand, she had something of a chamber music career (in 1970 she played in the ill-fated nonet I composed and conducted for the movie *Panic in Needle Park*) and died a suicide. There was the rubicund Abba Bogin, frisky as a pup with an infallible ear and a "way" with Haydn. And Jacob Lateiner, for whom Elliott Carter would invent a piano concerto, thanks to the Ford Foundation in the beneficent sixties.

Shall I add that mostly all of these pianists who were my new friends were also Jewish? That I mention this merely as a sociological datum is only partly true, or that I noticed it simply because I was Gentile, thus an outsider. For one thing, the pianists among themselves spoke not only the common language of pianism but of the Jewishness they shared, and which indeed dominated the performing world then, as distinct from the composing world. (Aaron Copland as a Jewish composer was the most visible exception since Mendelssohn. But he was also gay, which sort of makes him a Gentile.) In fact, I felt a bit like a cheat, as I had felt at Northwestern, in my passivity at not cultivating a more goyische milieu. Today this sense of . . . of *illegitimacy* could not arise, since the student pianists are mainly preteenagers from Korea or Japan who, for sheer technical proficiency, play rings around Horowitz, but who spend so much time practicing their instruments they never learn English. In 1943 the gap between a reticent midwestern Wasp and second-generation Russian Jews was casually spanned by the rambunctious magnanimity of the latter, with their stage mothers and extrovert brio that is part and parcel of the public performer's character. Besides, who else was there?

I don't recall having shared a single meal with any of the cowed composers, much less visiting their rooms. Was I reticent about wanting to discuss, say, Delius, fearing they might have found him superfluous, even facetious, if they even knew of him?

The famed harpist Carlos Salzedo was a vibrant figure around the halls, with a following of exclusively female blond angels who had all forgone the standard instrument—the golden triangle that is strummed in heaven—for the Salzedo harp. The Salzedo harp sounded effective for Salzedo's own works (the most popular, called "Scintillation," required striking the hollow case of the instrument) but looked like an ecru coffin. One of the harpists invited me, and I crazily accepted, to accompany a recital in her Virginia hometown. (What the program comprised, I've now forgotten, likewise the bus trip south. I do recall only that the angel's parents spoke of "Negroes" even as a Negro passed canapés.) Can one fraternize with harpists?

> The harpist needs a lot of pluck,
> A black silk costume and a truck.

wrote Gluyas Williams.

The singers at Curtis, by the nature of things, became staunch pals, and some remained so for decades. They were pupils of Madame Gregory's, of Richard Bonelli's, of Elisabeth Schumann's. Muriel Smith, whose mezzo was rich and slick as peanut butter, was the first person ever to sing my songs publicly. This she continued to do, recitalizing regularly along with her triumphs as the first *Carmen Jones,* later as a vedette in London, finally as a pawn of Moral Rearmament. She ended as a dietician in a southern college, where she died forgotten.

Ellen Faull, whose soprano of unlimited range flowed with unflawed naturalness from her larynx like a cloud of peridot chiffon, was also a disciplined technician with a wide repertory. She has become, via international opera houses, one of our classier vocal pedagogues. In 1963 at her behest I made a little book of Tennyson settings which she premiered the next year, and continues to promote. Remo Allotta (later called Kenneth Remo), a laughing Italian with diction clear as spring water, also inspired some psalm settings which he championed, until the song recital as a lucrative medium collapsed forever. Meanwhile he created a major role in Weill's *Street Scene,* vanished, reappeared in California as Aschenbach in *Death in Venice* toward 1974, and now seems again submerged.

Tenor David Lloyd, then David Jenkins, was, like Byron Hardin, in the army and showed up only on sporadic furloughs. Will I ever forget this seductive self-assured soldier as he opened his mouth to intone —Eugene at the ivories—a lied of Brahms's? David didn't so much change as instill my notion of Song: how it is sculpted, articulated, sounded. Four years after when we were all in New York I set a text of Catullus expressly for—not David himself but—his disembodied voice. In 1962, with Veronica Tyler, he created (as the French say) my cantata, *King Midas.*

Of the string players I remember many but befriended few. The image of cute Bobby LaMarchina does return, sitting on his haunches in the cloak room tossing jacks, regarding no one, seemingly illiterate, then in the evening, on the stage of Curtis Hall, concluding a sensually controlled version of Ravel's *Habañera* with that insidious upward glissando, so adult, so satisfying, and yes, so musical. He was Piatagorsky's pride who grew into a conductor, performed my Third Symphony in Washington, D.C., and again in Hawaii, had flings with two strong-minded female acquaintances of mine, and now I've lost track.

Although William Kincaid and Marcel Tabuteau (the latter's wife coached French at school) were in evidence, especially on Saturdays at the Academy at their respective desks as first flute and first oboe, and although I was in awe of the very fact of them, as one is with people one has long heard about but never seen (their solos on the three separate recordings, all led by Stokowski, of *L'après-midi d'un faune,* were, in calculated languor and tonal hue, nothing less than lewd), I did not mingle with or recognize any student wind players, even less the brass and percussion majors, if there were any.

For the record, I "minored" in piano with Freda Pastor, still on the faculty today with her wheat-colored hair, and treating me still like a child. At our first lesson she said, "You mean you're going to do it by heart?" as, with no music propped before me, I prepared to attack Beethoven's C-minor Variations, a piece I had mastered at Northwestern and felt professionally on top of.

(I am my ideal pianist. If I'd rather hear myself play more than anyone, it's not that I'm better than anyone—there is no "better than"; it's that my imagination fills in missed notes, the inner ear camouflages mere sloppiness. I play just well enough for perfection, while virtuosos play too well for perfection. Most Big Pianists perform the same repertory. They can't all be right. But I am right for me. Perhaps I should have said: The only pianist for my idealized performance is me. I have never needed to lament, "If only my parents had forced me to practice!")

The current landscape was stimulating and competitive. Curtis operated far closer to the professional bone than did Northwestern.

As to the sexual preferences of these enumerated categories of musician, I was not yet conscious of the generalities I was later to formulate in talks with Dr. Kinsey. Meanwhile, although I had a perfectly ample sex life during my one year in Philadelphia, I never slept with anyone connected with the Curtis Institute.

A few weeks after my arrival, I went upstairs to the Istomins'. There, sitting at the piano in a persian-lamb coat, legs crossed, one hand idly on the keys, was a girl who flashed me a smile of such radiance that it warms me even now. This was Shirley Gabis, aged eighteen, a protégée of Eugene's whom he was grooming for the May auditions at school. Friends on sight, we have remained so through thick and thin. Her silver laugh, like her golden smile, is all-embracing. (As a rule I dislike laughter, all laughter, but particularly the penetrating overreactive shrieks of girls impressing boys whose jokes they don't get, or the jerky cackle of mediocrities at the beach whose sole response to anything is this mechanicalization. A rare few have good laughs—Michael Torke today has a firm, round, male laugh—and Shirley was one of them.)

She lived on Delancey Place, number 2302, with her divorced mother, handsome Rae Gabis, who had been raised in London and enunciated in uppercrust British tones peppered with yiddishisms and goddamns. Shirley's speech, in turn, was an unnuanced mélange of high English and low Philadelphian, enjoyable but odd to my Chicago ears. She had inherited her mother's beauty and poise (Shirley's limbs and torso remain famous), as well as her willful, even combative, intelligence, often at odds with a plaintive vulnerability. Two older brothers were off at college; the father, a small, wiry businessman, lived elsewhere in the city but showed up occasionally to lay down the law, then vanished again. Rae Gabis, who loved music with the awed respect of the cultured amateur, was self-supporting as a furrier's assistant in Germantown, rising early to catch the commuter train, returning late, shopping en route at Horn & Hardart's, and making ends meet for the sake of her daughter's uncertain future as a pianist.

An hour after Rae Gabis had sized me up, she asked, with a smile of anxious ingratiation: "How much rent do you pay at the Gessells'? ...Fifteen a month?" Pause. "Would you like the back room here, for ten dollars a month, plus meals?"

So I moved in. The street-level apartment shared by this pair of adult females was a floor-through railroad, with three large rooms: a front parlor with sliding door which at night separated two sleeping areas for Shirley and her mother, and a back dining room, which was also my bedroom, overlooking Fitler Square. Smallish kitchen, one bath. Upstairs lived the Grossmans—Roy, the neighborhood's air-raid warden, and Mary, a retired high school teacher who drank.

We "children" went to bed late, got up late, evening meals were served by the *schwartze,* Lucy, during which Rae harangued us: "You goddamn kids, sleeping all day, while I work just to feed you." I had never heard voices raised at table, and found this as glamorously indigestible as the food, both here and in Latimer's delicatessen on Spruce Street: rare meat, corned beef, pastrami, sour cream, Jewish and Italian specialties. We went continually to movies (when not attending the almost-nightly recitals at Curtis), mainly at the Avon—*The Cat People, The Hard Way*—or at the all-night theaters on Market Street after bars closed, which was midnight in Pennsylvania.

Eugene, Shirley, myself, formed a triumvirate (except when Shirley and I went barhopping, which we deemed Eugene too young for), smoking a lot, talking unstoppably of subjects deep and gamy. I was uncomfortable with the local stress on classicism, especially on Beethoven. Yes, at Northwestern, and even before that with Belle, I had learned, even mastered—or vanquished, if you will—much of the standard repertory. But it hadn't occurred to me that Beethoven was the core of the cosmos. Now, with that Teutonic shadow over Curtis, and especially with Eugene and Shirley, I was made to realize that France was an unnourishing dessert, while everything east of the Rhine, with perhaps an added pinch of Italy, was Music.

I immersed myself in the late quartets, dissecting the scores, pondering the discs (mainly the Busch ensemble), and fearing that the lack was in me and not in Ludwig when his airs didn't click, when "it" didn't happen, when the involuntary mental erection impelled by True Art failed to materialize. I never got—still don't get—the point of Beethoven. Far from weeping, I nod; my guilty love of Debussy and (shame!) Poulenc was as disconcerting as my preferring sugar to pasta, or preferring men to women. Would Beethoven acquire new meaning when I "matured"?

Meanwhile I was subjected again to a draft exam, and was again rejected, as I would be still a third time in 1947 when Dr. Kraft, my analyst, wrote to the army psychiatrist that I had "not yet developed mature sexual impulses." (Picture the wise young privates in their barracks, ripe to defend the nation with mature sexual impulses!) But I digress. When I did mature I had not learned to appreciate Beethoven more intensely, though I did learn that Beethoven himself never developed mature sexual impulses.

As for that added pinch of Italy, it was intoxicating. Shirley was crazy about a dozen Monteverdi madrigals as recorded by Nadia Boulanger with four singers—the Comtesse (Marie-Blanche) de Polignac, Paul

Derenne, Hugues Cuénod, Doda Conrad—in Boulanger's own arrangements for piano and strings. This music "spoke to my condition," as Quakers say; one of the madrigals especially, "Amor," or "The Little Nymph's Lament," has, with its mounting melody over a four-note descending ostinato, lingered and resounded through my own songs more than any other musical experience from this period. Polignac's thin soprano—backed up, like a pop vocalist's, with a chorus of three commentators—was hardly lovely, but it defined expressivity at the highest level. Forty-five years later I found a copy of the old disc and played it again for Shirley. Oddly, though she recalled the other madrigals, she didn't remember "Amor," which, thanks to her, had been so seminal to me. (In 1954 in Rome, Bill Weaver played me the raucous Kay Starr's "Comes Along a Love," which throbbed in my head forever afterward. Recently I reminded him of this. " 'Comes Along a Love'?" he mused. "I don't remember. Was it on the other side of Kay's 'Wheel of Fortune'?")

Curtis had its claustrophobic side. Escapades were in order. Not having seen New York since the world's fair in '39, when I so savored the anxious sensuality of being far from home, I planned a return visit, with who knew what mischief in mind, sometime in late February.

"Then you've got to look up Lenny," said Shirley. She was forever talking about Lenny, Lenny this, Lenny that, and making comparisons between his talents and everyone else's. There's nothing Lenny can't do at the piano, she claimed, nothing he can't do with an orchestra, plus he's witty, good-looking, cultivated, bedazzling, hot stuff. Alvin Ross concurred. Alvin was Shirley's painter friend, gentle to a fault, winsome, wry, smart, and excruciatingly adept in his Balthusian portraits. He reminded me of Géorg Redlich, whose recent death was still unsettling. Alvin painted my detailed likeness (since lost) and we became staunch platonic chums, remaining so until he, too, died thirty-two years later of colon cancer. Alvin had a velvety voice, hooded eyes, and a single long white hair that sprouted from his forehead. He too raved about Lenny, who seemed to be a legend around Philadelphia, though but twenty-three when he quit Curtis the previous year. Lenny was one of those few who called Miss Hill "Jane." Both Shirley and Alvin were in love with him in their way, and so was Rae. His fabled gifts, where did they lie? I wasn't too aware of, or much interested in, what it meant to conduct, and no one had yet mentioned that Lenny composed. Why? He himself was not modest about his gifts; yet within the next twelve months, when three large, well-drafted works of his were unveiled to the world, even his intimates applauded as though he had suddenly grown a third arm. For the moment, though, he was a throbbing cipher.

If, as the French contend, beauty is its own calling card, so is chutzpah. So too, in my case, is ignorance. Leonard Bernstein must not have owned a phone, or else I didn't know you're supposed to call people before you go visiting—at least in New York—because my entrance into his life was a knock on the door.

I had never seen anyone who more exemplified Wordsworth's "bliss was it then to be alive," whose favorite works of art were so in sync with my own, yet whose acquaintance with these works had fomented in a milieu so foreign to mine. This I would realize in the next few hours, for to know Lenny at all was to know him immediately.

I had interrupted a rehearsal. Later he chided me about manners, but now invited me in and bade me listen. The piece being practiced was Lenny's own Clarinet Sonata. For someone not a composer his sonata sounded so much more seductive and well wrought than anything I—who *was* a composer—could come up with, that I felt, well, wistful. Already nineteen, with a scholarship at the world's most prestigious conservatory, what had I to show for it? For that matter, had any nineteen-year-old American, thriving in this youth-worshiping land of the free, composed a symphony with even half the strength and skill that Shostakovich had at nineteen in his repressive Russia, or a poem with even half the wisdom and nuance that Rimbaud had in his decadent France? I would delve into the matter at length with Lenny (who never delved except at length), because when the rehearsal ended and the clarinetist—whose name was David Oppenheim—departed, I remained for the weekend.

Bernstein, then twenty-four, subsisted as a music editor and piano teacher, working out of his second-floor flat in a Fifty-second Street brownstone, west of Fifth Avenue between Tony's Bar and the 21 Club. Since the block still glimmered with the same nightclubs as in 1939, the new residential pockets seemed incongruous. Yet in the four intervening years classical musicians, who once lived in Greenwich Village and who today haunt the Ansonia and environs, were already staking out flats midtown in their immigration to northern Manhattan. (That tinkling piano in the next apartment—said my host—is none other than Eugene List laboring on the Chávez Concerto, an image which moved me more than being with Lenny, because I had *heard* of List.) Lenny shared the place with a girl named Edys, who loathed me on sight. He balanced this, without apology or explanation, by his unpatronizing interest. If in later years I often saw him rude to a point of parody, it was always to peers, never to underlings unequipped to shout back.

We went over his little Clarinet Sonata, of which I especially adored the jumpy 5/8 motive. Learning that I'd been to Taxco two summers before, he seemed put out—*he* hadn't been to Taxco. That I'd met Paul Bowles, whom he apotheosized, while in Mexico vexed him still more—he forever combined generosity with competitiveness. Then he cheered up, declaring that the jumpy motive was his "Taxco tune" —that he *had* been to Mexico through his music. As for the "Taxco tune," it acted on me for years to come as Vinteuil's *petite phrase* acted on Marcel. Its serious frivolity, so vaguely low class and so precisely American, were traits I'd not known before.

"Shirley says you're the only one alive who can negotiate all those repeated G-sharps in 'Alborado del gracioso.' " "That's because I fake it by taking every third G-sharp an octave higher," and he showed me how. "Here's a better piece," he went on, and played "Une barque sur l'océan" from the same suite—*Miroirs* by Ravel—as the "Alborado." I'd often read through but never learned "Une barque," dismissing it as one of Ravel's rare duds. Now here was Lenny bringing life to those academic roulades, revealing a brand-new side of the one composer I purported most to know. His pianism was the most alive I've ever known, glittering in my mind still as I write. Those vital hands are now a skeleton's.

We talked of Chávez, agreeing that we were surely the only two people on the block who knew the Mexican's *Sinfonía de Antígona*. And how many others on the block could intone by heart the newly recorded French chansons of Marlene Dietrich, "Moi, je m'ennui" and "Assez"? (In the latter the orchestra suddenly halts as Marlene utters a deep *Ah!,* "the dirtiest single syllable ever etched in wax," said Lenny, echoing my reaction to Mae West five years ago.)

How had he avoided the service, and how did he deal with those complete strangers in the street—inevitably women—who point a finger to say: "Why aren't you in uniform?" Asthma kept him out. He dealt with the strangers by ignoring the hostile ones and cajoling the others. Left of liberal, like his friend Marc Blitzstein (who *was* in the army—pridefully so), Lenny was no pacifist, at least not then, but would come, over the years, in his fight for a better world, to believe in the wretchedness of the military. Would he today, with me, discourage the gay men and lesbian campaign for acceptance in the military, encouraging them rather to join in abolishing the military? (If I'd said this before, I repeat it here—my one obsession that bears repeating.)

He wowed me with his just-published version of *El Salón México*. But when I began sight-reading Copland's Sonata—rather well, I thought—he asked: "Don't you believe in observing dynamics?" I countered that the dynamics were in my head. He went on: "You

ought to go see Aaron. Aaron's always interested in *jungische* composers." Whereupon he picked up the phone and made a date for me
with Copland.

We stayed up late, drank scotch, I vomited, we finally retired on a
floor mattress in the front room, and arose next day at nine after Edys
had left for work. Since he had to give a lesson at ten (to an untalented
middle-aged priest) we had a quick breakfast on nearby Sixth Avenue
at the Faisan d'Or—gay bar by night, short-order joint by day—where
Lenny washed down his cornflakes with another shot of scotch (before
a lesson! I was impressed), and where he put nickel after nickel in the
jukebox to hear "Why Don't You Do Right?", because "it's all about
money."

We went to the Museum of Modern Art (my first visit), and when I
stumbled over the name Rouault, he corrected: "It's roo-ohl. Slowly
now: ROO-OHL." Music, too, must be "pronounced" right, he claimed.
"There's *the* inevitable performance for every piece." I can't agree.
There are as many right ways for any piece as there are good players;
even the composer's way isn't the last word (late note), and styles
change with the years, etcetera.

We went to the Central Park zoo (also my first visit) and examined
the camels, which resembled cartoon creatures who suddenly speak
English. Antelopeanly, Lenny leapt among the boulders, proud of his
New York.

Yes, we saw eye to eye, but from different angles, he from his
extrovert (Jewish, if you will) performer's perspective, I from my
retentive Protestant vantage. Thus, when he listened to *Les noces*—
which we both loved—through his ears, I through mine, what were
we hearing? *Les noces* is about ancient Russia by an orthodox Catholic.

When I said that a certain person had all the bad points of Jews but
none of their good points, Lenny coolly asked if I were anti-Semitic,
then promptly added (will I ever forget?): "You're a disconcerting
mélange of surprising sophistication and stupefying ignorance."

How do I sum up Lenny Bernstein after this first encounter? In
our country of self-limiting specialists, here was a jack-of-all-trades as
authentic as Leonardo. There seemed no area in which he did not
consider himself an authority—music, pictures, books, politics, cooking, lovemaking. His overreactive enthusiasms did not embarrass me,
even though they stemmed from someone five years my senior who
should have known better. Nor was I ever quite certain, during the
next four decades, how much of it was faked—like those repeated G-
sharps in the "Alborado." Still, each of us decides early in life on the
part he'll play; the role of enthusiast like the role of Protestant becomes ingrained, second nature, ourself. The fact that we were both,

by definition, a part of our century did not keep us from shivering with delight at the very thought, unlike (and this still holds true) 90 percent of classical musicians, who are trammeled by the past.

"What in the hell are you doing with Scalero?" he wondered.

What indeed?

Scalero now seemed dryer than ever. And so old. The fact that I, in his shoes today, will soon be as old as he was then, does not soften an interpretation of the past, though it does affect my way with the young. If my semiweekly intercourse with the maestro concerned nothing but counterpoint and more counterpoint, proffered in the abstract, an end in itself, I now avoid all emphasis on that craft with my students; should they need some tightening of their voice-leading, I suggest a refresher course elsewhere in the school. A teacher of composers, if there is such a breed, must himself be a composer, one who has often heard his own works well played, and thus has the practical sound in his veins with no cause to be frustrated. His point is made more through example than preaching. Indeed, looking back, I've learned as much from composers I never knew, or never could have known, as from scholastic discourse. Their work, not their words, provides the model, and a model is all that a student can build upon. I don't recall ever discussing *music* with Scalero, though we must have done so occasionally. I do remember his claim that the theme for *Essay for Orchestra* No. 1 by Samuel Barber—Sam, as he called him—was from his (Scalero's) own notebook; and that when the name of Virgil Thomson came up, Scalero said: "Silly man—he wears bracelets." Not being a practicing, much less an appreciated, composer, Scalero was damned if anyone else would be. To a younger pupil this approach could be sterilizing. But I was nearing twenty, and would bide my time. At least I knew who I was.

Who was I? Can a person be defined by who rather than what he is? By behavior rather than production? A composer cannot.

Was I composing on the sly? Absolutely.

Menotti taught a course called Dramatic Forms and I was enrolled, as was Wainright Churchill, plus a dozen singers. The purpose was to illustrate the theatrical devices of librettists and composers in every sort of vocal music, and the instrumental filigrees that embellished it. If art is the communicable concentration of some aspect of life that shows one or more persons what they did not know they knew, then surely the lyric theater embodied the theory more strikingly than other forms. I've also retained the term *chalumeau* as defined by Menotti: "This lowest register of the clarinet resembles a gurgling dark liquid, and that is just what Paul Bowles had in mind, in his wonderful background score to *My Heart's in the Highlands,* when a character guzzles liquor from a jug." And the class was beguiled by the teacher, singing both parts in his sweet little "composer's voice," when he performed a love-duet from his just-finished opera, *The Island God.*

Menotti got special dispensation from Scalero to allow Wainright and myself to compose similar scenes for presentation in class. My choice of text was gaudy. In Huysmans's *Against the Grain* the world-weary hero engages a ventriloquist and two mimes to divert him. As he lolls on silver cushions in a dark nook of his parlor, the carefully lit hirelings enact a melancholy scene from Flaubert. Toward the end of *The Temptations of Saint Anthony* Flaubert invents a savage conversation between the earthbound male Sphinx and the skyborne female Chimera:

"Hither, Chimera, rest awhile."

"No, never."

So it begins, winding a lurid path through such opulent pronouncements as, "I seek new perfumes, ampler blossoms, pleasures never tried before," and ends fifteen minutes later with the Sphinx's resignation to the impossible: "Thou dost escape me."

As sung by Remo Allotta and Ellen Faull, the well-rehearsed timbres and curving airs remain in the memory, and our teacher, whose rising fame was based largely on outrageous plots, professed titillation at the drama. Lately I've reperused the score: chunk after chunk of Ravelian harmony buttressing De Mille–type tunes make an effective display to the unknowing, but as a structure the piece is zero. I mention this little cantata, *The Sphinx and the Chimera,* because it is my first decently performed piece, and thus my Opus minus-one.

Opus minus-two was a Four-hand Piano Sonata contrived at the behest of, and recorded in a regular studio by, Eugene and Shirley. What wouldn't I give to retrieve that *cire perdue,* not for the beauty of the music but for the unduplicatable passion of the young performers! The music itself combined Hindemith's Four-hand Sonata with John Alden Carpenter's Concertino and pleased with a not entirely empty sparkle. I revived it on concerts off and on for the next five years, then consigned it to a forgotten trunk, where it shall forever remain.

My actual Opus 1, also dating from 1943, is a short psalm for men's choir and a few winds, about which I'll tell you in a few pages.

Shirley and Rae heard about my "Jewish generality" to Lenny, and were shocked. "What made you say such a thing?" I was not proud, but neither was I clear about "such a thing." Today's politically correct postures were differently focused yesterday. As a Quaker, wasn't I, by definition, without prejudice? (I note this here not to define but to describe.) If there were good and bad Jews, couldn't the same be said of Gentiles, of Negroes, of homosexuals? Lenny twitted me ever after for being anti-Semitic, and constantly repeated (if others were listening) his *mot* about my being a mixture of sophistication and naïveté. Alvin Ross, too, was bemused by my sweeping pronouncements which, when challenged, I would cover with a "Don't hit me, I'm a pacifist." Marie-Laure would soon declare that I—or at least my spoken French—was a cross between the princesse de Clèves and Jean Genet. Even JH today claims to be sometimes stunned at my various unreasoned *propos*.

Well, it is not given to us all "to see oursels as ithers see us." My parents, who had converted to the Society of Friends when their world seemed elsewhere so intolerant, were nonetheless capable of "remarks" about the Other. My rationale for Rae and Shirley would have been that, yes, for me Jews are the Other. But so are the Rich, the Chinese, all women, straight men, redheads, horses, and certain breeds of dog. Indeed, so is anything not myself. Generalities are risky, true, but they're sexy too. Opposites attract as well as repel, and similarities make a dull planet. Why else were we all so anxious to go live in France when the war was over?

In Yaddo in 1965, when he was more malleable than now, and was supposed to know about such things, Norman Podhoretz answered my "What is a Jew?" by saying he'd have to think about it. Next morning he said: "It's a frame of mind." This could be the case too for a homosexual (who could aver, and be believed, "I used to be gay, though I'm not anymore") but not for a black. To be black is, first and foremost, a physical state. The complication with Jewish is that it's sometimes a religious condition, sometimes a Semitic condition, sometimes both. But an anti-Jewish Arab is not anti-Semitic, and a Jewish convert—Elizabeth Taylor, say—can change her mind.

If someone told me that so and so had all the bad traits of a homosexual and none of the good traits, would I be offended? Probably. Less so, if that someone were gay.

In early adolescence I put away childish things and learned to understand T. S. Eliot. We all understood Eliot. He was the complex adult antidote to Amy Lowell. Today, three generations later, I cannot understand him, pondering Prufrock without a clue. But if the sense has vanished, so has an awe of his language-dropping. In Part V of *East*

Coker, for instance, Eliot speaks of "Twenty years largely wasted, the years of *l'entre deux guerres*—" which of course should be *d'entre deux guerres.* (Gore Vidal in 1985: "Tennessee loved to sprinkle foreign phrases throughout his work, and they are *always* wrong." Gore does the same, and they are mostly wrong—as in his many repetitions of *cri de coeur,* intending *cri du coeur.*)

Nevertheless, while still at Curtis, I sketched out a choral setting of *The Hollow Men,* opening with a male chorus in parallel fifths. I was pleased with this *trouvaille* until Shirley (unaware of my sketch) said that were she to set *The Hollow Men* to music she would open with the basses and tenors in parallel fifths. (In the contests I judged in the late fifties, many an entry was a choral version of *The Hollow Men,* each beginning with a men's choir in parallel fifths.) As late as 1947 I made a setting of Part IV of *The Dry Salvages,* which I called *Prayer:* "Lady, whose light shines on the promontory. . . ." Janet Lauren learned it, and the hue of her coppery monotone on the concluding words—"or wherever cannot reach them the sounds of the sea bell's/ Perpetual angelus"—lurks still in the back of brain, though the song itself, unprinted, lies dusty in the same trunk as the Four-hand Sonata. None of us knew that Eliot did not grant permission to composers. Only with *Cats,* posthumously, did his widow with an eye on the market concede the rights.

Not only Eliot, but all poetry today makes less and less sense. Did I ever know what it was about? Yes, in song settings. But no longer. It's not that I'd sleep till noon—I wouldn't go to bed till noon. The pith of a poem emerged during exhaustion in the seconds before sleep. But never *during* sleep: dreams have their own logic, which poetry ignores.

The logic of music was a stabler process, emerging during performance, despite our not being able to see in medias res, as with a picture, the outcome. With a painting that displeases we can look away, but we can't "listen away" from a piece of music. (However, it might be argued that a piece of music, on second hearing, is a hologram: we experience both the process and the outcome simultaneously.)

When Lenny phoned Aaron Copland on my behalf, he made a date for us to meet. Was that meeting the next day? The next month? Trips to New York had become so frequent that chronology derails, but the meeting itself, though natural, remains cleanly framed.

Copland lived at the Empire Hotel but had a loft across the way on Sixty-third, now Lincoln Center. There he received me, at the top of a narrow stairway on each step of which lay a carton of books. The studio itself had few amenities, no carpets, no pictures, no silken divans. Like Copland's music, it was lean. The long room contained nothing but shelf after shelf of music and records (the latter mostly air-checks), sensible chairs, and a grand piano on which lay opened a manuscript of the host's Short Symphony, which Stokowski was to conduct next week.

Copland was already the Great Man with his settled social style and candid laughter. Thanks to whatever Lenny may have told him in the interim, he appeared more interested in getting a look at me than at my music. Nonetheless I played him a bright unfinished trio, long since faded, and he asked if the tunes came easily. (Yes, I supposed so, wasn't that a composer's signature?) By implying that tunes came hard to him, he made me a peer with whom he discussed "problems." Eventually I learned that this was his tack with everyone—at least everyone male (he once told me he had trouble telling one woman from another). Such extreme amiability was in fact a wall—an American wall. At my request he played *Quiet City*. And showed me the score to *Of Mice and Men* so that I could check on the notation of the affecting moment when Candy's dog dies. (It's "Vissi d'arte" still in D minor but recast in *stile francese,* that is, in dotted rhythm with the dot on the weak beat, which transforms Puccini into Copland.)

We talked of Mexico, and of El Salón México—the place, not the piece. That's all I recall.

Did I go from there to Fifty-second Street? It never occurred to me during those Manhattan forays that if I couldn't crash at Lenny's pad, other doors wouldn't be open. I had only to visit one of the Eighth Street bars, or the 123 Club—a "piss elegant" hangout in the east sixties—to get picked up and offered a bed. The legal drinking age during the war years in New York was eighteen, as distinct from twenty-one in Chicago; even so, with my baby face, I was forever obliged to show my draft card to bartenders.

I do remember that on the second visit to Lenny (had I phoned ahead?), even before I reached his apartment, the landing resounded with the razzmatazz of a jazz chorus. It was "The Revuers"—Betty Comden, Judy Holliday, Adolph Green, Alvin Hammer—screeching a number by Lenny, with Lenny himself slamming and caressing the ivories in the same wildly accurate style he used for classical music. The number was to be tried out that evening at Café Society Downtown and I was allowed to attend. We would meet the others there at ten.

En route to Sheridan Square, Lenny stressed that Judy Holliday was considered the most beautiful woman in New York. (She *was* presentable, but "most beautiful"? "Christ, you're such a literal-minded schmuck," he said.) The nightclub act went shimmeringly, The Revuers doing some scenes (notably three simultaneous imitations of Lionel Barrymore) which I would see and see again over the years. Judy between shows downed gin from a shot glass, to my admiration, and claimed she had stage fright.

Again I went to Fifty-second, again vomited, and again went to bed on the front-room floor, just as Edys was coming home. It was dark. She and Lenny chatted about the success he'd had downtown, then she pleasantly asked: "Who have you got under the blanket? Adolph?" "No, it's Ned." She froze, then melted into the back room. Edys, a decent-enough-looking dark-haired tight-lipped long-suffering left-wingish type, was never less than hostile toward me. Nor did I ever inquire as to the circumstances under which the two shared the apartment. (I continue these sentences without the embellishment or poetry of hindsight, relying strictly on the summoning of dry fact, for the sake of history, of how one thing leads to another, of eternal return, how nothing advances, though things do grow.)

Next afternoon Lenny played me a transcript of the Clarinet Sonata, which he and David Oppenheim had performed on WNYC. Anew I was entranced by the "Taxco tune," renotating it in my head to bring back to Shirley and Eugene. (The process is familiar to many composers: we hear visually. If at a concert a new piece is played that I wish to retain, or if in the subway I'm grabbed by a melody I don't want to forget, I shut my eyes, sketch an imaginary staff on the brain, inscribe thereon the notes in question, photograph them with a fantasy camera and, upon reaching home, develop the negative in my notebook.) Then we went to see *In Which We Serve,* Noël Coward's patriotic movie, at the Ziegfeld on Sixth Avenue.

So domineering was Lenny that it's hard to picture him as shorter than myself, barrel chested, too, traits that would turn gnomelike with the years. He was in fact stunningly handsome, not least because he capitalized on his drawbacks, making them into alluring eccentricities as handsome persons always do. (Aaron on the other hand was stunningly ugly, but no one ever mentions this.) Lenny emitted a faint acrid odor, like sweaty almonds, not unpleasant, which went away, as it had with Don Dalton, when the cyst on his knee was lanced a year later.

I was not physically attracted to him. I should have been, he was my carnal opposite, dashing, dusky, undaunted. But he was too smart, too much the center, too much the brash straight-A kid from grade school. Our egos didn't jibe. My social and sexual role I've already noted (*Le bourreau au salon, la victime au lit*). To get away with such a stance precluded being loved—more, to being *in loved*. Anyone can love, I figured, it's a form of blackmail; but to be loved requires the manipulation of ingrained appeal. To sleep with the Famous seemed, by the nature of things, to sleep with self-lovers, that is, to sleep with myself—incest pushed to the nth degree. 'Tis idle to object that Lenny was not yet famous—he was famous before he was famous, he *acted* famous. So much so that when, overnight in November, he became famous for real and remained so forever, everyone said: Why, success hasn't changed him one bit!

Could Lenny love? Such a surmise is high-schoolish, no one knows answers except as they obtain to oneself. Yes of course he loved— that was the purpose of his life. He also slaved at being loved, and by succeeding changed the world. As to whether he was ever *in love,* who can guess the anxieties, so hidden in another, that inevitably accompany that deeply silly condition? I often saw him anxious, yes, but never suffering, except toward the horrific end.

There are no coincidences. What we need we find, especially when we're unaware of seeking. This morning, thumbing a biography of Copland, I fell upon an illustration labeled: "Manuscript, sketch of the 'Dog Scene' from *Of Mice and Men*." This magic page, last seen by me in 1943, is not in D minor but E minor, is not notated in dotted rhythm but in even eighth notes, and does not exactly outline the descending four-note motive of Puccini's aria. So much for my notorious total recall.

Ah well! Since originality is merely the imitation of something wrongly overheard, shall I use my blurred retrovision of Copland's motive and call it my own?

Meanwhile the little "Taxco tune" was recent enough for accuracy.

Back in Philadelphia I played *la petite phrase* for Shirley and Eugene, then on the spot concocted a paraphrase—a pastiche of a pastiche, so to speak. The paraphrase made us giggle, yet went on to serve as a kind of code, a liaison between the high gravity of Curtis and the dangerous giddiness that lay beyond. The pastiche, a mere four bars of syncopation, was something Eugene, with one eyebrow raised, might interpolate into a Chopin scherzo as he rehearsed it for us. It was a way of mocking Lenny for being...what? New Yorkish? Superficial? He represented another mode, especially for Eugene. French versus

German. (In 1957 I would incorporate the motive into my Third Symphony, which Bernstein, knowing nothing of our secret, premiered with the Philharmonic the next year.)

Such contemporary music as was approved in "our circle" was definitely Austrian or German. Shirley was "going with" a young Chicago cellist now stationed with the navy in Philadelphia. Tall, blond, affable, straight, Seymour Barab was an extremely versatile musician. Via recordings and sheet music as well as during the live string quartet sessions that occurred biweekly at the Gabises', he had already indoctrinated Shirley into the works of Schoenberg, Webern, and Berg, and of his Chicago friends, George Perle and Ben Weber. Nontonal or serial composition was scarcely in fashion, though when the war ended, and for decades beyond, it would seep over and damage the globe like a liquid tumor. For the moment, no one but Ben was writing twelve-tone music.

I'm not today, nor was I then, very taken with the subject of tonality, my own or anyone else's. I've always assumed that the whole of music —indeed, the whole of the universe—was tonal and that assertions to the contrary protesteth too much. All music, including Boulez and Babbitt, is tonal to my ear, and I'm convinced (but can't prove) that everyone, including Babbitt and Boulez, hears music tonally. Should a score appear wildly complicated, I listen simply by imposing a subliminal pedal-point beneath the wildness, and the complicated filigree falls into place. By tonal I mean, of course, derived from the overtone series, a cosmological given. To deny the inescapability of this series's power is merely to admit the power through denial.

As to the term "the new tonality," I am writing in the tenth decade of the twentieth century. I confess in good faith that I don't know about it. It seems to be a current trend but feels suspiciously like a reversion, and quite un-new. I am old enough to retrace the trends of my own generation and to realize that they recapitulate ontologically music's history for the past fifteen hundred years. The history is not one of progress—art doesn't progress, at least not in the sense of improving—but of continual back and forth: the Eternal Return. We evolve perpetually from harmonic periods into contrapuntal periods, then back into harmonic, into contrapuntal, into harmonic, forever. A contrapuntal period is always complex and is always superseded by the antidote of a harmonic period like the one we're presently enjoying. I would suppose this was common knowledge, and that "the new tonality" is but another incarnation.

Thanks to the nudging of Seymour and Shirley, Eugene, even before I knew him, was already dipping his toe into the shallower waters of nontonal music, fooling around with Alban Berg's bland Piano Sonata, and actually learning Ben Weber's accessible bagatelles, which came closer to wit than any atonal music I've since known. Humor, as couched in a joke, relies by definition on resolution, while the twelve-tone language by its nature avoids resolution. (Which is why twelve-tone music is ideal for dramas like Schoenberg's psychotic *Erwartung,* but fatal for chic comedies like his *Von Heute auf Morgen.*) Still, Eugene's interest was more intellectual than heartfelt, and perhaps a bit defensive. He seemed as wary of French repertory as he was of homosexuality, which did not prevent him from exalting at the "revelatory Gallic newness" of Debussy's early *Air de Lia* (actually a tame reflection of Massenet) when he was assigned to orchestrate it, or from vicariously plying me about my sex life.

If I used to be called good-looking I mention this only because my looks had an effect on certain people, and that effect changed the course of my life three or four hundred times. Once in passing Shirley mentioned my good looks. "Oh, is Ned good-looking?" asked Eugene, the idea not having struck him till then. My budding acquaintance with Lenny, about whom Eugene felt at once sardonic and intrigued as he did about my open homophilia, forced him to consider intermasculine sensuality as something more than "fairyish," as his friend Byron put it. Like Kipling's East and West, our French and German sensibilities nevertheless seemed not to mesh. As his naïveté was being chipped away, Eugene never tired of hearing about ghetto terminology. (Neither did I, for that matter, since Pennsylvania slang differed from Illinois slang: a minty was now a dyke, belles became queens, jam became straight, queer became gay, jacking off became jerking off.) But he was also convinced that if I just met the right girl, etcetera. He himself was dating an uninteresting creature named Lila, encountered like most of his extramusical contacts at L'Aiglon. Eugene's manner with Lila, meant to dazzle us as much as her, was based on the lady-killer tone of George Sanders, a suavity which rested quaintly on his childlike brow. Still today, world famous and, among performers, the most neurotically intellectual of musical psyches, Eugene likes to impress with his cool *mondanité.* And still today he feels it's okay for his friends to be gay so long as they stay in the closet. Back then the consensus was that Ned should lose his virginity before the age of twenty. So I agreed to go to bed with a girl before the end of summer, if Eugene would learn Ravel's *Gaspard de la nuit.*

. . .

Such sex as came my way in Philadelphia was easygoing, unsentimental, and generally found on the inroads of Rittenhouse Square or in
the various hot spots beyond Broad Street. Especially fun was the
Music Village on Juniper, where the bar was gay and the restaurant
was not, and where the music was strictly classical. Occasionally with
Shirley, often with Alvin, I would hang out there swigging beer among
the almost exclusively military clientele while *Tod und Verklärung*
rang from the jukebox. I seldom got incomprehensibly drunk, as I
had in Chicago and would again in later years, partly because of the
competitive discipline imposed by Curtis, partly because bars closed
early. As the witching hour approached we'd down three bottles of
Schaefer at once, maybe with a boilermaker, as the crowd grew restive
with the anxiety of "making out." Should *I* make out, where would I
go?

If Shirley were with me we'd sometimes take my pickup date to an
all-night movie on Market Street, where, after an hour, he, seeing that
the film was more urgent than sex, would vanish. This happened as
we viewed *Claudia* and *The Sky's the Limit,* wherein Fred Astaire sings
"One for My Baby." (Here is the moment to declare that I cannot
bear Fred Astaire. True, his early pictures with Ginger Rogers were
watchable, but his slightly nasty, much too old, self-assured come-on
was something I, even at twelve, could never stomach. Nor can I
stomach Groucho Marx. Yes, he's witty, but not *that* witty, and twice is
enough. I tend to resist cult figures anyway, and the more Groucho's
"cultivated" the more I resist. The same holds for boring Charlie
Chaplin, who, like every star comic, is quite humorless. Maurice Chevalier's smarmy *putasserie* makes my flesh crawl—although Pierre
Bernac, Poulenc's exemplary interpreter, cited Chevalier as his premier model. Insofar as everyone loves Beethoven, I despise him.)

If Alvin were with me we'd sometimes collect at one of the all-boy
parties organized at closing time in someone's nearby pad and dance
until dawn. If I were alone I'd sometimes go to a far-off hotel room,
with maybe the burly marine from Pittsburgh whose tense biceps and
clean-smelling khaki have stayed with me, or simply to the vacant lot
just off Spruce between Nineteenth and Twentieth. Once in a while
I'd bring someone back to Delancey. The only problem was not to
collide with Rae Gabis's all-night Saturday poker party, a round-robin
tradition which once a month occurred in her dining room, i.e., my
bedroom.

There was the French sailor, invited home from a park bench, who, when I coyly took his navy blue cap with the red pompon, said quickly: "Surtout ne le mettez pas" ("Don't put it on"). Instantly I realized the gaffe of my silly civilian predecessors and flung the cap onto a chair. Years later I recalled this admonishment while reading Colette's squirm-making *Le képi,* wherein the Older Woman commits the fatal error—in her elation after a good screw—of marching about stark naked with her young lover's hat on her head. That ended their affair.

Various others I would see semiregularly, on hot afternoons, quite noncommittal. I never said "I love you" in Philadelphia.

Then there were the bedbugs.

They began meekly enough. Shirley complained of itching one morning and showed us the ruffled pink of her scratched flesh. A day or two later, same symptom from Rae. My back room seemed immune for the moment; but to sit down in the upholstered armchairs of the front parlor was to rise up twitching two minutes later. Bedbugs. It's said they can survive unfed in a wall for years, only to emerge when just the right blood type shows up; like sharks they then go mad, eating even each other. Nocturnal, they act when the lights are out and bite only such parts of a human as are exposed—the face and necks and hands, never private areas under the sheets. Soon, though, our bedbugs shamelessly crawled down the wall in broad daylight. They look like flat ticks, have a nutlike odor, and the welts they impose resemble mosquito bites, but more virulent and longer lasting. We each had sequences of bumps like little mountain ranges along our arms which we clawed till the craters oozed red lava. (A decade later when I asked beautiful Nora Auric about her prematurely white hair, she explained: "When Georges and I were in Poland—that was in 1928—we stopped at a country inn. In the middle of the night we discovered bedbugs. We surrounded the mattress with vats of water, because bedbugs can't cross water. An hour later they had collected on the ceiling and were dropping down on us by the hundreds. Next morning my hair was white.")

Rae hinted that my god-knows-where-you-find-them friends had brought the vermin with them; the predicament was as embarrassing as the seven plagues of Egypt—what about her poker games? So the exterminator came to fumigate the two front rooms, which meant the whole building had to be vacated for six hours. That night the women slept easily.

Not so I in the back room. At 2 a.m. I awoke, writhing, turned on the light, saw a dozen glutted bugs trying to escape. They (and how many others!) had immigrated to the dining room during the exterminator's inquisition and had already set up housekeeping. Crushing as many as I could (it's not easy: they've survived a billion years thanks to an armor both slippery and uncrackable), I defied the wartime curfew and left the light on until dawn. Neighbor Roy Grossman, our local air-raid warden, fined me. And the exterminator was telephoned again.

If the provenance of the bedbugs was moot, the crab lice which now replaced them were clearly borne by one of the Philadelphians to whom I never said "I love you." If only the bedbugs could have devoured the crabs! Again, chemicals were the sole solution. When Rae found the bottle of Larkspur lotion in the bathroom she hit the roof, demanding that I be good, or she'd throw me out.

I was good.

In the light of present-day medical horrors throughout the globe, these benign annoyances now seem more innocent than measles.

The other day I asked Naomi Graffman if, when pouring tea for the Curtis undergraduates, she crooked her little finger the way Mrs. Bok used to. "Do I ever!" she said. "And what's more, I make them crook theirs."

Naomi's husband is the eighth director of the Institute, and although certain stresses have since veered slightly from right to left (composers are now admitted to be crucial to music), Gary Graffman has retained the protected luxuriant ambiance of yore: same thick carpets and high ceilings, same rigorous standards for the same limited cast of strictly scholarship whiz kids (they all know each other), and same Wednesday afternoon tea in the lobby, dispensed by important females. The third director, Efrem Zimbalist, was a dim presence in the hallways when I was a student, and Mary Louise Curtis Bok, who founded and endowed the school eighteen years earlier, was the chief hostess. During the scholastic year of 1943 these two, in their mid-fifties, married each other. We were all informed that Mrs. Bok must now be called Mrs. Zimbalist—no problem for me, since I never called her anything. From her kindly imperial height she spoke to me only once, to exclaim how pleased I must be that Scalero had taken me, for Scalero was her pride, while her joy lay in Barber and Menotti, whom she supported splendiferously in Mount Kisco.

It was a false situation, for I disdained the maestro and felt soiled at being identified as "one of his."

Nevertheless, for reasons that now elude me (possibly because the war was intensifying and who knew where tomorrow... etcetera), it was agreed that I would spend the summer in Philly and continue lessons with Scalero. The lessons, for which he now charged five dollars each, transpired at his home in the new bank of apartments on the Parkway, two miles away.

That summer was suffocating. Often hungover, semihallucinating, I dawdled en route to Scalero's, pausing to rest in the shadow of the great museum, with a paper bag of grapes and cheese. Sometimes I entered the cool galleries to commune with the beloved Rouaults. With effort I would detach myself from this spectacle to regain sanity —is that the word?—in the air-conditioned parlor of my reactionary mentor. Never, not once, did he show me a rapport between our thousand counterpoint studies and their practical appliance—their relation to the realities of Palestrina or Bartók.

During the heat wave I took a train to Washington, D.C., for a weekend with Paul Callaway. An electric change bloomed for me in the capital after the torpor of Philadelphia. Nothing poetic, everything erotic, in that purposeful proliferation of military motion on the steaming avenues. In buses, in bars, and in beds, all the citizens—the majority in uniform—were unquestioningly locked into the international tragedy.

Smiling little Paul, unchanged except for his soldier's apparel, short and cute and sinewy as ever with that squinchy smile, contrasted with the debonair and savvy style of William Strickland, with whom he shared a civilian apartment while serving—both of them—at the Army Music School. Except for, and even during, a steady ingestion of dry martinis during leisure hours, Bill (whom I'd never met before but had oft heard of from Sowerby) and Paul lived and breathed music. They *were* music, and reinforced my enthusiasm, as Lenny had done, about a need for *American* music. Reared, like Paul Callaway, in the Episcopalian milieu of choirmasters and organists, a milieu now as then more tolerant of living composers than any other group in church or state, plus his new alliance with the Army Music School, which trained bandleaders in the best of what there was of a specialized repertory, Bill Strickland was a first-rate conductor, avid to expand the catalogue. For hours on end, at the clanky upright, he played for me American works by the dozen, mostly choral, some orchestral, a few songs, including those of Ives who was not yet a cult, and Samuel Barber's enigmatic chant for unaccompanied choir, "Anthony O'Daly."

That night I went to a party. George Garratt, who earlier in the month had swung through Philly and failed to impress Eugene with his prodigal improvisations, had implored me, should I be in Washington, to look up his precious boyhood chum, pianist Earl Wild. Earl Wild, as it happens, had recently broadcast *Rhapsody in Blue* under

Toscanini and was a military star stationed in Washington in the line of military duty. I wrote him, he sent back a phone number which I now called from Paul's. Earl Wild seemed not to know George Garratt, but invited me to a party at the house of someone called Alison, if I had a dollar to spare for a taxi—it would cost that much to get to the suburbs.

At the party, besides the host in mufti, were a dozen soldiers and a Steinway grand. Among the soldiers were organist Virgil Fox (flamboyant yet old-maidish), Eugene List (simple and sweet, who would soon make headlines as the official pianist at the Potsdam Conference), and Earl himself, the epitome of raw talent honed fine. List played Poulenc's *Mouvements perpétuels*. Then Wild asked us to give him four notes—any four—on which he accordingly improvised for fifteen minutes in the styles of whatever composers' names were called out. Everyone got drunk and danced to pop records. Was this your typical army get-together? I note the episode only because in later years List and Fox and Wild would each perform my music, but none remembered meeting me in Washington, or even that such a party took place.

That night I slept in Paul's bed. Next morning, over waffles and bacon, Bill Strickland said: "Ned, if you write us a piece I'll conduct it here in September—something five to ten minutes long, for men's chorus and a few winds."

"Even if you don't like it," I stammered.

"Even if I don't like it."

That was my first commission.

A visit to Rosemary, who was spending the summer in Baltimore as a *bonne à tout faire* for a Mrs. Gilpatrick in exchange for keyboard lessons which this woman seemed to offer solely to female collegians on vacation. Gilpatrick had a "method," of course, stressing relaxation and closed eyes, allowing the body to be saturated with the meaning of sound, or something. ("Horowitz is a bad pianist because he's too tense.") Rosemary was not blessed with the aptitude of a public performer but was always, still is, an easy mark for therapists. She thrives on group spirit; I do not. Mrs. Gilpatrick and I didn't see eye to eye. But Rosemary showed me how to mash potatoes, and later in Philly she cleaned the Gabises' kitchen, to the horror of Rae, who felt that Shirley should have done it. We also went up to New York together for a sober day.

While lunching with Rosemary at an outdoor café near Rockefeller Center I saw Lenny for the last time before his permanent explosion into glory. He came toward us from across the street—with an older woman who turned out to be Helen Coates, though she wasn't introduced—and said (I remember the wording, because Rosemary later quoted him to Shirley): "I've just had some mildly interesting news. Rodzinski has appointed me assistant conductor of the Philharmonic. And this"—he designated Helen—"will be my secretary."

Lenny had moved to the Chelsea Hotel, an old-world edifice on West Twenty-third, possibly because Paul Bowles was there too. It was at the Chelsea that he showed me Bowles's ballet *Pastorela* with its haunting duet, originally a rollicking folk song in 3/8 based on the couplet "Pobrecito, huérfanito/Sin su padre, sin su madre," slowed down and reharmonized as an Adagio. Paul Bowles, man and musician, beguiled Lenny. In March, the latter had conducted the first (and only) performance of Bowles's zarzuela, *The Wind Remains,* at the Museum of Modern Art, and forever after, in salons and lectures, he lauded his idol as one of America's least-sung heroes. Yet he never again performed a note of Bowles's.

Bowles for the moment was an established light, but within a few months Lenny would outshine him a thousandfold. Just as in 1946 Menotti, with the success of *The Medium,* became and remained more renowned than his life's companion, Samuel Barber, who had hitherto been the star of the family and who grew accordingly sour, or as in 1960 Edward Albee, with the success of *The Zoo Story*, became and remained more renowned than his life's companion, William Flanagan, who had hitherto been the star of the family and who grew accordingly sour, so Bernstein, who had absorbed Bowles's jazzily perfumed modes by osmosis, eventually allowed himself to believe that he was their originator. (In 1954, at Jean Stein's on the Rue Bassano, I sat for a minute at the piano, noodling on a theme from *The Wind Remains.* Lenny stopped whatever he was doing and said: "O God, Ned, when did I write that gorgeous thing?")

Did it ever occur to you that Albee, Menotti, and Tennessee Williams each wrote only two works—a small one and a big one—from which all their ensuing works were pallider spin-offs. Albee never surpassed his early short *Zoo Story* and the long *Who's Afraid of Virginia Woolf.* Menotti never again equaled his early short *Medium* and the long *Consul.* Williams never afterward came close to the early short *Glass Menagerie* and the long *Streetcar Named Desire.* I'll speak of the reasons when—and if—I come to Tennessee.

Paul Bowles himself I would see soon again.

Forays up to New York grew more frequent, sometimes legitimate, sometimes not. With Shirley we made several six-hour round trips to cover the complete sequence of Beethoven's piano music offered, with snorting bravura, by Artur Schnabel at Carnegie Hall. (In preparation for these events I relearned all of the thirty-two sonatas, even as in the spring I had tackled all of Schumann. Tackled, not thrown.) On my own I went there mainly to cruise, bedding about, catch as catch can. I've no remembrance of how the days were spent beyond using the shining private washrooms of the Winslow bar on Lexington for my personal toilet (I didn't yet shave much, still don't), and subsisting on milkshakes and apples. Evenings I drank at the Old Colony, and accordingly ran into Arthur Weinstein, soigné and pretty as ever, who turned out to know everyone I knew, only better—Lenny, Aaron, and Paul Bowles too. Back at Arthur's Upper West Side apartment we called Bowles. (On the phone Bowles told Arthur that, yes, he remembered me from Taxco, but remembered my father more.) He came by in a mist of perfume, and we talked and drank until the wee hours.

Learning that Menotti had used his score of *My Heart's in the Highlands* as an example of how to use the clarinet's chalumeau register, Paul said: "That's flattering of Gian Carlo. But there is no clarinet. The score is for only trumpet and fiddle, with a Hammond organ doing most of the dirty work.". . . He spoke of his 4-F army status. The induction psychiatrist, dumbfounded that anyone could be a composer, inscribed on the sheet of findings: "Paul Bowles. Writes symphonies. Rejection recommended." (Elsewhere he had been labeled a "premature anti-Fascist.")

Three a.m. I had no place to stay. Paul offered hospitality at the Chelsea. Arthur's elevator being out of order we descended twenty gloomy stories on foot to the basement. "Good place for a murder," said Paul in the taxi—or was it the subway?—to Twenty-third Street. It was impressive when, on our arriving at his little room at the Chelsea, he immediately phoned his wife, Jane, in *her* little room at the Chelsea, and chatted for twenty minutes as though it were day. The room reeked of patchouli. He brewed mint tea on an electric hotplate, then played a record—by now it was after four—of Jean Cocteau declaiming his own "Anna la bonne," a singsong harangue by a hotel maid addressed to the corpse of the woman she has just killed. (Forty-six years later I set these verses to music.) When finally we retired I was limp and passed out, or pretended to. Paul was not thrilled. At noon he brought over cereal and corned beef from the deli across the street. Wasn't that a mundane repast for one so special?

Paul was never less than bewitching with that cold compassion, those cruel anecdotes, and bizarre tastes, stances he eventually nurtured into cult status. The stances were honest, however (no mere

whim led to a half century of self-exile from his loathed America in
the comparative discomfort of Morocco), but also off-putting. His affably smart conversation was identical with everyone, from concierge to
countess, serving as a neutral screen between him and you—not to
mention the active screen of exotic perfume which always enveloped
him. The allure of remoteness and of musk are sometimes used as
bait by certain females; but just as dark Lenny turned me off sexually
with his fame, so did blond Paul with his studied removal.

Eugene had graduated in June and decamped to New York with his
parents, but not before shepherding Shirley through the formidable
entrance auditions at Curtis, and settling her as a bona fide member
of Serkin's flock, to everyone's delight. Shirley was therefore practicing like mad in anticipation of school's reopening in September. And
I, prior to the reopening, took a hiatus from Scalero and went back,
via one of the always-packed wartime coaches, to Chicago for a month.

I hadn't forgotten the "virginity" pact. But who in Chicago could I
lose it with? Maggy was emotionally out of the question. Hatti would
laugh in my face. Now, Hilda Mary might be ideal. She was a casual
fag hag, and promiscuous, uninvolved, and flattered to act the role of
Lycenium. She agreed, taking the ritual as a lark, the ritual which to
me was a necessary evil.

Hilda Mary was nothing if not ample in form, powdery white in hue,
dyed blond, uncomplicated, good natured, perfect. The procedure
occurred, in his absence, chez George Garratt, who had moved back
from Kenmore Avenue to Bellevue Place. Hilda Mary bought a bottle
of champagne, then garbed herself in black chiffon, thinking that the
more feminine she became the more intrigued I would become.
"More masculine" would have been still worse: *une femme est une
femme*. As I wrote earlier, I love women—their intellect, their privileges, their force, their rouge, their passivity—in all ways but sexual.

Yet I performed the act, perfunctorily, to completion. All sex is
senseless, of course, even stupid, when viewed from without (the
pinkish hairy murkiness, unlovely grunts, imbecilic thrusts, the barrels
of sticky sperm and such slag spilling forth over the centuries), but
this occurrence in its dearth of passion seemed maximally devoid of
meaning. I felt no added affection for Hilda Mary. Contempt, rather,
because she had usurped my rightful role.

Yet there it was. I've had sex with one female once, as distinct from
hundreds of men! (Accumulation in itself is vain, but formidable with
hindsight. Consider how much of our own bodies we devour in a
lifetime—fingernails, snot, scabs, sweat, blood.)

Hilda Mary went on to set up housekeeping with a woman named Audrey, twice her size, with whom in the 1950s she was killed in a car crash.

Less flashy but more lasting, during this stay in Chicago, was a meeting with Ben Weber.

Once I quipped that some of my best friends were twelve-tone composers. That quip sounds senseless today, the Tower of Babel having melted into a pillar of magnanimity, and nobody minds what dialect you sing so long as you articulate. Two generations ago, however, our land was a diatonic prairie staked out by Copland where offspring of Schoenberg, not to mention the master himself, were unfashionable. One didn't have friends in both camps.

Who were the youngish musicians still hoeing the tone row? George Perle (at least in his prose works), Lou Harrison part-time, and Milton Babbitt. Anyone else? Only Ben Weber. I, a tonalist born, would soon know them all in New York; I wanted to learn how the world turns and didn't yet know that to be American was to be a specialist. Meanwhile, here was Ben Weber.

Ben and I had never run into each other in Chicago in former days, but Shirley and Seymour urged me to call him when I returned there. We met in a bistro on Adams Street and chatted for an uncomfortable hour. Uncomfortable because no one had warned me that Ben's sole subject matter was himself (anything else and his eyes glazed over), and that self was a fantasy of fatal beauty. The reality was such that at twenty-six Ben seemed middle-aged, pudgy, balding with a patchy roan fuzz replaced by psoriasis and an ivorine countenance dominated by shapeless over-red lips. But I already admired his music so was prepared to be patient.

That music remains always beautiful, and that's its flaw. Beautiful at any given moment—but the moments don't cohere, don't contrast, don't aim toward a target. The music was all conceived according to Schoenberg's twelve-tone method, yet one might suspect Ben of tweaking his row so that the acrid sevenths and mellow ninths of Impressionism would fall logically upon his staff; or inversely, he restricted himself to the method so as to legalize his alien corn. Ben's art seems compromised, as though inside that unsmiling Germanitude lurked a Frenchman itching to get out. His heart was tonal even as his society was humorous. Still, one cannot fairly criticize a language, only the use of a language. Had Ben written diatonic music, he would not have been Ben. Had Ben Weber been heterosexual, all other things being equal, his music would have been different.

Bill Strickland's commission was a hypodermic. Within a week after our meeting I composed a biblical work for male chorus and a few winds and mailed it to Washington. Before it arrived, I made another biblical setting ("Let them be turned away who say to me 'Aha! Aha!' ") for two-part men's chorus with oboe, clarinet, and two horns.

Bill responded enthusiastically to both, opted for the second, wrote that the parts would be copied by student soldiers, that he would program it in August and hoped that I'd come down for it. Rosemary joined me in Washington, we stayed at the Mayflower, heard a rehearsal and accordingly attended the world premiere of my Opus 1, under the title of *The Seventieth Psalm*.

How does it stand up today? I won't disown the craft which gleams with beginner's luck, nor the content which boasts a freshness of one who by definition is not repeating himself. But *The Seventieth Psalm* is a small work without much staying power. Back then, however, despite the watery acoustic at the National Gallery, the sound of years of work suddenly made sense, like a rose unfolding on speeded-up film; it affected me electrically. Those thousand flyspecks in the manuscript now quivered with a life of their own, brought to the fore through the lips of strangers. I could have been dead or in Timbuktu and the music would still be decipherable, communicative, existing in a continuous present tense. How pale were the rewards of a painter, whose work in its final shape existed alone in the studio, as compared to those of a composer, whose work is "realized" only when interpreted by middlemen—but then with such a controlled madness that listeners are literally (as opposed to figuratively, like painting) made to dance! This comparatively humble hearing became the standard against which I judge all other performances of my career. For here was what it meant to be a composer—to stand naked before an audience without the physical presence of one's own body!

Thus I lost my virginity a second time.

Around this time, before the fall term at Curtis, again in New York, I had two encounters that would soon alter both my mode and geography.

The first occurred at the Old Colony, where, long after midnight when I was feeling no pain, a brash, short, swarthy muscular presence invited me to his place on West Eleventh Street. Morris Golde was twenty-five, fourth child of immigrant Romanians, successfully self-employed (with his brother he founded a direct-mail advertising business), lover of the arts and friend of artists, with whom, as a consumer, he was not competitive. Morris had grown up in the (to me exotic) Bronx with actor Jules—later John—Garfield, whose toughish manner he shared, two-thirds natural and one-third pose. Which I suppose is the same with us all: unlike animals we invent our most useful role and play that role forever. I was attracted to Morris's East Coast accent with its dropped Rs and incoherent elisions—"A-hunt-fiff Street" for 105th Street. He reminded me of Hollywood mafia.

I in turn reminded Morris of Jane Bowles, apparently because of a use of non sequiturs and a knack for changing the subject when cornered. (My role depends on those I'm with, and on the age I first knew them. With old friends individually, I revert to a behavior of yore; with several people at once, known at different periods, I adopt the "several-at-once" role. The sexual role, however, remains stationary.)

Morris and I fit like hand in glove (I was the glove), contrasting in temperament, like-minded in artistic tastes. His near-manic but genuine concern with the political left echoed that of my Chicago bohemia, reanimating my never very vigorous sense of justice. Morris came down to Philadelphia often that autumn, and I now had an honest excuse for more frequent excursions up to New York, plus a place to stay. On one such excursion I encountered Virgil Thomson.

Learning that Thomson needed a copyist, and being proud of my own calligraphy, I called on him in his ninth-floor apartment at the Chelsea, where he had lived since his return to America in 1939, and where he would remain for the next fifty years. His first words, once we were settled on the sofa beneath the huge Stettheimer portrait, were: "So what's your sad story?"

I was prepared for the swishy voice because of the lively round table in Chicago a year or two back, but not for the patronizing friendliness and icy impatience, a mixture I later found to be native to uppercrust French females. His eyes were quick, his head balding, his cravat a hand-tied butterfly bow, his cigarette holder a nonfilter, his stomach already paunchy (he was forty-seven, a year younger than Father), his housecoat maroon, his slippers plush, and his manner sardonic and adult. I was intimidated. Not because he was a famous composer (I didn't know a note of his music), nor because he was a redoubtable critic of the *Herald-Tribune* (I never read newspapers, but *The New York Times*'s Olin Downes was more nationally known). I was intimidated because I'd never met anyone like him, so brusquely precise, so businesslike about music—and hence didn't know how to behave. The intimidation would never entirely go away and proved to be a good thing.

My "sad story" was that with Scalero I was unfulfilled and longed to spread my wings. Virgil sympathized. He gave me a few things to transcribe from manuscript to autograph which I was to return in a fortnight. If he liked the copy, we would continue the process by correspondence through the fall term at Curtis; then on the first of the year I would move to New York as his employee.

I was shocked by Thomson's music. Contemporary music then meant Prokofiev or Schoenberg, Stravinsky or Chávez, Milhaud and even Poulenc, maybe Copland, certainly Antheil, men with guts, sensuality, rhapsody, violence. But this: Here was a *Sonata for Flute Alone* and a couple of early songs on the French verse of Georges Hugnet. The script, in faded pencil on yellowing paper, was tentative and super-tiny like the work of an inexperienced child. The music itself— was it a joke? It sounded sappy and charmless yet pretentious in its false naïveté, above all untalented. Oh, well. I copied it dutifully, Virgil was happy, our deal was made.

Father was distressed. To abandon the security of a classy scholarship for the vagaries of Manhattan was folly. I may well have prospects for a definitive job and a place to live, he was against it. If I quit Curtis, he would stop financial aid. This was the only ultimatum Father ever made to me, and he held to it. For a while.

During the autumn quarter I no longer—I've forgotten why— roomed at the Gabises', but shared an unfurnished railroad walk-up one block away on Twenty-third with Paul Erlich. A swain of Shirley's, Paul was in turn a friend of my Chicago friends, David Sachs and Norris Embry, all graduates of Saint John's College in Annapolis. He was an amateur violinist with a touching devotion to music and a keen mind. But I hardly knew him—we went to different schools together. Alvin Ross helped furnish the dreary place by painting orange crates and beds from the Salvation Army and designing extravagant dragons in charcoal directly onto the walls. There was also a little piano lent by Curtis.

In October Margaret Bonds and Gerald Cook, who had joined forces as a two-piano team, stopped in Philadelphia for a three-week gig at some nightclub. Margaret and her husband, Larry Richardson, stayed with friends in the suburbs. Gerald moved in with us. They all were moving permanently to New York.

Like Paul, Gerald was out of sight much of the time. He had had some recent lessons with Nadia Boulanger, who was billeted here and there in the States for the duration. Gerald persuaded me to contact her. Thus began a correspondence between the greatest living musical pedagogue and the only living American composer who—despite an entente that would form after I moved to France—never studied with her.

The greatest living organist was E. Power Biggs, and since Paul Callaway maintained that Biggs performed every new piece he ever received, I wrote a piece for him—which he never played. But, as with Boulanger, we struck up a correspondence, and one thing led to another.

Weekends, Morris came down and we drank beer at the Music Village and the Walnut Street bars, sometimes going to movies at the Avon on Spruce Street, or to the huge museum on the Schuylkill River.

Philadelphia postscripts:

—Because Eugene was Serkin's undisguised favorite, it was a foregone conclusion that he would win the competition and debut that fall at the Philadelphia Orchestra's Young People's Concerts. Still, there was the formality of an audition. Eugene asked me to play second piano for the Brahms B-flat. So I practiced hard. On the morning of the audition he reneged and asked Eileen to play. I held firm. Attended only by Serkin and Ormandy, the audition took place in a studio at the Academy. After three minutes Ormandy agreed. Thus I played, and didn't play, but it was my first meeting with the conductor —and my last for thirteen years.

Ormandy always entered the stage adjusting his cuffs. I always enter a stage adjusting my cuffs.

—I saw Father in Washington. He suggested we take a taxi to Chevy Chase to see his old secretary, Miss Ring, who had retired there, and did I remember Miss Ring? (Yes, but didn't confess what Mother had told me and Rosemary years before.) We visited with Miss Ring on her front porch. She looked the same, plain, crippled, schoolmarmish, hair in a bun, like the woman with a smashed pince-nez in the famous still from *Ten Days That Shook the World*. I marveled once again that my handsome sire had had his "affair" with this reticent creature who resembled not at all Hollywood's notion of The Secretary.

—I asked Lenny if Mongolian idiots have Mongolian idiots. He considers this. "No, they have Caucasian idiots."

—The sole books I recall reading were *Buddenbrooks* and Henry James's *The American,* both at the prodding of Eugene, who chose well. Not so with his vending of Schubert's E-flat Trio. There are two sorts of Great Man I can't abide—or, more gently put, don't need: the ones whose Greatness I deny categorically (Bruckner, Berlioz, Elgar), and the ones whose Greatness I allow but can do without (Beethoven, Mahler, Schubert). With all his humble economy, Schubert seems, even in the songs, long-winded. The last movement of the Trio resembles a person who can't stop talking.

—With Shirley at the Museum of Modern Art, I briefly place my schoolbooks on the counter to adjust my coat before we venture into the winter fog. On the bus we discover that, along with my books, I'd picked up an expensive volume of Pavel Tchelitcheff. I know his name because Belle Tannenbaum's best friend in Chicago is the pianist Alan Tanner, Tchelitcheff's once lover, and because the painter's scenery— slate-blue and blood-red—for Hindemith's *Saint Francis* ballet in 1938 had shown an intoxicating world. Now here were reproductions of paintings of such excellent sadness—the freaks, the strawberries, the trapezists, and especially the image of the dismayingly sexual Lincoln Kirstein (who was he?)—that I became intoxicated anew, returning to the museum to see his pictures in real life.

—We sit around imagining the unimaginable. The faces of our mothers, being sliced slowly to ribbons while we are forced to look. During these same hours across the ocean, fifteen million gypsies, Jews, homosexuals, intellectuals, idiots, and other categories of European misfit are being sucked into a holocaust of which we are yet only dimly aware.

—Shirley's a fellow pupil now, we have classes together, including one with Menotti. She has a crush on Menotti, and we walk him to Thirtieth Street Station after school. We do the same with Serkin's assistant, Mieczyslaw Horszowski, whom she also has a crush on, and who plays Beethoven definitively, even I agree.

—Shirley's best girlfriend is Louise Elkan, scion of the Elkan-Vogel publishing firm that prints French music in America. Shirley and Louise do interpretive improvisations to Mahler symphonies, looking like kindergarten students of self-expression.

—In New York one weekend she and I both stay at Morris's. At the Carnegie Cinema we see a revival of *Crime without Passion* with its eerie montage behind the opening credits: liquid globules drip onto the screen, grow larger, and one by one turn into fearsome banshees who then dissolve in a cloud. Morris says: "Another drop of blood and we'll get the Rockettes." Such Manhattan sophistication! Is Shirley impressed, or does she feel this whimsy belies Morris's butch front?

Later in the street we pass an unfortunate woman whose left eye is higher than her right. "She lifted her eyebrow once too often," says Morris. Wow!

—Am I ashamed of Philadelphia friends that I don't juxtapose them with Chicago friends, and vice versa? It's too complicated. The Chicago friends know nothing about music, not at least from inside out.

Have I learned anything from a year at Curtis? Little academically, nothing from Scalero, but everything from the viewpoint (earpoint) of repertory, amity, concentration, execution.

People always ask: "When do you do your work? You're so prolific, yet you're so busy extracurricularly." Answer: I'm never not working. Every thought and action of my life pertains to my music. I'm working when I eat, when I sleep, when I cruise, when I read, when I say I love you. When I talk with you about the weather or when I type these words, sonic notions are fomenting, usually quite consciously. The time-consuming process of notating these notions is merely the tip of the iceberg.

—To a desert island I would take nothing but my own talent. My memory of great works is stronger than the fact of those works.

—I have failed to discuss my shyness (there's a memo to myself to do so, here on my desk) because, although I agonized for years on chances missed because of timidity or chances ruined because of liquor that camouflaged timidity, and although I recall it as pathological, I cannot reexperience it. Once I had convinced myself that shyness is a form of vanity and that those witty others opining loudly across the room were not so much wittier than I, I gritted my teeth, began to speak my own language, while trying not to be a fool rushing in. Anyone bright is shy, and anyone bright discovers that shyness doesn't get you far.

That said, I still shudder from shyness, as I still shudder from stage fright. No one believes me.

—Those Saturday-night chamber music jamborees at 2302 Delancey! Eileen Flissler, on learning that maybe the Brahms Piano Quintet would be played, *rehearsed her sight-reading* of that piece in the afternoon so as to impress us with her sight-reading in the evening. ("I swear I've never seen this music before.") But Seymour might substitute Bartók's First String Quartet, and leave Eileen hanging.

"The potency of cheap music." It's true that the pop songs of one's adolescence, perhaps because they were forever intertwined with situation—kissing, dancing, pining—are more evocative of time and place than classical music, which is generally imbibed in the pious restrictions of a hall. For Rae Gabis these artistic sessions were a prelude to all-night poker parties; for me they were a prelude to barhopping. To this day I cannot hear the Bartók without salivating in anticipation of beer and more beer.

—Once I defined a concert as: That which precedes a party.

Morris, not shy, had a way, after showering, of going around naked, with that tough ape strut of gangland types from Singapore to Saratoga, flaunting his triceps. Naked, except for always a towel over his shoulder. "Why do you always wear that towel over your shoulder," I asked, "when you're naked?" Long pause. "Because when I was little my mother accidentally let slip a pan of boiling oil that scarred me." "Can I see?" Yes, there was the angry, pink, knotted wound, healed and defiant. Five years later when I told this to Nell Tangeman, who had a similar scar on her shoulder and chest, she asked: "So what did you do?" "I kissed it." "And what did he do?" "He cried." "I'll bet," said Nell.

—At the Christmas party in the Curtis lobby, on the eve of my permanent leavetaking, Elisabeth Schumann sang a Schubert lied. Inconceivable, then as now, that she should sing a Poulenc *mélodie,* yet that *mélodie* on Judgment Day will be seen to be as important as Schubert's. (Why, then as now, do major music schools have no staff to instruct French repertory—much less American repertory—with the same relish as German?) Nonetheless I was moved to tears.

The decision was made. Against Father's better wisdom I would leave Curtis on 31 December for good.

Now voyager . . .

I have loitered in 1943, not knowing when to stop, because those four seasons mark the close of a side of youth to which I still clung, while aching to slough off. Philadelphia was a womblike hyphen between the not-yet-embalmed past and the plunge into New York's maelstrom.

Names sprinkled through the year, unrelated and casual, may ultimately crisscross. Yet dreams, like kaleidoscope patterns, cannot be passed intact between people. Indeed, our own childhoods will never be recaptured by our present selves without shattering and repositioning their fragments into new puzzles, like crests of bright waves which instantly melt back into shade. Everything exists while simultaneously ceasing to exist, so that "meaning," even to itself, alters incessantly.

Yet what else have we except art and bullets? Well, some try to communicate through what they call love, others through mutual nostalgia. These few thousand words have briefly served, for one person in one frame of mind on one autumn morning, to call back lost friends and reintroduce them here.

Part Two

Part Two

15. Virgil

Manhattan during the war and up through the early 1950s was governed by Aaron Copland and Virgil Thomson, the father and mother of American music. Young composers joined one faction or the other, there was no third. Both were from France through Nadia Boulanger, but Copland's camp was Stravinsky-French and contained a now-vanished breed of neoclassicist like Alexei Haieff and Harold Shapero, while Thomson's camp was Satie-French and contained a still-vital breed of neo-Catholic like Lou Harrison and John Cage. (The Teutonisms of Wolpe-via-Schoenberg were as yet quiescent.) A few lone wolves like me were still socially partial to one or the other. I saw less of Aaron than of Virgil, simply because the latter was my employer for a while.

With the hard lens of hindsight it's clear that, beyond an occasional letter of reference or a pat on the back, neither musician, during decades of fraternizing, ever lifted a finger toward my music, be it by performance, verbal recommendation, or through their copious prosifying. Naturally they were more important to me than I to them —they were older; to this day I recall every word that each ever said, and realize how their professional behavior stamped mine. Yet such awareness stems from tenacity: instruction is taken, not given, and they set an example just by being. Beyond those elements of themselves that were at the disposal of anyone, I owe nothing to either man. Still, with the soft lens of hindsight I cannot today recall either man without my eyes welling at the accumulation of affection that comes only from patience and the years.

On the face of it, entry to the Empire City through Virgil Thomson's door would seem the ideal route for a twenty-year-old, half Julien Sorel, half Alice Adams, anxious about a solid career in the shifting sands of musical composition. Thomson at forty-eight was the best English-language critic in the world; by extension he was one of our most-played composers. His daily reviews and Sunday sermons in the *Herald-Tribune,* although of smaller readership than Olin Downes at the *Times,* had larger cachet, and that cachet—the power to put a musician on the map and keep him there—had much to do with his own music being commissioned and performed. Virgil was shrewd as they come—about everything but Virgil. When in 1954 he retired from the paper, the performance frequency of his music plummeted overnight to the surprise of no one but himself.

Meanwhile, at the start of the new year 1944, he was at his peak, writing words and music nonstop, socializing, too, and with a presumably satisfactory sex life. There are three conditions of success to which we all aspire—success in work, in society, and in love—but nobody can juggle more than two simultaneously; to succeed in all three at once means that one of them is collapsing—we're dancing on a volcano's brink. For now he seemed blessed, at least from where I sat.

I sat at a long table in the end of the dining room between parlor and bedroom. The European tone of the Chelsea, which smelled of camphor and lavender in the old-maidish lobby and of cinnamon and citronella in Virgil's apartment, set me more or less at ease: it reeked of childhood. My duties as in-house copyist were to work under the master's guiding eye from ten till noon and from one till three five days a week. For these twenty hours I received twenty dollars, of which five went to Morris for rent, five to a savings account, and ten to concert tickets, music, books, groceries, subways, and beer. During the first week I had lunch with Virgil (I didn't yet call him that) while he taught me the ropes. After that at midday Morris would meet me at a Riker's hash house on Eighth Avenue, or I'd eat alone somewhere or maybe nowhere.

The copying tasks began with short pieces, graduating eventually to big ones, rendering everything in Virgil's oeuvre that had not hitherto been printed into legible fair copy. The problem lay less in making a readable facsimile than in deciphering the original. Virgil's penciled calligraphy, like the manuscript of Pierre Boulez—a man whose music was as fancy as Virgil's was plain, and who was in all ways except keenness remote from Thomson (the two would nevertheless become, a decade later, staunch friends for reasons of expedience)—was slapdash, almost as though he didn't want to be deciphered.

Every week my script improved. Reexamining the script today, it appears overly ornate, with scrolls and curlicues formed by the special music fountain pens that could write thick and thin in India ink, but it was a marked contrast to the original. Virgil, of course, showed me examples by his previous secretaries to use as models, and once sent me uptown to the atelier of Arnold Arnstein, dean of copyists, where five young people were bent over the scribblings of the Current Great (Schuman, Moore, Menotti, Barber) and transferring, by means of slide rules and compasses, rough drafts onto transparent paper—onionskin, as it was called—for photoreproduction. After a month or so of clarifying early works of Virgil—whimsical settings of Georges Hugnet or Jean Racine or King Solomon, for example, or the dumb sonata for solo flute, or the truly touching 1928 *Stabat Mater* on a text of Max Jacob (the only beautiful piece he ever penned), or sonic one-page portraits of friends that had never been inked—I graduated to bigger things. I did the score and parts of the First Symphony *(Symphony on a Hymn Tune),* scheduled for performance by the Philharmonic the next season. The responsibility was intimidating: Rodzinski would be conducting from my score, eighty men would be playing from my parts, and if someone sounded a false note, the error would not only be traceable to humble me, but expensive rehearsal time would be spent in correcting it.

More than the responsibility, though, was the instructive value. Yes, I was skeptical about, even contemptuous of, and mostly bemused by, what I felt to be Virgil's sappy stuff (and jealous that big-time performers should be hoodwinked), for I hadn't yet perceived sophistication in the simplemindedness. But the experience, for a young composer, of being answerable for every one of the myriad notes in this or that score was more vital than theory. The best way to learn how a piece of music is confected—be it Monteverdi or Charles Mingus—is to copy it. Not impersonate but reproduce literally, like Borges's mad (sane) antihero, Pierre Menard, who "translated"—from Spanish into Spanish, so to speak—all of *Don Quixote* word for word, then called it his own.

Among my chores as apprentice was to accompany the boss to rehearsals. Virgil-as-performer was insecure, hence feisty. In private his lucidity was exemplary since as a critic he could do the impossible—put into words that which can't be put into words, by describing one art in terms of another. When playing a Mozart sonata, for example, for friends in his living room, he would raise both hands high then let them fall with great authority onto all the wrong keys; yet he would accompany this action with such explicatory elegance about how all of Mozart's instrumental slow movements are really subliminal love-duets that he gave an illusion of virtuosity. But in public he could offend. Once when he was engaged to guest-conduct one of his affairs —I think it was *The Mayor La Guardia Waltzes*—with Stokowski's Youth Orchestra, his insecurity grew apparent not through reticence but through bullying. During the rehearsal he shrieked at the kids to play softer. He was hissed. Stokowski meanwhile, as was his wont, strolled coolly among the instrumentalists while Virgil ranted on the podium. "Leopold," cried Virgil, "how do I make them play softer?" Stokowski, all aplomb, turned toward his adoring orchestra, put a finger to his lips, and simply whispered: "Softer."

Another time, before the live Wednesday-night performance on WOR of the master's recently orchestrated *Five Portraits,* I became embarrassed more for me than for him. During the previous weeks, while copying the score and parts of this new piece and weary of Virgil's endless series of moronic tonic-dominant progressions, I spiced up a couple of chords with added sevenths. Hearing this at the rehearsal, Virgil had a fit. I realized my miscalculation (the "improvements" diminished the music, if possible) and it was my lot to go into the orchestra and correct each part while the conductor, Alfred Wallenstein, and players expensively waited.

I recall this evening for another reason. After the performance Virgil took me to Bleeck's Tavern, better known as the Artists and Writers Restaurant, a hangout of *Herald-Tribune* employees on West Fortieth. With us were Edward James and Yvonne de Casa Fuerte, both of Virgil's generation. Yvonne, a marquise, French and poor despite her rich Spanish title, was sweating out the war as a violinist in American pickup orchestras. Plain, even gross-featured, she exuded nevertheless a whiff of strong glamour with her copper hair and ostrich plumes, her gruff gallic authority which does not exist in American females, and her inability, despite long residence here, to speak English. (André Breton, asked why he never learned our language while living in New York, replied: "Pour ne pas ternir mon français." And Gertrude Stein, whose French was said to be rocky and accented despite the bulk of her seventy-two years on foreign soil, could have said as much, in reverse. Indeed, might not her clarity in English—in *American*— have been dimmed had she stayed home?) In the 1920s Yvonne had founded the Sérénade Concerts in Paris, which promoted Darius Milhaud, the young Igor Markevich, Henri Sauguet, Vittorio Rieti (whose mistress she was), Francis Poulenc and Nicholas Nabokov. Now in New York she was active in the League of Composers, a cousin of the French organization. In fact, besides Yvonne, there were four powerful women who, in this prefeminist era, ran the bureaucratic side of New Music: Claire Reis, who had invented the League in 1923; Minna Lederman, who started the dazzling *Modern Music* magazine, verbal artery of "the cause" until its demise in 1946, and who as I write remains vital in her late nineties; Louise Varèse, wife and biographer of Edgard the innovator, excellent translator of Rimbaud, and parental figure to all; and Alma Morgenthau, sister of Henry Jr. and mother of Barbara Tuchman, who gave money. What these women said went. Claire, Minna, and Alma were each touchingly, because hopelessly, in

love with Aaron Copland. Yvonne and Louise were not (they were also
not Jewish). Yvonne, my first brush with the dynamic of a continental
lady, remained an ally, especially during my Paris years when she
became cultural attaché at the American embassy. As for Edward
James, natural son of Edward VII, he was shortish and thin and married
to Tilly Losch, but queer, very, and a patron of the arts beginning with
the late Diaghilev ballets. He had written the text and paid for
Poulenc's first big choral piece with orchestra, *Sécheresses,* and otherwise sought the company of the highborn and of rough trade. I never
saw him again after this Wednesday, but Gavin Lambert eventually
wrote a novel about him called *Norman's Letter.*

Virgil invited me for a weekend to the New Jersey house of his
Harvard chum, art historian Briggs Buchanan (whose musical "portrait" I'd copied). Of this outing I recall the half dozen taffy apples we
bought at the bus station for the Buchanan children, a shimmering
garden with dahlias, the quarters shared with Mr. Thomson, and, most
crucially, Erik Satie's *Socrate.* Virgil sang me this little cantata in his
composer's voice (i.e., his nonvoice of definitive expressivity), and
during that half hour I felt my notion of the world's musical repertory
change shape, swell, shrink, and ensconce itself in my ken where it
would permanently lodge, along with *The Rite of Spring,* as one of
those three or four artistic experiences against which I would judge
all others in the coming years.

What can be said of *Socrate?* On that special morning I was most
struck by the second movement, wherein teacher strolls with pupil by
the river; the intonations are continual nondevelopmental iterations
of adjacent couplets, as in the line "Est-il rien de plus suave et de plus
délicieux?" Such contagious monotone chutzpah, honest and respectful. But when I later bought the score and rehashed it on my own
piano, the three scenes bloomed differently beneath my fingers. *Socrate* is, in a sense, without style—without immediate location in time.
Oddly, when you talk to confirmed Satie freaks who think of the
composer as "minimal," they've usually heard his every work except
the masterpiece, *Socrate.* (Although "master" is the one thing Satie
was not; it's what Germans are.) I've sung it to myself every week of
my life without getting bored, the joy of expectation remaining always
fresh. Satie's philosophy, in relating the conventionally unrelated—
equating wit with sorrow as a qualitative expression, for instance—
was not far from yesterday's pop culture, which made the ordinary
extraordinary by removing it from context. Elsewhere, conversely, like
the surrealists, he treated his eccentric subject matter straightfor-
wardly. In the margins of his compositions he inserted little verbal
jokes, whimsical advice to the performer or "impossible" directions

not unlike those Ives was employing at the same time in America. *Socrate* itself is fairly long as pieces go; as a program in itself, fairly short. Nothing "goes" with it, least of all other works by Satie since, in a way, they are all contained within *Socrate*. The texts from Plato's *Dialogues*, highly truncated in the French translation, are set to music without romantic gyration, even without vocal embellishment, almost as they would be spoken. They are set literally, so to speak, with respect. Respect—that is, humility—is not a quality one quite associates with greatness. Yet humility is precisely the genius of *Socrate:* Plato is not illustrated, not interpreted, by the music: he is encased by the music, and the case is not a period piece; rather, it is from all periods. Which is what makes the music so difficult to identify. Is it from modern France? ancient Greece? or from Pope Gregory's sixth century? Why the music seems never static I do not know, for in the academic sense *Socrate* has no development beyond the normal evolution imposed by the words. Hence the music moving forward seldom relates to itself thematically, though its texture remains almost constantly undifferentiated. The dynamic level hardly rises above mezzo-forte, with little contrast and no climax until the final page, when we hear forty-four inexorable knellings of an open fifth which denote the agony of the philosopher, who, in the last two bars, expires with a sigh. The harmony, mostly triadic, is rarely dissonant, and never dissonant in an out-of-key sense except in a single "pictorial" section, again from the end movement, when the jailer presses Socrates' legs, which have grown cold from the hemlock: here the words are colored with repetitions of a numbingly foreign C-sharp. So where lies the remarkability, the ever-renewed thrill of anticipation? It lies in the composer's absolutely original way with the tried and true. The music, written in 1919, is not "ahead" of its time, but rather (and of what other work can this be said?) outside of time, allowing the old, old dialogues of Plato to sound so always new.

What worked for Satie did not (to my ears) work for Virgil, for Virgil was a sophisticate faking naïveté, while Satie was a true naïf hoping for sophistication and achieving it despite himself. Virgil, like so many, misread the name Satie by inserting an *r* betwixt the *i* and the *e*.

In case you've been wondering, Virgil and I never "had sex," nor did he ever make a pass. Except once. One winter afternoon, when I had to stay late to make corrections in something I'd botched, Virgil said:

"I'm going to take a nap. Will you wake me at exactly four fifteen."

At four fifteen I opened the door into his darkened room.

"It's four fifteen."

"That's no way to wake Papa. Come over and wake Papa with a kiss."

Am I supposed to say no? So I leaned down, as upon a great lady—a great, *doughy* lady like, say, Nero—and kissed him on the lips.

"That's how to wake Papa," he said, quickly realizing he'd maybe done the wrong thing. I still hear the wistful voice now as he turned toward the south window through which the light was fading fast over our grimy city.

"It looks like Barcelona out."

Where is Barcelona? In Spain, the only country besides England that Virgil had visited outside of France during his long years abroad.

Six months passed before he was aware of Morris as more than a name I lived with, and who sometimes phoned to ask where the hell I was. The Second String Quartet had just been published by New Music Editions with, among its hundred-odd pages, one minor misprint where a flat was omitted. The thousand extant copies were delivered from the publisher. My job was to enter the missing flat into each copy, pack the whole into a footlocker and deposit this hundred-pound object at the American Music Center at 250 West Fifty-seventh, then bring the footlocker back to the Chelsea. I said that my friend Morris Golde would help with the cab. When Morris showed up, all tough and eager, he hoisted the footlocker like a feather onto his shoulders, and off we went. Virgil was thrilled.

That evening we dined *à trois* at Bleeck's. (Lucius Beebe was there and had a drink with us. He feigned remembrance of our Chicago orgy five years ago, especially when I mentioned that Frank—now in the army and whom I'd recently seen in a gay bar called Ralph's on West Forty-fourth, where he stole my new wristwatch—had stolen my wristwatch. "A l'ombre des jeunes filles en fleurs," remarked Beebe, blushing as much, or as little, as he ever would. "Du côté de chez les voleurs," added Virgil.) If, as Virgil said of his first meeting with Gertrude Stein, "We got on like Harvard men," he and Morris hit it off like long-lost Jewish cousins, and remained close—closer than I ever was with Virgil, or at least in a different, noncompetitive way—until the end.

Morris Golde lived and still lives on West Eleventh, but now he owns the ground floor, while then he rented the one-and-a-half-room flat on the fourth story back. The half room was mine, plus a rented upright, the décor was Mexican with a view onto a courtyard complex *en face* as in *Rear Window,* and the street remains one of the prettiest in the Village, with only eleven short blocks up Seventh Avenue to Virgil's to where I walked each morning. Each evening we ate out, usually at Drossie's, a good and cheap downstairs bistro on Greenwich

Avenue run by a Miss Jeanne Drossie with her two Americanized
Russian-born sisters who resembled the witches of *Macbeth,* only
shorter and oh so warm. All the waiters were gay and so was half the
clientele. The other half was high bohemia. Joe Gould, for example,
with his sweet darting eyes and bushy beard, toting the notorious
manuscript of his ongoing *Oral History of the Universe;* he was the
premier intellectual homeless bum who one early dawn came to pass
out on our floor. ("A myth is as good as a smile" wrote Cummings
about little Joe Gould's winsomeness.) Or Maxwell Bodenheim, author of *Replenishing Jessica,* who would descend the five steps into
the restaurant where, pausing among the candelit tables, he lit his
cigarette with a theatrical sweep of a wooden match up the back of his
pants, then danced a little dance and vanished. Or the bitchy and
likable Dougie who, like Dante Pavone (another patron), proclaimed
himself a "layer" of Djuna Barnes's Dr. O'Connor and who in fact
had been immortalized by Kay Boyle in her *Valentine for Alan Ross
MacDougall,* who had published a collection of Attic recipes called
And the Greeks, and who—though twice his age—was now Alvin
Ross's best friend (for Alvin, too, was now in New York). Or the
sculptor Zadkine with his white granite hair. There was no liquor
license, you could bring your own, but most people, even bohemians,
didn't drink on weeknights—*Americans* don't drink on weeknights
but make up for it on weekends, which the French find infantile if not
gross.

Morris and I were Americans, and he knew the city like the back of
his hand—not just the concert halls and baseball arenas but the drinking holes. Of a gloomy, snow-covered Saturday we might decide, before landing at Drossie's for the evening meal, to go pub crawling,
starting at noon and working up Sixth Avenue bar by bar. But we'd
seldom get beyond Fourteenth Street since the pub grew more crucial
than the crawling. Or we'd have a martini, or two or fourteen, in a
gorgeous orange-and-black Longchamps, perhaps the one on lower
Fifth, where the walls are banked with pink glazed mirrors into which
yellow lamps reflect their discreet heat, and you are in another world.
Outside the sleet pelts the late afternoon and slush accumulates on
the salt-strewn sidewalks, but here the gin in its funneled tumbler
protects you from reality—or rather, *becomes* your reality—and Morris tells me about Kafka. A sober Sunday, after such a Saturday, could
be no less unreal. Do you remember—we were *there!*—when the
airplane crashed into the Empire State Building and hung like a
maimed bat in a hole on the sixtieth floor? Elevators fell sixty floors
in six seconds. We were too distant to make out what the radio reported: a woman's head—she had red hair—impaled on a girder.

Energetic, Morris rose early, rushed to the IRT local which whisked him near the Forty-fifth Street office where he ran a flourishing direct-mail and printing-press business with his older brother, Michael, married with children. (A still older brother, Ben, a successful businessman, was gay.) Among their many musical clients was the Town Hall's series called The New Friends of Music. For them, thanks to Morris, I made fifteen extra dollars copying the parts, astonishingly unavailable commercially, of Ravel's *Chansons madécasses* directly from the full score, which Martial Singher accordingly sang with the Albeneri Trio. I emphasize "astonishingly unavailable," for in those days everything in music was available. You had only to walk into Chicago's Lyon & Healy store, Philadelphia's Theodore Presser store or similar sheet-music outlets in any medium-sized city across the country and buy the always-in-stock complete works of Gabrieli or Griffes, Praetorius or Poulenc, not to mention standards like Stravinsky or Schoenberg, all for sensible sums. Today printed music must be sent away for; six months later your Gabrieli may arrive from Milan in a battered photocopied facsimile, with a bill for $200, or more likely a memo saying "permanently out of print." So much for the age of quick communications in the high arts.

Evenings Morris and I would dine out, usually at Drossie's, sometimes at the more expensive ($2.50) Waverly Inn, where the chicken pie and the cinnamon apple tart à la mode were special lures, occasionally at the old Brevoort Hotel on lower Fifth Avenue, which had an outdoor café in summer months. Two or three times we dined at Morris's parents' in the Bronx. Romanian immigrants with marked accents, they lived comfortably on the Grand Concourse, doted on their three money-making male offspring and served gefilte fish, which turned me off. Mrs. Goldenberg was domineering. Her husband, stricken with Parkinson's, was not ambulatory. He hummed little folklike melodies of his invention, which I notated properly on music manuscript paper. His pride in this physical evidence of his talent was touching; he made scrolls of the sheets and kept them in a crystal vase to show the neighbors.

During the eighteen months of our cohabitation Morris and I were never unfaithful, although there was habitual teasing and flirting, especially at all those after-hours all-boy dancing parties we ended up at, after a dogged ingestion of beer on Saturdays at the Welcome Inn or the MacDougal Inn, identical gay bars side by side on MacDougal Street. We quarreled some, made love a lot—about eight times a week —and listened incessantly to music, usually all at the same time. The lovers' bed resembled a shipwreck, the room smelled of muscle, the phonograph heaved with *Der Rosenkavalier*'s horny evocations, as we fell panting to the floor, then rose to swill milkshakes with raw eggs and sherry. Often I'd copy my own work at home on the cedar table while Morris read aloud: Vincent Sheehan's *Personal History,* Denton Welsh's *Maiden Voyage,* Joseph Mitchell's *McSorley's Wonderful Saloon* about the landmark on East Seventh where we sometimes hung out.

Morris was friends with, and had been the lover of, harpsichordist Ralph Kirkpatrick, a patrician presence of massively organized intellect, already half blind and very tall. It would be hard to imagine two creatures more disparate, Morris with his darting, wiry verbosity, Ralph all calm and cultured as he sat at his Chalice-made instrument. Kirkpatrick's series at the YMHA of Bach and Mozart sonatas with violinist Alexander Schneider was a landmark of performing excellence, as were his solo clavichord series at the Carnegie Recital Hall. Harkening to the clavichord is a craft in itself, knowing how to stay still so as to hear each silver teardrop tinkle in an ever-growing necklace miles away.

Ralph loved Billie Holiday, even knew her a little (a little is all anyone knew her). We visited the singer at the Onyx Club, where I got drunk, and in adulation sank down to put my head 'neath her skirt, which smelled like a Catholic church. Bringing her back in the early hours to Ralph's small flat on Lexington Avenue it became clear that Billie, in all her uneducated glory, could attend as astutely as any trained musicologue. She admired the harpsichord, its construction, its repertory, became a silent audience to Ralph the executant. Billie was a jazz star, never a blues singer except for a few forays, notably into Bessie Smith's repertory, and in her own "Fine and Mellow." Like surrealism, which was a literary (sometimes by extension a painterly) movement that excluded the art of music as sissified and irrelevant, so the blues is a poetic form that can exist independently of the music that ornaments it—a series of AAB verses in iambic pentameter:

> My man don't love me treats me awful mean
> My man don't love me treats me awful mean
> He is the lowest man I've ever seen.

"Iambic pentameter," said Billie. "Yeah, that's it."

Had I gleaned anything during three and a half years at Northwestern and Curtis, other than some practicalities about the craft of formalized sound? Certainly I had mild crushes on this or that male or female teacher, but I never forged such scholarly role models as Father and Paul Goodman represented in the outside world, or Debussy and

Ravel from the evanescent past, or Virgil and Aaron in the very close future. But I did learn that, just as there's no one right way to play a piece (there are as many right ways as there are smart virtuosos, and even the composer's way is not final), so there is no one perception of any fact or concept or, indeed, "truth."

Having firsthand knowledge of homosexuality, and seeing that the world is mostly blind to, or wrong about, homosexuality, wised me up early. Jews are similarly wised up about their status.

I had a recurring nightmare which makes no plausible sense, and which began (again) in 1944. Today, putting myself in the Me then, the Me then puts himself in the Me of infancy when it all started. The dream does not concern human or animal rapports. Just a mass, immense, shifting with and against other masses, cloud shaped and lugubrious. The counterpoint of mass-against-mass is like the motion in Messiaen's music, as distinct from the line-against-line in Bach. No variety, no progress, no illumination. Only inexpressible fear.

And every year or so throughout my life I dream of being pregnant, literally. How I got in that condition, and by what route the child will emerge, I do not know. (Magritte's green apple fills a room.)

Seated for my daily stint between parlor and bedroom, I observed Virgil Thomson running the world. When I arrived each day at ten, he would have performed his ablutions, and now, in clean orange pajamas from Lanvin, propped up and surrounded by an ocean of pillows with a sharpened pencil and a big yellow pad (he never learned to typewrite), he conducted the musical life of Manhattan from his bed. If it were Tuesday the phone would be off the hook as he scrawled (his handwriting was as infantile as his musical calligraphy) his Sunday sermon, which he would then, with no revisions, dictate by phone to his secretary, Julia Haines, at the *Tribune*. The subject of the sermon, he explained to me, could materialize from anywhere: the previous month in concert halls (he reviewed three concerts a week), crank letters from strangers, reactions to the state of modern song in France, or from a question Maurice Grosser put to him en passant. On other weekdays he would spend the morning hours on the bedside phone, mostly on business for the paper: making assignments to his staff of critics (which included Paul Bowles), or telling them his reactions to their reviews from last night. He might otherwise extend or accept invitations involving Oscar Levant or Sir Thomas Beecham (whom he loved) or Ormandy, or simply gossip with his Franco-American cronies, who included the art world as much as the music: the brothers Berman, Sylvia Marlowe, Philip Johnson, Tchelitcheff, Peggy Guggenheim. Since the bedroom door was wide open as I labored, naturally I overheard all this, often with a lifted eyebrow (I was the *bourgeois* he was pleased to *épater*), unless he specifically asked me to close the door, an academic gesture since his shrill voice carried.

On one such occasion his mother, Clara May Thomson, then aged seventy-nine and in New York for the first time, was present. She slept in a room down the hall but arrived at Virgil's each morning at 7:30 to help the cook—a large and humorless old-world Negro woman named Leana—shell peas or iron shirts on the other end of the table whereon I labored. Toward noon I was asked to close the door, and we all cocked our ears as Virgil dialed Paul Bowles.

"I have to bawl you out, Paul dear, so have you had your breakfast?"

"Breakfast at noon!" snorted both women with midwestern righteousness.

As for Paul Bowles being chided, it struck me as . . . as against nature that anyone could be in the driver's seat with Paul; Paul was just not accessible. I hadn't seen him yet since living in New York, but still thought of him with vague awe if not respect. Virgil's reprimand concerned what he called Paul's "pose," going around saying he didn't know anything about nineteenth-century German music, for this made mockery of criticism and by extension of the *Herald-Tribune*. Of course, Virgil had no love for, or careful knowledge of, German music either, but when a review of, say, a Brahms symphony was needed it was assigned to Jerry Bohm or Arthur Berger or, *faute de mieux,* Paul Bowles, who was admonished to do his homework. Meanwhile Virgil took his mother to all sorts of recitals, including one of John Cage's for prepared pianos. Asked her opinion, Mrs. Thomson replied: "Nice, but I never would have thought of it myself."

Were I to dare interrupt a phone conversation with a query about some illegible smudge, Virgil would remonstrate either by amending the smudge to look worse than before or by declaring: "That's baby stuff, baby. Don't bother Papa with baby stuff." "Baby" was one of his favorite words. So was "amusing," which in English rings more preciously than in French. Everything was amusing: Macbeth, a cherry pie, his mother's heavy overcoat. When he said to the stony Leana before she went out shopping, "If you see any vegetables that look amusing, buy them," she came back empty-handed.

In the afternoons Virgil, dressed, would receive in the parlor. Again I eavesdropped as he rehearsed his Violin Sonata with Joseph Fuchs, or served coffee to the staff of *View* magazine, which wanted an article from him, or chatted with his most frequent visitor, Maurice Grosser, friend and longtime lover from Harvard days, a topnotch realist painter of people (Jane Bowles), landscapes (the coast of Maine), and foodstuffs (mainly eggs and rounded fruits and vegetables like eggplants and pears, all vastly enlarged). Maurice, a Mississippi Jew, was in physical stature reminiscent of Morris Golde, sinewy, short, excitable; in mentality he was, arguably, the brains behind Virgil's brains. Have I already mentioned that it was Maurice who took the raw sketches of Stein's *Four Saints in Three Acts* and superimposed a scenario which blossomed into the ideal libretto, even as Alice Toklas wrote Stein's famous autobiography? But neither Stein nor Thomson gave credit its due, and their paramours were willingly silent partners. True, Maurice did have an independent career as a painter and a cult public of sorts; he also wrote two intelligent and useful books about painting. True, too, that Virgil encouraged Maurice (his junior by a few years) by recommending him, talking him up, but only insofar as Maurice didn't grow too tall. Even long after, when Maurice Grosser died at eighty-three (of AIDS, astonishingly), Virgil was oddly mum.

Indeed, he was oddly mum about anything that might compromise him publicly, if not socially, especially sexual innuendo. Campy and gossipy and aggressively effeminate as he was at home, so was he circumspect in the world. This may have been due to the still-recent trauma of the arrest in that male whorehouse; more probably it was due to his cool rivalries and deluded notions of himself. Because my *Paris Diary,* published in 1966 a few months prior to VT's own autobiography, was unprecedentedly plain about my own homosexuality (it's not that I made a point of it—on the contrary, I didn't bother to pretend), he cut all references to me in his book for fear of being compromised. Who was he kidding! That book, an otherwise unique document on the economic history of the arts in contemporary America, has a faint but common stench, not just because he doesn't mention what Gide called *la chose,* but because, hypocritically, he does mention his passions for various women.

Virgil, who spoke as he wrote, economically and to the point, in whole sentences and paragraphs, had the wittiest English language repartee of anyone around. Even physically he had imitative gifts of cutting precision, as when he would rush across the room with tiny tight steps, imitating a Gibson girl in a hobble skirt playing badminton. But he was no less competitive than most artists, as well as imperious about his lore. How often I saw him alienate unalerted folk he was meeting for the first time—a professional photographer or a brain surgeon, for instance, to whom he'd explain the craft of soft-lens focus or the details of a scalp incision! For the young ("All young people look alike to me") he also had all the answers. What is this silly old fairy trying to say? they would ask. Of course, Virgil spoke always in French-style generalities, which are anathema to literal-minded American children.

After six months or so of secretarial work chez lui, it was thought I needed more formal training. He never admitted it, but Virgil felt a vague sense of responsibility vis-à-vis my father; after all, he had talked me into forgoing my scholarship at Curtis in midstream and moving to New York. And he was aware that the meager salary he doled out was my sole income. So he took it upon himself to give me lessons, no extra charge.

There is no such animal, according to Thomson, as the teaching of musical composition (do as your idols do, not as they say), which is an esthetic study best left to analytical Germans. Composers become composers not because they take lessons but because they beg, borrow and steal. Certainly I had learned counterpoint and harmony until they came out of my ears, while amassing a repertory was merely a question of answering to the heart (we wouldn't be musicians in the first place if we didn't like to hear music) and of attending a regular dose of concerts, thanks to the free tickets provided by Virgil. But academic instruction of the so-called creative arts is a nonexistent process. Good teaching, the imparting of extant knowledge, is a healthy infection which leads students to rich mineral waters and makes them drink; but no teacher can cause a piece of music to be, he can only criticize it after it exists; if he is a composer he can teach only by himself being—by allowing himself passively to be imitated. But there is a craft, if not an art, the lineaments of which can be imparted, even from one untalented person to another, and that is the craft of orchestration. Instrumentation is physical fact, not theoretical idea. That is what Virgil intended to show me.

At first I was wary. What, after all, did the maker of all these simple-minded ditties I'd been transcribing know about teaching? But during the eighteen months I worked with Virgil I was to learn more than during the long years, before and after, spent in the world's major conservatories. In mastering the art of calligraphy a young musician becomes answerable for every note among millions, for the need for clarity on the page (because music, before it can be heard, must be visibly communicable), and the copyist eventually knows the score better than the author of the score. Meanwhile, if orchestration, unlike composition, is the study of specific balances—a study available to any layman—then Virgil, in placing before me the principles of this study, explained once, and only once, the sonic results of every physical combination of instruments. Just as overhearing the phone conversations—and thus his manner of behavior in a professional milieu—

was an indelible instruction, so I can recall today as on a disc each word he spoke during our lessons fifty years ago.

His lucidity was due no less to an innate clarity of mind than to a voicing of that mind through an ideal language of thrift: he spoke French in English. Since he knew what he was talking about and didn't waste words, merely to be in his presence was to learn. And merely to think about him is to risk being influenced, as these pale phrases attest, for no one out-Virgils Virgil.

My ambivalence about both him and his work rose and fell with the years. I could live without his music, yet his two operas on Gertrude Stein's texts are arguably our *only* American operas. His music resembles, more demonstrably than with any composer I know, himself. It is impatiently terse, free of fat or padding, eschewing sensuality to a point of self-indulgence, and one absorbs it like an icy acid which bathes a core of hot prettiness. At its best his music is very, very witty —if that adjective makes sense when applied to nonvocal works.

I was Virgil Thomson's sole pupil, which makes me proud, and made him proud, too, so far as it went, especially when he eventually heard my opulent scoring—so much more opulent than his—but which retained a transparency that only his training could have produced. (Transparency means that no matter how many instruments you use at any moment, each one—each group—is heard, nothing vanishes in the fray. This is French, as distinct from German, where, since every instrument or group is doubled, nothing retains an individual stamp.) Still, Virgil, who was old enough to be my father, was always slightly jealous of whatever successes I may have had after I went to France, where hitherto he had been, or so he imagined, America's only musical representative.

One spring night at Drossie's, Morris and I ran into Paul Bowles. He was sitting in a corner with his cousin, stage designer Oliver Smith, eating the homemade apple cake for which the restaurant was renowned. Learning that I was now Virgil's copyist, Paul asked if I'd be interested in doing a copying job for him. So next night we visited him.

Paul rented a small penthouse nearby, at 56 Seventh Avenue off Fourteenth Street, with a spectacular view of downtown Manhattan. (Did you know that Seventh Avenue curves at a 110-degree angle while descending toward the Battery?) The larger of his two rooms was all in white: white sofas, a white piano, with long white curtains moving slightly in April's first warm breezes, and a white fur rug wall to wall. A white telephone with the number removed. Drums here and there. Like his room at the Chelsea a year ago, this one reeked of perfume, as indeed did Paul himself, wherever he went. He had spent the better part of his Guggenheim fellowship on raw ambergris which he combined with other basic essences to confect heavy oils that imbued the furniture, never to disappear. A luscious cage of scent for him to hide behind. He brewed the gooey incense in various flavors and titled them for special exotic friends: a vial of *Evil Eye* for Hazel Scott, *Green Devil* for Elsie Huston. Garish books, with a careful casualness, were strewn over the floor: a tome of Goya's horrifying *Caprichos,* a collection of Weegee portraits of murderers. Paul reinforced his effect when speaking of Man Ray, who once showed him photographs of slaves somewhere in North Africa, chained to pillars and living in their own excrement. (Eight years later, when Man Ray befriended me in Paris, I asked him about these photographs. He had never taken pictures of slaves, he claimed, never been in Africa, never heard of Paul Bowles.)

All this would be chitchat were it not relevant to another aspect of the man which grew clear in the next half hour, and which changed my life as *Socrate* and *Sacre* had changed my life. Paul asked if he might play for us a recent piece of his. This turned out to be an aircheck of a five-minute arietta from the zarzuela *The Wind Remains,* which had been recently broadcast with Maria Kurenko intoning the Lorca text. I was bewitched and remain bewitched after five decades. Would Paul enjoy comparing my state to that of Dorian Gray to whom Lord Henry lends a copy of *A rebours,* precipitating poor Dorian's descent into "esthetic corruption"? Alas, Paul's music is the picture of health. A more proper analogy might be the *petite phrase* of Vinteuil, like Lenny's "Taxco tune."

The *petite phrase* in this case was that most melancholy of intervals, a descending minor third, the "dying fall" that—I later discovered— threads all of Paul's music. This arietta was a mere bagatelle, after all, yet it had more impact on my thinking than any symphony of Mahler, who also favored the dying fall yet whose nature was the antithesis of Paul's. The little phrase was a mannerism which Paul is doubtless unaware of; we live with our signatures, so never think much about them. For me, though, it was a conscious expressive device which I appropriated and have retained. I have composed ten times more music than has Paul (with the 1949 advent of *The Sheltering Sky* he shifted, in the ken of the general public, from the role of composer-who-also-writes to that of author-who-used-to-compose), yet somewhere in my every piece lurks the rhythmic or melodic lilt, albeit disguised, of the invisible mentor. Influence, of course, is all art's fertilizer: thievery is embellished, then branded with the new owner's tic. Paul Bowles and I are separated enough in years for me still to wish, at this late date, for his approval. He would surely feign astonishment at this juvenile admission, especially since he might not see—or hear—himself in me.

If I stress Paul's musicality, it's because that musicality seems to have fallen away in our world. The bulk of his fans today are unaware that he ever composed, much less have they ever hummed his tunes: Americans are meant to be specialists. So for the record let it be said that Paul Bowles is, like Europeans of yore (Leonardo, Cocteau, Noël Coward), a general practitioner of high order. Unlike them, his two professions don't overlap—neither esthetically nor technically. Composers when they prosify (Schumann, Debussy, Thomson) inevitably deal with music or with autobiography. Bowles is the sole fiction writer among them, and his fiction is as remote from their prose as from his own music. His stories are icy, cruel, objective, moralistic in their amorality, and occur mostly in exotic climes; they are also often cast in large forms. His music is warm, wistful, witty, redolent of nostalgia for his Yankee youth, wearing its heart on its sleeve; and it is all cast in small forms. No American in our century has composed songs lovelier than his. None of these songs is currently in print. That fact echoes the indifferent world that he elsewhere so successfully portrays.

The only secretarial work I did for Paul was to copy an extract from a ballet, *Pastorela* (fifteen pages for fifteen dollars), but with the years I had occasion to examine piles of his music, including the beloved moment from *The Wind Remains*. If the sound of his music remains like the wind over an otherwise barren earth, the sight of it was like a beginner's. The manuscript was puerile in appearance, the spellings and placements on the staff were frequently incorrect, the orchestration seemed so unbalanced (according to my textbooks on instrumentation) as to sound like a smear. Hey, what was it with these trend-setting New Yorkers that they knew less than I about the basics of their profession!

Father came through town and stayed at the Waldorf. Having never met either the roommate or the employer of his son, he hoped to play host to the three of us. We would dine *à quatre* in Peacock Alley. Virgil was amenable. "I've met fathers before," he said, when I invited him, wondering nevertheless if the Waldorf might strike him as rather too snazzy for his presumably impecunious student's sire. Father was eager as a boy at the prospect.

Morris and I arrived first and went up to Father's two-room suite.

Father took me aside to announce the sad news that Don Dalton was dead. At boot camp Don had walked into an airplane propeller and been torn into a thousand shreds. . . . Poor clever, gentle Don, no death is dignified. His mother, Arleen, and my mother became friends then and exchanged letters for years. After Loren and Géorg, Don was my third death, and they were war casualties only indirectly. Yet the war was beginning to gobble our young men as AIDS gobbles them today. The thought of Don shrouded the evening.

Then Virgil showed up and had to use the toilet. Father showed him into the side room, where *The State of Music* was lying open on the bed. Before Father could hide the book, Virgil spotted it and was flattered. During the course of the meal Virgil found Father handsome and wise. Forever afterward he claimed that "Ned's father is in love with him." Rosemary ultimately met Virgil at the Chelsea, didn't get the point of him—the continental affectations, the specialization. Mother too saw him several times in later years, and never cared for him.

Unguided, I was composing copiously. Virgil, adamant about not being a teacher, nonetheless inspected the goods occasionally, to show off his technical advice. Among these goods was *Prelude and Adagio* for organ, flute, horn, and viola, which I wrote, unsolicited, for E. Power Biggs. Before sending it off, Virgil, who knew a thing or two about the organ from his youth as choir director in Boston's King's Chapel, gave me hints about pedal use and voice leading. I mailed the result to Biggs in Cambridge. This time he was more enthusiastic. I heard *Prelude and Adagio* first over the air, when Biggs eventually programmed it on one of his Sunday-morning nationwide broadcasts (on 6 May 1945, at 9:15 a.m., to be exact), assisted by three members of the Boston Symphony. I was enchanted with the glow of my instrumentation: how the real flute reflected the organ flute stop like shadings of blue in a Rouault gouache; how flute and horn, silver and gold, blended as echoes in a Hopkins poem; how the luxuriant rasp of the viola in its long sad solo was mirrored myriad times among the strands of organ piping. The work in the reality of retrospect seems stodgy and without contrast, but Biggs rehearsed it as amply as though it were, well, a Ravel premiere, and I ensuingly played the tape—I mean the old 78-rpm vinyl acetate—for anyone who would listen. Two or three organists have since performed the piece as a curiosity, but it remains as it should, unpublished. Biggs and I corresponded until his death in 1977, but we never met.

. . .

Norris Embry recited a quatrain of Jean Cocteau's called "De Don Juan":

En Espagne on orne la rue
avec des loges d'opéra.
Quelle est cette belle inconnue?
C'est la mort. Don Juan l'aura.

In one sitting I set it, steeped in the Bowlesian dying fall. (When in 1950 I first met Cocteau and quoted the poem, he, like Man Ray with the slave pictures, professed not to remember.) During the next weeks I wrote other songs on verses of my own, or by friends, or by an odd cluster of poets suggested either by Norris or by his colleague, blond Bob Anderson, both now settled, or unsettled, in New York after years at Saint John's College with David Sachs. "Doll's Boy," for example, on Cummings's famous words. Alvin Ross designed a blue and pink lithograph depicting the "eight and twenty ladies in a line" which Morris used as a cover for a limited edition which he printed privately. Also privately printed by Morris were *Three Old English Songs* on lyrics by Chaucer—did you know Chaucer wrote lyric poetry?—the first of which, titled simply "Song," came forth as follows:

Lenny Bernstein, already world famous from his overnight substitution for Bruno Walter at the Philharmonic, gave the New York premiere of his own *Jeremiah Symphony* with that orchestra in March of 1944. The soloist, mezzo-soprano Jennie Tourel, featured only in the third of the three movements, nevertheless sat on stage for a full twenty minutes—jet-black hair, deep-blue dress, uninflected gaze—before opening her mouth. When finally she rose and began the Hebrew lamentation, the skies opened. Her unique sound of nasal chocolate, enunciating the biblical text, was at once satisfying and nourishing; she was the first example in my experience of an ugly person who, through talent and sheer presence, becomes, while in the act of singing, the epitome of glamour. As for Lenny's music, this was the first of it I'd heard in public. It was nothing if not Jewish, while mine is nothing if not goyische. Yet this plaintive heady draft infused my creative consciousness, in both tone and texture, quite as intoxicatingly as Paul Bowles's arietta, so that I went home and notated the memory, literally. The Chaucer song, which is this memory, is as Wasp as Lenny is not. Or so I imagined.

If the notion of musicalizing a poem in French seemed chic, so did the notion of musicalizing poems by friends. Bruce Phemister, like most of the old Chicago acquaintances, lived in New York now. Less a poet than a novelist, Bruce had nonetheless written a nostalgic stanza named "Russian Spring," which I had used pleasurably a year before. Now I asked him to make a suite in three sections to be sung by soprano with flute, violin, and piano. This he did in a triptych of Sitwellian images called "Hell," "Noon," and "Spring." (Father, learning of these titles, urged me to change "Hell" to "Hades," imagine!) The seminonsensical word sequences were theatrical and quaint, and eminently singable. (Virgil did not concur: perusing the text he sniffed: "I think she stink," which made me titter uncomfortably.) I found good interpreters: Ellen Greenberg, a chum from Northwestern and now with Stokowski's Youth Orchestra, played fiddle; Leslie Oakes, a pupil of Francis Blaisedell's, who had recently recorded the Bowles Flute Sonata, played flute; Janet Lauren, a trusted soprano from Curtis, sang; and I was the pianist. According to a pretty promotional postcard printed by Morris and pasted in a yellowing scrapbook, we premiered this piece, now called *In Piazzas Palladio,* during a live broadcast from WNYC on 20 February 1945, between 4:15 and 4:45. Also on the program was my Four-hand Sonata, and an *Arioso* for violin and piano, of which I retain no copy and don't recall. The broadcast was part of WNYC's "American Music Week," which the radio director, David Stimer, was launching that year, and which continues still every February. Stimer, himself a pianist, acted pleased with my program, became a friend, and would pass through my life in various guises.

Virgil announced that I must resume piano lessons. He summoned his old friend, the French pianist E. Robert Schmitz, who had written a book on piano method, modestly called *The E. Robert Schmitz Piano Method,* which I perused with mixed feelings, having then as now an allergy to methods of any sort—one man's meat, etcetera. The doctrinaire study named all the arm and hand joints and how to use them properly (never put your thumb on a black key), despite flagrant evidence of improper use by a Horowitz or a Glenn Gould, who gyrate their torsos and flatten their palms with heaven-sent results. Nevertheless, I agreed to take lessons with Schmitz's star protégée, a Miss Betty Crawford.

I don't remember much about the lessons, in either method or repertory, but Betty was an affable and intelligent woman with an unexciting yet useful skill at the keyboard, and I "used" her often as an exponent in my own works during the next few years. She was also, although I couldn't know it then, a vital link to the next chapter in my life, as will appropriately be seen in the next chapter.

Drinking, so as to be able to have sex, defeats it purpose. Drunk, one's impotent. So drinking becomes an end in itself. Let me describe a hangover. With a hangover—assuming you're not planning to drink again soon—the mind is so riveted on the body that there *is* no mind. Is this self-renewal? the obstinate craving for oranges and soda water? the obsessive sex drive? With a hangover, only the body exists. In urinals, in back alleys, in barns, far from taverns, one glides from cubicle to cubicle, inspecting, rejecting, in the semidark, pausing sometimes at length, then starting all over again, like flipping channels on the TV.

Drink and recover in order to drink and recover in order . . .

Recurring theme, with no variations.

One morning out of the blue there sat another person at my worktable in the Chelsea. Tall and bigboned but somehow fragile, like Orson Welles on a tulip stem, effusive but shyish, obsessed with how music looked on the page, this was Lou Harrison. A California composer six years my senior, he had worked with Schoenberg and with Henry Cowell with whom he had founded New Music Edition for publishing what then was deemed experimental work. Now he was uprooted for the first time, about to begin a stint as a part-time stringer at the *Tribune* and meanwhile helping Virgil with extra copy work. More skilled than I (Lou's hand-drawn musical and prose artifacts are world famous), with a practical sense of performance broader than mine (he had formed his own percussion orchestra with John Cage in San Francisco), and with a grasp of intercultural workings that surely exceeded my grasp, Lou became Virgil's valuable colleague. Indeed, he may even have let me slide out of sight were it not for his devotion to my cause; nor was Lou interested in replacing me. As it was, we got along famously: Lou as a person was a total original, as a composer a total eclectic. His social style was Californian, easygoing, even oriental, but with more than a twinge of a daftness which led later to a turn in the loony bin, and a predilection for Negro males. His music style was anything that was asked for; Lou felt that one ought to be capable of all, and had earned a living from choreographers (twenty-five dollars a minute was his fee) of every persuasion, composing fandangos for José Limón, Coplandesque diatonicisms for Jean Erdman, Schoenber-

gian mood pieces for Charles Weidman. Lou taught me the whole bag
of tricks of the so-called twelve-tone system in about an hour, and I
applied them for about a week. Finally, however, his eclecticism was
original. Lou Harrison fifty years ago was concocting raga-type ostina-
tos identical with those today of Philip Glass and Steve Reich, with the
notable difference that while all three men prepare canvases that are
nonpareil, only Harrison superimposes a drawing—a melody—upon
the canvas which gives it a reason for being.

Weekends we would gather at Lou's pad on Bleecker Street, where
he lived with his black boyfriend, a clergyman, and while swilling
quart after quart of Schaefer beer, talk of his idols, Ives, Ruggles, and
Varèse, artists he pitted against Copland, whom he disdained. Lou
adopted me, was helpful in many ways, for he had his foot in every
door. It was he (I *think* it was he) who gave me entrée to certain
organizations that performed me, like the International Society for
Contemporary Music.

Impromptu Thanksgiving at Virgil's. We all go down to the store to
buy raw things which Virgil will then cook in his little kitchen. Maurice
Grosser, Lou, a couple of others, but not Morris. I recline on the
sofa, an odalisque with a flask of yellow wine, nursing an incredible
vagueness which had lately been remarked by Virgil, who declared
that my work was deteriorating and that I was too young for that.
Maurice shoves a couple of goblets into my hands and says, in his
tense quick way:

"Fill these with water and make yourself useful."

"No," pipes Virgil. "Ned doesn't have to work, Ned's a beauty."

Lou adored the retort and quoted it always. But whether or not I
played the lily of the field, I was waxing remote, unfocused, confessing
to Virgil that Morris and I were having differences, that the apartment
was growing smaller by the day.

Morris and I gave big parties in the small apartment, so big sometimes
that if a guest passed out, he would remain standing, bolstered involuntarily by the others.

Sometimes smaller parties, suppers where I'd bake sweet potatoes
because, since I'd loved them since childhood, I assumed you did too.
I would play the record of *In Piazzas Palladio* repeatedly for one and
all. Aaron Copland told Alvin Ross, who told Morris, who told me, that
he always heard the title words as "With Zaza's Fellatio."

. . .

The International Society for Contemporary Music, known to all as the ISCM, was the rival of League of Composers, though in 1954 the two groups merged. In the forties the ISCM represented the Germanic side of a spectrum on which the League was French. A junior offshoot, called the Forum, had charter members and gave concerts. Lou thought I should join. One evening at Miriam Gideon's on Central Park West I was presented along with Jacques de Menasce. Miriam, Elliott Carter, Dika Newlin, Mark Brunswick, Vivian Fine, and Kurt List were the hosts. Jacques and I offered our wares, then were asked to withdraw while members voted. Jacques was accepted unanimously, while I had one dissension, which to this day still leaves me guessing.

The first Forum concert on which I was featured took place in the upper auditorium of the old City Center on Fifty-sixth Street, 17 December 1944. Lou was featured, too, and so were the two veterans, William Ames and Johan Franco. I accompanied "Doll's Boy," "The Knight of the Grail," and "De Don Juan" as sung by Lys Bert (now Lys Symonette of the Kurt Weill Foundation), a German friend of Morris's with a light and smart soprano sound. Because I knew there would be a postconcert seminar in which each composer must justify his existence in words, I got sick a week beforehand, went to bed, and for five nights vomited black bile. What did I know of the clever repartee and biased dogma that governed factions and inspired edgy wit! In those days there were far fewer composers around than now, but those few were an accepted, if rarefied, fragment of general society; art, like education, was not anathema, and thus artists could afford to bicker about which language was holy writ and which was negligible junk. To the ISCM the writ was twelve-tonish and the junk was Coplandiana. My music was diatonic, even nonmodulatory in the extreme, and thus would fall under the Coplandiana label—a music conceived without any system beyond that of economy, and which must sink or swim solely by the persuasiveness of its expressive content. Since the ISCM weighed in the direction of the highly methodic twelve-toners, and since they, being less in vogue than the tonalists and hence more adept at verbal self-defense, I felt like a fish out of water. Today, of course, art is not even a peripheral concern. Composers of classical music are not despised pariahs, for to be a pariah one must exist. Being invisible, living classical composers are safe if powerless and poor, so they band together and write each other recommendations. The aleatorics, the dodecaphonics, the minimalists, the neoromantics, all are mutually tolerant bedfellows.

Well, I survived the postconcert seminar, even acquitted myself without embarrassment by stating that music must defend itself—or something equally obvious.

. . .

I produced more and more music, mostly songs on words of Donne and Blake ("A Burnt Ship," "The Sick Rose"), and settings of Old Testament prose. These were sung at the frequent "new music" concerts, usually with myself accompanying Muriel Smith.

Muriel had quit Curtis a year ago to become the overnight star of *Carmen Jones*. This all-Negro updated English-language version of Bizet's opera, unlike *The Swing Mikado,* left the original score intact. When Muriel Smith bolted on stage, a smoldering Vesuvius, to sing the "Habañera,"

> Love's a baby that grows up wild
> and he don't do what you want him to,
> Love ain't nobody's angel child,
> and he won't pay any mind to you,

she threw back her head with its blue-metal hair, strutted about on her mocha legs, cajoling cast and audience alike in a contralto as insidious as hot golden rum, the house went wild. Nothing like her had ever been seen on a New York stage, her picture was on *Ebony*'s cover with interviews in *Look* and *Life,* desserts were named for her at Sardi's, and she was mobbed in the streets. At school in Philadelphia, as a student of Elisabeth Schumann's, she had proved bigger than life, uncontainable, a born actress of the histrionic mold. Yet, like so many professional vamps through the ages—not just stage people but *femmes du monde* and business women—Muriel was innocent in matters sexual. She lived with her mother in a railway flat on Saint Nicholas Avenue. Whenever I went there to rehearse, our work would be succeeded by lunch (mashed potatoes stick in the memory), during which her divorced father would show up and quarrel loudly. If Muriel had a crush on me—a crush that would endure for years, with a smile through her tears—it was assuaged in those days only by proxy. After a performance of a Saturday evening she would come downtown and talk until dawn, whereupon she would expire in the little bedroom and I'd sleep with Morris in the parlor. Sunday, using the multicolored canes which Father had bought in Mexico, we would investigate the Empire City, strolling through the Lower East Side, and try to speak French. We never kissed. Like most of us, Muriel was nourished by the necessary obstacles of love.

The sound of Muriel's mezzo was the closest thing to dying or, rather, to a suspension of living, when time stops except for the hallucinogenic concentration on the immediate: it was like listening to red, to cake, to the ecstatic smell of tuberoses frozen in amber. This is not an informative way to describe music, I know, but Muriel resisted sensible criticism. (All singers do, unlike instrumentalists, for a convincing voice is irrelevant to intelligence, even to practice.) Indeed, I could never speak to her about "meaning," about the sense of this or that poet, for she would only agree with her beautiful eyes, unaware of intellect, then open her lips and prove a point merely by song. This could have been fatal—performance by instinct alone. It eventually was. For the present she drifted on.

We made home recordings together, thought about opera possibilities, even straight acting. We collaborated until the end of the decade, when she moved to London to become an even bigger cult figure, and certainly—as a black glamour girl—a weirder novelty than at home. In England she had regular jobs on the stage in *The King and I, South Pacific,* and in movies, notably *Moulin Rouge,* where she rips open the screen in a fight with Colette Marchand, then gains a sort of "unsung" immortality by dubbing Zsa Zsa Gabor's singing of Auric's famous "Valse." Elsewhere she made pop discs by singing fast songs slow, like "Come Rain or Come Shine," as Streisand would do years later with "Happy Days." She also gave sober recitals in Wigmore Hall in programs of a surprising complication considering how unskilled she was at just reading notes. Muriel had the exasperating habit of learning by rote, not untypical of singers then but rare today.

Her decline began with Moral Re-Armament—how vilely that rings to my pacifist ears—a fundamentalist sect that salved Muriel's sincere but sometimes misguided notion of civil rights. (In 1956 she turned down an offer from Samuel Goldwyn to star in the film of *Porgy and Bess* because "it doesn't do the right thing for my people.") Her entire energy was now spent propagandizing for that sect through films and concertizing worldwide. Returning to the States finally, she visited me, proselytized, brought sentimental poems of her own making, hid little tracts between the sofa cushions. She became a dietician in Mount Kisco, then in Virginia, where she continued gullibly to champion Moral Re-Armament, where she lived still with her mother, and where both women died within a year of each other, the mother at ninety-one, Muriel at sixty-two of an excruciating postmastectomy ordeal. She vanished in limbo, forgotten.

Since writing the above I've gone through her file of old letters. So much more intensity and confusion than what I recalled, it's heartbreaking. Muriel felt strongly about what she felt strongly (race relations, the power of song, salvation through prayer) but saw as through a glass darkly and was used. Did I too use her? We all use each other continually, animals and humans, it's the design of existence, a chain reaction.

. . .

John Cage was very much around, and we met often, mainly at Lou Harrison's dark loft on Bleecker Street. Like Lou and Virgil, Cage spoke in a high-pitched démodé whine which belied his craggy features framed by a manly "German" haircut. Already tireless in the promotion of his selflessness, he seemed a dime-store Descartes pushing "Je pense, donc je suis" as though he'd coined the phrase. If everything's art, as Cage would claim, then anything's art; and if nothing is truly ugly (a heap of corpses at Belsen?), as he also would claim, then is anything truly beautiful? His undefined terms make for easy chuckles and a soft-centered coterie, while his nonegoist stance makes for lasting publicity of that stance. All contradiction is brooked with a permanent smile, like that of so-patient Mormons who, because they're going to heaven and you're not, can afford magnanimity. Cage today has grown dogmatic, oversimplified, a bit pinched, awfully boring. When a Laurie Anderson claims that she can't mistrust anyone so funny, I'd counter that continual laughter is idiocy. Half a century ago his style had not yet congealed into cliché, nor indeed had he begun to work with Merce Cunningham in their mutually independent collaborations. ("We're doing different things simultaneously," say they, validifying this as art because "that's what happens all around us in actual life." Then why not three, or seventeen, or five million things on stage simultaneously?) His reaction to my work, specifically to *Prelude and Adagio,* which Lou called Bogey Man Music, was of hearing what was not in it, while what I heard in his prepared pianos was a seductive tinkle, if it didn't last too long.

But how does anyone hear anything? My dearest friends don't hear Bach, or see blue, or taste lemons as I do (at least their adjectival emotional reactions never synchronize with mine). John Cage, who's favorite piece was my favorite too, *Socrate,* gleaned from it what I never heard. Where for me Satie's quips were plaintive, to John they were campy, and to take at face value Satie's designation at the end of his three-minute piano piece, *Vexations,* "to be repeated 486 times," and then to rent a hall plus a relay of pianists and to do precisely that for twenty-five hours, is to take Satie literally where he was being merely whimsical. Elsewhere Cage links Satie and Webern because, he contended, there has been only one new idea since Beethoven in the field of structure, and that idea is couched in their brief pieces: brevity as definition. Why, then, perform *Vexations* 486 times? As for *Socrate,* it lasts over half an hour, and indulges in heartwarming harmony—a trait John would eschew. Webern and Satie were in fact opposites: Satie's page was minimal, but that minimum was perfect, and he stopped when he was through (unlike Beethoven). Webern's music, equally short by the clock, was more densely packed than a hydrogen bomb.

Ankey Larabee had a fling with Cage. She told me that he liked to make love to the accompaniment of a metronome. Once when a spring got loose, the metronome began ticking faster and faster. The lovers stopped, breathless, when it reached the maximum 208 beats to the minute.

I was bowled over when one evening John brought forth *Either/Or* by my piquant landsman Kierkegaard, of whom I'd never heard, and began to read aloud: "What is a poet? A poet is an unhappy being whose heart is torn by secret sufferings, but whose lips are so strangely formed that when the sighs and the cries escape them, they sound like beautiful music." Could this be shortened to "An artist when he cries makes music"? Less overwhelming was the premiere a few years later of Cage's most notorious piece, "4'33"," scored for a performer who remains silent by his instrument for four minutes and thirty-three seconds. Hadn't Harold Acton, in one of his novels from the twenties, proposed the identical philosophy? (The music dwells in the audience's fidgety thoughts and in the random outside din during the prescribed minutes.) John has been dining out for two generations on Acton's uncredited notion.

What a fake! Yes, but a fake what?

There is no fatalism except for the True Believer, but there is coincidence, especially if you seek it. The foregoing paragraphs were written yesterday. This morning, 13 August 1992, John Cage's death is announced on the *Times*'s front page. Immediately perception softens. How could I not feel moved at knowing we'll never never never meet again? He was *someone,* after all, and prevailed for half a century. Only last March we spoke on the phone, during my incapacitating siege of sciatica and herniated discs. John gave me the number of his chiropractor ("She's black and tough and lives on the Lower East Side, and though I imagine I feel better I don't really feel better") but I never called her, although I felt concern for his concern and for our mutual plight, which now I view with the warmth of retrospection. This will happen no doubt often as I advance through these pages: opinion shifts as old friends die. I've gotten out his few letters which will now be filed in the obit drawer (yes, I'm Order personified since renouncing spirits and tobacco in 1968 when first I heard Time's wingèd chariot), and feel honored to be featured in John's book, *Notations* (admittedly along with 268 other composers—we pick up crumbs where they're scattered), with a replica of my manuscript for *My*

Papa's Waltz, and with this uttered wisdom typeset eccentrically according to I-Ching chance operations: "September '67. Just as illegible handwriting means semi-conscious bad manners, so slovenly musical calligraphy signifies a disordered composer. . . . I learned more in 6 months as a professional copyist than during 4 years at the conservatory. Ned Rorem."

John Cage's lavish posthumous publicity is as inane as the emperor's new clothes that swathe him still. My magnanimity ebbs, nor will I anymore change horses in mid-page.

So when the Academy asked me to write the memorial tribute I answered "No, and neither probably would any other composer. John never had an audience from among the musical cognoscenti, get one of the poets." Am I jealous?

Allen Ginsberg gave the tribute last Tuesday, ending by "playing" "4'33"," during which the Immortals sat stonily. I later heard one of them state how dazzled he was once at a 1963 performance of *Radio Music,* when amidst the static came news of Kennedy's assassination —what a coup for John's genius. Well, anything comes to those who wait, while washing their brains. But Cage's coup was unearned, as was his long-lasting fame. Unearned at least by standards of craftsmanship, of originality, and even of wit.

No one can see his own century. No one, indeed, can see the back of his own hand. We can't see ourselves or know what purpose music serves. Music-as-expression-of-the-age is an excuse for shapelessness, convulsion, and horror. Every age thinks it's the only and final age, and every age is horrid, convulsive, shapeless.

Eugene Istomin had moved to New York in June of '43, and the following November debuted, age seventeen, with the Philharmonic in the Brahms B-flat. He was now living with his parents on West Seventy-first, atop the little hill between Broadway and West End. We went there often, to encounter the flavorsome solidarity of White Russian expatriatism. The language, the relatives, the kissing, the samovar, the extrovert tears, the pathological adoration of music, the heterosexuality, the Slavic melancholy which was only partially Jewish— all that lent new vigor which was not just emotional but useful. Useful because among the throng appeared one Harold Brown, a hermetic, opinionated composer, not young (maybe thirty-five), whose music was adored by Eugene, who felt I should study with him. What Betty

Crawford did for my piano technique, Harold did for my interpretation of other people's music: if black and white ivories are approached
as *conveniences* for the fingers, the Chopin etudes are approached as
evolutions of Gregorian chant. This would be gobbledegook did not
Harold's own pieces purvey a mysterious appeal (and a solid scaffolding) that I've never seen or heard since. His lessons, imparted through
study of plainchant mixed with an exegesis of Cocteau's movie *Sang
d'un poète,* were a salubrious contrast to Virgil's no-nonsense orchestration lessons down on Twenty-third Street. Harold Brown's Quintet
for Strings and his eerie songs (especially "Alysoun," on an eleventh-
century English lyric) had much to do with the medieval modality of
my own early songs. If forty years later he died unknown while ever
superior to many an interferer, some of us feel that in his surly urge
to avoid the reeking herd—in his not playing the game which is part
of the rat race—he sailed above the storm but, unlike The Eagle of
Rock, he sailed quite out of sight.

A more amicable example from among the émigrés was the Sibe-
rian Alexei Haieff, he of the perpetually worried smile and ingratiating
stutter, ten years my senior, and the very definition of what was already
named neoclassical, being one of Stravinsky's tight entourage—with
Arthur Berger, Harold Shapero, and Irving Fine—until they were each
traumatically dumped at the end of the decade with the advent of the
remarkable Robert Craft in the life of the genius. Alexei was an intimate of Kiriena Siloti, who had been Eugene's first piano teacher, and
was herself daughter of the legendary Alexander, Liszt's chief pupil,
still thriving now in New York. Alexei's music was crisp, elegant, play-
able, nonvocal, fun to hear because it "sounded" (what you saw was
what you got—very French), but there wasn't much of it. He invited
me one afternoon chez Siloti where Stravinsky was to be guest of
honor. This was the first of three times (in thirty years) that I met the
man, and being intimidated, never said more than "How do you do."
Stravinsky remained seated, seemed hunched (as indeed he seemed
always during the various magical times I watched him on the podium), and nodded with a childlike grin in eager silence as the other
guests, one by one, ventured to sit beside him for an allotted five
minutes. After a while he left, just as Aaron Copland arrived. The two
greeted each other at the elevator. Can one forget Aaron's first words
to the rest of us as he took off his coat?: "Imagine! Stravinsky's going
down just as I'm coming up."

Eugene, now eighteen, still liked to be thought of as a roué, though
in fact he was an overweight apple-cheeked prodigy, perhaps even a

virgin, who steeped himself in classics. In giving me Leibniz which flowed over my head, and Henry James which filled me with tears, Eugene changed my perspective on literature. I wouldn't read more than *A Turn of the Screw* before moving in 1949 to France, where I would devour dozens of James's novels and canonize him along with Proust and Simenon, but already the master was ensconced.

Last night, punchy from five hours of television, I decided to crack Henry James again. But the preface to *The Golden Bowl* seemed so impenetrably arch—like a satire of James—that I burst out laughing. Isn't life too short for such madness now, or am I just stupider?

Then this morning, in the line of dutiful research for these pages, I rummaged in old storage boxes labeled 1944–45 and found pieces I only dimly recall, beautifully copied and fading, pieces not even listed as NR's "unpublished juvenilia" in various reference books. An *Overture for GIs,* for military band, which had been sent to Bill Strickland, who gave it a reading in Georgia but which I never heard. Two suites for piano solo, and a *Portrait of a Young Girl,* dedicated to Shirley Gabis. I phoned Shirley to talk about this.

Didn't I remember, she asked, when she used to come up to New York to spend weekends with me and Morris? On one such Saturday she retired at midnight, while Morris and I continued drinking at the Welcome Inn where a soldier made a pass at me and socked Morris hard on the chin, ripping his lip open. We came home bloody, and Shirley was not amused. A rift. I composed the *Portrait* and sent it to her. Which eased the rift, somewhat.

Tragedy with a happy end is true to literature if not to life. A *Room with a View,* for instance, or maybe *Middlemarch* (which isn't a tragedy, though it is a drama of a self-made woman, as I recall). Comedy with a sad ending is true to life but not especially to literature. *Les parents terribles* comes to mind.

The storage boxes contain also a Suite for Orchestra, and penciled songs on verses by Jackson Mac Low, Conrad Aiken, Frederick Prokosch, and a collection of *Five Portraits for Oboe and Piano* (the portrait idea I stole from Virgil), which Josef Marx performed with Betty Crawford on an ISCM concert, and later on WNYC. Of this mass of material I marvel at the worthy energy, and at the mostly worthless outcome. Certain of the songs written then, and during the next five years, are as excellent as any I'd ever write (during the next forty years sometimes I'd try to imitate the élan and professionality that the young Ned unaccountably possessed), but all of the instrumental stuff—*all* of it!—is duller than that of many a teenage applicant rejected today by me from Curtis.

I apologize, sort of, for enumerating these unknown works. They're for the record. The only justification I have for this memoir is the prestige, such as it is, of a composer.

The power of silence. The power, for example, of a lover who doesn't answer letters, a critic who never reviews you, a famous artist who adds to his mystery by ignoring fan mail. The power Quakers invoke, of course, is the inner silence of a group meeting—he who talks too much seldom says anything. . . . But is this true? Cocteau, Tallulah, Anna de Noailles, never closed their mouths but were worth attending, while a lot of quiet fools are foolish in their quietness.

The wheel turned, the spokes fanned out now toward such diverse stimuli that it's a matter of selection. Several events in the spring of 1945 immediately precipitated a new direction, which, all told, was a nice direction.

Morris kicked me out. After eighteen months of cohabitation he longed for a change of scene, a room alone, a lack of me. (Once when Morris was away I brought a sailor home "after hours" and played the phonograph full blast with the window open while making love. Billie Holiday's voice moaned in the courtyard, "You follow me around, build me up, tear me down," and the neighbors were not amused.) Morris was kind but firm, wanting me gone by tomorrow. Since I couldn't yet move into the little flat on Twelfth Street that had been promised as soon as a friend vacated, I stayed at George Garratt's big apartment on East Fifty-third. Morris and I remained close, saw each other nearly as often as before, and he was concerned about the adventure, attractive and frightful, of my living completely alone for the first time.

Then Father persuaded me to return to school. He would pay tuition, an allowance and rent (twenty dollars a month) if I would aim for a degree at Juilliard. A degree, as distinct from a diploma, meant attending various nonmusical classes. At the entrance exams in April, I passed the musical tests with such flying colors that I was not required to take most of the theory courses. Still, to qualify for the "secular" curriculum at Juilliard I had to enroll for eight weeks of summer school, in general history and English lit., at NYU. Which meant commuting from Garratt's down to Washington Square five mornings a week.

The upcoming school plans precluded further work with Virgil, with Harold Brown, and with Betty Crawford (at Juilliard I would be a double-major in piano and composition and would continue orchestration with the comp teacher). As with Morris, my new and strictly social role with Virgil would continue on the best of terms. My last day as Virgil's lackey, he took me in a cab to the Mary Chess Boutique on Park Avenue and asked me to pick out the biggest bottle of any cologne I fancied. I didn't fancy any (Paul Bowles had gifted me with a lifetime supply of patchouli oil), but chose the Russian Leather because it brought back the past.

Virgil also suggested I contact soprano Janet Fairbank. Having looked over my songs, he concluded that Fairbank, who specialized in arcane Americana, would love them. So I became Miss Fairbank's rehearsal pianist.

As for Betty Crawford, she was soon to leave New York anyway, as a bride. Her parting gift was to pass on her job playing for Martha Graham. This seemed too interesting for me to forgo.

How I juggled these friendships, academic deadlines, and pianistic responsibilities while still finding time for the semiweekly binges of a newly divorced narcissist, I cannot imagine. My body of today has shifted its resilience, and so has the century. But with my back to the mirror I can't always tell the difference.

16. Martha

Everyone called her Martha, but no one was her confidant. She tore through society wearing blinders, looking neither to left nor right except to ferret out samples of what she would call "truth": children in the subway, a gazelle at the zoo, buildings, boulders. She had no urge for small talk or broken hearts, and thus, like most obsessives, lacked humor. (Actually, we all have humor, but yours may not be mine.) Yet her works, half of them, are about prefeminist strong-minded females, victims as well as predators, often embarrassingly horny; the other half are about transcendent saints or silly geese and can be genuinely funny. Being a genius, she fit no definition. The personal coldness, couched in a guise of extreme cordiality, was pure self-protection. Remoteness is the coin of involvement's flip side. She was Garbo's mirror—Graham acted, Garbo danced.

I had seen the Graham company years earlier, been impressed, found it agreeable with its seductive scores of Paul Nordoff, though not all that different from Chicago's own Ruth Page Company with its seductive scores of Jerome Moross. But in 1945 Martha, aged fifty-two, was at her peak (the redoubtable Sol Hurok had just signed her), and even I realized that there must be a discombobulation when one meets the original after one has already known the imitator.

So here I was, sitting across from the original, being interviewed for the position of classroom pianist—not, as I had hoped, of rehearsal pianist, which would have meant playing the new scores being choreographed for the coming season. She was all affability, now a flirting girl, now a grande dame, now a businesswoman, now a fellow musician. She did like me, or why put on such a show, yet I couldn't tell what was expected of me. "You know," she announced, "Leonard Bernstein once worked here. He really *was* 'On the Town' in those days. It didn't work out—he couldn't help playing 'real music' and mooning around at the keys, rather than playing rhythmic incitations."

Virgil once summed up the whole dance world in a phrase: "They are autoerotic and have no conversation." About Martha in particular, Agnes De Mille wrote: "No one can remember exactly what she says." Well, I can remember exactly two things: "The pay will be three dollars per class; and you will need a Social Security number." Thus Martha Graham became my first official employer.

The Graham studios were on Lower Fifth Avenue, number 66, above the Cinema Playhouse, which showed a perennial double feature, *Blood of a Poet* and *Lot in Sodom*. Classes then, not unlike Yoga sessions now, built gradually from the floor to the ceiling systematically over ninety minutes, entirely on counts of eight, barefoot, stressing contraction and release. Six or seven girls, three or four boys, some of them students, most of them company members, began the session prone on the uncarpeted parquet. With lowered heads betwixt hunched shoulders, they exhaled to a beat of eight; then with head and shoulder thrown back they inhaled to another beat of eight. These sequences were replicated in different postures for half an hour, until, with a lovely sweep of arm and hip the assembly rose in unison to an upright stance, and the routine was repeated. For the final half hour, still on counts of eight, the class hopped about the room in various postures and at various speeds. Or so I recall. Current practitioners of the Graham Method (the method that rocked the world in one generation, it has been asserted, as opposed to the three centuries it took for ballet to evolve) would say I've got it wrong. Yes, probably. My fingertips are eidetic, but my torso is not kinetic; I never took a class, and improvised on the keyboard only according to what I thought (or vaguely felt) the class wanted. "Play any old notes," Martha advised, "as long as you keep the beat."

I performed for three classes a day, five days a week. The first was taught at 8:30 a.m. by Martha herself, whom we all agreed was "inspiring" ("we" being myself and the dancers, who had the souls of children and were easy to empathize with). She would talk a lot. Example: "Yesterday while wandering through the Museum of Oriental History I came across a Buddha of cobalt alabaster. His shaved pate was lowered in profound meditation and I felt a clash of East with West rush through me like slow lightning, a respect tinged with envy, an attitude it would be well for us all to emulate. It is such meditation—such *dynamic, fruitful* meditation—that I could hope each one of you might absorb." Then she would approach the thrilled and baffled youngsters and one by one stretch their limbs with her magic hands ("do as I do, not as I say"), while my improvised pianistic drumbeats, or sighs, orgasms, always to a throbbing count of eight, and sometimes using music of old masters—Prokofiev's *Visions fugitives*, for instance —tried to impel their movements.

The second class was led by Erick Hawkins, whom Martha loved (they would be married—briefly, catastrophically—shortly thereafter, during which this unique monster would legally become Martha

Hawkins, a role from one of her hillbilly creations), and who was her company's romantic male dancer, with Merce Cunningham as comic or evil relief. Erick often joined the students as a warm-up in the earlier class, but everyone else was new—except me. He, too, would talk a lot. Example: "Recently I visited the Oriental Museum and came across a Buddha with a shaved head. This Buddha represented the rift between West and East, and I wish you could emulate him." Poor Erick, he longed to be taken for a thinker. But in appropriating Martha's nonanecdote (though he might well have been with her yesterday at the Oriental Museum—wherever that may be), he diminished himself in my eyes. Still, to watch him leap, or gyrate, or touch with such gentle formality a fellow moving body was to see Nijinsky converted to modern dance. Like most people, he resembled his name, with that aquiline nose, those chiseled cheeks, the Tom Cruise gaze, a craggy ramrod. He was less intimidating than Martha, easier to follow.

Easiest to follow was Margery Mazia, who conducted the third class. She didn't talk, at least not about "meaning," and never criticized my playing.

Quickly I came to worship with the entourage. As regular worker, Martha became a model of Spartan self-denial, sometimes scheduling classes for Sunday mornings when normal people should be abed, hungover. As exceptional artist, she showed us how to wander from the beaten track, but only *she* found her way back. Then as now she was America's first female, yet had to solicit subsidy despite the fame. The fame was such that all her girls wore their hair tight in abject adoration, their mouths slightly open, their thighs at odd angles—but only *she* brought it off. Then as now, or so I contended, Martha Graham was one of the four most significant influences of any sex, of any domain, of our century. (The others? Billie Holiday, Djuna Barnes, Mae West.) My dream was to compose for her.

In April, Roosevelt died suddenly, leaving a perilous and jangled world in the hands of Truman, whom we had seen pictured playing a piano on which the young Lauren Bacall was seated. While Rome burned. Morris and I were crossing Eighth Street when the headlines of *PM,* exceptionally printed in white on black paper, announced the tragedy.

A week later the Germans surrendered. You can't imagine the released elation that spread across the city on V-E day. America had not, after all, been occupied, yet the ubiquitous jubilation, the dancing in the streets, the camaraderie celebrated a sympathy with Europe's relief. Morris and Alvin Ross and Dougie and I strolled through the Village and the Lower East Side, not drinking, or hardly, but drowned in good will. From the upper floors in the Women's Prison on Sixth Avenue and Eighth Street came shouts of "What's happening down there?" Cops relaxed their vigil. In Drossie's a glow emanated. We all went to bed late, rosy and sober. A few weeks later came a revived exaltation as Eisenhower, looking like Paul Callaway, was whirled up Fifth Avenue (we caught him at Washington Square) in a ticker-tape parade.

Nor can you imagine the talent that seemed to mushroom from the fertile ooze of war. After the opening night of *The Glass Menagerie*—heightened, or rather, delineated, by Paul Bowles's background score, which came later to be known among musicians as "the Tennessee sound"—it was clear that *something* had happened, a hypodermic for American theater which could already be called postwar art. A queer goyische flavor was sprouting out of the war and would burst in a few years. For the moment the overall optimism, plus the specific acceptance—unimaginable today—of High Art, was the electric tone in that madly healthy air.

True, with relaxation came bad realities. Within weeks the German concentration camps were reproduced on newsreels with odd reactions. I recall with distaste, as Morris and I sat in Loews Sheridan watching the ghastly scenes of Dachau and Buchenwald, how a girl behind us let out shrieks and sought protection in the strong arms of her boyfriend, as though the spectacle had been designed, like a Frankenstein movie, just to scare her. It struck me that absolute silence would have been more proper.

In June I shuffled the Graham schedule for afternoons so as to attend two morning classes at NYU. In history I sat next to a fat boy whose smell gave me a headache. English lit. was taught with some panache by a stentorian virago, proud that Lauren Bacall—whom she called Betty—had once been in this very class.

The first four days, beginning on a Monday, went swimmingly. Then Thursday night (for the call was stronger than my will) I got drunk at the Old Colony on Eighth Street, left the premises at 4 a.m. to head for the subway, was surrounded on MacDougal Street by a bunch of thugs in mufti and armed with broken bottles. Too bleary to realize quite what was occuring—"il n'y a de dieu que pour les ivrognes"— I did detect the voice of "dieu," who spoke authoritatively: "Leave him be." The voice came from a soldier—a knightly sergeant literally in armour—before whom the thugs recoiled, their intimidation by the military being stronger than their contempt for fruits. The soldier, whose name was Bill Smith and whom I saw off and on for years, returned with me to East Fifty-third and we spent the dawn, the morning, the afternoon and the evening in bed. Morris phoned me there: "Are you alive? Are you all right? People saw you downtown in trouble last night. What a hell of a way to begin your schooling. Are you a composer or a bum?"

In August the war stopped. Again I was with Morris walking across Eighth Street and again the headlines on *PM* were printed in white on black stock. A new kind of bomb had razed Hiroshima.

V-J memory seems less exhilarating than V-E. Domestic events dominated. By now I was living alone unsupervised.

The composer Noel Sokoloff, denizen of Drossie's and member of the Sokoloff clan (his father, the conductor Nicolai, in 1955 would commission and premiere my Second Symphony with the La Jolla Symphony; his cousin, the pianist Vladimir, was Zimbalist's accompanist and on the Curtis staff, where he today remains as my colleague), had inherited from Norman Dello Joio, and now ceded to me, a tiny apartment at 285 West Twelfth Street. This space, three steps up from the street and directly over a basement restaurant called the Beatrice Inn, involved one unfurnished 12- by 18-foot room, a bath, a closet, a nonfunctioning fireplace. Rent: twenty dollars monthly. This would be home for the next four years.

From the Salvation Army I purchased a single bed, a bookshelf, a red armchair. Literally for a song I bought Muriel Smith's Mason & Hamlin upright. (The song was a setting of Sir Thomas Wyatt's "Appeal": "And wilt thou leave me thus?/Say nay, say nay, for shame!") On the floor were bamboo mats soaked in Paul Bowles's patchouli, a mere phial full, which gave off an acrid, oriental, dizzying, spermy stench for the full four years. There was an old enamel table, a hot plate in the closet, a radio, a phonograph that worked when it wanted to, and a filthy tub and toilet which, after a month or two, Maggy Magerstadt scoured thoroughly on the same day that, for a fee, she painted the walls and ceiling lemon yellow. For Maggy now lived in town, at 88 Horatio, as did Hatti Heiner Martin, with her infant son, David, at 105 Greenwich Avenue.

Somewhere along the line I got rid of Muriel's piano in exchange for another upright belonging to Virgil. This was a European import, garish, with two copper candlesticks protruding from the music board. Since Virgil had his own Baldwin grand chez lui (courtesy the makers), he boarded this one out with friends. The piano was good but cumbersome and lacked the low E below that staff. This note was simply not there. With the result that nothing I composed the next four years contained that low E.

Like most self-respecting musicians I do compose at the piano; means are less vital than ends. To the layman, nevertheless, music is *the* intangible art because it is heard and not seen; he is more intrigued by a musician's workshop than by that of other artists. He accepts without question the poet's rhyming dictionary, the painter's prefabricated brush, but has a notion that there's something amiss in a composer who writes at the piano, even if the composition is *for* piano. The notion stems from the Hollywood portrait of composers strolling with the muse down a country lane and notating their inspirations on the spot as full-blown symphonies. Of course, music used to be simpler, harmonies could be heard by the inner ear without need to confirm them at the keyboard. But today's more complicated sonorities can't rely on imagination alone. Stravinsky maintained that it is unmusical to write *away* from the piano, for since music deals with sound, a composer must always have access to *la matière sonore.* Well, musical composition, though it does always deal with sound, does not *primarily* deal with sound but with the organization of ideas eventually expressed through the direct language of sound. Ideas today can occur on country lanes as they did yesterday, but as they seldom occur fully realized, their final utility might not be ascertained until they are remolded at the keys.

The books on the new shelves were by Kierkegaard, Calder Willingham, Isak Dinesen, Proust, and Melville. The only wall decorations were the wonderful large cork mask from Mexico, and Alvin Ross's unframed portrait of me, done two years before in Philadelphia, plus a large wood crucifix, for even at this late date I affected the Catholic paraphernalia of yore.

One morning, returning from the NYU class led by the stentorian virago, I bought a black-and-white hardcover notebook and began to keep a diary, a practice maintained ever since. Why? The virago had uttered the phrase "Happiness is an answering to the heart," and suddenly I felt that if I did not verify my ruminations in ink, nothing would remain. With a blush I confess that the first entry, dated 6 September 1945, 1 p.m., begins: "Happiness, then, is an answering to the heart (pity the poet at the stock exchange), and those many who say 'is there a ham sandwich in the writing of music, or 2¢ out of the dreamer and Shelley-reader' are hideously true." I concur with neither the grammar, the sentiment, nor the style: What is "true" in what "those many say"? Isn't happiness a state for idiots? How many poets do you know who are languishing at the stock exchange? And isn't Melville a mortifying influence?

But other entries have more solidity, and certainly the information will be helpful for this book. A few pages later I noted: "Good dancers are rarer than good pianists, for the same reason that great performers should never be called 'genius' (if anyone is still called such a thing) —that being reserved for inventors alone. The more of himself the executant exhibits the vulgarer his resolution. But the *dancer,* choreographer or no, Ah! . . .

"Having just come from Graham's where I watched the heavenly Mae O'Donnell especially, it was again revealed how personal, how out-and-inwardly primal the medium is, even if only to raise an elbow with anguish or laughter behind the shower curtain. Dance is the individual's ultimate expression—a dangerous quality for the instrumentalist. However, it is more difficult tastefully to control one's own mode of expression (the peak of divine creation) than diligently to adjust the renderings of someone else's bright ideas. Everyone could dance with a certain beauty if impossible barriers were smashed, but not everyone could play someone else's music with beauty under the same conditions. So Dance, being more universal, produces necessarily less of the Great. But anyone who dances creates, no matter the formal impediments to his style. Motions of the very young are often overwhelming lovely, but their piano playing is never pleasant. When Mae moves she has no instinctive sense of rhythm, no motive of musical line, but on or off beat she's exciting all the same for her body's an electric wave with no brain. Were the same true of an instrumentalist we'd squirm in our seats. And there is only one Martha, but a plethora of flawless pianists. . . .

"It is amusing to see the kids during class, their lips half-parted in ecstasy, their contractions and releases propelled by desire to rid themselves of what they feel to be 'ancestral frustrations.' But after class a too-close awareness of their sweet sweat provokes self-consciously coy joking, mindful of scenes in stations when men-friends greet after long absence with a heartfelt embrace, then start to spar and punch good-naturedly, embarrassed by the previous demonstration unbecoming to the American male."

Was this a pastiche of Martha-speak, or was it my mode of writing then? Her most apt and oft-repeated *mot* was: "The body never lies." Which is why, after many a month, she fired me. Oh, quite nicely, because, as she rightly explained, improvisation is clumsy discipline for young composers. Her unspoken reason was my lack of the pianistic thrust needed to impel collective contractions and releases. Dance accompanists, to be good, must take classes themselves.

I have always loved bad weather, the snug feeling of being inside while outside the elements rage, myself an anonymous island in a flood of people. It snowed continually that fall. The room had two windows, casements of four panes each, opening onto the street. One pane had been shattered by an insane pickup, and replaced permanently by a square of cardboard scotchtaped to the frame which never quite kept out the cold. Next to this frame were stored quarts of beer, butter, and perishable groceries. I had no refrigerator. Nor was there a telephone until late in 1947, so friends left notes or knocked on the window—the habitat was vulnerable. The permanent snow magnified the permanent *va-et-vient* of demilitarizing freedom. In one of her lesser films, Rita Hayworth states: "Armies have passed over me." Of the uncountable numbers of servicemen with whom I dallied indiscriminately (inevitably as the "bottom") and through a haze of alcohol and sleet, I still harbor every lock of hair.

During a blizzard I gave a party. Virgil was there, and Muriel Smith with a photographer from *Ebony* (I still have the pictures), and Cecil Smith, who was now running *Musical America,* two marines, and Frank Etherton, Paul Goodman, plus a dozen others. We decided to light a fire. Noel Sokoloff had warned me that the grate was sealed off, yet it functioned admirably. How could we know that the neighbors upstairs were gone for the weekend? Next day I lit another fire. Down came the neighbors black with soot. My flue ejected straight into their room. "Our baby is dying," they said.

A week after Martha summarily fired me, Erick Hawkins knocked on the window. In he came, stomping the snow from his boots, and made himself at home. They hadn't found a workable substitute pianist, he explained, and now the holidays were upon us with dozens of new students enrolled. Would I consider coming back, at least until January? I would have said no, salving my wounded pride, if Rosemary weren't due for a long Christmas in New York with a former classmate from Beloit. They planned to take a course from Martha Graham.

I never had sex with anyone from the studio, except Donald, the receptionist. Louis Horst, the queen bee's mythic Svengali, roamed the premises aimlessly from time to time, like a lost elephant, vaguely sinister but impotent, spying on his mate's possible indiscretions; beyond this there was no emanation of real eroticism in the classes, only the make-believe—the symbolic—which is never a turn-on. Martha herself could sometimes seem dull. An evanescent celebrity in daily contact soon grows solid, susceptible, clay-footed.

Agnes De Mille, who in a recent 500-page document on the Great Lady, has not one word on how Martha used music, does advance an amusing stupidity: "...[Martha] came to prefer men who were not demanding, who were not wholly men but only part-time males, and who could make way in their own psyches...for the greater dominating infatuation: *the work.* Again and again and again, as time went on, she chose to fall in love with a homosexual man." If a homosexual man is only a male when he's screwing Martha, what is he the rest of the time—a female? That would make him a lesbian. (Genet: "Un homme qui en encule un autre est deux fois homme.")

Closing tight the eyes and thinking back on that faraway season I am less stimulated by sights and sounds than by smells intensified by the constant snow. Odors of dry sherry, of vetiver, of rye toast, of blond cedar, espresso, citrus, incense, male corduroy: upper-class taste (or aroma). Lower class: odor of ale, of semen, of snake, of salami, of locker rooms, lank blue hair, and pectorals. Have I confused the classes?

People (interviewers) act surprised when I profess insecurity. They don't see the perishability of it all. Satisfaction of increasing appreciation is paralleled by vulnerability of simply aging. As he grows more famous—or less famous—a person grows more frail, until he just disappears.

A pupil gets most of what he will get during the very first lesson.

To make an extra buck I asked Juilliard to send me a pupil. This turned out to be a sixty-five-year-old well-garbed German refugee who dabbled in tunes. He called me Doctor. What could I teach him, beyond the structure of a Beethoven quartet? I could teach him Song, since Song has a preexisting skeleton (the poem) upon which to hang our melodic flesh. I can teach literally anyone to write a "perfect" song, although the song may lack the blood of life which only God can provide—the God I don't believe in. (Buñuel: "Thank God I'm still an atheist.")

Martha thought Rosemary was the prettiest thing she'd ever seen. "It doesn't matter that she can't dance—just to look at her is enough." If Rosemary were taking a class I was accompanying, Martha never chided me for playing too slow or too fast or too loud or too soft. The mythical collective therapy of the rhetoric, which I found sophomoric, struck a chord in Rosemary which she retains to this day, and which is retained too in Erick's choreography with its Native American earth worship. Erick currently has a big enough fan club to withstand my doubts. Despite various confabs over the years, I simply cannot collaborate with Erick because I cannot believe in his nursery-school tactics of releasing the soul through group movement, etcetera. When I asked Edwin Denby, "Do you take Erick seriously?" he answered: "Mustn't one?"—meaning, I guess, that Erick took himself too seriously to leave room for doubt.

He made one theatrical misstep. Martha allowed Erick to introduce one of his own works into her programs. Now Martha, when she had used melodrama, i.e., the spoken word, in her dances (utterance of Dickinson's verse in "Letter to the World," for example), took care to keep her own mouth shut, preserving her aura while fellow cast members talked. But Erick, in *Stephen Acrobat,* not only spoke himself but did so right after executing a strenuous turn, breathless, panting, incomprehensible. Again he reflected Martha in a distorting mirror, and the already loathsome device of speech-with-music became, with him, merely *à côté.*

In 1946 Father was transferred to Philadelphia. My parents for twenty thousand dollars bought a fine four-story house at 2213 Delancey Place, just half a block from Rae Gabis. In 1946 Shirley Gabis married the cellist Seymour Barab, and they settled into a ground-floor flat at 242 West Twelfth, just half a block from me. Rae and my parents became friends and remained so. Shirley and I recemented our friendship, which remains strong unto the moment.

In 1946, I met a physically charismatic psychotherapy grad student at the Astor Bar, one Fabian X. Schupper. We had a stormy romance for about six weeks until the center could not hold. I cried and cried. This resulted in a little song, just four measures long, but perfect in its wedding of text to tune.

> Love's stricken "Why"
> Is all that love can speak—
> Built of but just a syllable
> The hugest hearts that break.

Which tells it all. I've run across Fabian in later years; unless they die, old lovers always cross one's path again. I may yet in these pages describe my sexual acts, fantasies, preferences, habits, for I think this important to any portrait. Then again I may not. The image I choose to present might be dispelled by specifics. There's nothing like an unexpected detail to demolish the best-laid plans of newlyweds. (The little song, incidentally, was incorporated sixteen years later into a cycle named *Poems of Love and the Rain.*)

In April 1946, at Drossie's, I met the author Herbert Kubly, and we too had a stormy affiliation for about fifteen months. With his play, *Men to the Sea,* running on Broadway (Frank Etherton had a ranking role), Kubly was also music critic for *Time* magazine. Conceited, handsome (the William Holden type), and blustery, he was equally insecure and defensive, having little technical knowledge of music, and a dramatic gift dwarfed by that of Tennessee Williams, whose spectacular (and permanent) star, like Bernstein's three years before, had just risen. Kubly (everyone called him that, though he preferred Nic), eight years my senior, lived on a floor-through at 247 West Thirteenth, got up late and worked all afternoon with the kind of zeal he felt necessary to The Artist. (The Artist must Live to the Hilt so as to have Material.) Evenings he went to concerts or operas, maybe taking me along to explicate some nuance—not that *Time*'s then-unsigned articles, all in the same amorphous voice, dug very deep. I would have liked to attend, but wasn't invited to, the after-theater parties given by people who might find me "suspect"; for Kubly's image of himself was that of Ladies' Man, an image which, along with his pose as adroitly polyglot when in fact he had slight talent for languages, undermined his credibility, at least for one observer. When his prizewinning, well-researched travelogues on Italy came out in the fifties, with himself portrayed as a multilingual bounder, it seemed clear to me that The Artist, to be The Artist, can be a hypocrite in everything but his work. Of course I was jealous. Not jealous of his other "affiliations" (as *Time* critic, his cachet provided access to such catches as Whittemore & Lowe and to my old professor, Gian Carlo Menotti, whose flashy new fame as composer of the "Broadway opera," *The Medium,* was comparable to Tennessee's, and whom I was, in my inexperience, now shocked to see buttering up Kubly) but of his female intimates— notably Lotte Lehmann and Maria Jeritza—that in my madness I felt might be "useful" to me as a songwriter. I was mostly kept under wraps.

And yet, do these caustic sentences appear excessive, in contrast to the palliative file marked HK which now I draw forth? Here's a penciled scrawl on his notebook paper slipped under the door and still stained with a footprint when I stumbled home one snowy dawn: "The pain in my heart is too great and the hours are sleepless so I wander the dark streets searching but all I find is a dismall [sic] hell of loneliness and I wonder why life must end like this." Ah, the expense of spirit is indeed a waste of shame when such effusions (I myself would pen a book full of them a decade after) seep over into middle age. Energy spent on the horrors of love is better spent on writing about the horrors of love. "Si vieillesse savait!" as Beckett quaintly put it.

It was my pleasure to unite Herbert Kubly with Janet Fairbank, Wisconsinites both. Janet lived on the then uniquely tree-lined, almost rural, block of Fifty-fifth between Lex and Park. The tone of that street is as vanished today as the viewpoint evinced in the soprano's apartment. Janet Fairbank, a plain but stylish well-off "bachelor girl" (her term), chose to inhabit a two-room walk-up with a hot plate and an upright, and to spend all her allowance on "modern music." If her voice, though firm, was neither agile nor very pleasing, it did possess a more infecting drama than many another nonvoiced specialist since. Unlike the others, she neither deluded herself about her voice nor thought of herself as granting a service to American music literature. Without sanctimony, she performed from sheer affection, mildly astonished at the small but solid public she drew to her annual concert of always new songs. Also, she had no competition. Oh, there *was* a host of terrific professionals around—Povla Frijsh, Mack Harrell, Nell Tangeman, Jennie Tourel—but theirs was a generalized vocabulary of the unhackneyed, whereas Fairbank had a specific monopoly on Americana. From floor to ceiling her rooms burst with manuscripts begged from or bestowed by live composers. For twelve months, replacing her regular accompanist, Henry Jackson, I served as her rehearsal pianist, daily sorting through this morass.

Janet and Kubly hit it off. Early that summer, before Mother and Father moved east, I took my first airplane ride ever, to visit them in Chicago. The plane was purposeful, exciting, and scary. (I still love being in a plane: the takeoff has an inexorable *reason* about it, like an erection, and the journey, no matter how crowded or tedious, represents a suspended animation during which one stops pondering suicide.) While on board I composed "Alleluia" for voice and piano, the title intoned forty-three times, fast, on a meter of 7/8, formed on a jagged nota cambiata which may or may not have been inspired by the untroubled view on this virgin air trip. After a few days in Chicago, I proceeded to Lake Geneva, where Janet had invited us both for a weekend at her family's estate. I was given a guest room all in azure, with a mahogany night table on which reposed a fat book of photographs from the Belgian Congo, inscribed: "To the Fairbanks, remembering a frantic cocktail and a peaceful blue room. John Latouche." How effortlessly chic! My own house gift was the new "Alleluia."

Janet premiered over a hundred songs, mostly American, of which the manuscripts now lie in Chicago's Newberry Library. More important, nearly all were printed, under her aegis, by a minor company named Music Press. Songs, being an even less marketable commodity than squid eggs or poetry, it is creditable that these publications, later sold to the major company of Presser, remain to this day in stock, many bearing an inscription to their Onlie Begetter. For Janet *was* American Song.

That December she opened her annual recital with "Alleluia." To his credit, Kubly, who was not at the moment speaking to me, reviewed her in *Time,* stressing that she was not crazy (and mentioning me en passant as one of the unknowns on the program). Surely the pull of responsibility to her vocation acted as a revivifying serum. At forty-four, stricken with Hodgkin's disease, she had already crossed the deadline set by doctors. Janet did not, however, survive to behold her certain mark of permanence, the lovely brown-and-green Music Press editions.

I recall the afternoon in October 1947. Doorbell and phone rang simultaneously: a messenger delivered the thrilling complimentary copies of my new published song, "The Lordly Hudson," on Paul Goodman's poem, dedicated to Janet, while on the wire Eva Gauthier was saying that Janet had died that morning.

Madame Eva Gauthier, she of the blue hair and endless supply of satin hats, inhabited a tiny flat in the now defunct Hotel Woodward on Fifty-third east of Sixth Avenue, with crates of scores and a yapping Pekingese. She was four feet ten inches of opinion, always precise, sometimes precisely wrong. Gauthier became the third of my three simultaneous female employers. Was she already seventy when I began playing for her coaching sessions, mainly for students on the GI Bill? Certainly she was from an era of inexpert sight-readers—from when prima donnas did not decipher. Debussy had taught her the role of Yniold by rote, she claimed. She also claimed intimacy with Ravel and Gershwin, showing us her song programs devoted exclusively to, and accompanied by, this pair. During those programs she changed garb with each group, involving vast swatches of stuff from Java, where for years she had lived with an importer husband. Her tendency to the graphic, or to getting things slightly off center, titillated those youngsters who came to her after the war. To a young tenor after singing Fauré's "Prison": "Keep in mind that this poem was conceived by Verlaine in jail where he was put for cutting off Van Gogh's ear." To another tenor excusing his high A's because of a cold: "Be glad you don't have to hit them during your period, with blood seeping onto the stage." To me, about to accompany her in the demonstration of a scene from *Pelléas:* "Skip the rests, it's mood that counts."

But what a fantastic teacher, if teacher means one whose enthusiasm is transferable—who leads horses to pupils and makes them drink. Gauthier's enthusiasm was for the *intelligence* of music, and though she couldn't read music, she could talk it.

We couldn't know it then, but that was an era of very delicate dinosaurs. Song ascended, thrived, then collapsed forever in a span of about thirty-five years, from 1920 to 1955. The quality of American song after World War I mellowed considerably, and by 1950 had turned to pure gold. We composers were not yet clearly aware that the normal display for such gold, the song recital, was already a losing proposition. Nor was pocket money any longer fair exchange. It would not occur to a singer, not even to Janet Fairbank, to pay for a song. Song was for love. So we continued to bring live nosegays to ghostly stars, courting a moribund breed. We were (to switch metaphors) young mothers lactating for their dead offspring.

Quick flashbacks:

—What do I most covet among the vignettes with Kubly? Going to Uptown Café Society to hear his friend Susan Reed sing folk songs, and finding ourselves next to Lana Turner's ringside table. Breathtaking in a tight black blouse, little black hat with black veiling, black chiffon scarf, black skirt with the below-the-knee New Look just launched by Dior, and black spike-heeled pumps. Sitting with a loutish gent (he turned out to be Greg Bautzer), she was sensationally arrogant, prettier than a rose, glancing neither to left nor right but only into his eyes, even when she signed an autograph. They got up noisily and left during one of Susan's songs.

—Finding John Latouche at "The Beggar's Bar." The weird German actress Valeska Gert, who in 1925 destroyed Garbo in Pabst's *Die freudlose Gasse,* and in 1963 would portray a witch in Fellini's *8½,* was now proprietor of this dive on Bleecker Street where she entertained tiny audiences as cackling diseuse, and where Norris Embry in adoring masochism waited tables for no pay. Latouche sat there, looking for Negroes ("Où sont les nègres downtown"), and drinking with a friend. We had met over the phone one day when Virgil was out, and later at a party chez Bu Faulkner, where I said: "I'm a composer," and Touche said: "I didn't know that people who looked like you did anything." Now here he was, moaning. "Sex has reared its ugly head for everyone but me." He imbibed no less than did I, was maybe thirty, feistily stylish, as befit an uncontrollably gifted Broadway *arriviste*.

John Latouche and I became friends (to know him five minutes was to befriend him) and would remain so until his early death. He was one of a kind, not a chip off the old American assembly line, and, as Wilde said of himself, put his genius into his life and his talent into his art. The art as I saw it never quite jelled, or maybe it just wasn't my sort, being a sort of preface to Sondheim (the way Marc Blitzstein was an afterword to Weill). The theater pieces with Jerry Moross had a jazzy panache, *Ballad for Americans* was patriotic to a turn, *Cabin in the Sky* still has original lyrics, and the libretto for Douglas Moore's *Baby Doe* remains a model for today's composers to lust for. But that's not enough. I find myself sitting in an East Side boîte with silver walls watching John Latouche watching Mabel Mercer with the intensity of a crucifixion, as Mabel, seated in an armchair, sang "While We're Young." She did not, I felt, merit this devotion.

Touche (as everyone called him) mingled with the upper crust but catered to the middlebrow. That, plus hard living, sullied his craft—his point of view. Or did it? We can't be other than we are, and what we are we do. Besides, if the tough little charmer seemed to die at thirty-nine, he was actually 117, since he lived three lives in one.

—Cerutti's, a piss-elegant Madison Avenue clipjoint where Margaret Bonds and Gerald Cook, known now as Bonds & Cook, played two pianos while everyone sang, and where, now that I was free to roam, I picked up Lucius Beebe's boyfriend and went back to their suite at the Madison Hotel, where we more or less coited *à trois,* which they took pictures of.

—Paul Bowles, when Gertrude Stein died in 1946, underwent, he claimed, a purge. Gertrude had long ago said, after scanning his poetry, "As a writer you're a good composer," and the words stuck in his craw. Now he began writing freely again as he had in the twenties, mainly for *View* magazine, stories that contrasted starkly to his light, exquisite, nostalgic, café music. The fiction was—is—unrelentingly cruel, humiliating, unbearable. (The nonfiction, as expressed in music reviews, as I recall it, was raw, a bit glib, inexpert, he didn't really care. Or am I wrong? He did, after all, care about the huge research he pursued on North African folk song, subsidized by the Library of Congress.) As the prose grew in structure, his musical composition dwindled. Not that he stopped composing; in fact, his arguably best works were coming, to be destined always for Fizdale & Gold, the most important two-piano team that ever was, not only for their diamond-sure executions but for their causing major new works to exist for their odd medium. (Arthur Gold and Robert Fizdale set up a web of interaction between the hitherto—at least in the USA—independent worlds of music and literature. Their commissioning over the years of Stravinsky, Cage, Boulez, Haieff, Auric, Poulenc, Thomson, Tailleferre, Milhaud, Barber, as well as Rorem and, of course, Bowles, plus, for the last two, poets Frank O'Hara and James Schuyler to provide singable texts, resulted in *the* repertory for two pianos, a mode of expression which has now, alas, gone the way of the dodo and the song recital.) And he did continue creating incidental music for plays, now also an extinct vocation. But mostly it was books that preoccupied him.

—*View,* a first-rate avant-garde bimonthly, rarefied and arty, stressing French surrealism in writing and painting (but not in music: music can't by definition be surrealist; music was banned by Breton, founder of the surrealist party; and music is never, or almost never, one of the arts in so-called magazines of the arts—it stands apart, even as opera stands apart from music), ran for seven years during the war and just after. *View*'s directors were three giant graces with swishy voices, like those of Virgil and John Cage and Lou. Charles-Henri Ford, like his beautiful sister, actress Ruth Ford, was a southern belle, curt and bossy, out to conquer Manhattan in the shadow of his life's partner, the great Pavel Tchelitcheff. Parker Tyler, also a southern belle, black haired and languorous, was a pretty good poet, as was Charles-Henri with whom he had written a "dirty novel," *The Young and Evil,* in the late 1920s, as well as coediting a magazine called *The Blues* out of Mississippi. Their whipping boy, chain-smoking John Myers of Buffalo, was much too tall and plump to be so effeminate, not unlike George Sanders disguised as Watteau's "Blue Boy" with an impish smile and perpetual drink in hand. The magazine contained raunchy experimental prose, poetry and art reviews by mostly Americans (Clement Greenberg, Paul Goodman, Edouard Roditi, Harold Rosenberg, Marius Bewley, Paul Bowles, Borges, Henry Miller, Camus, Durrell) and black-and-white reproductions of pictures by mostly Europeans (Max Ernst, Man Ray, Miró, Duchamp, Klee, Breton). John Myers was the one I came to know best. He fancied himself a sort of Diaghilev, and within ten years became, if not the most powerful, at least the most curious of American art dealers as well as a theater producer and matchmaker. For now, besides running *View,* he was a professional puppeteer.

Was it through Maggy Magerstadt that we met? Maggy was working with John's puppet theater. In any event, John, without knowing a note of my music, without indeed knowing music, decided I was the greatest composer this side of Paul Bowles, and asked me to write—real quick, honey!—some songs for *Fire Boy,* a playlet by Parker's boyfriend, Charles Boultenhouse. This I did, for voice and piano, although the songs were sung by John accompanied only by drum. John, who had a tiny nonvoice, learned the notes by rote and later intoned them most affectingly while manipulating the puppets. (They were published years later as *Three Incantations for a Marionette Tale.*)

During these weeks I also set to music a lush poem of Parker Tyler's called "Dawn Angel." Of the three or four hundred songs I've produced over the decades, this is the only one composed according to how the poet declaimed his own words. I invited Parker over to Twelfth Street precisely for this purpose. There he is still, seated in the red armchair, eyes closed, head thrown back, lisping softly, caressingly, affectedly, as I make notes. Each rise and fall, each loud and soft, each hesitation and accelerando will be incorporated into the manuscript. At the end

> and the black bloomed with black that sings,
> skying the distance with a twinkle of birds—
> when the angel speaks now plumage garbs his words:
> his light wears birds.

Parker bangs out "black bloomed," swoops up to "skying," pauses in the center of "twinkle" (which becomes "twink–kle"), sinks into "now," and sighs on "his light wears birds." It's all there on the page: rather than setting the words, I set Parker's voice. I've never heard "Dawn Angel" sung, and it remains in manuscript.

With John as go-between I collaborated with Charles-Henri Ford, providing incidental music for his strange little puppet drama, *At Noon upon Two.* Two vicarious persons take turns looking through a keyhole and asking one another about "What's she doing now? What's he doing now?," while those being spied upon dance, copulate, writhe, burn and perhaps die. My background score was for flute and piano, plus two chopsticks hit against each other and against the echoing strings inside the piano. With flutist Ralph Freundlich playing for free, me at the piano (and chopsticks), John Myers's squeaky voice as one of the watchers, and Lionel Stander's gravelly voice as the other, we recorded the playlet in a studio, and the recording was used as soundtrack during the live performance. This took place as part of a fund-raising bash for *View,* at the Old Knickerbocker on lower Second Avenue. The puppets were manipulated by John, with costumes and sets of Kurt Seligmann, while the sound system boomed out the voices of these tiny creatures. I salvaged some of this music for my Violin Sonata.

Kurt Seligmann designed a startling cover for my "Alleluia"—an armored angel, gaudy and embryonic, seen from behind, trumpeting toward the heavens. I did not know Seligmann well (though I warmed to his smile, his atelier overlooking Bryant Park, and his wife, Arlette, whose naughty eyes were weighted in blue kohl), perhaps because, like all surrealists in principle, he was heterosexual—homosexuality, like music, being taboo. (Charles-Henri had been granted, he claims, "special dispensation" by Breton, while Lorca and Dali were simply banished.)

Pavel Tchelitcheff was alluring. I met the artist at the puppet performance but had seen pictures of him long before. Also he had been the lover of Belle Tannenbaum's "dangerous" friend, the Chicago pianist Alan Tanner, who spoke of his genius. And I had been spellbound by Tchelitcheff's décors for Hindemith's ballet *Noblissima Visione,* all in dark red and dark blue illustrating the world of Saint Francis. Who in New York was not closely acquainted with his works at the Museum of Modern Art—the freaks and acrobats, the basket of edible strawberries, the portrait of a sexy Lincoln Kirstein, the exhilarating and painful universe in that magical tree called *Hide and Seek?* Parker arranged a meeting with me and Pavlik (as he was called) at a time when Charles-Henri was away. A *dîner à quatre,* with the three of us plus a rich parasite named Perry Embiricos at the Russian Tea Room. Pavlik had an electric charm, plus a bracelet of red yarn to ward off evil spirits, which I never saw him without. If no sparks resulted from this electricity, the fault was, according to Parker, mine. Parker reproached me always for frittering my youth away, not by drink and not by sex, but by combining sex and drink. Maybe he was right. I did ultimately dally with Perry Embiricos during an initial visit to the Everard Baths, after which we attended *The Respectful Prostitute,* Sartre's political play then running on Broadway. Did I mention that Charles-Henri's sister, Ruth Ford, starred in Paul Bowles's translation of Sartre's previous play, *Huis clos* (rendered as *No Exit* by Paul, who took the title from a subway stile), which ran on Broadway the previous season? Ruth, tough, gorgeous, mannered, was somehow too intelligent for an actress.

Footnote. After living for sixteen years on Sixteenth Street in one room smaller than mine, Parker and Charles Boultenhouse moved to 15 Charles Street, the same building my parents would eventually inhabit for twenty years before moving to Cadbury. They all became neighborly, and after Parker died, Mother and Father and Charles and Charles's mother grew close.

• • •

Lenny now lived on West Tenth in the same bank of houses as Oliver Smith's, into which Paul and Jane Bowles had moved. One cold spring dawn after closing time, Lenny, standing in a doorway on Eighth Street, hailed me as I passed by with giddy Frank Etherton smoking what was then called a reefer. What was then called hep (now still referred to as hip) describes Lenny at all times, so he, too, took a puff. Frank, intimidated by the Great Man, vanished. Lenny guided me chez lui, where I vomited. "Is that all you ever do?" Next morning, when Helen Coates arrived, Lenny unapologetically reintroduced me (we had met often through Muriel Smith) then invited me back that evening to dine. Served by a black female cook we had meat loaf and salad and homemade cherry ice cream, which I bolted down but which Lenny didn't touch, nursing a fever but hating to slow down. We strolled around the Village, tense and sober, stopped at my pad, where he glanced disapprovingly at some new songs on the piano ("Town Hall encores," he called them), then went back to his place. The intensity with which he empathized! "I am all that exists for him"—we all believed. He had just returned from Paris, where Poulenc (O brave new world!) had gifted him with the score of the *Les mamelles de Tirésias*. At the piano he sang for me the wondrous choral scene, bluesy and languorous, "Comme il perdait à Zanzibar," and we both burst into tears. Whereupon Lenny placed both hands on my shoulders, studied my features in that way of his, and said: "The trouble with you and me, Ned, is that we want everyone in the world to love us. And that's impossible—you just don't *meet* everyone in the world."

Other nights, if I returned home alone from the bars, in my wooziness I might phone Madame Povla Frijsh, the Danish soprano, to whose art Morris had introduced me. Of a breed that no longer exists, Frijsh, without much of a voice, could do anything. She sang in—could *think* in—eleven languages, starting with that from her native Denmark, where she was born in 1881, and wrenching your heart in each one. Stageworthy to the core, she was a cult, bigger than life, and for encores accompanied herself in Grieg and Stephen Foster. Her forte was the comprehensible projection of texts (if she forgot a word, she would substitute that word's parallel in any tongue—a practice maybe less spontaneous than she, an actress, might admit); her main mannerism was the swoop, whether it was needed or not; and her pride was in finding the *mot juste* for her program notes. ("The only words in English for the untranslatable 'O ma délaissée,' " she once explained about Aragon's poem *C,* "is 'Oh my hapless one' " a solution—not bad —that no one born to the English language would probably have found.) Because she launched, hot off the griddle, the songs of Barber and Bowles and Virgil and all, I wanted to know her before I knew her, and in impotent rage would call her in the early hours. I said nothing—just listened to her accented anguish as she repeated: "Who is this?" I confessed the ruse to a young tenor student who found it wonderful. Then I myself began to receive late-night phone calls with a scary silence at the other end of the line. (The calls were from the tenor, I later learned.) Meanwhile I mutely phoned Kubly a couple of times. One day I told him I was getting late-night calls from silent callers. "I've been getting them too," said Kubly. "I thought it was you. Now I know it's not."

Before he moved to Tenth Street, Paul Bowles lived in the notorious Middagh Street pensione in Brooklyn, where Auden played mother hen to various renters: Benjamin Britten and Peter Pears, George Davis and Gypsy Rose Lee, Golo Mann and Carson McCullers, Richard Wright and Oliver Smith. It seemed only proper when the beauteous Teru Osato came to the city with her new husband, Vince, that I should ask Paul to find lodgings for them there. Frances Osato had for some time been working as a seamstress in the East Fifties; her chief mannequin was Sono, now a star in *On the Town,* who was pictured in *Vogue* modeling Frances's pearl-covered skull caps. Frances was a surrogate parent not only to dozens of Japanese girls loose in the city but to myself needing a meal and loving to play as she sang. She took me to plays and to concerts too. Teru, she said, had cancer. The least I could do was to find her a home.

Some time later I was sitting, exhausted, in the lobby of Juilliard when one of Frances's Japanese girls, a violinist, came up to say that Teru had only four months to live. Under my arm was a book of American poems. I whispered to myself, Why not write a song while waiting? Composing as a craft can be a permanent release—but not emotionally, only technically—it keeps you busy. Still, a few of my songs came as temporary emotional release, for instance "On a Singing Girl." Elinor Wylie had made a rhymed transliteration from Greek of an epitaph for a musical slave girl who had died young. I plotted out the vocal line right there on my lap, overtailoring the prosody as was then my obsession. So the voice was complete in itself, though I had no idea of how the accompaniment would go until I reached home that evening. I'd learned that if a vocal line is conceived alone it will take on the rambling curves of nature rather than the artificial curves—square curves, you might say—of folk song: for coherence, a systematized accompaniment is indicated. (Contrariwise, sometimes in our piano improvisations we hit upon a figuration so pretty that any silly tune can be successfully superimposed.) I needed square curves. Having just come to know Paul Bowles's song "David," I decided to disguise some of the piano part of that into a background fabric. Such conscious plagiarism is safe, remorse leads us to sabotage innovators, we sign our name. Who is the wiser? Certainly not Paul. Artists, by definition innocent, don't steal. But they do borrow without giving back. By the same token, after the fact, they may follow a singer's suggestion. The closing words, "dust be light," were originally an octave higher. Povla Frijsh, whom now I knew, lowered them to their now inevitable position.

This song, like most of mine, was made in a couple of hours. To be exact, my diary (from which the above facts are culled) indicates it was finished at 9 p.m. on 29 April 1946. Four months later Teru, aged twenty-five, died.

The passionate angles of the Kubly affair dissolved into the way of all flesh. After the requisite years of spiteful mourning we became true friends, nontactile, bizarre, wary.

Love is impossible. If it were possible it wouldn't be love. The *égoïsme à deux* sung by our poets since the start of time depicts what the Greeks called a sickness—the time-warp fantasy still believed (I think) by the young. Consider the Gershwins' pentametrical couplet with its internal rhymes:

> It's very clear our love is here to stay,
> Not for a year, but ever and a day.

But ever and a day equals, in the real world, no more than those three years of Tristan and Isolde. Still, those three years can contain pleasures and tortures like no others. While they last.

Love is a recent invention. Not love of mankind, better defined as mutual respect (loving thy neighbor as thyself is hardly one of the lesser commandments), but Romantic Love, so possessive, so dramatically selfish, so short-lived.

I set to music a little poem of Kubly's called "The Anniversary" about the death of romance. For the record, in these drawn-out months of 1945–46, I finished several other songs, including two psalms, called "A Psalm of Praise" and "A Song of David." The fact that everyone was reading Gladys Schmidt's "historic" novel *David the King* accounts for the biblical settings, as well as for another song called "Absalom" on Paul Goodman's sad verses. A piano piece called *Prayer and Paraphrase,* influenced by Lou's obsession with Carl Rug-

gles (who leaves me cold), was premiered at an ISCM concert. There
was also a setting of Whitman's "Reconciliation" about the poet's love
for a dead soldier. And another setting, "Spring and Fall," on the
Hopkins poem Norris had read into the machine at the Chicago museum so many years before, may be the most touching song I ever
penned. Built on the descending ground base of Monteverdi's "Amor,"
it spins a tune of an adolescent girl's first menstruation and the pangs
thereof, mounting gently ever higher as the bass line reiterates its four
notes ever lower.

More astonishingly, during this same era of cruising and liquor,
school and dance classes, vocal accompaniment and lovers' quarrels,
I also completed the following works:

Five Portraits for Oboe and Piano, "pictures" of composer friends,
performed by Josef Marx and Betty Crawford at an ISCM concert, and
then on the radio.

A big affair called *The Long Home* for chorus and orchestra, on the
final chapter of Ecclesiastes, which Paul Callaway conducted at the
Washington Cathedral. (Ben Weber, now living in the Village, a stone's
throw from me and from Shirley, was, like me, eking out a living as
copyist. I still retain in a treasure chest Ben's beautiful autograph of
this work.)

A bigger affair called *Cain and Abel,* a musicalization of Paul Goodman's operatic play wherein Cain is represented as loving his younger
brother and sacrificing that brother as his most precious thing unto
God. (Only the penciled first draft exists, never orchestrated, never
performed.)

A still bigger affair, *That We May Live,* a three-hour pageant on a
script by Milton Robertson celebrating the new state of Israel. A huge
cast of actors, dancers (choreography by Lillian Shapiro, one of Martha
Graham's troupe), speakers, and an orchestra (conducted by Isaac Van
Grove) interpreting my evocative set pieces, including a hora and
other sung pastiches based on Hebrew tunes, and an apotheosistic
march invented for the dance classes—all this combined to perform
in Madison Square Garden. I, the only goy in the enterprise, was paid
five hundred dollars, with an extra hundred for a later Philadelphia
performance. For the glossy program Kubly wrote up my bio in *Time*
style, very snazzy, recalling the white boy in short pants with his Negro
piano teacher in Chicago. During the months of preparation a good
deal of camaraderie fomented, and Robertson's wife, handsome Marie
Marchowsky (also a Graham dancer), commissioned a piano score
for her already choreographed solo titled *Lost in Fear* (twenty-five
dollars).

None of this music was later incorporated into other works. But what I learned in terms of practical instrumentation was inestimable. The pageant brought in the first money I ever earned as a composer.

It was David Diamond who, having turned down the job, recommended me.

David Diamond had become a friend during the summer of 1944.

One dull August Sunday, as Morris and I drifted through Washington Square during the undistinguished annual outdoor art show, we were suddenly dazzled by a display of portraits as remarkable as the sight of their author, who was standing beside them. This was Allela Cornell, tall, gangling, and grandly ugly (like Mrs. Roosevelt), who, in charcoal, limned your likeness as you sat there, gaped at by passersby. We chatted. Learning that I was a musician, Allela invited us to her studio, a vast flat above Ruby's Garage at 544 Hudson which she shared with the composer David Diamond.

David was as unusual-looking as Allela, aged twenty-nine, with his flat, sad, ashen face, like Petrushka's, his balding red hair, his slightly puckered lips. Incapable of small talk, even of medium talk, he plunged immediately into the large meanings with anyone—Einstein, Garbo, the plumber—and *tant pis* if you weren't on his wavelength. But mostly you were on his wavelength—he had a way of making his interlocutor feel worthy (especially the plumber), a way of leveling distinctions between castes and types. He beguiled not through beauty (which he lacked) but through equanimity, talent, and a certain charisma. He was also a little crazy.

My role in David's life, and his in mine, will swerve and crumble and rise and flex as the decades mount up. For now our rapport as sometime drinking buddies was governed by a Socratic discipline. I was impressed by David's fame. Of those in Copland's milieu, David was surely the most successfully prolific, having since eighteen been a creator of symphonies performed regularly by Koussevitzky, Mitropoulos, Reiner, and Rodzinski. But he was also known to be a problem, chiding his guiltless seniors with righteous indignation at parties, proffering deep love to those who by their very nature cannot reciprocate (rough trade), and withdrawing his own works from execution because of an imagined slight. There was a quasi-suicidal disorder to his comportment which I found glamorous, all the more that it was balanced by a rigid, almost religious, discipline regarding his work. His intimates shared his predilections. Allela, for one, was possibly a great painter, but final proofs never grew manifest. For in the fall of 1946, out of unrequited love for a beautiful drunken rich woman, she swallowed strychnine and died a slow death in the gloom of Saint

Vincent's hospital. (The rich woman, out of remorse, gave David her Steinway grand and joined AA.) Despite his connections, his pull, he, like most composers, earned a scattered living. Currently he played violin nightly in the pit orchestra of *On the Town*, thanks to Lenny Bernstein.

David meanwhile was impressed by my eagerness and naïveté, and by the fact that I was copyist for Virgil, whom he dismissed as "a phony." It was agreed that I do some copy work for David too. During the next months I would transcribe his Third Symphony, his Fourth Symphony (score and parts), his Second Quartet, and various smaller works, mostly songs.

Again, as with Virgil and Paul, I felt a jolt when actually *seeing* this music—the bareness. Is this what sophisticated New Yorkers were up to? The Modernity we Chicagoans were weaned on was complex— not the brainy, decarnalized complexity of the Austrians (who were out of vogue then to all except the milieu of George Perle) but the corporal complexity of the naturalized French: that is, of Stravinsky and Bartók. I'd not yet heard of the lean, *dépouillé* mode of the eastern seaborders, of the dominating Copland, who spent a life slicing off extra fat. True, their scores were sprinkled with "wrong notes," but these were mere maquillage, a cross-hatching over C major.

Nobody composing in America then had more technique than David Diamond. By technique I mean know-how, métier, ability to cope solidly and persuasively with whatever dictates classical French-style, Boulanger-imparted craft. But craft can be damaging, too; it sometimes caught David up short. Too much expertise per se, too much working out, ends up treading water in undifferentiated color. The worst of his later songs are dull by being too correct, the prosody too careful, too talky.

David's early songs were stuffed with appeal and melancholy of the highest order, meaning that these qualities are transferable (we bask in them) rather than static, like Narcissus' charming sadness, which we merely admire coolly. The later songs retain the melancholy, but the appeal is edged out by a portentous, declamatory dead-seriousness which is at best dramatic (though not theatrical: they have motion but no action—they don't lead anywhere, as theater must), at worst pompous. Of sobriety there is plenty, of humor little.

But where *is* humor among composers? Can one prove that this essentially verbal virtue even exists in the "abstract" art of music? Humor is demonstrable only in vocal music, that is, in sung texts, in song, the bastard which in its multiple guises accounts for four-fifths of music history.

I've reexamined his lovely "Epitaph," composed in 1946 on a Melville poem. My own "Reconciliation," written that year, comes too close for comfort to his "Epitaph." The influence is flagrant, not least in choice of texts—I read what David read. But though the keyboard configuration in each song is virtually the same, our vocal lines are undisguisedly our own. Innovation in itself, of course, is meaningless. (Radiguet: "A true artist is born with a unique voice and cannot copy; so he has only to copy to prove his originality.") David and I wrote our songs on top of each other; Debussy's "Fleurs," too close for comfort to Poulenc's superior "Fleurs," predates the latter by forty years.

When I told David I'd seen Lana Turner at Café Society, it turned out he had *lived* with her. He tutored Artie Shaw in counterpoint when he was married to Lana. "What was that like?" I truly wondered. "Oh, Baby Snooks [he called me Baby Snooks], Baby Snooks, your endless questions. Well, it was exquisite."

He took me to the midnight WOR broadcast of *Perséphone,* with Stravinsky conducting, and Madeleine Milhaud as the dynamic diseuse. Which is the first time I saw that sacred man in the act: the musicality of his physicality, moving up and down, as though he were joggled slow-motion in a tumbril, his sinewy back, his desiring arms. David brought beer for everyone.

He was responsible for my first publications, the two psalms, which were accepted on his recommendation by Associated Music Publishers and printed immediately.

We ran into him, Morris and I, on that somber night of Roosevelt's end. David had written music for *The Tempest* (starring Arnold Moss, with Zorina as Ariel and Canada Lee as Calaban), an extensive score for sizable orchestra which he himself conducted every evening. "Tonight," said David, "Moss broke down during the closing speech, 'Our revels now are ended.'"

His songs from *The Tempest* revolve still in my brain; I listen to their echo. Sometimes I wonder if the frisson of hearing again a long lost piece is due less to the music's power now, than to a remembrance of the music's power when first discovered. Can one, in other words, enjoy the madeleine for its own sweet sake?

George Perle, still in uniform, resurfaced from foreign parts during this period and was often visible at intermissions of ISCM concerts. He had thickened and virilized since his lean Chicago days, an equivocal sensuality beneath his unflappable stance. I took to spending Saturday evenings chez lui, where he analyzed Bartók's six quartets for my illumination. He admired my perspicacity while remaining immune to my gifts, if I had any, nor did he play me the results of his own gifts, which I came to savor only years later.

It is tempting to compare Diamond with Perle, if only for their jeweled proper nouns. I do abhor metaphor in musical discussion (music's "meaning" is not too vague but too precise for words, thus untranslatable), but I might suggest that the *oeuvres* of each man are mutually exclusive except in resembling the other's name. Perle, with all his in-built emotion, nonetheless incises his staves with a diamond stylus. Diamond, with all his academic exactitude, nonetheless sculpts tunes creamy as pearls. Their one other point in common is the birth year, 1915.

Apropos wit, George's nonvocal music does possess it, but don't ask why. He can also write fast music that is inherently, kinetically fast, not just slow music speeded up. I used to contend that there is no fast twelve-tone music, since fastness depends on dogged repetition (hoofbeats) which twelve-tone music cannot by its nature have. But then, though he is the world's foremost authority on Schoenberg's so-called twelve-tone system, George himself doesn't compose in that system.

There is not, however, any *witty* twelve-tone music, because twelve-tone music is German. Earlier I emphasized that to be French is to stress proportion; to realize that humor and horror are not mutually exclusive; to be profound while retaining the levity required (at least in Paris) to get through life without collapsing; and to discover the depth on the surface of things. To be French is to show three sides of a coin. French is witty, and wit, as exemplified by that most stylish of French composers, Franz Joseph Haydn, is ellipsis—knowing what to leave out. Wit depends on tonality, and all French music true to the name is tonal.

To be German is to dig in rather than to spread out, to get to the crux of things obsessively. That which under other circumstances seems funny gets drowned by the very terms that offer it, like Schoenberg's *Von Heute auf Morgen,* a suburban-type wife-swapping farce mired in Bavaria. Serial music, especially in the theater, lends itself ideally to themes of injustice and dreamlike madness because the system depends on irresolution. But where Schoenberg uses this lugubrious language for his "comic" opera, stultification ensues.

A case could be made, though I shan't make it, that Schoenberg's science, like Freud's, while being irreversibly branded on the globe, can now be viewed as a blind alley. Freud entered a cave which expanded toward ever deeper shadows rather than narrowing toward a ray of light. Schoenberg, in "emancipating" dissonance, ultimately justified flaccidity. Dissonance by definition resolves, otherwise it is not dissonant (dissonant to what?); but where all is dissonance nothing is dissonance—no relief, and at the same time no tension.

Shirley and George knew each other too, both being friends of Ben Weber's, as was Shirley's new husband, Seymour Barab. They all moved in the same then-isolated twelve-tone circle of fifths. George, now a widower, would marry another sculptor, even as Shirley would marry twice again, before Shirley and George, forty years later, would marry each other. Quite like Madame Verdurin and the prince de Guermantes. Well, maybe not quite.

Back to Martha.

Early in 1946 we moved out of the studio and into the theater when she opened for the first time under the splashy sponsorship of Sol Hurok. This meant she now was on Broadway with a thirteen-piece orchestra and a three-week run. It meant too that certain students who had been drafted into the troupe would make their debuts, and that I would finally see the new Chávez score, whose sounds (fairly nondescript) had been filtering from one rehearsal room while I played classes in another. I'd already seen the costumes, such as they were— loincloths for the boys, red scarves for the girls—when they arrived two days earlier to the childlike glee of all. I'd already heard, too, Copland's *Appalachian Spring* in its full orchestra version, which had just won the Pulitzer Prize, and which Martha had premiered the previous year, along with Hindemith's *Hérodiade,* in Washington. These dance works, with the new *Dark Meadow,* were now before us in New York. The excitement resembled what a Diaghilev opening must have generated forty years earlier. I've never felt anything like it.

When the curtain rose on *Dark Meadow,* those daily faces—the lighthearted kids from dance class—were suddenly unfamiliar. Four boys squatting on their haunches clutched from behind, between their knees, four girls, also crouched, and like amoebas in slow motion they glided awkwardly about the stage in contradiction to Chávez's disappointingly precise but useful-enough score. Amid this octet Martha, as She Who Seeks, lay on the floor and rolled herself up in a rug, then unrolled herself, then rerolled herself, then reunrolled herself, while we, deep into Freud, were chilled to the core. (The next season Iva Kitchell, the comic mime, performed a hysterical parody of this behavior.) Though I must have seen it a dozen times, I recall no more of *Dark Meadow* than the close: a Noguchi tree suddenly sprouts tin leaves as the chorus moves obliquely to the front of the stage while Martha, back to audience, slants off to the wings, staggering slowly, arms raised and clutching a bright red menstrual rag.

Appalachian Spring, a ballet extolling family values with music by a man who never slept with a woman (Martha told me beforehand that the score was crystalline—her word—and apt to a tee, while Aaron explained to me afterward that it was composed "in the abstract," according to cues and lengths, and that he never knew the plot, much less the title, until the final rehearsal), is called a masterpiece, the right meeting of talents at the right time. Martha was perhaps a bit old for the role of Bride, and less enthralling than as another bride in *Hérodiade* where, with only Mae O'Donnell as lady-in-waiting, she prepares to marry Death while only a bassoon—Hindemith's bassoon—prods her magically.

At the peak of her fame (like Lenny Bernstein, she had always been famous, even before she was famous), Martha was nonetheless past her prime. What one now recalls is not her technical prowess—the swirled kicks or the hard heel resonantly crashing into the floor repeatedly like a flamenco—but the sheer presence, the morbid visage, the stillness. Immobile as a pillar, a liquid pillar, a pillar of brandy, she moved mountains.

Later that spring, at the old MacMillan Theater on the Columbia campus, she premiered yet another grand contraption to Samuel Barber's maybe best score, *The Serpent Heart*. Again Mae O'Donnell, in her cool blond beauty, provided the perfect foil as the chorus who graciously raises the curtain, again Martha with a snake in her mouth has a hair-raising solo on a boogie-woogie bass, and again Noguchi provides the ideal prop when Medea, as the curtains close, rides toward the audience madly in her shining chariot. (Parenthetically, the three most unforgettable décors of my experience are Noguchi's for *Diversion of Angels,* Balthus's for Ugo Betti's *L'île des chèvres,* and Félix Labisse's for Claudel's *Partage de Midi.*) I retain another memory of that May night at *The Serpent Heart*. During intermission a woman, perhaps forty, very blond, all alone, overly made-up but saved by her singular theatrical beauty, dressed all in beige, including a beige pillbox hat, except for a flame-colored chiffon scarf ("cheapness that only money can buy," as JH once put it), was pacing the aisle angrily. This was Stella Adler, whom I would see from afar for many years, and who would come to recognize me only after a dozen meetings ("All goyim look alike to me," was her excuse), and whose daughter, Ellen, became a friend in Paris. Stella, age ninety-one, died yesterday as I write these words.

I shall round out this chapter called "Martha," which would have little raison d'être were it not for this:

After the stint of working at her studio I did not meet Martha Graham for eight more years. Ah, the fact of her was forever around Manhattan—and much of musical life centered on that fact; composers were rated by some according to whether they had collaborated with her. By others, notably John Myers & Company, who felt Balanchine rightly ruled the roost, Graham was rated zero. But her myth advanced, aided by Hurok. I kept up, as young composers always do, if only to see what the competition consists of. But after moving to France in 1949, the fact of her dissipated.

In May of 1954 I wrote in my diary: "Martha Graham's company is here for the first time. The French who, if only on their deathbeds, do take their freewheeling birthright Catholicism for granted, do not therefore know how to take the implacable no-nonsense of Martha's pagan Jocastas or protestant Emily's. We had that with Kurth Jooss, they wrongly clarify (they, who ask with brave discovery if you know Brahms's quintets!). The French are still for toes and fairy tales, so they have put her down.

"Yesterday afternoon, emerging from the Eglise Saint-German into green sunlight, I spotted her at the Deux Magots terrace seated gauntly before a cold demitasse and a pile of dry brioches. For a moment we spoke—if indeed speaking is how one communicates with her, if one communicates—and I wandered off, caught again.

"Caught by the past when I was as young in New York as now I am in Paris, as enamoured there then of miraculous Frijshian ladies as I am here now of my Marie-Laure. And Martha again today, so out of context! How far, on this warm warm evening, were those nervous mornings during the war's end, of banging to a count of eight loudly, while in silence I worried that she choreographed *Dark Meadow* to Chávez's tunes, not mine. How far, those Grahamesque explications we all understood without understanding, that vague speech on mental landscapes of primeval ritual, which did somehow compel the dancers! For we were moved, it worked. . . .

"Tonight I took in again her *Night Journey,* dying. Afterward, alive in the wings, I asked Martha (hugely tiny among her winged Noguchis) how long she'd be in town, if we could have iced tea together, or could I show her Versailles. 'Yesterday would have been the time for that,' said she, 'when you passed by the Deux Magots. From now on I haven't a minute to myself.' "

Twelve years later. In the fall of 1966 her conductor, Eugene Lester, having read my recently published *Paris Diary,* felt he should bring me and Martha together again to discuss a collaboration.

I see her moving toward me across the immensely echoing floor of the rehearsal room, now up on East Sixty-third Street. Each step disintegrated the clock until her scarlet mouth was close, uttering the identical phrases of years ago, but which inevitably took new meanings according to occasion. We chatted only briefly. (She spoke disparagingly of Nureyev, whom she had just met, and who had flung his whisky glass across the room into the fireplace. "The arrogance!" said Martha, though it was a gesture she would have been capable of.) Then to business.

Stock still for twenty-seven minutes she listened to the tape of my *Eleven Studies for Eleven Instruments.* When it was over, she'd all but choreographed it in her head. We shook hands, kissed, it was a deal. Already she had a title, from Saint-Jean Perse, *The Terrible Frivolity of Hell,* and I recalled that, of course, Martha always spoke, ever so softly, in iambic pentameter.

Because I had to leave for several months in Utah, that was that. I knew she was working on "our" ballet for the winter season because she phoned occasionally—those inspired midnight calls with ice cubes tinkling through the wires across the land. (Her drinking, which was known, now seemed a crass contradiction of that earlier Spartan self-denial.) The ballet was evolving, but possibly because the music wasn't written for her, my feeling of high honor was coupled with disinterest. Also, the music had been used by others before her, though Martha didn't know it and I certainly didn't tell her. Valerie Bettis, Norman Walker, others . . . In her two hundred-plus creations, a mere handful were choreographed to already existing music. Just as American Song wouldn't be quite as it is without Janet Fairbank, so Martha Graham caused to exist a great bin of first-rate music. Would I have written something especially for her?

But in a sense, it *was* written for her, as I realized on returning to New York and, like Maldoror, seeing for myself. In the past, it's been shocking how dancers seem unaware of what composer they're dancing to. With Bettis and Walker and the others I'd been pleased but not dazzled: mostly they Mickey-Moused the music, doing what it so obviously told them to do. Not Martha's troupe: they demonstrated how I'd made *Eleven Studies in Search of an Author.* How unright that music was without this sight. How Helen McGehee's hops were inevitably correct against the amorphous trumpet! the group's immobility when my little orchestra goes wild! Robert Powell's rhythmic trance behind the screeching clarinet! Virgil's epithet was wrong, at least for now: for now, though they never stop talking but still with little conversation—meaning they hover over facts while avoiding ideas, except when approaching ideas as though they were sacred or (what's worse) new—they are so eloquent with their autoeroticism that speech grows superfluous.

Because she was unliteral, and knew how to design *counter* to the yet indispensable music, Martha is my only collaborator (though she never once asked my advice) to have been right, all right, turning my disinterest to satisfaction.

I seldom read dance criticism, mostly because critics nearly never mention the music, much less how the music is used. Yet without the music the dance would be without its spine. A good choreographer goes against the sound in a manner that only the sound could provoke, finding in the music's potential more than even the composer is aware of. No critic has yet written an essay on the interaction—on how music, because it has no specific meaning, can make or break a given "meaningful" scene. Music's power lies in an absence of human significance and this power dominates all mediums it contacts. When Georges Auric composed the score for *Blood of a Poet* he produced what is commonly known as love music for love scenes, game music for game scenes, funeral music for funeral scenes. Cocteau had the bright idea of replacing the love music with the funeral, game music with the love, funeral with game, which gives the film its surreal correctness.

The sea reminds me of Debussy's *La mer; La mer* never reminds me of the sea. But if a picture recalls the sea, the sea conjures up no picture of anything beyond itself. In this sense, water is as abstract as music, but a picture of water *represents* an abstraction. Whatever title Debussy may have chosen, his work is finally enjoyed as sheer music. If a novice were told that the three movements of this piece illustrated three times of day, not on the sea but in a city, he wouldn't know the difference. Paintings also present different impressions to different people: as many interpretations exist as spectators. Etcetera.

Maybe I'm wrong. Reexamining *La mer* tonight it occurs to me for the first time that all three movements are essentially fast, yet one's memory of this sensuous experience is—as with all sensuousness —slowness. And the harmonies, which constantly revolve but never resolve, do imply the hopelessness of the sea, at least for a human lost in it. The hopeless chords.

Arthur Miller ends his autobiography with a beautiful three-word verbless sentence: "Even the trees." He tells us that all living entities on earth are interrelated, are continually looking at each other, are looking at us, even the trees. Couldn't the reverse be as true? I cannot know you. No Arab of yore can know us, nor Noah, nor Lana Turner. Even our mothers. We are each alone in the hopeless chords of the sea.

17. Ned's Diary (II)

Betty Crawford and NR, 1945.

Was liquor the canvas upon which all else was limned, or was the "all else"—sex, music, death—the canvas upon which liquor was limned? The postadolescent creature who once I nourished, but who is disappearing round the edge of the universe, can perhaps depict himself more succinctly, if not more accurately, than I can. Here are some scattered entries from his early diary.

1945

29 September, Saturday afternoon. Had an orgasm last night which coincided with a splitting in the head where the whole world seemed shattered into ten thousand lavender leaves. Afterwards I went to sleep and dreamt a dream: At home in Chicago there were many many people collected in the front and dining rooms, all with sad faces and all waiting to be hanged on a gallows in the elevator hall (which I never saw during the course of the dream). Hard to believe so many could get into the apartment. I too was waiting to be hanged for some unspecified mistake (I vaguely recall Bruce Phemister negotiating some of the sinister proceedings). At first it seemed to be a joke, but soon, sure enough, we could hear the hazy but sharp sound of a neck cracking in the next room, followed by a sort of dull cheering and a groan. I thought of escaping through the side windows but the streets all around were filled with people guarding the house. I was sweating and terribly frightened, and a person from the hanging room would come in every 5 minutes and say "Your turn" to one of the assembly, and then we could see in silhouette the horrible act through shadows moving on the wall. In the dream I had a vision of a soldier in an endless field. He was about to be hanged (perhaps he was German). He was very alive, with tears in his eyes, and then very dead—and there was a close-up of the tears which I seemed to go into like in a mirror and then I awoke.

I had to weep a bit on the bus along Riverside Drive coming from school yesterday. The river was covered with hot mist which led to the ocean & to Europe. And felt I wanted someone to be nice to me. I want a house with Negro servants. . . . Stopped by David [Diamond]'s to pick up my table, and he was depressed, having come from Bartók's funeral. He said of course that that was the end *utterly*, but said some pleasant things too, and cheered me up somewhat. I delight in him. . . . I got drunk with Remo and E. (the latter had arrived in N.Y. unannounced). . . . A letter with a 10 dollar mail-order from Bill Smith who's seriously wounded in a plane crash (8 months surgery). Letter from Paul Callaway—also in an Okinawa hospital. Homesick messages. These soldiers—how can they be reasonable now, or even trust in anything? Oi!

Tears came to my eyes again after a few drinks in the Belmar bar where I sat alone to do my "fantasizing" of the past & future. Last night I was a white prince in the Belgian Congo, but other times I'm married to Maggy & a success or not a success, wondering what the people around do in or out of bed. Death's been around a lot and I think I'm afraid of it. Virgil writes of Olivier Messiaen in Paris. Glory to Jesus & the war-torn "grand pathétique" composers. But here comes the ice man.

David said it's immature of me to allow myself to be so upset by the atrocities of Irma Greise (the mistress of one of the concentration camps) who tied the legs of pregnant women together so that they couldn't give birth and died in agony. For adjustment and a striving toward a certain happiness is reconciliation to loneliness which is universal, and which is present at all times in all things no matter what one seeks to do or think or feel. So says David.

I don't like Chinese art for the same reason I don't like high school girls: little tiny wristwatches, microscopic handwriting, inaudible stupid voices in class (though occasional hysterical shrieks in the lounge). But while oriental water-colors do have some imagination, the girls are not to be considered. I want a vigorous slash, some energy in the wilted stance, some violence in the delicate, bright or dull, but no pastels.

3 October. . . . discovered crabs again last night and have exterminated the place with DDT to take care of the scorpions too. . . .

The whole war and its aftereffect seem to be smacking us in the face for the first time. Now that it's over we can look back clearly and feel afraid. In photos the Japanese faces burned by the atom bomb are impassive. . . . The war and the world seem on a scope too big for me.

. . . more settled if only I could stop drinking, & stay home, forgetting about romance *en ménage,* & try to get my goddamn schoolwork done.

Last night had my yearly before-sleep dream which would be like the DTs except I've been having it for at least 12 years. A sensation of heaviness and distance, unpleasant, not airy as a dream should be. With eyes open in the dark I know that I could touch the chair, yet it's miles away, the room is enormous, the curtains are monoliths on the horizon. With all that space there's still pressure. Then it goes away and I finally sleep.

No desire for hearing music, none for the actuality of sex (on my mind constantly, it seems); would throw out every last bit of my music if it weren't for the excess of shit around that is being played. . . . *The Long Home* appears a bit too ecstatic as far as I've gone (laziness); will have to wait and see, if ever, how it sounds . . . must stop announcing so vehemently how much I hate everyone & thing. E. said I was overcritical, & so does everybody else. Sick, maybe, of myself, and that's a state. Should I go to bed now?

The bed is a foot beneath the sill, the sill is a yard from the sidewalk where passersby at noon do not suspect the writhings so very close. Conversely: the gibbering idiocy of good sex, three feet away from the banal sounds of the city.

. . .

... having an hour to kill between classes I took a ferry ride to Jersey at 125th. What a restful excursion for a nickel! and the chugging and the salt smell like the Brittanica to Southampton nine summers ago. Was piqued at turning around, at which time the view was of the huge stone rampart in an altar-like sunburst (the weather was unseasonably stifling), so naturally I thought of medieval pogroms in the broad afternoon. Like screwing by day—something that is traditionally nocturnal. Why is the river always so slow, so misty, so indefinably sunny?

Don't know now what to begin composing having finally assembled most of my scraps & made them into pieces (the last is *Prayer & Paraphrase,* two inseparable piano studies for Virgil's birthday next week). And how does one get one's music played? That, I must say, is depressing.

Tomorrow—a little adventure. I'm to meet at 7:30 and dine with Pavlik Tchelitcheff—Parker's conspiracy—so of course I'm anticipating in a hopeful & dubious manner about something, but I'm not sure what.

Sunday nite. A really lost weekend. Ill, vague, uncoordinated, with a poison stomach. Haven't eaten in 2 days, since Friday with Mr. Tchelitcheff as a matter of fact: wonderful shaslik at the Russian Tea Room. Liked him better than I thought I would, charming and witty and vain. Alcohol—been mostly day and night steadily with strange physical people and my whole system seems burnt out. It's hard to care that I didn't go to Philly, and didn't do any work, and didn't clean the filth-encrusted bathroom, but only had my ego flattered by dumbbells and saw Lou somewhat thru a fog and all the talented fairy friends. My hand being still unsteady, I find it difficult to write, even to turn the page, or to think at all. Rainy, rainy day, dark moody river on which I speculated while retching this afternoon as I walked.

13 November. Nothing's more leveling to a jangled mind than to discover finally by Tuesday that normal thinking, diet and demeanor are again in keeping. . . . For a long time, even in my soberest moments, I listen with incredulous envy to whoever says "I cleaned the house today," or "I bought some dandruff remover," or "I saw the Yiddish melodrama on Second Avenue," or "I will attend such and such a lecture," even "I read a book." For I wonder how there's time for such acts plus drinking too, both being extracurricular to the fundamental principle, writing music, which is an endless proposition, especially if time is taken out here & there to notate in a journal. Sunday I was really nauseated at bedtime, and lay thinking of the fatal dose, and how gray my face would look to friends after three days of death, during which no one worried much, assuming I wasn't in after ringing the bell or trying the door.

It seems that personality differences are pure chance, like the cards that offer 4 million possibilities for a suit from a deck of 52. And if there're billions of gene cells the results are unimaginable, so that which is personality—the moral gorgeous spirit of the mind, the glum or joyous heart—is only the result of a nervous internal disturbance. If this is true then David has to be right when he says the grave is the very, very end (or is that simply Jewish?). Could some order be found in the genealogist's fumblings, so that we aren't forced to conclude that great works are the result perhaps of stomach ulcers?

Later. An acquaintance, a disarming one, having just dropped in, I've finished ¾ of a gift jug of wine, good wine too, on this my night for work, fugue-writing and history study. And it's late and still Tuesday but I'm to go out—forever it seems—and have a drop or twelve of beer, though tomorrow's my early day. But I didn't fail for a moment to run through the sermon in *Moby Dick,* reminiscent of the one in *Portrait of the Artist,* or Hemingway's "Today is Friday." A line about the rock: "Yes, the world's a ship on its passage out, and not a voyage complete; and the pulpit is its prow."

And even later. To come home and find the ink bottle still open. And I'd wanted to say only *shit shit shit* & icicles [handwriting illegible]. The rain is horrible & there's a consolation. The icicles are me goddamit, with a progressively bad complexion. O, O, O.

Wednesday. . . . I'm horrified when I read now what I wrote last night, and remember that withal I was crying when I put it down. [Etcetera . . .]

Virgil being back from France, Morris and I went up to the Chelsea (after hearing Landowska play less well than expected) to a little party he gave for the usual people, the most offensive one there being the vomitous Peter Lindamood (whose very name I shudder to inscribe lest it associate me with him), and the most delightful being Lincoln Kirstein although I didn't talk to him (whose name sent a tremor through me, owing to the innocent crush I've had on him for years). Virgil is quite as brilliant as ever, more so in fact, a little louder, a little thinner, still too severe and always completely lovable. But the effect of such gatherings necessitates a purge, and that I take out on Morris, who, no matter what he thinks, is stubbornly wrapped in fadism, artifice. My whole body aches, I itch, and am cold. Scabies.

My dear parents are in Puerto Rico and my guilt at not writing them hurts. For Mother's upset and Father's famous, and both hence need consolation. Also love from their loving son.

. . .

Before I go out to get a haircut, a line or two concerning my love life, which is to say a thought on sex. . . . Just wrote the parents asking forgiveness for the delay, but said I loved them utterly and no one else in the world; that I'm in a sort of neo-pubescent era of being pummeled by so many bright influences that it's hard to know which to trust, or in which to stake a claim. Silver frosty autumn days! Also that I need a period of abstinence from composing, in which to consider my talent, the style and the proper method of approach toward creation. For the making of music is filled with personality pitfalls (at least for me). . . . [Etcetera] . . . —an omnipresent shyness (of which most people seem fortunately oblivious now that my social life is linked so much to drinking) obviously is directly relevant to my eccentric sex habits. . . . [Etcetera . . .]

24 November. Why not die! Last evening had a harrowing lecture from Morris on what a shit everyone thinks I am, and it came as a shock. I shall try to be nicer, but how? Then to come home and buy beer and wait three hours for Arthur with the house smelling like a church and me playing Ravel to myself. And if no one turns up . . . ? So then I must go to commune at the Belmar. And did, sitting there in the lovely aloneness before going to solicit a partner for the chore of dubious sex. . . .

If I'm not nice to people, no one will come to my funeral.

Wednesday afternoon. Fuck my Id. Spent an extra hour alone with Giannini this aft, while he told me I showed promise, etc. (I'd just written an *Agnus Dei* in the shape of a fugue), and of course we agreed on superlative craftsmanship based on the prerequisite of at least an implied tonality.

And it's true that just when the evening's moral resolutions are of the most resolute, there's an interruption. For last night I'd planned to finish the reading of the sea-novel, when over trotted Ben Weber with his thin cerise lips, bald head, eczema and flabby belly, and — it's hard to believe—for 4 full hours we talked (⅓) about the proper Local 802 payment for professional musical calligraphy, and (⅔) about the gory details of his sex with "gorgeous numbers" who, if you ask me, vibrate with an ever-present nonexistence.

Why is it that lately—well, the past 6 months—I have such inclinations to weep, not real salt, but to be moved, if not deeply, at least once a day? Not over a bleeding drunk in the subway, but at the sight of a happy family; not over a Greek tragedy, but at a sweet line there in any book; over a sunset of course, but not at a dribbling moon when I must draw my coat up about my ears (though this recalls that surrealist warmth that used to invade me when outside alone on a winter day I would examine the furrows in a porous brick wall at point-blank range, and see there a microscopic world I could and could not enter, and want to swoon).

Money is as false a standard as a sailor suit. Mother and Father took the sum set aside to advance Géorg in his education, and used it for his funeral.

A slight remark on a dream between the moment the clock rang and when I got up 10 minutes later. An intersection of streets in a none-too-crowded European city—the beggars' corner. About 8 or 10 heads were moving about in the road, and were regarded as a phenomenon, yet were more or less casually accepted by the inhabitants. All the heads were of old men, bearded, and with hats, jewish (I think), and some even Rabbis. They would talk amongst each other, never smiling, but not especially sad-looking either. Certain of them were mounted on little boards with wheels—the easier to get about—but most sort of glided along, the bottoms of their heads apparently being like the suction tentacles of the octopus—no necks at all. They had all been in an accident at the train station, and had been miraculously saved by a certain hospital, eventually to be liberated in this form. One in particular, a gentleman about seventy, was pointed out to me as being an honored freak among freaks, having only ⅔ of his head left (and still lived). This one fainted frequently from lack of food, or from loss of temper if an automobile happened to run over the tips of his long hair. He was subsequently carried back to the hospital, though against his will, by a normal acquaintance.

I'll finish merely by saying that this was first shown to me in a photograph: The Town with Living Heads in the Street. But during the course of the dream the scene became animated, and I was incorporated into the bizarre crossroads.

Liquor is a lovely thing. . . . Here I am unreal, but there I grow real and vibrate, thriving in misery. I fear work, for human life seems endless, an unrewarded climb. What's there to reach for but love? how pacify the energies but dream? Constant dreaming.

1946

Mother writes dismayedly about her ever-present problem: feeling unessential, subordinate to the family talent, etc. Papa ends a note thus: "In some ways we live in a very sorry world, but of course it's the only one we've got right now. Let's hope it improves, & that we all help a little toward the change."

Today is the first literature class. The instructor, Joseph Lane, is young and cute. I sit in the front row. Instead of taking notes I draw a picture of a hand pierced by a dagger, four weeping women, a nude floating from a huge incense pot, and Christ on the cross. The instructor sees this and makes a witty comment to the class. They laugh. I am embarrassed to my innermost fibers.

Standing on the perilous embankment at 122nd & Amsterdam, I realize again that *I am in New York*, the Empire city, the Chicagoan's goal. The weather being warm and wet (though the January sun emerges for a minute over there in Jersey, aquamarine and sumptuous), I go into Riverside Church where the green & orange stained glass is more enigmatic than in a peacock's fan.

The aim of life is nonexistent, or a sublimation to God. Platitude: True joy can come only through mysticism, not the past, it's too dreary, but perhaps something of the utter future away from this earth. Earth is vile, the scope of man is all vile, this earth will always be vile so long as man is here, and even after we are destroyed and have disappeared. The water and the wind are all that will stay—unless the water explodes too when the world is broken in two. But the wind will be blowing over the unphysical remainder, and will be glad not to have a brow to fan. What can God be thinking?

Teru Osato is dying. The young and the beautiful. Her mother and I are going out to Brooklyn tonight.

4 June. Marie danced *Lost in Fear* last night & it was ghastly. Music unrecognizable, and the whole recital gave the impression of lovely married women playing at being lesbians in modern dance. Lacked the wholesomeness of the true neurotic....

Most of the men in the Serious Music field are queer, while the women seem more on the straight and narrow. Conversely, the men of Jazz seem better-balanced than the women who go hog wild.

Wasted days, drinking half the day but only enough to impair work, not enough to get soused. Also the impending irony of perhaps being inducted into the army now that the war's over nearly a year. Father writes: "The heart of man seems to be intent on evil, or to be guided by short-sightedness." How it rains tonight....

· · ·

Maggy and Kubly offer a conflict: they don't like each other, while I like them both. . . . Charles Mills' wife tried to make me at a party Friday night. She was stinking drunk and unabashed in declaring that every artist in the room was full of invalid shit except her husband, the biggest genius of modern times. . . . Speaking of shit, Virgil remarked, apropros of my upbringing and with inconsistent silliness, that running around naked in front of other family members was straining the progressive idiom to the limit, & (contradictorily) would cause inhibitions in later life. This is an effect, but is it a cause?

Kafka's writing and Berg's music have an affinity. Both derive from the same . . . credulous skepticism about this eerie world, and frame the result, like the wounds in the hands of poor Saint Francis.

Two cats beneath the window keep my drowsiness from succumbing with their human screaming. True sex should envelop like a wind. How I want it! (I was going to write miss it—but my inhibited fancy always withholds me from excess)—want to be kissed for hours on and in the mouth, from hair roots to toenails. But this [illegible] is dismissed for a slight touch, a hasty climax.

Kafka's K and Berg's white virgin are life & death, neither having outward concern with the manageable details of sex. The cats can shriek thru eternity for all I care, while I walk the streets & ponder the imponderables.

Blue is my favorite color. Life Blue, as in the tale. Death Blue, too. Let me be put in a dark blue coffin to be always surrounded by the oceanful of whales and sailors—the vastest expanses and the raunchiest bars. There's no hope really, when happinesses are interpreted as truths (& all memories of previous minutes *are* truth) then everything goes, and everything is gone. Probably what I'm looking for is Enthusiasm, a trait which so turned my stomach for ten years past. But perhaps that zest on which all expound may be an answer in the form of Device. Who can do anything that can help anyone? Or who can have the infernal presence of mind to declare—pleasant escape!—what *could* be? Maybe some worldly gain stands a bit away as my half-hearted insensitive. That *had*, I'll yearn to cuddle with the hills like Émile. Of what use? For there is always the golden anticipation of the homecomer's smile which makes me think—but just for a moment—that I can't be sure that this is not the end. Yet the hoped-for never materializes, and God plays around with his chessboard, bored to a frazzle. One can never be positive of quite knowing when the End's around; who can say whether doubt might not be the ultimate joy? I am aware only that, for me, the world has become as far away as in a dream—as almost to disappear.

18. Aaron

NR and Aaron Copland,
Tanglewood, 1946.

La joie est bien plus fertile que la souffrance.
—from Ravel's letters, 1905

For a change of voice, and to offer a bird's-eye preview of a path that will later be strewn with closer specifics, this section, the transcript of an interview for Vivian Perlis's oral history series at Yale, recapitulates some of what was noted in chapter 13, then hurries through the decades to settle in 1988, when the interview occurred, two years before Aaron Copland died.

. . .

The first of his music I ever heard was *Quiet City* in 1940, and it bowled me over. Except for Chicago composers, Sowerby and Carpenter mainly, the notion of American Music hadn't quite taken with me. Now here suddenly was Aaron Copland's gem, at once so French like all I adored with its succinct expressivity, yet so un-French with its open-faced good will. So I tried to find as many of Copland's records as possible, although except for *El Salón México* (and I had visited that nightclub during a trip south of the border with my father) there wasn't much available.

We first met when I was nineteen and a student at Curtis. I used to go up to New York each month to seek various modes of art and fun unavailable in Philadelphia. I knocked on Lenny Bernstein's door (I didn't know you were supposed to phone people first), and we hit it off. He had the Copland Sonata on his piano, and played it for me, and again I was bowled over, despite—with its almost mean angular aggressivity—its difference from *Quiet City*. So Lenny picked up the phone and made a date for me to visit Aaron. That would have been February of 1943.

I went next day to the West Sixty-third Street studio, which I recall as a single narrow room as long as the block and compartmentalized by shelves heavy with air-checks and acetates of his various scores. Aaron was affable, immediate, attentive, with that wonderful American laugh; in the four-plus decades since that day I've seen him behave with the same unaffected frankness not only with other young unknowns but with countesses and Koussevitzkys. He played me a tape (only it wasn't called a tape then) of *Of Mice and Men*, of which I was especially touched by the super-simple D-minor moment for solo strings illustrating the death of Candy's dog. I played him a juvenile trio, my Opus minus-one, which I still have in a drawer somewhere. We talked about whether tunes came easy, and gossiped about Mexico and Chicago. That was that. When I moved to New York the following year Aaron was a regular fixture at New Music concerts, and always surrounded. A few times he came to dine on West Eleventh Street where I lived with Morris Golde, once with our mutual friend, the painter Alvin Ross, who did both our portraits. But it wasn't until 1946 that I really grew to know him.

In the summer of '46 I got a scholarship to Tanglewood and became one of Aaron's six protégés. The protégés were billeted in one huge stable in a Great Barrington girls' school (now a golf club), along with Martinů's six protégés, and Martinů himself. But Martinů fell from a garden wall during the first week, was badly shattered, and had to be replaced by Lopatnikoff. The twelve student composers had two lessons a week with their respective maestros, plus two group sessions, plus access to all kinds of rehearsals, notably of *Peter Grimes*, which received its American premiere there. It was the happiest summer of my life. Aaron lived in Pittsfield and invited me to dine once or twice, and to see *Señorita Toreador*, an Esther Williams movie that used *El Salón México* as background music. He also offered me scotch and sodas (he was never a drinker, but I was) which quite went to my head: Aaron was my teacher, after all. "Don't tell anyone," said he, "because one can't make a habit of inviting students out." But what did he really think of me?

I was always a lone wolf and never became one of Aaron's regular flock anymore than I became one of Virgil's, except that I worked as a copyist for Virgil, so I knew him better. Aaron had an entourage, so did Virgil; you belonged to one or the other, like Avignon and Rome, take it or leave it. I left it. Or rather, I dipped my toe in both streams.

Virgil's "Americanness" predates Aaron's. Virgil's use of Protestant hymns and, as he calls them, "darn fool ditties," dates from the twenties. Aaron's use came later, filtered through Thomson's. One may prefer Aaron's art to Virgil's, but give Virgil full credit: Aaron knew a good thing when he saw it. Although he's had a wider influence, he'd not be what he is without Virgil's groundbreaking excursions. Virgil invented his own folk music (a little as Poulenc and Ravel did, with their Polish and Italian and Greek pastiches) and left it rough hewn, while Aaron took actual folk music and revamped it into sheer Copland.

I gleaned less from the one-on-one meetings at Tanglewood than from the classes. The class in orchestration was most canny. Aaron had us all score the same passage—five or six measures—from a piece of his. We did this, each in our own corner for an hour, then regathered to compare the results against the original. Very instructive. *Appalachian Spring* had just been published, and we all carried our own little score around like holy writ, the way the Latin-Americans carried around the Falla Harpsichord Concerto and the French students *Pelléas*. (This, please note, was five years before the Boulez backlash.) But Aaron, sly fox, had us orchestrating sections of *Statements*, which we couldn't possibly have known beforehand. Sometimes he would invite outsiders. For example, Britten came to talk about *Peter Grimes*, and Harold Shapero analyzed his Classical Symphony. We had a class in movie music, and one in modern vocal music. Aaron had yet to write the Dickinson songs, and didn't yet feel of himself as a song composer.

He was more interested in other composers than any composer I've known. That was the season he imported youngish geniuses from all over South America: Tosar from Uruguay, Orbon from Cuba, Ore-

go-Salas from Chile, Ginastera from Argentina, Buenaventura from . . .
Aaron listened patiently to every note of every one, then commented
in a very general way. He was less a pedagogue than an advisor—a
sort of musical protocol expert. Exhilarating on the spot, but I recall
the details less accurately than with my Virgilan contact. Virgil was
more naturally verbal. Also Aaron, although in theory unbiased as to
your style, was in fact disposed to praise music that most sounded like
his own.

The next summer I went back to recapture Paradise. You never
quite can, can you? And yet I did. In 1947 the guest composer-teacher
was Honegger. Like Martinů before him, Honegger was stricken during his first week and spent the rest of the time in the hospital. So
Samuel Barber, who just happened to be on campus, agreed to replace
him. I was still in Copland's class, but Barber's chief pupil was Bill
Flanagan, who thereupon, until his death in 1969, became my best
friend (platonic) in the music world. By then I had already published
a few songs and had a firmer ego than the year before. Aaron seemed
to repeat himself with the new class, even as I doubtless do today at
Curtis, hoping no one will notice.

I returned to Tanglewood for a few days in 1948 when Hugh Ross
introduced my Sappho madrigals. Then I stayed away until 1959 when
I stopped by for lunch with Aaron and Harold Clurman. In the shade
of the shed I shed a tear and haven't been back since.

I have never been able to squeeze a compliment out of Aaron.
He was always willing to write recommendations, always willing to
socialize, but my music was nothing he would include on programs.
Perhaps I lacked a musical identity (except in the few dozen songs
from the mid-forties which are inimitable) until I went to Morocco
and started thinking bigger and writing symphonies. Yet even then,
although he flatteringly scoured everything I showed him, he never
enthused. What I learned from him was not what he taught me per se.
Rather it was through observing how he did what. Aaron stressed
simplicity: remove, remove, remove what isn't needed. That stuck.
The leanness!—particularly in his instrumentation, which he himself
termed "transparent," and taught me the French word *dépouillé*:
stripped bare. The *dépouillement* was certainly something he got from
Paris, from Boulanger—but he was *not* seduced, as I was, by so-called
Impressionism. Our respective Frenchnesses were at opposite ends
of the scale, and that, I think, put him off.

Aaron brought leanness to America, which set the tone for our
musical language throughout the war. Thanks largely to Aaron (via
Virgil, of course) American music came into its own. But by 1949 there
started to be a give and take between the United States and Europe.

Europe woke up where she left off in 1932, like Sleeping Beauty—or Sleeping Ugly—and revived all that Schoenbergian madness, now perpetrated ironically not through the Germans but through Pierre Boulez, who was a most persuasive number. The sense of diatonic economy inseminated in us by Copland was swept away in a trice, and everyone started writing fat, Teutonic music again. It was as though our country, while smug in its sense of military superiority, was still too green to imagine itself as culturally autonomous; the danger over, we reverted to Mother Europe. Aaron never really survived the blow.

In 1949 when I was living in Paris, Shirley Gabis (now Perle) and I invited a half dozen people over to hear Boulez play his Second Sonata, and Aaron came. At least one of us left the room in the middle, so discombobulating was the performance, but Aaron stuck it out with a grin. On the one hand, he was aroused by the nostalgia of his own Parisian past, when everyone tried to *épater les bourgeois*; on the other hand, Boulez was appealing and sharp as a razor, and Aaron would like to be taken seriously by the younger man and his mafia. Artists, even the greatest, once they achieve maximum fame, are no longer interested in their peers' reaction so much as in that of the new generation. Who knows what Boulez thought of Copland's music? The French have always condescended to other cultures. Except for Gershwin's, names like Copland and Harris and Sessions were merely names when I first dwelt in France, and are still (pace Carter and Cage) merely names there. Anyway, that same day, Aaron sat down and played his *Variations*, no doubt to prove he was just as hairy as Boulez, but the effect was one of terrific force and form, and, yes, inspiration, thrown at the hostile chaos of the enfant terrible.

I came back briefly to New York in 1952 and visited Aaron in one of his hundred sublets (this one deep in the south Village). Patricia Neway was there, rehearsing the Dickinson songs which she was to premiere with the New Friends of Music. I was terribly interested (and, as a songster myself, maybe a bit jealous) that Aaron kept the verses intact without repeating words not repeated in context, and impressed at how sumptuously, even bluesily, melodic the songs were despite the jaggedly disjointed vocal line. He had already—hadn't he? —written the Piano Quartet, his first leap onto the tone-row bandwagon. But here now again was the pure old master, clear as mountain dew.

During the fifties we saw each other less, since I lived in Europe for that decade. But whenever he was in Paris I invited him chez Marie-Laure de Noailles, where I lived, or chez Marie-Blanche de Polignac, who "received" on Sunday evenings. I can still see him in these two extraordinarily beautiful houses, amid the fragile Proustian society. Renoirs all over the walls, breast of guinea hen all over the table, the dizzy scent of Lanvin perfume pervading the salons, and Aaron so down-to-earth with his famous contagious giggle, so plain, so—dare I say it?—Jewish, and at the same time cowboyish. For it's notable, maybe even something to be proud of, that the first truly important American composer is a Jew, yet a Jew who never, as Lenny did, wrote Jewish music. Except for *Vitebsk*. Always at these functions he was duly impressed, but anxious to get to the sonic core of the situation, meet whatever musicians might be there, or listen (especially at Marie-Blanche's) to Poulenc, or Jacques Février, or maybe Georges Auric playing four-hands with the hostess. Mostly, though, he was probably unexcited by the tone, anxious for something more current, more vital.

In the spring of 1954 I saw him often in Rome. *The Tender Land* had just failed in New York, and he seemed anxious for a change of air. Also, Nicholas Nabokov had organized a huge international festival of modern music there, as he had in Paris two years earlier (funded by the CIA), and Aaron's Piano Quartet was to be played. Now, although this piece predated Carter's First Quartet by at least a year, and Stravinsky's Septet by at least two years, its seriality came off as bland compared to the other two works, which were also homages of defection to the enemy camp by their respective creators. Aaron's succumbing to the new mode was not so much dishonest as desperate— a falling into the trap of the young whom he still hoped to lead. But how could he remain a leader when he was in fact being led? In Rome that spring, although he was continually surrounded by interviewers and hangers-on, it was clear that Elliott Carter, involuntarily, was usurping the throne, at least in the ken of the brash young Turks.

As Aaron's fame swelled during the sixties and seventies, his influence waned. In January of 1966 when he came to Salt Lake City, where I was teaching, to conduct the Utah Symphony, I told the university that, sure, I'd invite him to give a talk if they would cancel all classes and guarantee a full house. There was a full house, all right, but strictly of faculty and townspeople.

What else? It all now seems so long ago. In the past twenty years we've met fairly often, but as you know, Aaron is receding into his own world. And any "world feels dusty when you stop to die,/We want the dew then, honors seem dry"—as he depicted in his most beautiful song. But the honors that accrue to him ever more vastly appear so often to be simply praiseworthy, a touch standoffish, treating the man like a saint. Now, to be a saint, you must once have been a sinner, and I feel that it diminishes Aaron to avoid discussion of his various temptations. We all recall his friendly reticence, his hunger for gossip, although he himself was not given, as Virgil was, to gossip. Aaron never said nasty things to others, but I've seen him cool to people who wanted something out of him or who were too clinging. And I've seen him lose his cool, as when he nearly expired while listening to Auric's awful Piano Sonata, and actually swearing when it was over. Or when I referred disobligingly to Boulanger in *The Paris Diary*, he wrote me that he would simply not endorse a book that was so vindictive about someone he had always loved and needed. (That slap did me good and reversed many an exhibitionistic stance.) I've seen him elated, especially when a new piece was being played (you never get blasé about that first performance). I've seen him struck dumb by the beauty of a passing human being. I've seen him depressed, dark, near tears, about the plight of an arrogant friend we both loved. But he never actually talked about his carnal life, except elusively. His rapport with Victor Kraft was ambiguous, and in any case, pretty much deromanticized by the time I knew them both. It's not my place here to speculate on later loves—his generation even including Auden, was circumspect. Indeed, Aaron was the most circumspect person I've ever known, considering how he encouraged others to let down their hair.

I am thrilled and I wish Aaron could be thrilled too, to discover how cyclic our world becomes if you live long enough. In just the past two or three years, I've heard any number of scores by young men and women in their twenties, scores which do more than emulate the wide-open spaces of Aaron's most beloved works—they actually sound (in timbre, tune, and hue) like steals from the master. Always admired by the masses, he's becoming readmired by fickle youth.

Nevertheless, I asked three members of this youth recently: "Is there any composer whose next work you just can't wait to hear?" They had to stop and think. They were not agog as we once were about how the Clarinet Concerto was going to sound, how the new Nonet was going to sound, or how *Inscapes* would be received. These were *events*. Aaron Copland wasn't the only one, but he was the chief one whose new works we were all avid to hear. I don't think it was because we were specifically younger. It's that the whole world was younger, there were fewer composers around, the repertory of American works was slimmer, so any new addition was a thrill. Aaron was the king and in a sense still is. There hasn't been another man since then from whom all young composers await each new endeavor with bated breath, and whose endeavor usually doesn't disappoint.

19. Juilliard and Tanglewood

Shirley (Xénia) Gabis with NR, Paris, 1949.

Amid the diffusion survive these facts, used as *points de repère*: Scholastic year 1945–46 I went to Juilliard and got a bachelor's degree. Returned to Juilliard for 1947–48 and got a master's. Summers of 1946 and 1947, Tanglewood.

If memory merges and blurs—blurges—the Juilliard years as it does the seasons at Tanglewood, it will accurately recapture episodes as on a camera's plate, so that I can remember who and what smelled how and where. But not when. The diary begun in 1945 is some help, though not in chronology. While typing the extracts of chapter 17, after I became used to the *pose* (all books are posed), it grew clear that the young Ned was less concerned with history than with states of mind—and states of body. Daily agendas—engagement calendars—which I have kept from 1947 until the present, though also of some help, were, especially the early ones, dashed off in short-hand.

I'll continue as before, letting the present reshape the past.

For Juilliard I retain neither nostalgia nor affection. I made acquaintances, participated in the Tuesday Composers' Forums, enjoyed some courses, but never quite knew what I was doing there, the standards seemed geared to a lower mean. To get a degree one needed non-music courses. Having passed the entrance exams with flying colors I wasn't forced to attend music classes except in piano and composition. The most pungent recollections of that illustrious music mecca are studies in sociology, American history, physical education, and yes, hygiene, which taught that the human diet needs copper as well as iron—copper being obtained both through milk stored in brass vats and through apricots. (Apricots again! shades of the nursery-school fare.) Also two semesters of world literature—imparted by the learned Elbert Lenrow—which, if nothing else, inspired some musical output including songs based on texts sacred and profane. Among the latter were *Four Madrigals,* my first attempts for unaccompanied vocal ensemble. Written in the autumn of 1947, they are dedicated respectively to Hugh Ross (who conducted their premiere at Tanglewood the following summer), to Rufus my father, Gladys my mother, and to my teacher Bernard Wagenaar. The C. M. Bowra versions of Sappho fragments were from *Greek Literature in Translation,* in the tattered margins of which I tenderly find scribbled my almost-completed melodies. Since then I have composed vastly for chorus in every size and shape, but never with that svelte flamboyance of beginner's luck.

Any phrase, not just in a slim volume of verse but in a newspaper or on a subway poster, was food for song. On my birthday Morris gave me a book of Donne's *Epigrams* containing the enigmatic paradox called "A Burnt Ship" with these closing lines:

So all were lost who in the ship were found,
They in the sea being burnt, they in the burnt ship drowned

from which came a song, then a home-recording with Remo Allotta, long since vanished, whose voice haunts no less than the couplet which revives yet again Enobarbos's image of Cleopatra's barge: "A burnished throne burned on the water." This perfect ditty in the Lydian mode was thought up on the banks of the Hudson, and the tune now evokes the groves of academe far more than does any careful instruction of yore.

Bernard Wagenaar, my chief raison d'être, was a delightful man. But

of his teaching I remember nothing, not a shard. Others in his flock
—Robert Starer, Robert Craft—may remember more. Yet I was a
"major" in composition. As a "minor" in piano, I played that instrument better than my female teacher, whose name has faded. Vincent
Perischetti taught form, and Robert Ward taught conducting, which I
audited.

I had flings with one or two students.

When the Greenwich Village bars closed at 4 a.m., my custom was to
invite stragglers—four or five, sometimes more—back to my room,
stopping en route at an all-night deli for a case of Schaeffer's ale.
Toward 7 a.m. I'd say: "Everyone out. Everyone ... except *you*"—
pointing to a favored soul. Thus Chuck Turner, who in fact was a
colleague at Juilliard seen in the halls, but met now at Mary's Bar on
Eighth Street. Byronically appealing in both mien and garb, with ruddy
Wasp features and straight ebony hair combed in a leonine swirl, an
open collar and erect posture, Chuck emanated neither narcissism
nor ferocity, preferring the role of courtier to courted, and speaking
quietly of all things cultured. He majored in violin, which he played
well for a Gentile. He was also a year or two older but had none of
the hauteur upperclassmen will show toward juniors, nor the envious
condescension performers will show toward composers. I was the
sophisticate, he the cornball, the roles were defined. But despite his
ingenuousness he was more canny than I in the instrumental world
and was helpful in special ways.

My First String Quartet (long since scrapped, thank you) was capa-
bly sight-read by the chamber group that met at Chuck's on Sunday
nights, and this taught me a thing or two. We often took walks together
between classes along the riverfront. (Juilliard, it will be remembered,
was then located where the Manhattan Music School is today, at 124th
and Claremont.) We remained colleagues, dispassionate but staunch,
long past the yearning college days. When I wrote violin music, he
would "confirm" it on his fiddle, deferential but firm in his suggestions, as Seymour Barab was with my cello music. When in the late
1940s I needed performers for the backstage music being churned
out for productions by the ANTA experimental theater, Chuck volunteered his services gratis. I thought of him always as handsome, green,
unpretentious, smart, more than presentable, a mensch. When I
moved to France we lost contact for a while.

A year or two later, sometime in 1950, who should stroll toward me
at Saint-Germain-des-Prés on the arm of Gore Vidal but Chuck. An
unlikely duo, and one I vaguely disapproved of. I do not like catego-

ries to overlap, and Gore Vidal was somehow my property, as was Chuck on the other side of the stile. I had known Gore, sort of, from, of all things, those Pyramid Club parties (take-a-chance-on-a-chain-letter-and-win-a-fortune—really an excuse to meet people) which were the rage in the mid-forties. I knew his work and his social demeanor and couldn't connect him with Chuck. But then, opposites attract—not that Chuck and Gore were opposites, at least not in their physical urges.

A year after that, also at Saint-Germain-des-Prés, Chuck reappeared, this time with Samuel Barber. Chuck had become not only the violinist laureate of the Barber-Menotti entourage (Sam was on his way to Copenhagen, where he would record, at his own expense, various of his orchestral works, including the Violin Concerto with Chuck as soloist), he had also become a composer. Barber was of those who must make geniuses of their swains, and had coaxed some not-bad pieces out of Chuck, including an orchestral poem called *Encounter* in honor of Spender's recently founded magazine. Chuck was more of a true creator than many a performer-turned-composer (Casals, Casadesus) but was lazy, not prolific, and gave up writing music after the intimacy with Barber lessened ten years later. To his credit, he continued thinking of Sam as our century's greatest musician, defending the mentor against all slights real or imagined.

In later years Chuck turned into a teacher. When his parents visited from Detroit in the late 1960s they became friendly with my parents. All was cozy and Juilliardy except for one thing: Chuck had inherited Sam's faults but not Sam's virtues. The virtues were, of course, the undeniable gifts and the ability to sculpt and disseminate those gifts in convincing, sometimes deeply moving, forms of every size. And Sam had a debonair wit and a way with mimicry that was devastating. He could also be imperious, dismissive, snobbish, petty, and just plain mean, especially after a few drinks. These last qualities were acquired unearned by Chuck, on whom they did not sit well. At an all-boy meal chez Henry McIlhenny in Philadelphia, early in 1981 on the evening after Sam's funeral, Chuck, who had earlier that day warmly lamented the good lost years, suddenly turned on me and said: "What are you doing here? You always despised Sam." In fact, Sam and I had a love-hate rapport, such as it was. Sam felt slighted that my songs were sung as often as his, for who was I in his ken but a shrimp. But we sparred and were affectionate. (Now, posthumously, his songs are heard far oftener than mine.) A month or so before he died, Sam phoned to ask if I could get Chuck a job at Curtis, where I had been teaching for a year, and where he—Sam—had been the fair-haired child in the 1930s. I promised to try, and did.

Since then Chuck has blown hot and cold with me, now "defending" me from my "enemies," now sending me letters of such vituperative loathing that I no longer see him. His reasons are his reasons.

I used to say that I forget but do not forgive. This is false. I cannot hold a grudge, and as the century closes am ever more baffled at the relish with which whole nations torture each other. It's growing worse. I will be friends with anyone who is not a fool, beginning with Chuck Turner, although I am frightened of madness and bored with drunks who show no signs of attempted recovery.

On 11 March 1946, Father had his picture in *Time* magazine:

> The fastest-growing experiment in U.S. social medicine is the Blue Cross, a nationwide organization with the laudable purpose of helping members meet hospital bills in advance.... In 1938 a medical economist named Clarence Rufus Rorem, using the remnants of a Julius Rosenwald fund grant, made a survey of the scattered hospitalization plans, sold them on forming a national organization. Rorem is now the $15,000-a-year national director.... For a maximum of $24 a year, the average Blue Cross subscriber, or any member of his family, gets: (1) 30 days semi-private care in the hospital.... As an obvious and partial answer to socialized medicine, Blue Cross has worked well ... all that can seemingly stop Blue Cross from snowballing still more is state-controlled medicine.

Another time—was it that season, or a year or two earlier? (it seems to me the war was still on)—early on a Saturday evening, around nine, in the Crossroads Bar off Times Square, I caught sight of Tony Romano, whom I'd met in passing at a party somewhere when he was with someone, me too, and we'd eyed each other with hopeless shrugs, at least my shrug was hopeless. Now he was alone. To myself I said what the alcoholic says in his better moments: Don't mess this up by getting drunk. Tony Romano resembled everything his name implies: Italian from Brooklyn, husky biceps, army uniform but with neck unbuttoned since he was no longer in the service, wisp of black fuzz peeking from out the white T-shirt, semieducated with a destructive smile, masculine to the core with not a shred of the queer's wily subterfuge, tough, a paragon, my opposite, my type.

Once in my room he declined a drink, but said: "You've got an orange"—designating a platter of oranges "can I have an orange?" After the orange he pinned me to the mattress as a lepidopterist pins the moth to his board.

Tony, with whom I had nothing in common, whom I "dated" only three or four times (always the result of a spur-of-the-moment call from him), and to whom I was merely a roll in the hay, became during the next decade a totem—like the unshaved man in Jackson Park during my teens—an ideal provoking a stimulating languor to which I would succumb in waking dreams and look for on every street corner, while knowing it could not be rediscovered.

In the mid-1950s, during a brief trip back to the USA and a briefer hike to the Everard Baths on Twenty-eighth Street, I spotted Tony in the morass of the steam room, where tears are not distinguishable from sweat, and he didn't recognize me as I sank to my knees. He was the dedicatee of the little opera *A Childhood Miracle,* but of course he never knew.

Irritation. Like the sound of chewing and swallowing in someone you no longer love.

An artist doesn't see things as they are, but as he is—so runs the age-old saw.

Leo Sowerby came through town to hear Hugh Ross conduct the world premiere of *Canticle of the Sun.* He had been to Manhattan twice before, introducing me to David McK. Williams, H. W. Gray, and others of the specialized field of organ and church music, but never hobnobbing with the more cosmopolitan milieu, i.e., Aaron and Virgil. Instead, Leo seemed aloof to that which he would name modish, the very milieu I longed to be accepted by, and which today would be called the Power Elite. Leo had met these "powers" on committees, but they were as little aware of him as he them. If when *Canticle of the Sun* won the Pulitzer that spring of 1946 he felt vindicated, he didn't let on. Vindicated of what? Joaquín Nin-Culmell recently wrote me that "Virgil was a smart critic who tried to quip his way through music." Leo would have concurred. As for Aaron, wasn't he just chic?

On this occasion I took him to Drossie's, where his so-ultra-bourgeois aspect—rimless specs, thin necktie, worried frown—only confirmed his membership in high bohemia to those at neighboring tables. (Parenthetical remembrance, apropos glasses, of Virgil's pragmatic query to his surgeon, circa 1985, after emerging from anesthetic: Virgil: "Am I going to die?" Surgeon: "No." Virgil: "In that case I'll need my glasses.") At one of these tables sat composer Sam Morgenstern, to whom I announced: "I don't know what to do this summer." "Why not," said he, "go to Tanglewood?" So life changed again.

For the first time since the war Tanglewood reopened like a great flower in June of 1946 with a vigorous sense of liberation and fertility rife in all the arts. I have never ever felt such a collective purposefulness and camaraderie as was displayed during those six weeks on that handsome campus. Since Aaron Copland was not only the chief composition professor but co-director with Koussevitzky, my scholarship was assured.

The mansion at the Great Barrington school lodged twenty students, ten boys being quartered in the adjoining barn, and ten girls in the mansion proper. A bus took us each morning after breakfast (pancakes), via Stockbridge, to Tanglewood near Lenox, about thirty minutes away, and returned us in the evening, unless there was a concert, which there usually was. In our dorm I recall Howard Shanet, Earl George, Vladimir Ussachevsky, Louis Lane, and Danny Pinkham (all students of Martinů's) bunking demurely in a row, and of the girls Sarah Cunningham plus two auditors—Grace Cohen and Paula Graham, a singer. Also the morbidly seductive—both his music and his person—Heitor Tosar.

Bohuslav Martinů was staying alone in the mansion too. His terrible accident happened during that first week. I had visited his small New York apartment on Fifty-ninth Street the previous winter when David Diamond was subletting, but had never met the man. Aaron now admonished me to be nice to Martinů ("those Europeans are always at loose ends without their wives, you know"), and when I asked Aaron what the Czech's music was like, he answered: "Like a Chinese nightclub under water." One evening, when Paula and I were savoring lemon meringues at a Barrington bakery, in wandered Martinů, at loose ends without his wife. We invited him to our table, chatted amiably for an hour as darkness fell, then returned down the avenue to the jasmine-scented gardens of our communal school, and said good night. Five minutes later, a crash, a yelp, a groan. Martinů had fallen from a fifteen-foot parapet leading from the mansion to the nearby golf course. Ambulance, hospital (Nikolai Lopatnikoff was quickly called to substitute for the remainder of the season.) We never saw Martinů again, but he lived in continual pain until his death thirteen years later.

Along with running the whole show at Tanglewood, and giving his six pupils two private lessons a week, Aaron Copland in his classes gave lectures on instrumentation (for one of these he took us to the shed and had each first-desk man of the Boston Symphony demonstrate his instrument), on other composers' methods, and on how to write movie music. During the war Aaron had been the only "serious" composer to go to Hollywood, first to score *Of Mice and Men, Our Town,* and then Samuel Goldwyn's *North Star.* He introduced a new esthetic—"the Copland sound"—to films, which dominated sound-tracks until the late 1950s, when all cinema, here and abroad, stopped using anything but pop. In off hours Aaron mingled with the Hollywood intelligentsia, mainly European refugees, and heard his chamber music played on special recitals. At one of these he performed his own brittle Piano Sonata, after which who should come backstage but Groucho Marx. "Groucho, what are you doing at this kind of concert? I have a split personality, so don't tell Mr. Goldwyn." "Oh, he doesn't mind," said Groucho, "as long as you split it with him."

Preparations for *Peter Grimes* dominated every segment of Tanglewood during that summer of 1946. Rumor had it that Britten himself would be there, and Koussevitzsky had already stated: "There is *Carmen.* And there is *Peter Grimes.*" Britten was only a name to me, one I assigned to the preset blancmange notion of British music. England had produced some pretty good authors and painters in the past 250 years but had not, for some reason, a single composer of any weight since the death of Purcell in 1695 (except for maybe Sir Arthur Sullivan). Suddenly issuing from every rehearsal hall on campus were the most persuasive tunes imaginable, long and inevitable and strong and mournful. Over there in Studio B was Phyllis Curtin (then Phyllis Smith) with two fellow sopranos and pianist, venerable Felix Wolfes, going through the trio that closes Act II and, with its soaring other-worldliness, putting *Rosenkavalier* to shame. Over here in the espalier terrace was Hugh Ross and his large chorus practicing the vast a cappella ensembles which, as fully as any of the soloists, will propel the opera's tragedy. Down in the main shed was Lenny disciplining an orchestra which, though standard in make-up, emitted, thanks to Britten's unique ear for checks and balances, noises that were more than music—that *were*, literally, chalk cliffs and waves and stifled lust and fear. So English music, like Sleeping Beauty, now with Britten's kiss, had awakened after two centuries. The odd aspect: Britten was no innovator; he was as conservative as Poulenc in pursuing the tried and true, and, like Poulenc, his every measure seemed traceable to another composer. He was *better than*, not *different from*, speaking the same language with a more singular accent. Because in the next decades Britten would become the brightest light in English music, and by extension the strongest influence on the young, those young emerged writing conservatively. England did not, like America and France and Germany and Italy, have to suffer the convulsions of serial experimentation.

A great work is one you never get used to. *Peter Grimes*, like *The Rite of Spring*, was one of my milestones. Before opening night I bought and brooded over the score and befriended as many of the cast as possible. (Though not Phyllis Curtin, whom I scarcely met and would not come to know until 1959, when she turned into, and has remained, the most important soprano of my career.) Not the least of my motives for this detailed study was the report I made to Kubly (for yes, our friendship was still on) in his capacity of reporter. Since he could not attend the premiere, I sent a detailed telegram, and this was published, scarcely edited, in *Time*. Kubly did show up the following week, and Aaron gave me permission (but I was already twenty-two!) to quit the Barrington confines and lodge with Kubly at the Hotel Lenox. There I also gave him a review, musical and gossipy (Lenny's acrid comments at rehearsals), of the American premiere of Shosta-kovich's new symphony—I think it was the Eighth. Lenny pretended to be not amused, and during lunch on the lawn, in full view of everyone, knocked from my head the tan beret which I then sported, but kissed me afterward as was his flagrant wont.

Britten did come. I spoke with him *à deux* only briefly, at the postopening party. He smelled somewhat of digested champagne. I was inhibited. A month later I sent him a sycophantic letter, a copy of "Alleluia," and (since David Sachs had once told me that Prokosch had introduced himself to Spender with a nude photo of himself) I en-closed a snapshot, taken by Kubly, of myself stripped to the waist and picking raspberries. Britten didn't answer. For the record, we did conduct for many years a two-sided correspondence which I later initiated from Morocco, not coquettishly but apropos of his work with pacifism. (Also for the record, I mentioned the seminude picture in my first published book, *The Paris Diary*, and received a dozen letters —not just from men but from *women*—whose senders enclosed nude pictures of themselves. You can't imagine what people think they look like!)

Oh, the fragrance of those giant elms, especially in the rain, when sounds like odors carry pugnaciously and the last movement of Sibe-lius's Third spreads through the winds, conducted first in the morning by Seymour Lipkin, and in the afternoon by Gerhard Samuel, Kousse-vitzky's chief new pets. Koussie (as he was called)'s chief regular pet was, of course, Lukas Foss, who, because the eminent Russian conductor couldn't read scores, acted as literate assistant, playing all music, new and old, submitted to the maestro.

Lukas, about my age, was more flamboyantly facile and versed than me. A German refugee—and retaining even today a crusty accent—his music was virulently non-European, meaning lean, angular, muscular, diatonic, unromantic, and using folklike tunes and jazzy rhythms, either foursquare or in ⅝ meters. Lukas and Lenny were intimates, vying amiably for their simultaneous reputations as triple threats. Lukas was surely as good a pianist as Lenny, a thoroughly trained conductor, and a composer (at twenty-two) of large-scope works that were conspicuously performed by major orchestras.

That he was at this time more American than the pope (Aaron) reflects the yearnings of the naturalized citizen—yearnings to be accepted, to be in the swim. In ensuing years Lukas has leapt onto so many bandwagons (the wide-open-spaces vehicle, the twelve-tone vehicle, "chance," "happenings," the "masterpiece" syndrome, neoromanticism, minimalism, always using the "right" poets if vocalism was called for—in sum, so up-to-date that his music grew dated with each fashion change) that if all the art of our century were wiped off the earth save that of Lukas, the next century could reconstitute our musical history through his scores alone. Those who criticize this bent chez lui miss the point—that cultural promiscuity *is* Lukas, even as spreading-himself-thin is Lenny.

He was socially promiscuous too, and, being heterosexual, for all practical purposes, made passes at various girls including my friend, the beauteous Grace Cohen, whose Nefertiti features, long lilac hair, and the plangent torso of a modern dancer pleaded for defilement, even as her Bronxy voice pleaded for mercy.

Lenny brought Lukas and a guest, Marc Blitzstein, to a party one night in the great hall of our Barrington school. We all sat on the floor while Lukas played and sang—or rather, bleated as composers do—a spacious *Parable* he was composing for Todd Duncan and orchestra. I was jealous not only of his inspired technique for manipulating so large a canvas, which I'd have been incapable of despite my narcissistic act of self-assurance, but of his cool ability to show his cards so expertly in front of everyone. I resented my own reticence, my lack of exhibitionism on the grand scale, and rationalized that, well, I wasn't Jewish.

Blitzstein was even more of a performer. Drenched in the gold dust of reputation, he was part of American history with his leftist operas of yore, his army stint in Europe from whence he'd just returned, and his recent huge piece of patriotic gore, which Lenny had just con-ducted in New York, called the *Airborne Symphony*. Now here he was in the flesh, about to show *his* cards.

It is a truth universally acknowledged that inside every composer lurks a singer longing to get out. What is known in the trade as "the composer's voice"—that squeaky, unpitched organ with which com-posers audition their vocal wares to baffled sopranos or uninterested opera producers—may explain their becoming composers in the first place, out of frustrated vengeance. The human voice is, after all, both the primal and the ultimate expression, the instrument all others seek to emulate. I have known only two American exceptions to the rule that the composer-as-singer sabotages his own work. One was Samuel Barber, who had a true, gentle baritone of professional class, albeit with the rolled *r*'s of upper-crust Philadelphia. The other was Marc Blitzstein, who, true, had a "composer's voice," but who composed specifically for such a voice. With his wheezy larynx he could put over his own songs because of a fearless, horny conviction that I've never heard elsewhere. Indeed, during the long run of *Threepenny Opera*, all of the regularly changing cast seemed to be hired according to how much they sounded like Blitzstein.

Now here he was in Barrington, cajoling, whispering, rapping his new song, which Lenny was calling a masterpiece, and which in fact was called "Zipper Fly." We could not then know the dancer from the dance, for with Marc at play, his song (to his own text) seemed irresist-ibly witty. In retrospect, heard through "real" voices, one realized that his left-wing ditties are lessened by standard beauty.

I wanted to know Marc Blitzstein, and would, but not then.

The fellow student composer I came to know best and longest was Daniel Pinkham, he of the eternally even temper, ingratiating smile, roving eye, biggish ears that were maximally experienced for church music. Like me, Danny wrote songs, indeed, specialized in songs, although choral music and little operas were very much in his cata-logue too since in Cambridge, where he lived and had a church job, he had access to all sorts of professional singers. We weren't quite aware at the time that all composers didn't write songs: the icy truth is that songwriters are as rare among composers as composers are rare among football players, and this specialty within a specialty proved a bond between Danny and me. By Song I mean: A lyric poem of moderate length set to music for single voice with piano. (A lyric poem is an expression of its author's feelings rather than a narrative of events. A moderate length is up to five minutes. Single voice means the instrument of one singer. A piano is a piano.)

Danny, protégé of Piston's and Boulanger's, grandson of Lydia Pinkham, and a proper Bostonian with long *a*'s and soft *r*'s, did not show feelings other than optimistic ones. One can't picture him weeping. Blazingly intelligent, his culture was—is—nonetheless restricted to music. He *is* music. Reading matter, no matter how abstruse, seems cogent only insofar as it serves his muse. His conversation, though clever, is nondevelopmental, almost strictly anecdotal, as though he feared where an evolving *entretien* might lead. He remains a major American harpsichordist and organist, and a confector of—at its best—delicious and sometimes touching *Gebrauchsmusik*. He has never shown envy, and attributes his smallish reputation to his not being in the swim. He has always lived in Massachusetts.

Danny had a station wagon, the better to cart around his ever-present harpsichord. He was always going somewhere or coming back, saying good-bye or saying hello, transferring hitchhikers, unloading students at the nearby lake where we swam at noon, sometimes tearing off a piece in the back seat. Our relationship was platonic. We remain faithful colleagues and mutual champions.

Remnants:

—Have I mentioned that Aaron called me Boy?—he called all of his boys Boy. Or that in his speech on movie music he claimed that in Hollywood you could score for anything you wanted, although the actual orchestration, for legal union reasons, was farmed out to hacks? That, for example, in the snow scene of the horseless carriage in *The Magnificent Ambersons* Bernard Herrmann used fifteen celestas. That last point scintillates, but the fact was belied years later when I saw—heard—the film on television. No celestas.

—Did I drink at Tanglewood? Not much, and not problematically. Did I have sex (other than with K)? Just once, with an oboe player in the woods, followed by a violent headache.

—Paula Graham presented a group of my songs with me at the piano, at one of the composers' concerts, and was, as the saying goes, a success.

—On the lawn by the shed we were likely to see Paula's visiting friend, Patricia Neway, gaunt but firm with a businesslike stride, fierce deep eyes, an unfunny approach to music and drama, a tragedienne with, it was said, the most beautiful voice in the world. That winter she would star on Broadway in Britten's *Rape of Lucretia*, would give recitals all alone and make you think they were operas, and would finally create the role of Magda Sorel in Menotti's *The Consul* internationally, and have flaming desserts named for her at Maxim's. More of her later.

—On the raft in the lake we were likely to see Arthur Weinstein, Lenny's chief hanger-on, yet with his own identity as interior designer, and a pretty amateur tenor voice with which he interpreted *recherché* repertory, i.e., Poulenc and Britten and sometimes me.

—On the cash register of the music store we were likely to see Robert Holton, energetic in his promotion of living art, ambitious in the publishing field, soon to be important at Boosey & Hawkes where, some years later, at his behest I would be welcomed and remain until today.

—On the grass behind the rehearsal hall, Robert Shaw was putting a group of madrigalists through their paces. The work was Hindemith's unaccompanied set of *Six Chansons,* on Rilke's French lyrics sung now in English. Shaw was a handsome hypnotist who, by merely rocking the cradle, could entice lovely tones from shrieking babies.

—So enamored was I of Britten that I pillaged every available score from Bob Holton's bookstore and discovered, for the first time, that originality as a virtue is only relative. The opening song of the *Michelangelo Sonnets,* for instance, is, in the piano accompaniment, not even a plagiarism of Ravel's *Le paon* but a carbon copy. Yet one never hears of an affinity between Ravel and Britten. The two works, given their contexts, are independent.

—For the composers' meetings we each had to analyze a short contemporary piece from top to bottom. I chose Samuel Barber's *Essay for Orchestra* No. 1 in which I accounted for every note in its formal, harmonic, contrapuntal, melodic, rhythmic, and instrumental context in relation to every other note. I still have the marked-up music, which I know better than my own.

—Father drove through Lenox, met some of my pals, renewed acquaintance with Aaron, and told me that Mother was edging into another period of darkness.

After the stint in Tanglewood, my parents and I went to New Glarus. It was their last local sortie before their permanent remove from Chicago to Philadelphia in the fall. Herbert Kubly, proud of his Swiss origins and of his Wisconsin home town, a cheese-making center, where every August the Wilhelm Tell legend was acted out in Switzerdeutsch before a huge audience *en plein air*, invited me and my parents to witness this pageant and stay as guests in the family house. The show was endless and incomprehensible, but Mother was moved to tears by the ending, when Tell shoots the apple from his son's head, and the two fall into each other's arms. She couldn't stop crying, and continued off and on through the night, imploring me to remain with the family forever. Kubly, not amused, felt we were a neurotic clan right out of *The Silver Cord*. Mother, when I told her this, was offended. As for me, wasn't I the picture of stability?

Wasn't the "artist," in fact, the most sane of citizens, saner than generals or moneymakers, since he and he alone knows what he wants to do and how to do it? (Money and war merely bide the time.)

Back in New York that October the ties with Kubly weakened. I recall myself as passive observer, touched by but indifferent to Kubly's flailing, his anxiety, his landing in Bellevue. A truly unhappy person is tiresome, his misery being so all-consuming that he relinquishes his personhood. Nor is another person (thought by the unhappy person to be not a person but a monster) ever responsible for the unhappy person's unhappiness. But neither of us reasoned that way then.

20. Paul · Sam · Marc

No no.
A miracle works more than the spell of spellbound music.
It works life;
it awakens a dead body to behavior
and my poor heart to love such as I did not know I knew ...
—from *A Sermon on Miracles* by Paul Goodman

Time oozes on—at least for those of us who are alive (as the euphemism has it in English)—sometimes swift, sometimes stagnant, always forward and flexible. Ten minutes spent being burned at the stake are not comparable to ten minutes in line at the bank, or waiting for your lover's phone call, or at a lousy movie. The condition anterior to being alive and the condition after (even rocks are alive, even lava and salt; Earth is a panting organ coated in rubicund slime—*us*) are the same, that is, no condition: nonexistence. Though the very term "nonexistence" implies a tangible finality, a *something* that is there. The poet Freud knew that our own death is unimaginable; when we try to imagine it, we perceive that we really survive as spectators.

Anyway. If chronology has been often unverifiable hitherto, I now have before me the first of four-dozen agendas kept since 1947, and they are explicit. Alas, except for the page of January 1, which contains but one word, "Chaos," many of the other notations throughout the year are in shorthand, referring to forgotten Christian names, and to appointments without direction, sometimes several on a day. There's a seemingly limitless sprinkling of boyfriends (Al, Sunday at 6; Eddie, Tues. at 2 a.m.; Fabian, Carl, O'Malley, Dick Stryker, Max T., John H., Tony, Gary) some of whom reassemble themselves in the mind's eye with their smiles, their threats, their uniforms, and I tingle as I type this. Janet Fairbank's name recurs throughout the year, always at 11 a.m., so I must have been still working for her. George Perle, Pavlik, Alfonso Ossorio, Grace Cohen, Shirley, Ben Weber, Leo Rost, Seymour Barab, are names that turn up weekly. On 25 April I note that my journal was stolen by an overnight visitor. (The visitor phoned often to say we—he and I—could make a bundle by publishing it. When he finally brought it back, hoping for a reward, I asked Grace and Seymour to be present, in case of any rough stuff.) Romolo di Spirito, Eva Gauthier, John Heliker (Lou's dear painter friend who's line drawing of me remains in my treasure chest), Joan Lewison, Christopher Lazare, Jennie Tourel. Buy lotion for crabs. Write Rome Academy again. 26 May, *At Noon upon Two* at the Old Knickerbocker (I'd thought it was at least a year earlier). Read Gide. Read H. James. John Lindsay (who became John Wingate), Howard Moss, Ankey Larabee, Zeller at 9 p.m. (this was Robert Zeller, picked up at the Old Colony Bar, who eighteen years later would conduct the premiere of my opera *Miss Julie*, and fifteen years after *that* would perish from AIDS, before AIDS had a name), Paula, David Stimer, Hennig (my elderly German pupil), Mae O'Donnell, and Rae Green. *The Mother of Us All. The Eagle with Two Heads.* Kimon Friar. Muriel. 18 June leave for Martha's Vineyard on train with Paul.

Why have I not written of Paul up to now? Because I couldn't know how to start? Outside of my family, Paul Goodman was the strongest nonmusical influence of my American life; and his influence, as a poet and thinker, on my music—literally on my music, not on my thoughts about music—was inestimable. He was my Goethe and Heine, my Apollinaire and Eluard, my Boïto and Hofmannstahl, my utterly American source, my spring; the poet, among the hundreds I used and sometimes abandoned, to whom I most often returned, even after he died in 1972 at sixty. To paraphrase Auden: He was my North, my South, my Night, my Light,/I thought that love would last forever,/I was right.

A decade earlier he closed his journal thus: "I am not happy, yet as of today I would willingly live till 80. I have already lived longer than many another rebellious soul." *Growing Up Absurd* had finally brought him major prominence, although he had been preaching (and practicing) its contents all his life. If he was not happy, nobody wise, with imagination and open eyes, can stay happy for long. But he was vital and fertile; more important for an artist, he was appreciated, even ultimately "understood," when he died, twenty years short of his goal. Happily—if that's the word—he did not survive to see his reputation fade, to be replaced by flabbier savants. Even at the end, in the melancholy of fame, Paul Goodman was admired by thousands who, paradoxically, did not know his name. His original notions, having become general knowledge, crumbled into slogans which the liberated youth of the 1960s spouted at him—to set him straight.

To say that he became my most pertinent influence, social and poetic, would be to echo many a voice in the young groups who felt themselves to be as important to Paul as he was to them—the inevitable covetousness that comes when great men involve their entourage not only through their work but through their person.

My first good songs date from the mid-forties, most of them settings of Paul Goodman's verse. I may have written other kinds of songs since, but none better. That I have never in the following decades wearied of putting his words to music is the highest praise I can show him; since I put faith in my own work, I had first to put faith in Paul's. Through Paul I wrote not only songs to celebrate Sally's smile, or Susan at play, or prayers for the birth of Matthew Ready (who died before his father, mountain climbing), but the opera *Cain and Abel*, a ballet (with Alfonso Ossorio), choral pieces, backgrounds for the Beck's theater and nightclub skits.

On 18 June when we took the train to Martha's Vineyard, Paul and I were headed for Menemsha, where Shirley's mother, Rae Gabis, had taken a house. There were eight of us: Shirley and Rae, Eugene Istomin and Byron Hardin, John Eustace (a friend of Norris's from Saint John's), Paul, me, and Miriam Gideon, with whom I shared a room as well as a birthday (she was born 23 October 1908). Paul brought his just-published *Kafka's Prayer* and was the guru of the fortnight. I read Sartre's just-published *Chemins de la liberté*, and everyone else read Reich's just-published *The Function of the Orgasm* (in a plain brown wrapper) because Paul was a devoted Reichian. This literature was absorbed on the beach, where the poet Edward Field often joined us. I was jealous of Field's good looks. Paul had solutions for everyone.

Me: "I don't like the way Ed Field talks."

Paul: "Then cover his mouth with kisses."

Byron: "I don't have dreams like 'Gene does, of coming onto the stage stark naked."

Paul: "You're probably not as good a pianist as 'Gene."

Rae: "Well, I still think Roosevelt was a great man, even if he did get us into the war. Great men can make mistakes."

Paul: "Then what makes them great?"

On the beach, at Eugene's request, Paul wrote out a pretty good translation of Alyosius Bertand's three medium-class poems which Ravel used as epigraphs for his virtuosic piano suite *Gaspard de la nuit*. Eugene reprinted them in his programs throughout the world. I was impressed at Paul's grasp of French, though of course he had the grasp of anything. (A year later, when Jean Cocteau passed briefly through New York, we all went to gaze upon him at the Gotham Book Mart. Paul, who worshiped Cocteau and who was never intimidated, was intimidated. He spoke to the maître only in English—"My translations of your works are better than these," gesturing toward a display— which Cocteau didn't understand. "Tell him in French, Paul," we all prodded, but he didn't. We knew French then, but not how to speak it.)

Homely but sexy, big nose and glasses, his broad New York accent belied his vast education. He made passes at literally everyone of every age, sometimes even at dogs, because he felt that repressed Americans deserved fulfillment. Despite his two common-law wives, Ginny and Sally, and his children, it was not girls but boys, 95 percent of the time, that made his eyes shine and his heart break. Since everyone on earth, whether they allow it or not, is bisexual, why shouldn't Paul himself be the answer to any man's secret gay yearnings?

To John Eustace, on the beach: "Give in to your feelings."

John: "I do give in to my feelings. I just don't think you're attractive."

When Paul died, no one denied him as a serious mind: there were homages emphasizing his contributions as sociologist, city planner, psychotherapist, linguistic theoretician, political and educational reformer. All mentioned *Growing Up Absurd*; some talked about his diary, *Five Years*, which juxtaposes tracts on creative method with carnal encounters; a few applauded his novels (is that what they are?), *The Grand Piano, The State of Nature, The Holy Terrors*, and *The Dead of Spring*, a tetralogy on an iconoclast's passage through the Empire City. But if he was that rare thing among radicals of the time, an educated poet, no eulogist brought up his poems. A disconcerting number of fans, even among his friends, did not realize he wrote poems.

That was partly his fault. Hardly modest, Paul nevertheless did not stress the sheer variety of his talents. Like Cocteau, who classified his own output—fiction, movies, plays, ballets, drawings, paintings, criticism, and pure life—under the one heading *Poésie*, so Paul called himself a humanist. "Everything I do has the same subject," he would say, a quite European nonspecialist attitude for one so American—or rather, so New Yorkish.

Yet his poetry is not the same as his other works. It rises higher, and will be viewed as individual long after his thrilling but didactic ideas, pragmatic and doctrinaire, are absorbed, as they already have been, into our anonymous culture.

His poems, a third of them, complain loudly of his loneliness, how no one returns his love. (The love, physical and moral, addressed perhaps twelve people a day!) Yet he wasn't a particularly giving person, except as therapist. When the objects of his affection grew up, he lost interest. I went to bed unsentimentally with Paul as long as he wanted but never initiated it. He smelled of his baggy sweater and pipe smoke. Out of what he thought was duty, he'd make a pass at, say, Shirley, an hour after me. He felt—and was probably right—that humans didn't fuck enough, or with the right relaxed purging pleasure. But he wasn't every man's ideal.

Paul, a couple of years after his son's birth: "Sally and I don't know what to do. Matthew doesn't yet seem interested in masturbating."

To the always circumspect Aaron Copland, meeting him for the first—and last—time at a party: "A lot of cute boys here, don't you think?" Aaron walked away. Paul found him hypocritical.

Let me stress his frivolity, a quality contained in all artists, since all art is made from the contrasts formed by an ability to express relationships between the superb and the silly. Paul's was not the simplistic sexual frivolity of a Mick Jagger, nor the thunderous German-joke frivolity of a Beethoven (whom he adored), but the high-camp, spiritually practical yet sad frivolity of, say, Haydn, Voltaire, Gogol, Auden, Billie Holiday.

Did you know he actually wrote music too? Not very inspired, sort of Brahmsian, and technically childlike. Like fellow composer Ezra Pound, he confused homemade discovery with professionalism, though any well-trained nonentity could have done better. Still, his writing *about* music, critically and philosophically, was less dumb than any layman's since Thomas Mann.

With all his heterogeneity he never became (though for a time it threatened) a pop figure with catch phrases, like McLuhan or Buckminster Fuller. He was too compact for love at first sight.

He was aloof and cool—traits not unusual with philanthropists, beginning with Freud. He never ceased to intimidate me because he was, and remains, The One whose stamp of approval I seek; childhood idols never have clay feet. When the demands of glory grew, his warmth was directed more toward groups than toward individuals. I received his new poems then only through the mail. We had grown so apart that, on phoning in late May of 1972 to ask about his health, I half hoped he wouldn't answer. But he did.

"Should we be worried, Paul?"

"Yes, we should." Yet gently he added: "Nice to hear your voice, kiddo." I sent love to Sally, and we promised ourselves an autumn reunion. But in August he died.

If Paul can die then ànyone can die, even God, and whom can we fall back on now? In 1939 he concluded an epitaph for Freud:

> . . . suddenly dead for all our hopes and fears
> is our guide across the sky and deep,
> this morning a surprise for bitter tears,
> a friendly dream now I am asleep.

Paul Goodman was a household poet, a poet who did not rework verse into Eliotian cobwebs of intricacy but composed on the run, for immediate occasions, in the manner Frank O'Hara would make popular. Two examples:

In 1947 John Myers madly tried to turn Mary's Bar on Eighth Street into another Boeuf sur le Toit. For the opening Paul and I concocted three blues which John and Frank Etherton at 11 p.m. intoned in the styles of Mistinguett and Stella Brooks. Heartbreaking. But hardly the speed of that clientele. Then at 1 a.m. Eugene took over the keyboard of an upright casserole and amid the fumes of laughter and beer performed *Gaspard de la nuit*. Incredibly, that *was* the speed of the clientele. (Those blues today? In the back of a trunk. But maybe the words and music would be the speed of our new clientele!)

Janet Fairbank, that youngish soprano who during the war years gave concerts of new American music, a specialty no less rare then than now, was our sole voice, our outlet. We all collaborated on many a song that Janet sang; indeed, it was she who premiered my setting of Paul's soaring words, "The Lordly Hudson." The evening she died, Paul appeared on my doorstep with a poem. "Here," he said, "make some music out of this." Three short stanzas describe how Janet sang our songs because she loved to sing, how we loved to make up songs for her to sing, how she is now mute and we are dumb. Too soon the final lines evoke Paul Goodman himself, with their question from the impotent survivor confronted with a dying fellow artist:

... If we
make up a quiet song of death,
who now shall sing this song we made
for Janet not, because
(no other cause) she loved to sing?

I did once bring Paul together with Samuel Barber—Redskin and Paleface—probably late in 1947. They were so busy not trying to impress each other that the evening lagged. This took place at Paul's somewhat shabby pad on Ninth Avenue where he lived with Sally. No amenities except books. The oeuvre of the two men was as diametrically opposed as their personalities, Sam all stylishness, Paul rough-and-tumble. Opposites don't always attract. Paul clearly resembles his writing. But does a composer resemble his music?

Words are symbols for what isn't there at the moment. Painting depicts three dimensions in two dimensions. But if music is symbolic or representational, I don't know what of, and I've been dealing with it all my life. Assuming we can define what music "means," what humans are made of, or even the four humors as they pertain to art, then certainly a composer resembles his music, since by definition one cannot exist without the other. Still, biographers often disengage the two, as though the animal source were a necessary evil to be shunned or purified. Art is not True Life, to be sure, but it *is* distilled life, and who else's but the artist's?

I had met Sam that past summer. Once again I was among Copland's flock at Tanglewood, and once again the guest teacher, this time Arthur Honegger, suffered a collapse and had to be replaced. Barber happened to be on the premises—he was touring the Cape and had stopped by for the weekend to hear Koussevitzky conduct his overture to *The School for Scandal*—so he was drafted. Again too that summer were the composers' meetings, and at one of these Sam and I first shook hands. Those Tanglewood bull sessions were knotty, long-winded, theoretic, "meaningful." But Samuel Barber, as America's sole songwriter (a fact that awed me, as well as Danny Pinkham and Bill Flanagan, who were in his class), had access to "real" singers. Avoiding the nonvoiced American specialists with lunatic reputations—the Janet Fairbanks that *we* relied on—he understandably favored divas with big, gorgeous sound boxes. True, he had written "Monks and Raisins" for the bizarre Frijsh (who could deny her?), and soon would be sculpting his *Mélodies passagères* for the one-of-a-kind Bernac (whose link with Poulenc had grand cachet), but they were Europeans. Mainly, however, one then thought of Barber as the composer of

"Nuvoletta" and *Knoxville* for the established Eleanor Steber, even as he would later compose *The Hermit Songs* for the up-and-coming Leontyne Price. Sadly it was not to songs but to stars that the public was and is drawn, and without arias even stars aren't certain magnets. If foreign composer-singer tandems like Poulenc & Bernac or Britten & Pears once had box-office appeal in the United States, the famous home-boy, without an orchestra behind his soloist, did not. When Barber & Price, as pianist and soprano, were offered by Columbia Artists as a package during the early 1950s, they had too few bids to continue. (When Donald Gramm and I were offered as a package by the same management in the 1970s, the only recitals we pulled off were those we got ourselves. Today, even those would be unprocurable: nobody any longer knows, in our philistine world, what a song concert is.)

But back to the bull session. When in deference to the songwriting Sam the question of Song was solemnly broached, how tantalizing to hear him say: "Yes, all composition is difficult, but why song more than 'straight' music? Why the fuss about prosody and diphthongs and declamation and word quantities? Why not write as you speak?" which is the reason vocalists enjoy him, and why my dim guilt was assuaged. When I showed him my analysis of his *Essay* from the previous year, he found it absolutely faultless and (like most analyses) absolutely beside the point.

One hears Sam in his songs as unmistakably as one tastes Julia Child in her recipes, not least because he was himself a true singer. Yet is firsthand knowledge a prerequisite of first-rate work? At parties Sam would, if coaxed, accompany himself—though never in his own music —in some dear goody of yore, "Pale Hands" being a favorite. What he mocked was precisely what he once most "felt," for his own early efforts were close to the bone of Carrie Jacobs Bond. Which explains their popularity on safe recital programs. Despite his classy choice of authors (Prokosch, Hopkins, Horan, Lorca, Rilke), his most famous songs lack profile; they could have been written by anyone. I once proclaimed the paradox that Barber has no identifiable style, yet has identifiably influenced Chuck Turner.

At Tanglewood Sam was not interested in his female students, nor in fact the heterosexual ones (and they were, oddly, in the majority). He took a shine to Bill Flanagan. Also, I suppose, to me. We had the habit of gathering for martinis at the Lenox Hotel's garden bar at six, of listening to the church bells while Sam spoke magically of the Angelus in Rome, his second city, where beauty was unproblematically available, and of skipping the evening concert in favor of some roadside restaurant. One midnight we all went swimming in the violent moonlight. I was adamant about not taking my clothes off for the plain reason, comprehensible to any male of any age, that cold water shrinks the sex, and I didn't want to be judged accordingly. (I am, in erection, far better than average hung—let's leave it at that.) Sam nevertheless phoned in the fall to invite me for a weekend at Capricorn.

Capricorn was the house in Mount Kisco which he shared, and would continue to share for years, with Gian Carlo Menotti, and with a (to me) unexplained poet named Robert Horan. Sam picked me up at the entrance to Juilliard and off we hied. Capricorn seemed the ultimate luxury, rambling and isolated, with studios at each end of the property where Gian Carlo could write his Catholic dramas like *The Saint of Bleecker Street* and Sam his Protestant tracts like *Prayers of Kierkegaard* without there being internecine friction. Perhaps Robert Horan was the buffer. Horan, known as Kinch, turned out to be hand-some and heavy drinking. He played the host on our arrival and remained—soft-spoken and alluring—for the evening meal, after which he left for the city and I never saw him again. Gian Carlo was away. Leaving me and Sam to play cat-and-mouse for forty-eight hours.

Have I already·said it? I'll say it again: I can't sleep with famous people. Or for that matter with rich people, or people in power, used to being the center of attention. I have been in bed with four *Time* covers—Lenny Bernstein, Tennessee Williams, Noël Coward, and John Cheever (included among three thousand proportionately anonymous souls, including one woman)—and I performed out of a combination of duress and politeness. However, I grow uncomfortable when in other people's memoirs I read of this sort of thing (maybe this will be excised when the time comes), especially when embellished by the writer's smug sense of his charisma, boasting how he wouldn't put out for some star. Still, it's integral to this story to say that Sam wanted to and I didn't, so we didn't. He was thereafter standoffish in my regard.

I had the impression—we all did—that Sam Barber in his heyday was the only musician in a land of iconoclast cowboys for whom elegance was the defining virtue; when he left us in 1980 at seventy he took with him, for better or worse, a concept of craft stemming from that virtue. Now insofar as it means control and taste, is *elegance* quite the noun for the Barber's art? Does one confound the product with the person, well wrought in shape but overwrought in content, coolly French on top but Brahmsian beneath? And insofar as it means aloof and unruffled, is elegance actually the term for the person, and is his product so inevitably suave? Listen again to the First Symphony, frantic and—if you will—ill-bred throughout its nineteen minutes, or to the trivial and vulgar *Excursions* for piano. Then think back to the man himself, as Apollonian a creature who ever stopped chatter on entering a room, as canny and cultured a companion as one could desire on his good days, yet with on occasion the cutting manners that only those born rich can get away with (or think they can) and with the *terre-à-terre* opportunism that every composer, rich or poor, has harbored since before Haydn. Yes, Sam resembled his music, quite literally, as Paul resembled his writing.

Paul wrote a beautiful text for me to set to music according to terse specifications given by Danny Pinkham. Danny wanted something, about ten minutes long, that he could premiere in his Boston church that autumn. Paul, heartened by my previous settings of his words (notably "The Lordly Hudson" and the little opera), had written the campy poems screeched, with me at the piano, by Myers & Etherton, first at Mary's Bar and then at The Little Casino: "Jail-Bait Blues," "Bawling Blues," and "Near Closing Time." These were, so to speak (or so to sing), Reichian ditties:

> So often near closing time
> desire overbrims
> and comes off in the head
> instead of in the limbs

Now Paul felt that his pseudo-Bible style would be apt for the Pinkham commission. This was *A Sermon on Miracles*, which I arranged for unison chorus with four solo voices and small string orchestra. The performance, on November 30 in Boston's Second Church, was a great reward: the music sounded as I'd dreamed. (Among the soloists was Janet Hayes, blond and stagey, whom I would come to know better in Paris.) After the postconcert party I got drunk in the wilds of Cambridge and awoke in a sordid hotel bed with an Irish bartender who had a cleft chin.

I used to see Sam most frequently at George Bemberg's at 24 West Fifty-fifth, where we would dine *à trois* and sing our songs at each other. Before I sailed for France in 1949 Sam tried to coach me in how to behave with this or that countess once I got there. What would I be doing with countesses? I wondered.

Diary: Paris, 1950. Barber loathes the imputations of the serial elite. He persists in addressing the perplexed René Leibowitz as Mr. Ztiwobiel. "Well, if a composer can't recognize his own name in retrograde, how can his listeners be expected . . ."

1958. The day he won the Pulitzer for *Vanessa*, Sam Barber came, along with me, to dine at Lee Hoiby's. "Have you heard," I asked, "that Poulenc's writing a monologue for Callas on *La voix humaine?*"

"Francis is an opportunist," said Sam.

"Still, what a swell idea."

"Because Maria's an opportunist too—she can't stand other singers on stage."

"But still, it's a swell idea. Admit."

"You think so because you're an opportunist. Everybody says so."

"Yes, but still—wouldn't you have wanted her for *Vanessa?*" And I got up, collected my coat, and left. Before the elevator arrived, Sam came out to the hall and sort of apologized.

"It's just," said he, "that you punctured me where I was most vulnerable."

Between these dates, 1950 and 1958, we met often in Paris, usually chez Henri-Louis de la Grange, a mutual friend, though I took him also to Marie-Laure's, and they hit it off, more or less. Early in the decade I was seated on the terrace of the Flore with my girlfriend, Heddy de Ré, both very high on *fine à l'eau*, when Sam and Virgil and two or three others materialized at the table next to ours. For no reason I called Sam a shit, and for a year was ashamed at this gratuitous folly. I wrote a song for him—one of six ecologues on poems of John Fletcher, and mailed him a dedicated copy. He acknowledged this decently, and never referred to my misbehavior. He was a great solace, too, when I was in anguish about my Italian friend, P., whom Sam knew and liked.

In New York during the 1960s he came to dine chez moi two or three times. In the 1970s I don't remember seeing him except at parties, where he was icy. Like many, he liked at first, and then didn't like my *Paris Diary*, which caused a flurry—so innocent now it seems! —among those in the closet. Sam was outraged (according to Chuck Turner) because I recounted an anecdote he'd told me years before, maybe at Tanglewood. "When you get to Italy," he had said, "you'll find the Italians acquiescent. But even when they say I love you they still want to be paid. A friend of mine was hiking in the most remote region of the mountains above Torino when he came across a peasant boy who'd never seen the city. They made love. After which the boy asked for money." That's all.

If I declare that although I in a sense am among Sam's audience, I never quite cared for the person, nor did I need the music: both were too rarefied, unpredictable, neurotic, and, well, too *elegant* for me to deal with. No sooner is that last sentence written than I'm assailed by contradictions. If I do not need Sam's sounds, how to account for his ever-haunting "Anthony O'Daly" smiling through my most-sung song, "The Silver Swan," which no one has pointed out in the forty-five years since that swan was hatched? For what reason have I kept over the years those dozen letters I now reread, finding in each a generosity somehow mislaid?

In 1978 a disc was issued on New World Records called *Songs of Samuel Barber and Ned Rorem.* The liner notes by Philip Ramey included separately taped interviews with each of us answering parallel questions.

Ramey to Barber: "What do you think of Ned Rorem's songs?"

Barber: "I like one, 'The Lordly Hudson.'"

Ramey to me: "And Samuel Barber's [songs]?"

Me: "Quaintly enough, I find Barber's songs the weakest part of his otherwise strong output. They work, but they work in a turn-of-the-century way. They present few problems, and that's why singers sing them. Understand that I'm not criticizing Barber's language, only his tradition."

On this disc is Barber singing his own *Dover Beach,* recorded in 1933. Why am I covered with gooseflesh when the live voice of this dead acquaintance fills the room, as now it does, lending a patina of precious antiquity to the furniture?

If frequent contact plus sharing of victory and woe are what make for friendship, then I'm not the one to recall Sam Barber in any formal fashion. We moved in different circles. Also, being almost the only ones whose catalogues were colored by Song, that fact in turn was colored—at least for me—by a certain rivalry. One may question the propriety of one composer publicly discussing another, especially when that other lies underground.

My falling away from Paul Goodman (beyond the fact that he grew less interested as I grew more independent and lost my baby fat) stemmed from an incident. *A Meeting in the Lobby* is the title of a skit he devised in 1947 for me to set for a now-vanished soprano. I scoffed to someone about Paul's marginal notes on how the music should be composed, saying that he erred as poets often will by "helping out" their musician, and that anyway he seemed to have thrown the words together. The "someone" told this to Paul who (maybe rightly) felt it was not for me to broadcast how he worked, that the skit emerged from special experience, and that I was ungrateful to the very person who had put me on the map. Actually Paul was no more known than I in those days, and if "The Lordly Hudson" is now the famous title of his collected poems, it was then strictly a song by me, not us. But I *was* ungrateful. I learned far more from him than he from me.

In *Seven Little Prayers,* my first cycle on texts of PG, I was still confusing prosody with "gracious sounds." For example, knowing that long open vowels are easier to sing high than tight *e*'s and *u*'s, I took the word *son* as an arbitrary climax to one of the prayers.

Paul: "Why did you put *son* on that long loud B? Because you knew the poem was really about my daughter? Or because it's the same as *sun* shining high? Or from love or resentment of me? Why?"

"Because it's a good word to sing high."

"That's no answer."

Paul actually had a pretty fair ear, but was somehow too—well—too *intelligent* to let his ear lead, rather than follow, his idea. Thus in his fiction when a character speaks colloquially, any given phrase rings true, but the sequence of phrases degenerates into didactic philosophy. Elsewhere, as in chapter 4 of *The Dead of Spring,* the conversation is silent, and the respect in his description of manual labor is so gently contagious that it's hard to imagine such writing outside a novel. Paul did not follow the rules, he made them, and he made them only after the fact of finding them in his own pieces.

His theater does not work. He knew all about it except how to make it.

Nearsighted but refusing glasses (they aren't medical), he continually crashed into the furniture. He did not think women equal to men.

The difference as guru between Allen Ginsberg and Goodman is that one catered to the feelings of the young while the other catered to their minds. Obviously Ginsberg won out.

I can't recall ever seeing Paul Goodman and Marc Blitzstein in the same room, though they can't help but have met at one of the billions of parties we all were giving. As lurid left-wingers the two would have had more in common ideologically than with the blander Sam Barber, yet Barber's and Blitzstein's origins were akin.

Like Barber, Blitzstein was raised in a well-off pre–World War I Philadelphia milieu, but veering thence in opposite directions, Sam toward the anxieties of mandarin individuals (Cleopatra, Prokosch, Kierkegaard, Vanessa), Marc toward the collective woes of Everyman.

During the Second War they did both serve in the military, resulting in a jingoistic bomb from each one: Barber's Second Symphony, known as the *Night Flight,* which he finally withdrew, and Blitzstein's *Airborne Symphony,* which finally withdrew itself. Beyond this coincidence, they had nothing in common. That one was Episcopalian, the other Jewish, surely figured.

A more cogent comparison is between Pasolini and Blitzstein, both upper-crust Communists murdered by rough trade, the first in the outskirts of Rome by one of the very *ragazzi di vita* he had spent a lifetime nurturing, the second on the isle of Martinique by three seafarers of the very type he had spent a lifetime defending. Though communism may have been a mere touristic escape for each man's life, it nonetheless formed the core of each man's art. "A scholar and a master of the Italian language, [Pasolini] picked up no grounding at all in the life of the proletariat," wrote Clive James recently. "He never did a day's manual labor then or later.... This is standard for revolutionary intellectuals and can't usefully be called hypocrisy, since if there is such a thing as proletarian consciousness then it is hard to see how any proletarian could escape from it without the help of the revolutionary intellectual—although just how the revolutionary intellectual manages to escape from bourgeois consciousness is a problem that better minds than Pasolini have never been able to solve without sleight of hand."

As for Marc, how might he have reacted to the "liberation" of Communists thirty years after his death? By seeing them as eager consumers, no better than they should be, "born of poor but dishonest parents"? Today we perceive a lopsided focus in certain visions of the golden past. Marc retained that focus to the end, though his friend Lillian Hellman wrote: "A younger generation ... look upon the 1930s radical and the 1930s red-baiter with equal amusement. I don't much enjoy their amusement, but they have some right to it."

Like most young composers in the 1940s I knew Blitzstein's worth solely from hearsay. Textbooks were full of him as America's embodiment of Brecht's "art for society's sake"; he himself decreed that the creative artist must "transform himself from a parasite to a fighter." A parasite on whom? I wondered. A fighter for what? If I was not political, I *was* impressed by those who were, like Lenny Bernstein and Aaron Copland, who constantly sang Marc's praises, making me feel guilty. Even Virgil Thomson, a sometime foe of Blitzstein's and an aristocrat to the toenails, had declared years earlier: "*The Cradle Will Rock* is the gayest and most absorbing piece of musical theater that the American Left has inspired ... long may it remind us that union cards can be as touchy a point of honor as marriage certificates."

Beyond the force of these dynamos, Marc had the added mystery of *one who had been there*—of one now unavailably away in the wars. The music was no longer played but the spirit held firm.

Then suddenly he returned, a hero in uniform, and Lenny premiered, in April of 1946, the ambitious *Airborne Symphony,* with Orson Welles as narrator, eighty male members of Robert Shaw's Collegiate Chorale, and Leo Smit as pianist with the New York City Symphony. Who was I to express a purely artistic dissension among these committed intellectuals? Yet I was appalled. What I intuited then I affirm today: the piece was patriotic smarm. Admittedly I have an allergy to melodrama—to, that is, speechified music—unless the verbalism is tightly rhythmicized, as Walton so cannily rhythmicized Sitwell's *Façade.* (If the sung voice is the most musical of instruments, the spoken voice is the least.) Thus masterworks like Debussy's *Martyre,* Stravinsky's *Perséphone,* Honegger's *Jeanne* go against my grain even as I revel in their sonic superstructure and fairly classy texts. But Blitzstein's text for *Airborne* gives new meaning to overstatement, a *Reader's Digest* tribute to our air force, preachy, collegiate, unbuttressed, as Copland's corny *Lincoln Portrait* is buttressed, by a less-than-trite musical background. The few nonembarrassing moments in the score are too close for comfort to *Histoire du soldat,* and in the libretto, to Whitman's diary. Bernstein was to appropriate Blitzstein's sentimentality—the boyish belief in Man's essential Good—and to use it better. "Better" always means better tunes. (Of music's five properties—harmony, counterpoint, rhythm, color, and melody— melody is sovereign; without a sense of contagious melody a composer is not a composer.)

Yes, a great work is one you can never get used to; but I grew used immediately to the *Airborne Symphony,* which went in one ear and out the other with no trace of residue.

Yet on that famous July evening in Barrington four months later, when Marc played and sang for us with such tough and telling charm, suddenly everything fell together, the pudding was in the eating, the components of his art meshed. Harmony churned, counterpoint spoke, the rhythm was catchy and the color luminous, the tunes came across, all precisely because they spewed from Marc's own body, then lingered like a necessary infection to love and not get used to, at least for one evening. Next morning, if the songs were gone, Marc's fragrance remained.

During the fall, as a student at Juilliard, where to qualify for a degree one had to take sociology, I phoned Marc for an interview about his ideas on Art and Society. What do I recall of our talk that November afternoon in the one-room flat at 4 East Twelfth, where he lived until he died, I who felt no relationship with—much less a need for divert-ing—the masses? I recall that Marc called Poulenc a sissy. That he called Cocteau a *true* artist, while claiming that anyone who could turn a fable of Love and Death into something as "chic" as *L'éternel retour* (all the rage then in New York), especially by labeling the love potion "poison," was hardly a *great* artist. That all music to him was political. That he looked like Keenan Wynn. That he said: "Admit it, you didn't really come here to interview me for your class."

During the next sixteen years we were friends, even when far away, friends, that is, as much as quasi mentor and reluctant pupil can pla-tonically be. I sense that, while never saying so, Marc always misguid-edly felt I was too much the prey of the upper class to write important music. As for the lower class, I never saw that, except for sex, Marc was a mingler there. He liked good food and drink and shunned the reality of deprivation.

Why, I recently asked a person who knew them both, was Lenny such a devoted admirer of Marc? Because, said the person, Marc was a failure. Well, Lenny worshiped Aaron too, and Aaron was a success. Yes, but Aaron was that much older (b. 1900 as against Marc b. 1905), and a monolithic idol for us all. True, there are cases where two friends, one famous and one not, are switched overnight in the world's eye, as Lenny was switched in rapport with composer Paul Bowles, and later with Marc. Bowles went on to plow (successfully) other fields, while Marc persevered in Lenny's shade. But if Marc could ever have been deemed a failure, he is not that today, and his renaissance, as well as his historicity (he's been gone for nearly two generations), now allows him to be judged in perspective.

The first of his few letters came after I had moved to France in 1949, and was in reply to what must have been that bane of all "older" composers: a young composer's request for a recommendation.

July 14, 1949   Dear Ned: Yes, you may use my name as reference for a Guggenheim. . . . I envy you Paris, and I remember that gone feeling. Me, I just sit chained to the desk, getting the orchestration of the new opera done in time for a deadline. . . . As ever, (signed) Marc Blitzstein

The new opera was *Regina,* his first in twelve years, which was premiered four months later. Eight years later, this time to New York, came this:

November 8, 1957   Dear Ned: I was charmed and impressed with the tribute, and with the quality of the song. But when you go to the trouble of making a fine piece and dedicating it to me, why the hell don't you present it in person? My love   Marc

The "tribute" was a setting of Paul Goodman's "Such Beauty as Hurts to Behold," which I would have felt worthy of Marc. Earlier that year I had written a one-act opera, *The Robbers,* to my own text based on Chaucer's "The Pardoner's Tale." Marc was dismayed—he said I'd got lost in "libretto land" with my arch and archaic locutions. He undertook to rewrite the entire text: without changing a note of the music he refashioned each verbal phrase so that it fell more trippingly on the tongue. This was a voluntary two-day job for which I thanked him with the little song.

Jan. 6, 1959   Dear Ned: Here is the piece, and a note to Bill Flanagan, which I beg you to deliver. I despair of reaching you by phone; my hours are a mess of disorganization. . . . Love, Marc

The "piece" was a 500-word essay, "On Two Young Composers," contributed at my prodding to launch a program of songs by me and William Flanagan (whom he'd never met) that took place on 24 February. The first general paragraph, beginning "Songs are a tricky business" (even more apt today than then), is wise, original, and bears reprinting. Of Bill he concludes: "A certain modesty dwells in his music; it should not be confused with smallness." Of me: "Ned Rorem makes thrusts, each of his songs is a kind of adventure. . . . It is a long time since anyone brought off the grand style, outsized sweeping line, thunder and all, that marks 'The Lordly Hudson.' He will one day write an impressive opera." (So concerned was he about "an impressive opera" that he brought me together with his beloved nephew, Christopher Davis, who had made a libretto called *Mario* for the occasion. Nothing panned out. But Christopher's powerful and responsible writing—on capital punishment, on the sociology of rape, on his uncle— has held my interest over the years, and our "impressive opera" may yet be born.)

Libby Holman, torch singer and art lover, had contributed financially to the 24 February event (the first of a series of "Music for the Voice by Americans" which Bill Flanagan and I produced in those years). She had become a friend. I was young enough still to be dazzled by my legendary seniors, and smug enough to feel a power when introducing, for the first time, one of these seniors to another. Libby had never met Marc but would perhaps have enjoyed playing the role of Pirate Jenny in one of the myriad productions of *Threepenny Opera* which at the time had made Marc (ironically, because he was only the translator, and because the late Kurt Weill, a homophobe, never cared for Marc's "cashing in") a rich star. One evening I brought them together in a Village bistro. Libby, exonerated from maybe having murdered her husband years before, had inherited that husband's fortune but spent a fat chunk of it on civil-rights groups, especially after her only son died—as Paul Goodman's son died—while mountain climbing. There now I sat, silent, as these two conversed intensely with their violent theatricality, their true unusualness. There I sat with her who had killed and who would later kill herself, and with him who would be killed.

Libby never once mentioned Pirate Jenny. Marc paid the bill.

Soon after, it was his turn to go to Paris, this time with *my* letters of recommendation.

August 6, 1959   Dear Ned: It was a glorious trip, from all points of view —including *amours* and the business aspect. And I want to thank you for your letters—although I never got to use the Auric or the Veyron-Lacroix; and Marie-Laure, after a series of *contretemps,* wired me to come see her in Hyères, which I couldn't. . . . I've tried to reach you by 'phone; now Golde tells me you are in Wis. I have decided to accept the song-cycle commission from Alice Esty (who tells me your Roethke songs are nearly finished, you dog); and it is in line with that that I write you now. . . . Did you make some kind of deal with Roethke regarding the commission? and if so, what? Do you mind telling me? I want to do the right thing; at the same time I am puzzled as to how to share the commission with the poet (of existing poems), if at all. So do write me here, outlining your own procedure in the matter. And love. Marc.

Alice Esty, an adventuresome soprano, commissioned, between 1959 and 1966, three composers a year to write cycles for her, starting with Marc, me, and Virgil T. My cycle was on poems of Theodore Roethke, who sent me several lively letters, not at all about esthetics, but setting forth in canny paragraphs exactly what he wanted in residuals, and asking for equal billing on the printed score. (We met only once, not at the concert where the songs were premiered but at the party afterward, where he showed up drunk.) I don't know what kind of "deal" Marc finally made with *his* poet, E. E. Cummings, but his group of seven songs, *From Marian's Book,* is, for my metabolism, his very best work. Just as Tennessee Williams's best stories are better than his best plays, precisely because he knows that those stories will never be known by the vast philistine matinee public and can thus be impuniously as convoluted and intimate as he feels, so Marc's concert songs do not, by definition, pander to the big audience. Not that such pandering is in itself wrong; only when an intellectual aims for the hoi polloi. Marc was an intellectual where Lenny Bernstein was not (although he tried to be and was, in fact, smarter than many an intellectual). Lenny, like Poulenc, wrote the same *kind* of music for his sacred as for his profane works; Marc tempered his language according to whom he was addressing.

> February 24, 1960   Dear Ned: A sweet wire, for which I thank you. I feel badly that our rehearsals didn't allow me to get to your concert . . . I have just come from Carnegie Hall, where Poulenc stubbed his toe flatly in "La Voix Humaine." A comic "camp" is bearable; a serious "camp" is utterly phony. Love. Marc.

Clearly Marc was on the German side of my universal spectrum. Morris Golde had, as with Virgil, become closer to Marc than I was on a purely social level, offering no tension or rivalry but being that ideal fan, the Maecenas *désintéressé*. Morris was—is—a go-between, and very useful when I got involved with the Brecht-Weill estate.

> June 29, 1960   Dear Ned: How good to hear from you. The name Yaddo awoke all sorts of fine memories. Do give my warmest to Elizabeth [Ames] and any others who remember me. . . . "Jasager" *is* a beautiful piece. As to copies of the piano-vocal score: I'm sure Lehman Engel must have at least one. He did it way back in the thirties, with the Henry Street Settlement chorus, I think; and I seem to remember it was in English, so he . . .
>   . . . Incidentally, what about the Brecht estate? They'll raise a fit if it's known that an "unauthorized" translation has been made and used, even if noncommercially. Lenya, I have found to my sorrow, isn't enough when it's a Brecht-Weill work. . . .
>   I had Shirley Rhoads to my place for a swim yesterday. She is fine, still living (according to her) in a dump, this time in Lobsterville on the other end of this divine island. Maybe sometime in August you'd like to come visit me for a couple of days? Although I warn you I'll be lousy company; all work and swimming, that's me this summer. The opera is hard, hard. I do nearly twelve hours a day. I suppose I'll look back on this period of struggle with love and envy. All affection.

That would have been mailed to Yaddo. The opera he speaks of was the uncompleted *Sacco and Vanzetti*. References to Kurt Weill's *Der Jasager* concerned my project of producing it at the University of Buffalo. This I eventually did, with my own translation, and with nobody's permission.

Two years later it was Marc who was in Yaddo, I in New York. I planned in February to come to Yaddo, which would have meant my taking over Marc's room there, but changed my mind, remaining in the city instead to rehearse for another of the American song concerts with Bill Flanagan. From Yaddo, then, came this postcard, the last written communication I had from Marc.

Feb. 22, 1962   Dear Ned: Thanks for the aviso. I shall probably stay on, as Elizabeth has asked me to. But I must come into town for some days: probably around March 18-19. Will you be seeable? Work goes fine, if slowly. I wish I could come to your concert, no soap. I enjoyed the leaflet —but I wish you and Bill would stop those arty-arty Harper's Bazaar photos. Still, it's your face, and a beauty too. My love to Bill and you. Marc.

I have no copies of any letters I may have sent to Marc. But before he left for Martinique I made this entry in my diary:

3 October 1963. Last night the Rémys came to dine, with Shirley and Marc Blitzstein. Marc gets pugnacious after two drinks, interpreting virtually any remark by anyone as either approbation of or a threat to some dream version of the Common Man who hasn't existed in thirty years. But the Rémys were bewitched, having never encountered this particular breed of American, probably because Marc is a breed of one, who, like John Latouche in the old days, when on his best behavior, is the most irresistibly quick man in the world.

I never saw him again. Three weeks later he left for Fort-de-France in Martinique, and eleven weeks after that he was dead. On 22 January 1964, the world received the news, via *The New York Times* front page, announced as an auto accident. Next day it was learned he had been set upon by three Portuguese sailors who, with drunken promises of sex, lured him into an alley where they left him moneyless, naked, battered, and screaming.

Beyond the horror and dejection, how did I react to Marc's death? With a sort of surprise? He had led, on his special terms, an organized and exemplary life and was critical of those who hadn't. With me he was avuncular, and vaguely protective esthetically and hygienically: Don't listen to too much Ravel; be sure to do this or that after sex with strangers. This grown-up, this model—how could he have . . . well, *allowed* himself to be murdered? And in midstream. His opera was definitely scheduled for the Met (although Bing is said to have asked, Were Sacco and Vanzetti lovers, like Romeo and Juliet?). Again the diary:

27 January 1964. Except for Bill Flanagan, whom I see every day, Marc was the only composer I frequented *as a composer,* someone to compare notes with. When we'd finish a piece we'd show it to each other, as in student days, hoping for praise, getting practical suggestions. Our language, on the face of it, would seem to be the same (diatonic, lyric, simple). In fact, we barked up very different trees. Marc was nothing if not theatrical, and precisely for that he showed me how the element of theater was integral even to remote forms like recital songs.

Malamud is an author with whose subject matter (Jewish poverty in Brooklyn) I'd seem to have little in common, but with whose *Assistant* I identified wholly. It's discouraging to realize that Marc's best work was his last, *Idiots First,* which he played me just weeks ago. Malamud would have continued to be his ideal collaborator.

My charm, if I have any, is economized for occasion. Marc's was squandered freely. When as a Juilliard student I first knocked on his door for an interview, Marc Blitzstein received me with a—a sort of Catholic Impatience, worn like a cloak, as he sat at his piano criticizing Cocteau for being fashionable. Have been going through my diary of that period, which talks of the slush in the gutters, Marc's postwar indignations, etc. . . .

I've always felt it, of course, but more and more I've come actually to see that happiness not only precedes but accompanies calamity.

I have just listened, without intermission, to the new CD of *Regina,* all 153 minutes of it. Here are some notes taken during that experience:

I am not a reviewer, I am a composer and a sometime critic; but I do read reviews and see how they shouldn't be done. (Is the reviewer's description of a new work, for example, succinct enough to show whether he likes it without his saying "I like it"? Does he describe the work, or the performance of the work?)

Much has been made about Lillian Hellman's continual interference —how she forbade Blitzstein's numerous embellishments on her play. Playwrights, if still alive, can be a thorn in their composer's side (so goes the received opinion); why don't they just shut up, the play will survive on its own, and a composer's domain is a separate dimension. During the lifetimes of Blitzstein and Hellman the opera was never produced as the composer envisioned it. Am I a minority of one in believing Hellman was right about the musicalizing of her play? This first complete version proves that more is less.

When Poulenc expands Bernanos's *Dialogues des Carmélites,* from a filmscript made on Gertrud von Le Fort's German novella the text stays intact, though with an overlay of five ritual numbers from Latin liturgy. Four of these serve as prayers-without-action to close scenes;

Season's Greetings!
John Heliker.

NR sanctified by John Heliker, 1946.

Morris Golde, New
York, 1944.

Docteur Guy Ferrand, Fez,
Morocco, 1949.

3

NR with Janet Fairbank, Lake Geneva, Wisconsin, 1947.

Billie Holiday.

Marc Blitzstein.

David Diamond.

NR with Maggy Magerstadt,
Chicago, 1946.

Aaron Copland's class at Tanglewood, 1946 (NR second from left).

Nell Tangeman, 1948.

From my autograph book (1956–57):
Marc Blitzstein; Robert Veyron-Lacroix; James Baldwin; Kenton Coe, NR, Jean-Pierre Marty, and Aaron Copland; Edward Albee; Samuel Barber; Henri Sauguet; Lukas Foss; postcard signed by Marie-Laure de Noailles, Oscar Dominguez, and Jean Genet; Ben Weber; Francis Poulenc; Truman Capote.

Pencil manuscript, fair copy, and printed publication of 1948 song "The Youth with the Red-Gold Hair," words by Edith Sitwell.

Shirley Gabis and NR, 53 rue de la Harpe, 1945.

Samuel Barber.

Marie-Laure de Noailles, 1949.

17

Jennie Tourel and NR, Venice, 1951.

18

Georges Auric and NR, Hyères, 1953.

Virgil Thomson, William Flanagan, and NR, 1959.

Jean Marais and NR, on Marais's houseboat, 1952.

21

Julius Katchen and NR, Paris, 1951.

22

Paul Goodman.

NR and James Holmes, Nantucket, 1978.

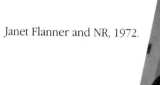
Janet Flanner and NR, 1972.

24

23

NR and Leonard Bernstein, 1986.

the fifth, the final *Salve Regina,* impels the action when, with each crunch of the guillotine, the music modulates upward, thinning out bit by bit, until all sixteen nuns are dead. These interpolations do not "open up" the story; they intensify a basically motionless drama by entering, as only music can, the mute interior of monastic life. The play is tightened into a necessary opera, there is something to sing about.

When Blitzstein expands a densely plotted story about "the little foxes that spoil the vines," the text is widely revised, and with the addition of jazz bands, Negro spirituals, party music, "set" numbers on his own doggerel. The play is loosened into an unnecessary extravagance, because otherwise there would be nothing to sing about. True, certain non-Hellman parts of the piece—such as the "Rain Quartet" and the terrific Dance Suite in Act II—make arguably the best music in *Regina,* just as the Latin choral numbers are the most beautiful parts of *Dialogues;* but where these are extraneous those are integral. Whatever else Hellman's play might be, it's economical: the power of her craft lies in the claustrophobia of greed, her principal characters are hopelessly naughty and unpoetic. Even without the composer's accessories, it's questionable whether any opera can depict unalleviated evil. Music, the most ambiguous of the seven arts, lends sympathy to aberration. Are not Scarpia, Iago, and Claggart, as repainted by Puccini, Verdi, and Britten, raised from mere loathsomeness to a sort of tragic pathos? To hear Regina Giddens and her relatives at song is to defang them, our vines still have tender grapes, and gone is the hard compulsory shell of Hellman.

Add to this that *Regina* is Blitzstein's only large work not designed around his own singing voice, using instead the tessituras of operatic professionals as *Porgy and Bess* uses them, and you have a watery version of the grandiose. Indeed, the tunes and texture are often pure *Porgy,* but without the seductive guile of Gershwin's melody. Nor does Marc, with his frequent spoken interpolations, solve the unsolvable puzzle of how to set pedestrian matters to music. The all-northern cast has great fun whooping it up with southern accents, but their bite is diffused, wilting. Nor can I seize the sense of some of Marc's text (what does the much-repeated "Naught's a naught" mean?), while I cringe at the rhymes ("Greedy girl, what a greedy girl,/Got a greedy guiding star./For a little girl, what a greedy girl you are"), and at the anachronisms ("A bang-up party, and quaint withal,/to call the Hubbards the honored guests at their own ball").

This said, something in the sound grows occasionally touching, echoing a far past, as Monteverdi and Puccini echoed too, except that this past of Marc's is mine too. It is easy to dub him the poor man's

Kurt Weill in his Common Man works; here lies no trace of Weill, but Copland rather, laced with Kern, insolently corny and gorgeously scored. Nor can I deny that I pillaged boldly Birdie's grand lament about the old homestead, Lionnet, for an aria in my own *Miss Julie*. The recurrent "dying fall" of a minor third, rising higher and higher, I owe utterly to Marc.

And I owe to him the recurrent motif (also a drooping minor third, this time fast and nasty) in my 1958 orchestral poem, *Eagles*, filched from *his* orchestral poem, *Lear*, of the previous year. But this borrowing is of a device (Strauss used it too, in *Salomé*), not an esthetic. For Marc did not even superficially influence me.

Which is a good point from which to recapitulate about Marc with some leftover notes:

Lenny Bernstein would never have been quite what he was without the firm example of Marc Blitzstein, yet there's nothing Marc did that Lenny didn't do better. A like analogy may be drawn between what the giant developer, Aaron Copland, borrowed (and glorified) from the midget pioneer, Virgil Thomson—or between Britten and Holst, Debussy and Rebikov, Wagner and Spohr. The greatest masters are not the greatest innovators. Marc Blitzstein, oddly, was not even an innovator, except geographically: what Weill stood for in Germany, Marc stood for in America: the sophisticated soi-disant spokesman of the people. His biggest hit was the arrangement of Weill's "Mack the Knife" which infiltrated even *The Fantasticks*.

Marc, the populist, hung out with aristocrats; Poulenc, the aristocrat, hung out with bartenders.

Good reviews don't make me feel as good as bad reviews make me feel bad, but no reviews are worst of all. This sentiment, which all artists feel (don't they?), was rejected haughtily by Marc. Yet in 1955 when *Reuben Reuben* (on that hopeless subject: lack of communication) was so roundly loathed by the tryout audiences that they spat upon him, Marc was reduced to tears. Out of context I recall the songs, as he sang them to me, through my own tears. Indeed, so moved was I by the composer's wheezy intoning of "The Very Moment of Love," meant for a chorus in an insane asylum, that he copied it out in my little autograph album which lies before me now. That song, like the songs in *Marian's Book*, like the "Letter to Emily" in *Airborne*, like Birdie's aria—they stick in the mind.

Yet I am not a fan. I state this advisedly, knowing most of the music pretty well, and giving the man—because he was a friend—the benefit of the doubt (a benefit not accorded to, say, Glass or Carter). Of the fifty-odd essays I've written over the decades about twentieth-century matters musical, just one—about Virgil Thomson—has been a harsh reaction to the work of a friend. We both lived to rue this. In 1972, after thirty years of mutely despising Thomson's music, and figuring that he as a major critic who dished it out regularly wouldn't mind a taste of his own medicine, I presumed finally to voice my feelings in print. Virgil was not thrilled. When he deigned to speak to me five years later, I vowed never again to weaken a friendship by attacking the vital organs. (Contrary to some opinions, it is not pleasant to write unpleasant reviews.) In retrospect, probably it was better for my soul to have said my say and be remorseful than to have stayed mute and be regretful.

With Marc my ambivalence is by definition removed. I loved the man and hated much of the music, hated the man and loved much of the music. He can't defend himself today, but the music can. That music can shout me down. Still, I can live without it. For artistic if not for moral reasons I am unable to discuss it persuasively, and thus should not perhaps have penned these pages. It's too soon to know if my soul is the better for it.

Great events do not impel great works, but they do alter method and certainly attitude.

Paul Goodman when his son died, stopped.

Samuel Barber when his second huge opera failed, stopped too.

Marc Blitzstein, frantic about his past operatic failures, and drunk with doubt about the wall of impending work, stopped as well, before the fact.

21. Ned's Diary (III)

You're too old to understand.

Yes, but I've been young while you've never been old. Anyone can be young, you just have to get born; but to be old is an accomplishment of sorts—of patience, if nothing else. The old are just as dumb as the young, but slightly cannier, which is why they get the young to fight their wars.

When JH asked me last night if I'd ever had a close male friend who was straight (recalling Copland and Harold Clurman), I realized that the question had never occurred to me. No, I guess not. Though in the old days, when we all saw each other socially every day, many of my male friends were straight—Eugene, Seymour, the husbands of girlfriends.

Are you too young to understand?

The diary of then, with its endless blather about loneliness and liquor, is no worse written than this now, and paints the scene better than "I" could. Samples:

1946

Town Hall with Morris to see (hear) Wanda Landowska. The curtains are half-drawn toward the center, leaving an intimate frame for the harpsichord, the lighted lamp beside it and the Louis XV chair upon which lie seven golden cushions. Landowska enters like a crippled crow, each step measured to last five seconds, and, leering hypnotically at the audience lest they stop clapping, takes a full ninety seconds to reach the chair. She sits down. Then immediately gets up, removes the top cushion and throws it on the floor. Then sits again. In slow motion she extends her right claw toward the keyboard, suspends it for a moment, then withdraws it into her lap. And turns toward us. "Last night," she announces, "Bach came to me and presented the fingerings and registrations of each of his pieces which you will hear tonight. My labors have borne fruit." (Shades of Rosalyn Tureck's first words to the great lady: "We have something in common; we both play Bach." "Yes," answered Landowska, "you in your way, and I in his.") She begins to play. Her introductory speech would have been a pretentious camp had she not delivered the goods. But every minor nuance is the atom of a major scope, while the digital prowess is in such service to the composer, that, yes, we hear Bach speaking.

Then she played Mozart, and *on the piano,* that same D-major Sonata I used to bang out for Belle Tannenbaum. This commenced with a grand rolled chord, and continued with freedom and chutzpah à la Chopin. Who is to say that Chopin himself might not have played Mozart thus? Landowska, after all, is closer to the ways of Chopin than to ours: she was born only thirty years after he died, and he was born only nineteen years after Mozart died. True, 129 years separate Bach's death from Landowska's birth; but styles of playing alternate between the pristine and grandiose from generation to generation, just as styles of composition shift between contrapuntal to harmonic (the latter being simple, the former complex) from era to era. There is no one right way to play a piece; there are as many right ways as there are true performers. There is no progress (or if there is, progress cannot be always equated with the Good), there is only the Eternal Return. Landowska is a true performer, her "act" stops when the play begins. Bach does inhabit her.

• • •

7 May. Tel jour! Telle nuit! Suicide doesn't solve all problems, for this dawn I was rejected again from the arms of the nation. A release, like some clotted growth clipped from the soul. Tribulations are always approached alone. Each of my 3 sweetest loves—David & Maggy & Kubly (with whom last night I had a homemade meal conceived with heroic ingenuity)—failed completely to indulge my apprehensions about the ordeal of this morning; the one for his concern with other problems; the next for her former knowledge of my breastbeating; the third for a chronic fussy boredom of humor. Nor are they pacifists: they felt I *should* be in the army. After the homemade meal David and I went to *Petrushka* (conducted with inelegance and mimed atrociously, the magician especially; and the mob scenes quite lacking in that glistening coordination I remember from the good old days as mass psychology in miniature with that quick change-of-interest from diversion to diversion, jealousies, sweet jubilance and melting disdain) & then across the street with Zeller and Jerry Robbins (the former an angel and an ass, the latter possessor of a winning face and living proof that dancers aren't all incorrigibly ignorant of the "musical line"). How I wish it were an inspiration to return home. . . .

. . . Gauthier remarks that my songs are all concerned with coffins or religion and indeed that's true. Consider King David, of whom I now read, who became *not* more elated but more pessimistically sterile with age. But those were the days when pogroms were a matter of course, as the unseen ankle was blessed by Victoria, and as inversion runs rampant today. . . .

Kubly's art is different from mine, and he defines it too minutely. But all who produce are alike. If loneliness is a prerequisite, it will present itself despite our looking for it. If to write a good book one must be always "observing people" (with the excuse that human nature is being absorbed into technique)—which I don't believe, though for the playwright it may be more imperative than for the painter— then how can he leave them suspended to go off to his loneliness and discuss them, while they continue to resolve themselves more fantastically than he might conceive? . . .

David's been around overly much, disrupting my domesticity and pestering hell out of both of us. Seems drunk & under hypnosis (to a childish degree) to the point of hurling a wine glass (half full!) at me. But he came back 6 hours later to apologize, with Ed [Stringham]. I will not be pulled down by him, he's killed too many already.

• • •

... a certain divineness fires the artist's imagination [but] this is not discoverable in female writers. With Miss Dickenson [sic] as example of much high caliber talent, it's seen that she conceives in miniature, like all women, dealing with small ideas that are part of great ones, but never great in themselves. Is it because she employs short verse —tetrameter—which is coy by definition & bad for music setting? When women venture (I was going to say intrude) into pentameter, or more sophisticated meters, they sound either like Miss Millay whose deplorable sentiments are only slightly disguised in the sonnet, or like Miss Moore whose commendable output is too foolproof (in device) and frigid for grandeur. Women may feel the godly life intensely, but are too subjective, hence cannot be great. Uncontrolled subjectivity is fatal to art. Feminine invention is generalized. Their path is unalterable. They cannot subject or object themselves. They also bear children.

... Tomorrow, off to Tanglewood, thence to Wellesley to hear Bill [Strickland] conduct my *Prayer of David*. Will the summer provide sentiment unerasable in loveliness? I shall miss K. for affinity rises, but I must close green eyes and try to adjust and grow older. For despite the evil wished upon me by all, there is also a wonderful warmth upon ...

Instrumentation is the one craft in which practical experience is dangerous. A composer who spends each semester learning to play badly, one by one, all the instruments of the orchestra, will compose according to his own limitations, not according to his theoretic fancy. Even if he learns to play the instruments well, it goes without saying he can't play them all at once. So what use is his knowledge when he comes to orchestrate?

In destroying Nazis, were we attempting to kill what we suffered as our own evils?

... Repentance has the longevity of a hangover.

Now Teru and Allela are both dead. (I remember a year & ½ ago introducing these two), and Kubly passed a straight-jacketed night in Bellevue. A moody universe, and a violent mother.

"... for so hard I think on man/the thought crumbles into absolute un-Nature ..."

I don't like *Peter Grimes* anymore, nor Messiaen either. Flash in the pan stuff, G. Perle calls it.

11 November. Early this afternoon Paul Goodman stopped by to see me for the first time in a year, and we went for some coffee while I told him my 2 dreams of last night, one about copulation with a police dog, a new baby brother!—the other about a 3rd degree trick of firing a rifle into the rectum of the victim, instilling ferocious pain but leaving the period-till-death uncertain—not telling him (lying) that the 2nd one's subject was he himself—after which he left, but promised (tho not shyly) to return tomorrow nite at 10.

The Penal Colony petrified me. Temporarily . . . am convinced that should I ever approach a significant penetration (no reference to Paul's advice for alienation of infantilism) it will be alone in vocal setting. . . . The *Cembalo Concertino* in form, and in negotiation of the instrument's virtues. . . . Ralph [Kirkpatrick] is indeed surprised and pleased, reading it for me stylishly, but does not pretend to other than intellectual comment. But then, since my shallow profundity shall never be realized except through the voice, I shall confine my soul's commitments (like all Frenchmen) to a tiny sequence (allowing the poet to worry before me on the ultimate forms of my larger endeavors), and should I succeed, thru enterprise, to an even slightly enviable technique, my prolific output will none-the-less (in other than programmatic music) be constructed on folk tunes or some such (which they say is valid) to amuse the passerby. Having thus rationalized my misgivings, social and inspiration, I shall go out.

The Pauls, Callaway and Goodman, are eminently lovable. The second could have my whole heart. As we said tonite no inhibitions can occur for me where respect's absent (i.e., for the brainy! i.e., my smug lack of chagrin at the $7 whore-payment) but where the playmate is a lettered person the liaison may be regarded—& *during* the act— literally, no matter how heart-felt the passion. Accordingly I can't but feel, enigmatically, that the sexual—true—intellectual is making fun of me (tho not Paul who's an angel utterly—"destroyed utterly," as he declared after twice emitting, & with what pleasant scent). Hence the writer has the better Out: for can a Reminiscence (the most cherished of all sensations) be reported accurately in a piece of music, or on a canvas?

I compose what I need to hear because nobody else is doing it. Yet I feel guilty about what I do best—setting words to music. Because it comes easily, meaning naturally, I feel I'm cheating.

. . .

Thanksgiving. Back from Philadelphia the 2nd time this week. *The Long Home* [at Washington Cathedral] was beautiful and moving even if the Theater Inc. people and Ballet Society don't like my music. Mother went too, bustling about like Jenny Petherbridge. In myself I find a disarming similarity to Prince Mishkin—though my questionable qualities are indistinguishable from Natashya Fillipovna's.

[*17 December, after playing a recital with violist Enrico (?)*] Except for the ceaseless languid snow, Stamford, and the bus trip to it, was unbearable. Each little town identical to the next and recalls the anonymity of the one in *The Killers.* The Empire City becomes an isthmus of coherence. My conduct fractious as it unfortunately always is with hicks who hold no physicality for me. But my stage comportment exemplary & I'm 50 bucks to the better. And love sprang eternal from glances at the daily unknowns in the small hotel dining rooms.

Landowska phones out of the blue. Christopher [Lazare] gave her my number. . . . I visit her with the *Concertino da camera* under my arm. She is the mesmerizing witch we've seen so often on Town Hall's stage. To Danny Pinkham her first words had been:
"Jeune homme, vous avez l'air bien sympathique. Est-ce que vous êtes pédéraste?"
"Oui, madame."
"Très bien. Maintenant, quant à la musique."

To me: "Grab my hair and pull." I do. "Now don't go telling people I wear a wig." This quite affably. Like a strikingly ugly cat who has swallowed an indigestible canary, but won't admit it, she speaks gutturally of various things which I can't understand, staring at me fixedly all the while. Then sitting in an armchair next to the piano, feet propped on an adjacent stool, score in her lap, she commands: "Play." So I play, messily, the long harpsichord piece on the piano. She says my French accent sounds good, and that my sensitivities are French, which, coupled with my phenomenal memory, paves a way.
There are those who sleep not for the tactile, but as a social function to promote hesitant egocentricity.

1947

2 January—The New Year. Three days of suicidal chaos, verbal demands for death. Paul always does wonders for me with his saintly element, and his new little pamphlet of poems. Eating offends me. Our bodies are smashed easily. Paralyzing sensation to lift the receiver of a ringing phone and say hello to silence, but to know an ear is listening out there.

I fear sleeping for nightmares.

Prefer the Russian idiot to Camus', though he's no nihilist.

Those few of whose conversation I cannot get enough see me mostly as "a friendly sort." How is it? I want 3 dear friends. But I feel good, am writing. My publications [two psalms, Associated Music Publishers] look nice enough, though there was no thrill involved. And it's pleasant to fix my own meals (a momentary but complete and blissful loss of connection with the world) in my own room, which is warm.

Later. HK now says he loathes me with "the profoundest of human hate" (which is obvious). I dislike the word enemy. Incessant proximity is dangerous. . . . His destruction is only partly my blame. I'm not of Wagner's magnitude.

Got robbed again last night: this time by an Italian baseball player with shoulders like the golden bull of Egypt, who took my new sweater & all my change—promising to return everything. The latins and the jews between them are draining me dry. . . .

. . . drinking over-much lately so that I can't even hear an approximation of what I play on hungover-Janet-mornings. For reasons of suicide prevention, it's imperative to retain my pretty features or become psychotic—the opposite from what I am—without the O-so-superficial insistence of Italian praise.

Picking my nose this morning was like applying a small sharp shovel to a shredded velvet carpet, the dehydration. E. didn't mind, even gave me a dollar. He's a longshoreman from Jersey and not articulate. David says my tastes are masochistic but I feel even the cruelest people need loving. I have half a bottle of Calverts left, but as usual spent all my money again. I'll stop drinking now for a few days to finish the organ piece for Paul [Callaway]. Everyone comes around but Tony.

Monday night, 4 a.m. Yes yes yes I have come to that state I feared most. Nothing, sex, nothing is so important as alcohol. And yet coming back here alone I don't drink. How I envy. And overcome the hideous shyness drinking, drinking.

Thurs. . . . when I contemplate suicide as I do daily there's an element of I'll show them. I don't know why I want to do it. I've been drunk every night for a week. All I want is to cry. I'm jealous and dishonest. If I don't get screwed soon I'll collapse. Yet I won't allow it. I don't like people, really. When I go out tonight I don't care if I come back dead.

Tues. Was interrupted (at 3 a.m.) in the above by Eddie's arrival directly after the soldier left. As far as returning dead, of course I didn't, but we all went to see Billie Holiday & I practically went down on her in front of everyone because of that extravagant beauty, but I only played with her legs for in her shallow grandeur is an austere intimacy. I find Alfonso [Ossorio] quite charming.

So of course I hinted my troubles to Mother & she is worried. Having been raging drunk for over ⅔ of the time for the past 3 weeks, I've almost completely lost my looks. To stabilize the family I say that I'll discipline myself without the aid of an analyst....

Amongst those *we* know, suicide is more frequent than insanity—neuroses vs. psychosis. 2 cases for freedom: *Jude the Obscure* and *The Function of the Orgasm.*

Even the soap is dirty!

Horrid smell of sausages 12 hours ago. Harlem! They stole my money. ...*If only my family would die* so that I too could with a clear conscience ... when sober all I can do is sleep.

When Picasso comes to an impasse he does not borrow from friends but reverts to origins. Do I? Is the style a friendly one? Or is Monteverdi here with me, more than a friend?

I am the only caricature. Why are you others so flippant? I take you seriously.

I will not pass Bacchus. The other vices, though less harmful, are less sociable....

Quick photo vs. slow screen. My conflict.

She (my dear friend S.G.) declares herself sans neuroses. Then where am I if in all the revels I cannot equal her in discontent knowing already even love is a task.

Thunder, it's snowing, and the sun is out. Is there a snowbow? an *arc-en-neige?* It's 5 p.m. and I just got up. Why do I avoid eating even at starving times like this (Alfonso having demolished the cab driver)? [sic] Of course there's nothing wrong that a good screw couldn't fix. And I get too drunk for this and that's the vicious circle. How my head aches!

•   •   •

To make music foremost, life secondary. To become my own slave . . .

Yes, the composer does write for an audience. This doesn't mean he necessarily writes what the audience wants. . . .

Promiscuity of affection—where it is redeeming and where it is a question which pains me most when I am in love. Always I model my standards on my parents' marriage and accordingly achieve a form of morality which rationally I don't sanction, nor do my contemporaries. . . .

Dreamed of a thing called a Reich-bomb, though we did not associate this name (nor did I until awake), which had to be loaded beneath the sea. It was huge, but not so much so that the sharks had assumed a minute proportion as they swerved amid the various fixtures and (we held our breath!) almost collided with the significant one. Yet we had no cause for fear, as this machine was entirely artificial and could not be exploded by animal contact. But soon a shapeless buglike device was attached to a slim protrusion which immediately began to work and for exactly an hour ("only an hour" impressed me when I realized the ultimate result) it whirled faster and faster until invisibility; and then the bomb went off from under water (space?) aimed at the earth which was the size of a parlor-globe in the perspective from which we beheld it. When it hit, a vast amount of white custardlike fluid slowly gushed into the side of the sphere. It was meant to destroy one-third of the world. And very soon it had actually decayed such a portion as to make the earth seem quite lopsided and distorted. The net impression was one of shock and depression.

I can remember the day and time of day, especially the weather, even my apparel, what I said, during every episode, every fragmented occasion, of my life. This phenomenon is distracting (like the "gift" of perfect pitch when you just want to enjoy a piece rather than notate it while listening), when I observe some tantalizing face or figure on the momentary subway or passing barroom, for a week later (the week being the smallest cyclic segment of the average routine) to the hour —or two weeks, or 3, or 7—I'm sure to be there again & waiting. Sometimes they return. But if I'm not there, I must wonder. . . . Now I will find myself in a given public place subconsciously attracted, on the same day & hour, by the most incidental occurrence of perhaps years before. If this regularity of sympathies could be directed toward something more than Transient (melodrama of former faces), then maybe the shape of my etudes could be solider, more coherent, patience having been applied.

· · ·

Nowadays technique may provide a beginning and an end, but the middle is where art is truly tried, the middle is where we bog down. I dream of a work with no start or stop, just a forever ongoing middle....

Phenomenally drunk last night. Results of a fall: a shattered jaw still shredded with blood; a tongue destroyed, purple & white with pus, dirty-gold from iodine. But if I seldom look the worse for wear, is it because I don't think of myself as a dissipator? A sinner perhaps, but I can't connect alcohol with ill health.

The world is covered with snow. Wish I were dead.

Had made a mental note for weeks to write a bit on Order, but have been kept from it by a frenetic Disorder, and now am too tired. Yesterday I organized finally a scrapbook of my accomplishments. This I can do, and keep diaries, though not clean the room or stop drinking. But there is a regularity to carousing, so that I live by formula if not by schedule.

It smells like Vermont today....

Alarming that it's felt Billie Holiday must go to prison....

8 June, Sunday, 1 a.m. Benzedrine! What a night! Went to bed at 10 this morning with a girl named Winnie who's black as the ace of spades and 6 feet tall, with buttery breasts and a perverse psychology, but a bizarre charm and an air of culture. So it has been a short day. ... Dreamed elaborately that I was pregnant. Also of death by falling from a high trapeze, unnoticed by the audience. Erection visions! Exhilarating if melancholy.

When I play through *Cain and Abel* I can weep with myself. But I am in no ways an experimenter.

It has become a roadhouse evening. Summer smells are the only sentimental ones. It's so beautiful out that shopkeepers' wives have set chairs on the sidewalk while they knit, and after midnite Fifth Avenue is still full of strollers & lemonade-drinkers at the Brevoort café.

I love my family, though they are not my type....

Tonite I returned from a strenuous week in Martha's Vineyard where yesterday I took a Rorschach test. A long strain, and at the conclusion I all but fell apart. What pictures! I couldn't find a pleasant one: human distortion, vaginal chaos, lonely bugs, underwater societies with heaven & hell, demented mammals. Perhaps Tanglewood again will be a diverting solace. I look beautiful now from a week of abstinence and sun. But I am transiently back into city ways & here I sit with a glass of bourbon. . . .

2 July, Wednesday nite (Tanglewood). Although I haven't had a drink since Sunday and have been living in a pastorale climate, I still think in alcoholic terms, and tonite at the quartet recital a parallel struck me. When I get drunk, it lasts a long time but never long enough (neither the binge—3 to 5 days—nor the individual night). Should I begin at 3 in the afternoon, I'm still unsatisfied by 4 the next morning when the bars close, and must continue, if possible, until 8 or 10, with or without friends. The day is too long, but not long enough. Even so I fear will be the hours of my whole life. . . .

The sky and poetry are French, the earth and prose are German. German is literal, French figurative.

Don't judge others by yourself.

Then by whom shall I judge them?

Driving yesterday (15 January 1993) through the sleet from Hyannis to Manhattan, JH at the wheel, I observe: "It's weird when you think that Charpentier died in 1956. Because he—psychologically and actually—is a nineteenth-century composer." This morning JH observes: "No offense meant [none taken], but that remark dates you. Charpentier's only 'recent' from your older perspective." Still, Charpentier was born in 1860, two years before Debussy, and I was thirty-three when he died in Paris. I could have known him—technically we were colleagues. I could *not* have known Debussy, who died five years before my birth but who was, actually and psychologically, a twentieth-century composer.

This afternoon I ask my students (David Horne, Eric Sessler, Jonathan Holland, who came for lunch): "Am I a twentieth-century composer in your eyes?" Silence. Then tentatively from David: "That depends on how active you remain. We are twenty-first-century composers." "Not," I am quick to append, "if you die in the next six years."

22. Bill, Howard, Kraft, Nell, and Others in the Theater

Bill Flanagan, whose name has already perfumed these pages in passing, was the one composer among hundreds who would become a close friend (platonic), though that didn't happen suddenly. True, during our first hour we—what's the word?—*understood* each other, he sizing me up warily like the Cat Lady who stage-whispers across the café to Simone Simone, "Moya sestra," I gazing in disbelief at his incongruous bleached hair, tanned cheeks, china-blue eyes, weak chin, all set off by a lavender crew-neck sweater. Yes, we eventually became "sisters," but during the beginning years I liked and disliked Bill, he disliked and liked me.

It was Grace Cohen who brought Bill round to West Twelfth one noon in early 1947. We were the same age (he actually two months older), though he later lopped off three years when his bio began appearing in books because, like Tennessee Williams who did likewise, he felt those three years had been lost in a mist of mediocre jobs and boozy immobility. We thought alike, talked alike, were built alike (though I was handsomer), and composed alike. Grace had known Bill at Eastman, and both had recently immigrated to Manhattan along with a nucleus of several classmates: Charles Strouse (known as Buddy), Noel Farrand, Larry Rosenthal. They all spoke adoringly of their shy former mentor, Bernard Rogers, and disparagingly of director Howard Hanson, who had fostered homosexual purges.

I would visit Eastman myself for a weekend the following winter, on a consortium whereby undergraduate composers from all over would have their wares displayed in that illustrious Rochester conservatory. A bunch of us from Juilliard bunked in one hotel bedroom, reading *Hamlet* aloud and huffily criticizing the other schools—all good, clean, postadolescent fun. My new *Mourning Scene,* for voice and string quartet, was performed glowingly by the able baritone Warren Galjour, though the Flanagan contingent had warned me that the "gay" text (young David bewailing to Jonathan: "Thy love to me was wonderful, passing the love of women") would outrage the faculty. I never met Hanson, then or later, though on three occasions he conducted my music with the school orchestra. I did, though, have lunch with Rogers, a radio performance of whose opera I had recently been dazzled by (*The Warrior,* based on the story from Judges, contains one memorable line, when Delilah, pungently sung by Regina Resnik, puts out her lover's eyes with a poker: "How do things look now, Samson?"), and was pleased to tell him so. How I, a student, came to be sitting tête-à-tête with this eminent creator, aged fifty-five, I don't recall, though I do recall his endearing lisp, possibly because of my own speech defect. Seven years later his little opera *The Nightingale* would be premiered on a double bill with my first opera, *A Childhood Miracle,* in New York while I was in Paris.

Meanwhile, Bill Flanagan and his clan, plus George Garratt, followed in my footsteps with David Diamond, studying in his Hudson Street loft, privately and en masse. I attended some of the classes. David was a stickler for analysis, and not a bit lazy about assigning—and thus being obliged to correct—basic counterpoint and harmony conundrums, as well as the rigorous "deconstruction" of Beethoven symphonies and original composition according to prearranged forms. Bill was technically sloppy. Raised in Detroit, the only son of lower-middle AT&T employees, he had had a solid Jesuit education which I always envied since it enabled him to verbalize a subject and to speak of various philosophies where I flailed affectedly. But where I did not flail (I'd had counterpoint till it flowed from my ears), Bill was at loose ends; his training at Eastman and earlier had been slapdash. Nor was he prolific. He would balk at dotting the blank page with notes (the Jesuit logician?) for fear they might not come out right. Rather than err and be rueful, he would refrain and be frustrated. His overriding—and to an extent paradoxical—problem was this: the kind of tonal language he wished to speak was the stripped, lean, diatonic dialect of Copland whom he worshiped. Of course, it's hard to be simple—to commit to paper only that which needs to be committed. Still, the "simple" composers (Schubert, Poulenc) are generally generous; their music, after all, isn't challenging technically; they've either got it or they don't, and "it" is quickly apparent. Bill's contradiction was that he somehow mastered the rules backward. Like a dog who learns housetraining in reverse (who can't wait to come in from outside so as to shit on the carpet), Bill had got it into his head that the *inner voices* of four-part harmony periods should be kept moving disjunctly while the soprano and bass remain static. He was stymied where I was free, and I found his musical utterances, despite their sometime beauty, always amateurish.

Bill resented my ease, on paper and in the world. I envied his cultural balance (he knew all about music except how to write it, and could discuss it more persuasively than I could). He likened us to Bette Davis and Miriam Hopkins in *Old Acquaintance,* the hardworkingly serious authoress versus the giddy maker of potboiling bestsellers. I called him Blanche, because like the heroine of *Streetcar* he played the manipulating victim, and he called me Scarlett, because I played the manipulating vamp. We retained these cognomens even in solemn converse, sometimes veering to Belinda and Dorothy. The nomenclature was according to Malcolm Cowley's "Convolution" game of freshmen. (Man comes in from the storm and says the obvious: "Gee, it's raining out." First convolution: Man comes in from the storm and says with irony: "What a lovely day." Second convolution: Man comes in from the storm and, eschewing the irony as itself obvious, says: "It's raining.") Bill and I were not exactly birdbrained drag queens; thus our quaint ways were not meant to be campy, except that they *were;* not meant to be serious, except that they *were.* Our correspondence when apart was forever in the style of eighteenth-century pornography ("Ah, sage Belinda, I tremble to state . . ." "Most precious Scarlett, prepare for a shock . . ."), with no foul language but much data about our respective careers, carnal and musical.

Was I actually at ease in the world? Hindsight is blinding. Was Ned a suave sophisticate who got what he wanted? Is that what people now believe? Just last week a lackey from ASCAP (an elderly lackey, I assume) phoned me about some technical inquiry, then added: "By the way, I used to know you—at least from afar—at Tanglewood in 1946. You know what most struck me then?—it was how removed and shy you seemed." And just this morning a letter from someone at the BBC, about some technical inquiry, closes: "By the way, we were both at the same time in Paris (1950–53). I was a rather shy and bewildered German student, standing sometimes in the last corner of Marie-Laure de Noailles's salon without uttering a sound. . . . No one ever talked to me; you did once. You were deliciously rude and wore a black polo-neck sweater."

Ourselves as others see us . . .

For the record, Grace Cohen's daughter, Nina, owes her existence to me. One midnight in the Astor Bar a likable boor named Leo Rost picked me up, and with the passing weeks purported interest in my music, my "mind," my friends. Did I, he asked, know any girls as cute as me, to introduce to his straight friend Marc Jaffe? So Grace and Marc got married, Marc became a redoubtable publisher, and today they're divorced, but Nina remains.

What was I composing so copiously that Bill felt wistful about? In 1947, besides the three blues tunes with Paul Goodman, I also wrote (on his poetry) "The Lordly Hudson," which won the Music Libraries citation as "best published song of the year," and which, except for "Alleluia," was my most-sung song for decades; "Catullus: On the Burial of His Brother" (Aubrey Beardsley translation) designed specifically for David Lloyd's tenor voice; two more songs on Goodman poems about Janet Fairbank; "Mongolian Idiot" (Karl Shapiro); a prayer from T.S. Eliot's *The Dry Salvages;* a loathsome setting of a loathsome patriotic poem by Paul Engel, "The Freedom Song," commissioned for a never-produced "Sports Spectacle"; settings of Hopkins ("Spring" and "Spring and Fall"), of Frost ("Stopping by Woods" for my father's voice, unaware that several hundred other settings already existed); my first song cycle, *Seven Little Prayers,* again on Paul's words, never published but used in part much later in an oratorio. Besides these works for voice and piano, there were also the *Four Madrigals;* the *Concertino da camera* for harpsichord and seven instruments—the piece I showed to Kirkpatrick and Landowska, and then put in a trunk and forgot (until a few months ago, when one of the few copies surfaced in Minneapolis, where it has been scheduled for a world premiere, forty-five years after the fact); the *Mourning Scene;* the *Sermon on Miracles;* the unfinished String Quartet; another work for chorus and strings called *Out of the Depths,* which Bill Strickland conducted at Wellesley and which has since vanished; and a ballet for piano called *Egress* commissioned (twenty-five dollars) by a lanky modern dancer named Louise Holdsworth. In 1947 I also made sketches for songs on words of Melville. And of Howard Moss.

Howard and I met at a Village party and woke up next day in the same bed. The affair, if you can call it that, lasted three days, but the friendship lasted until he died in 1987. At twenty-four he looked forty, at sixty he looked forty; he was never young, never old. Nor was he an erotic object to my taste, possibly because, frozen in Freudian analysis as he had been and would remain forever, he emitted that flavor of worried superiority of one who has all the answers while knowing there are no answers—a desexed anesthetic intellectuality. But he also *was* intellectual, a true poet to boot, with the added queasy stigma of being, all his life, the sole poetry editor at *The New Yorker.* Howard wore a constant concerned smile, like Noël Coward's, brow furrowed above steel-rimmed specs, lips tight, incapable of being parted except to utter clever repartee. He had become his magazine. He could not speak without being memorable. Sometimes he was memorable. So were his poems, each one, even the less good ones, being unflawed in their facets if often self-conscious. The only thing wrong with Howard Moss's poetry is that nothing's wrong with it. At its best it soars. He was also the only poet I ever knew who could write *about* poetry in a manner that made a difference, that explained, without pedantry. A rhyming metricalist, he had little use for—nor they for him—the surrealist, lewd, heart-on-sleeve vagaries of *View,* or of Paul Goodman, or, in their early years, John Ashbery and Frank O'Hara, though he later came round, even published Ashbery and Kenneth Koch too.

So I used one of his poems, "Tourist's Song," from which to make an accompanied tune. With the years I used a dozen more.

Early in 1956, when I returned to America briefly and performed in Town Hall with Mattiwilda Dobbs, who included, in a large group of my ditties, the new "See How They Love Me" on Moss's spacious lyric, he wrote:

> I did enjoy enormously the songs of yours sung that evening, and it made me want you to have more poems of mine set by you. . . . We might spend an evening or afternoon together, going over poems to see if there's anything that interests you. . . . I was particularly impressed with the Browning, and hoped she would sing it as an encore. But I loved the encore, too, the gondola song, which she sang better, it seemed to me, than anything else on the program. *You* sounded good, too; in fact, an accompanist I was with said you were a fine accompanist, and so you are, as you probably don't need to be told. Also, for what it's worth, I thought you *looked* fine: humble, dangerous, and dashing.

(For what it's worth?) What poet today is concerned any longer with serious collaboration as Howard was then? What composer today can afford to think about voice-and-piano ventures when there is no longer an outlet?

Soon after, Bill Flanagan too made a setting of "See How They Love Me," very beautiful, and from then on Howard preferred Bill's various musicalizings to mine, tacitly. When, four years later, I wanted to use Howard's *King Midas* cycle—ten poems in all—Howard wrote:

> About *Midas:* it's Bill's and I just called him to make sure. He says he's set two or three and has sketched out some of the others. . . . What I wish you'd do, *Midas* being unavailable, is a cycle made of other poems.

In fact, Bill never wrote a note, and the *Midas* poems eventually fell to me.

> How is Yaddo and who's there? Do you have enough citronella? And, dear boy, the two months need not be either sexless or silent. Take a *long* look around, and plan accordingly. There is no desert without its trickle. (Great thoughts division.) And, if worse comes to worse, I'll *fly* up. Love, Howard

My taste in live poets during the 1950s veered from the grayish formality of Moss toward the redder freedom of Frank O'Hara, and so did my circle of friends, if I had a circle. Paths crossed less with Howard, then finally hardly at all. Yet in 1975, after my so-called *Final Diary* was published, Howard wrote a parody of it for *The New Yorker,* called "The Ultimate Diary," which I found unfunny, though everyone else roared. (I've just reread it, and I, who never laugh, laughed.) Howard did have a mean wit, and satire is, they say, the truest compliment. But his spoof now makes it hard to continue these navel-gazing memoirs.

My friendship with Bill was cemented on my definitive return to the United States in 1958 after a decade in Europe. We also became professional partners, organizing concerts—as Copland and Sessions had organized them in the twenties—of contemporary music, songs specifically, before the art of song perished forever. Bill now lived with Edward Albee, as yet unknown, but whose sudden sparkling ascent would lead to a firm change in all of our lives, and to Bill's downfall. More on that later; for now, just this: Bill Flanagan was the smartest person (beside Father and Paul Goodman) I've ever known. But his intelligence—the ability to analyze his art *avant coup*—stifled his gift and led to a form of blackmail—sweet blackmail, to be sure, and flattering and victimized and hopeless, but blackmail all the same. He told me once that he had based his life—at least his professional life—on mine. He decided systematically to look as I looked, eat what I ate, say what I said, write the same sorts of letters to conductors and prima donnas that I wrote to conductors and prima donnas, phone whom I phoned, dye his hair the same hue as my dyed hair, all this so as to attain the identical goals that he assumed I was attaining. Yet since he was smarter than I, and plainer than I, how could my goals be his? Nor were his sexual yearnings like mine, nor his sense of France, nor his childhood. There is only one category of behavior that cannot be correctly generalized: the care and feeding of the creator. No sooner do you claim that all great artists are thus and so, than along comes a great artist to stand that claim on its head.

I am not responsible for Bill's death.

Howard was the first of us to acquire the complete recording of *L'enfant et les sortilèges,* which came out that spring of 1947. What intoxication! The "Five O'Clock Fox-trot" had long been familiar, but its very frivolity precluded imagining that the context from which it drew breath was Ravel's chef d'oeuvre. Here now, blooming like a fiery orchid out of Howard Moss's phonograph, was the whole piece, a mere half hour, but which has throbbed through every minute of my life since then. One couldn't do better than to quote Colette about *her* first hearing of this little opera (is it an opera? a ballet with words? a visual cantata? probably the latter, for no staged production ever provides more than distraction from the music's careful charisma) for which she had furnished the libretto five years before. "I had thoughtlessly titled it *Divertissement pour ma fille* until the day Ravel, with icy gravity, said to me: 'But I have no daughter.' How can I convey to you my emotion at the first shake of the tambourines accompanying the procession of shepherd boys, the moonlit dazzle of the garden, the flight of the dragonflies and the bats. 'C'est amusant, vous ne trouvez pas?' Ravel said. But my throat was knotted tight with tears: the animals, their swift whispering sounds scarcely distinguishable as syllables, were leaning down in reconciliation over the Child. . . . I had not foreseen that a wave of orchestrated sound, starred with nightingales and fireflies, would raise my modest work to such heights."

Colette, to my ignorant ken, seemed nonetheless a sort of Gallic Beatrix Potter, a woman-writer and thus superficial; she remained so until I sat down and read her, inspired by the details of her death in 1954. On 3 August, at about 8:30 in the evening, she died in her bed ("after a small sip of champagne"—Janet Flanner), overlooking the Palais Royal gardens. Immensely famous, and given a state funeral, she was scandalously denied burial at the Eglise Saint-Roche by the archbishop of Paris, because of her divorce and wicked ways. Although I had seen her picture almost daily in French papers, I did not discover until too late that the all-knowing Colette was our century's greatest stylist—too late, that is, to have sat at the foot of her bed. In the mid-sixties I set to music, for chorus and small orchestra, Janet Flanner's telling depiction of Colette's funeral, thereby posthumously allying myself to that grand woman with the same gorgeously specious syco-phancy that even a Schubert or a Strauss or a Debussy allied himself to Heine and Hofmannstahl and Verlaine.

David Diamond was the first of us to acquire the full score of *L'enfant et les sortilèges,* and Bill the first (no, I am not a leader, etcetera) to acquire the piano reduction with the English translation mawkishly made by Catherine Wolff, so we all memorized each mea-sure and Freudianized each Oedipal scene, and have used the mem-ory and the Freud ever since.

Speaking of Freud—which everyone did every day back then—it was thought by "everyone" (mainly Shirley, Eugene, and especially Paul Goodman) that my profligacy made me ripe for analysis. Indeed, friends wouldn't answer for their friendship if I didn't submit. Through his brother, architect Percival Goodman, Paul (who himself would become a lay analyst in the 1950s) recommended Dr. Erich Kraft, a refugee who resembled Dr. Nolte, my so-called composition professor back at Northwestern: thick German accent, dwarfish, frail, ugly, old (probably fifty but looked seventy), and rigorously hard line. He practiced, along with other Freudians, in a beautiful old whitestone across from the Frick Museum. While waiting in the lobby before our first interview, who should be seated across from me, waiting for *her* doctor, but Martha Graham. We greeted each other, then attended in stony silence (she's good at that) for a full quarter hour. Whereupon Kraft's door opened and out walked Ed Stringham, patient and poet. Was one supposed to see one's acquaintances at one's analyst's? Nei-ther Martha nor Ed nor any familiar face was ever again in evidence during the semiweekly sessions of the next eighteen months.

Father and Mother came up from Philly to check the scene, staying at the Marlton on Eighth Street. I did not formally begin with Kraft until after Father met with him. Father harbored mixed feelings, thought of the process as maybe chic and unnecessary, but grew con-vinced, halfway, by my pleas. This was a switch on the ridiculous single session with that female Freudian long ago, when my plea to the parents was to spare me. The evening after his visit to Kraft, Father and I beheld the unstable Elizabeth Bergner in *Cup of Trembling,* a Broadway potboiler about a woman who unwittingly drinks too much too often and ends up on many a morning not knowing where she is. Father was impressed that I admitted to the same experiences.

Mother over the past year had been, off and on, in a Pennsylvania hospital for three series of electroshock treatments. The bedraggled spectacle of her in pale blue robe, hair unkempt, confused aspect, and pathetic confidence in a certain doctor so-and-so, like Olivia de Havilland in *The Snake Pit,* caused Father and me to fall into each other's arms and bawl. Every few years Mother would repeat the process—of being strapped to a table, of crying No, of losing her memory, and of emerging eventually optimistic if childlike—which on the whole seemed to turn the trick, the trick of going on. (By 1965 when she underwent her final series, the technique was improved: instead of six weeks in the loony bin, it was six days of hour-long visits to an office where the treatment was brief and painless. In these six days she passed from inert dejection to a purposeful worker for civil rights, and the cure lasted ten years.) My purpose for psychoanalysis was to be cured of uncontrolled drinking and maybe of homosexuality, abetted by Father, who would pay the agreed-upon fee of ten bucks a session. He didn't wish me to follow in Mother's path.

Today, of course, we know there is no cure for the malady of alcoholism, though one can recover permanently through abstinence; the abstinence may be a torment if a question of will, a pleasure (as now for me) if a question of tenets and logic and desire. It is wrong to be constantly drunk, but psychoanalysis (the possible investigation of *why* you drink) is of no help, none. It is not wrong to be gay, nor did I ever truly believe it was, so this did not figure much in the sessions with Kraft.

At the first of these, on 19 November 1947, at 3:15, lying on the couch, with Kraft and his scratch pad out of sight behind my head, I began to transfer right off the bat. He was a mean little parrot, stunted and smart, trying to rape me. Could I translate that into flattering terms? What was the routine? Would he never squawk a word? be insulted? succumb to my wiles? allow that I was his favorite pupil? With the months, so as not to waste Father's money, I invented situations, perversions, dreams (such invention was the same as reality—it was, after all, *my* invention, hence my concern). That first session over, I emerged onto East Seventieth and headed west toward the setting sun. Elmyr Hory, a Hungarian painter I'd met recently at Stewart Chaney's, was giving a cocktail party nearby. I immediately got drunk; it seemed the proper thing, since I was now under an analyst's care to stop drinking, and it would provide conversation with the other guests, none of whom I knew: jazz pianist Joe Bushkin and his wife, who were intrigued, or said they were, by Dr. Kraft; actor George Sanders with an expensive blond who spoke Hungarian with the host, was garbed in a brown taffeta sample of Dior's just-launched New Look, and who called herself Zsa Zsa Gabor (Eugene would be thrilled to hear about Sanders, his ideal); Anita Loos; and other Europeans crammed into a basement flat with a stairway leading nowhere. (Years later Hory gained notoriety as the world's slyest criminal in exile, for his Van Gogh forgeries.)

That's what I feel that I felt at the start of analysis, forty-six years after the fact. (What I felt during the fact is in the next chapter.) Did the ongoing procedure have its effect? Can one know? I was six seasons older when it stopped, and age brings its own rules, with or without Freud. I learned to like Dr. Kraft's gentle obduracy, his parental force, though he never expressed an opinion until I announced a projected long trip to France. (He said, You'll be taking yourself with you, and I said, No I won't. And I didn't.) I learned to dissect dreams, even to create dreams designed for dissection, to sleep on the surface where dreams most vibrate, and to describe their madness in order to hide firmer madnesses which were none of Kraft's business. I learned to believe in the poetry of Freud without ever really giving credence to its efficacy.

When Nell Tangeman was found dead in her Washington, D.C., apartment on 15 February 1965, she had lain there friendless for some time. Nor was there an obit next morning, nor in the weeklies, nor in the many musical monthlies which were then prevalent. She sank without a trace. I heard of Nell's death from Newell Jenkins on the phone three days after, but it wasn't until several years later that I was saddened if not surprised to learn from Oliver Daniel that Nell's body was broken, that she had brought home a stranger who left her for dead. (Bill Flanagan seventeen seasons later would expire likewise— not from assault but from an overdose—and lie putrefying for a week before police broke down the door.) Nell was forty-six. Who besides a few old acquaintances remembered her as the most interesting mezzo-soprano of our mid-century?

Before we met I had often heard Nell Tangeman in song. During 1946 she introduced America to Messiaen's *Poèmes pour Mi,* then sang Jocasta in Stravinsky's *Oedipus Rex* under Lenny Bernstein. In 1947 she performed the hard solo role against an unaccompanied chorus in the premiere of Copland's *In the Beginning.* Her handsome appearance, her violent eyes, her aggressively passive delivery and opal-colored décolleté dresses (*gowns,* as singers call them) were balanced by a brand of vocalism that no longer exists: a true contralto that passes from a velvet growl to a clarion purr, or descends from a heady altitude to a golden chest-tone, all in the space of a breath. But only if the music asks for it, for instance, in Milhaud's *Chants populaires hébraïques* or Bernstein's *Afterthought* or the Monteverdi madrigals mastered under Nadia Boulanger. So I was pleased when she phoned out of the blue to say she was looking for an accompanist.

Our ensuing close relationship lasted until her death. She was the most formative singer of my life: everything vocal that I composed over the next six years (until I began to be commissioned by other singers of other sexes and other timbres) was composed for her specific capabilities, for I knew no other capabilities. Her example determined not only how I wrote for the voice but that I wrote for the voice at all. (It was never the voice per se that drew me to song, but the naked words that would be clothed by my notes.) Which is why, when I wrote my first high coloratura song, "The Silver Swan," it was actually a mezzo piece transposed up a fifth; and why even today sopranos and basses say that my inclinations seem to swerve around the mezzo tessitura.

Nell was the recently divorced mate of Robert Tangeman, my current musicology professor at Juilliard and as stuffily academic as Nell was a free soul. They had forged careers together at Indiana University and were now wending their separate ways. Nell's way was one of devotion to today's music; she had by far the best vocal métier from among the "modern music specialists," who mostly attracted an audience through novelty rather than beauty.

On 24 October 1948 Nell made her Town Hall debut and got a rave from Virgil in the *Tribune* ("an artist right off the top shelf . . . with brains, beauty and skill"). With flutist Carleton Sprague Smith and violinist Maurice Wilk, I accompanied her in the disinterred *In Piazzas Palladio,* retitled *Three Pieces for Voice and Instruments,* and wore a tuxedo for the first time since high school. (Eugene: "You looked and sounded divine," but no word about the music itself.) The postconcert reception included both my parents as well as Dr. Alfred C. Kinsey, the latter a friend of Nell's from Bloomington.

Kinsey, Father's age exactly, was persuasive, even seductive, which may account for his successful question-and-answer sessions. Would I, he asked, consent to an interview (he was planning a book on the sexuality of artists, which was why he was in New York visiting Juilliard and other sacred conclaves)?, and could my parents consent, since they were so conveniently in town as well? ("To record a whole family makes for useful crisscrossing," said he.) I would and they could. So he quickly assigned Mother and Father to his assistant, Dr. Pomeroy, and made a date with me himself.

He was staying at one of those sordid Times Square hotels, it could have been the Royalton, where we got straight down to business, a business that would last, he announced, exactly forty-seven minutes. His questions, as read from a clipboard on his lap where he also made notes, were designed to forestall inadvertent fibs and hesitations.

("When did you first masturbate?" "I never masturbated in my life." "How did you have your first ejaculation?" "Er..." "Are you heterosexual?" "Er...") Though shy, I was not devious, so we proceeded according to Interview I, as opposed to II or III, which were for different categories of victim. More than the interview, which remains vague in the memory, I recall our later off-the-cuff talk. Since I knew more than Kinsey about who "was" and "wasn't" among musicians, I generalized as follows:

Harpists (of whom, like hairdressers and cooks, most are women though the best are men) are all homosexual—the males, that is. Male string players are all Jewish and all heterosexual. Male brass players, wind players, and percussionists, though not necessarily Jewish, are also all heterosexual, at least those in orchestras; among soloists the percentage wavers. Of male pianists, also mostly Jewish, half are gay. ("Gay" was not standard usage then, at least among straights.) Male organists, all gay. Of classical singers no tenors are gay, most baritones are, but few females. In jazz the reverse obtains: the woman are lesbian, the men are macho—but alcoholic. Choir directors, all gay. Among composers, who until the war had been mainly Gentile and defiantly effete (Thomson, Griffes) or defiantly virile (Ives, Sessions), the ratio was fifty-fifty. The ratio remained fifty-fifty. Stravinsky's flock of Americans, which overlapped with Aaron Copland's, was straight and Jewish, Virgil's was mixed. (Rumors still abound that Aaron championed mainly his gay entourage. What entourage? Leo Smit, Irving Fine, Arthur Berger, Harold Shapero? For a gay goy like me he never lifted a finger.)

Then I went abroad and, until his death in 1956, began a correspondence with Kinsey. His famous study, *Sexual Behavior in the Human Male,* needed "American" inserted between the last two words. The interests, obsessions, and embarrassments of French, German, and English males did not at all jibe with ours; and in Morocco, where virtually all males practice what we call homosexuality, virtually no males are homosexual. *Autres lieux, autres moeurs.* As for music milieux—possibly for reasons of Catholicism in France, where the organ is a manly instrument, or of no sissified implications in Scandinavia, where choral singing is part of the family—homosexuality is as rare among organists and organist-composers as among choral conductors, and the ratio with other instrumentalists, including harpists, is the reverse of ours. As for male orchestra conductors, they were and remain married worldwide, though most of them fool around: being absolute monarchs, anything is permitted them, provided they are protected with a wedding ring.

Dr. Kraft was not impressed by my meeting with Kinsey, whom he found superficial. But he did go to Nell's recital and found it "very lovely."

Nell Tangeman liked to give the impression of being bisexual (lesbianism had a certain naughty cachet in those days, while male inversion was simply a stigma). She could drink as much as I could and behaved worse at parties. The drunker she got, the hornier, making passes at everyone (even Ben Weber), while growing ever less comely. At a postconcert party in, say, Bowdoin College, where we gave a recital together that fall, she would swill the punch, gulp the shrimp, then, with crumbs on the edge of her smeared lips, begin pawing the president's wife. Because someone had once told her she had an infectious Irish laugh, she cultivated this into a too-frequent guffaw, bursting forth unprepared, and no one knew which way to look. Her artistry on stage was rehearsed, more than tasteful, exquisitely controlled, in a word, anal (as we Freudians liked to say): her social comportment was cheap, messy, dangerous, oral quite literally. I never drank on tour, but because I was Nell's escort at such times, I was perceived as being somehow responsible, and resented, rather than sympathized with, her behavior. In fact, though I loved Nell, I never really liked her.

If Bill Flanagan modeled himself for a while on me, Nell did the same with her friend Martha Lipton, a pulchritudinous ebony-haired mezzo with good manners and a contract at the Met. She never drank. Nell envied Martha the Met, her worldly know-how and chocolate voice. On stage Martha had everything but temperament. Nell was more vocally compelling if less technically radiant than Martha, though neither woman was intrinsically an actress. Nell found Martha guilty of everything that she, Nell, was far guiltier of: overweening ambition, overriding jealousy, overdressed négligée. Martha in fact was the epitome of sobriety, planned her rather traditional career with common sense, was calmly garbed. Because we were soulmates, I perhaps recognized myself in Nell and found myself wanting. Her dumb pushiness embarrassed me. Would I have abandoned her had she not been what I deemed a great singer on the edge of a cliff, and, like me, a disreputably unfocused dissipator harboring a repentantly compulsive worker? That chemical balance produced unique results in both our cases, though with Nell the dissipator won out early. Our good years together were few but fertile, during which she premiered three of my spacious pieces shaped expressly to her gifts.

The first of these was a cycle of six songs called *Penny Arcade,* based on evocative verses about Forty-second Street penned for the occasion by young Harold Norse, a feisty little Brooklynite sexpot who claimed to be the simultaneous lover of Chester Kallman and Wystan Auden. These unpublished songs, assessed coolly today, remain exemplary in their economical trashiness: individually they are honed to display the female middle voice, collectively they cohere while contrasting, and their virtuosic color appeals to listeners. To have let them remain in manuscript is due maybe to my discomfort at their dated vulgarity, or maybe because I used elements from each one later and better. But they flourished for a while when Nell and I performed them at the drop of a hat, and one of them even entered the repertory of the luminous Mack Harrell.

One evening we did them at a party chez William Kapell. Who among those who have known Willy can forget his electric vitality? Of all first-generation North American pianists (a notable preceding generation does not, for whatever reason, exist; the mentors of this first generation were at least twenty-five years older and inevitably Central European), Kapell was the most successful. His fame when I knew him rested on his so-adroit championing of Khachaturian's Piano Concerto, a blockbuster that wriggled and swooned and did what you wanted it to do. Eugene had befriended Willy and brought us together hoping we'd show off for each other. Even as I write I can still hear his *way* with a keyboard: that purposeful, shining, pliable strength, like Damascus steel, yet gentle as a child, a *good* child. I never grew to know him well (though what does "know well" mean? Willy seemed so dynamically alert that an hour with him was like a month with anyone else) but retain as in a snapshot the powerful almost-sexuality of his attention. It never occurred to me, when Eugene urged me to play, that Willy would call me a good pianist, but when I finished he knew the music better than I did, plied me with questions, not letting me off the hook. He cared. He would demonstrate at the piano, ubiquitous cigarette between the lips, or expostulate from an armchair while brutally scraping the eczema on his forearms with the teeth of a comb. Somehow his too-short career, given his violent concentration, did not seem "too short." Willy was only thirty when, one month after Jacques Thibaud died in a plane crash, he died in a plane crash. I was at the Boeuf sur le Toit on the rue du Colisée that autumn night when Sigi Weissenberg came up to announce the news. Neither then nor in the following weeks was there anything but sorrow in the air: no sense among pianists of competition eliminated, only the weird realization that the more concerts can be packed into a jet-age international itinerary, the more chance the devil will take revenge.

Anyway, Nell sang *Penny Arcade* at Willy's party. As usual she was exemplary during the performance, passionate yet precise. As usual she was insufferable after the performance, incoherent and trying too hard. Arthur Judson, the redoubtable impresario, was there, impressed with her vocal style, appalled at her society. Nell never got a big-time manager.

It's not that I'd sleep until noon, wasting half a day; I went to bed at noon, rose at seven, and began all over again. This would occur once or twice a week. But the interims were as positive as the binges were negative—frantic work and careful diet balanced desperate play and near starvation.

When in the late 1950s I first dipped a toe into Alcoholics Anonymous (but it would take another decade before the tenets took), I was struck by the logic of the formal meeting but bemused by the lack of self-analysis. I didn't realize that appraisal required sobriety. Erich Kraft, of course, felt that sobriety was a matter of willpower, and that willpower was a result of the piercing glance at one's childhood.

Eugene was the first of us to go to Europe. The grand tour was the goal of American graduates then, as it had been in the nineteenth century and as it is not today. For us the reflection of Paris's postwar aura from the twenties was forceful enough to impel an equally forceful mystique in the fifties. We would supply the mystique, awakening France like Sleeping Beauty of a long-war's nightmare. Eugene, giddy with his success as a young pianist and abetted by the funds of the Leventritt Foundation, went abroad early in 1948 and wrote us about how the newly released ferment of intellectual activity was more purposeful there than in the States. He rented a villa in Cap Ferrat where Shirley and I and maybe Norris Embry planned to meet him that spring. Shirley, in fact, went (hoping never to return), while I, despite a paid-for boat ticket, remained in America for another year. Here is why:

Seated one afternoon in a booth at the San Remo with pretty Sally Goodman, Paul's wife, discussing how Jewish thinkers never take us goyim seriously, I grew achy and overwarm. Even as she watched, Sally saw blotches spread over my face. "Looks like chicken pox," said Sally calmly. Sure enough, the symptoms were diagnosed next day.

Of all things, for a twenty-four-year-old! Canceling France, I went to Philadelphia to convalesce with Mother and Father. There was nothing worse to the disease than a fortnight of itching so exquisite that even a saint with fiery fingernails could not resist ripping—slowly—the luscious thick scabs from his forehead. To this day I retain a crater above my right eyebrow.

During that May in Philadelphia I composed my first Piano Sonata, a short three-movement affair with a rousing finale called Toccata.

Returning to New York, I collected a master of science degree (as did four other composers and sixteen instrumentalists) in the hallowed halls of Juilliard. My reaction, as the handsome new president William Schuman berobed me in dark velvet, was: Such fuss for so little. What had I learned there, at the parents' expense, but an affirmation of what I'd already taught myself, and a confirmation of the still-throbbing fact that performers and composers face in opposite directions? Yes, I did compose, under the hazy tutelage of Bernard Wagenaar, an Overture in C for orchestra, which won the George Gershwin Memorial Award. The piece didn't deserve the prize, but I did. According to the terms of the honor, the Overture would be premiered the following season by the New York Philharmonic under Michel Piastro, representing my first hearing ever in Carnegie Hall. The prize also included a thousand dollars—which would pave the way toward the postponed trip to France—plus whatever copying bills might be incurred for preparing the materials. (I didn't tell the Philharmonic, but the materials already existed. Seymour Barab, the mensch, had helped me copy the parts prior to Hanson's doing a run-through at Eastman. Nor did I, in turn, tell Seymour that I was allowing the Philharmonic to prepare a whole new set of materials. You won't tell them now, will you?)

Besides the Overture and *The Chicken Pox Sonata,* I composed in 1948 two perfect songs: "Requiem," on Stevenson's famous verses, and "Echo's Song," on Ben Jonson's "Slow, slow, fresh fount" for a party to honor Eva Gauthier. (When "Echo's Song" was published in 1953, the dedication was changed to "To Xénia Gabis," which had become Shirley's name. She had divorced Seymour Barab meanwhile, and while in France, where "Shirley" was unpronounceable, adopted her middle name, Xénia.) Also a suite of ten simple piano pieces called *A Quiet Afternoon,* dedicated "To my sister's children." Rosemary had gotten married in January to John Marshall, a tall, good-looking, paternal, humorous but solemn conscientious objector and biochemist. They lived in Chicago and were expecting a baby. (By the time the suite was published they had three babies—and three more would emerge with the years. Hence the dedication.)

Along with these works was a ballet titled *Death of the Black Knight* on a scenario by Paul Goodman. Music and words were commissioned and paid for by Alfonso Ossorio, but the work was never performed.

Two other songs, both on poems of Edith Sitwell, saw the light that summer. Though forced to call them "early works," I can recall so clearly the Manhattan heat wave during which "You, the Young Rainbow of My Tears" was composed, and later that same August the sea air at Truro which was the background for "The Youth with the Red-Gold Hair." Not till next May did I leave America for eight full years in France, yet these songs now seem Frencher than anything I later wrote in Paris. They also seem like lost children found again. The considerable delay in their publication was due strictly to legal complexities.

(Cautionary tale: When I completed these Sitwell settings, my publisher, which was then Peer-Southern, said: "Fine. Get the poet's okay and we'll print them." I'd hitherto musicalized any words that appealed to me; my few songs already published had been to verse in public domain, or to Paul Goodman. It hadn't occurred to me that living poets might have opinions, much less objections, about having songs made on their words. I mailed a genteel request to Sitwell, and received no reply. After four months I wrote again, and again no reply. In France a year later I stated the case personally to the poet's brother, Sacheverell, and to Stephen Spender, who, after hearing the music, promised to intercede. Still no answer. Once more I wrote, taking care, as Spender had advised me, to say "Dear Doctor Sitwell." Silence. Eventually I received from the Sitwell editors a note to the effect that Walton was the only composer the lady favored, but if I could persuade him to make an exception in my case, they might consider. Walton's secretary answered me from Ischia stating that the master was deep in *Troilius and Cressida,* but if I would write again in six months, etc. I wrote again in six months, and so did my publisher. No reply. Finally, exasperated, four years after my first inquiry, I sent off a note to Sitwell calling her a selfish old dragon—I'm not proud of this—from whom I had demanded a simple yes or no, and that I'd go ahead and publish the songs with or without her permission. By return mail her attorneys responded:

> Dr. Sitwell ... has referred to us your astonishing letter in which you complain that she has ignored your request to be allowed to use a poem of hers of which you had in fact made use before you asked. Dr. Sitwell receives a constant stream of requests from unknown persons who wish

to hitch their wagon to her star and has in self defense been forced to a policy of ignoring them.

They threatened suit should I attempt to publish. Thirty years later my current and permanent editors, Boosey & Hawkes, applied for and immediately received permission to print the songs.)

And Truro—what was I doing there? In June I met, at MacDougall's Tavern, a compelling young doctor named Ralph Teicher who, like all doctors, was a music lover. Did I want—he asked—to drive up to Tanglewood next morning? Since Hugh Ross was planning to pre-miere the *Four Madrigals* in Tanglewood that week (although I'd not planned to go), I said sure. Off we went on a mock honeymoon. Ralph treated me as Glenn Ford treated Gilda, using me to meet other people, leaving me to writhe at his getting drunk and driving out of control. Hugh Ross, recalling a Jacques Callot woodcut with his bony features and Harlequin gestures, performed the *Madrigals* amiably (as he would perform other of my works through the years), after which I left Ralph Teicher to stagger back to New York on his own, and proceeded to Truro. My host was Jordan Whitelaw, an oafishly lan-guorous music-loving pal of Danny Pinkham, and a Bostonian to the core, who had rented a house there. The other guest was John Ash-bery. Overplump and a touch too effete for my taste, John seemed encouraged by my disinterest. Under my door he would slip messages which I mislaid (how could I know he would become John Ashbery?) and I forsook both host and guest for regular forays into Prov-incetown. From one of these I returned one morning bleary eyed in the car of a guy whose name I didn't know to find Father parked at Jordan's house. Up until the end, Father had a way of showing up unexpectedly under circumstances he couldn't help but have intuited would be painful to both him and me.

In 1960 at Buffalo University a pupil brought me a song based on an Ashbery haiku:

> I placed flowers on your path
> because I wanted to be near you.
> Do not punish me.

Ralph Teicher? That autumn, in penitence perhaps, he introduced me to one G., a full-lipped sinewy man, with whom I had what's called an "open affair." Just writing this, I can again feel his attraction. Ralph himself was killed in an auto wreck.

The Poets' Theater, an honorable and hopeless undertaking, rose and fell in the space of a season. The premise, rightly or wrongly, was this:

"There is no song in the theater of today because the earliest voice to speak from a stage has been estranged from it . . . the voice of the poet." John Myers, billed as liaison and publicity director, procured me (as well as Varèse, Ben Weber, and John Cage) for the music committee. But the nominal mastermind was the exotic Maria Piscator, who was propounding, undigested, the theories of her estranged husband, Erwin. I liked to watch and smell her, as she floated about in gold lamé pyjamas and Chanel cologne, during the many meetings on East Seventy-sixth. But I never understood a word she uttered. The actual masterminds were the painters: Seligmann, Max Ernst, Cecil Beaton, Roberto Matta ("the matta of others mattas to me matta" was his slogan); and the poets Lionel Abel, Parker Tyler, Cummings, Stevens, and of course Paul Goodman. Maria was the sole female in the enterprise.

Two programs were envisaged, one for spring and one for fall, at the YMHA auditorium on Lexington. The spring program contained Genet's *Les bonnes*—mistranslated as *The Servant Girls*—directed by Richard Fisher (a friend of Roditi's who would later marry Maggy Magerstadt), and two Noh plays of Goodman, directed by Maria herself. One of these Noh plays, *Stoplight,* had music by Ben, the other, *Dusk,* had music by me, and silver scenery by Corrado Cagli. Four performances were presented, in May and in June. I remember the sensation of greasepaint professionality while snacking in the nearby coffee shop with the hero of *Stoplight,* fair-haired Dan Scott, Richard Fisher's lover, with whom I had a fling that endured the space of the run, and whom I'd see years later in Hollywood where he turned into Simon Scott. I do not remember the cast of *Dusk;* but my instrumental music, for flute and piano, was performed live backstage, by myself and Leslie Oakes, and was effective—or so said Tom Prentiss.

Tom Prentiss, Cagli's apprentice, was a boyish dishwater blond, quite male (the Sterling Hayden type), with a singular mind. He could look at a tree and make you look at it through his eyes by describing, in few phrases, how this knotted artery, that stretch of bark, these frightened veins of syrup could seethe and suffer in silence, and speak without words to other trees, maybe even to us. Tom, a Thoreauvian loner, was highly sexed (as most loners are—sex is not social, nor even necessarily sentimental), but also highly concerned with music and books and painting (all of which are replacements for sex, as our analysts daily informed us), and was himself the most expertly meticulous draftsman this side of Annibale Carracci. Tom despised John Myers as only a landsman (they were both Buffalonians) can despise one who has moved to the same new city where both ply rival trades. Tom was not tony and timely like the *View* contingent; he eschewed surrealism in favor of a bent for botany and a knack for transferring that bent, visually, to paper. Which eventually brought him a permanent job as staff artist for *Scientific American.* For the moment he was a mysterious decoration. He would, for example, sidle up to me at the San Remo, and hum the motto of my music for *Dusk* into my ear, then glide away. He had the layman's adoration for the composer (the breed has died out), and years later would continue to hum the same tune. Which is why, no doubt, in 1984 I reintroduced the distant theme into my Violin Concerto.

Paul Goodman was not a playwright; he was not, arguably, even a novelist. His philosophical didacticism precluded realistic dialogue, yet he was always writing realistic dialogue—or so he thought—as philosophy issuing from the mouths of babes. His dramas weren't flops (a prescheduled run of four performances can't be billed as a failure when it was an artistic triumph for us all), but neither were they dramas. *Stoplight* does have one terrific speech that begins:

> For all admit the wages of sin is death,
> come! let me waste no time to freely sin

and ends:

> how may I lure this horror to my home?
> the grisly death by what adroit mistake?
> Beware all travellers who ride with me!

A man whose name I've forgotten invited me to Cherry Grove some-time that summer. The first glimpse of Fire Island was disconcerting. Like Nantucket, where I'd visited with Morris in 1944, this spit of land seemed deprived, exposed, bereft of the opulence one connects—or does one?—with gay males. Anthropologist Claude Lévi-Strauss, in one of the funniest boners since Freud, claimed that homosexuals were drawn to the island because, like them, it was sterile. Aside from the facts that (1) "sterile" is hardly the word, and (2) I myself was not drawn to the island, I would agree with him. In later years, as with Nantucket, I learned that these unusual and somehow definitively American outposts have all the beauty of Shakers and svelte surfaces and complex hymns. They are not *tape-à-l'oeil* like Provence or Ant-arctica; like Debussy's *Pelléas,* these islands contain arias galore, but in microcosm.

Anyhow, the man whose name I've forgotten was involved with theater, as a small-time agent or producer or something. Immediately I drank too much, disappeared from the beach house, wandered wherever the ocean tide pulled, and at dawn knocked on a door and said I'm lost. As it happens, the person behind the door was George Freedley, head of the Theater Collection at the New York Public Library, and also a friend of the man whose name I've forgotten. As always, one thing led to another, and Freedley, who was gray-haired, pot-bellied, and uppity, decided, on learning I was a composer, to introduce me to ANTA once we were all back in the city.

The American National Theater and Academy, of which George Freedley was chairman, and whose committee contained Aline MacMahon, Alexander Kirkland, and Herbert Kubly, among others, functioned to produce "top theater" on a shoestring in small venues —what would later be termed Off Broadway. Midtown plays in those days nearly always had incidental music by living composers, performed live nightly. Paul Bowles was the most in demand of these composers, having inherited the mantle from Virgil in the WPA days, and achieved fame with *The Glass Menagerie.* Obviously Paul wasn't going to touch ANTA's small fees, but I needed what is known as Experience. I agreed to supply the score (a few songs to be sung by actors untrained as singers, and "mood music" for four instruments) to a new translation, by Leighton Rollins, of Euripides' *Hippolytus.* John Reich, an old-world German, would direct. The role of Phaedra would be taken by Muriel Smith, and the role of Hippolytus by Donald Buka, whom I'd never met but had seen in the movies, notably as Bette Davis's very cute son in *Watch on the Rhine.*

Muriel, by a stroke of casting genius, was the only one of ten actors who would not be singing. Yet her vocal presence on stage emitted the power of a prima donna, and, like Callas in Pasolini's nonmusical film of *Medea,* Muriel strode and declaimed, breathed and expired, in the mode of the nineteenth-century greats. Better still, she had a way of standing still, of not breathing, of projecting a pulsating inertia that I've never seen, except perhaps with Martha Graham.

The premiere on 20 November was followed by three other performances. The musical group consisted of flute, cello, trumpet, and piano, of which I recall only Seymour Barab on cello and me on piano. (I remember, too, that at one performance when the trumpeter was ill, Chuck Turner stepped in at the last minute, unrehearsed, and played the part on his fiddle.)

Three months later, on 26 February 1949, *Cock-a-Doodle-Doo* opened, also for a run of four performances. This new play by Iris Tree was directed by Margaret Barker, known as Beanie, who would become a lasting colleague. Beanie, already in her mid-forties, had been central to the old Group Theater, but now was drifting. She lived with Ann McFarlane, the same Ann McFarlane for whom Allela Cornell had ended her life and who now was a big wheel in AA. So was Beanie. I was not. Nor did I sometimes show up for rehearsals. Beanie lectured me, but the lectures incited me hopelessly, as though to prove my good I had first to prove my bad, so as to be worthy of your good, a vicious circle.

The play was a hillbilly confection about magic and love and crops. But the cast was dynamic. Charlton Heston and Darren McGavin were febrile and sensuous, born for the stage, and so was Peggy Feury. The Stylized Movement by Felicia Sorel involved, among the overall choreography, a little jig for Heston accompanied by a cello solo, all pizzicato. He came to my dreary room one Sunday morning to rehearse this, and seemed so warm, so comradely, that I felt we'd be brothers forever. (His movie career changed that. The only time we ever met again was at the White House for a "Festival of the Arts" in 1965. He was chatting with someone Important, and responded to my greeting with an unfriendly shrug, like Prince Hal with old Falstaff.) The music, for just piano and cello (intoned by me and the trusty Seymour Barab), was based on a Kentucky folk tune, eventually published as "Mountain Song," and still played from time to time on other people's recitals.

23. Ned's Diary (IV)

Two weeks ago I dreamed I strangled to death a woman who had no name.

1947

July, Tanglewood. If I fall in love a hundred times, requited or no, the cycle is complete each time. If I love 7 a week, each day has the same gamut, the same tender tortures, as a year. We cannot fall. Suffer daily for someone new I have never seen. . . . Tanglewood is frightful, not the happy memory of last year. Too social for concentration, but I am happy when I am the center, thereby overpowering shyness. The haircut makes me bullnecked. . . .

Headaches at orgasm. Sensation accumulates, becoming more and more intense so that at the climax I grow blind with an unendurable crunch in the temples. Takes nearly 36 hours to abate totally. Not always does this happen, but often enough, especially when sober. . . .

If I am passive, the earth is more so. I do make things, which is more active than lying fallow. Man grows passive through lack of craft; the imminent mass suicide looms because he cares no longer. The strong of the earth—who are evil—know this. "Follow me to your destruction," they say to the jew who reports with mathematical docility to the gas chamber. Until individual man is rendered incapacitated (arms chopped off, presenting a rational excuse for non-aggression) he will continue to vent his vicious insecurity upon the poet. . . . My strength is extraordinary, being creative—next to the bartender who petrifies me.

18 August, New York. The longest binge ever: 7 days. Robbery again, and six days ago I woke up with this snapshot in my hand [photo of a wedding couple being photographed, pasted in diary], from somewhere on First Avenue. . . . Smattering of love last week when Latouche administered some African therapy to my overboard condition of emergency.

Martha's Vineyard. . . . dreams: often of lions. (Wrote a poem called *Lions.*) . . . Made up a movie as we drove to Chilmark. During the credits, behind the written word, face of a boy comes closer. Credits finished, all we see filling the screen are his lovely head and naked shoulder, perhaps tears. Hair of a woman perceived descending from top of screen, face upside down, she glances at boy, disappears. Only his head & shoulder. He screams, loud, and fades. Everything is black. Movie begins.

Suicide by injection of a fork into the eye, revolved into the brain. This is done at a café table.

Sartre's trashy novel: "One could only damage oneself through the harm one did to others. One could never get directly to oneself."

Dream: Huge boa-constrictor, with a dog's nose of elastic & vast manipulatory power, hangs in a lone tree above an empty highway. A fast new car approaches upon which this snake means to drop & encircle, demolishing. But the car's too fast and the snake falls just short of it onto the road. In anger he makes jerking gestures with his jaws, as though to swallow the car—which has vanished. It has become night, the road now a city street in silence. I walk with a friend, but the boa squirms behind; he becomes an auto. The auto nears now, slows down, and from it 3 rough men appraise us. Solicitous? The car makes a U-turn, follows slowly. Street dark and quiet. I am in the foyer of a slum-house, a house of danger—or rather of unpleasant mystery. My family's? Darkish red glow. A distant room like that of a medium, screens, messy canopies and lace, people without faces fade in and out, never close, always across the black room. (Yesterday I saw 3 movies: in a cartoon a dog's nose was detachable. Later in Mary's bar, 3 gangsters frightened me.) I have been drinking again.

11 September. Every afternoon on awakening I have turned into some new kind of animal, a lobster, a hound. Today in a haze I sat with the sober world of Stewart's cafeteria at 32nd and 6th Ave. Spastics, snarling cashiers, senile stupidity, general un-beauty. Is this the real world I emerge into? . . .

16 September. Weird things are happening. Why will not burglars leave notes? My house, flimsy thing, is inhabited at nights when I am gone. . . .
. . . Now the suitcase is stolen. Heart hurts. Today the postcards of apology. Close to alcoholism. Nosebleeds, the sheet smeared with blood clots. An alarming letter from Janet [Fairbank] about how my reputation as a dependable musician is going down the drain. I can explain nothing of the world to myself. Am I a failure? What difference does it make?
An evening with Frank Etherton is inevitably odd. Last night he pried open the iron safety-door of Café Society, and down a long flight of steps, through a porthole, we saw Nellie Lutcher, stark naked, powdering her breasts before a mirror.

5 October. The piano is in the same condition as myself, poor battered thing. . . . I was robbed *again* last night, but had only 7 dollars.

2:30 a.m. Have begun Gide's journals. What shameless sincerity! How is he to be admired this day? Yet he has become the Great Man with the speculating fruition behind him. Will we who are young be able one time to turn back to decades of recalling? There looks to be another big war soon. We will never have known middle age, but will have been here for the world's end. . . .

8 October. Louise Holdsworth woke me yesterday noon (I'm writing a dance, *Egress,* for her) and asked me out to lunch. My eyes are bigger and browner, she says, than before she went to the coast. She cannot work, discussed her divorce. Does she mean to seduce me? . . . Then after school had tea with Chuck Turner: same problem. Dined with Janet Lauren who proferred some slight but solid advice, from her singer's vantage, on the new songs. We saw *Marked Woman,* the old Bette Davis farce. At midnight Eugene and Seymour came by with ice-cream and ginger ale; and at 2 Shirley called all laden with marital woes. This busy manner diverts the ego, but is hardly solitude.

28 October. Is will be was. There's more room where people aren't than where they are (age 7).

I'm 24 now, and hygienically have begun to die. Tonite the 3 of us (Gene, Sh. & I) ate at Chambord—50 bucks! Christ, I can't even touch rum-cake or fruit in wine or brandy sauce without going askew. I shall see a doctor?

Does a man who has spent years in a concentration camp recall any moment of this with the nostalgia indigenous to the past, or is such sentiment beyond human nature?

31 October. Don Giovanni this evening, that perfect thing. Talked to Sally Goodman at intermission; she had come by yesterday afternoon at 3:30, but I (having just awakened) was sitting in bed with a jet black man & woman, drinking vermouth and eating baked beans. I didn't think to invite Sally in for fear she'd be shocked: she wouldn't have been, except by my face which was ashen.

Last night an hallucination. Having retired with the remnants of a shattering hangover after only 8 waking hours, I found it difficult to fall asleep. Room in total darkness. After tossing for a while, I opened my eyes. Blazing light! I could make out some exquisite snow-white buildings in the shimmering distance, but immediately a hand passed about a yard above my vision and dropped a flower on the pillow beside my head—or was it a crumpled note, a message? This all took but a second. I trembled, and after an hour dropped off.

When I come home (alone & sober) late at night, I'm always afraid someone is in the room, until I turn on the light.

5 November, Wednesday. Now that autumn's here (frail rain falling, soon snow) I have all of my breakfasts home, in a part of the room called the Yellow Corner: 3 yellow rugs, chair with a yellow cloth, lemon-colored table-spread on a box and a bowl of golden apples, bananas and oranges. And the chair's wood is blond. Very insane.

Saw Dr. Kraft today. Am I sure about this? Therapist = the rapist.

Last night at George Bemberg's, as we talked, I suddenly heard a bird singing. When it sang again an hour later I asked if there was a canary in a nearby apartment. He said no, but his own pet finch died a year ago & a certain few of his friends can hear it sing now (he can't, because he lives there). George has a European charm, a cross between Gian Carlo and Alexei Haieff, but being literary his style is more complex.

Tiger's Eye. Why must each new little-mag format be lavish & extravagant, boxing vacuum? The story I read by Anaïs Nin an hour ago is already forgotten. And New York seems to host a surplus of modern dancers, all à la Martha, popeyed, longhaired, rich-lipped, vastly facile and utterly monotonous from a relentless hammering on the least amusing of the overdone psychoses. These girls are naïve in their urge to express—to project—their little troubles. It's obscene.

10 November. There's no such thing as good or bad taste—only taste.

Saturday George Bemberg & I played through French songs all evening, mostly Fauré, Poulenc, Milhaud. Then today I get a new ditty from Danny Pinkham who sends me everything he does. He puts it this way. "Also I send you a new Fauré song I just wrote (maybe it's Teddy Chanler instead). I think it's pretty hot stuff myself, in its own quiet way. Hope you don't disapprove." Does he feel he's weak, or is he being sophisticated about the derivitiveness inevitable to the young?

John Lindsay [Wingate] & Christopher Lazare each phone about once a week (when I am most busy) and talk forever, wittily, about their own troubles (no mention of mine). Who cares? Even my closest friends are conversationally selfish. So I have always tried not to be except with bores. The word "I" always makes me feel strange.

I no longer bring 15 or 20 people home every nite to continue drinking after bars close at 4 (and then throw them cavalierly out at 7, bottles and all). I will be quiet for a while—calmly bacchanalian, as I wrote to Danny about *A Sermon on Miracles.*

16 November, Sunday, 2 a.m. Just left Christopher with whom I spent the entire evening (after having passed a sober afternoon at the movies—French—with Fabian). He gave me a hypodermic of dealudite (?)—opium and morphine. An eerie, shifting, languorous sensation quite opposed to liquor, which cannot be drunk with it. Being of oriental derivation, the drug when injected is placid and sensual, not conducive to erections. Impossible even to urinate. Perception made sharper, all is apricot-colored, like drowning slowly in chiffon. Fingers shake, though the brain stays crystal clear, eyes grow leaden, shoulders tingle. At best it makes one feel like snuggling beneath the wing of an angel. But it fatigued me formidably (though conversation stays acute), made me itch & sweat, and finally vomit. Fortunately effects wear off pretty thoroughly, except for hiccups, unlike liquor—and then, appropriately enough, we had a midnite supper at a Chinese restaurant on 48th, although hunger disappears with drugs.

Jackson Mac Low stops by to leave some children's poems he just wrote for me to set. Nice separately, but as a cycle they're too much alike. Influenced by Paul Goodman and (of all things) *Wozzeck*—hop! hop!

Violence all over New York now, and murders, especially in the Village. Awakened at 4 a.m. by gunshots and the squeal of an escaping truck. Afterwards the local gin-mills empty their blinking tight customers onto the sidewalk where they unsteadily discuss the crime. It's the second recent gang slaughter in the neighborhood.

A few dark mornings later I am again wakened by 2 people fucking right outside of, and against, my door. This disturbance lasts 25 minutes (I hear each word and motion climaxed by the wastebasket being kicked clatteringly over) and then they leave. Rushing to peep through the window, I wonder should I have asked them in. No, hallway fornication is a sacred tension. Instead I pray they won't wake the neighbors, and long to throw them 2 white roses.

17 November. Yesterday I ate an orange, today also, and so will I tomorrow. Last Thursday noon, too, after a night of puking. Why are we not so organized that food-fuel is only needed once a week? Or if it's daily, then eating should not be infinitely replicated (like vestigial male & female organs contained eternally within each other) but become an untried alluring taste every one of the thousands of times. Food, and discussions of it, bore me.

Bumped into Peter Briggs, and later Aaron Bell (who came to the city to see *Medea*) at Julius's bar last week. How can such bright boys be so tediously opinionated? And yet, each time I leave Dr. Kraft, I realize that for an hour my voice has droned without shading—that I have been unwrapped. Then back to the world where, with our dearest, the gaudy veneer is reassumed. Is this our personality, our charm, that vanishes at the analyst's? At birth we enter our disguises.

18 November. This afternoon Zelda Goodman and I did 4 songs of mine (twice) at Juilliard. Nice reception. But to call my religious music undignified, as was the case in the post-performance confab, is naïve. A pile of shit could be construed as exalted. I answered all questions with canny wit, & said that while a poem or symphonic etude is complete in itself, a song is a 3rd thing, to be considered greater than the sum of its parts. And religious meanings are much broader today. (My fingers shook from last night's beer.) Jacobi was enthralled.

Thursday. The silent bed. Awoke fully clothed. I have never been drunker. . . . What we absorb we later impart. . . .

Friday. . . . so I tell Kraft some of this, but withhold some too. . . . Last night Shirley and I went to *Tosca,* all dressed up and hungover. Horrible production; Tibbett a disgrace. But such music—the Frenchified splendor of those ubiquitous lowered sevenths and parallel fifths! How does a composer, without being drunk, let go enough to write such schmaltz? Can a world exist without alcohol, people work and sleep together without being high? Afterwards a strange 2 hours at Tony's Café on 52nd where I'm allowed, being with fashionable girl, etc. Later I hear from Bobby, the waiter at Mary's, that I had announced the nite before that I came there just to insult people (this is important!). We run into Alfonso Ossorio, with whom I make a lunch appointment and then oversleep. He is with a circle of wealthy asses, but Shirley finds him appealing all the same. (He has done a pretty good cover for Rimbaud's *Illuminations.* Maybe I'll have him do one for "Mongolian Idiot.")

Saturday afternoon. Awoke this morning with a cold. Lesson with Wagenaar who finds *Cain & Abel* expressive but sluggish. . . . Session with Kraft, the third one, and I blush from the strain of telling my dream of resentment about him. . . . Ryder exhibit at the Whitney with Shirley: pungent, gloomy, inspiring. Today is like Ryder: deep, mellow, glimmering rain. Very Saturday. Tonight Billy Masselos' remarkable program at Carnegie.

. . . Finished 14 Greek plays: 11 tragedys [sic], 3 comedies. And Gide's nice book. Must resume Proust (also Kierkegaard's Mozart essay), *Ulysses* (who stole it?), *War and Peace,* & Rimbaud. . . . Probably, in my horror of order, I keep this journal as unacknowledged anal-eroticism (also my constant nose-picking to the discust [sic] of all). But my spitting, smoking, fingernail-biting & drinking—are oral. . . .

Jennie Tourel: her green silk negligée is expensive but tawdry; she's very pretty but her elbows are a little crusty, her lipstick is inclined to be cracked, smeared; and there are chunks of vaseline in her iron-blue hair. She is tired: very Oral. . . . On the stage she is immaculate, a coquette, bewitchingly clean. She can do anything—as Virgil puts it, she can sing "high and low and soft and loud." She is impeccable: very Anal.

Claude et Maurice. Genius vs. talent; little boys, one simple, one suave; ninths vs. sevenths; oral vs. anal; sensual innocence vs. sexual wit; outdoor painting vs. hothouse restraint.

4 December. Uncanny weather, not conducive to setting into a 4-part round the little carol Paul sent. . . . Jackson [Mac Low] stopped by, said nothing. He seems a frightened boy.

Blazing drunk last night at Julius's (saw Stud Ruml who's gotten fat, and his new Stalinist mistress who's not as attractive as Bobbie James. He's trying, like all the others, to publish his novel), and at the San Remo where a girl named Marjorie R. propositioned me (she liked my green sweater), but when I phoned today I find she's left town. Alas! Woke up at 2 this aft. having wet the bed. Went with S.G. to put the deposit down for Times Hall; then to see the luscious Viviane Romance in *Panic,* a pleasant French film on murder & deception; then had my cards read badly for a dollar in a creepy Village tea-house; then to the analyst; then met Muriel Smith for a late & long supper. Muriel is heavier and appealing, excited by her recital at which she is *not* singing my songs.

I've always liked women with long hair, bangs, berets, very high heels, even as I'm fascinated by people who don't drink, men with hair on the back of their hands, people who don't need glasses, and eating *in.* Closely related to my aversion to the words "pie" and "cake" is the feeling of guilt when I eat pastry, which I love.

Spent evening accompanying fiddle sonatas with Chuck Turner: 2 Mozart, 2 Beethoven. Then read all the plays in Paul's *Stoplight,* hoping to find one for music. (I must have him "lucidify" 2 of them.)

The stained glass of Riverside Church is all in bird colors: cardinal red, parrot green, diaphanous bluebird blue, canary yellow. The luminosity too suggests fluid: orange crush, the deep blue of sunlit sea-depths, green of crème-de-menthe, red blood.

How happy are the doctors' names: Kraft, art; Freud, joy; Jung, youth; Reich, state.

Have never encountered in literature this situation: A good man in high place, an evil man in low place. Through their interactions the good man is caused to sink, the evil man to rise until the scales are balanced. The left side then continues up, the right side down; the good man is destroyed, evil triumphs. The Good has a flaw of course; and perhaps Evil's "flaw" will be a trace of good. But Evil will not be punished, and Good will go unavenged. How real is the logic of this dénouement. Still, we leave the theater filled with pity and fear, struck by the circumstances around every corner. Othello?

Aaron says that with all the rapid and liberal advancement (particularly in jazz which has furnished a complete new system of orchestration), only in Love Music has there not been a change since Wagner.

...been snowing lavishly for a long while this evening. Supper with Tom Stauffer, just over from Germany. (Snow has always reminded me of him.) He's plumper, looks well at thirty, same fierce pontifical manner, grand height, short hair, childish aggression, wears glasses, still stutters....

Paralyzing interview at Kraft's, all from the flimsiest dream-fragment: Alone in a huge empty pillared marble hall, my sister enters in Grecian mourning. Associations total and terrifying....

Rimbaud last night made me sad, it took a long time till sleep.

Glassy, cold, yellow, bright, snowy. I was the only one with spectacles, without a tie, and who didn't say a word in Sociology today, but I learned that a Stradivarius's comparative high quality is fiction. A pertinent point.

Pointless session with Kraft. Tense supper with Papa.

15 December, Monday afternoon. Refrigerators: nasty food-houses, civilized traps, how I hate them. Anything concerning food offends me.

Saturday. Lunch at Muriel Smith's. Fine supper and alcoholic evening again at Alfred Auerbach's. David Lloyd recorded 2 of my songs.

Last night, suicidal evening of bourbon with Bill Flanagan & Billy Johnson; later with Will Hare, in whose house I collapsed.

Man created God in his own image. Except for me.

2:15 a.m. Hangover's finally worn off, and I'm better. Tom's Texan just left. 4 hours!

Ate at home here with S.G. tonite; hamburger weirdly done. After, we went through the Couperin twice—the Third Tenebrae Service. I could expire to that piece.

Baudelaire: "Drugs can only reveal to man what is already there."

Dream of a butterfly the size of a peacock, trembling and transparent, fringed with silvery crimson. How nice to own a peacock the size of a butterfly.

Winter's here, with black astonishment from the sky. The need for love is more real than love. Worst blizzard since 1888 (the year Debussy wrote the *Arabesques*). Streets still piled high with sick ocher sleet. Subways jammed, yet male members of the Blind (indistinguishable from one another) persist in parading from one end of the cars to the other, soliciting money for their lack-of-talent by playing not only the accordion but trumpet and saxophone and snare drum, singing popular songs devoid of style. Everyone is embarrassed.

Visit to Central Park Zoo last week before meeting Grace at her dance class. What a clever diversity of fauna fellow the earth with us. Entering the lion house I quiver and recall my dreams. The amber cast on a lady panther's bristles as a jailor plays a hose on her; she spits, eyes straining back as she seeks to recollect her forest home a thousand years ago. I see that she is called "Chicky."

1948

14 January. Went to see Marc Blitzstein this aft. He says we are all political whether we like it—or know it—or not. In his work he feels he must speak directly, not being a subtle person. . . . But aren't most of our historic masterpieces direct?

M. Blitzstein also said that Cocteau (he knows him) is an unhappy man: that each new work is to be the chef d'oeuvre, but never quite is. That Cocteau has made the broadest and most basic of human emotions—love & death—into chic vogues.

But the danger with reporting is that, often as not, the reporter's own spirit is projected more than that of which he reports. . . .

Though healthy people are seldom heard from. The unadjusted (adjusted to what?), if they have anything to say, make, by definition, our great men. . . .

Even our most advanced societies have their noses in the ring of God. None is to be trusted, even the Quakers, when they speak in the name of the Lord. But how by logic are they proved wrong?

Calm evening, after a drastic weekend, at Sid & Joan Simon's. Sam Kramer and his wife (who looks like Madeleine Solonge) were there, also Frances Osato. Nice meal. I sang my blues songs, and Frances her Basque folk songs.

Didn't want to go to Kraft's today, but as usual in such cases the "lesson" was more than regularly edifying. Certain fears become illuminated, as I start to understand alcoholic compulsion.... Made a reservation for Antwerp, May 26th. I'll find the money somehow. France and Italy will make a crucial change in me; the American strain is my background but not my milieu....

24 January. 3 a.m. Fierce insomnia, which always comes with a hangover, and I must get up at 7:45. I'm told that on learning the bars were closed, I charged purposely into a lamppost head first. Now I feel it.

Read 2 awful books: *The City and the Pillar* and *Other Voices, Other Rooms.*

Each meal eaten hastens me to death; each word spoken binds me tighter to the world. If I denied myself consciously, would I live longer than in the abandonment which leads to nothing? Let's concern ourselves with differences of technique less than with sameness of motivation in the making of music as in the making of a good world.

I itch! God, but I itch! For weeks I've itched on all parts, and at night the itching turns insupportable. Before I finish scratching deliciously one section, another section commences; I am an octopus in a multiple self-embrace of scratch and wrench from the ceaseless tantalizing tickle which attacks all places reachable and unreachable. Pink warts, bleeding hives, crabs, ringworm of the crotch, scabies—all of it itching, itching like a hair-shirt 24 hours a day, and nothing to be done.

6 April. I shall not write here for a long time. It's partly the impact of this recent murder which prompts the hiatus. I may still spend more time in destroying myself than in constructing fine things. But when I return from school to be phoned by the Charles Street Police Station (asking about a man with whom I had a one-night stand; whose name, Victor Trerisse, rings no bell; who was found with his skull crushed in his apt. on Perry Street; who had noted my number in his address book), I am stunned into recalling the thousands of hours these past years wasted in squalid—no, dangerous—company. Happiness and love count less than an even keel for work. The analysis must become my *raison d'être.* Delights which ornament the weeks, sweet or sour, must remain in the head. Talk now, don't journalize.

6 September. The 6-month interim contained my giving a good party, an M.S. from Juilliard, meeting Nell Tangeman, Rosemary's marriage, inebriated orgies, suntans, haircuts, Shirley in Europe, a sick mother, lack of love, and also piles & chicken pox.

. . .

Because of Dr. Kraft's current vacation, my thoughts return to these pages. The holiday consisted of a miserable 4 days at Tanglewood (though Hugh Ross did the new *Madrigals* exquisitely: he knows them better than I do). Then 2 weeks at Truro with Jordan Whitelaw, than whom it is inconceivable that anyone could be more monotonous, but the last evening there Paul Cadmus came to dine (by way of contrast), and we saw a great whale spouting out there in the bay. Next day I returned, slick and tawny from the haughty sun, to the problems of this magic city.

At Provincetown, Julius Monk quickly spread the tale of when I threw the full beer bottle at his white piano; I had forgotten that when the police asked me "Why?" I replied (with lowered eyes), "Because I'm unhappy." I'd gone to his boîte with Bob Olsen, Stella Brooks and Ellis Kohs—an incongruous trio.

Although I wrote two songs (to Sitwell poems) I spent most of the time careening through the countryside swilling stingers with the coyness a suntan allows. And I feel in my vacuum of boredom that, despite my genius, I shall compose nothing great until I am no longer beautiful. . . . Van Gogh, in a letter to his brother, quotes Richepin: "L'amour de l'art fait perdre l'amour vrai."

Today, hungover, went to the plangent new French Dietrich movie with Nell Tangeman and Martha Lipton (Marlene striding toward Gabin with a steely urgency that one half her age can envy). Then to a party and had our handwriting analyzed (spooky). Later, Nell and I watched a man undress from her back window.

15 September. Finally visited Mother at the hospital this afternoon. It was pathetic. With Father, we spent an hour walking through the grounds which are endless and paradisiacal: forest, formal gardens, rocky streams which truly gush beneath Japanese bridges, arbors, benches, occasionally a nurse with a strolling charge. But poor Mother remembers nothing. Or rather, she seems scatterbrained. Still, it is good to find her as happily manic as she was melancholic before. Later I felt like crying, and did, and hated to leave Father. Mother had kept asking us for cigarettes and wanting us to meet all her friends (which is against the rules), and even the nurses, though she says some of them are cruel (she meant cold, or businesslike).

It is *not* "human nature" to wage war. When a fascist leader of strong personality woos the crowd which longs to follow, he's not addressing an instinct of self-preservation, but a desire for self-expression which is stronger.

A funny day. Got up early for Kraft and accomplished nothing. Phone rings incessantly: spend an hour a day talking to people I detest. But I can't seem to write a thing, which has never happened before. Visit from Warren Hassmer (who came all the way from Boston to see me—a disappointment), and from Chuck Turner (we lunched on his sandwiches in Bryant Park). . . . Harold Brown, despondent as ever, stopped by for a short while, but I had to leave for a silly cocktail affair at Nancy Reid's, so we took the subway together (I seem to spend *another* hour a day underground). . . . Nancy wants me to compose a "one-man" cantata for the instrumentation of Sauguet's *La voyante;* I think I will, if Paul'll write me a groovy enough text. The guests, except for Nancy (the world's most affected woman, who looked beautiful—from a distance—in a long scarlet skirt), were all male (queer), mostly snobs, and included Stanley Bate and pleasant Colin McPhee, neither of whom I'd met before. Left with Oliver [Daniel] and we talked of living together which got me back a half-hour late for my dinner date, and was detained still further by bumping into ra-ra Gene Fuller. Being stood up, I went alone and hungry to the Billie Holiday film which was degrading and bad for jazz. Billie looked fierce. Then to the San Remo for a coke (I drink liquor only on Tuesdays, Fridays and Saturdays, as the 4 weekly psychoanalysis sessions are at 10 a.m.). MacDougall's with Tony Clark, since I had been an hour late meeting Sally. . . . Strange to walk those streets sober, those bohemian streets through which I generally reel, seem pointless and drear. Values askew. Indeed a stupid day.

The room crawls with tropical roaches, dust by the barrelful, rust in the sink, scum around the tub thick enough to slice and serve as *consommé madrilène.* All my music in spectacular disarray. Despondent fatigue caused by the ceaseless parade of the inevitable pair: drunken night, shaky day.

Friday finally cleaned the house and smeared the last of Paul Bowles's ambergris (which has lasted a year and ½) into the wood, & then got drunk at Julius's bar with a bunch of Bostonians; later, limitless gin-&-tonics at Morris's where it was good to see Alvin Ross after months. Last memory: Harold Norse lugging me home in a taxi and tucking me in.

Saw three movies today with a new friend, a jet-haired cross between Dana Andrews & Robert Cummings, named Frank Bland. I introduced him to Howard Moss who said, "And I'm Howard Exciting." Now I am alone. Tomorrow begin again the job at Mme. Gauthier's, which means a little money and a lot of experience, but still anxious at not being able to write.

Frank Etherton just phoned (it's 1 a.m.) from his seat of monstrous repose at the Algonquin, and for 15 minutes mouthed squalid whimsies, mostly gossip, about the frightful impression I had made on Alec Wilder at some snobbish audition months ago where I was not yet too tight, but sincerely told Wilder, in what must have been honeyed rhetoric, how much I admired certain of his songs. Important item: Frank, calling me in the company of a paratrooper, flatters me in porcelain accents, reiterates the phrase "successful young composer." But this is self-praise, for he throws famous names around like chicken-feed, to substantiate himself in the eyes of his friends. Does he exist for himself, or for anyone else, when alone in a room? Do I?

Never heard a peep out of Mrs. Lucie Bigelow Rosen after sending her a bread & butter note, hoping to solicit a commission but apparently insulting her by saying the sound of her Theramin was like the faraway moan of a dying dinosaur. I seem either to strike people as an utter bitch or a cloying adolescent. . . .

The statement that irks me most is: "What have *you* to be frustrated about? Why, if *I* had a method of self-expression I'd certainly find nothing to be unhappy about." Art is not a screen to hide behind but a job like any other. Having a talent, one takes it for granted; it's not a blessing but a responsibility. Having both legs, I can't imagine being without them. (But I do have dandruff and am shy). . . .

Cocktails with George Freedley whom I want to champion me. Wore the green bow-tie Stella Brooks gave me one unreal morning at a gage-party and tried to impress him with my charm and talent. I want to write the score for *Hippolytus* with Muriel Smith. . . . Henry Jackson came over tonite & we went through Britten's *Rape of Lucretia*. I played him my Piano Sonata which he said he liked (no one else does). But we were interrupted by herds of old friends, Richard Stankeiwicz and a Juilliard violinist with a Chinese concubine, then John Wingate (with his Marshall) just back from Nantucket, and as usual articulately depressed—this time about his young friend's Roman Catholic ties. Returned nine beer bottles to buy a late supper at the Sevilla, then we sat in Abingdon Square awhile. Now it's 2 a.m. No wonder I don't work. . . . Reread the scary section on execution in *The Idiot*. . . . 3 hours later. Can't sleep. Eyes heavy and aching, like golf balls made of blood, gelatinous yo-yo's.

21 September. Another full day of accompanying for Eva Gauthier's students. Politically she's a formidable reactionary for a woman of her wide acquaintance, travel, culture. Only the nostalgia for the old lush days, inevitable for one of her years, can excuse her. For she is not a Catholic like Stravinsky or Boulanger, the former so devout that his colleague Messiaen's devout offerings are mere "crucifixes of sugar," the latter so cocksure as to claim that if Gide had not been raised a "Huguenot" he would not have made a career out of continual rationalizing. Gauthier's musical reputation must be based on her repertory, for as a coach (than which few are better, which says little), she offers nothing that any other coach couldn't. I abhor her squealing Pekingese and squeaking Siamese enough to throttle them, yet am beguiled by this 70-year-old with blue hair and a jade collection, glamour-fetishes which always trap me and which Kraft may or may not understand.

Yesterday on the subway, which was fairly full, I sat reading and quietly picking my nose. A woman across the aisle said audibly, "Mister, please use your handkerchief." I melted with shame and did not look up. If I'd had one, would I have used a handkerchief after such a request?

Today on the uptown 6th Ave. bus which was fairly full, I sat in the back reading when my right ankle began to itch. After scratching, the annoyance moved upward, though I thought little about it. But by the time I reached Gauthier's my whole calf was a vibrating mess of welts, so that I had to apply a soothing lotion. Sure enough, an hour later in the presence of the rich and haughty Cathleen Parker Bernatschke, a bedbug big as life appeared crawling on the knee of my trouser. Eva, with regal calm, plucked it and deposited it shining into the toilet ("Brightness falls from the air"). But we all squirmed uncomfortably long after.

23 September. Over ten years since my first sex experience. Nine years since first meeting Géorg, the first of so many dearest friends to die unquietly. Eight years since first I came home drunk. Autumnally cool tonight—going-back-to-school weather that smells of pencil shavings and starched skirts. Reading Rosamunde Lehmann's *The Ballad and the Source.*

Another opulent feast last night chez Cathleen Parker, who's to concertize in Italy & wanted to see some more of my stuff. Gypsy Rose Lee was there (who recently married Julio De Diego, of all people). At first I was disappointed by her looks, then found that the famous physicality is couched more in vitality than in prettiness. She talks incessantly with a certain flare for comedy and sparkle, but exclusively of her own affairs which concern mostly backstage vagaries. I contributed nothing to the conversation, forced and dull, which terminated when they all took off to Karen Horney's lecture (significantly on "The Shallow Personality as Caused by the Neuroses of Our Time").

26 September, Sunday. High on benzedrine and whisky with Christopher Lazare for 10 hours last night. As usual the pattern was expressionist, blurred. We went to the 111 Club to see T.C. Jones (backstage, *complètement la grande dame,* T.C., like all drag queens, makes me feel comparatively masculine when he bats his painted lashes and speaks of Luise Rainer in breathy tones); then to the Ebony for Billie Holiday but were barred because of no necktie. . . . At the Pink Elephant I see Tony R. for the first time in a year and a half, and he's forgotten my name, *quelle farce!* Trouble sleeping (3 hours in all, retiring at 8 a.m. finally) because of the benzedrine. Christopher was literally loaded with his morphine, shooting up every 3 hours, but remained always articulate. . . . Mother phoned early and bright from Philadelphia this morning, out of the hospital, sounds fine. . . .

28. Another tiring but pleasant 4 hours with Madame Gauthier. When she speaks of her past, especially the years in Java and the sound of the Orient, I am transfixed. But when she sings through a song (with her still-expressive equipment) I am so outraged at her rhythmical ignorance that I would scream reprimands if it weren't for making her seem incompetent before her pupils. She takes far more than "a singer's liberty": she's oblivious to note values, rests, clefs and proper entrances.

In the 6th Ave. delicatessen I come across John Cage at lunch and pause for a shallow chat. Then meet C. Turner to see the Gide film at the lavish new Paris Theater. Somewhat moved, but on the whole disappointed. Gide is almost dull with his perverse wholesomeness. I do like striking truths but need new effects too. And isn't it unforgivable that a brainy film like *Symphonie pastorale* should not experiment with the camera to amaze the eye as well as to satisfy the reason? Instead we're given the same white series of flashes.

A touching letter from Mother—now out of the hospital—enclosing snaps of little Christopher and Rosemary still looking pregnant. (My dreams remain full of RR when not of lions.) Also, finally, the pictures taken by *Ebony* magazine at my party last June (forty people in one small room), showing Virgil looking sly, Donald Fuller plastered, me coy, Flanagan surprised, Frank Etherton idiotic, Muriel friendly and patronizing, Reid Arendt vacant and handsome. Quelle collection of accurate horror!

3 October, Sunday midnight. . . . As a child I murmured the word "magnolia" before going to sleep, and on awakening "gardenia." The idea was to start and end the day well, no matter what came between. Why? And why flowers?

Eva, always the rabid politician, shows me, with gloating elation, an article from *American* on how communists have infiltrated even such venerable institutions as the Guggenheim Foundation. There, among former fellowship-holders, we see the names of Aaron Copland, Marc Blitzstein, Douglas Moore as leaders who wish to "overthrow our government." Is this scare that's flooding the country a desire for liberty accompanied by the stronger fear of the responsibility of liberty? Nevertheless I erase Blitzstein as a reference in my Guggenheim application and substitute Eva Gauthier. Incidentally, Douglas Moore, whom I've never met, gave me an unsolicited recommendation based on the *Hippolytus* score. Challenge: to be more concerned about what I think of others than about what others think of me.

In Philadelphia this evening. Very pleasant. Rae brings along Teddy Letvin, living as an undergrad in her house as I once did, and he monopolizes the piano with a rather good sonata by a new Curtis composer, Rochberg. Cousin Olga, who must be terribly lonely, answers, "But Aunt Gladys, my friends are in the movies." Mother seems much better.

29 October. Indian summer. Tonite David Sachs and I went to the Gotham Book Mart to hear Rexroth read his pseudo-butch poetry. Paul Goodman in society now acts like a blind man (his vision is 20/300 and he hasn't worn glasses for years because they're "unmedical"), for he says things when nobody's looking, so nobody hears. He says: "By the time I've finished a work I haven't the energy to think of the audience." . . . Rexroth's verse, like Saroyan's prose, hoists the everyday into rarefied ether, which makes it more singable.

1 November, Monday, 2 a.m. Tonight, yearly lecture from Eugene apropos my behaving disgracefully two nights ago and alienating all my friends. And he asks what am I doing with analysis anyway when I make no effort to eliminate the grizzly combination of self-adoration and self-humiliation?

Every popular song today is concerned with money.

Tomorrow we vote for president. Last week Nell and I saw Truman on Broadway: Times Square was a bedlam of anticipation, sirens for minutes heralded his approach preceded by 300 cops on motorcycles and several double-sized funeral autos. Terrifying and unreal, for a single simple man. (I have added a portrait of the young Schubert to my collection of beautiful and monstrous faces.)

3 November. A long time ago I read in Ripley of a Persian prince whose total behavior from birth to death was recorded by a relay of secretaries always in his proximity: his every gesture, spoken phrase, each time he scratched his ear or kissed or read, or smelled a rose or dreamed or shat. But in the end, how monotonously incomplete this must all have been. . . . Maybe I shall dispense with the compulsion to notate daily every whim I glean. My essential anguish—linked with ambition, passive and enthralled—I find difficult to clarify, even to Kraft.

Words from the dead: Where are your secrets now? The suicide, finally all effected, did not succeed. For you carried the trial here, followed by what was meant to remain, trouble being deathless. Therefore do not die for yourself, each world's the same. Had your confessor vanished in suicide, where then would be your most secret dreams? . . . Suicides that fail are the ones that kill you, since you're no longer here to savor them.

Last night Donald Fuller and I drank *spheres* of Manhattans, becoming so ravenously high that he didn't vote, but we laughed raucously all through the ballet. It deserved it too: what a disgrace to perform multiple entrechats in metered mimicry of Ravel's icily impeccable orchestration of *Empress of the Pagodas.*

2 a.m. Having completed the first two lacerations, I'm about to begin "—and in the open air." I now like Russians (especially dirty ones, perhaps crusted or sticky but youngish, healthful, vodka-soaked and garishly handsome) since the "oppositeness" of Italians no longer satisfies, nor offers sufficient mystery. Stavrogin's confession.

8 November, 1:30 a.m. Terribly upset by the recent murder at the Waldorf, and by the pathological beauty who did it. It's all I talk or think of, and collect clippings and pictures. Apparently he was punishing his father by this symbolic gesture. His name is Barrows.

I find cats in my room. When I come home they have crawled through the broken window pane (it's been out for two years) to elude the cold. Finally they vanish slowly with somnolent arrogance. And I hate cats.

Depression persists with a taut expectancy. But it's still *general:* my whereabouts in this ill world.

28 November, Saturday, 2 a.m. Well, I'm still waiting for love more earnestly than ever, having completed a blistering 3-day binge over the Thanksgiving holidays, during which I won the $1000 Gershwin prize, and though Wagenaar swore me to silence, I've already told 50 people. What humiliation if it should be a sweet dream merged in with the nightmares of these days.

David takes an hour on the phone to say how insufficient my writing technique is (Sylvia Marlowe's recital tonight. Jesus Christ!). I write such silliness to keep myself company this cold sad morning. Whole body aches from drink.

1949

11 January. Lindaraja. Last night at Herbert Weinstock's I heard this for the second time—the first was 8 or 9 years ago when the Bartóks played at Northwestern—and retrieved with perfect accuracy that tantalizing motive.

Needless to say the holidays were hysterics untold, embellished with benzedrine and bile. . . . I've stopped analysis, and for the basest reason: to save money I might afford to spend elsewhere. And the movie Carl Goldman has made of me is almost completed.

Rosemary's son is an angel. *Arc-en-ciel d'innocence.*

Winter rain. The evening sun makes lavender reflections in the pavement. Ansermet: "In music the present is extended."

24 January, 2 a.m. Gieseking's recital tonight was canceled at the last moment. There was battling with the pickets, and he was carried away to Ellis Island. And Billie Holiday's been arrested again. If Gieseking is partly wrong, certainly another part of him is great and thus untouchable. Can we afford to deny ourselves the rarity? Billie to me is of equal importance. An artist should be always the exception.

Supper with Father. Over a month now since I've seen Kraft. I am the same. But busy—little commissions, many performances. Working fairly well, though middles are hard (anyone can write beginnings and ends). Reading Stravinsky's *Poetics.*

27 January, 12:30 a.m. Tony came to see me today for the first time in 2 years *(quel type extraordinaire!)* and I bought him $5 worth of opera records. The mere proximity, that lank hair, the ungrammatical accents, the knowledge that he could crush me in a trice, all that's enough to set me on fire. So I've gotten an Italian primer and have begun to study. . . . Tonite we finished the film on me. Chichi, but

I look beautiful. . . . *L'enfant et les sortilèges* remains my chief sonic infatuation. Now that I've actually seen Ravel's instrumental score, I recognize my talent as one long shortcoming. I would die to have composed it.

29. Last night we penetrated deep into the negro section of Brooklyn to hear Margaret [Hillis]'s choral program, and once again the perfect Schubert Mass. Brooklyn! I had been . . . is *apprehensive* the word? . . . and it was well founded. Never having ventured past the Bridge and Sand Street, I was overwhelmed with a sentiment that comes only with *neighborhoods,* neighborhoods on warm and rainy nights. O I can only fall in love with someone from Brooklyn, the simple lives and simple loves. The streets there have the names of all the streets in America—presidents' names—though they seem to cut through this huge borough with the quaint irregularity of a child's knife in a square gingerbread. Couldn't we name streets nostalgically: Street of the Dream, of the Black Strawberry, of Weeping, of the Family? This sounds Spanish.

Sunday night, 2 a.m. Again benzedrine! I swear I've never been so concentratedly concerned with sex as since the analysis stopped. All my waking hours—and, of course, the sleeping ones. But I *do* it too, sometimes twice a day. Possibly I've been involved with a thousand souls, but the summery idylls seem gone forever. I don't even want to talk to the partners. Shall I go on the wagon for six weeks now that I'm working again? Donald Fuller has done it and is no longer a zombie.

I miss Shirley. Word reaches us that in Sicily with Norris she is miserable as ever. . . . It would be impossible to write worse than Tenn. Williams's *Desire and the Black Masseur.*

7 February. Carleton Smith tells me that "The Lordly Hudson" has been voted "Best Published Song of 1948" by the Music Library Association.

Now it's Dexedrine! But it was needed to fortify against a working day, after drinking so much at Louise Holdsworth's sweet party yesterday. Laden with contrite sorrow I dined at the Calypso with my new friend G., a reactionary middle-westerner of whom I seem to be fond—full-lipped, well-hung, with the charm of right-wingers when they're charming. My energy was expended solely through playing Lena Horne on the jukebox.

Reading Balzac and more Melville.

I don't give myself time to do anything, satiated like the hero in *The Girl with the Golden Eyes*. Possibly only an American is so nervously blasé as to find no pleasure in long seduction but drinks so as to speed up what of course can't be accomplished when drunk.

13 February, Sunday night. Robbed of a wallet & good overcoat.

Tepid, almost sultry weather. Night oozes with perilous calm. . . . Ralph and Jim rout me out of my unhappy bed, and we drive to Wall Street, steeped in deserted Sunday terror. The sky's been sweaty and black all day. I come home and screw from 5 to 6, then meet Alfred A. at 7 for a lush steak and the new Sartre movie. Return and try to finish the *Knight* music for Tuesday, full of remorse for having taken Eugene to a strange party last night to see my film. I got drunk and we wept over Shirley, who's almost destroyed in Sicily now. Then to San Remo, later the thievery. Also more benzedrine tablets. Finally they're all gone.

My broadcast went well enough yesterday, but nobody heard it. Also Beanie is satisfied with the play's music. Eugene's convinced I should return to Kraft. Reading Joseph Conrad.

16 February. After the Stravinsky concert tonight I met Aaron in the Tap Room. Why am I worried that I looked so ugly? I've never liked my character when with Copland, but I can't forever be a child, wearing the maroon Christmas T-shirt Nell gave me, sitting with Dick Stryker. I want Aaron to think me a good composer. . . . I have concluded I am the best accompanist around.

A moving letter from Dr. Kinsey today which I must treasure. He says I can bring joy to the world, that society must learn to appreciate a musician for his contribution.

But there is so little time. The day has only 24 hours, and I hear so many wild things within that they cannot possibly all emerge before I die. Fifteen more years and I am forty. To look upon my work season by season, how little it seems. Some of it's good, even very good. But importantly good? or great? What's great? how few seasons are left? How many lives are wasted more than mine? What's waste, when self-destruction becomes the very fertilizer of creation? How I despise the teutonic image of Beethoven, glum and mean, plowing his way over the countryside. Is the *in modo lidio* where his illness led him?

Laundry is the most daunting of nuisances if you're drunk for weeks. I want summers when Hatti and I dined at International House, outdoors, dressed up in sheets drinking gin in sunlight, but mildly. That was 10 years ago, and in another city.

Temperature yesterday over 70°.

27 February, 2 a.m. I like movies more than anything. I would rather see a good movie than hear my own music. I've never seen one I haven't been completely absorbed into. Transference is total, and impression sticks for several hours. How then can I be expected to get in bed afterwards with the person who went to the movie with me. This was the case tonight, and I managed to alienate another new acquaintance. But now that this seafarer has just gone, I have space for regrets.

Have finished, copied and orchestrated *Death of the Black Knight.* There remains only the production chaos, which can be other people's worry for a change. . . . Slept through the *Cock-a-doodle-doo* rehearsal yesterday, refusing to answer the phone, causing 7 other souls inconvenience, nay paralysis. At least Beanie belonged to Alcoholics Anonymous and understands.

The monotony of the necessary time it takes to notate, after one is already bored and thinking of new ideas. . . . Reading Hardy again *(The Mayor of Casterbridge)*; also Camus in French *(La peste).* Rehearsals every day this week.

7 March, a.m. Back from Philly. Can't say no, so I make dates, then break them by mail. Tonight I phoned Fred Keating's hotel and left a message that our appointment was canceled. Too weak to call him at Spivy's Roof. . . . And now again I've sent someone off into the very cold night and already regret it. (A person connected with the FBI.) . . . I deny myself sex, but can't resist blueberry pie or gin or Dexedrine or hair bleach or morphine derivatives if they happen to be lying around.

Finished *The Scarlet Letter.* If the amazing chapter "The Minister in a Maze" were written today it would no doubt occur that the things he believed himself to have only thought & felt (as he went down the street after the forest interview) really took place, whereas the things of disguised innocence which he spoke, were actually in his imagination. This might have been disclosed in the last chapter as a kind of revolt of the people who now understand his profane meanings after he has shown his scarlet letter.

6 April, 1 a.m. Began smoking again after 5 days of brutal strep infection like barbed wire in the throat. I haven't gone a day without tobacco since my tonsils were out at 19. Maybe the illness was due to being between the devil and the deep; for behind is a month of unchecked drinking (which is why I've not written here), and ahead is the concert with Nell. Jittery. In rehearsal my piano tone has always had the silky glow of distant rubies, but today it was like swine at untuned harpstrings. My chest is strung in taut rows of unrelieved snot! (Went to Mel Kiddon's to have my ass shot with penicillin.)

Till recently the weather was unseasonably Edenic. Now 12th Street is a smear of cold drizzle without personality. Oh for the sunsets which closed like a dusty spray over Chicago—a sad amber peacock folding his fan.

3 May. Dined at George Bemberg's with Sam Barber, just the three of us. George sang for us, with his accurate toneless tenor, an attractive song of his, "Elizabeth the Beloved." Sam sang for us with his true, true baritone, an unpublished song of his about a swan in French. And I sang with my wheezing howl, all of *Penny Arcade.* Sam, so suave, ah so suave, always ribs me good-naturedly (because he, being 156 months older than I, feels wistful about the two of us being the only songwriters in the land?) and now offers a vocal lesson on how to intone for what he calls "all the countesses" when I land in France next month.

As I orchestrate, the radio blasts the all-male chorus from *South Pacific,* "There Is Nothing Like a Dame," which, considering the percentage of queer chorus boys, seems as incongruous as an assembly of female gym teachers lustily apotheosizing the masculine form.

Bill Flanagan calls them Rat Ladies, that brand of movie star with a stunted torso, soulful eyes in a huge wilful head, football shoulders tapering to the toes which are only four feet below the scalp: Swanson, Crawford, Shearer, Colbert. Now our own Stella Brooks is a baby version of these, the poor man's Lee Wiley, ungifted and brassy in her own repertory ("I'm a little piece of leather, don't you know,/So well put together, don't you know,/Just a little piece of leather,/Strip off the skin of life"), but within a radius of one square mile, from Sheridan Square to 14th Street, she's everyone's favorite fag hag. So we went to hear her yet again last night, at the Little Casino, and, well . . .

4 May. Photographic session at Oscar Hammerstein's on East 63rd, as sort of a warm-up for the concert Saturday. Avon Long is there too, cutting capers, and Alec Templeton who will play *Rhapsody in Blue,* and who is a very warm man, as the blind are wont to be (like Hattie's father), unless they're cranky—there's no middle ground. Hammerstein, despite being pockmarked, paunchy, and old as Father, is sexy. I hardly spoke.

22 May, Sunday, 12:30 a.m. It has been raining for 72 hours.

Today I had 5 orgasms, 3 in conjunction with the author of a fan letter received a week ago from a sailor, yes a sailor, who'd seen the picture in the *Times*. . . . These last days in New York have been a cycle of unreality: a great deal of sex and booze, fear about depression and as always about war. Though (also as always) I rationalize that I work more than any other composer, so am happy. Then Alfonso points out: one's character cannot be segmented, we are the sum of our parts, and art can result from an unhappy drive.

Well, on Wednesday I'm off to the ocean and will leave the unhappy drive on dry land. Europe will transform the illnesses into blessings.

24. Envoi

In their published memoirs, various acquaintances have evoked the Ned of this period as either a drunk, a narcissist, an unstable musician, or a mix of all three:

Harold Norse: There I met the nineteen-year-old composer—Ned Rorem—whose luminous beauty and heavenly music were irresistible. But he was intoxicated on more than music: he drank too much. Dreamy and self-absorbed, he would smile his crooked little smile and in a languid foghorn voice remark on how "delicious" I looked, as if he could order me for dessert.... During the five years we had known each other I felt an affinity with Ned's music. I wanted a *Lordly Hudson* success (he had won his first prize for a song he set to a Goodman poem).... Coaxed into existence by Ned's urgent demands (he had specified the subject, *Penny Arcade*), the six hastily dashed-off lyrics were with equal haste set and a performance given—by mezzo-soprano Nell Tangeman, with Ned at the piano—at the MacMillan Theater on May 19, 1949. Virgil Thomson, who sat in front of me, never turned his head. Onstage Ned handled questions smoothly (I admired his poise) and called out "Harold, are you in the audience?" when they referred to the poems. . . . When sober, he had a sardonic wit, but too often he was a falling-down drunk.

Virgil Thomson (1948): . . . full of talent and spontaneity, but lacking, like much of this composer's youthful music, a hard, plain, expressive core. (1970): Ned Rorem . . . has aspired to produce in English a vocal repertory comparable to that of Francis Poulenc. . . . Certainly it is in solo songs, of which there are literally hundreds, that Rorem makes his bid for consideration beside the creators of German and French lieder. Consideration in this company one can grant him for his taste in the choice of poems and for grace in the melodic line. But no such intensity is present as in the German masters from Schubert through Wolf and Mahler or in the French from Duparc and Fauré and Poulenc. In fact no such intensity exists anywhere in English song. . . . Consequently Rorem's effort, no less than that of Barber, of Douglas Moore, of Ernest Bacon, David Diamond, William Flanagan, the great Copland himself, and of Ives in concert songs, remains nobler for its persistently setting out on what may well be a hopeless errand than for any world's record achieved. When Poulenc, as a friend, discouraged his vocal efforts and praised the orchestral, Rorem sincerely believed him to be jealous. What can one say of so impregnable a stance? Nothing except that the English art-song is not yet a major form, and that even Benjamin Britten, with all his great gifts, has come no nearer.

Paul Bowles: I remember Ned Rorem rushing here and there, always in a mist of alcohol.

Judith Malina: I liked his perverse attractiveness. He listens to music holding a yellow rose with his head thrown back in a pose as effective as he believes it to be. He is almost entirely turned inward; but if someone more his type had not been determined to possess him, I might have found a way.

Anaïs Nin (1966): The Ned Rorem diary had brilliant moments and he could have written a fascinating one, but remained on the surface . . . and also in spite of appearances, indiscreet but not open, not really. Some parts are striking. He never went fully into anything. He falls apart. Certainly his life is in shreds, and willfully superficial. Scattered. No courage and no core. A shame. I don't know his music. I am sure there was more there than he gave.

Larry Rivers: Swimming down Eighth Street one afternoon with Frank [O'Hara], I was introduced to the good-looking, all-smiles Ned

Rorem, the composer. (Good-looking? Ned was considered one of the beauties of New York and had the pick of all the lesser beauties!) I was also introduced to the ever-critical pipe-smoking lay analyst Paul Goodman, who told me I must be sick for refusing to go to bed with him.

John Myers (Late June 1946): ... I opened at Spivy's room ... [and] the room was jammed with friends. ... When I went out to the terrace for some fresh air, a friend beckoned me to a table, where I met Ned Rorem and his companion Maggie [sic] von Magerstadt. Ned said he too would like to compose some songs for puppets if I ever did another show. I felt flattered, since I hear Ned is talented. ... (1948): ... Boultenhouse who wrote three lyrics; and Ned Rorem who set the lyrics to music for voice and tympani. ... During the winter [Herbert Machiz and I] would give several Sunday afternoon musicales, always organized by my old friend Ned Rorem. Baked Virginia ham, pumpernickel, and white wine, Mozart, Schoenberg, Ben Weber, and Ned Rorem were the bill of fare on a few such occasions.

Tennessee Williams [To Maria St. Just]: Will you please ask Jean Stein to send me the Paris address of that young composer, Ned Rorem, that I promised to send a short work or libretto? I think it is ready for him, and perhaps I may go up there a week or two this summer. Please send me this address right away as I'm not sure I can stand Rome much longer. [To Dotson Rader]: I remember Ned Rorem once invited me back to his room. He lived in one room then. Oh, Ned was very drunk. Now he doesn't drink anymore and so isn't as interesting anymore. Some people are very interesting when they are drunk, and total bores when they're sober. Ned Rorem was so beautiful when he was young. I stared at him all night long. So when he invited me to his room I thought I'd hit the jackpot! He pulled off his clothes and lay down on the bed and pretended to pass out. I just caressed him for a few minutes, and then I went home.

Postscript. *Virgil Thomson again* (1974): Ned Rorem's reprint of formal pieces from *The New Republic,* along with bits of more improvisatory material, is frankly titled *Pure Contraption.* The essays themselves, less penetrating musically than [Robert] Craft's and less learned than [Andrew] Porter's, are nonetheless better made for easy reading. They are more gracefully written, for one thing; their English is meaningful, picturesque, idiomatic, in every way alive. And their malice is far less seriously intended. He pays off a few scores—against Copland and myself, for example—without bothering to make any musical point at all. And he pokes equally harmless fun at Elliott Carter's tendency toward "the big statement," a sort of music-writing that we used to mock in French as *"le style chef-d'oeuvre."* ... Actually Rorem is not a dependable critic, in spite of a good mind and a pretty good ear, his egocentricity gets in the way. It prevents his seriously liking or hating anything. He is scarcely involved anymore even with his private life, which for some years furnished him with literary materials as well as a devoted public. In a recent interview published jointly in [Boston and] San Francisco, his burden is how little he cares about his prose and how devotedly he indites his music. Actually it is his lack of literary ambition, I think, that gives to his writing so much charm, along with the eight years' residence in France that firmed up his mind and his manners. His music has no such ease. But the writing reads, as our black friends say, right on.

On rereading the preceding chapter, and the other three diary chapters, I must blush, if not apologize, for the perceptions that elude the mind as they are drawn through the eye back to the navel, the humorless scope of A to B, the generalities on lower-case "jews," the moaning vanity. All this, believe it or not, in only one fifth of the extant journal of the 1940s! The diary reads like Howard Moss's parody of my diary. Why not omit it? For two reasons:

First, since those entries by definition lack perspective, it seems literarily useful to juxtapose them upon what I remember (by definition with perspective) of the period; I was curious to verify how near to or far from the fact my memory landed. Second, the journal served as an anchor which I could either occasionally draw up, dripping with scum, or let lie in the depths, secure in the knowledge that it served its own invisible purpose. Finally, although I've kept a journal up to the present day, I must now nervously bid it farewell as a reference for this book. My *Diaries,* in four separate volumes from 1951 through 1985, have been published. True, they are all currently unavailable, except in libraries. Still, as a writer of songs who has always felt queasy about obliging poets to say twice what they have already succinctly said once, I don't wish to feed on myself anymore—at least not with the same menu. From here on these pages are on their own.

Before sailing for France, a few loose ends:

Because I am convinced that one's esthetic taste, like one's religious stance, is fixed before the age of reason, I'm bemused to read that I hate cats (I love them), and that I granted such short shrift to Gore Vidal, Tennessee Williams, and Truman Capote. Surely my *taste* embraced them, so it must have been friends who squelched that taste. The boiling fertility of all the creative arts in the United States between

1945 and 1950—in theater, in novels, in music—was perhaps not as apparent then as with hindsight. It was also, if not in music at least in literature (as with the three authors named), suddenly Gentile, nonheterosexual, non-*Partisan Review,* nonpolitical.

Truman, Gore, and Tennessee were as famous then as they ever would be because they were young, and to be young was an American thing—still is. Of the three, though I met him first, I knew Gore least: he was the least stunning (so far as "the madness of art" is concerned), but the least difficult to talk to—he could follow a subject to a conclusion that was generally illuminating (like Paul Goodman, he revealed the brightness of the obvious—of what was always under the eye but too close to see), and cared for human rights beyond his own needs. I never worked with him professionally so our paths crossed, and continue to cross every few years, strictly socially. With Truman I wrote a ballet. With Tennessee I composed incidental scores for two of his plays; but though I saw Tennessee daily for months we never had a coherent conversation. Later I'll speak of his dramas, which have come to sag. For now—for then—I was enthralled by his artistic preoccupation with victims and their shattered hearts (he was in reality the selfishest man alive), and his preoccupation with how the bad turn good as the good turn bad. *Summer and Smoke* is a rewrite of Maugham's *Rain* which is a rewrite of Anatole France's *Thaïs.*

The 7 May premiere of Overture in C, led by Michel Piastro in an otherwise all-Gershwin program in Carnegie, was not an event. I attended with Nell Tangeman, who asked, when I joined her in the lobby, what I'd been doing all afternoon. (Writing a concerto for Eugene.) My agenda notes that the family was there, that Bill Flanagan threw a party afterwards, that I visited Lazare Saminsky and then took a sunlamp treatment the day before, that I sent Rosemary a note for her birthday the day after, that I paid bills (to Elkan Vogel, etcetera), made phone calls (to Donald Fuller, and to Irma of the travel agency), and that I made a date with Victor Kraft. Yet of the concert proper I recall nothing. My piece was neither flop nor success, nor can I recall today the sound of it. With astonishment I retrieve these reviews:

Noel Strauss in the *Times:* "The 'Overture in C' by Mr. Rorem, a special feature of the concert, had been judged by a committee consisting of Leonard Bernstein, Marc Blitzstein, Aaron Copland and William Schuman. It was richly and imaginatively scored, with novel and striking percussion effects, and possessed emotional intensity as well as strength and vitality. Tighter construction, however, would have kept it from making an impression of being somewhat fragmentary."

Francis Perkins in the *Tribune:* "Mr. Rorem, who is twenty-five years old, shows talent and inventiveness in this work, which runs for a little under ten minutes. The style is homogenous; some of the musical ideas had a slightly Gershwinesque turn and flavor, but not to a degree which obscured a sense of individuality which was also apparent in their treatment; their harmonic investiture and the orchestration were skillful and effective. Various pronounced rhythmic patterns are one feature of the overture, another is a series of short episodes both before and after a broad central theme; this gives a certain sense of discontinuity in music which gave a general impression of much ability and promise. . . . Mr. Rorem received the Prize from Oscar Hammerstein 2nd, just before the performance." Irving Kolodin in the *Sun:* "This year's honors and emoluments of the Gershwin memorial concert . . . went to Ned Rorem, who enjoyed, as well, the experience of hearing his prize-winning 'Overture in C' played by an orchestra under the direction of Michel Piastro. He might have wondered, however—along with such previous prize winners as Peter Mennin, Harold Shapero and Ulysses Kay—whether the pleasure was one wholly unalloyed. On either side of his earnest, skillful and not very vital work were [sic] one after another of the Gershwin favorites which, whatever they are not, are certainly vital. Rorem, of Juilliard and Tanglewood background, has a full complement of musical tricks at his disposal and might eventually organize them in a manner more distinctive than one heard in this 'Overture in C.' While pondering that possibility, he might also note well the freshness and spirit, the untricky components of the Gershwin music."

Twelve days later I shared a Composers Forum at the MacMillan Theater with Leon Kirchner. Four years older than I, Kirchner, a Schoenberg protégé, had just arrived from California and was quickly paired with me as a foil, by the current powers, on this prestigious recital. Arthur Berger in the *Tribune:* ". . . both offered ample evidence of their musicianship in the compositions through which they were represented, but they also provided tangible confirmation of this by appearing as composer-pianists. Mr. Rorem's participation was confined to the accompaniment of his song cycle, 'Penny Arcade,' to which he brought the needed fleetness, nimbleness and sensitivity. Mr. Kirchner, playing his massive and uncommonly impressive Piano Sonata, naturally had more occasion to reveal his performing talents. . . . Rorem, recent winner of the Gershwin prize, is far less a stranger. His many works have been appearing on programs with greater and greater frequency. His enormous facility is no news, and he has become, quite inevitably, a young composer to rely upon where a job must be completed neatly and elegantly for almost any musical occasion at hand. The Four-hand Sonata, composed at nineteen, indicated that this facility has been there for some time. Facility is a good thing to have, but it is also a good thing to struggle with, and last night's music seemed to have done little of this . . . if Poulenc and Satie are admirable sources for any young composer, it seems important for Rorem now to elaborate on them more than he has, to find some dialectic for his undeniably charming and engagingly languorous vein. He is a very well endowed composer indeed, and it would be good to see him be more severe with himself, to do more to transform his rich sources of popular song. . . . Yesterday's forum . . . had such excellent participants as Nell Tangeman, mezzo soprano [and] Eugene Istomin, pianist." Carter Harman in the *Times:* "Mr. Rorem's music is at once easier to take—it is pleasant-sounding—and harder to describe (it is also innocuous) than Mr. Kirchner's. Mr. Rorem has a gift for spinning a sweet melody, but it is loaded with clichés and it sometimes simply stops instead of ending. 'Penny Arcade,' a 'cyclical melodrama for voice and piano,' had moments of charm and cleverness, a busy accompaniment of little variety and many words that were often so misaccented as to be unintelligible. It had also the benefit of Nell Tangeman's lovely mezzo-soprano voice and Mr. Rorem's own piano accompaniment."

On Wednesday, 25 May 1949, the SS *Washington,* a single-class American liner, drifted from pier 61 on West Twenty-first Street toward Le Havre. Mother and Father saw me off. As they grew ever tinier on the receding wharf I sobbed quietly. I occupied berth 2 in room B-32 which otherwise contained seven elderly Czechoslovakian gentlemen, whose wives were in an adjoining barracks, and who snored and farted through the night—I, who cannot to this day, share a bedroom with even the nearest and dearest. Two smart girls on the boat, Betty and Judy—whose surnames unforgettably were Rubinstein and Horowitz—remained ideal companions for all the wistful bingo-playing voyage. On 1 June, Shirley (now Xénia) met the boat-train at Gare Saint-Lazare, and with elated exhaustion we taxied through the orange-canopied metropolis—none of which resembled, try as it may, the Paris of 1936—to the rue de la Harpe, where another, utterly severed, life began.

Part Three

The Emperor's form is so gorgeous he doesn't need any clothes.

25. 1949:

Harp Street and

Saint-Germain ·

Nadia and José ·

Poulenc and Guy

> If one of us should die, I'll go to Paris.
> —Freud

> It is just possible to imagine God speaking French.
> Christ never. His words do not function in a language so ill at ease in the naïve and with the sublime.
> —Cioran

With a shock of nonrecognition one peruses the growing number of studies on "The Left Bank in the Fifties" by Yankee memoirists and vicarious sophomores, studies that seethe with anecdotes about Americans among themselves: Jim Jones told Plimpton to tell Styron about Herlihy who told Southern that Vidal had told Keogh about Baldwin who told Richler. Nary a whisper about local culture.

But there *were* French people in Paris then. I *saw* them.

Not that they were any more interested in the monolingual *Paris Review* than Americans were interested in the monolingual *Les Temps Modernes*. Indeed, the French ignored non-French culture in general, and American culture in particular; what they knew of us then was what they know of us now: Hemingway and Jerry Lewis. Major American intellectuals have resided in Paris for centuries without the French acknowledging so much as their names. Oh, an occasional sport might flicker in the Gallic ken—Truman Capote, Richard Wright —but it is their oddness, not their talent, which enthralls for fifteen minutes.

Musically the scene was similar when we, apple-cheeked and credulous, stepped off the boat. The witty French quip—"America is the only country in history to have gone from barbarism to decadence without an intervening civilization"—was, at least musically, based solely on their knowledge of Gershwin as strained through Milhaud, and on the frenetic Negro chic launched by Josephine Baker. The ascending warm popularity of actual postwar Americans now on French soil, with their guileless sexiness as military saviors, was means of entrée into any circle (at least until the backlash provoked by the Rosenbergs' electrocution in 1953), but nobody wanted to hear what these children had on their minds. This said, France has never been an especially musical nation. She has produced great musicians, but no viable musical public. The French are nimble at talking *about* music, but at listening they are at best polite.

I had come abroad ostensibly for three months, and stayed eight years. To the question, "Did all that time in France influence you and your music?" the answer is: I went to France because I was already French, not the other way around. It is not the going home (though we may never have been "home" before) that makes homebodies of us; we are homebodies, so we go home.

Of course, none of these glib—these *French*—truisms yet shaped my perspective as the cab moved through the city that June morning of 1949. Shirley's voice was telling me, as I gazed at the passing awnings and pigeons (*French* pigeons, *French* awnings), that the apartment we would be sharing was already shared with her lover, Jean-Claude Maurice. She hadn't written me this for fear I'd blab; she was, after all, still nominally wed to Seymour Barab, and her mother would have a fit, etcetera. Jean-Claude, she assured me, would be my perfect teacher, since he spoke no word of English and was the greatest poet since Baudelaire.

The building at 53 rue de la Harpe was five stories of white stucco and huge slanting windows à la Cézanne. The ground floor, or *rez-de-chaussée,* was a jazz club called the Rose Rouge run by a middle-aged Senegalese who was also our landlord—none other than Benga, onetime actor who played the silent role of the Black Angel in Cocteau's *Sang d'un poète* nineteen years before. We had the front flat on the third floor (second floor to Europeans) which consisted of a piano-filled parlor overlooking the street, a back bedroom (mine), a claustrophobic entrance hall, and a bathroom-kitchen containing a bidet (I'd never seen one) in which carrots were presently soaking. No bath, no shower.

The sight of Jean-Claude was a surprise. Willowy without being exactly effeminate, he resembled Fantin-Latour's portrait of Rimbaud. Shirley vouched for his genius (her swains were always geniuses), for his heterosexuality (not my type in any case), and for his affability (certainly true). The rent was 20,000 francs, roughly sixty dollars, most of which I paid in cash to Benga during the months I lived there, off and on. Rue de la Harpe runs one crooked block (mostly North African in those days) parallel to boulevard Saint-Michel, and debouching onto boulevard Saint-Germain across from the Cluny Museum which, during all those years, I never once entered. Thus we were at the heart of the student quarter, and a twelve-minute hike to the vices of Saint-Germain-des-Prés. Everything—a park bench, a filet of horsemeat, a public urinal—seemed a valued relic to be absorbed and retained.

From my first day, as with any first encounter with another person, I began testing my effect on the city—on "her"—as much as her effect on me: flexing my intellect, looks, speech, shyness. Was it then, or five years—or thirty-five years—later that I discovered shyness won't get you far? It came to be clear that those loudmouths across the room were no smarter than I, and if I didn't say my say, nobody would say it for me. Quakers are taught not to interrupt, nor are they known for their repartee. The French don't interrupt either, but even the humblest concierge has a way with words, speaks in complete sentences, and if she doesn't always mean what she says (unlike we earnest Americans), she always says what she means.

The Huguenot tourist's notion about the French and wine (every Frenchman is slightly drunk all his life because of the obligatory *coup de rouge* with each meal, but no Frenchman is a binge drinker like Americans who, between weekly bouts, abstain utterly) troubled me. When I was good I was very very good: sobriety was a state to be coveted like a clean shirt while it lasted, just as drinking was for the purpose of getting drunk. Would I be able to order Badoit water instead of *vin blanc* with the noonday meal, without being thought a hick or—more likely—a sufferer of chronic liver trouble?

And what about sex? Having always functioned on the principle that Beauty is its own calling card, I was not used to being rejected, and knew the ropes in the States. But was I a type for French tastes?

Certainly they were different from us, not just conversationally but physically: shorter, swarthier, less obsessed with antiseptics than with home remedies, and, in intercourse, less obsessed with fellatio than with buggery. I managed. Shirley, the wise old European ensconced with her true love, felt such preoccupations were frivolous for one new to the Louvre, the Opéra-Comique, the Jardin des Plantes. "Oh, you boys!" she expostulates, when I ask Norris, who's lived abroad for ages, how and where one gets laid in the city, where are the gay bars, how are the men in Pisa, in Greece. "Aren't there more important things than sex?" asks Shirley. The answer is No. The best way to learn a foreign language is in bed.

I had brought, duty free, six quarts of Gordon's gin and a dozen cartons of American cigarettes which were ingested over the next weeks, by all of us, not least by Jean-Claude, a penniless voluptuary thrilled by the ways of the world. "Us" consisted of a Franco-American nucleus that had formed, long before, around the little apartment: Norris Embry (who had come clear from Crete, he said, just to see the revival of *The Blue Angel),* Gary Samuel, Arthur Weinstein, Fizdale & Gold, and a raft of Jean-Claude's pals who, when they spent the night, spent it in my bed.

Atop the heap of mail waiting at American Express was the first of 150 letters from Nell Tangeman.

May 26, 1949
38 W. 69th

Darling Ned:

By now you will be well on your way, riding in fine freudian frenzy on the ocean waves, and my thoughts and heart are with you. I would not have it otherwise than to see you off and watch with a mixture of agony and pride as you stood at the ship's rail and waved until I couldn't see you anymore—but it was with a sinking heart and dribbling eyes-nose that I turned away. Maggie [Margaret Hillis, choir director, Nell's roommate] and I, after terrible difficulty in getting the car extricated from the mess of parked trucks, went wandering down 8th Avenue for a place to eat and I remembered the Sevilla; it was with wonder and nostalgia that we realized, when we got out of the car, that we had parked exactly in front of 285 W. 12th and I wept anew at the forlorn looking window pane. . . .

Nine days later:

Your letter this morning was so unexpected, and sounded so free and happy that it has added the necessary wine to this already miraculously beautiful June day. . . My heart did honestly sink at the sight of your boat & and the people on it. I can tell you now that you are safely across. It

looked so crowded and so incredibly dull. I hope you can come back on
something more exciting, altho the Irish lad undoubtedly made life a joy
in the moments available. . . .

(Irish lad? And did I come back on something more exciting?)

These are samples of communication from another era, the necessary leisure, the sole means. Today I have forty-five filing cabinets of
correspondence received mainly from the 1950s. My longhand re-
sponses to this correspondence are dispersed throughout the world
in other cabinets, or in ashes long since consigned to fertilizer. I wrote
to everyone—mainly to my family, but also to Dr. Kraft and Dr. Kinsey,
to cousins and lovers, to performers I'd never met—and relied as we
all did on this slow form of love and duty. I still write letters, a habit
which even old friends find quaint.

The yellowing agenda. That June was five hundred months ago. The
interim can sometimes show France as an inactive absence. But if I
close my eyes, a single hour can evoke a presence so acute that reality
—indeed, Being itself—becomes "that which was."

The second day we saw the French version, *L'opéra de quat'sous,*
of Pabst's film on Kurt Weill's opera, with Margot Lyon (an acquaintance of Shirley's) in the Lenya role. Whereupon we bought the sheet
music at one of the well-stocked kiosks along the quais, and learned,
in French, every one of those so-German songs, singing them in unison at the Steinway to all the permanent guests. I also played and
bellowed solo lush arrangements of "Stormy Weather," or of "Lover
Man" and "Good Morning Heartache" and other Billie Holiday favorites, filling the pad with American nostalgia. We saw *Le chevalier à la
rose* at the Palais Garnier with a now-forgotten cast, and Franju's new
Le sang des bêtes, an unbearably sad film about a Paris slaughterhouse
where the panicked sheep are shown anthropomorphically and the
cows are killed with crowbars, while the background music—*le fond
sonore,* as the French call it—is the happy voice of a little girl intoning
Trenet's "La mer" to an accordion accompaniment.

We walked, we walked. Not just to the upper Right Bank where the
grown-ups lived, but to the black market ghetto of the rue Vieille-du-
Temple to turn dollars into francs (the legal exchange of 345 became
400), thereby memorizing the twists and turns of the eerie Marais.
Mostly we ferreted out our own fifth arrondissement, a town in itself,
memorizing every *ruelle* between the oldest church, Saint-Julien-des-
Pauvres, to the newest tobacco store, Le Mabillon, all squirming on
the soil of the ancient Lutèce which, because two thousand years ago
when it began to grow from a riverbank settlement into a center as

beautiful as the vanished city of Ys—*pareil à Ys*—became known as Paris. On the afternoon of Tuesday, 7 June, loitering in the place Sainte-Geneviève where children used to throw rotten fruit at the drunken Verlaine (not really so long ago), we heard a choir rehearsing from the nearby church, repeating, repeating, a modal five-note refrain. The sky clouded over. We returned to Harp Street. Norris, looking as always like a hyperthyroid version of Picasso's *Blue Harlequin,* thin and wistful, mixed gin and sodas. Then, leaning by the great window and gazing down into the darkening street where neon was beginning to reflect in the newly wet pavement, he pronounced these verses:

> There fell a beautiful clear rain
> with no admixture of fog or snow,
> and this was and no other thing
> the very sign of the start of spring.
>
> Not the longing for a lover
> nor the sentiment of starting over,
> but this clear and refreshing rain
> falling without haste or strain.

I felt, still feel, that no poet, certainly not our habitually perfervid Paul, had ever more prettily stated the absence of anxiety. That evening, using maybe that five-note refrain, I made a song out of the Goodman lyric, my first music written away from home.

The second or third reason for many of us to magnetize toward Paris —along with the need to stretch and molt after the quarantine of war; to slough off parents in order, ironically, to seek grandparents, our *roots* as we called them (though were Jimmy Baldwin's roots really in Paris, or were mine, for that matter, rather than in Dakar or Oslo? Yes, artistically; although his beloved Gide was filtered through Harlem while my Gide grew up in Chicago's Hyde Park)—was to pay homage to Nadia Boulanger, arguably the greatest teacher since Socrates, certainly the greatest *music* teacher. Charles (Buddy) Strouse was idling in Paris that spring. We made a date to attend together one of Boulanger's Wednesdays, on 8 June at five o'clock. We would give each other moral support.

A few years after her death at ninety-two in 1979, I ended a review of Nadia Boulanger's biography thus: "If she did not change the planet's shape, she shaped some who did. Was her emphasis on technique only one of many 'techniques'? Do the French with their machine-gun-solfège accuracy necessarily produce better musicians than the more flaccidly reared Americans? At least Nadia knew that to be moved without métier is insufficient, while with métier inspiration falls into place. Her contagious enthusiasm was no tacit agreement for grooving, but a demonstration that structure, art's sovereign ingredient, need not always be dull, and that to write down your dreams you must be wide awake."

To arrive at rue Ballu, you walk due north from Trinité Church, either on rue Blanche or rue de Clichy. (If you take the latter you will find, at the halfway mark, the Cité Monthiers Cocteau describes in the opening words of *Les enfants terribles,* and which later was transformed into the snowball-throwing soundstage in *Blood of a Poet.* Do you remember? The scene where, during the card game, Lee Miller says: "If you don't have the ace of hearts, my dear, you're a goner." And when the Poet seeks to retrieve the ace of hearts from the breast-pocket of the dead youth—that is, himself—beneath the table, Benga, the Black Angel, has invisibly removed the card. Does the Cité Monthiers still exist, or has it too been quietly covered with snow forever?) At 36 rue Ballu you will find Nadia's building—on what is now named place Lili Boulanger—where you must take a rickety elevator (which, as Cocteau says, dates from before the age of elevators) to the fifth floor where a male servant, Italian, will take your coat and show you into the grand salon.

The moment I saw Mademoiselle, as she was known to all, I was confirmed in what I would write so many years later: that musical composition is a no-nonsense deal—that inspiration is a matter of conscious control. The hostess was surrounded by supplicants from all over the globe, she in an armchair, they in straight-backs, or maybe on the organ bench, for yes, there was an organ in that room. Buddy and I had come up in the elevator with an American lady bearing a bouquet of white roses, duly offered to Mademoiselle who exclaimed: "What lovely *marguérites!*" Then to the Italian servant: "Would you take these *marguérites* and put them in a vase *sur la table dans la salle à manger.*" (Didn't *marguérite* mean daisy? Buddy and I wondered later, or was it also a generic term, like posey?) Boulanger, despite a long stay in America during the war and her proliferation of English-speaking students, never quite learned English. An ear for music does not mean an ear for language, and vice versa. Nor does intelligence enter in. Many bores speak many languages expertly and without accent—and are just as boring in every one. To master another tongue (unless you are raised bi- or trilingually) means first of all to *want* to, and second to be blessed with a certain extrovert hamminess which perfectionist musicians, who hate making public mistakes, refuse to summon.

The routine at the Boulanger Wednesdays was to wait your turn. There was no general converse, and no food. Mademoiselle addressed, from left to right, the chairs surrounding her, while you, plus attendant celebrities, waited your turn. At my turn she claimed not to recognize me, wasn't my hair blonder than in the photos I'd sent? The event seemed so unreal, so somehow unmusical, that I was at a loss. At the same time her voice, husky and low as Tallulah Bankhead's, emanating from an ashen mouth surmounted by steel-rimmed spectacles, hair coiffed in an antique bun, severe suit and bow tie, sensible shoes, seemed theatrical yet true. That this *vieille fille,* who may still have been a virgin at sixty-four, could give off a sensuality to me no less than to a long-lived array of pupils was no more incongruous than the lightning that was said to have passed continually between Hemingway and Gertrude Stein. I came back the following Wednesday, whereupon we made a date to meet tête-à-tête and go over my wares.

Even as a painter will, at the last minute, add the "telling" little patch of scarlet that makes his landscape suddenly breathe, Boulanger will change one note—just one—in your song, that makes the hitherto leaden page suddenly flow with a fortunate breeze. She had the knack for nosing out the one rotten apple in the barrel, and for replacing it with one of gold.

Yet she didn't want me to become her pupil: I was already twenty-five, she pointed out, not seventeen, and my character was formed, *tant bien que mal*—my *nature bête,* which her prodding could only sterilize.

But we loved one another. She arranged for me to receive the annual Lili Boulanger Award, and performed my works in public, which provided much needed prestige and finance to impress my parents and supplement their allowance. She also invited me as a peer to her table (I recall especially a lamb stew with Lennox Berkeley and Kathleen Ferrier whereat three languages—French, English, and American—were foils for discussion), and to her occasional rehearsals whereat she solicited, and followed, my suggestions. Later, when I lived chez Marie-Laure de Noailles, of whom she took a dim view, partly because both had loved Igor Markevich long ago, and partly because she tacitly found Marie-Laure superficial, Nadia nonetheless promoted me, wrote to me, worried about my gaudy self-destruction, nurtured me from near and far, until she died.

Why, then, was my attitude so righteously huffy? In 1965 when my *Paris Diary (1950–1955)* was being prepared for publication, a set of galleys was sent to Aaron Copland from whom a blurb was hoped for. He answered:

... I'll be very curious to see how your Diary is received. I myself had 2 different reactions: reading it as if I didn't know you or the parties concerned it definitely has fascination, but reading it as an "insider" I had complicated reactions—too complicated to go into here. I couldn't supply your publishers with a blurb because of your plain nasty treatment of N.B. It isn't that I consider her beyond "reproche" but I just don't feel it's my role to "O.K." a book that belittles her.

Indeed, on rereading my two dense pages on Mademoiselle ("... Only a female, and uncreative, could have built within herself the most spectacular musical métier in the world today. Hers is the search for a true spark among those crackling in her synthetic electricity, a shimmer attacking others who fear to make love...."), I blush for my unearned sarcasm. I was not being daring or original, but following a vogue for putting down Nadia. I was a pretentious coward.

Is it more than coincidental that the names of Boulez and Boulanger contain the same first four letters? These were the two foremost French musical powers of 1949, Boulez in ascent, Boulanger in decline, and both representative—though who could see it then?—of the decay, the *blanche agonie,* that was clutching French culture and that would bring it to what it's become today. As recently as 1972 Boulez recalled with customary charity: "After the war, Messiaen and Leibowitz were the important figures and no one had any use for Boulanger." Like Boulanger, Boulez in his early years was a prophet mainly in foreign lands. Unlike her, he returned in triumph to Paris where to this day, for better or worse, he reigns supreme.

Indeed, so intimidated was I by both presences that for twenty years I felt guilty at loving tonality while retaining a built-in revulsion for serial music, was threatened by the very fact of it—and so by Boulez —as though I'd been forever missing the point of something which finally had no point.

George Bemberg suggested I look up his cousin, Philippe. As it happened, Shirley knew him already, so we went together to his big house in the rue de Grenelle. Philippe was a gaunt version of George (they both resembled the Hollywood villain Henry Daniell), and we liked each other right off. The rooms were vast and lavish and, like all the rooms of the continental rich, slightly crumbly. Philippe gifted me with an illustrated edition of *Les enfants terribles* which I treasure still. A true romantic, he committed suicide a few years later, in Holland, for a story of love. Or was it because, having refused to receive Eva Peron when she passed through Paris (the Bembergs were Argentinean), he was unaccountably taxed to the tune of two hundred million dollars?

Philippe's nearest friend was an Italian composer incongruously named Raffaello de Banfield (his father was Austrian, his mother Triestina), every bit as rich as Philippe but with a rather more purposeful routine. With a thick but fluent accent, wavy blond hair, and a constant feline grin, Raffaello could charm the birds off the trees. A sometime pupil of Boulanger's, he had a ballet, *Le combat,* currently in the Roland Petit repertory. I saw it. Amateurish but appealing music, overwrought choreography, with costumes by Marie-Laure de Noailles, made out of Ping-Pong balls because, she would later explain, Ping-Pong balls are buoyant and propel dancers. Raffaello was close to this woman of whom I had heard. Indeed, he was *mondain* in the extreme, knew everybody, went everywhere, and had enough money (despite a mother who doled it out) not to have to work with any regularity on his chosen craft. Wealthy artists are no better or worse than poor ones, but they don't need to listen, and that dearth of need is discernible in their work. During the years I knew Raffaello, sometimes even living in close proximity with him, I never saw him take pen to paper. Leonor Fini once claimed that Raffaello's music was written by a little man in Trieste. Well, that little man hadn't much discipline.

Anyhow, Raffaello in those days had a darling robin's-egg-blue Maserati which was his signature. He invited me to Versailles, perhaps just for the ride. But when he picked me up on Harp Street, Shirley's mother, Rae Gabis, visiting in France for the first time, appeared with me. Raffaello's face fell. He rallied, and Rae never forgot. He lived at 21 rue Casimir-Périer, two steps from the Bains Deligny, a huge pool on a public barge docked in the Seine. Raffaello took me there. I had already acquired crabs, that is, pubic lice, which the French call *morpions* though they look just like the North American species. Because my new swimming trunks were the minimal *slip de bain,* the crabs were visible. Raffaello plucked them, one by one, in view of everyone. This was Paris, *après tout.*

I mention him at such length because he adored my music, because he had the effervescence of his country which I'd never previously experienced, and because he will return peripherally through these pages. (Currently Raffaello is director of the opera in Trieste. We've not met in many years.)

From whence the crabs? During my exactly two months in Paris (I would leave on 30 July for Africa) I slept with perhaps a dozen people, some of them several times. These people were found mainly *dans le quartier*—the byways of Saint-Germain-des-Prés, a classical cross-roads, flanked by the medieval church (forever under scaffolding), between the rue Bonaparte and the rue des Saints-Pères. The Flore is where you sat from six until midnight, because Sartre had founded existentialism there during the war rather than in his apartment where there was no central heating. From midnight until 4 a.m. you went to the Reine Blanche, a strictly gay bar just across the boulevard, run by a fat harridan, Madame Alice, who never quit her seat at the cash register while shouting orders to the bartender and bouncer. When the Reine Blanche closed you moved down to the Pergola, open twenty-four hours and catering to all types. This triangular foray could be shifted imperceptibly by starting at the Deux Magots, thence to the Fiacre, and ending at the Bar-Tabac. There was also the Montana, a more discreet gay bar on the rue Saint-Benoît next to the Flore, or, for a daring change, the Boeuf sur le Toit, across the river on the rue du Colisée. This was my routine about thrice a week. Even on sober nights I never retired early at Harp Street because of the clatter of voices and drums downstairs at the Rose Rouge. Likewise I avoided returning there at 9 a.m. from the Pergola, because Shirley, who was preparing a debut recital at the Salle Gaveau, would be practicing. As a new face I did not lack for beds here and there.

It never occurred to me that an obligatory rapport existed between sex and love, that these two experiences could not thrive independently. Though impelled sometimes at the idiotic instant of climax to utter *Thanks,* or *Yes,* or *Go to it,* the moment after brought an equally strong impulsion to utter *Get out.* I was not owed, nor did I owe, any commitment to another person for the act of sex. Swans and geese will die of broken hearts, but not mammals. Of course, such notions sometimes backfire.

Rum-soaked hours spiraled to such a force that, between 1940 and 1968, there were perhaps a thousand blackouts—days so blurred as to be scraped from memory. Although, quaintly, sometimes what I blocked out during one spree might be recalled, not during periods of recuperation, but only during the next spree. Those periods of recuperation, meanwhile, especially with hangovers, were usually spent in the tingling anonymity of Turkish baths and urinals—"looking for love where it can't be found," but where, in fact, love, lasting love, *could* be found.

Well, what *should* I have been doing? Sitting forever at the desk, pen poised? Listening to Beethoven until the cows came home? It is good to be a *recovering* alcoholic if only because of the adjustment and clarity this implies. At least he knows what he is, if not quite who, and can act accordingly.

The unthinkable horniness of a hangover when reason is stifled as the body reawakens from last night's lacerations! The whole town seems erect as you walk—blinded by an equinoxal sun—through it, and any male passerby becomes a possibility. A new city, mapped by its *pissotières*.

Meanwhile, as a one-night stand in one of the dozens of dark hotels in the quarter, nothing had changed. Except that now it was French knees knocking at your rump, French teeth tearing at your nape, French verbs entering your ears as hoarse nothings in these dangerous hours of early morning. What would happen if you suddenly lost the need for equilibrium despite the unending maelstrom all around?

Yet the resilience! An ash can in Paris was no longer an ash can but the Holy Grail. If bad things happened, they became good, because they were French, thus instructive, for this was the land of Jean Gabin, northern too, where the summer sun rose at 3 a.m. I never found (as the anguished Foucault did) that the French were intolerant of homosexuality, or Americans either for that matter. Admittedly, the only people I've ever known have not been the stone-throwing bourgeoisie, but artists, the idle rich, and similar misfits.

Bobby Fizdale and Arthur Gold somehow already knew everyone in Paris. Even Jean Cocteau. Indeed, they had been hired to record the backgrounds for the film being made on *Les enfants terribles*. Cocteau hoped they would improvise around "The Japanese Sandman," the song he had listened to, over and over and over again, while writing the novel in seventeen days during his 1928 disintoxication at the Saint-Cloud clinic. "But we don't *know* 'The Japanese Sandman,' " they told him, "and besides we can't improvise." "Mais comment ça!" He seemed startled. "Vous êtes des américains!" (The director, Jean-Pierre Melville, eventually used, to haunting effect, Bach's Concerto for Four Pianos, played anonymously.)

Meanwhile Bobby and Arthur were planning a two-piano recital at the Salle Gaveau on 24 June, including Paul Bowles's clangorously delicious Concerto, with a small orchestra that Gary Samuel would conduct. Paul came from Tangier for the occasion, though he claimed to hate France where he'd not been since before the war (nor would he return for another thirty-five years). The instrumentalists were not quite up to the rhythmic complexities of Paul's piece, though when I examined the score the fault seemed as much Paul's as theirs. I remembered from my days as a copyist how Paul's music, so forthright to the ear, looked devious to the eye, as only the music by someone unversed in proper notation could look. But Fizdale & Gold played nobly as always, and "everyone" was there. A postconcert party was given in the rue des Saints-Pères, chez Edmonde Charles-Roux, who was editor of *Vogue*'s European offices. And there, late in the night, I met Henri H.

Henri H., known to all as José, was music critic for the monthly *La table ronde,* an employee at the music division of UNESCO on the avenue Kléber, and most significantly, the amanuensis and official biographer of Francis Poulenc. Would I, he asked, like to have a drink later at his place, he lived just down the block? I would. It was a Friday night, no need for him to rise early next day, so we stopped by the Reine Blanche on the way. It was 2 a.m., we were both a bit tipsy, and there ensconced at the bar in all his fat glory sat Georges Auric, to whom José introduced me. It goes without saying that a fifty-two-year-old French composer, distinguished member of the Groupe des Six, would not have heard of any American composer, much less me, but when I whistled to him through my rosy lips the key themes from various movies he'd scored—the Black Angel's tune from *Sang d'un poète,* the morose waltz from *Les jeux sont faits,* the swooning love song from *Le diable aux corps*—it must have been a heady dose for him, from this nocturnal barbarian with bleached hair. (I had just learned the term for peroxide: *eau oxygénée.*)

José H. rented a floor in a *hôtel particulier* at 66 rue des Saints-Pères which belonged to the Comte Anne de Biéville, a supercilious fop who modeled himself on Montesquiou—that is, Proust's Charlus —and whose sole claim to fame, besides money, was having done the argument for one of Diaghilev's ballets, *Errante.* I spent the first of many nights with José, of whom I became very fond, and in due course he became the dedicatee of the new song, "Rain in Spring." At thirty-three José was slight of build, biblical in aspect with tight curly hair, and a paradoxical demeanor that was laid back but concerned, literal-minded but poetic. A *pied noir* raised in Algeria, José soft-pedaled his Jewishness and was sometimes unearnedly imperious (as when berating his cook, Susanne, in front of guests), a trait learned, I assumed, in imitation of his classy friends like Marie-Laure de Noailles. He owned a lovely looking clankety-sounding Pleyel piano which he played with a certain skill but no "feeling," and he knew French repertory like the back of his hand, especially Poulenc, for whom I shared his abject adoration. José grew, he said, to be in love with me, but was more protective than jealous of my amoral wanderings. I used his place as an occasional crash pad, once even showing up at five in the morning of the same day I was scheduled to come to lunch with Norris and Shirley and Jean-Claude, all of whom then arrived to find me still in bed with their host. Other times he forced me to eat, when he found me staggering around the quarter looking for drinking pals. His only serious anxiety was when I went off with Guy Ferrand. He wept then on Shirley's shoulder, as even, years later, on Marie-Laure's shoulder, for what he felt were my dangerous indiscretions. I cured him, he claimed, of love.

More important, at least for me, was José's entrée into musical circles. He considered me a protégé, a "find," was intrigued by my music, especially by *Penny Arcade* which, in its skewed Frenchified sonic language, depicted the arch-American milieu of Forty-second Street where he had never been. He showed me off to everyone.

The night after the Fizdale & Gold concert we gave a party on Harp Street for Paul Bowles. I seem to remember Bill Flanagan (passing through Paris with an effete companion en route to Italy), Shirley, of course, and a bunch of Jean-Claude's companions. The crux of the evening, however, did not rely on people but on a hideous nutrient.

Paul had brought a wad of *majoun* from Tangier, a figlike pudding, gummy and nutty, but tasteless, derived from kif, Africa's marijuana. As a drinker, I'd never cared for drugs; they're not legally social in the same way, and you need to wait too long for the effect. With liquor, of course, comes puritan remorse (". . . they have beaten me, and I felt it not: when shall I awake? I will seek it yet again." Proverbs 23:35), while with hallucinogenics there seem to be no aftereffects. Still, was it quite proper of Paul to pass his vice around to us children?

How could I know that you don't mix hash with alcohol—business with pleasure? So I swilled wine while skeptically ingesting the more nuanced and leisurely gift. Suddenly everything in the room froze. Each person became a statue, mouths puckered or opened on a word never finished, total stillness. Except for me. On a different time-wave, I walked among these Pompeian statues for whom time had stopped.

I left the party, made it to Saint-Germain, ran into Charles-Henri Ford at the Reine Blanche. He had just come from seeing Arletty in Cocteau's adaptation of *Un tramway nommé désir,* but Charles-Henri's French was so weird I couldn't comprehend. Wasn't Arletty an ostracized *collabo*? I wondered. But just as the French were currently sleeping with American tourists (it was an alluring convenience), so they had slept with Germans, at least until the last year of the occupation when things turned menacing. But sex with the enemy was not collaboration, merely a venal sin, and Arletty was apparently now back in the business of acting. Anyway, Charles-Henri and I had a few beers. Then I returned to Harp Street. Nothing had moved. All were still posed as I'd left them, like George Segal plaster figures. Then the *majoun* hit me too. I collapsed into a dream, had sex with Jacques (one of Jean-Claude's straight friends), succumbed to a deep sleep, and woke into a stream of afternoon sunshine, none the worse for wear.

Ralph Kirkpatrick was around, with his likable intelligence. "You must see *Ondine*," said he, as we sat on the terrace of the Deux Magots, munching grape tarts and sipping our *café filtres* thick as slush and sweet as Cointreau. We were observing with amusement the *ratés* parading back and forth. The *ratés* (failures) were unapologetic spin-offs of the public existentialists who disported themselves in a manner they felt that Sartre (whom they'd never read) would approve of. They had the accoutrements of sophisticated despair but no talent to choreograph it. "*Ondine* is Giraudoux's greatest play," said Ralph, "and remote from this display."

Next evening with José we saw *Ondine*, which contains the most touching curtain line in all theater. "Comme il est beau, comme je l'aurais aimé" ("How handsome he is, how I would have loved him"), sighs the water spright at the final sight of her mortal lover whom she has been obliged to forget, a lovely sample of the conditional tense for me to try out here and there. Louis Jouvet and Dominique Blanchar inhabited a transfixing décor of Tchelitcheff, in as many shades of blue as the ocean had depths, and an incidental score of Sauguet, lilting and eerie.

The following night I saw Raffaello's ballet, *Le combat,* and Roland Petit's vulgar *Carmen,* then went to a sleazy hotel in Clichy with C. (another friend of Jean-Claude's) and fooled around. The weekend of 2 July was spent in Fontainebleau with José. We stayed at an inn on the edge of a park filled with moss-covered statues, and didn't drink. We walked and talked, and José, who knew all about English except how to speak it, was a literate and patient teacher of the French which I had vowed to vanquish. We all speak our own dialect within our mother tongue; I was anxious to master French sufficiently to speak a Ned-French as I speak a Ned-English. Marie-Laure would later say my French was a mélange of the princesse de Clèves and Jean Genet, as I, chattering with the duchesse of so-&-so, conjugated *enculer* in the imperfect of the subjunctive.

The calendar shows me, the following Monday, having cocktails at the American embassy, then meeting Roger, a movie director, at the Flore at ten o'clock. On Tuesday, Tom Stauffer, blustery and crass, on leave from Germany. And on Wednesday: Francis Poulenc.

. . .

Over the years I have written five essays on Francis Poulenc, the twentieth-century composer to whose work I feel most akin. These essays, at least in theory, are still available; they deal mainly with the music, and the man shines through only by implication. So as not to repeat myself, here I'll talk mostly of the man.

Scrubbed and shined, thrilled and expectant at this prearranged tea party, satchel beneath my arm and escorted by José, I appeared on Wednesday, 6 July, at his door on the fifth floor of 5 rue de Médicis, overlooking the Luxembourg. Poulenc, garbed in a peignoir, opened the door halfway, peered at us from the shadows and spoke: "I implore you to forgive me, my dearest Henri [he was the sole person to address José as Henri], but I can't receive you now. Please come back instead on Friday. Please." And he closed the door without explanation. Thus ended my first meeting with the master.

José assured me this was proper conduct, that Poulenc was a gentleman. Still a bit taken aback, we repaired to an outdoor bar on nearby rue Corneille, to decide, over a glass of Cinzano, how to spend the next hours. We talked of Poulenc, how he was the only queer member of Les Six, that group so-named by Cocteau, who were too young for the First War and too old for the Second, and who were knit together in name only. In later years, when people asked if I knew any of The Six, I always answered yes, all five of them. The sixth, Louis Durey, abandoned the clan two years before I was born and was the least psychologically glued to the effete anti-Wagnerian clarity of the others. His name is not listed in these alexandrines of Cocteau:

> Auric, Milhaud, Poulenc, Tailleferre, Honegger,
> J'ai mis votre bouquet dans l'eau d'un même vase.

(I eventually knew Auric by far the best, but adored Poulenc the most, though Honegger would be my professor when I had a Fulbright, and Milhaud and Tailleferre were stable acquaintances.) José explained that Poulenc and Auric were intimate (platonic) friends, that the former never showed his music to anyone before getting the latter's approval. Auric, the most cultured, the most "brainy" of any Frenchman I would ever meet (though he knew no word of any foreign language), was, by that token, a bit stymied creatively. True, he was France's most experienced composer of film scores, but when it came to concert music—to "serious" ballets—he struck me as, maybe, pompous. Out of fear of making mistakes, Auric ended up empty-handed, while Poulenc, less intellectual, rushed in where angels, etc. A true artist errs and then rues; a less true artist refrains and then weeps. The difference between remorse and regret. I would liken Auric and Poulenc to Bill Flanagan and me, if it didn't imply that Bill was less of a "true" artist. Anyhow, José went on to explain that Poulenc liked rough trade, and that he had a permanent affair with his married chauffeur, Raymond. I still felt that José, after what had just transpired, wasn't quite as . . . well, on the *inside* as he let on.

Whereupon Henri Sauguet passed by, with two others, and paused to chat. Learning that I was an American composer and knew Virgil (for Sauguet was Virgil's dearest musical friend in France), he invited José to bring me around and intone my tunes, any time will do. Then off they went to dine around the corner at La Méditerranée.

Let's us go there too, said José, it's *the* restaurant of the Left Bank. So we did. La Méditerranée, in place de l'Odéon just across from the Théâtre de France, was indeed *the* place, expensive and non-American. Again I felt, vis-à-vis José, that his bark was bigger than his bite as we sat at our little table like poor relations, while way over there, laughing, were Sauguet with his friends and other witty monsters. But José told me about them all, and I told him that yes, I did know Sauguet's music, especially the lean, enchanting *La voyante* which Danny Pinkham had played for me long ago.

Brooding today over "La reine de coeur" from 1960, perhaps the last song Poulenc ever wrote, I hear how much less perfect it sounds than, say, "Une ruine coquille vide" from twenty-three years earlier, according to how I teach my children (quit the key in the midsection so that the return to familiarity will "tell"). Yet who am I to criticize the maître from whom I learned all? In its two pages "La reine" may move nowhere, yet it's moving as hell. Poulenc here used the same air as in the contemporaneous Clarinet Sonata, and the same harmony as he'd been using all his life ("all so quite new," as Cummings would say), yet the recurring tone B, leaned upon, with a major seventh dangling below, rends the heart. I imagine it orchestrated, with that rending B sounded far off on a French horn, among the strings in the Théâtre des Champs-Elysées perhaps, perhaps in 1922 before the song, or I, existed, and intoned by a horn player with dark gray hair, melancholy, with firm torso, monolingual, and uncircumcised.

(I have been given a quadrillion dollars. Bring me that horn player for whom I lust. No? Then why am I rich? But wait—here he comes— you have brought him. Why does he look over my shoulder at the beauty behind me? Oh, why am I rich? That beauty is me as I once was. You are banished.)

As a maître Poulenc was dangerous, a converse dybbuk. Using no mask, he sang through his own lips with other men's voices. His very lack of originality became the unabashed signature of unique glories. The signature cannot be passed on.

．　．　．

Friday then, José and I dutifully returned to rue de Médicis. This would be the first of a dozen visits over the years whereat Poulenc and I, with José as cheering section, played for each other. Poulenc's interest in me was, of course, my interest in him: like all the French, he knew nothing of the United States (although he'd been there twice on tour with Bernac), so was impressed that a young American could be so well-versed in his music. He tutoyéd me straightaway (I said *vous* to him until the end), and we talked not just about music but about "men." His taste in the former was biased toward everything French, except Fauré for whom he had an allergy, perhaps because he was so clearly influenced by him (an instance of imitator improving on original); his taste in the latter was toward *sergents-de-ville,* lower-class types with handlebar mustaches, long winter underwear, and a slight pot belly. The exuberance of such types shines through virtually all of his oeuvre, not just the *Chansons villageoises* and the *Mamelles de Tirésias* but in the jollity of his grave religious works. His *beau idéal* was our Governor Thomas E. Dewey. "How can you Americans not have voted him for president? *Il est divin.*"

At the end of this first visit he left the building with us. We walked him to the métro (he never used taxis, only his chauffeured car or the subway), passing the little square which now bears his name—appropriately next to a police station—down the rue de Tournon to Saint-Sulpice. Directly across from his doorway, skirting the garden with the high iron fence, were two *pissotières* about twenty yards from each other. Poulenc told us he often peered from his window at the comings and going between these two *tasses*—or teacups, as the slang has it. He even frequented them himself. Why, just yesterday morning he went into the first *tasse,* where he observed this *garçon qui bandait.* Five hours later he stopped by again and there was the same *garçon qui bandait.* When we arrived at the subway he bid us good-bye, calling José *mon cher grand* and calling me *mon petit,* all this with the nasal twang so characteristic of both his voice and his music, his upper-crust elegance (he was born rich: Rhône-Poulenc pharmaceutical products), his barnacled nose, his ugly beauty.

José explained what Poulenc had been talking about, the speech having been too rapid and colloquial for me. Public urinals, called *pissoirs* or *pissotières,* were for cruising, as I would eventually learn only too well. There was one on nearly every block in Paris, typically shaped like a Tiffany lampshade or tea cozy, with space for three human males whose six legs—like a gigantic insect—were visible from outside. These venerable art-nouveau institutions, which Djuna Barnes called "confessionals," were abolished as eyesores in the late

1950s by de Gaulle's wife. As for the *garçon qui bandait,* or "guy with a hard-on," how did you translate this verb? *Bander,* literally "to tighten," in semiargot meant "to get an erection," but could apply to women too, as in English a woman can be said "to get horny." José told me, with solemn pride, that Gide had legitimized the word by using it in *Thésée.* Such was my French lesson for the day.

Between the two appointments with Poulenc came an occurrence that changed my life. (Well, yes, any occurrence, even daily ones of buying the *Times* or brushing the teeth, changes our life, but not necessarily geographically.) Did I mention that the Reine Blanche is a quite small establishment—a narrow twenty-five-foot-long bar with a dozen stools on the right as you enter, and on the left a four-foot-wide walkway— made to look bigger with mirrors? There at midnight on 6 July, while chatting with Alvin Ross as we swigged Pernod, I leaned toward the reflecting wall and kissed my image on the mouth. From behind me a voice in accented English said: "I could do it better than that." I turned around to a *coup de foudre.*

Guy Ferrand, twenty-nine, stocky with a salt-and-pepper crew-cut and a hint of five-o'clock shadow, bad teeth (like everyone in France), and keen oriental eyes, immediately struck me as very sexy. A Bordelais by birth, he now lived in Fez, Morocco, where, as a professional doctor he headed a plan at the Hôpital Cocard to inoculate indigenous tribes and rid the land of malaria. For the moment he was on vacation, so why shouldn't he come home with me? I hesitated to bring him upstairs. Instead, in the dark before dawn, we made love on the mildewing hallway stairs, and next day motored to Chartres in his Citroën 4-chevaux. The cathedral seemed then, as on every subsequent visit, dingy and cheerless. But the apricot sherbet in the medieval café *en face,* accompanied by Guy's descriptions of North Africa's lunar landscape, remains indelible, as does his singing of raunchy French folk songs as we drove back to Paris at dusk through the flat and prosperous be-poplared countryside.

Norris did see *The Blue Angel*—we all did. We also saw (heard) *Tristan* with Flagstad who filled the Salle Garnier with tragic gold.

One night the Reine Blanche was raided. Within thirty seconds, like a black hemorrhage, the place filled with police—*les flics*—who, without explanation, herded every client, including me, into a waiting paddy wagon as the *consommateurs* from adjoining café terraces gathered to jeer. At the préfecture on the Quai des Orfévres (site of so many Simenon novels) we were ushered into a huge room where hundreds of customers from other bars were already waiting. There we spent the night, to be released, again without explanation, around 6 a.m., into a cloudless dawn. Harp Street being a stone's throw across the Saint-Michel Bridge, I got home in five minutes only to find that the Rose Rouge had also been raided the night before. At least I learned a new word: *rafle* (noun, fem.), police roundup or raid.

Ubiquitous in the quarter was the staggeringly beautiful Juliette Gréco. Nothing like her had ever been seen before. She came to represent the very icon of existentialism when she sang, in a throaty baritone, the world-weary chansons of Kosma and Quéneau in a boîte called the Tabou. Straight bangs surmounting worried black eyes, long hair in a jet stream down her back, long limbed and svelte in her boy's pants and a rapid stride. Usually she was alone, though occasionally in the company of the equally stunning, equally tall, Annabel. Like animals or vines the two women walked intertwined, laughing, carefully ignorant of their staring fans for whom they legitimized the lure of Sapphism. Gréco was a marvel of the natural world, until she got her Jewish nose gentilized (by Dr. Claoué, father of composer Yves Claoué), became famous, changed her slacks to pink chiffon skirts, appeared as a fury in Cocteau's *Orphée,* and married various semi-celebrated males. (Annabel too got married . . . to Bernard Buffet.)

I saw Guy daily, introduced him to everyone, went to museums and concerts (but not to bars since drinking to him was anathema), and learned more and more French. He turned out to be an avid music lover, even had a piano in what he called his "very agreeable house" in Fez. Head cocked, as always, to one side, he asked that terrible question, to which I gave the only possible reply:
    "How would you describe your own music?"
    "By playing it."
    Whereupon he invited me to Morocco.

José took me to Henri Sauguet's in the rue Truffaut. Sauguet, aged forty-nine, had been a protégé of Satie's and Koechlin's; his calm, economical, ultramelodic, and rather featureless music appealed to me hugely. His personal homeliness—big nose, weak chin, pop eyes, and pince-nez—worked to his advantage as a wit, as when he imitated Landowska lecturing on the harpsichord, or Raffaello de Banfield discussing high art with a duchess. He was the wittiest man in France, quick and savage; but like many satirists he was the soul of kindness. On that Monday of 18 July were also present Jacques Dupont, Sauguet's lover for the past twenty years, aged thirty-eight, painter and portraitist of the quality of Bérard, and whom I found seductive with his laughing eyes, old-fashioned mustache, and habit of chain-smoking; and another composer, Jacques Leguerney, a somewhat tamer version of Sauguet in whose shadow he perennially flourished. I showed off for them, since José H. was "launching" me as a mascot in society, and they were warm. When I mentioned Guy Ferrand they wondered could this be the same Guy Ferrand who was the *ami* of Reynaldo Hahn, that is, of Proust's lover?

They talked continually of Jean Cocteau, since Sauguet had been once launched by that poet as I was being now launched. As usually happens when an artist's best days are behind him, Cocteau was currently more famous than ever merely for being Cocteau. Surely to Americans he was, after Gide and Jean Gabin, France's chief export. In 1949 Cocteau decided that fame was too much for him, and withdrew. Everywhere were signs of his withdrawal—of Cocteau in the act of not-being-famous. Newsreels showed him walking away from the camera, then turning to wave farewell. Americans (i.e., Paul Goodman, Norris Embry) had memorized his serious side, but in Paris his trashier and more beguiling side was omnipresent. He had been paid, said Sauguet, 500,000 francs to write this slogan for Lanvin: "Ladies, your legs are poems. Bind them in Lanvin hosiery." And when Marlene Dietrich came through town, he introduced her from the stage: "Madame, your name begins with a caress and ends in a whiplash."

From Paul Bowles, returned to Morocco, came this letter in red ink out of the blue:

> British Post Office, Tanger, Maroc 8/vii/49
> Dear Ned: A word to ask you what you're doing, what you're going to do, where you are, where you're going to be, and when. I hope this will reach you and that your friends will forward it to wherever you are. Truman C. is here; Gore V. left the other day. Perhaps one of these days you will show up. I think you'd like it. I looked for you at the R.B. on Blvd. St. G. my last night. No sign. best, Paul

But where exactly *is* Morocco? I asked Shirley and Norris. It's down under the Mediterranean, they said, just across from France. Do you think I should go? I asked. What else have you got to do? they answered.

On "22 juillet" Paul sent another note, black ink on powder blue:

> Your letter came this afternoon, and it was exciting news to hear that you might be coming so soon. Of course, this is the best time of year in Tangier. It is incredibly beautiful now. We are living at the Farhar, which

is on the mountain overlooking the sea, Spain, and the Riffian Mountains. The house is being built, but is by no means finished. It *could* in a pinch be lived in, but I don't think it would be comfortable for you. Perhaps in another week our maid will be out of the hospital and could cook for you. I may of course be completely crazy in thinking you expected to live there in any case, but actually you *could* in the salon (about 6 feet by 4) and the maid would prepare your food. The rest of the house is full of Arab workmen. Let me hear from you about all this. The hotel where we are is well out of town. Be sure and notify me in advance if you come so I can meet the boat. It's hellishly confusing to arrive alone and not be met.

best Paul

What made him believe I was coming to Tangier, let alone to lodge in his unfinished house, when my plans were clearly to go to Fez, 150 miles southeast, to spend the rest of the summer? I had decided to accept Guy's invitation. He had now gone to Bordeaux to visit a brother, and hoped I would meet him in Avignon where we would begin the trek southward. I would need a typhus shot, he said, adding that he loved and missed me. (I miss you = *tu me manques,* i.e., you are lacking to me, one of those convolutions an American needs to get the hang of.) Was I getting into hot water? I scarcely knew him— though what does "to know" mean? It has to do with intensity, not longevity. I knew Guy during the last fortnight more deliciously than others I'd seen daily for years. Still. Opposites attract, but this very opposition may become the source of bickering, then of divorce. Unless, like Jack Spratt and wife, you lick the platter clean.

Meanwhile, I was carousing as much as ever, and not working, unless work is the ingestion of a novel culture, and trying, like the leopard, to change your spots, just at the moment when those very spots are your trump card.

Comte Anne de Biéville sought to beguile me with pornography, mainly Cocteau's equivocal drawings for his own *Livre blanc.* Pornography is fun or dull according to an artist's skill, but when concocted to excite, it works only if the *dramatis personae* are your type. If one character, although physically a turn-on, behaves as you feel he should not (behaving passively instead of actively, for example), the intended bonfire acts like a wet balloon. Still, how healthy, how natural! What Great Master did not produce his percentage of the genre? (Webster's: Gk *pornographos,* adj., writing of harlots, fr. *porné* harlot + *graphien* to write.) Maybe all writers are whores. Witness the "dirty" sketches, gay and straight, of Jacques Callot, of Goya, of the Renaissance glories in the secret drawers of the Naples museum and of the Vatican, of Picasso and Balthus and Paul Cadmus. Music cannot be proved to be pornographic, though Shostakovich did his best to subvert the Wagnerian convention of Love-as-Violins, by using the belching thrusts of drum and trombone to represent a wedding night.

You cannot imagine the odoriferous nostalgia evoked as I sit at the dining room table with a magnifying glass, curved over a great map of the city retracing the promenades of nearly a half-century ago, streets whose names have changed, cafés and hotels long since demolished, boarding again with José (now dead) the Bâteau-Mouche, that little riverboat, at nine o'clock (the summer sun of northern France does not set until midnight), and dining with two carafes of white wine while the scenery of the Seine changes kaleidoscopically as you glide the lazy kilometers between the Pont de Tolbiac and the Pont d'Issy, and being young and in love and in Paris. I took the same Bâteau-Mouche trip with Guy (now vanished), and the limits of being-in-love seemed boundless. Eternal love lasts as long as it lasts: sometimes, as the clock ticks, an hour or two, sometimes a lifetime.

We bought a ton of music at Durand's (now also vanished) in the place de la Madeleine—Messiaen, Ravel, Debussy, all their complete works in those memorable editions with the composers' monograms on creamy vellum. Music publications were still artifacts.

1949 saw the agonized climax of French culture; we got there before the rot. The Great were still there; some of them, like Poulenc and Messiaen and Genet, had their grandest works ahead, while others, like Honegger and Sartre and Gide were already in a twilight. No one would replace them, but this perspective was as yet unfocused.

France knows all about music except how to listen to it. Italians sing with their singers, Germans sit with head in hands, while the French attend nicely and whisper, "Comme c'est beau." Not an auditory breed, they are culinary, visual, excel at dress design and pictures and literature. No French composer has been prophet in his land, and no French performer can stand apart from his sacred repertory enough to interpret it with necessary scope. Whether they could govern another country as remote from their rational Catholicism as North Africa with its violent Islamism would be soon determined.

Guy met the train in Avignon on 30 July, two months to the day after my arrival in Paris. (Those eight weeks had laid a foundation to which I could return.) From Avignon we drove through the Midi, honeymooning in Cannes (at the little Westminster Hotel on the other side of the tracks, far from the maddening Croisette), La Turbie, and Monte

Carlo (where we saw an octopus on the beach), thence to two days in Marseilles and Cassis. In the underground bars of these towns I—in the black turtleneck given me by Jean-Claude—was taken for a mute and local hustler, but only in the dark. In the light, even the most debauched American in a long-rehearsed disguise will never be mistaken for anything else: his eyes may be bloodshot, but they will forever reflect innocence—albeit sometimes an evil innocence. On 4 August we drove the car into the hold of a small liner named *Sidi-bel-Abbès,* and made the twenty-six-hour crossing in first class, dining on the best filet mignon I've ever tasted. On 5 August we sighted the Algerian coast, with behind it six thousand miles of a raw new ancient steaming continent.

So there was Africa, which would be my intermittent home for the better part of the next two years.

26. Morocco ·
Paris · Morocco

Just as my inverted basic education—that of being inadvertently exposed to the works of today before being indoctrinated into those of yesterday (classical music thus becoming as problematic to me as "modern music" to you)—turned out to be correct while the scholastic veneration of the past seemed wrong, so Morocco would represent during the next twenty-eight months, esthetically and professionally, the right place at the right time. Gertrude Stein: "I like a view, but I like to sit with my back to it." For a narcissistically ambitious Chicago boy, aged twenty-five, the sudden isolation of Africa was a refuge against the competitive rat race of Paris and New York. With no rivals to impress, I could either implode with boredom or work concentratedly. During this period, therefore, I composed my First Everything.

An artist works because there's nothing else to do; whatever else he tries will make him sick. However, one might add that much of the "else" feeds his art: brandy, sex, and oversleeping, as well as books and paint and country sunshine, not to mention procrastination—all this serves as fodder.

In Marseilles, that huge old grimy port to which the penitent red-haired Mary Magdalene retired after the Crucifixion, we visited the Château d'If, and consumed apéritifs on the Canabière, the most splendid avenue in France. Our last night there, after a bouillabaisse at a waterside bistro of the so-called *ancien vieux port,* we saw Louis Jouvet's sadistic *Fantomas après Fantomas* in a *cinéma du quartier,* then roamed the nontouristic byways of that metropolis of crime, of Fernandel and Mistral and Raimu, and of the rippling italianate accents voicing the nonetheless Gallic homilies of a logical race, then returned to our dumpy hotel to make love.

Imagine now Oran, a thousand wet kilometers to the southwest on the hilly Algerian coast, identical to Marseilles (at least in my inexperienced ken) yet peopled with Arabs: the jolt of another language, another continent, another spooky culture where I too now am the Other—no longer an American in their eyes (what is America?), but a Nazarene from Europe. Oran was Marseilles in reverse, the site of Camus's *La peste.*

It must have been an afternoon landing, since I remember driving west for a hundred miles, arriving in darkness at Oujda on the frontier, and passing a bedbug-ridden night at a somber auberge. The landscape was indeed lunar, but purposeful somehow in its barren yet masculine grandeur. And now Morocco, more mountainous than Algeria as we began the descent toward Fez, seemed maybe sweeter despite the lack of France's color, the stark emphasis on silvery tan and cactus green. The countryside of France had been squared off, neatly parsimonious, each acre accounted for; this was extravagant without generosity, without ownership. League after league of unchanging biblical—Koranical?—décor which had little to do with me. Yet I did not feel like an interloper, much less a hostile witness, for I simply did not exist. Nor would I have suspected Moroccans themselves existing in this lifeless plain if we hadn't had engine trouble and stalled; whereupon a dozen djellaba-garbed men materialized (we, how silly! were in shorts, and thus prey to a trillion flies which also materialized) to slit our throats—no, to give us a helpful shove.

Approached by motor, Fez is first glimpsed, like Mexico City, as an oasis way over there in the valley. Founded in 808 by Mohamet's brother, it is the holiest Moroccan city. You gaze down upon a hundred mosques jutting from three centers: the Ville Ancienne, the Ville Nouvelle, and the Ville Française. Guy's "very agreeable house" was situated in none of these *villes,* but within a dusty medical compound outside the wall, a hundred yards from the great Bou-Jeloud gate, a savage arch of blue mosaic, and abutting an Arab cemetery. Since Muslims are buried uncoffined and upright, hyenas sup on available scalps and shriek their pleasure in the moonlight. Outside at night, sounds of other animals I didn't know combined in a sad, thrilling canticle that made me ill at ease: owls, dromedaries (which were called *chameaux,* or camels, despite their single hump), sometimes jackals. By daylight flies, flies everywhere, snarled between your toes, in your hair.

The one-story house was a concrete affair with modern bath, big kitchen, big L-shaped parlor-dining area with grand piano, and big bedroom with big single bed shared by me and Guy. (In those days, and up through 1957, I could sleep in the same bed with another; since then, not—not even in the same room.) Big porch, big windows, tile floors, fans everywhere. Outside, no greenery, just a few smaller abodes here and there occupied by the personnel. Sand, parched gardens, skinny dogs, palms, tarantulas.

On the second day, Sunday, 7 August, Guy gave me a labyrinthine tour of the Old Town. Street of Tanners where bleached hides reeked. Street of Dyers where shimmering skeins of scarlet stretched endlessly. Street of Coppersmiths where pots, vast and wee, were fit for pantries of giants or pygmies. Each street claustrophobically narrow, flowing with loud women in veils, hawkers, and screaming kids. A mosque doorway now, in whose shadows lurked the lepers, one of whose facial cancer had caused her cheekbones to protrude like some undersea creature with eyes on the ends of stalks. (I thought of Lana Turner, so perfect in black chiffon that night at Café Society.) The utter misery. Then the utter peace of mint tea in the rich gardens of the Hôtel Jamai in the heart of the Médina. Street of the Whores, where we drank more mint tea, and where the fake *houris,* unveiled and middle-aged, seemed decorous and indifferent. Street of the Jews, the Mellah, where all doors are painted blue to discourage the flies (flies hate blue), in contrast to the Médina where the Arabs, who despise the money-lending Jews to whom they are indebted, don't paint their doors, and so have flies.

The tour was too quick, indigestible, remote, with forbidden flashes of some incomprehensible truth. Through it all had come glimpses not just of the result of a mores, but of those who had fostered the mores over millenniums and were rushing now past us, alive, foreign, yet breathing the same air as us. The glimpses were discombobulatingly erotic. While there was scarcely a sense of the hidden female, the ubiquitous male gave new sense to the word "virility," each one a sort of hologram of that unshaven far-ago man in Jackson Park. This was virility in the abstract, in the absolute: the Arab male was the Other by nature, and desperately attractive. I was doubtless the sole American inhabitant in the whole of French Morocco (decadent Tangier was still at this point an international port), certainly the only American *composer* on the entire continent. How was I to make contact—was I morally *meant* to make contact?—with this mysterious breed which was unanimously homosexual in practice but not in theory (thus overturning Kinsey's hard-earned premise)?

There were too many hurdles with the French language to start from scratch with the Mohgrebi dialect of Fez. Besides, I was here because of Guy, not to get laid indiscriminately, and needed to work hard, having not penned a measure since "Rain in Spring." Nor was there often a question of drinking. Morocco is not equipped to deal with hangovers. (Just as in Rome—which is also no land for drinkers —where if you venture forth too soon the morning after, you'll grow dizzy at the sight of a yard-long marble foot, so in North Africa, a country of legal cannabis where alcohol is religiously proscribed, if you drink you will drink alone.) Since I knew that, chez moi, one drink leads to twelve, I preferred not having one. (Not even wine? people always ask, as though wine were some inoffensive pap.)

Guy had a servant, Messaoud, a lean appealing thirty-year-old jack-of-all-trades (will he rape me? why not?), illiterate, serious, married, who showed up each dawn and departed at dusk. He ironed, washed, cooked oddly but well, was forever barefoot, spoke French badly. I was bemused that Guy would *tutoyer* Messaoud, the same as the policeman had tutoyéd the prisoner in that Jouvet movie. Guy said to listen: Messaoud also addressed *him,* Guy, in the familiar second person singular; the Arab language has no *vous* (just as English has no *tu*) except in the plural. Messaoud said *tu* to me too, of course, and called me "M'siou Nit." He seemed to accept me solemnly as part of the household. When Guy occasionally was away for twenty-four hours inoculating some tribe in the far country—the *bled,* as it's called— Messaoud would stay at the house overnight, sleeping outdoors on the moonlit threshold to protect me (symbolically—but then again, realistically) against intruders. Which moved me. He never asked questions.

What Guy's colleagues thought of the fact of me, I have no idea. It was as though he had come home from a bourgeois summer vacation with a bride. Such a situation is more relaxed in the colonies. No one pried. Of course, I was on an intellectual par (to say the least) with the French intelligentsia of Fez and, being a young American musician, I was more presentable than most colonials' lovers, who were generally Bedouin houseboys.

When do you work?

I'm never not working.

Everything pertains, one thing leads to another, you can even eat ambrosia abstractedly if your mind's on a modulation. But outsiders want a tangible routine.

In Fez the routine was tangible. Once settled in, Guy was gone all day at the hospital, except for the de rigueur midday meal (which I loathed), even in the Saharan heat (which I loved—I eventually spent three summers in the dry furnace of Africa, laboring continually, without fatigue: the weather report—No Relief in Sight—being ever a cause to rejoice), after which came the de rigueur siesta when we made love while the frowning Messaoud clattered in the kitchen.

Between August and October I composed two sonatas, one for piano solo (the second), and one for violin and piano. The Piano Sonata was in three tightly crafted movements. The Overture, one of my few works in classical sonata form, contains a first theme sounding (to me) like a Provençal chant, and a second theme cribbed from an Arab lament overheard on Messaoud's radio. I was, after all, in Africa—weren't composers supposed to absorb the folk elements from the environs? The Nocturne is a lush blues skewed, as though pictured in a fun-house mirror. The closing Tarantella, copied from a remembrance of something by Rieti which Bobby and Arthur had played in June, is frothy virtuosity at its most delicious. In this version the sonata would be premiered by Leon Fleisher at the American embassy in Paris the next May. Soon after, I changed the order of movements, added a knuckle-breaking Toccata, and gave the new version to Julius Katchen, who played it all over the world. As such it was printed, under the title *Seconde sonate pour piano,* by the French publisher Pierre Noël (now Billaudet), and dedicated to Guy Ferrand. Katchen recorded it in 1952 on London/Decca, my first record ever, and it sold well everywhere to nice reviews.

The first of the Violin Sonata's four movements was already finished in 1948, and now served as a curtain-raiser to a languid Waltz, a passacagliac Dirge, and a Final Dance. I mailed the twenty-minute result to the only violinist I knew, Maurice Wilk (he had played in *In Piazzas Palladio*), who premiered it in Washington in 1950. Now titled *Sonata in Four Scenes,* it wasn't published for another twelve years (by C. F. Peters), at which time it was dedicated to Edward Albee, mainly because Albee had just dedicated to me his play *The Death of Bessie Smith*.

Evenings, which is when I prefer the main meal of the day, we dined in one of the three restaurants of the New Town, preferably À la Légion, a European bistro frequented by, among others, an old queen who surrounded himself with légionnaires, while we obliquely observed the *manèges*—the supposed vying for favor with royalty among these rugged semicriminal foot-soldiers. (Is it offensive to refer to that customer—with the unearned disdain used for a fellow member of one's own minority group—as an old queen?) The khaki-clad légionnaires, with their Yugoslav accents and rustic joshing, were objects of mystery. Unfaithful lovers by definition, they also reeked of the sand, as Piaf moaned from every jukebox.

> Il était mince, il était beau,
> Il sentait bon le sable chaud,
> Mon légionnaire. . . .

After our *yaourts au citron* (I had never before heard of, much less tasted, yogurt) and powerful *cafés espresso* we would either go home and listen to records and play the piano (Guy had subtle catholic tastes but, like my mother, banged the instrument with reckless abandon), or go to the one cinema in town, queuing for tickets while the sun, the size of a circus tent, collapsed over the rusty gravel. I noted seeing that summer *La femme en rouge, L'amour autour de la maison, Echec au roi, A chacun son destin* (during which we were again assailed by bedbugs), *Halte, Police!, La rivière rouge,* and other French films not made for export. Also the Swedish *Appassionata* with Viveca Lindfors flailing at the keyboard, and American films with Abbott & Costello or Paulette Goddard jabbering in French. These forays proved culturally instructive, if only because the jargon issuing from the screen—especially the dubbed American movies I'd already seen—represented a usefully vulgar counterpart to the rigorous grammar I was elsewhere studying.

Because in grade school I was a lazy student, albeit from a cultured family, I spoke correct English without knowing why. Because in Morocco I devoured a French grammar until it oozed from my ears, I ended up knowing the "whys" of French more than of English. To this day I don't know what a declension is in English, but can conjugate the imperfect of the subjunctive in any irregular French verb. The fact that the French speak in alexandrines as naturally as Americans speak in iambic pentameter affects their music too; the waves of their alexandrines, being longer, flow smoother than our choppy iambics. Indeed, the French language, being the only Indo-European tongue without a tonic accent in any multisyllabic word (*solitaire,* for example, or *tablier,* can legitimately be set to song with a stress on any of the three syllables), French music, even the nonvocal music, is the least rhythmic of all Indo-European musics. Which is why, no doubt, Ravel composed *Boléro,* that most doggedly on-the-beat piece in the repertory, to show that "I too got rhythm."

My verbal grasp of French hitherto had lain in the repetition of the Verlaine and Eluard texts used by Debussy and Poulenc. But the ecstatic recitation of such phrases as "Dans le vieux parc solitaire et glacé" or "Une ruine coquille vide pleure dans son tablier," didn't get me any farther with Parisian taxi drivers than the query, "Driver, what stream is it?" got me with Manhattan cabbies as we skirted the Lordly Hudson. To an anglophone's eyes the subway announcement, "Il est défendu de cracher et de fumer" quickly translates into "It is defended to crash and fume," until he eases, day by day, into another basic meter, the meter-of-logic. The meter-of-logic, now juxtaposed onto the Arabian meter-of-frenzy and broadcast daily to an American who has hitherto spoken in his native meter-of-impulsiveness, became a heady mixture that in retrospect I realize in no way affected my music. I read the Bible—meaning *L'Evangile,* or New Testament (the French have no concept of the Old Testament)—and *Phèdre* and *Madame Bovary* and *Pompes funèbres,* as well as the daily paper called *La Petite Vigie;* listened to quotidian chitchat at the hardware store, and succumbed to the *language des fleurs* nocturnally as pillow talk. Months later, when I again heard English spoken at the consulate in Casablanca, the sound was at once crass, warm, and embracing, like awakening into a familiar dream.

What was I doing at the consulate in Casablanca? Guy had received a letter typed in bureaucratic French from that institution. It had come to their attention that an American, Ned Rorem, was residing in Fez. Would it be possible for Mr. Rorem (or, in the event that he's one of your patients, a representative of Mr. Rorem) to visit the consulate in the very near future? Apprehensive, we trekked the 200 kilometers almost immediately.

The consul, a backslapping Yankee, hemmed and hawed before getting to the point. Had I ever, he wanted to know, heard of an Arthur Lee? . . . Well, yes: Arthur Lee was an acquaintance from nine years ago in Chicago, when we were both sixteen, a student at the Art Institute, friend of my friend Géorg Redlich, and a protégé of a social worker named Rosabel Velde. (I didn't add that we'd had sex.) . . . Did I know if he was a Communist? . . . (Pause.) Well, everyone in those WPA days, you know, was sort of left-wing around the edges, though I personally had never been much interested in politics. Where is Arthur now, by the way? . . . The consul didn't know; nor did he tell me how my name, after all these irrelevant years, had drifted from Chicago to this wilderness on the wings of a half-forgotten fancy. The consul was jocular, knew all about "artists," had even been a bit lefty himself once, you know how it is.

Something about my own vaguely conciliatory stance smelled bad.

Casablanca, with its million inhabitants, bore no relation to Ingrid Bergman's version—it looked like Detroit—but did have a great pastry shop (sugar is manna to drunks on the wagon), and some good movie shows. Once or twice a week I'd accompany Guy on his excursions into the *bled,* sometimes with Messaoud in the back seat who would help if the car got stuck while fording a desert creek, or ferret out scorpions beneath the seats. Thus we would embark toward Ouarzazate or Tinerhir, southerly towns halfway to the Sahara where in the summer there were no idle excursioners at the luxury hotels hemmed in by jasmine gardens. After inoculating fifty frantic Berber children in a nearby village we would return to the hotel and be served—alone in the dining room beneath a casually revolving fan— by fifty liveried youths with a menu as opulent as that on the boat from Marseilles. Or we might dine on a whole sheep in the astoundingly plush home of the local *caïd,* serving ourselves greasily and without utensils from the various communal pots of couscous, embellished with lamb or with cinnamon, washed down with the obligatory mint tea. I never felt comfortable with these all-male confabs, encouraging at once the (to me) barbaric practice of eating with the hands and subdued belching, and the oriental formality of restricting conversation to smug nodding. I remember a Sunday picnic with Messaoud and one of the nurses from the compound, the plain Mademoiselle Bursier, in Guy's brand-new Buick, near the cool falls of Ifrane, and of being stung by a wasp, and then of visiting Meknès and taking pictures near the emerald cloisonée walls. Fragrance of honeysuckle, the dying sun, taste and touch of oranges, and the sad smile of the unloved nurse. I mention that afternoon for no other reason than to clear it from my head onto the page, and to include the name of someone, among billions who have died since 1949, that will have otherwise vanished without a trace.

Almost daily we visited the Royers, Guy's substitute family consisting of mediocre and trusting colonial parents coincidentally named Fernand and Fernande, and their two children, a homely homosexual extrovert son and a chinless unmarried daughter who had a crush on Guy. Madame Royer—Fernande—made fudge and smiled. Monsieur

Royer was retired, Michel was eligible for the draft and sometimes dressed in drag, and Jeannine was studying English. Guy always made me play and sing whatever I happened to be working on. Since I can't perform my own piano music unless I practice it as I'd practice any other composer's music, and since I can't sing except for imitations of Billie Holiday which only other Americans of that period might appreciate, there wasn't much to offer. I had, however, along with the two big sonatas, written three new songs. One was a three-page rendering of Apollinaire's "L'automne" which, except for the little Cocteau poem of years before, was the only French setting I'd done; another, "The Call," was a ten-measure vignette on anonymous fifteenth-century verses ("My blood so red/For thee was shed...."). "L'automne" has never been heard and hides somewhere in a trunk. "The Call," an echo of Frances Osasto singing Basque airs, was later arranged for unaccompanied chorus and woven into a suite called *From an Unknown Past* (1951). Both versions are printed, and the solo version was movingly recorded in 1962 by the incomparable Donald Gramm who, with his bass-baritone beauty, turned this forty-second bonbon into a heartbreaking masterpiece. The third song, "The Sleeping Palace," on an enigmatic stanza of Tennyson sent on a picture postcard from John Edmunds, was, fourteen years later, incorporated into a suite of Tennyson settings for Ellen Faull to sing.

The weekend after that Sunday picnic with Mademoiselle Bursier we finally went up to Tangier, taking the train. Our compartment contained an officious trilingual female who kept up a nonstop monologue in Spanish, French, and Arabic for 200 kilometers, a distance of five hours, with three separate customs formalities at the border. My first impression is less intense than the conglomerate impressions from various visits over the years. Tangier, after the instant red panache of Marrakech, the green of Fez, and the blue glittering coastal capital of Rabat, seemed white and seedy and ominous. In 1949 this was still the International Zone, and would remain so until the revolution of 1956. To converse quietly in English at a café in the Xoco Chico meant that some denizen at a nearby table, looking like Henry Armetta, would cock his ear and take notes. A nest of tenth-rate spies.

Saturday night we wandered the town, assailed by boyish beauties peddling unlimited wares. Sunday Paul Bowles picked us up at our quaint English hotel on the waterfront—the Mimosa, I think—to guide us back to his pensione, El Farhar, on a hilltop for lunch. His entourage was somnolent and disorganized, having been last night to a masked ball thrown by Cecil Beaton; hung-over hangers-on came and went around our table, mainly reliving the party. These were Jane

Bowles, Truman Capote, Themistocles Hoetis, Brion Gysin, plus lesser lights at other tables.

Jane, *toujours égale à elle-même* with her ski-jump nose and her stiff game leg propped up on a chair beside her, was not eating, but sipping pink gins which she reordered every twenty minutes by yelling to the bartender in the corner, "Encore un pink gin, je vous prie." I found her, as always, endearing and scary with her imperious vulnerability, her complaining, her giggle, her indifference.

"Do you know a girl named Mugsy Phyllis?" she asked, referring to the lesbian who had married my sister's Japanese boyfriend, Chino, a decade before. "She was here last week and asked if I knew you. She called you Neddo." She went on at length about how lesbianism was the one worthwhile route to follow on this troubled globe, then called for another pink gin, this time in Spanish. Paul, a proud audience for Jane's prattle, had the patience of a parent. His literary career, except for the stories in the specialized *View,* was for the present nil to the general public, but in another month would dazzle the world with the advent of *The Sheltering Sky.* Jane for the nonce was the Family Author, still resting on the laurels of her six-year-old novel, *Two Serious Ladies,* which I'd read and admired.

I'd read and admired *Other Voices, Other Rooms* too, but had never met Truman who was less puckish than his pictures, mainly because of his glasses. He had a way of sizing you up through those glasses, bestowing a quick plus or minus, without appeal. He took more to Guy than to me, I believe, but his French was nonexistent, and Guy was perhaps baffled by this supposedly famous gnome. "You're a musician," whined the gnome, "just like Paul. Well, then you must know Jennie Tourel. Jennie Tourel came to Yaddo once when I was there and I was told to show her around. She was wearing a green gown and high heels, right in the middle of the afternoon, and I was supposed to be working, but we went for a walk in the woods, and she wouldn't take off those shoes, so she got stuck in the mud." End of story. This, I surmised, was the Wit of the Great. Jane and Truman made a pair, cuddly and snotty, playing their insulated game inside a time capsule—they could as well have been in Omaha. Writers, I guessed, didn't have to be profound except when they were writing.

Themistocles Hoetis, an American who spoke no Arabic, sat swathed in a burnoose and on his haunches despite many available chairs. He was silent, sexy, surly, not up to the banter or not interested. His claim to fame was as editor-founder of a pretty good literary review called *Zero* published right there in Tangier.

Brion Gysin: I had awakened one morning in his arms after a boozy night the previous summer in Provincetown. Then he had said he was writing a treatise on slavery in eighteenth-century Canada. Now here in Tangier, tall and Anglo-Saxon, suave and open and educated, an informed dabbler, he had become a painter. Brion's pictures, all on foot-square canvases, represented the entire Sahara rather the way Jean Hugo painted Côte d'Azure landscapes on postage-stamp-sized enamels. "You cannot," said Brion, "find a canvas even half the size of the Sahara. You have to stop somewhere, so I stop here."

Whereupon we all quit the dining room to see Jane's sick kitten. Jane had an apartment separate from Paul's in the pensione. A veterinarian was to visit her pet at three o'clock. I retain, after forty-four years, a vivid picture of the huge Spanish doctor hovering over the curled-up kitten, and shaking his head.

Paul took me and Guy, along with Themistocles, for dessert in town, at Madame Porte's. (Brion and Jane and Truman remained, to nurse their hangovers and kittens. All three planned to live in Paris next winter.) I had come, after all, to Tangier to see Paul, but he typically pretended I'd come to change money, the exchange rate for the dollar, even on the "white market," being higher than anywhere in Europe. Nor am I sure what he thought of Guy. They both had a proprietary interest in me, but since Guy was there to show me around, what good was Paul? As for Guy, he never took to Paul—found him precious and vicarious about this strong land, whereas he (Guy) was doing something practical to improve the lot of the *indigènes*. Paul, in fact, funded by the Library of Congress, had spent months in the *bled,* recording every shred of still extant folk music before it perished forever.

For the moment, there we sat, sated on pastry and Turkish coffee, smoking our cigarettes: Paul with his ivory holder and British Sweet Caporals, Guy with his three-pack-a-day Gauloises *bleues,* and I with my Moroccan brand Koutoubias, named for the minaret at Marrakech, which were almost as good and twice as cheap as American cigarettes.

Our host had recently returned from a stay in Ceylon, where he had quite simply bought an island. A hilarious mimic, Paul spoke to us in the skittering high-pitched monotone of the colonialized natives of India where male whores use the verb "to enjoy," without a modifier, to mean "have sex" (rather like the French "jouir"). Example: "Shall we enjoy on the beach?"

I never heard Paul say anything "important," though as with Jane and Truman, I supposed he put his important thoughts into writing. Still, I was young enough to find Things more superficial than Ideas, not yet realizing that gossip—*high* gossip, to be sure—was more nourishing than philosophy after a certain age.

Next morning we changed money, and returned to Fez.

. . .

Ramadan fell in September that year, which meant the faithful must
fast from dawn to dusk through the lunar month. Also a suffocating
heat wave had set in, so that if you wrapped your naked self in a cold
wet sheet, the sheet would be dry as a dead leaf in minutes. Everyone
drank twenty Cokes a day—or rather Pepsi-Cola. The Pepsi-Cola manufacturers had created a monopoly in North Africa by advertising their
product as *not* being brewed, like Coca-Cola, from pig's blood. (Arabs,
like Jews, are not pork eaters.) Guy felt it would be cruel for Messaoud
—who, as a Moslem, fasted from dawn to dusk during Ramadan—to
have to fix our midday meal, and that we should lunch out as much as
possible. I felt this to be inconvenient—which Guy in turn felt was
petulant and *American* of me. Summer intensified. The sky turned
bone white. Tempers flared.

Guy asked if I'd help toward buying a goat so that Messaoud could
sacrifice it, according to custom, by slitting its throat. This I did for the
unsmiling but grateful servant who, with all his virility, was nonetheless repelled by the slaughter. His reaction, in its protected haze,
disturbed me: Messaoud was an Arab, after all, thus indifferent to
cruelty. I note this with embarrassment. Am I being quite honest?
Certainly I was impatient, used to getting my way as pretty people are.
Could I also have felt, beneath the uncivilized patina of Morocco, a
certain ennui in what Paul Bowles found so urgent? An annoyance that
the Arabs couldn't behave as Arabs, leaving me more time for work—
a work which, by its nature as Art, would be paradoxically indulgent
of the Arabs as Arabs? Was I tired of the astonishment of Morocco? I
am no traveler.

Raised to believe in equality, Rosemary and I never questioned the
difference between white and black. But the difference of Arabs was a
novelty which I greeted with frustration. I was tempted by, hence
resentful of, the Arab male's swarthiness. Opposites attract. Yet I am
not attracted by the Balinese, so where is the moral?

Back in Fez, the agenda reports more movies attended, more meals in
and out of the Médina, more books read (Anouilh, Sartre), and a feast
prepared for the Royers featuring roast rabbit and a *poire belle Hélène*
made from poached pears, homemade vanilla ice cream, whipped
cream, poire liqueur, and homemade chocolate sauce. More trips,
notably to Marrakech again, to the Roman ruins at Volubilis, and to
the festival at Moulay Idriss of horsemen shooting into the sky at full
gallop. I noted too, on 28 September, that "Monsieur Vachet, the
restaurateur, went insane today, leaving his wife free to carouse."

(On 6 October my First Piano Sonata was premiered in New York's Town Hall by David Stimer, he who five years earlier had initiated the ongoing series on WNYC of American music. The final Toccata was eventually published separately by Peters in 1961 with a dedication to William Masselos, and the whole three-movement work came out ten years later.)

There are notations about tailors, haircuts, banks (scrupulosity of small sums changed), and frequent references to Cooks. I must have cashed in my return boat ticket and used the money, $185, to spend instead in Paris. For yes, I went back to France, after nine weeks in Morocco, flying from Tangier on 12 October. Guy said he was ethically constrained to let me go back into the fray, that he had no right to force me to blush unseen, all because he loved me. What I did not note in the daily agenda was that, above all, Morocco had meant being alone, hour after hour, day after day, hatching eggs in a cocoon without time, without tears, without much sex, but with the intense focus on chiseled self-expression that only the young have the energy for.

Did I plan to stay away indefinitely? Was it a mistake to leave and break the spell? (There are no mistakes.) I didn't know it then, but I would return to Fez in less than three weeks.

My first act in Paris was to gather the precious new manuscripts and, before they could be burned alive, deliver them to the Néocopie-Musicale. This was accomplished with the same juvenile enthusiasm as in 1936, when returning to Chicago after the long vacation in Europe, I rushed to the grandfather clock to see if the cache of robins' eggs still lay within. The Néocopie-Musicale was an establishment existing solely for reproducing in multiplicate the results of labor on a craft; nothing therein pertained to other than music printing. I liked this room whose very ugliness was functional: the presses, the flickering blue lights, the reams of transparent onionskin paper of every size printed with from eight to thirty staves, some with clefs and some without, the stacks of envelopes, india inks of various hues, pen nibs of various thicknesses, rulers long and short and made of cedar or glass. The address was 9 rue Foyatier, near the upper exit of the funiculaire leading to Sacré-Coeur. The owlish Monsieur Vadot, who for decades plied the now-obsolete trade of blue-printing music manuscripts incised upon his special stock, made several copies—and bound them—of the new Violin Sonata and the new Second Piano Sonata. I remained his client until the business folded.

. . .

Shirley said that John Cage was in town and wanted to bring Pierre Boulez (I wrote "Boulaise" in the calendar) over to play his newish sonata. Our apartment, rue de la Harpe, was the only place that John knew with a good piano.

There were eight of us—me, Shirley and Jean-Claude, Cage with Maro Ajemian, and Boulez with two cronies, a cute sandy-haired painter named Bernard Saby, and a less cute type whose name has vanished. Boulez himself intimidated me, though on the face of it he should not have. The face of it was that, being composers of the same age but from separate lands, we should have ideas to exchange. Yet beneath the face—which in his case was sexy (I am seldom intimidated except by persons I find sexy)—lay an imperious self-assurance that was all work and no play. If he was not yet the superstar he soon would internationally become, Boulez was nevertheless preceded by a reputation of enfant terrible buttressed by a huge intellect, a quick mind, and a vicious wit. Cage had already told us that the Frenchman was anything but French—that he had gone on where Webern left off, serializing not only the sequence of pitches but of every variable in music including rhythm and dynamics. Nothing was left to chance, to crass inspiration. All this Germanitude was Greek to me, as to most Americans who had been liberated, during the quarantine of war, from Europe and developed a language of their own. This language would all too soon be squelched by none other than Boulez, who would intimidate not only little me but Copland and Stravinsky and anyone who crossed his path. All this, as Antigone said, for a handful of dust.

Preliminary niceties dispensed with, Boulez sat down to play. I still picture Miss Ajemian, who, as America's premier pianist of the avant-garde, knew a thing or two about these affairs, and now assigned herself as page-turner for the maestro. Wearing a scarlet Dior dress, she stood to the left of Boulez and, with an expert hand, pinkie crooked, plied her trade with the incomprehensible score. The music meant nothing. It simply wasn't music—worse, it was painful. And endless. When Boulez finished we were at a loss for words.

"C'est très beau," Maro allowed, breaking the silence. Whatever else it was, the sonata wasn't *beau*. Nor surely was it meant to be. Boulez gathered up his music and his friends, bade us a perfunctory au revoir, and was gone.

Jose was taken with the new Violin Sonata, particularly the penultimate movement which he loved. Not so Shirley. She found it inferior, but liked the new Piano Sonata which she thereupon decided to include on her upcoming recital in the redoubtable Salle Gaveau. This would be her debut into the professional realm of soloists and she practiced continually, while Jean-Claude lolled about scribbling verses, as I, if I had been out late the night before, groaned in time to her slow arpeggios.

The word "cuite" is inscribed many times in my datebook. Binge! Sobriety's exquisite placenta had been rent; the discipline so carefully cultivated in mind and body over the productive North African summer had been ripped apart by my alter ego. One drink is too much, and never enough. Since the virus of a single martini is already polluting the system, why not have sixteen? (Drink and recover in order to . . . etcetera.)

One seldom entered the Reine Blanche at any time of day without bumping into James Baldwin, known to all as Jimmy. We had known each other back home in scenes of similar tonality on Bleecker Street: my leading him on at midnight, then changing my mind near closing time; him, drinking as though he had a hollow leg but never showing it, except by speaking high philosophy and looking hurt with his bulging wet eyes. Jimmy was intensely serious, at once credulous and canny. Like everyone else he talked of the novel he was writing, but unlike everyone else he actually coughed up that novel four years later to worldwide success. For now he was earnest, a good listener, nearly always with white Americans, though when he wasn't at the Reine Blanche, who knows? Jimmy Baldwin's problem, and also his springboard, was not that he was black and queer, but that he was black and queer and *ugly*. He had every right to behave like a beauty, and did, and it often got him farther than it got me. Patience is its own reward.

After Jimmy became famous he remained as always a good listener, indulgent of white friends' folly, or so he pretended. But he was also busy, and his days were spent mainly in the humdrum marketplace of art and politics. His problem then became how to fit drinking into the professional schedule. During the late 1950s we renewed our acquaintance as neighbors, he on Horatio Street, I on West Thirteenth. I introduced him to Marc Bucci, composer and expert jazz pianist, with whom he had an affair. There remains a vision of Marc accompanying on my battered upright, as Jimmy sang spirituals with a small and beautiful voice, tears streaming down his cheeks. We visited my then-agent Audrey Wood: he hoped she would obtain Marlon Brando for the movie of *Giovanni's Room*. Instead, she presented us to another client, Dorothy Heyward, who with her husband had written the book for *Porgy and Bess*. Mrs. Heyward had also written the play *Mamba's Daughters,* in which Ethel Waters had so majestically created the role of Hagar. Audrey felt this could make an ideal opera, if Jimmy wrote the libretto and I the music, and she procured the rights from Mrs. Heyward. Jimmy was enthusiastic, the story was his to the core, he took me to Harlem to hear gospel singing, he throbbed with lyrics. (I still have one, scribbled on an envelope—"There is a scorpion in my heart"—alive with anxiety about insoluble injustice.) But gradually I saw that the project was not me. Would it not be hypocritical—condescending—to presume to write a work around a suffering I had never endured? I withdrew from the project. Surely I erred. Gershwin, after all, hadn't done badly with *Porgy and Bess*. Where was my imagination? It was a mistake not to have persevered. (But there are no mistakes.)

Summer lingered. The sky glowed with diaphanous yellows, and the Paris oxygen contained no hint of autumn frost—the sort of weather that makes students nervous at having to return to class. I too felt nervous at having decided to stay indefinitely abroad. There were the parents to placate; I had subsisted thus far on their largesse, on the remnants of the Gershwin award, and, in Morocco, on Guy's benevolence. Nadia Boulanger now proposed me for the Lili Boulanger Award, five hundred dollars granted in the name of her late beloved sister, which I duly received. This impressed my parents, as did the possibility of a Fulbright. They were proud of me (especially Father; Mother sometimes felt I was "no better than Rosemary" and shouldn't get special dispensation), but knew no precedent about the care and feeding of a composer in the family. I explained that they had spawned an exceptional child whose treatment must therefore be exceptional. Father agreed to send me a monthly allowance of one hundred dollars for a year.

In this ambiance of silken weather and semisecurity, Shirley and I one afternoon took a walk along the quais where we bought two green balloons, and brandished them conspicuously around the quarter, as behooves proper bohemians, while I sang Apollinaire's refrain: "Tes yeux ressemblent tant/A ces deux grands ballons/Qui se tournent dans l'air pur/De l'aventure." Settling in the Montana bar, we had lemonade, and released the balloons which floated to the ceiling where we abandoned them. Passing in front of the Flore we heard a shrill voice cry Ned. It was Truman Capote, who recognized me from our so-brief meeting six weeks before. He was seated with his American agent, they were staying at the Hôtel de Nice. We made a date to dine that evening, and would meet in the Pont Royale bar.

A liquory evening, during which I took at face value everything

Truman related, and so did he, since he invented his own truth which he announced always as fact. He asked what I thought Paul Bowles did for sex "with all those Arabs." My silent reaction was that he should know better than I: didn't "they" all know about each other? I hadn't yet learned that famous people are as mystified by each other as we mortals are by them; nor do they have more powerful inklings, only the power to illustrate communicatively such inklings as they do have. Around midnight we lurched into La Librarie, an existentialist bar across from the Montana, rue Saint-Benoît. Someone tapped me on the shoulder.

It was Bernard Saby, the cute sandy-haired painter who had been with Boulez a few days before. Bidding goodnight to Truman, I went off to Bernard's, somewhere in Passy, where we smoked some pot, as we Americans called it then. We sort of made love all night, passed out, awoke in the afternoon dehydrated and conversational. Bernard at my request phoned Shirley, care of the Rose Rouge, to say he'd found me *ivre noir* the night before, that I was in safe hands, and that we'd all meet that evening at the Petit Marigny to see *Le procès*, Gide's dramatization of Kafka's *The Trial* for which Boulez would conduct the incidental music by, I think, Honegger. Boulez was the protégé of Jean-Louis Barrault and Madeleine Renault, the Lunt & Fontaine of the French stage, to whom the government had lent the Théâtre du Petit Marigny for their experimental whims.

Bernard was vaguely insane and clearly endearing in the informal blur as we lounged naked, inhaling the still lurking fumes of yesternight. On every wall of this rented room were his paintings, what passed as abstractions to Parisians of that time, benign pale colors, ungeometrically wavy, nonthreatening. We talked, I in still-faltering French, he with his appealing stammer.

"French music means everything to me," said I. "Honegger, Poulenc, Milhaud—I was raised with all that."

"C'est du petit pipi," was his reaction. "Small potatoes. That stuff is passé, nobody does it anymore."

These convictions sounded secondhand. It grew clear that he was under Boulez's thumb—Boulez, who had the week before referred to Stravinsky as *merde* on the radio. Bernard reiterated the tired canard of Rimbaud, "Il faut être absolument moderne," as though it were new—as though each one of us were not *absolument moderne* simply by virtue of being alive today, and whatever derivative art we produce is still, by definition, the art of today. Weren't the French, if not conservative, at least *conservateurs*, naming their parks and squares after Balzac and Greuze? Why, your very concierge will proudly drop the name of Proust though she's never read him. Imagine that in America.

"Oh, America," said Bernard. The French didn't think about America. Boulez didn't think about America. (Decades later he became our Philharmonic's chief, with his no-nonsense interpretations of the artists he now decried, including the beloved Debussy whose *La mer*, I reluctantly admit, has never sounded more properly fearsome, and gelid than under Boulez's baton—if, in fact, Boulez uses a baton.) For the moment I felt despondent that this chic and predictable disavowal of the past, as urged by strong personalities, would lead us into a new dark age where hidden masterpieces would need to be preserved by monks over the centuries. At least these "strong personalities" knew the masterpieces they were repudiating. Europeans were not, like us, oblivious to culture. (I type these sentences in May of 1993, the day after the terrorist bombing of the Uffizi Gallery in Florence.)

Bernard and I pulled ourselves together, met Jean-Claude and Shirley for a cup of soup at the Rond Point, then proceeded to *Le procès*, starring Barrault as Joseph K., arch and un-Kafkian. I saw Bernard Saby again a week later, but the blush was fading. In the middle fifties Pierre Souvchinsky, ghostwriter of Stravinsky's Harvard lectures and now a promoter of the avant-garde, brought Saby to lunch at Marie-Laure's where he seemed drugged, extinguished, out of place, full of smiles but unequal to Souvchinsky's sales pitch. Eventually he died ambiguously, still young, broiled by the icy light of a one-track-minded captor.

I saw quite a bit of Truman, who used me as decoration and as translator. He came to Harp Street to entertain Shirley and Norris Embry, after which we went to the Deux Magots for him to be interviewed for *Paris-Match*. The interviewer was Yves Salgues, star reporter on that weekly, whom I'd met at the Boeuf sur le Toit a few nights earlier. Yves, tall and blond, unstable and handsome, was also an author, a fine one, influenced by Giraudoux. I will bring him up later.

I will also bring up James Lord, whom I came to know well, and with whom I now note a lunch date Aux Ministères, familiarly called Madame Garde's, where everyone ate, good and cheap, in the quarter in those days. (Virgil: "I decided that if I was going to starve to death, I'd rather do it in Paris where the food is good.") I don't recall how we met, probably through José, and of this meal I remember only that we discussed a character in his novel-in-the-making.

"The character is very beautiful," James explained, "and could walk into any bar with the aplomb of the very beautiful, knowing that heads would turn."

"But beautiful people don't have aplomb," said I. "I'm terrified when I walk into a bar."

On 23 October I turned twenty-six, the age at which male citizens of the USA are no longer eligible for military conscription. On the terrace of the Flore that evening, with José and Jimmy Baldwin, surrounded by other tables of Franco-Americans, I drew forth my draft card and ostentatiously burned it. The gesture, like the throwing of that pearl rosary into the murk, had no point beyond theatricality. The draft card had long served as proof to bartenders that I, with my perennially juvenile features, was old enough to drink. To have burned it in the old days, on American soil, would have been a jailable offense, and admirable, if you will, that a pacifist was announcing his convictions and willing to pay the price. Now it was perhaps merely an inconvenience. Yet until I was forty, the age at which one no longer needed to register, I was hounded by the notion that sooner or later I'd be asked to show the card under some legal circumstance. I never was. But Father still carried *his* draft card.

Whenever Norris, always in a cloud, would start to cross the street against the light, or tell us about last night's dangerous adventure with some workman in Les Halles, Shirley would say, "Dear Mrs. Embry," a shorthand reprimand for the letter she would have to write announcing his death. She now took to reprimanding me as well. "Dear Mrs. Rorem," she would sigh when I shakily returned to the fold ever later.
    Shirley did have a knack—exasperating and final—for letting us know that her liaison with Jean-Claude was rare as Francesca and Paolo, while our one-night stands were bagatelles. Her French was thorough and colloquial, incorporating the broad slow Parisian twang of Arletty's. I adored her. But the apartment was not large, three's a crowd, I had no routine, and was getting on her nerves.
    One morning she confessed she'd come across a letter from Guy on my bed and couldn't help reading it. Her heart bled for his lonely words, and for the closing phrase, "Tu es ma vie tout entière"—you are my whole life—in which I had noted only that the two adjectives did not agree with one another, although the first one, *tout*, because it was followed by a vowel, would, although incorrectly masculine, *sound* like the feminine modifier of *vie*.
    "I think you should go back to Fez," said Shirley, taking a puff of her Gauloise, "and get some work done."

On 2 November, when I boarded the night train for Marseilles, I had been back in Paris only eighteen days. Beyond the occurrences already mentioned, I note the following: There was a certain Pierre Pichon, bony, blue-collar, and fair (as a rule I prefer the somber), with whom, for the next year or two, I had harmless amourettes before he disappeared completely, no doubt returning to prison somewhere. We saw twice Clouzot's movie of *Manon Lescaut*, updated, a quasi masterpiece, with the disturbing Serge Reggiani and Cécile Aubrey, the latter a persuasive pre-Bardot slut who would eventually give it all up to become the mistress, it's said, of the Glaoui of Marrakech. We dined, with José, at Philippe Bemberg's, rue de Grenelle. David Diamond passed by for lunch; then, it being Wednesday, we went together to Boulanger's about whom he was acidic, and a few days later we took him to dine chez José. Yves Salgues's name appears in the agenda repeatedly, as do the names of others I can't now place. Janet Hayes, the soprano who had sung in *A Sermon on Miracles* in Cambridge, was now in France, married to choral director Charles Walker; we talked of giving concerts. With infinite pleasure I met, through José, Monsieur et Madame Heitor de Azevedo, a Brazilian couple of whom he was José's superior at UNESCO, and she—Violetta—was among the most beautiful women in the city, with her imperious posture and carmine lips, her electric warmth and charcoal eyebrows.

But I did miss Guy, his stability, his touching traits such as not knowing how to swim, his un-French devotion to the straightforward, his innocent trust in the power of music, and his sexiness, which was, so to speak, free.

On the train to Marseilles I slept not a wink, caught the boat at ten on Thursday morning, and arrived at Oran on the 4th barely missing the train to Fez. But I got there on Saturday and collapsed, as though I'd been gone a year.

Everyone has experienced the sometimes unpleasant surprise of seeing a new lover nude for the first time. The reverse obtains too. More than once, in a public sauna, I have swooned in the ideal grip of some stark-naked grimy Apollo, to discover twenty minutes later, when we meet at the exit to go home together, that now, clothed, he is all wrong.

Things were the same with Guy, and then again they weren't. Fez itself had altered, as any place alters with the seasons; the heat modified, the daily storms, and the intellect of the town—the Ville Nouvelle —revived after the fallow holidays. Yet life in the house remained stationary. If the itchy carnality that had joined me to Guy was fading —not least because he was less an object, more a person, and as a person had foibles, gentlenesses, even a wisdom that did not turn me on—love and habit were taking its place. Habit and love—but especially habit—are the vitamins of art.

In three days, from 24 to 26 November, I composed, appositely during a watery surge from above, three Barcarolles for piano solo. These I copied on transparent paper, mailed off to Monsieur Vadot, and he in turn forwarded copies to Shirley and a few pianist friends. Shirley decided to include them, along with the sonata, on her upcoming Paris recital, and asked me if Guy could wangle a tryout on the concert series in Fez.

The elite of Fez, like most intellectuals in colonial centers, are, by virtue of their isolation, more doggedly cultured than their more relaxed cousins back home. Avid for learning, they grab at every bone. My journal shows that in the six weeks before Christmas we went out perhaps twice a week to high-toned vocal and piano recitals, to plays from the road companies of various professional theaters in France and Brussels, all with first-rate artists, and to the "better" movies. Yvon le Marc'Hadour, who sang on the recording of *L'enfant et les sortilèges*, gave a concert; so did Vlado Perlemuter, after which Guy, as a board member of the concert series, gave a reception at which I was urged to play the new Barcarolles; so did the svelte baritone, Camille Maurain. On the stage we saw Cocteau's *Les parents terribles*, which I remembered trying to read when Father was studying it, hoping it might be a sequel to *Les enfants terribles*, and finding even then, despite my having no experience beyond Chicago, that it convincingly extracted surrealism from that least surrealist of phenomena, the French middle class. Edouard Bourdet's *La prisonnière*, with Pierre Blanchar, which had also burned bright on my parents' shelves in translation as *The Captive*—daringly about lesbianism, gee whiz!—came daringly to Fez.

We visited the Piscines des Malades at Moulay Yacoub on 16 November, and the Fête du Trône in a thunderstorm, during which the sheltered Europeans paid no attention to the "natives" seeking shelter.

Among lesser films (the frightening *Daisy Kenyon*, *Fabiola*, and *Key Largo* dubbed in Arabic) were two French masterpieces. Vercors's troubling *Le silence de la mer* concerns a provincial father and daughter obliged, during the Occupation, to house a German officer. This they do, while vowing never to speak to their guest. Thus, during each evening meal, the educated and sensitive officer speaks in monologue of his childhood, of his love for France, and of the tragic ironies of war. He then retires, saying, "I have the honor of bidding you a very good night." (This remark, repeated as it is a dozen times, becomes a refrain which the audience of roughnecks echo in unison, making a joke of what they could not seize. Or so I assumed, poet that I am.) Daughter and father listen in silence. Only at the end, when the officer announces that he will be billeted elsewhere and will never see them again, does the young woman, depicted by the ineffable Nicole Stéphane, utter the word "Adieu."

The other masterpiece was *Patte blanches* by the director Jean Grémillon, starring Suzy Delair, with Claude Romain in a minor role as a rough gamin.

Life is a spider web. During the next twenty-four months I would know intimately both Grémillon and Romain (the latter becoming a short-time swain and long-time friend), while, for what it's worth, Nicole Stéphane would become the companion of Susan Sontag.

I've always, like all Americans, ached to be a movie star, maybe even an actor. Or actress. Trouble is, I can't act. Yes, I know our lives are our acts: unlike animals without an oral grammar we humans constantly reinvent our persona by choosing series of words never before uttered. Yet I cannot convincingly read aloud a line I haven't written.

Also in the six weeks before Christmas I made extensive sketches toward a Second String Quartet as a fitting thank-you to Boulanger for granting the award, and toward a Two-Piano Suite as a fitting vehicle for Fizdale & Gold. Both works were coldly plotted to get me out of the rut (if rut it was) of small-scale songs.

Cecil Smith, now editor of *Musical America* and living in New York with Perry O'Neil, wrote to say that Perry had received the new Piano Sonata and had already scheduled it for a radio performance. Would I, by the way, like to write an essay on North Africa for his magazine? I did, calling the article "The Real Musics of Morocco," and Cecil duly published it, along with a quaint photo of me in white shorts on the day of the picnic with Mademoiselle Bursier. I blush at the presumption: What did I know, or really care, about local folklore compared to the vast and loving research Paul Bowles had gathered for the Library of Congress?

With fairly naïve chutzpah I sent the same quaint photo to André Gide along with the "Alleluia" and a letter congratulating him on his eightieth birthday. His address, 1 bis rue Vaneau, was given me by Truman Capote, who claimed Gide as a dear friend, assuring me that the Frenchman "would adore that sort of thing." Young people don't know that their very youth gives them entrée. Indeed, Gide replied immediately, claiming he was now too old, alas, to do more than shake my hand across the sea, and suggesting I look up his young friend, Robert Lévesque, who had just been named professor at the Lycée de Fez. Lévesque turned out to be forty, licentious, smart as hell, and eventually became a valued associate, especially of Guy's.

I tried my hand at writing stories in French.

On 20 December, with Nell Tangeman's mezzo timbre in mind, I wrote one of my best songs, based on a sextet of Spenser, sent to me, like so many marvelous texts, by the caring John Edmunds, copied in his ornate scrawl on the back of a postcard depicting the head of a Vermeer girl:

What if some little pain the passage have
That makes frail flesh to fear the bitter wave?
Is not short pain well home that brings long ease,
And lays the soul to sleep in quiet grave?
Sleep after toil, port after stormy seas,
Ease after war, death after life doth greatly please.

I can understand a poem only by setting it to music. Thus it becomes mine, and I grow anxious should someone else admire the poem alone, though it may be a thousand years old. I don't know anything about the human voice except how to compose for it; the gracious vocal line is common sense. We are what we sing. (Edward Albee, after he became famous overnight, gave classes in dramaturgy. Bill Flanagan: "What does Edward know about writing plays?—he just writes them.")

Someone must have been telling lies about Ned Rorem, because he awoke one morning to find himself arrested by a communiqué from Shirley which ended thus:

(Paris, Dec. 22, 1949)
... Ned Darling, I'm suspicious of you. Your letters have that ever-so-content-with-myself quality which chez toi is treacherous. My sweet boy, you're *not* the best American composer—& if you're going to follow in Paul Bowles's footsteps there's no expecting you ever will be. Instead of writing a bad novel why don't you write a good last movement to the sonatine? Or work on the first sonata? When are you going to face the difficulties of your work and solve them? It's not easy to be a composer. If you continue doing this like falling off a log your music is going to sound that way. This African idyll is fine but it's bad too. You forget so easily even when you're surrounded by reminders. Very little of what you have written is worthy of you Ned. *For God's sake remember that.* Remember too that mama & papa don't know anything about music & their approbation has nothing to do with the quality of what you write. Oh if you knew how badly I want to see you fulfill all that's golden in you—& frankly I'm sick of the trash. Think Ned, all that gold!!!
Bruce & JC send love. My best to Guy.
I love you—
S.X.

Shirley's letter disconcerted me because in some way I felt she was right but didn't know what to do about it. After all, I did work hard, and yes, some of the work, like the Spenser song, came like falling off a log. But was the song less good for that? Maybe it's *not* easy to be a composer, but neither is it hard—at least not for a composer, which is what noncomposers are loath to realize. Shirley entertained a notion about Great Art and Dedication that was, if not Hollywoodian, at least German in its head-in-hands solemnity. She was asking a cat to be a dog. I was losing it both ways.

(There's a gag about the fraternity man whose roommate's parents visit the frat house unannounced. While waiting for their son to appear, these proper folks engage the fraternity man in small talk, when suddenly he sees, coming down the stairs behind them, the roommate stark naked and very drunk. To divert the parents' attention the fraternity man yells, "Hey, look!" and points to the window, not realizing that out on the lawn are two dogs fucking.)

Nor had it yet grown clear that there are in this world two basic genres of composer: the mad extravagant Teuton who thinks big and is complex, and the logical thrifty Gaul who thinks small and is simple. Mahler's Ninth can be cut in twain and remain Mahler, but change one bar of *Daphnis* and you no longer have Ravel. (Reptiles are French, canines German, though some reptiles, like crocodiles as distinct from garter snakes, are German, while some dogs, like whippets as distinct from Newfoundlands, are French. Crocodiles, however, become French when compared to alligators.)

Well, Schubert could write five songs before breakfast, "like falling off a log," while Poulenc labored for months over one ditty in order to make it *sound* easy.

The art of music does not improve with the centuries but swings like a pendulum forever between contrapuntal eras and harmonic eras. Contrapuntal eras are more complicated (Bach, Schoenberg) than harmonic eras (Ravel, Poulenc), nor has France ever produced a contrapuntist of note. Shirley was trapped, through her instincts and friends and background, in a contrapuntal era; I was trapped in a harmonic era. We could thus each not grasp what the other was driving at. Still, if her words made me feel impotently guilty, my miffed resentment forced me to state: I will, in the next year, compose at least one of everything, submitting to the disciplines of big forms as well as small. Whether or not the result sweats and shrieks and breathes and bleeds—lives, in short—at least no one can say it's ill-formed. God herself is not always on target.

This statement, of course, was not what Shirley had in mind. She wanted me to ponder, philosophize. Which was not in my nature. Still,

I have her to thank, *tant bien que mal*, for whatever larger scope ensued.

The word "symphony" was still cause for awe. Friends and relatives bowed in respect, while orchestras were more likely to program a new American work, whatever its shape, if it were called symphony than if it were called *Nude Descending a Staircase*.

In a little more than three weeks, beginning 22 December and ending on 17 January, I composed and orchestrated and copied my Symphony No. 1. The last of the four movements incorporates a fragment from a Berber wedding tune as a binding motif. The first movement is a stately curtain raiser; the second an Andantino in the lilting ⁶⁄₈ meter I was overexploiting at the time; the third a Franco-Hindemithian lament. Copies of the full score, via the Néocopie-Musicale, were duly mailed to hopefully interested parties. One of these must have been the American embassy in Paris, because Jonathan Sternberg, director of the Haydn Society in Vienna, wrote that he had borrowed the score from Miss Herle Jervis, then the cultural attachée, and would like to do the premiere with the Vienna Philharmonic. I agreed, provided he pay for reproduction of the instrumental materials, which I could not afford. The first performance accordingly took place in February of 1951, though I did not attend. (I have never to this day set foot in Austria.) Following this there were many hearings elsewhere, particularly in the United States, but I never heard a live one until Alfredo Antonini conducted the symphony in Carnegie Hall exactly five years later.

How all these performances came about strikes me today as astounding. I, a complete unknown, was living far from the political centers, and had no agent (still don't), much less a steady publisher, as representative. Yet everything I wrote was performed almost as soon as it left my desk. In our current philistine age no composer, no matter how famous, would dream of writing an uncommissioned symphony just for the love of it, without a down payment, a deadline, and a guaranteed premiere date. Things were easier long ago. There were far fewer composers, and far smarter audiences in the homogenized classical world.

I made a transcription of the Andantino movement for organ solo, called it *Pastorale*, sent it to Peer-Southern, who printed it in 1953, at which time I dedicated it to Henri Fourtine, the lover who would succeed Guy. The full symphony would not be printed until 1972.

"What If Some Little Pain," incidentally, was published by Hargail in 1952, and dedicated to Julien Green, who by then would be a persuasive influence. Dedications, as every poet knows, can veer from manuscript to galleys. After the journey, sometimes years long, one may finally be indifferent to the initial inspirer, while owing something—a kiss, a dollar—to someone new on the scene.

The weather during the last week of 1949 was tepid, even sweaty, although it had snowed on the 13th, leaving ridges of ice on the edges of the huge palm leaves. According to the book I got drunk on Cinzano cocktails in a bar alone, the night before the snowfall, and didn't know how to behave. This was almost my sole encounter with alcohol while with Guy in Africa. . . . Young Michel Royer, now doing his obligatory *service militaire* but stationed at home, had for some reason to be circumcised (aged twenty-three!), and we visited him at the clinic, his mother, Madame Royer, armed with her fudge squares and a worried mien, his sister Jeannine expressionless. Michel's virile member appeared infected and wormy. In two days he was released.

On 22 December, the symphony's seminal day, I note that we purchased a parrot and a backbrush. . . . On Christmas Eve we shared *réveillon* at the Royers with Robert Lévesque, and with their oldest son and his pretty wife and infant, visiting from Casa. . . . On the 28th Zelda Goodman was to broadcast my two psalms from Jerusalem; and I studied the score of *Boléro.* . . . On New Year's Eve, which was also the eve of Guy's thirtieth birthday, I made Jell-O (a recently introduced novelty, which, I correctly explained, was made from horse's hooves) in three different colors, red and green and yellow.

Thus ended a decade, and also my first seven months away from America.

27. What Truman Capote Means to Me

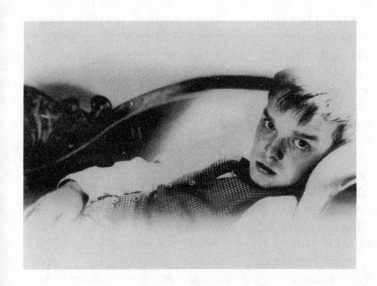

When famous artists die, nine times out of ten their fame dies with them, particularly in our century when glory is extra to what is glorified. If this is true with, say, Gide or Hindemith, who were not products of the American publicity machine, but whose vast reputations relied on their physical presence on the planet, and whose works became all but unavailable the morning after their deaths, how much more true it is of pianists and actors and ballerinas and bestselling authors. Bartók was a rare exception in having died needy and becoming immediately rich posthumously. Likewise Sylvia Plath, maybe Jackson Pollock, and of course Scott Fitzgerald. Mostly, though, we strut our fifteen minutes on the stage, then vanish.

Truman Capote would have seemed—before he died—an ideal candidate for oblivion. Like Warhol, he was famous for being famous;

but how many of the gawking fans, who witnessed him drunk and incoherent on talk shows, ever read a word he wrote? The last half of his life was so cheap, so dissolute, so vulgar, so public, that, like a sort of reverse Rimbaud, he renounced writing (while advertising himself as the greatest author since Proust), and vanished into the spotlight.

Insofar as she exposed me to a new and invaluable mode of thinking, and insofar as I admired her as much as any friend I've had, the most crucial "older" woman in my life, after my mother, was the Vicomtesse de Noailles, known as Marie-Laure. Long before I moved to France I'd heard about her as a creature of flamboyant mind, eccentric mien and endless wealth. When I first glimpsed her I was struck, not by how far but how near she came to the pre-set image. I recall that glimpse like yesterday. It was at the start of what would be a gin-soaked night, during the unbearably satisfying minutes of a Paris dusk, on 29 October 1949, in the Pont Royal's basement bar. She sat a few tables away with a redhaired man (he later proved to be the American painter Tom Keogh); I was with Truman Capote, who had greeted her as we entered: she *stood up* for him, as gentlemen stand up for ladies, and kissed him on the lips. "That's Marie-Laure de Noailles," whispered Truman, "the most powerful woman in Europe," but he didn't introduce us. It would be a year before we actually met (with her melting, like most legends when you get to know them, into a vulnerably interactive intelligence), and another year before her mansion in the place des Etats-Unis became my home, which it remained—even after I'd quit France—until her death in 1970.

Truman Capote, meanwhile, I'd met only six weeks earlier at El Farhar in Tangier, but his notoriety, like Marie-Laure's, preceded him. Indeed, the previous year when *Other Voices, Other Rooms* made headlines, I had devoured it between classes at Juilliard, finding it, as I still do, though dangerously influenced by, superior to Carson McCullers. (Superior because, unlike McCullers, each word, as with poetry, was unextractable, and the words together formed inevitable chains, like perfect wreaths of roses, which in turn formed themselves into paragraphs, pages, chapters.) The notoriety lay, of course, less in the surprise that the book was good literature (even rarer then than now on best-seller lists), than that the back cover was adorned by a photo of the author gazing at us, doe-eyed 'neath yam-colored China-doll bangs, from a prone pose on a Victorian settee ("it assumes I'm more or less beckoning somebody to climb on top of me")—scarcely the stance of our Hemingways hitherto. If in real life he was not so cutely passive, he looked every bit as infantile—physically, that is

—although his utterances, in that much-mocked voice, were always pointed, disarmingly honest and, I suppose, adult. Still, Truman wasn't like you or me. He was a conspicuous sissy, and not one bit ashamed. When I had asked Bowles how such a specimen coped in the actual world, he said that, well, Truman didn't often venture far from his geniuses and dowagers, but when he did (showing up in the Casbah maybe, or on the Lower East Side, or indeed in the plains of Kansas where a decade hence he would be documenting the Clutter murders), he was the source of disbelief rather than of scorn. Fame and chutzpah were his shields. He graced the odd side of Quentin Crisp's coin: being unreal, neither man posed a threat, but whereas Crisp as defiant victim got bashed now and then, Capote as defiant lord seemed immune to battery. This was clear in Paris now where I saw him every day. *Other Voices* had just appeared there, under the weak title of *Domaines hantés,* and I served as translator during interviews (like many good writers—and composers, too—Truman Capote lacked the gift of tongues) which were conducted in places like the Deux Magots, where strangers gaped approvingly. The rest of the time we talked.

What about? Not art, certainly. Do professionals after twenty ever talk esthetics (exhausting both their energy and their secrets) rather than money, sex, and contracts? Nor did we talk music, since Truman like most literary types knew nothing of that. (His impression of Jennie Tourel: high heels and silk pyjamas, even when hiking through mud at Yaddo. His impression of Esther Berger: "I think she's sweet"—I lifted an eyebrow—"like a cobra.") Mostly I listened as he improvised around, for instance, his "dear acquaintance," Denham Fouts, an American who in the late thirties slept with just everyone—Jean Marais, King Farouk, the Maharajah so-and-so—everyone, that is, except Hitler. "Had Denham Fouts yielded to Hitler's advances there would have been no World War Two, and Denham would not have had to slit his wrists in the bathtub of that Roman pensione." Truman talked of the long poem he was making, *The Postman's Lantern,* which would surely be settable to music (where is it now?). He speculated on why Paul Bowles stayed for so long in Morocco, then put it down to the available sex. He was stirring in a description of Jack Dunphy, who had left his wife, dancer Joan McCracken, to live with Truman forevermore. Jack's modest but true gift as a playwright Truman praised to the skies, but he praised too Jack's wise eyes, pale hair, and virile nape, and claimed to *need* the color, taste, and smell of each segment of Jack's body. Still, I seldom saw them together. Truman's life was compartmentalized. The two men were as unlike as Topsy and Eva, characters they had portrayed at Cecil Beaton's costume ball the night before I met them in Tangier.

In early November Truman left for Sicily and I returned to Africa. In March 1951 this was mailed from Taormina to Marrakech:

Dear Ned, Your card was forwarded to me here where I have been for over a year working on a novel. Am leaving in three weeks for Venice and late in July sailing home. Would so like to see you; I hope you *will* come back to N.Y. I hope you are *working*. I think of you often. My love to Marie-Laure—my love to you

et mille tendresse [sic]
Truman
In N.Y. my address is still 1060 Park Avenue

But our paths didn't cross until two years later when he turned up again in Paris. Meanwhile, his reference to "sailing home" impressed me (most expatriates in those days repudiated America), and his emphasis on "working" influenced me; a short story collection and *The Grass Harp* had just come out, and I read them with pleasure and envy at his knack for unstilted metaphor and structure, virtues I sought to impose on my music. On 28 November 1953, he came to lunch in Marie-Laure's blue marble dining room, and told us he was taken with the rich because they *were* rich—he wanted to *use* what made them tick, if in fact they ticked by being rich. Ostensibly he swapped his fame for their wealth. But did the rich ever in fact coolly sign checks to him? and can it be seen, looking back, that he ever "used" all that research in his books? He was vicarious in the sense of being a prudent watcher, moralizing about, without participating in, the global gangbang (nonpolitical department). On 17 December he dragged me to one of those loud caves in Saint-Germain-des-Prés (sober, I loathe nightclubs—the din!) where we sat for hours watching the young dance the Java. He said, "You have an innocent profile, at least from the right."

He never came to France again, not while I lived there. In New York we met from time to time, generally tête-à-tête, though sometimes with his famous flock. I do treasure an evening with Dietrich, another with Gloria Vanderbilt. Still another in a Third Avenue cinema, theoretically watching *To Catch a Thief*, actually refereeing an onanistic exchange between a male couple in the row ahead, after which we supped at Johnny Nicholson's now-defunct café where, over a chocolate soufflé, I heard about the chores of celebrity. "Yesterday, five minutes after my new phone had been installed, and nobody could possibly have known the number, it rang, and a voice said, 'This is Speed Lamkin.' Talk about opportunism!" (Speed Lamkin was to have a brief run as the poor man's Truman Capote during those distant years.) I remember also the first television production of a Capote oeuvre, "A Christmas Memory," and Frank O'Hara's guffaw when Geraldine Page appeared on the screen, looked mistily out at the country dawn, and uttered the script's first line, "It's fruitcake time." In 1959, with Valerie Bettis, I composed a dance called *Early Voyagers,* based on *Other Voices, Other Rooms,* which toured the U.S. with the Washington Ballet Company. And so forth. If Truman and I weren't quite friends we were staunch pals, always casual and mutually respectful.

But the nature of our rapport was to sour horridly.

On the eve of my fortieth birthday in 1963 Glenway Wescott gave a dinner party. There were five of us, with Truman doing most of the talking. Luridly he recalled his recent stint in Kansas, detailing for our amazement the qualities of mind and body of two young murderers (one of whom he was clearly in love with) standing trial there. He was making a book out of it—a nonfiction novel, he called it—"but it can't be published until they're executed, so I can hardly wait." Truman's position vis-à-vis those poor boys was admittedly unprecedented; he'd spent more than a year living near them on death row (and would eventually return to Kansas to witness their execution). Still, I remember asking myself later that night if he had quite the right attitude. Did he believe what he said? Or was I—as he called me, when I objected to his repeated use of the word "nigger"—a hick, who missed the finer points. (Truman was not a racist, but he did possess a personal vocabulary.)

On 14 April 1965, Patrick Smith and Richard Hickock were hanged. Immediately *The New Yorker,* in four long installments, published Capote's account which came out as a book at the end of the year under the title *In Cold Blood.* Even before the first printing the author was said to have earned, with subsidiary rights, etc., two million dollars. In February of 1966 I sent this letter to *The Saturday Review* which printed it:

Capote got two million and his heroes got the rope. This conspicuous irony has not, to my knowledge, been shown in any assessment of *In Cold Blood.* That book, for all practical purposes, was completed before the deaths of Smith and Hickock; yet, had they not died, there would have been no book. The author surely realizes this, although within his pages it is stated that $50,000 might have saved them—that only the poor must hang.

Auden, in his libretto *Elegy for Young Lovers,* portrays a poet who, for reasons of "inspiration," allows two people to perish, and from this act a masterpiece is born.

Now I am suggesting no irresponsibility on the part of Capote other than as a writer: I am less concerned with ethics than with art. Certainly his reportage intrigued and frightened me, and certainly he presented as good a case against capital punishment as Camus or Koestler. But something rang false, or rather, didn't ring at all. His claim to an unprecedented art form gives cause to wonder.

An artist must, at any cost, expose himself: be vulnerable. Yet Capote the man, in his recent work is invisible. Could it be that, like the Ortolan-eaters so admirably depicted in Janet Flanner's recent *Paris Journal,* he is hiding his head in shame?

(The Ortolan reference is to the tiny yellow sparrows which, according to old French engravings, are roasted alive and consumed, bones and all, "with napkins hoisted like tents over [the eaters'] heads to enclose the perfume, and maybe to hide their shame.") A month later Kenneth Tynan took up my tack in the *New York Post,* Truman retaliated—and became more famous. I was not invited to his fabulous party at the Plaza, the high point of which was reportedly the entrance, not of such guests as Tallulah Bankhead or Candice Bergen or Janet Flanner herself, but of the law enforcement contingent from Holcomb, Kansas.

In 1967 I and three other composers were honored at the American Academy of Arts and Letters. I duly noted the occasion in my diary, and concluded the entry thus:

What I shall remember, however, is not the glamour of the ceremonies proper but the appearance during the earlier informal festivites of Truman Capote, with dark blue shirt and coral tie, as he approached me with an uncharitable glint in his eye. Beginning softly, he crescendoed to a point where a crowd gathered, and finished off with frenzy: "I've liked what I've read of yours lately, Ned, etc. etc., I didn't see it, but friends told me you'd written something in *Saturday Review* against my book. Now I worked hard. You didn't go through what I went through. I produced a work of art, and you have no right to attack it. . . ." This! twenty-eight months after the fact.

Anyone has the right to attack a work of art, especially when the work is self-advertised as documentation. An author who claims his facts are unassailable because they're art wants it both ways: Don't hit me, I'm a lady.

I never saw Truman again. Two years later I was doing a "signing" at the Gotham Book Mart for my new *Critical Affairs.* Truman was invited, and apparently got as far as the shop downstairs. Andreas Brown, who runs the Gotham, later said that Truman picked up the book, found his name in the index, read the reference, and decided not to come upstairs. I had written:

> Truman Capote, in adapting for other mediums his goodies of the past, gets a lot of mileage from a comparatively meagre output. His art becomes his life. Like record producers, he glories less in creation than in distribution. But distribution is *the* art of today. Nor will there be, in any case, posterity for anyone.

Time passed. I didn't think much about Truman, there was nothing much to think. He appeared oftener on the tube than in type, talking about writing rather than writing; what he declared was, in essence, that he was good and "they" were bad, but he offered no proof. I did, however, enjoy two or three visits from his biographer, Gerald Clarke, for whom I dredged up scenes of childhood. Suddenly one morning in May of 1976 a friend phoned and told me to rush out and get the current *Esquire,* for in the second installment of *Answered Prayers,* called "Unspoiled Monsters," Truman Capote had immortalized me. (He is writing here of "the leathery little basement bar" in the Hôtel Pont Royal:)

> Another customer of this bar, whom I met there and who was friendly enough, was the Vicomtesse Marie-Laure de Noailles, esteemed poet, a *saloniste* who presided over a drawing room where the ectoplasmic presence of Proust and Reynaldo Hahn were at any moment expected to materialize, the eccentric spouse of a rich sports-minded Marseillais aristocrat, and an affectionate, perhaps undiscriminating, comrade of contemporary Julien Sorel: my slot machine exactly. *Mais alors*—another young American adventurer, Ned Rorem, had emptied that jackpot. Despite her defects—rippling jowls, bee-stung lips, and middle-parted coiffure that eerily duplicated Lautrec's portrait of Oscar Wilde—one could see what Rorem saw in Marie-Laure (an elegant roof over his head, someone to promote his melodies in the stratospheres of musical France), but the reverse does not hold. Rorem was from the Midwest, a Quaker queer— which is to say a queer Quaker—an intolerable combination of brimstone behavior and self-righteous piety. He thought himself Alcibiades reborn, sun-painted, golden, and there were many who seconded his opinion, though I was not among them. For one thing, his skull was criminally contoured: flatbacked, like Dillinger's; and his face, smooth, sweet as cake batter, was a bad blend of the weak and the willful. However, I'm probably being unfair because I envied Rorem, envied him his education, his far more assured reputation as a coming young fellow, and his superior success at playing Living Dildo to Old Hides, as we gigolos call our female checkbooks. If the subject interests you, you might try reading Ned's own confessional *Paris Diary:* it is well-written and cruel as only an outlaw

Quaker bent on candor could be. I wonder what Marie-Laure thought when she read that book. Of course, she has weathered harsher pains than Ned's sniveling revelations could inflict.

My first reflex was to dissolve in disbelief. My second was to retaliate, not so much in my own defense as in Marie-Laure's—she was dead and couldn't fight back, but I was alive and could. Still, fight back I didn't—not because as a Quaker I was wont to turn the other cheek, but because my lawyer, Arnold Weissberger, explained that his business was to keep clients *out* of court; also, that the Pulitzer Prize (which came to me the following week) would deflect public focus from Truman's bitchery.

Between 1977 and 1982 I kept a column in *Christopher Street* wherein the next paragraphs, separated by years and lodged in apposite contexts, glimmered.

I've occasionally admired the Coctelian rightness of Truman Capote's off-the-cuff repartee, and for years have retained in my treasure chest of wish-I'd-said-thats the following from one of his long-ago interviews: "When I throw words in the air I can be sure they'll land right side up." This noon, thumbing the Goncourt journals, I come across this from Gauthier: "I throw my sentences into the air and I can be sure that they will come down on their feet, like cats."

Suicide as an art form. Mishima at his peak dies publicly for what he feels to be truth. Truman Capote at the ebb of his power kills himself publicly for what he knows to be non-truth. Whereas Mishima grows ennobled, Capote shrivels (if a toad puffed up with hot air can be said to shrivel). His sketches of others are ultimately harmless, but the unwitting self-portrait is putrid as Dorian Gray's. All that Truman touches turns to fool's gold. A book may or may not be a work of art, but it's not for the writer to say so, or even to know so. An artist doesn't "do art," he does work. If the work turns out as art, that's determined by others after the fact. Art and morality aside, Truman's work can't work. A work which names real names but whose author is fictitious? An author must be true, his characters fictitious.

Today Truman's is a name uttered in hushed tones by the likes of Cher and Johnny Carson: he's the poor man's thinker, *le savant des pauvres* who are mostly quite rich. Not that the real intelligentsia is contemptuous, they just have nothing left to say. Truman sold his talent for a mess of potage.

On Dick Cavett's show Truman Capote, looking like that extraterrestrial embryo from the end of *Close Encounters,* posits the same defense of his upcoming nonbook as he posited last year and the year before: "Well, Marcel Proust did the very same thing." One might quickly reply: Yes, and so did Hedda Hopper. Every writer—or interpreter or conversationalist or archeologue (to avoid the word "artist")—depicts reaction to milieu; there is literally no other material to work with, on or off the earth.

Those extracts are as much as I've ever said in print about Truman Capote. However pertinent, they grieve me today. Were we kindergartners flinging mudpies? Is there a special ethics to friendship with public figures? Truman was confected of three disparate characters: private person, public person, writer. Are friends still friends when they publish what they feel about each other's professional claims or social fame? Truman hurt me, I did the same to him. Now it seems silly, benign, reparable, and it's too late. Last summer when his picture appeared on the front page of the *Times,* "Truman Capote Is Dead at 59; Novelist of Style and Clarity," I felt a sense of pride and of loss. Pride, because America cared to mourn a poet as it celebrated politicians. Loss, because, like Marie-Laure, Truman could no longer fight back.

After his death I reread most of his published work. He often speaks of the datedness of others, making his own datedness loom larger still. Of course, everything dates: Bach and Tolstoy date no less than jitterbugs and hula hoops—or you and I. Our exquisite viewpoint toward love and death this morning is, by virtue of afternoon trials, reslanted and thus dated—though maybe more intense—this evening. All things date: they date well or they date badly. I went through the early stories with the hoped-for exhilaration of finding long-lost friends. They're very 1940s, all about coy adolescents, doppelgängers and little else. Split personality was the rage after the war. Technically though (especially the remarkable "Children on Their Birthdays") the tales are flawlessly professional in that they're neither too short nor too long, the sentences sound inevitable, the images apposite. *The Grass Harp* cloys. *Other Voices* holds up (maybe because it's about queers? and they were the long-lost friends), although Gore V. contends that the most ravishing vision therein—the little country train being so slow that butterflies float dreamily in and out of the windows —is swiped from McCullers. But I never saw it in McCullers. *The Muses Are Heard* remains original, informative, funny. So does the 1956 etching of Brando. The rest seems dispensable. Still, what remains is his alone, an oeuvre tinier than his reputation, about the size of Duparc's in song, Beardsley's in pictures, Jane Bowles's in fiction.

Jane Bowles is nowhere mentioned in the printed interviews (although Truman contributed a preface to her Collected Works); nor is

Bill Archibald, who wrote the film script for *The Turn of the Screw,* which Truman signed for his "name" value and then took credit for; nor is Harold Arlen who, as composer, was solely responsible for *House of Flowers.* Like most American literary types Truman knew and cared nothing about classical music (though his instincts are elsewhere sound: "Streisand's great fault as a singer, as far as I'm concerned, is that she takes every ballad and turns it into a three-act opera. She simply cannot leave a song alone"). As for his last projects, notably the snippets from *Answered Prayers,* he forever reviewed them, instead of writing them—telling us what to think instead of letting us decide. The fault with *Answered Prayers* is not that it's gossip, but that it's cheap gossip, and Truman must have known this on some level of his consciousness. We learn nothing potent about the world's most interesting hearts and minds to which Truman alone had access, only their dirty little secrets. We never *are* told how the rich tick.

I weary of my efforts here. We are forever wishing our artists were something else, rather than what they are. It is too easy to say that Truman frittered his gifts away. The very frittering *was* his gift. The very fact of him, even in those first bright years, was never what our academics deem "serious," but who cares for them. Like Sibelius, like Rossini, Truman ceased composing long before he died, and was what he was.

He might not be quite out of my heart, but Truman is off my chest.

28. 1950: Morocco · Italy · France · Morocco

Shirley Gabis, Cap Ferrat, 1948.

New structures can be made from the same blocks, but the blocks are all ready from childhood on. Only in childhood are we destined to collect them and pick them up.

—Mahler

Ses emprunts? Igor [Stravinsky] ne songe pas à les nier. Il est architecte de la musique; les architectes n'ont pas à inventer les pierres dont ils se servent. Ils les prennent là où elles se trouvent.

—*Paris-Match*

> ... the power of invention seems rarely to accompany great ... genius; it is the minor [workers] who conceive the brilliant ideas which they drop carelessly by the wayside for the greater [artists] to pick up.
>
> —Enid Starkie, *Rimbaud*

The first month of the new decade was spent knowing I would be visiting Italy in February. Italy was the standard goal, after France, for every American on the grand tour; my route had simply deviated more than most. The purpose in heading specifically for Torino seems to have been Nell Tangeman; she was stationed there, incongruously for a singer, on a Fulbright fellowship, and longed for us to meet again.

On New Year's day I read *Corydon*. On 2 January was the dancing Fête de Jésu in Meknès, after which the Royers came to dine. On the 4th, Jeannine's birthday, with lunch at the Renaissance. Haircut on the 5th. On the 6th, Lévesque at his Hôtel de la Paix beneath the arcades, his mischievous smile and high education which he never took seriously. (He treated us all like his semiliterate Arab pupils.) Then a familial celebration of Epiphany, when Madame Royer made the traditional Galette des Rois, a Twelfth Night cake, rather dry, containing one gold ring. From the 7th to the 9th a tour with Guy of the south, the paradise again of Tinerhir at dawn with sacred fish in the Blue Spring's source, the cliffs and gorges and the crazy café at Midelt, the trustful smiling Berber children, and the long lunch at Boul Malne with François and Hélène Rémy—he a bearded doctor, she a pregnant painter—who would become our friends. Frequently a certain Madame D'Ernancourt is noted in the agenda, but who was she? The 12th, party for the pianist Flavigny. Meetings with Lévesque's English friends; visit to the barracks of Michel; attendance of Jean Gabin's new film, *Au-delà des grilles*, pretty strong, with Isa Miranda as a French-speaking Italian waitress who serves him *marc*. The 17th, finished symphony. The 19th, proofread the symphony, then saw Garbo in a dubbed *Ninotchka*. The 20th, saw *Manon* again, then bought more *eau oxygenée* so as to bleach my locks prior to invading the Italy of black-haired males. (For years, off and on, I dyed my hair, to a point where, in 1957, I wrote: "My latest affectation is to leave my hair its natural color." That color, observed Nora Auric, was like the better Swiss chocolate.) The 21st, town of Bahlil, and cold! The 22nd, Ifrane and Azrou with the young Royers. The 23rd, "arose at 10:30, as usual." The 24th, made a broadcast interview on Radio-diffusion Marocaine, with one Christian Houillon, handsome, of the *Courier du Maroc,* my first-ever live interview in French which, in a land where English is unknown, seemed less disturbing than had it been in France. On the 26th, dined in the Médina with Lévesque's well-off bourgeois friend Jean Bertrand, very effete, whom we picked up at the Hôtel Jamai. He had visited Chicago. The incongruity of evoking Oak Street beach, so far and so long removed, did not escape us, an incongruity which today seems negligible. The 27th, Guy in Taza, listened to broadcast of my Tuesday interview on Radio Maroc at 19 hours, then to a concert of native music at the palace. The 29th, press clothes, visit to Immouzer and again to Azrou. Apértifs with music lovers, M. et Mme. Bachelet, later the strange Madame D'Ernancourt again. Ticket to Oran.

Guy was my Great Love, this was understood. With tears welling in his oriental eyes, he made me vow that on next Tuesday afternoon, 7 February, in the early afternoon I would take the Superga funiculaire to the mountaintop church in the outskirts of Torino. He had been there during the war, and would think of me. He admonished me not to drink too much once back in civilization. Guy was, for a French Protestant, quite sentimental. (Was he a Protestant?) I promised to come back soon. (It would be four months.)

What today would be a two-hour hop by plane, was then, by land and sea, an Event. Bleak train trek through the cactus-laden plains of Morocco to the Algerian border. Customs. Change Moroccan francs into Algerian. More mournful scenery to Oran where, at 6 Boulevard Charlemagne, spent the night at Hôtel Royale. Ten a.m., embarked from Oran, on the Sidi-bel-Abbès, for twenty-four-hour crossing to Marseilles. Boat eighteen hours late. More customs. Change Algerian francs into French. On the Cannabière had croissants at a café where a youngish man in a fedora at next table summoned waiter with a "Garçon," mellifluous and nasal, then, without so much as a glance my way, pocketed his change and walked away forever. Have thought of him daily since. Train to Lyon, Hôtel Bristol near the station. Secret city of bridges, large, where the Black Mass was rumored to be still celebrated. In hotel café, man in black stands at the bar. I look again, and he is gone. Have thought about him daily since. Telegraph Nell about delay. Ten-hour train ride, Lyon to Torino, more customs at border, and changing francs into lire.

Nell greeted the train, ensconced me in the tiny Albergo Genio under the arcades (like Lévesque's hotel in Fez), after which we repaired to her pensione on the fourth floor of 23 Via Pomba and, in her ordinary bedroom, downed a quart of cognac.

First impressions were disconcerting. An oversized industrial agglomeration on the Po, Torino was even less romantic than Casablanca, surely nobody's notion of sunny Italy during this ugly time of year. Add to this, Nell. The personal coarseness and gnawingly misguided ambition were the most visible dark side of this otherwise unique mezzo, who as an interpreter of Mahler and Milhaud and English-language repertory was second to none. She resided, boarding-house style, with five other students, all Italian, who had meals (which I shared during my week there) at a round table, governed by a self-consciously maternal Magnani-type harridan that everyone loved and told their troubles to, and whom I loathed. Like many "lovable" people, like Nell herself, she was lovable on her own terms, and could turn in a trice if countered. Nell was the life of the party, drinking too much wine, singing at the old upright in the parlor. She was also sleeping, so she said, with Uberto, who wasn't too attractive but apparently possessed "iron thighs." How Nell, as a Fulbright recipient and already a well-known soloist, landed in Torino is anyone's guess. Rome and Milano were doubtless overbooked. She seemed to have some connection with the reputable conservatory there, and was also using the city as a jumping-off place for singing dates south and north.

The second evening we dined with the vice consul, a Mr. Shenfield, and wife, who fed us martinis and showed home movies, then served (it was Sunday, and we were Americans) waffles. When Nell asked for another drink, perhaps a tiny glass of wine, they apologized, they were all out. "What about that over there?" said Nell, pointing to a decorative little flask. Reluctantly they uncorked this, but didn't share the contents.

On the plus side: Nell had been engaged to sing with a sinfonietta in Florence on the 15th, and asked me to orchestrate a couple of my songs to include. This I did, finding manuscript paper and india ink at a local *magazzino,* and in the course of two afternoons instrumentalized "Little Elegy" and "The Lordly Hudson," then copied the parts. These were duly photostated, with the aid of Gianni, one of the pensionnaires, who served as interpreter at the photography store. We also gave, for a fee, a private concert at the home of a Signore Lessano for the Turinese elite. And yes, I did scale the Superga on Tuesday, and thought of Guy.

Nell had brought Paul Bowles's *The Sheltering Sky* from America where it had just come out with enormous critical and public success. Alone in the little albergo I read it in one swoop. Paul's stories in *View* had always struck me as willfully cold, but readable and satisfying to the cruel streak in us all. *The Sheltering Sky* was quickly interesting, not least because of its Saharan setting which I had quit only days before. But I found it unsettling too, in the wrong way; a touch vulgar, as though catering to a slick-magazine audience, and also a touch facile. I neither believed it, nor in it. I've since come to respect, without adoring, Paul's other fiction, but have never reread this novel. Twenty-two years later I had occasion to write: "If he is not a human portraitist, he has, like some filmmakers, created character from scenery. Deserts, jungles, city streets are personages in his book as in his life, and he causes them to breathe and suffer and threaten us as only a god can do. But when discussing real people the effect is desperate, touching, even sad, sometimes humorous, though only secondarily the effect he intended, that is, a pose of noninvolvement. That effect, which fills the novels, no longer seems viable for our troubled world —perhaps precisely because the world has turned into a Paul Bowles novel."

More immediately, Nell lent me another book. She was as continually guided through life by a sense of her tragically bawdy Irish forebears as I by the Norwegian stillness that preceded Father's fathers. She carried everywhere a thick volume called *Irish Poetry*. This contained many texts which spoke to my condition, and which would be set to music during the next months.

The train from Torino was a pagan deliverance out of Piedmontese gloom into Tuscan sparkle two hundred miles nearer the equator, each hill and dale of which was a background for a Botticelli portrait. Suddenly here was the Italy one had bargained for.

Detraining in Florence on Saturday, 11 February, we were met by our host, Newell Jenkins, his friend Jack Murphy, an interviewer, and a photographer. Whether my presence was expected, or even that my songs were meant for inclusion on next Wednesday's program, seemed moot; clearly I was an unknown quantity—one they would have to be nice to, for Nell's sake. During the unloading and picture taking I noticed a uniformed guard, exaggeratedly macho with a dashing casquette, staring undisguisedly at me. "Why is that guard staring undisguisedly at me?" I asked Newell. "Because," said Newell, "he thinks you're pretty." Yes, the Italy one had bargained for.

Newell Jenkins was then, and remains today, a specialist in forgotten Italian musical masters, but he veers on occasion, from duty if not love, to modern composers. He lived in a villa with his mother and with Jack, an impresario, in nearby Fiesole where we accordingly repaired and began to drink. There was talk of the huge hit Menotti had just struck, back in New York, with *The Consul,* the Kafkian opera which had made of Pat Neway an overnight star. There was talk, too, of the local fauna we would be meeting, and of the public concert coming up. We dined then, with more liquor. Newell seemed an adoring amateur.

The evening developed badly, with Jack driving me into town around midnight to show me the bars, then back to Fiesole where he and Newell quarreled, and where I was coldly assigned a room next to Nell's. At 4 a.m. she appeared at the door, said she couldn't sleep, got in my bed and pressed her body against mine from top to toe. I was repelled. Repelled by the unfamiliar softness, still more by her silent implication that if she, the female, took the dominant role I would be seduced. The fog of Chianti was no help. Nor did Nell seem more appetizing through a blazing headache next morning, when I registered at a hotel.

The Albergo Berchielli is a congenial inn at the tip of the Ponte Vecchio on the right bank, convenient to the Teatro Communale where rehearsals took place. The concert itself, on the 15th, was neither here nor there. Nell confided later that when she appeared on stage in the turquoise satin gown she'd worn in Town Hall, faced the audience, and struck her singery pose in preparation for the start of "The Lordly Hudson," Newell, his back to the public and baton raised, leaned imperceptibly toward her and whispered: "How fast?"

The most indelible impression from the postconcert dinner, served in Nandina's Kitchen near the Santa Trinita, was when my table companion, a lean, humorless woman with a flapper's bob and a man's necktie, turned to me and announced in medias res: ". . . so then John said, 'Darling, we're broke. We'll have to sell your jewels. We'll have to sell everything, and go on the dole.' " John turned out to be none other than Radclyffe Hall, author of *The Well of Loneliness,* the book which Mother, so long ago, had said was about thesbians.

"I was married to John," continued my dinner partner, Lady Una Truebridge, "and am the feminine protagonist of that great novel. When John died, I changed my wardrobe forever and became a man."

Next morning I left the too-costly Berchielli for the Pensione Bartolini, right across the river, at 1 Lungarno Guiciardino, where rent was 350 lire, or fifty cents, a day. My first thought was of the railway guard. I walked back to the station, and there he was. Later that day when he came off duty we met at the pensione. The language barrier was no problem, but the occasion was not earth-stopping, merely a one-afternoon stand.

Three and a half years later, when I fell in love with Pino, I vanquished the Italian language in a two-week crash course. For now, it was easy to get along in French, although the more opportunistic *ragazzi* had a smattering of either German or English, depending on which way they thought the war would be turning when they were kids in school.

Nell returned north. She would be going to France in a few weeks, to work with Boulanger, and needed to prepare in silence. I stayed on in Florence for another fortnight. The casual love was inebriating, as was the off-the-wagon reaction against the luxuriant prison of Morocco. Then, too, there was a nucleus of agreeable Americans, most of them, like Nell, Fulbright honorees in their early thirties, or Norman Douglas–type driftwood with funds and wit and no pretense at talent. The agenda as usual contains many a male Christian name—Gianni, Hugh, Franco, Walter—evoking an ebony curl or swarthy visage if not a conversation. But it contains, as well, the names of Milton and Evelyn Gendel, of Jean Purcell, of a Miss Suzy Hare and someone named Countess Valeva, bohemians all, whom I would run across repeatedly during the coming years in "the American corner" of various hangouts around Europe—Greco's in Rome, the Saint-Germain in Paris, the Club in London—and always be greeted with an intimate whoop. There was David Kimball, who had been one of Scalero's stars at Curtis, now here, a Jamesian fixture. And Barbara Howes with her then-husband, William Jay Smith, eager, intelligent, gifted, original. (In 1987 I would finally set one of Smith's poems—"A Nursery Pavane" for treble chorus—and shall do so again when the occasion demands.) These people, like the Little Gang of Madame Verdurin, were daily and useful, with whom I'd visit the Uffizi or the Bargello or stroll with along the Arno and through the parks, exercises which seem now de rigueur but which were then so exhilaratingly new. Movies, concerts, parties, plus the "gay" milieu, also American, which did not overlap with the Little Gang.

Accepted everywhere because I was good-looking and not stupid, I still felt at the edge, warmly tolerated. There was a political shimmer around the Little Gang which I could not transcend, partly, I suppose, because I didn't choose to. Why, at this time in history when the planet appeared less troubled than at any hour since 1914, intellectual bull sessions should center on politics as, during adolescence, they centered on art, was a depressing speculation. I was bored by politics and felt guilty about it. Guilty, in the same way as about loving rich desserts, passive buggery, and Impressionist music, as if these loves, and hence my own talent, were unmanly, not "important." The same inadequacy that had rottenly flourished in Chicago circles a decade earlier reemerged, which is why I drank too much. Nor was I center stage, as in Morocco. Not to be political—right or wrong—was not to be alive. But wasn't politics general, where art was specific? Hadn't I yet reasoned that the strongest political propagandists among artists, from Richard Wagner to Mary McCarthy, had never been more significant, as creators, because of their shrill beliefs, and that some of the biggest statesmen had never been artists at all? Hadn't I yet heard Auden's "Poetry makes nothing happen"?

Propped in bed one noon, reading *The Prancing Nigger,* who should enter without knocking but Bob Faulkner, everybody's favorite hanger-on, an unpleasantly pleasant surprise. Bu. When had we last met? Here he now was, flouncing around Europe on a frugal allowance. Hang-dog expression, upper-crust accent, the palest pose of being a writer, funny company. So that afternoon at five we went together to hear *Le martyre de Saint Sébastien* which Inghelbrecht was conducting at the Communale.

If the most fundamental musical expression is the pitched voice on prearranged tones, the least legitimate is melodrama, that is, the spoken voice against a through-composed sonic background, unless, as in the Sitwell-Walton *Façade,* speech is rhythmicized, in which case the piece becomes rap, a formal mode, unvarying. Otherwise the spoken voice gets in the way. When Ida Rubinstein, Russian and rich and ravishing but not a great ballerina, commissioned *Le martyre* for herself to intone for the first time as an actress, not as a dancer, Debussy, late in his life, wrote his most opulent music. But the text, in archly archaic French by D'Annunzio, though stunning, obtrudes: who wants France upstaged by Italy? Yet on this Sunday afternoon, with Alain Cuny as speaker, I was so moved by the sound of the French language again after three weeks in Italy, and of the familiar-since-childhood French score, that I felt I was back home.

"Let's go to Paris," I said to Bu. "Yes, let's," he answered. So we, on Wednesday, went.

Monday I bought the train ticket, wrote Shirley, had a mess of laundry done for 250 lire, visited the Palazzo Pitti, then met a person named Leo Feritti at nine o'clock at Lungarno Vespucci. Tuesday I tried to collect a debt from someone named Hal. That afternoon, in the bar of the Excelsior Hotel, Bu and I had eleven stingers, during which various friends sat down and stood up. Bu said, after the eleventh, "Now let's go concentrate on wine," as we wended our way to Nandina's Kitchen. But we made it to the train next morning at 10:17. It was snowing. At the station, there stood my uniformed guard on duty. He grinned, came over and shook hands, then saluted and clicked his heels. "Who's *that?*" said Bu, agog.

All of a sudden it seemed morally wrong to leave this beautiful city in this beautiful country after exactly one month—one incomplete month in an impermanent world.

The chief focus of the next seventy-eight days in Paris would be the joint concert of our music which Douglas Allanbrook and I would present at the embassy on 4 May. Douglas, a Boulanger product dwelling on nearby rue Monsieur le Prince, wrote pieces which in their comparative acidity were enough different from my own to provide a contrasting program. Between us we also knew enough first-rate American executants in situ who would donate their services. My half would consist of a song miscellany, myself accompanying soprano Janet Hayes; the *Four Madrigals* on Sappho lyrics which Janet's new husband, Charles Walker, would conduct with an unaccompanied choir; and Shirley, still known locally as Xénia, playing the new sonata. The embassy's cultural negotiator, one Simon Copans, and his associate, a Miss Herle Jervis, were capable of sponsoring and amply publicizing small recitals at a moment's notice in their little hall at 41 faubourg Saint-Honoré.

Meantime I was floundering for a place to stay. Bu and I had arrived at the Gare de Lyon three sheets to the wind, having swilled cheap wine for the entire eighteen-hour trip from Florence. Gordon Sager had booked us into the dumpy Hôtel Tarrenne, at 153 boulevard Saint-Germain, directly above the Reine Blanche. On the agenda leaf for that day, 2 March, I wrote just the one word "drunk." On the following day, the words "déjeuner chez José," then "Bu—champagne!" For the several days afterward, simply the indications "drunk" or "déjeuner et dîner chez José," plus frequent jottings about borrowing cash from Inez Cavanaugh, a friend of Jimmy Baldwin, who was opening a restaurant in the fifth arrondissement, or from Yves Salgues, the reporter-novelist from *Paris-Match* with whom I lay down with willing dissatisfaction every few days (we didn't quite fit), and who had just published a troubling fiction titled *Le jeune homme endormi* with an enthralling inscription which I still covet. We were all continually owing each other money. Gordon Sager, also a novelist, American, who had preceded me in cohabitation with Morris Golde years before, took us to see Bill Lieberman, the art curator now staying at the Pont Royale. There was also Robin King, a Londonian literary critic, and how many others!, with whom, abstractedly, night after night after night we hung out, making the rounds in the quarter, going to bed at noon, getting up at eight in the evening, and being very witty, self-congratulatory, blurred. Except for Yves, the sex I half enjoyed was

with Arabs, guileless and ever willing, who adorned the neighborhood, waited outside the bistros unsmiling, and led me to their shabby
rooms where we were lost dogs together. Although in Morocco I had
never slept with an Arab, or indeed with anyone but Guy, in Paris the
habit grew tender and natural. Other than they, José was my benefac-
tor and guardian angel.

After eleven days of this plotless routine, I lurched back to Harp
Street and asked Shirley to take me in. Which is when we began
making plans for the embassy concert, which would serve as a tryout
for her solo affair scheduled for June in the Salle Gaveau. Guy had
also arranged for her to come to Fez for a fortnight in early April, and
try out her program on the series there.

Jane Bowles was in Paris for the winter, staying at the Hôtel de l'Université, an amiable center for profligate Americans. Although an ideal
drinking buddy, having, in deed if not in word, no sense of responsibility, I recall her in the sawdust oily odor of restaurants more than in
the anisette zinc smell of bars. Jane loved to eat, or at least to talk
about eating, and could spend hours in an inexpensive café, sampling
this and that dish, sending it back to the kitchen, ordering white wine,
no we should have red instead, or perhaps rosé. Perusing the menu,
her adorable retroussé nose *en l'air,* her ever-still leg (from infantile
paralysis) stretched on an adjoining chair, she would run her cute
pink tongue over her pretty lips, frown, then grin, and never get to
the point.

What did I think of her?

Before we came to know each other well, people had said I reminded them of Jane, because apparently we both labored to be contrary and out of focus. Naturally I didn't see it this way. Jane was
(reticently) Jewish to my Wasp, anti-intellectual (she talked about
things, not ideas) to my literary ostentatious, insecure to the point of
shortchanging her gifts to my conceit about being the only songwriter
after Poulenc. True, she had at this point, except for the one not-at-all-
ordinary novel, published only a few stories, and agonized over her
silent typewriter (the sound of Paul's machine forever clicking down
the hall of El Farhar had driven her from Araby—as she called Tangier
—and brought her now to France), so she had cause to downplay the
cultural world. Yet she was already swathed in myth. I persuaded
myself that I was indispensable to her milieu. We both did look
younger than our years (she was already thirty-three), as heavy drinkers will, at least at the beginning. We both did bounce back fairly
quickly. We both did doubtless appear to function as non sequiturs in
speech and in act. And we both did share a taste for love objects that

were large nonverbal creatures who perhaps babied us in the boudoir but whom we dominated in the parlor. There was, however, a crucial difference, though we could not know it then: Jane was a victim, I a survivor.

Sober, I found her annoying, her rhythm obstinate, not slow but willfully counter to yours—whoever you were. Perhaps her bum leg was the source of this. Though Jane never left the sixth arrondissement, she took taxis everywhere, even to the dress shop one block away. Yet she could be the soul of generosity. If at 8 a.m., after a night out, I dreaded going back to Harp Street where Shirley would be pounding out scales, she would let me pass out in her silent room while she limped around the quarter, glad for an excuse not to work. Or she would come back with a friend—Wendell Wilcox, Stanley Bate —and sit silently by the bed, watching, lest I kill myself, for I had been crying so uncontrollably an hour before. (Wendell was a South Carolinian professor; Stanley, an English composer, still at this time married to Peggy Glanville-Hicks, an Australian-born composer living in New York and in love with Paul Bowles. Stanley Bate, back in London eight years later, was arrested in a public rest room. The night before his case came to trial, he committed suicide.)

Like her personality, Jane's oeuvre is one of a kind. Other writers are greater—whatever that signifies—if only because of their wider scope. Her own husband, or Gore Vidal, or even Faulkner are, as prosifiers, wiser but less special. Still, they are vast where Jane is narrow: her complete works fit into a single volume of 476 pages, including the preface by Truman Capote, who calls her "that modern legend." Every decade I reread the odd three-acter *In the Summer House,* with the notion of turning it into an opera. And every decade I again realize that there's something indefinable there that doesn't click. A case could be made that all masterpieces are graced with a tragic flaw. Something is "wrong" in the torsos of Michelangelo's David or the Nike of Samothrace, in the physiognomies of Greta Garbo and Marlon Brando, that renders them grander than the more perfectly featured lesser stars. But the flaw in Jane's play was not tragic, merely an ambiguous unworkability.

(One morning in Hyères I slashed my foot on a stone. That evening, as I moved ever so slowly down the stairs, Georges Auric said, "La beauté boite," comparing this scene to the one in *Sang d'un poète*— for which, of course, he had composed the score—where Benga, the Black Angel, falters on the courtyard steps. "La beauté boite." Beauty limps. Those words became a motto.)

Jane herself was somehow unworkably ambiguous. Like Frank O'Hara, who would rise up in a year or two, Jane Bowles is a person I might not have taken to had not a cult proclaimed her as special. Jane and Frank were narcissists, like me, and their inadvertent insistence on being-the-center at first alienated rather than propelled me. They were always great company, but on their terms; I grew to love them through conditioning—it was the thing to do—but the love stayed always tense.

Jane was fond of a dreary eatery in the rue Mabillon where at any time of day one saw seated among the wooden tables a gentleman, always alone, said to have been Apollinaire's valet. One night the waiter brought to our table, where I was seated with Jane and Nikita Waterbury, a carafe of Beaujolais on behalf of Apollinaire's valet. What were we to do with it? We'd had enough. Jane called out a thankyou to Apollinaire's valet, adding: "J'ai déjà drôlement bu de vin rouge, cher Monsieur." "Comme vous parlez bien le français," he called back. (They always said "You speak French well," never simply "You speak well.") I made a note of Jane's phrase.

Nikita Waterbury, a Junoesque American blond, lived down the hall at the Hôtel de l'Universife. Jane was in love with her, had her often in tow. Nikita garbed herself in black satin and struck poses, but her conversation belied her exterior charisma. She was no more intriguing than a high school gym teacher—was, in fact, a lugubrious appendage.

More sparkling was Sonia Orwell, an offering of Barbara Howes and William Smith, all of whom resided at the Hôtel des Saints-Pères where on 10 March they asked me to dine. Sonia, née Brownell, resembled Nikita Waterbury to a T, except that she was stimulating, and sang for her supper in a loud English accent. Her claim to fame was in having married George Orwell on his deathbed, but she had also for years been the peripatetic backbone of the recently defunct *Horizon* magazine, and now acted as free-lance editor out of her native London. Sonia was vivacious, grand, grossly pretty, zaftig, with long fair hair coiffed all in a swirl over her left ear, leaving her right ear free for a bangle. She was smart without depth, cultured without creativity, heterosexual but with mostly gay friends, and was, within limits, respected not only because she proved ever-useful as a literary go-between but was awfully good company. She drank too much and was bitchy, knew everyone and went everywhere. Her ubiquity mirrored Bu Faulkner's: you could leave one or the other of them slumped over a table at the Reine Blanche, go to your hotel, pack, catch a train to Rome, unpack at your hotel, go over to Greco's Café where Bu or Sonia would already be slumped over a table.

In America I had never been aware of intellectual females who were also chic. (Mary McCarthy would become the first exception that by the sixties established a rule; Sonia ultimately became an intimate of Mary's.) Sonia, with her left hand running nervously through her sumptuous hair while her right hand rapidly effaced and inserted words on a manuscript, biting her lip and furrowing her beautiful brow, was something to behold. Yet she was not agreeably beholdable at all times: she veered toward fatness, was insulting, narrow, and biased in her boozy pronouncements, a Difficult Woman, as David Plante has expertly portrayed her, in his *Difficult Women.*

Why do I go on about her, whose conversation, like Jane's, revolved not around idea but anecdote, and who was colorfully peripheral where others I've not mentioned were more quietly crucial? Because she had that rare gift of, when you were with her, making you feel there's only you. And because, like Jane, when I was destitute or, more calculatingly, in need of a presentable escort, Sonia was there.

Some winters later she showed up in New York for the first time and immediately had an affair with the cartoonist Al Capp, which seemed as inevitable for an English lady as Simone de Beauvoir's affair with Algren. I ran into her, incongruously, at Virgil's (like most literary people she knew nothing of music), where John Latouche adopted her. She wore her hair, said Latouche, like Valerie Bettis; and Valerie, when I came to compose a ballet with her in 1960, reminded me so much of Sonia with her unrestrained extrovertism that I often didn't know to whom I was talking. Still, it could only have been Valerie; by then Sonia was an out-of-control eccentric, grading erstwhile acquaintances with total plusses or unappealable minuses. I was a minus. Because by this time Sonia had married—commendably perhaps—a Mr. Pitt-Rivers who, like Stanley Bate, had been arrested *in flagrante,* and served a prison term, England's laws being no less virulent than those for Oscar Wilde. During one of my infrequent mid-fifties visits to London I had attended a party at Sonia's, and given her details of our mutual friend Ellen Adler's marriage to David Oppenheim. For no especial reason I said: "And David's absolutely straight." Sonia never spoke to me again.

When did we ever take baths? Except for Guy's house in Fez, none of my lodgings since the previous May had a tub or shower. Room-&-bath was not a standard requirement for young visitors in those days. Even on Harp Street, even in José's apartment, all we had was the sink and bidet. Not until January of 1953, when I moved into Marie-Laure's, do I recall taking a full bath in Paris.

· · ·

José more than once brought me to a bourgeois meal at the Azevedos'. The beauteous Violetta announced that Jeanne Gauthier would be performing my Violin Sonata on her upcoming tour. I was pleased, for Gauthier was France's leading female string player after Ginette Neveu, who had recently died in an air crash. (Aside to José, with her alluring Portuguese accent: "Ned was a young Apollo when he arrived in Paris. Now look at him. What can we do?")

Noted are other dates with American composer Irving Fine; with Casablancan composer Maurice Ohana; with Robert Olsen; with Jean Bertrand and with Paul Demarest; with Jean Téchoueyres; with Paul Tertian "whose sky-blue eyes seem untroubled by thought." I remember little of this.

I do remember returning often to see Henri Sauguet. An emblem of generosity *à mon égard,* he was patient with my still-hesitant French, and with the raft of new music I thrust on him. He treated me as a colleague, asked my opinion of his own new pieces. The best of those pieces, as it happens, had for me the flaw of greatness, the "limp of beauty," with its personal aching poignance. Never a presence in America, as were Les Six, even though Virgil pulled considerable strings, Henri Sauguet was nevertheless a big shot in France. Like all French composers he was, unlike Americans, a nonspecialist; for financial reasons they adapt to all aspects of their métier, from string quartet to popular song. He had just rearranged the little waltz from *Les forains* as a "complainte" for Edith Piaf who, with her gigantic larynx in a ninety-pound body, bellowed it beautifully like one who had lost her greatest love. (That love was prizefighter Marcel Cerdan, who had died in the same plane as Ginette Neveu.) As such, the song remained high on Paris charts, simultaneous with Sauguet's new ballet, *La rencontre,* on the sensational choreography of David Lichine. Can one forget the equally sensational angoras, Parsifal and Miriflore (later killed by a fox near Sauguet's farm in Coutras) and the Comtesse Patapoufna, who sat upon the dinner table with their own plates among ours? Will I forget Jacques Dupont, his dashing smile? his painting in which all that is curved becomes square, square clouds in pink and gray? and my gray and pink portrait with square cheekbones? And after the portrait the carousing of artist with model? Jacques was the Frenchest of persons, meaning that his interests were utterly contained within the frontiers of his country and language; and his joy-of-living, which was maximal, revolved around the economical *esprit* of visualizing all things violently *as they are,* only more so, rather than whimsically as they are not. We made love twice, once in his studio, then many months later at the Hôtel du Bon La Fontaine in the early dusk. But Sauguet never learned about it. Even today nobody knows except you.

On 23 March, visit to Madame Jane Bathori, 7 rue de Lanneau. Why has this faded to nothing? Bathori had created in 1907 Ravel's *Histoires naturelles* on the prose texts of Jules Renard who, like Maeterlinck at the premiere of Debussy's *Pelléas,* fell asleep on hearing the music. (Renard it was, author of *Poil de carotte,* who said to his diary: "My fortieth birthday. Can no longer die young.")

Clearer remains the wild sight of Madeleine Grey in the rue Blanche, she who had premiered in the mid-1920s Ravel's *Chansons madécasses.* The visit was remindful of the one to Landowska, when Madame Grey partially lowered her bodice to expose her left shoulder whereon gleamed a scar. "That," said she, "is where D'Annunzio bit me."

Clearest of all shines the company of the old violinist Hélène Jourdan-Morhange, for whom Ravel composed the Violin Sonata. Frizzily hennaed and coiffed à la Colette, she talked (as did Poulenc) with an outmoded Parisian inflection, drawling the nasal vowels in such locutions as "un vrai beau gosse"—"a real cute kid"—as deliciously outmoded as "twenty-three skidoo." More than once was I invited to tea, when she brought forth a manuscript of the sonata, stashed in a file with Ravel's letters which asked in detail whether the violin was capable of this glissando or that triple-stop, accompanied by diagrams. She gifted me with an inscribed edition of her useful, if harmless, biography, *Ravel et nous,* and we met innumerable times at entr'actes here and there.

I mention these women for the sole purpose of mentioning them. They had known Ravel, and that knowledge rubbed off on me. (Howard Moss, on a visit to Lamb House, picked up the hand mirror on the master's dresser, and gazed and gazed and gazed into it.) To have kissed each one on both cheeks was equivalent to a draught from the Holy Grail.

On the morning of the 24th I picked up Nell at the Gare de Lyon, waited while she unpacked at the Hôtel Bisson, then brought her to nearby Harp Street where we drank and sang from noon till midnight. Jean-Claude and Shirley were mesmerized by Nell's vocal stamina and precision as we performed for them, hour after drunken hour. But my energy flagged, and I saw Nell as a disheveled sot with smeared lipstick and a vanished voice.

Next day, fresh as a daisy, she brought me along to Nadia Boulanger's initial choral rehearsal in the rue de Londres. Nell had come to Paris—her first visit—to work up a program with Mademoiselle on the occasion of Prince Rainier's coronation. Nadia had been named official musician to the throne, and would bring her whole cortege to Monaco next month to perform on the palace steps. Or something.

The cortege contained the elderly tenors Hugues Cuénod and Paul Derenne and the bass, Doda Conrad, three of the great madrigalists featured on that treasured Monteverdi disc of yore. Also Gérard Souzay who, at thirty-one, with his vital diction, was Europe's premier baritone (Fischer-Diskau had yet to impose himself). Doda and Gérard and I immediately became friends, although they took a dim view of la Tangeman whom Souzay, who did not then know English, always called "la Tante Germaine." Doda, who never had a lovely voice and now sounded like a foghorn, though he got by from devotion and chutzpah, may have been jealous of Nell's natural métier, and of Nadia's all-out endorsement. Nadia and Nell had met in Bloomington during the war when the former had publicly called the latter "America's Kathleen Ferrier." As for Gérard, who was handsome and self-assured—but not *that* handsome and really quite vulnerable—he thought la Tante Germaine was, where I was concerned, overbearingly possessive.

When the singing began, with these soloists against a choir of sixteen, the mystery of perfection reigned. They practiced Debussy's *Trois chansons,* sections from Berlioz's *L'enfance du Christ,* and the new Stravinsky *Mass* about which Mademoiselle seemed unnecessarily proprietary. She had been Stravinsky's principal pal in France since before World War I, but now, with the advent of Robert Craft as chief advisor, and of Stravinsky's gradual defection to the enemy camp of atonality, she seemed edgy, defensive.

I didn't especially care for the *Mass,* found it willfully dry, yet felt a need to say something, if only because Nadia had granted me the Lili Boulanger Award.

"A well-wrought piece," I ventured. "How much do you suppose he got for it?"

"With Stravinsky one does not conjecture in dollars and cents," said Mademoiselle stiffly. (Her image of Stravinsky as he-who-can-do-no-wrong endured to the end. In 1964, when I visited Mademoiselle on her return from Berlin where she had heard the master's latest excursion into twelvetoniana, *Abraham and Isaac,* and asked how long the piece lasted, she replied: "Can one speak of temporal data where Stravinsky is concerned?" I later understood: the piece, thirteen minutes by the clock, seemed like a numbing hour.)

Still, with Stravinsky one *must* conjecture in dollars and cents, to counter the know-nothingness of our age. Serious music in its evanescence is nil, as distinct from painting which is a commodity any rich Texan can display on his wall. When Stravinsky and Picasso, the last of our sacred monsters, both died at near ninety in the early 1970s, the composer's estate was rated at four million dollars, the painter's at four billion.

Misapprehension of the faraway. Once during a trip back to the States I was asked by Marc Blitzstein if I knew Sartre, since sooner or later all queers meet each other. I had never heard, before or after, that Sartre was queer, despite his fraternal alliance with both Cocteau and Genet (the kind of alliance which only a heterosexual might see as revealing), and wondered how Marc could hold to such a touristy notion. All I could say was that Sartre was straight, the proof being that, no, we had never met.

As Charles Ives, when in the 1930s his rugged music finally began to be recognized, predated some of his manuscripts to make them seem even more "advanced," so Jean Genet exaggerated the relatively benign criminality of his youth, to increase the moral—or immoral—force of his self-referring fiction. (Have these two names ever before appeared in the same sentence?)

The present book is a biography by myself about the youth of someone who bears my name. It does not fantasize but seeks solely to retrieve facts, so the excitement of art is absent.

Anyway, that tingling cliché, "Art is a lie that speaks the truth," is skewed. Art never purports to be Truth. Art is art—though sometimes it clarifies some aspect of fact hitherto blurred, even to the artist.

Inaptness of metaphors comingling the arts, like "architecture is frozen music." Is music, then, liquid architecture? If the seven deadly arts could express each other, we'd need only one.

Innocent civilians. As distinct from . . . guilty soldiers?

In due course Nell migrated south to crown the prince in Monte Carlo, thence back to her studies in Torino, but not before trying to impress impresarios in more ways than one. Nell would kiss the hand that slapped her, as well as try to seduce "important" people even after contracts were signed. She made an indiscriminate pass at every class, at the hotel maid, at Shirley in a taxi, even, for all I know, at Boulanger herself. Her aim was less to slake a lust than to prove her existence (maybe it's the same thing)—a need to be reacted to. I understood, because it takes one to know one, and I despised her for it.

The day after she left, on 3 April, Eugene Istomin showed up with Leon Fleisher under his arm. Eugene, en route to Perpignan, would figure as performer and organizer in the first of what became an ongoing yearly celebration (later moved to Prades) centering around the personality of Pablo Casals. The chromatic tendency of this celebration, although transpiring in the French Pyrénées, leaned toward Casals's mostly Germanic repertory—what Virgil Thomson used to call the Fifty Masterpieces. Eugene was ripe for this milieu. It's not too early to announce that Eugene would become, through the years, a fixture of the festival, an intimate of Casals, almost a *fils adoptif.* In 1973 when the grand old cellist died at ninety-seven, Eugene married his young widow, Martita, the beauteous and canny. Together they've kept the flame while pursuing separate but adjunct careers, he as a soloist and she as director of minor musical empires internationally, with a loving elegance.

As for Leon Fleisher, ex-pupil of Schnabel's, now at twenty-one already a well-launched pianist, I had heard him play the Brahms B minor in Carnegie Hall, but never met him. Here he was on vacation, planning to spend the summer in France. As can happen with a person one has perceived first from afar, up there on the stage (an artist at work is always beautiful), then later meets socially, Leon now emanated a pristine aura. After five minutes, like anyone else (except actors), he was just like you or me, or rather, like all pianists, a bespectacled extrovert. Leon at Shirley's Steinway that month of April was a delight. He made the unvarying Brahms-Handel Variations and the interminable Schubert B-flat Sonata sound like real music. The Mendelssohn *Song without Words*—the one in E-flat—under his fingers bloomed into a song *with* words, an effusion which in its joy made the hearer long to sing out with some improvisatory verse, the way other great music, even including Beethoven, moves the hearer to dance. Leon accomplished this, I think, not by approaching the score as sacrosanct, but as the blueprint for a pleasure that all music inherently is, albeit sometimes dark pleasure, as in a Mass for the dead.

On the 12th Shirley flew to Casablanca, thence to Fez to spend two weeks practicing, culminating in her first public recital ever, at the Cinéma-Théâtre Lux of Fez. While she was away I noted: "April 13th, the Arab and the concierge. . . . 14th, drunk with Douglas A. & the ugly English girl, later Jean-Claude & Jessie. [Jessie lived upstairs with an American couple, Fern and Ken O'Brien, who took pictures.] . . . 15th, dîner avec Alberto Esteban. . . . 16th, Leon & Margie at 7. Stephen

Spender and Jim Lord at 9. Later, Elliott Stein and Daniel Mauroc. . . .
17th, see M. Vadot, call Doda, call Souzay, Inv. 62-79. . . . 18th, Souzay
à 16 heures, 18 av. de la Motte-Piquet. Guy & Shirley will call—6:30.
Onion soup at midnight with Eugene's horrible friends (au Royale). . . ."

Yes, on the 18th, Benga's bartender from Rose Rouge summoned
me to the phone, the only one in the building, two floors down.
Shirley and Guy's voices sounded plaintive and distant. Then came a
letter from Shirley, quite different in tone, now that our geographical
locations were reversed, from her previous one in December:

> Nedo chéri, it was divine to hear your voice last nite. Both Guy & I were
> very sad afterward. We miss you so. I love you more than I ever did. I feel
> that we're so close & right together now & that nothing is hidden. Heard
> "L'enfant et les sortilèges". I was so upset by it I cried. Saw you at the
> piano & singing, I never missed you so much before.
>
> I'm terribly upset about J[ean] C[laude]. I've only one letter since I'm
> here. These stories about 3 in a bed & his not coming home (he would
> never be at his mother's) have disturbed me profoundly. I don't know
> what to think. I'm quite miserable!
>
> I practice, wanting so much to play well despite the low caliber audi-
> ence. Your music is giving me a headache!! And the last movement of
> Opus 78.
>
> Guy is marvelous.
>
> Please write *often*. And tell me the truth about Jean-Claude.
>
> How am I going to work with these horrible thoughts in my head?
>
>   Love X
>
> Best to Leon & Eugene. Did he meet Casals?

Elliott Stein and Daniel Mauroc, the American and the Frenchman,
were coeditors of a bilingual little mag called *Janus*. Each was a poet
and, as poets go, generous to their brethren by keeping their periodi-
cal alive for several years. Partners in crime if not in love, they cooper-
ated at the office, but socialized individually. Daniel lived at home as
do all unmarried French males until middle life, while Elliott lived at
the Hôtel de Verneuil.

Of Daniel, whom I brought to see Jean-Claude with the successful
hope that he'd print J-C's poems, I retain most clearly a balmy afternoon smoking kif on the terrace of Café de la Mairie, place Saint-
Sulpice, the café of Dr. O'Connor in *Nightwood*. After awhile we began
to see two of everyone passing by. But we were not seeing double:
the identical pairs were talking to each other. In fact we learned next
day that a Congress of Twins was currently meeting in the vicinity.
Moral: Unlike liquor, which distorts reality, *in cannabis veritas*. Daniel

was a plain man with a perpetual grin and a conspiratorial tone. If you would prefer to listen to the general conversation in a given group, Daniel always managed to draw you aside with details about his big toe.

Of Elliott, whom I came to know more solidly in a frame lasting to the present, I retain most clearly the one-room fifth-floor walk-up and communal hall toilet (the kind you squat in, supporting yourself upon cement footprints), his permanent residence in France. The walls were plastered with portraits of starlets, comic-strip personages, crocodiles, Tiffany lampshades, muscle men, and a font for holy water. (Susan Sontag told me, circa 1966, that Elliott's room, no less than his *pince-sans-rire* rhetoric, was the chief source for her "Notes on Camp" —camp being a glorification of the garish-as-high art, or the queen getting them before they get her. Since there is no record of Susan telling this to anyone else, I'll give Elliott credit where it's due.)

Elliott, twenty-one, was the precocious Jewish kid forever. There was nothing he didn't know about Clara Bow or about Henry James. Unlike most literary thinkers he loved music, especially opera with its extramusical theatrics. Within a year Elliott would become my first librettist, with his richly free adaptation of Hawthorne's "The Snow Image" turned into a whimsical tragedy called *A Childhood Miracle,* a half-hour opera for six singers and thirteen instruments.

Stephen Spender and James Lord. . . . Like Leon Fleisher, Spender was preceded by his fame, specifically by his story "The Burning Cactus" which in 1940 I devoured and redevoured in an already ancient copy of *Hound & Horn,* and wrote tales myself with ambiguously sexed creatures named Tyl. I met Spender first when we lunched *à trois* in the tiny dining room of José. Naughty French tongues had even referred to them, using George Sand's title, as *Elle et Lui.*

"Every time I meet Americans, that's what they tell me—how they identify with Tyl in 'The Burning Cactus.' "

This left me silent. Silent I remained later when just the two of us were on the street, and Stephen confided that he now found José "rather triste, with that air of seeming in the know, when really he's never made it either as a thinker or a doer despite the grand people he rubs elbows with." Did Stephen know me well enough to put down one of my closest friends? My naïveté could not reconcile this attitude in a person known for his right-thinking—that is, his left-thinking—during the Spanish Civil War. Of course, just as a dictator coldly slaughters a mob but hotly weeps for his ailing daughter, so a philanthropist defends the masses while bitching his peers. Yet I myself wanted to rub elbows with Stephen, if only because he might put in a good word for me with Edith Sitwell. So I invited him over to Harp Street the following week, to hear me play and squawk "The Youth with the Red-Gold Hair."

Stephen arrived with James Lord, he of the square jaw and la-di-da accent out-Englishing the English despite his New Jersey roots. Even his French, which was grammatically and colloquially irreproachable (he'd been an interpreter for the army), was anglicized. Yet James's affected and sarcastic quips about all that's sacred belied his gentleness in human relations. He was the opposite face of Spender. He too rubbed elbows with the great. And why not? The great are, on the whole, more intriguing than the non-great, and James clove to them not for their greatness per se but for what the greatness stemmed from. One could argue that this very cleaving eventually rendered James himself as great as a *petit maître* can become. His depiction, in words, of what it means to be a Giacometti or a Picasso is unlike anything: he describes what cannot be described—the process of creation as it occurs, the finished product while it is becoming. If the actions toward monumentalizing Cézanne's studio in Aix-en-Provence rated him a Légion d'honneur insignia, his printed words on the painter's milieu during the middle third of our century are beyond price. Like Elliott Stein, James Lord also prepared a libretto for me, based on his disturbing story "The Boy Who Wrote No," but it never panned out. We did become uneasy friends, especially late in the decade when he replaced me as token American in the retinue of Marie-Laure de Noailles. And once, in August of 1954 when I was agonizing as only the young can (but I was already thirty) over a love affair, James slipped a poem under my dinner plate. I set it to music. Called "In This Summer," the poem contained this line, obvious but consoling: "... and human nature was not conceived to conform to human needs."

That song was perhaps not as persuasive as the Sitwell settings. But on this special Sunday, knowing Shirley was away, James and Stephen seemed less interested in my music than in sizing up Jean-Claude whose prettiness had been bruited about the quarter.

When Shirley returned from Morocco, order was not restored. Fifty years hence I may fill in the blank. For now let it be said that her tryst with Jean-Claude was waning, that she felt weary, and that she canceled her part in the upcoming embassy concert. When Leon Fleisher was conscripted to replace her, he agreed, on the condition he could have daily access to our piano to learn, in two weeks, my new Sonata and the three Barcarolles.

During these same weeks I practiced with Janet Hayes while Charles

Walker assembled singers for the Sappho madrigals. (French choristers who sing English do not grow on trees.) Added to this, in a pre-Xerox age, were the problems of photographing rehearsal copies (printed scores never arrived from the United States), of finding appropriate clothes (I borrowed José's old-fashioned tails), and of spacing the requisite binges so as to remain fresh and witty. The agenda is stuffed with rendezvous: April 19th, *L'homme de cendre* d'Henri Léger à la Comédie-Française. . . . 20th, Yves Salgues 3:00 au Montana, Jane & Nikita & Jean-Claude au Mabillon. . . . 21st, haircut, Doda Conrad at 3 rue de Bruxelles, Pierre Pichon au Colisée. . . . 22nd, Robert Kanters and André Fraigneau. . . . 24th, Snow. Dine with Gérard Souzay chez Francis in place de l'Alma, then all five Beethoven piano concertos by Julius Katchen, Cluytens conducting, au Théâtre des Champs-Elysées.

Doda Conrad was to be a crucial colleague. Already in his late forties, he was the only child of Marya Freund (b. 1876), a humorless, self-important Polish soprano who, true to her generation, could scarcely read notes but was Europe's answer to Eva Gauthier: a specialist in contemporary song who had not only created the Wood Dove role in Schoenberg's *Gurreleider* in 1913 but was the first to "speak" the French and English versions of that composer's *Pierrot lunaire*. She dwelt and taught in the same flat as Doda, who also shared his mother's pomposity, but with dollops of what might pass for whimsy. (His code word for homosexuals was Egyptian Royalty, and his knowledge of their soberest members was limitless: that the tragic pederast Pierre Bernac had a corkscrew-shaped sex, for example.) Tall, overweight, multilingual, Doda had become an American. Like all naturalized citizens he was unduly patriotic—proud beyond the line of his battle scars from World War II, and uncomfortable with my Quakerism. In the world of music he claimed not only to know everyone but to have been instrumental in everyone's basic career, not least that gifted boy, Arturo Toscanini.

He demanded his pound of flesh, but it was ever for favors rendered. Doda was tireless in promoting what he believed in, and what he believed in was always first rate. For Chopin's centennial the previous year, he commissioned Louise de Vilmorin to write six poems—a Nocturne, a Scherzo, an Etude, etcetera—and six composers to set these to music, including Sauguet and Poulenc and, for the Etude, one Leo Préger, whose name was new to me. Préger's song was haunting with its poignant curves, its every pearly note in perfect place.

Doda was right-hand man to Nadia Boulanger, as to Marie-Blanche de Polignac, the beautiful countess who sang "Amor" on that immortal Monteverdi record. He gave me three rare scores of Stravinsky and a carton of Chesterfields from the army PX for rehearsing *Winterreise* with him, and he was always good for changing dollars. Continually on the lookout for someone to champion, I was that someone for now. He introduced me to valuable people and commissioned works (through praise, not money) which he sang all over. If, sixteen years hence, Doda ceased to speak to me, a silence maintained for twenty-five years (the period in France paralleling our statute of limitations), he then at eighty-five wrote to say that all is forgiven. My crime was apparently something said about his mother. For the record: At Doda's request, on 29 September 1955, I composed a nine-measure master-piece based on Gertrude Stein's quatrain "I Am Rose," "dedicated to Marya Freund on her 80th birthday."

Robert Kanters and André Fraigneau were smart literary critics, both with regular jobs reviewing for monthlies, and both responsible for thoughtful studies on art and literature, though not music. I went to bed several times with Kanters, who was comparatively masculine and quite good-natured, in his little pad, rue de Beaune, but not with Fraigneau who was effete to a fault, and had composed an illustrated monograph on Jean Cocteau, whom he was the poor man's version of. To his credit, Fraigneau had also produced a collection of stories called *La grâce humaine,* the first of which describes the author in a train compartment also occupied by a prisoner handcuffed between two guards. The author and the captive glance furtively at each other for hours. Without a word they reach an understanding, then are parted forever. I asked Fraigneau what *La grâce humaine* meant. He answered: "La grâce humaine, c'est toi." (Is this a gracious paragraph?)

Julius Katchen would one day say: "Be nicer to Fraigneau and Kanters. Think of them as your audience. Everyone is the audience."

Backstage after Katchen's extraordinary demonstration I had said only "How do you do?" Not until late summer did we meet again and begin the passionately platonic friendship that would endure until Julius died at forty-three in 1969.

April 25th. Rain. Dine with Douglas Allanbrook, Leo Préger, Paul Demarest. . . . 26th, terribly cold. Postpone Jacques Durand-Dassier. . . . 27th, Charles Hathaway (champagne) and Leslie Egleton. Grémillon!!! 28th, do music for Mauroc's play. Kanters 5:30. José 7:30, and Poulenc's violin sonata concert, Ecole Normale. . . .

Préger turned out to be Romanian with a squat physique and beady eyes who lived with his sister. His music resembled my own. Despite warm feelings toward this music, I never warmed to the man, not least because he would next year win first place in the Prix de Biarritz, when I won second.

Charles Hathaway and Leslie Egleton were American fixtures.

Charles was a well-off supplier of opium, through his rich lover, Hubert de Senoch, to the artistic members of the Tout Paris—Cocteau, Tony Gandarillas, the Aurics—as well as an idle reconteur. Egleton was an obstreperous swish of a now-vanished vintage, like someone in Waugh. It was they who, seeing Jean Grémillon, the plump, surly, glorious, fifty-year-old movie director seated alone at the Montana, suggested I introduce myself, for he liked handsome boys. Since I'd never heard of him, there was nothing to fear. I was wearing Jean-Claude's black wool turtleneck (which I still have), had injected Privine in my eyes to make them shine, and was afloat in sparkling wine. Approaching this monolith whose head was on the bar, I murmured: *Monsieur Grémillon.* He groaned the groan of he-who-is-forever-burdened-by-strangers, then turned toward me, and his face lit up. "Alors, vous voulez faire du cinema, vous aussi," said he, and ordered us both a drink. We ended up in bed in Harp Street, where I changed my mind in midstream and wouldn't put out. He got dressed slowly and lumbered away, cursing Americans. Months later we met again, again at the Montana, and he laughed and introduced me to a friend as "that Yankee I told you about." It wasn't until after his death in 1959 that I learned what a uniquely key figure he was for French movies. (It was also in 1959, back in America, that I brought someone home from Julius's bar at 4 a.m. That someone turned out to have an artificial leg which he laboriously unscrewed. Whereupon I asked him to leave, and pretended to pass out. Cursing, he screwed the leg back on and clanked off into the dawn.)

Daniel Mauroc asked me to compose background music for his playlet called *Il n'y a plus rien à vivre,* a dark comedy and quite good. This I did, simply by having Leon Fleisher play the slow middle Barcarolle over and over into a recording machine. Jean-Claude's pretty blond sister Josette was strong as one of the three characters when the piece was mounted.

April 29th. Sarah Cunningham at 12:45, c/o Doll, 90 rue de Varenne. Janet at 2:00. Radio interview, M. Blesdoe, at 4:30, 118 Champs-Elysées. Brion Gysin and Peggy Fears, 7:45 at Pont Royale bar. . . . 30th, Rohini Coomara. Barman at the Hôtel Metropole, rue François-Ier. (Miss Rohini Coomara was a cellist friend of Sam Barber. . . . The bartender was someone José recommended, but I waited there shyly for an hour without seeing anyone who fit the description.) José at 5. Marie-Blanche de Polignac. Robert Kanters, 6:15 au Montana, then Maugham's movie, *Quartet.*

Sarah Cunningham was a prim Boston composer who had shared the Barrington dorm that first summer in Tanglewood. Our main point in common was that we had both rendered the same Hopkins poem into song, "Margaret, are you grieving." On this Sunday we had a brief lunch, blue cheese and peaches, in a corner bistro of the rue de La Planche where a svelte black-haired waiter with a filthy apron winked at us. . . . Brion Gysin, like Jane Bowles, was away from Tangier for the season, and had incongruously latched onto Peggy Fears, an ex Follies beauty now thickened with a husky voice who, a generation later, would inaugurate the successful Boatel at Fire Island Pines. . . .

Marie-Blanche de Polignac, née Lanvin (her mother founded the still-famous house of dressmaking and perfume; her father made a fortune in champagne), had a childless but loving marriage to the Comte Jean de Polignac. How this marriage evolved I do not know; the comte did have affairs with many another female, notably Denise Bourdet, but died before I came on the scene. Marie-Blanche was made of a successful sugar-&-spice mélange I'd never sampled before: wealth and beauty did not weaken, through laziness and vanity, a considerable love for music; and the considerable love for music was demonstrated through a sweet soprano of unequaled expressivity and through an educated comprehension (rare for sopranos in any era) of the art. The education was enhanced by her dinner parties for an international array of musicians every Sunday of the winter for thirty years, at her *hôtel particulier,* 16 rue Barbet-de-Jouy. The dinner, always at a table for twelve in a circular dining room with ceiling and walls decorated by Bérard and generally offering pheasant with the house champagne, was followed by a musicale upstairs where other guests would arrive to a room full of Vuillards, some to play at the two Pleyels, or sing, or present a new violin sonata—Les Six (except Honegger, who found the ambiance too rarefied), Menhuin, Lenny Bernstein, the nucleus being Jacques Février, Henri Sauguet with Jacques Dupont, Denise Bourdet. Or sometimes everyone would join in charades, or truth-or-consequences, or simply chat, as Marie-Blanche, always in a new *création de chez Lanvin* of chiffon as pinkly secret as the inside of a seashell through which her shapely legs were outlined, would move among the guests, a bit vague (she too smoked opium in the late afternoon), trailing a faint breeze of expensive perfume, and uttering the understated effusions in which only the French excel without blushing—"Comme c'est beau! Comme vous avez raison." On more auspicious nights we would adjourn to the concert hall in Marie-Blanche's garden pavilion where, while listening, we could look at the Renoirs—a process which always struck me as unmusical, if typical of the visual French who would pay Chagall a fortune for his murals on the ceiling of the Opéra.

Do not confound her with the much older hatchet-faced *Princesse* de Polignac, née Winaretta Singer of the American sewing machines, lesbian spouse of Marie-Blanche's husband's uncle, and the greatest musical patron of the twentieth century who caused to exist Satie's *Socrate,* and many a Diaghilev ballet plus slighter works of Stravinsky, Poulenc, Fauré, and Falla. The comtesse did not commission works, but she did participate in their realization. She had been Boulanger's chief supporter in the 1930s, and chief soprano too. To see those two together now was to see the eternal feminine and masculine, Marie-Blanche all passive, curved and spoiled, Nadia all business, square and rigid. (In 1935 Nadia ordered a no-nonsense gown from Lanvin for her conducting dates. Twenty years later Marie-Blanche suggested Nadia order a new dress. The new one was identical to the old.) Doda it was who brought me to Marie-Blanche's on this Sunday night. She made me welcome ever after, until she died so ignominiously—for even the rich die ignominiously—after an unconscious year in an iron lung in 1958.

Maugham's film, *Quartet,* contained a scene wherein a young man dreams of becoming a great pianist until the day his teacher, imperiously played by Françoise Rosay, decides he doesn't have the stuff. He asks her, during their final lesson, to play for him. She does, somewhat cruelly choosing the most difficult of Schubert's *Moments musicaux* (glitteringly dubbed by Rubinstein). After which he goes home and commits suicide.

Leon Fleisher would not commit suicide. His performance of my two pieces was the perfection by which I judged all ensuing performances, and his eventual recording for Columbia of the Barcarolles remains a collector's item. The embassy program of 4 May launched Leon in Europe, not least because Doda, bedazzled, nabbed him on the spot as accompanist, and then persuaded him to enter the Brussels Queen Elizabeth competition the next year. Leon won first prize (a million francs and solo dates throughout the Continent), to emerge as one of America's four leading virtuosos, with Eugene, Gary Graffman, and Julius Katchen. His glory would be grotesquely restricted in 1964, as would Gary's some years after, by a neurological affliction of the right hand.

After the concert we threw a large party in the two small rooms on Harp Street. The whole audience showed up, including José with Marie-Laure de Noailles. For a year José had been trying to bring us together. Most of the guests inadvertently entered the building through the Rose Rouge. When Benga caught sight of Marie-Laure, whom he'd not seen since *Sang d'un poète* in 1930, our cachet as his lessees soared. Marie-Laure had, of course, with her spouse, the Vicomte Charles de Noailles, subsidized this first film of Cocteau. The pair had even been filmed as part of the world-weary audience applauding the suicide of the young poet as he lies in the snow under the card table. But when, because of this blasphemy, Charles was threatened with excommunication not only from the Holy Church but —far worse!—the Jockey Club, the scene was reshot with Barbette and Arturo Lopez.

Marie-Laure ignored me utterly, but made eyes at Jean-Claude, even stroked his cheek and, in an effort to beguile him, danced a hula while Leon and Eugene played their four-hand arrangement of Falla's *Dance of the Miller's Wife* which set the crowd afire with its throbbing swirls. I was embarrassed that this famous forty-nine-year-old Vicomtesse, the most powerful intellectual in France, would sink to such sophomoric ruses. She gave Jean-Claude her phone number, but he never called.

I dawdled on in Paris when I should have returned to work in Morocco. This pious reflection now sounds facile, as I turn the calendar leaves of which each is a barricade between a mass of tomorrows, all simultaneously visible as I gaze down, like Marcel, from mile-high crutches treading gingerly between one field of corpses and the next. But to the young Ned, the future lay in the moment. The next fortnight would be a blur except for what is noted in the diary. I do not remember experiences as well as what i have written about experiences.

Paris then was the Paris upon which I most frequently reflect: Lutèce, the sixth arrondissement, from the rue Saint-Jacques to the rue de Sèvres, bordered by the boulevard Montparnasse on the south, and on the north by the Seine. This precious township contained the only friends, bakeries, bars, and cinemas needed to make the world turn. The coincidental but never mutual tonalities of the serious Sorbonne and the frivolous Saint-Germain, plus the sinister intimacy of the sinuous *ruelles* with their dozens of student hotels which I learned like the back of my hand, seemed unchanged since Villon, since Balzac and Proust (though did the great Simenon ever write of the area?). Later, during the years I lived with Marie-Laure in the sixteenth arrondissement, I would return here mostly, to fall in love and otherwise get into trouble.

Far more than New York, Paris is an outdoor city, even in winter. Not just the sidewalk cafés and tobacco stores but the art-nouveau urinals, one to a block. The *quartier* reeks of sex. Behind this doorway, down these alleys, up in that room of the now-vanished Hôtel Saint-Yves, over in the little Square du Vert Gallant at sunrise, I left parts of my body—sweat and sperm and suntan peelings—in the fugitive arms of green-eyed strangers, sometimes with eternal loves, all of them dead, and that village weighs like a tombstone, as does this book.

On 5 May, Doda and I dined at La Régence, saw *Fric Frac* au français, then strolled through the Palais Royale where Doda, while pointing out landmarks, invited me to write a cycle for him. During the next days I seem to have had rendezvous at the Flore, or at movie theaters. How many times a week did I repeat the *traversée* from rue de la Harpe to Saint-Germain-des-Prés, holding my nose in passing the Café Odéon which forever smelled as foul as its counterpart in Manhattan's Forty-second Street shuttle! The weather turned seraphic. José had a new boyfriend, Richard Négroux, a Romanian with a thrilling accent and a vigorous stride, with whom I made love in the rue Cujas during the early evening of 8 May, my sister's birthday.

On the 10th with Robert Kanters, a reception for Thomas Mann. Shaking hands with the great Mann, I wondered: Did he remember me from the front row at his Northwestern lecture in 1940? That night, informal dinner at M. et Mme. Laidley's, from UNESCO, whose guest of honor was Louis Beydts, composer of operettas and current director of the Opéra-Comique. Offered a glass of bubbly by my hostess, I demurred, echoing Jane Bowles's phrase to Apollinaire's valet, "J'ai déjà beaucoup bu de champagne, Madame," which Beydts praised as a flawless alexandrine, inviting me to his office next afternoon to show him my wares. I never made it. Leaving the party drunk, I passed a chaotic, even dangerous, evening, crashed at Jane's, and slept through the appointment.

George Bemberg was around. Also the Azevedos. And Jean E., a cute French boy Shirley had found in Tangier, with whom I visited the Assyrian room at the Louvre, had a duck dinner, and went to bed. Milhaud's grand opera, *Bolivar,* on the 15th, starred the slick soprano Janine Micheau intoning with accuracy the stratospheric lines. On the 16th, lunch chez Jean Bertrand, avenue Hoche; then Doda's concert at the Cercle Interallié; later José at Café Weber at 7:30, and a postprandial visit to pianist Nadia Tagrine. On the 17th, Sauguet had a concert at the Ecole Normale featuring his many settings of the surrealist Max Jacob. There were seven of us in the audience.

Thursday, 18 May, lunch with Henri-Louis de la Grange, an uppercrust bourgeois pal of Sam Barber now writing a biography of Mahler, in his mansion at 208 boulevard Saint-Germain. At five, picked up laundry, packed a huge suitcase (enclosing, as a gift for Guy, several of Norris Embry's extraordinary brown and black lithographs), caught a 9 p.m. bus at the Gare des Invalides which headed toward Orly, then boarded an old-fashioned plane for Casablanca.

For a composer of songs the problem lies not in finding a sonic impulse (if he did not feel the impulse hourly he wouldn't be a composer), but in finding a text which somehow asks to be musicalized just by him; if he plans a connected series of songs, he must find a *group* of texts, sometimes by various authors from different centuries, which can be joined in an inevitable-seeming sequence.

Leon Fleisher suggested Herrick as a sensitive source for Doda's cycle. Already on the airplane I was making notes in the margins of a Herrick reader, bought last week at Brentano's on the avenue de l'Opéra, and by the time we landed in Africa had even, in the little notebook on my lap, set one of the poems to music ("Comfort to a Youth That Had Lost His Love"). Before the month was out the cycle was done, nine songs and a piano interlude, titled *Flight for Heaven* after the last line of the first poem, "To Music, to Becalm His Fever." The words seem born for singing, every line plotted with Doda's booming bass in mind. The manuscript was duly sent to Monsieur Vadot at the Néocopie-Musicale, who then forwarded two copies to its only begetter. Doda, with Leon Fleisher as pianist, accordingly tried out the piece during the coming autumn in various salons, and on a European tour. As early as 19 November he gave the USA premiere at a League of Composers concert in the Museum of Modern Art, David Garvey as accompanist.

Flight for Heaven, lasting fifteen minutes, is my first cycle, one I am not ashamed of. Through Doda's connections, the work was published by Mercury Music Press, founded by Leonard Feist and his brother, Milton. (Milton Feist, the Stephen Hawking of music, was a withered tiny creature who lived in a wheelchair, had an astronomical IQ, and could expound, without making you blush, on all matters cultural. His love life, if he had one, was discreet, though he had a seemingly tough constitution. I once at midnight wheeled him into the San Remo where he was the belle of the ball, then wheeled him home at 4 a.m. During his short life he welcomed my works into his firm, which was eventually transferred to Theodore Presser.) When the cycle was in proof during early 1952 I naturally dedicated it to Doda, although, since by then I was living with Marie-Laure, I inserted a dedication to her too, above the last song, "To Anthea, Who May Command Him Anything." In 1963 Donald Gramm recorded two of the songs on Columbia Records.

It seems astonishing now: during this same period I completed not only a sizable Suite for Two Pianos for Fizdale & Gold—which they never played, nor has anyone else (although I orchestrated the overture years later for my Third Symphony)—but the *Six Irish Poems* for Nell Tangeman. True, I had made sketches during odd moments, ever since leaving Italy; still, the fomenting period exploded when I reached Fez again, and it was merely a question of getting the notes down on paper. These songs, on stark northern texts, were sculpted around Nell's strong points, and were the first pieces I wrote for voice with orchestra.

Those first weeks back in Fez were industrious. Like a pet cat who when you take him to the country assumes another personality from that of the city, so my patterns in Fez and in Paris were in differentiated counterpoint. Promiscuous binges of France were balanced by the Protestant remorse of Africa, the cause and effect of an oeuvre, the Jekyll and Hyde, the rising and falling and rising again. In Fez, with its routine, regular sex, and no alcohol, that which had come to a head now burst. The emission is how you see it: spewed pus, a baby, art. I can't relive it. (Just yesterday they were sitting on that yellow sofa. Today the sofa remains, but they aren't there. Like the master's face vanished from the Lamb House mirror.) I was playing roles in separate ongoing plays, plays without plots, but developing nonetheless.

By day Guy was overwhelmed in the line of duty. Beyond the rural tribes to which he ministered, he had private patients at the Hôpital Cocard. One of these was a woman who, having over the years crammed her apertures, front and back, not just with standard dildos but with carrots, hairpins, and lightbulbs, was now bleeding between death and life. Another was a Berber matron whose son had lately been attacked by a rabid dog; he had not been bitten, but his trousers were ripped. A month later his mother, mending his trousers, placed the darning needle in her mouth and was stricken with hydrophobia. Which demonstrates the demonic, that does not pall with time. Guy meanwhile had adopted a dog (nonrabid) of his own, a stray female mongrel which in homage to Shirley he named Xénia. This dog adored me but I despised her. (Why? Until puberty I lived only for animals. The overnight aversion stemmed, as I view it now, from pets monopolizing the attention I felt was my due, with their mute-cute demands encroaching on the work habits of their betters.) Animals were drawn to me inversely as I was repelled by them. Had I an unbeknown saintly side, like the evil Loeb—or was it Leopold?—to whom in his prison cell birds swarmed? More likely, since animals have no appreciation of human morality and "goodness," the answer lies in something like pheromones. As James Hamilton-Patterson, England's most articulate living fictioneer and amateur naturalist, puts it:

"Animals flocked to Saint Francis not because he was a saint but because they happened to like the smell of his glands."

I practiced a good deal, inventing, then perfecting, long programs of short works. Webern's wispy piano pieces, some lasting only ten seconds, were used in this regard: a popular quip had it that if a projected concert of new music seems too lengthy, just add something of Webern to make it seem shorter. But my ideal program consisted of thirty-six preludes, twelve by Bach, twelve by Debussy, twelve by Chopin, all intertwined. In relearning the forty-eight preludes and fugues from *Das Wohltemperierte Klavier* in a gorgeous new edition from chez Durand—I had cursorily grappled with them in the 1930s—it became clear that the preludes were superior to the fugues (preludes are French, fugues are German), if only by their sensually controlled freedom as distinct from the more predictably developing fugues. Also, the three composers meshed cozily, like prosciutto and melon with vin rosé.

In the evening when Guy came home exhausted, I would play for him either what I had composed or had practiced. After a brief nap together, we dined in the Ville Nouvelle at the Renaissance where a huge ceiling fan revolved casually, the wide blades better at dispersing flies than in creating a breeze, and I felt there was no one in the universe I'd rather be with than Guy, as we consumed our *veau à la crème* with watercress salad, habitual peach melba, then adjourned to the Légion for slow-filtering coffee. There was an incongruity to this portrait of a French doctor cohabiting with an American composer in the colonial milieu of darkest Africa, an incongruity which enhanced the bourgeois tinge of fidelity that stabilized our housekeeping.

Sometimes Lévesque joined us. As a patient professor of literature proud of his knowledge not only of classical French but of the purity of argot, he was the perfect mentor for me, who am relentless about linguistic parallels. How do you say "fairyland" or "armpit" or "they are disgusting" in French? What is the difference between *être* and *se faire* when conjugated with *baiser?* Why is there no direct equivalent of "shallow," or no future of the subjunctive, as in Spanish? Multisyllabic adjectives that look the same in French and English are weaker in the former tongue. *Sinistre, formidable, vicieux* are best rendered as "dreary," "terrific," "horny." "Il est mort de sa belle mort" does not mean "he died for his beautiful one," as I once impotently heard the all-knowing Jennie Tourel explain to a class of sopranos apropos of Poulenc's setting of Vilmorin's poem "Dans l'herbe," but "he died a natural death." Well, any fool knows that. Yet some, less foolish than I, persist.

Lévesque lent me *Le sabbat,* and spoke about its author, Maurice Sachs, the self-destructive protégé of Cocteau, whose autobiography was shatteringly alluring but necessarily unfinished because, like other queer French thinkers, he disappeared beyond the Rhine during the war and was never heard from again. I sang Poulenc's setting of Robert Desnos's "Le disparu," which begins:

Je n'aime plus la rue Saint Martin
 depuis qu'André Platard l'a quittée,
 Je n'aime plus la rue Saint Martin,
 je n'aime rien, pas même le vin . . .

for Desnos too, like his fictional Platard, vanished one morning without a trace. Lévesque also gifted us with his red leather copy—still in my shelves—of Stendhal's *Promenades dans Rome,* because Guy and I planned a train trip next month in Italy, where he had never been. Had a year passed since we first met on his last holiday?

Other evenings were passed with the Royers, or at the movies. Recent films of Wyler or De Sica seemed all the more trenchant dubbed into French. *L'héritière,* with the Jewish Copland's music depicting Bostonian frustration now spilling from the theater onto the Arabian sidewalk, had a poignance all its own, as did *Le voleur de bicyclettes* whose Roman urchins emoted in the tongue of Voltaire. We swam often in the sacred pond of Sidi-Hrasem (where one dawn parts of a woman's dead body were found), and made nocturnal tours of the Médina with Guy's medical colleagues, drinking almond milk at the "bar" of the *quartier réservé.* One afternoon, on the terrace of the Jamai, I ran into Louise Holdsworth, of all people, for whom I had once composed a dance score. First-class French films: *Le corbeau* and *Rendez-vous de juillet,* the latter starring Daniel Gélin, whose poems, believe it or not, I would set to music in 1953.

Up in Paris on 2 June, Shirley finally gives her recital in Gaveau, and sends the program. She will return to America in August. (Years pass before we meet again, when she will have divorced Seymour Barab, then married and divorced a Chicago dentist . . . named Guy!) Leon Fleisher takes over the apartment in rue de la Harpe. On the same night as Shirley's concert we, across the Mediterranean, see Esther Williams in *Señorita Toreador* (*Fiesta* in English), also with Copland's music, *El Salón México,* stupidly incorporated. Haircut. More swimming. On 8 June we dine at the Royers, then leave for Oran on a late train which had bedbugs.

Bedbugs were everywhere in those days.

29. 1950: Italy · Morocco · France · Morocco

Among the pleasantest memories of this second trip into Italy is a picnic near the Leaning Tower, on our final Sunday, with Arthur Gold and Bobby Fizdale who could plot and execute a meal as gracefully as a program of two-piano selections. Bobby and Arthur had been our hosts a fortnight earlier during a stop in Florence, and had planned for us—like a meal, like a program—the rest of our trip meticulously. Now, on our way back north, they were curious to learn how we may have veered from their itinerary.

Two weeks earlier our crossing from Oran to Marseilles—a habit by now—was aboard the *Ville d'Alger*. In Marseilles we saw a revival of *François Ier* with Fernandel who, as that city's most cherished native son, with his long droll melancholy features like Adolph Green's, had his movies continuously recycled to SRO audiences. Afterward we went to a huge gay bar, Les Trois Cloches, near the Corniche, filled to the brim on this sweaty Sunday midnight with queens in feathers screeching in meridional accents at the butch sailors, short and muscular, posing in their tight culottes and little pompon caps, very Genet. Sometimes the *matelots* and the *folles* danced together to a bouncy accordion-accompanied java. If you've never been to a gay bar, start with this one, though you may be forty years too late.

From Cannes (again at the Westminster Hotel) to Pisa by train the route is not scenic because of the tunnels, but I read the whole way, mostly Graham Greene in French, *La puissance et la gloire,* without pleasure, and the Stendhal travel guide. What in my mind's eye do I first conjure up from Florence? I conjure the actual statue of Lorenzo, whose image had graced the green history book of U-High when I pondered how a mortal could be so beautiful and yet so great. Now here in "real life" sits his marble replica, brooding in profile through the ages in the Medici Chapel, with those well-formed calves 'neath a metallic armor whence the equivocal smell of musk clots the atmosphere. Are such thoughts allowed with Guy present, seeking facts in the little guidebook borrowed for a moment from a female tourist from France? It filled me with sadness that Lorenzo was so unavailable; I am sad today knowing that four hundred years hence other men's eyes will still fall upon Lorenzo, as they did four hundred years ago, and he will never return their gaze. The sadness is not wholly unpleasant.

"Here comes Bu Faulkner," said I without surprise, as we awaited our pasta that evening in Nandina's Kitchen. Guy recognized him immediately from my description (melted face of a humorous Newfoundland, guilty from a drunken night on his knees beneath the San Nicole bridge), and from the tone of his letters. "Hold onto your cloche hats," whined Bu as he approached our table and sat down, instantly regaling us with local gossip. We invited him to join us next evening for the dress rehearsal of Gluck's *Iphigenie in Aulide* with Edwin Denby in the Boboli Gardens. Afterward we would sup at the Caffè Arno, the Flore of Florence, with Bobby Fizdale and Arthur Gold, whom Bu called the Fizgolds. He knew them all of course—was more than tolerated as mascot by his betters, a court jester, like John Latouche without the talent. Denby, skinny and witty, deep-eyed and sad, was now a guest of "the Fizgolds" in their suburban villa. He was your typical destitute artist, much loved, living for decades in other folks' nests, or alone in his Twenty-first Street walk-up where, in his seventies, he killed himself to forestall the pain of incurable cancer. Edwin had retired as dance critic of the *Herald-Tribune* where Virgil attested —others concurred—that he was America's *only* dance critic.

Guy and I too became, for a night, guests in the villa. Probably Arthur and Bobby felt they owed me this, in exchange for the big Suite for Two Pianos which they would never play. Also Bobby got a sort of crush on Guy, who was on his best behavior as leveler between dissipated America and extrovert Italy. We told them of our plan to reach Rome slowly, by bus and by train, and they, who knew the terrain, proudly drew up a schedule.

In Siena, thanks to their recommendation, we stayed at the Palazzo Ravizza, an intimate pensione run by the ancient Contessa Grottanelli, right off the main square and two blocks from the children's fair where we rode around in little bumpy cars. Even as the sensation I most remember from Chartres is the apricot sherbet, and from Florence is the Lorenzo marble, the one sensation from Siena is the children's fair. Yes, there were medieval walls, the Gothic Baptistry, verdant backgrounds, the unrecuperable scenes of war, but when you're in love you remember games and bedrooms more than history. You also quarrel a lot and worry about money.

Rome. Depending on your first view you bless or damn a town. Emerging from the Stazione Termini I breathed a stifling dusty air and the stink of Cinzano, sulked for a day in our pensione, the Fogetti in Via Marche, while Guy sightsaw. Steady hot rain. Then we visited Alexei Haieff and the weather changed. He resided with the Igor-Aaron klatch, still serene in their crisply well-made neoclassicism before the ignorant armies of integral serialism clashed over their careers and turned them into school teachers. On 22 June I wrote in the diary:

"Yesterday we went out to the American Academy to visit Alexei. A lovely site as sites here go, and far from the center of the world's noisiest city, but overly tranquil and almost sad. It seems too bad to be stuck in the suburbs with nothing but creative people for companions: there's no real conversation, no social energy, not even any real competition (though these people are now grown-ups) such as we used to get at Tanglewood. Alexei, whom I hadn't seen in five years, has gotten fat. He seems cheery and naïve as ever, and as much in love with Stravinsky. His French is the oddest ever spoken, so we talked English all afternoon and Guy was bored.... After an outdoor lunch in an expensive trattoria (Alexei paid) we visited the composers' studios which are ideal. Ulysses Kay and Jack Beeson, both on Prix de Rome, showed us around; both seem blissful, both married.... Leo Smit played Stravinsky wonderfully for us ('Ragtime,' the piece with the marvelous Picasso cover); then he and Alexei played a two-piano version of the latter's new concerto, dedicated to the former—a most charming work, but so à-la-russe as to be nothing else. Finally Leo played Harold Shapero's C-Minor Variations (dedicated to Igor Stravinsky) which is long and wants very much to be Op. 111. . . . It's all a closed little successful clique living off the various American foundations to which letters of recommendation have been written by older members of the same successful clique. (Alexei's music is dedicated to Arthur Berger, whose music is dedicated to H. Shapero, whose music is dedicated to Stravinsky, whose *Symphony of Psalms* is 'dedicated to the glory of God and to the Boston Symphony.') I have nothing against someone's music sounding like someone else's, but none of these people is as *good* as Aaron or Stravinsky, whereas they ought either to be better or different. . . . As for Jack Beeson, the poor dear has finally finished a very thick and gorgeously copied opera (Paul Goodman's *Jonah*), and it makes my heart bleed to behold that patience dissipated on an effort that will never see production. Reminded of Boulez (for whom my heart doesn't bleed) whose manuscript literally requires a microscope to decipher. At no cost does he want to be understood. . . . Alexei & Mrs. Kay (Barbara, quite pretty, friend of Margaret Bonds) walked us to the bus, and we came down into illuminated Rome to drink coffee on the Excelsior sidewalk (around the corner from our pensione, 14,000 a day for two) and watch the disarming Italian population trot by."

Two days later I wrote: ". . . Walked around some. I like the new buildings, the broad thoroughfares, the Mussolini architecture. But the city as a sentimental whole has been a big disappointment. I loathe the streetcar, despise the parks, detest the people in the streets, and convulse at the 'averageness,' the dearth of strangeness. There's not even any heavy Catholicism. I want to leave."

Back to Florence, a weekend with Bobby and Arthur and Edwin. They had the coarse unwitty Chester Kallman, plus an exotic woman named Toto, in tow, Bulgarian perhaps, handsome, multilingual, hard drinking. Everyone was reading Ivy Compton-Burnett. Fireworks at the San Giovanni festival, after which the Fizgolds played *Epigraphes antiques,* the pedaled sonorities wafting into the garden where nightingales gurgled. Next day, 25 June, Bobby drove us all to Pisa where we had the picnic, me and Arthur and Edwin and Guy and a young Italian, on the surrealist unornamented lawn flanking the Leaning Tower, one of the seven oddities of the modern world. The menu has faded. But Edwin gave me a very American poem, on a soiled yellow sheet, called "First Warm Days," which ends:

We all are filled with an air like of loving
Going home quiet in the subway shoving

which I put to music. The song was mislaid, then surfaced in 1989 to be refashioned to fit a poem of Whitman's called "Are You the New Person?"

At dusk our fellow picnickers brought us to the bus for Genoa where we spent the night, took a train into Marseilles, a plane to Oran, and arrived by train back in Fez in time to see, on 28 June, *A Letter to Three Wives*.

Edwin Denby at our picnic had said: "One comes to see the monuments of European towns. Next to these monuments the towns can look ridiculous, which in turn make the monuments ridiculous. But in Fez are no monuments: or rather, the city itself is one vast wonder, and so there is no call for impatience when one resides there."

My immediate project, on retrieving this routine African peace, was to finish the String Quartet. Since it was to be dedicated "To the memory of Lili Boulanger," these words from Elinor Wylie's translation of a Greek octet called "On a Singing Girl" would serve as epigraph:

> She, whose songs we loved the best,
> is voiceless in a sudden night.
> On your light limbs, O loveliest,
> may the dust be light.

The last of the four movements was written first. (Have you noticed that composers always say *to write* for their action, never *to compose?*) Its slowly growing Lento aped both mood and device from David Diamond's beautiful Third Quartet wherein the viola provides a ladderlike pedal over which the other strings climb to heaven and disappear. The second movement was written second, a Pastoral in 6/8, very Gallic. The first movement was written third, an Allegro Moderato preceded by an Introduction drawn from the last movement. And the third movement was written fourth, stolen like a whisper wrongly overheard (though if the goods are transformed, is it a steal?) from "The Voice of the Virgin Erigone" in Debussy's *Le martyre* which still rang in my ears. All four movements were realized between the 10th and the 27th of July. The piece was quickly programmed in Paris, as well as in Philadelphia, thanks to my parents who lent it to a New Music group there.

To get the juices flowing for the quartet, I wrote a seven-page *Sicilienne* for two pianos on 29 June ("Thought up in Siena, written down in Fez") which, since Fizdale & Gold never performed it any more than they performed my other two-piano music written for them, I dedicated "To Pino Fasani" when it was printed (as was the quartet) by Peer-Southern some years later. Whittemore & Lowe finally premiered the *Sicilienne* on the Dave Garroway morning radio show. The Lento movement of the quartet, swelled into a string orchestra like Barber's *Adagio,* was eventually recorded on MGM label. The whole piece is titled String Quartet No. 2, which technically it is, though the first quartet has been, as the saying goes, withdrawn, and lies with the First Piano Concerto in a trunk whose whereabouts remain secret.

Six Irish Poems, the first of five works for solo voice and orchestra that I would write over the years, was pretty much sketched out in Paris; I now finished the orchestration and sent the whole to Nell Tangeman. The texts by George Darley (1795–1846) are bleak, and so are the songs.

I renounce none of this work, though maybe would exclude most of it in a two-hour retrospective concert.

Also during the summer I composed—I mean *wrote*—three other three-page songs: "Lullaby of the Woman of the Mountain," culled from Nell's Irish collection (words by Padriac Pearse); "Philomel" on Barnsefield's poem; and a bawdy ballad called "Whiskey, Drink Divine." And a *Slow Piece for Cello and Piano.* This last was described in my diary as "a string tune the note-lengths of which are twice as long as those of the piano, thereby making a deep blue design against a pale blue fabric. The two instruments never get together in their note denominations; the cello has no stopped chords; the tone is sad; it takes about 5 minutes. What do I call it?"

The diary, forsaken when I left America a year before, was now resumed with an overall title, *Journal de mes mélodies,* because Poulenc was keeping a similar journal. Written mainly in French, it purported to be a blow-by-blow account of my new music as it was being born. Soon I reverted to English, and dealt with more mundane matters, neatly inscribed in fountain pen with nothing crossed out or edited (unlike the present book, painfully typed and crosshatched with revision). The pith was incorporated into *The Paris Diary.* Some dross remains, which I'll quote from time to time as an indication of the times. For example:

"Write a story about a parental suicide pact. They decide to kill themselves because of the guilt inspired by the vigorous accusations of their enlightened child, who happens to be undergoing psychoanalysis for which they have paid."

Or:

"Write an article on the naïve art endeavor of the United States.

Young Europeans are less good; they're restrained by staleness. Still, America, after an initial impetus, is going nowhere. Call it *A Child Is Dying.*"

Or:

"What will happen today that I'll dream about tonight? 'And all those useless orgasms!' says the dying pederast." (Today I'm inclined to dream of what happens next day. Most orgasms by heterosexuals seem useless too.)

Or:

"A French musician of the 18th century . . . 'left the theater only to go to the tavern, for at that time musicians got drunk with the approval of the state, and perhaps were musicians only by that favor. A musician who did not drink was held in worse regard by his confrères than one who played out of tune or out of time. But customs are greatly changed.' (from Adolphe Adam, *Memoirs*) . . . Remarked to me at Michel's party last Saturday night: 'I hear you won some sort of Gershwin prize. Do play us the *Rhapsody in Blue,* you must know it by heart, it's my favorite.' They also asked for *Intermezzo.* This has been going on for years, yet always makes me weak in the stomach, especially during this unspeakable heat wave when I have just had my first drinks in three months. What a teeny-weeny walled-up little métier I seem to have chosen myself: no wonder composers are bohemians, not to mention alcoholics & sometimes all kinds of other things."

Or:

". . . Raoul Dufy has been cured of his paralyzed hands. What *is* this? The same happened to Rembrandt. And Beethoven, Bach, and Brahms were deaf, blind, and dumb. What are they ashamed of? They should all play Mendelssohn's 'Song without Words' in E-flat, Opus 67 number one."

Or:

"The first and only time I ever saw Ned Rorem was in the marketplace of Marrakech. He wore a chocolate-brown shirt, filthy tan pants, and black shoes. But what a face—like an angel's! Tall and artificially blond. He was shopping, Ned Rorem, and in his left hand was a bunch of many-colored roses, and under his left arm a pineapple wrapped in newspaper; in his right hand an unlit cigarette. He was before a kiosk of caged parrots which were shrieking at full speed. For a while he spoke quietly to the merchant, but then all of the sudden he grew agitated. Although I could not hear him because of the din of the birds, I knew he was quarreling at the top of his lungs, quite surprising in one with a demeanor so calm. Then he began to cry, and I turned away, not liking him anymore (though I'd felt a certain nonphysical attraction at the start). For I dislike tears to a point of loathing, especially tears of shyness which certainly these were. I therefore hope never to encounter him again."

Memoir is style (French). Diary is content (German). A diary is too close to the fact to be stylish (does one write of one's breaking heart with style?), while a memoir is too far from fact for substance.

Chronology is to the autobiographer what a poem is to the song composer: the skeleton's there, it just requires flesh—the *recall* of flesh—without need for inventing a plot. Aware that nobody wants to read about other people's childhoods, much less their progenitors' childhoods, I've nevertheless recollected early affinities for Mother and Father. Now that I've decided to stop this book by 1952, well before my thirtieth year, and subtitle it "A Memoir" rather than "An Autobiography," I'm indulging in detail, since I *have* the detail. The problem: there's no climax, there can't be, even with autobiography, unless the author slits his wrists on the last page.

It was my second summer in Morocco. This time I would stay until nearly September before heading up to Paris. The season was a duplicate of 1949, so far as society is concerned. Movies weekly, books daily (*Tropic of Capricorn, Wings of the Dove,* Paul Goodman's new *The Dead of Spring*). Arab concerts monthly. Endless letter writing, mainly to parents, and to Monsieur Vadot of the Néocopie-Musicale. Evening picnics in the cool hills of Immouzer. Twice we dined in the very humble abode of Messaoud and his mother, touched by their effort to prepare a stifling meal in the stifling heat, and of the rigid yet barefoot hospitality.

But a sad fog had settled over the planet. The war in Korea seemed incomprehensible, coming as it did so soon after the armistice, menacing what everyone thought would be a third world war. I hadn't yet learned that people don't learn, that mistakes are repeated, violence sanctioned, love mocked, hate relished.

Ramadan ended on 16 July, replaced by rain, and more rain. Add to this the intimations of hemorrhoids which had brewed for a decade, injections Guy gave me for allergies aggravated by the weekly ingestion of a carton of Koutoubias, and the wet heat that encouraged nightmares (mainly about Martha Graham, for some reason), on the occasions when persistent narcolepsy could be said to be *blessed* by bad dreams, and you have the mood from which I recoiled daily to write music. Attempting now to see myself through Guy's eyes, I must have been insufferable. He said so frequently, yet reticently, torn between awe of the general situation and impatience at the particular self-indulgence of a spoiled American. The French may pamper their pet dogs, but with each other they are stoical; even the rich practice the sensuous reticence of peasants. Guy's affection was bemusing, as when he suggested I dally with one or another of his confrères (I never did) on the grounds that I shouldn't be wasted just on him. . . . Was I insufferable? People still say so. Why they suffer me, I do not know. Yes, I do.

The confrères were many, mainly straight young couples like the Rémys and the Millets, always intelligent with a conflict of interest: dedication to sanitizing this not-yet-independent and very foreign culture, yet nostalgic for their native soil. Piaf on the radio, or Charles Trenet singing "Revoir Paris," was enough to dissolve them. The male homosexual medicos were decorous if outspoken, as is the case with colonists, not just because they're far from home but because the "natives" have nothing against the practice, if not the Greekish emotion, of same-sexuality. Typical and rather mad was the bald Dr. Salme, now retired, who in his unqualified love for a Berber boy sent the lad a sheaf of Mallarmé sonnets. East and West were no less remote in those days than Romantic Love and perfunctory sex in the current curriculum of young Americans. (Not that perfunctory sex is not love: simply, it's love telegraphed, perhaps more poignant than long-lived cohabitations which, by nature, collect passionless barnacles.)

On the weekend of 12 August, after serving as witnesses at Millet's wedding in Ifrane, we proceeded to Tangier to change traveler's checks and to visit Paul Bowles in his as yet unlivable house in the Casbah. Next day Paul and Brion Gysin showed us the house: four narrow stories, one room to a story, a smell of damp plaster, no furniture except for a box of sapphires. We went for lunch to the beach of the Hercules Grottos, chauffeur-driven in Paul's new Jaguar paid for by royalties from *The Sheltering Sky*.

Paul showed no interest in ever composing again unless this were bolstered by a healthy commission—"But nobody remembers that I ever wrote music." Brion painted fervently, and would become something of a cult for the beatniks in the sixties, with his strobe-light images which I found infantile. He lingered in Tangier for another ten years, where he eventually opened a fancy restaurant, then moved to Paris, wrote infantile music, lived in a little Moroccan-style flat overlooking place Beaubourg, where saltimbanques turned handsprings day and night, and maintained a canny good humor until he died of rectal cancer in 1985.

On the roof of the house Brion took snapshots of me, peroxided, and of Paul's teenaged Spanish boyfriend. (Paul said: "The light one and the dark one, as Jane would say.") Then we returned to Madame Porte's for some divine pastry which, after the creamed-topped pear tarts of Italy, now seemed, in the Spartan plainness, unsatisfactory.

More movies, books, music copying, swimming, quarreling, cooking, and heat.

Then on 28 August I took the night plane for Paris, arriving next morning at Orly, bus to the Invalides, taxi to the Hôtel de l'Université. Now that Shirley had gone, Leon Fleisher had taken over the lease on the Harp Street pad, so I had booked a third-floor room-on-the-street (toilet down the hall) of this agreeable "artists' inn" at 22 rue de l'Université. Phone number: Littré 93-97.

The second evening, a Wednesday, quite mild, I was seated on the Reine Blanche terrace, bored, with friends, when I spotted Julius Katchen striding rapidly among the tables, then entering the bar, alone. I'd not seen him since that brief meeting last spring with Souzay. Nor had it meanwhile occurred to me he was queer. But the Reine Blanche was *the* gay hangout of the quarter and here he was. I went into the bar, found him surrounded by fans, ordered a beer, and reintroduced myself.

Much later that night we went to his place at 3 rue Cognacq-Jay. Julius had a bedroom there, plus access to the large apartment of an elderly *bourgeoise*, one Madame Ponthès, known as Tante Marthe, whom I never cared for—too smarmily calculating with her cold, knowing eyes. Julius had just turned twenty-four. He had also just come out of the closet. With all the guileless conviction of the newly converted he was as determined as a Saint Bernard humping your leg in public. Julius, who had lived in Europe since the end of the war, was both a grand pianist and a successful one—surely the most successful *American* instrumentalist on the Continent and in Britain. His professional assurance helped lend authority to his lovemaking, for he thought of himself, with his gross features and hairy back, as physically ugly, which he was, but sexually so. We nevertheless never did it again. Next morning a young student was ushered into the bedroom by Madame Ponthès, a Belgian who had apparently written Julius about coaching sessions. Julius immediately brought him into the bed. I was understandably horrified, and left.

Julius was everything that I was not. Warm, welcoming, self-assured, loud, nonalcoholic, patient, concerned about others, a performer, nearsighted, muscular, with a footballer's quick pigeon-toed walk. We became close friends and professional collaborators within the week. During the next month and a half we were inseparable, Julius modeling his notion of both homosexual and composer on myself; me modeling my notion of the virtuoso and knowledgeable interpreter on himself. He was the prodigy grown up, with 150 concerts a year, a repertory of—at a day's notice—fifty concertos and twenty recital programs, and a recording contract with London FFRR which gave him carte blanche.

His repertory, like that of most postwar Americans residing by choice in Paris, contained no French music. These pianists, mostly Jewish, liked the food, art, love, language, and freedom of France; but while they would not have dreamed of living in Germany, whose language they loathed, they played mostly German classics. If what we term "classical" can be linked to a school of French literature, the term is nil in French music. Musical classicism originated, developed, and decayed in the Austria of the late eighteenth century. The opulently controlled Impressionism which France introduced to the planet through her four great masters, Debussy and Ravel and Poulenc and Messiaen, was anathema to these virtuosos, who thought great meant big, and for whom the three Bs were doppelgängers. Julius once confided that while playing the Andante from Brahms's F-minor Sonata at a London recital, he got an erection and quite literally climaxed.

He liked to go out with mobs. Usually these were other pianists who would request, at the Café Saint-Germain, that two tables be shoved together. The mob would then gather round, eating *croque-monsieurs* with coffee or chocolate, and vie happily among themselves about the high prices they commanded, about some little restaurant discovered in Omaha or Osaka, about the SRO audience in Manchester or Munich (or about—this was a brave admission—how in Antwerp only nine people showed up), and about the digital failings of less successful competitors. Food, fees, fingerings, and foes: such was the subject matter of public performers who had never had a "normal" childhood, because their youth had been swallowed by the practice room. They were all educated and acquisitive, loving the literature of the lands they visited, and furnishing their homes with artifacts from these lands. But their conversation, after a long day at the keyboard, relaxed always into gossip.

The mob consisted of stars—Americans with their European counterparts—who met off-duty during summer sessions in Paris with their acolytes or legal mates. With Julius presiding, there were likely to be on any occasion Jacques Abram, Abbey Simon, Willy Kapell, Miriam Scriabin with Bobby Cornman, Eugene List and his new wife, Carroll

Glenn, Gary and Naomi Graffman, plus outsiders like Larry Adler or Janos Starker, everyone sober and screaming, except for the composers who, like me and sometimes Jean-Michel Damase, were quiet and drunk.

If these jovial confabs are now gone with the wind, like the Café Saint-Germain itself, it's not because performers no longer convene self-congratulatorily but because composers are banished from the convocation. Interpreter and maker now face in opposite directions, seldom turning around to join forces.

Julius differed from his three *frères semblables* by being even more monstrously to the manor born. His sound never equaled the melted gruyère sumptuousness of Istomin, his comprehension never had the aristocratic precision of Fleisher, and his fingerwork lacked the platinum incisiveness of Graffman. But his scope was more expansive than theirs, and his technique shamed Horowitz's. His grasp of repertory and of virtuosity was transmittable, and he enjoyed teaching.

The chief protégé was sixteen-year-old Jean-Pierre Marty, a pupil of Boulanger's. Julius's interest in Jean-Pierre was no less for Jean-Pierre's serious gifts than for his pomegranate physiognomy and athlete's form housing an intelligent but frightened spirit. Jean-Pierre, half Jewish, had during the war avoided arrest by the Germans through the intervention of a well-placed French lawyer, le maître O., who for this protection demanded his pound of flesh from the boy. Jean-Pierre later suffered traumatic relapses. During one such crisis he imagined himself the Saviour, and informed me that I was chief among his sanctified angels. I agreed, but advised him not to shout it from the housetops, the world might think him crazy. He took the advice. I eventually dedicated one of the Barcarolles to him. His next forty-five years have been no less problematic for him than for us all: he passed through phases of professional musicality as pianist, conductor, even composer (not bad), and currently directs the Fontainebleau School of Music, a job inherited from Boulanger. Surely it was Julius who had put the bug about my sanctity in Jean-Pierre's ear. He did the same with his other protégé, a young painter called François Jèze, for his puppy love was contagious.

He assumed that because he found me appealing, everyone else should. We organized an impromptu party for Lenny Bernstein at what was now Leon's pad on rue de la Harpe. Lenny's high-powered sister, Shirley, came too, and Yvonne Loriod, and Lukas Foss, plus other American geniuses, mostly performers, all showing off. It was understood that Doda Conrad and I would perform *Flight for Heaven*. (For that reason I did not drink beforehand but dined with Doda at the

Ministères where we laced our carrot soup with mustard—it's a stimulant.) When the room quieted down, we gave the private premiere of the cycle, after which you could hear a pin drop. Julius whispered that the roomful of people was so enthralled by my magical presence there was no place to go but home. More likely the people were so embarrassed by the inexpert roaring of our performance that no one dared show us up by further presentations.

Julius took me to dine at the home of Pierre Fournier, France's preeminent cellist, rivaled in the world only by Piatagorsky. Besides the cello, the two men had in common a wife, Leda, currently Madame Fournier. She had an unidentifiably throaty accent in her theatrical blond body, and an opinionated amateur notion of music buttressed by the assurance of her marriages. Pierre's social elegance contrasted with Leda's aggressive interest in anyone male. They had a drab-looking thirteen-year-old son who, Leda guaranteed, seemed to be turning into a veritable Adonis with each bath she gave him.

We dined also at the home of Philippe Boergner, editor-in-chief of *Paris-Match,* who with his wife owned an apartment off the avenue Foch. Julius was anxious for the magazine to do a feature on me, which it did the following February, written by Yves Salgues.

Since my real home was Fez, Julius planned a visit there during the coming winter to maybe give a recital as Xénia had done before him. He planned also to program the new sonata all over the world if I would add a fourth movement to bring down the house. While we're at it, why not write a concerto for him?

Julius's indefatigability, like Lenny's, seems breathtaking even today, as though he were making up for lost time—not just time lost by not avowing his homosexuality until twenty-three, but the time he would later lose when his life ceased at forty-three. Did he ever sleep? He practiced eight hours a day, socialized wholeheartedly with everyone in every city in the world, and consorted with at least one person a day, sometimes two or three or four. He would meet us every evening toward eleven in the quarter, returning by foot at dawn to the rue Cognacq-Jay, pausing at every pissoir en route. Not that my own routine was less strenuous, but it was accompanied by alcohol which, by definition, impelled a certain relaxation.

His learning capacity, as a valedictorian at Haverford, had always been evident. Though vulgar (i.e., extrovert, as distinct from Quaker), he was widely cultured and quadrilingual. He could also tune pianos —a virtue born of need, as when appearing in, say, Burma, to find himself confronted with an off-key upright. These traits I chalked up as merely Jewish, making light of his rare accomplishments. Julius, laughing, would pretend not to be hurt.

. . .

As with Poulenc, I have over the years written five essays on Jean
Cocteau, the twentieth-century poet to whose work I feel most akin.
And as with Poulenc, these essays in theory are still available. They
deal mainly with Cocteau's work in ways that seemed hitherto unex-
plored, at least in English (his relation to music and musicians, for
instance), although the man shines through inevitably, for there are
few examples in history where the worker and his work seem more
inextricably linked. The man alone (though Cocteau would be the first
to agree that he did not exist except in his art) was so public as to be
the intimate of the universe, although this "man alone," being also the
artist, could not be an intimate of the universe, since the universe by
its nature ignores art. He was endowed with the knack I've cited
before (in connection with Boulanger, Jane Bowles, Frank O'Hara,
Sonia Orwell, Lenny Bernstein, and *no one else*) of making you feel,
when alone with him, that you were not only the sole person to
understand his work but that he was the sole person to understand
yours. The knack cannot be faked or bought. I don't have it.

What can I say then, outside the essays, of this too-famous paradox
whom everyone knows, and whom I alone know?

And what did I write in the letter of self-introduction to which I
appended, as was now a habit, a picture of myself, that it should evoke
so quick a response? "You must invent a way to see me," answered
the poet by return mail. "Miracles succeed better than formal appointments. I do have a phone number and an address . . ." which he indicated with arrows swirling toward the bottom of the plain sheet of
paper. I dialed the number, made a formal appointment, and showed
up at the address, 36 rue de Montpensier, at 11:30 a.m., on 6 October,
wearing the green sweater Mother had bought at Wanamaker's.

The succeeding two hours comprised the most time I would ever
spend alone with Jean Cocteau. My report of these hours in *The Paris
Diary,* written the same day, is accurate so far as literal fact is concerned, but exudes an unearned snippiness in keeping with the tack
of outsiders who thought they were insiders. It was stylish to mock
Cocteau as being a chic liar, since that was precisely what he termed
himself. Anyone who passes the line of permitted glory is due for bad
press, prefiguring immortality. I fell in with the vogue. His every gesture I put down as an affectation (e.g., that he remained standing for
the entire visit, while I sat; that he gesticulated upward with his thin
famous hands, letting the folds of his azure peignoir fall to the elbow;
or that he had opinions about America which, because they were
drawn from a different perspective than mine, were false), without

asking myself why I had come there in the first place. In reality, Cocteau was the soul of kindness. Why else squander his morning on a complete stranger? (I was to learn months later, through André Fraigneau, that Cocteau had found me serious and candid, but that when he heard I'd taken up with Marie-Laure he despaired of my future.)

My cachet rose in Saint-Germain, thanks to that sole brief time with the master. Julius asked if I'd send reproductions of François Jèze's pictures to Cocteau, which I did, and which were duly commented upon (unfavorably). Over the years I never spoke to him with other than intimidated respect, addressing him always as *vous* although he said *tu* to me as he did to everyone—even whole groups. Our letters were raunchier than our conversation, and more to the point.

No, we never slept together, which answers the first question Francis Steegmuller put to me when preparing his biography. Because Cocteau never publicly denied his homosexuality, it was assumed by post-Victorian heterosexual Americans that he was indiscriminately promiscuous. But to be outspoken does not mean to be outrageous. I don't know about his sex life beyond what others have hinted, and what his own drawings (though not his writings) imply. Nora Auric said that, as a parlor trick, Jean Cocteau used to lie naked on his back, and surrounded by a cheering section, with no manipulation, no friction of any kind, would achieve ejaculation through a penis which, in erection, curved not toward his navel, but toward the scrotum. Jacques de Pressac said that because Cocteau's many disintoxications from opium rendered him impotent, he played the passive partner to the ministrations of his heterosexual adopted son, Doudou Dermit. My instinct suggests that, like most flamboyant personalities, Cocteau was more interested in facts than acts, and that, like most hard workers who couldn't stop talking, Cocteau never shut up enough to indulge. He was even modest and mannerly about such matters, more so certainly than the Protestant Gide. As for Steegmuller, he was fascinated by a phrase in Cocteau's second letter to me: "Je ne crois guère aux hommes de petites verges" ("I don't believe in men with small members"), which he mistook to be an affirmation of Cocteau's life-long obsession with big cocks (unlike most people?). In fact, I had told Cocteau that Professor Kinsey, at the end of each interview, gave the subject a card to be filled out and returned, stating the dimensions of the subject's "member" in repose and in erection. Cocteau's full reply was "Kinsey must have quite a file, and I don't believe in men with small members," which I take to be metaphoric, like his admonition that a true work of an art will inspire in the viewer an erection of the spirit. (What about female viewers?) Cocteau was not a lecher. His interest in people, distributed equally between women and men, was more clinical than carnal.

Whatever I asked of him he granted. That he may have done as much for the next young fan who came to call—but were there that many, really?—does not lessen his value. I treasure the many drawings he dashed off to my prescription (he could only "dash off," could never mull, although, as he said, his "hand does not have wings every day"), from the first 1951 portrait of a boy at a keyboard to be used as a passe-partout music cover, to the last line drawing limned shortly before his death, representing my setting of Elizabeth Bishop's poem about Ezra Pound in the booby hatch.

Other than the little 1945 song, "De Don Juan," I have used his words only twice. For a 1955 oratorio, *The Poets' Requiem,* Paul Goodman translated a speech from *The Knights of the Round Table* ("Look Segramor, you know the language of the birds. . . ."), which I set for two male voices, chorus, and orchestra. And for a Cocteau memorial in 1990, I made a seven-minute opera for soprano and piano out of the early monologue he fashioned for Marianne Oswald, "Anna la bonne." I also in 1967 prepared a background score for Auden's translation of *The Knights of the Round Table* which Herbert Machiz directed in Southampton.

I type these words on the kitchen counter of an empty house in Pittsburg, Kansas, on 7 July 1993. Hot, flooding rains. Jim Holmes, my reason for existing during the past twenty-six years, and I have stopped here for several days. JH's parents, like my own so recently, have receded into a retirement village called Sunset Manor. The family property has been sold, but before new owners take charge next week, JH and his local siblings swab it from stem to stern. He wept, seeing the old home again, deserted now like "The Cherry Orchard," when we arrived yesterday. From the basement where he vacuums he plays Carissimi's sad cantata, *Jephte,* on the new portable CD machine. A fifteenth-century Italian chorus echoes through this midwestern house as I write about the Paris of a half century ago. I have never been in Kansas before. After Friday, when we drive on to Aspen, I'll never see Kansas again.

We gave another party, this time at Julius's. I am amazed, today when I see so few people and am uneasy in full rooms, how natural it seemed yesterday to summon enthusiasm for perpetual reunion. Jennie Tourel was in Paris and longed for fans. This we arranged in a trice. Nell Tangeman was in town too (she had arrived on the 9th and we immediately celebrated—but what were we celebrating?—with Robert Kanters) and curious to meet her more successful colleague. Mezzo-sopranos were prevalent then, but Jennie possessed the most disturbingly lustrous sheen on her nasal diction, and the most intelligent repertory. Was she forty-eight? Nell, far younger, was still a shadow, though with a no-less-special instrument. She would never become a star, if only because of her personal instability. (Singers are a breed apart in the world of executants. A pianist, a violinist, can theoretically perform convincingly with a strep throat or measles. Not so singers, whose every physical indiscretion shows in their delivery, which is why singers are such backslapping, self-pampering, uncomplicated bon vivants. They suppress an inquiring nature, lest that nature warp their artificial gift for communication.)

At the party Lukas Foss took over. Seated at Julius's Steinway, he accompanied his own convincing "composer's voice" in his own huge vehicle, *The Song of Songs,* which he had recently conducted in Israel with Jennie as soloist. As Lukas belted out the entire score Jennie mouthed the words semiaudibly. "Why doesn't she just sing it herself," whispered the jealous Nell, while I felt small in the light of all this virtuosity. Doda, for his part, deemed the piece "bloated," admiring it, but sensing not only my inability to write but to *want* to write such a fat piece. Lukas was not a French composer. One year later Nell and Jennie became congenial coworkers when they shared the stage of Venice's Teatro La Fenice in the world premiere of *The Rake's Progress.*

During these same six weeks I saw a good deal of Norris Embry and Bruce Phemister, of Alvin Ross and Homer Keller, of Gerald Cook and John Coleman and Todd Bollender and other Americans passing through. Of Americans in situ there were the pianists James Shomate (Souzay's accompanist) and Noël Lee, the latter being the only one of us to have stayed on to this day, and who has turned into a composer, one of haunting singularity. And always the tireless Elliott Stein.

Of the French, I saw regularly Doda Conrad. Doda took me to dine chez Pierre Bernac in the avenue la Motte-Piquet, same building as Souzay. Bernac's odor as Poulenc's chief interpreter, unlike his flamboyant English counterpart, Peter Pears, seemed permeated by a pathos stemming from maximum know-how couched in minimum métier, which is what made him the greatest vocal teacher, at least for French repertory, of our century. . . . Doda took me to dine chez Marcelle de Manziarley in the rue des Plantes. Manziarley's fragrance as France's chief female composer, unlike her perhaps drier American counterpart, Louise Talma, was replete with the astounding technique that all of Boulanger's flock acquired. They solfège with machine-gun accuracy, a training unrequired in even the most expensive American conservatories; the training may not result in better composers, but it does result in quicker ones. Marcelle had a no-nonsense directness, culled from Mademoiselle, which made her attractive. . . . Doda took me to dine chez Boulanger herself, to whom he had explained that alcoholism (his word, and hardly a French concept) was a vital ingredient of my singular gift, providing the guilt requisite to all creation. I didn't buy this notion any more than did Nadia. Nor did she ever bring it up during my visits when, after a critical and unpaid perusal of my latest Moroccan outpourings, she would grasp both my hands in hers, look weeping into my weeping eyes, and say: "Our poor perishable body is the sole vessel for a lasting gift, and must be tended with care" —making the sentiment sound like philosophy. . . . And Doda took me to dine in the underworld of Pigalle, the rough bars of Barbès, villages within villages ruled by an autonomous apache mafia. (I say "mafia" for lack of an apter term, since the Italian word is an acronym for "morte agli francesi.") I was too shy to rent a room in a hôtel-de-passes with any of the presumably loomingly available gangsters toward whom Doda nudged me.

But I did have four regular lovers that brief September: a raunchy *voyou* named Marcel G. (Norris called him Legs Diamond) who stimulated himself twixt the gray sheets by reading the new issue of *Cra-poullot* ever-so-daringly devoted to homosexuality. Maurice H., a Dutch student from the University of Leiden, handsome and clinging in the Germanic mold, perhaps too clinging and too handsome, for he bored me (when Julius played in Holland a month later I arranged for them to meet; they hit it off in the dressing room during the intermission of Julius's recital), but when I reread his letters now and look at his snapshot, like the snapshot of Marcel, I acknowledge the wasteful haste of childhood. Their very European smell is evoked this morning in Kansas, and the destructive squeeze of their caramel biceps. . . . Less pungent because more intellectual was the ongoing flirtation with José's Romanian, Richard, and of Doda's friend, André B., who, after our tryst in those same gray sheets, lent me (I never returned it) the wittiest pornography since Petronius: Apollinaire's *Les onze mille verges,* an insolent pastiche of the insolent Sade, and the most deliciously readable incentive for anyone studying French.

My only other reading seems to have been Gide's funny—really and truly ha-ha funny—*Les caves du Vatican.* But we went often to movies: *Noblesse oblige, Monsieur Verdoux, City Lights* (Chaplin was then what he remains—a humorless clod who can *épater le haut monde*), *Kismet,* and, perhaps most importantly, our friend Kenneth Anger's *Fireworks.* Made when the good-looking Kenneth was a mere seventeen, *Fireworks* is a prequel to Genet's *Un chant d'amour* in its California depiction of rough trade, a sailor, the crotch from which explodes a Roman candle, and the bemused adolescent exploring. (Kenneth makes one error, which is not an example of "Beauty Limps": for the soundtrack he superimposes Ernest Schelling's *A Victory Ball.* I am possibly the only creature on earth to know this music; my preestablished associations for it don't jibe with the filmed images which are accordingly weakened. Unlike Kubrick's use of an archfamiliar Strauss waltz to jolt us with its odd juxtaposition in *2001,* Anger's use of Schelling jolts only me. Still, one is too many.) Cocteau once brought a group of pals to the Cinématheque to view this young American's daring new movie. Unbeknown to the late-arriving Cocteau, Lily Law (as Elliott called the police) had confiscated the film, since even the French have moral standards, substituting a documentary on the brothels of Budapest.

Cocteau's own new film, *Orphée,* came out on the Champs-Elysées. I saw it just two days before I saw Cocteau himself and was bowled over. The film does weather badly, seems a touch dumb today, but fun, and better than the 1928 play on which it's based. The music of Auric passed for hip, but dates too, except for one inspired moment: when Death (portrayed by Maria Casares) turns on the radio, there issues forth a magical flute which happens to be a quote from Gluck's *Orphée aux Champs-Elysées.* Silly me, the only musician in France who didn't know this reference! When I exclaimed to Auric about his original score for *Orphée,* I added: "Especially your inspired moment when Death turns on the radio and we hear that magical flute."

What else? With José to the ballets *Parade, Les forains, Le boeuf sur le toit,* after which we went to Le Boeuf sur le Toit bar, on rue du Colisée.... Tea chez Herle Jervis, where Serge Koussevitzky, whom I'd never met before, said: "You must come to Tanglewood." When I said I'd been there, he answered, "Well, then you must be given a Fulbright." We never met again. But two months later, without having applied, I was offered out of the blue a Fulbright fellowship "for further study in Paris," which I accepted.

Visit to Henri Barraud of the French Radio, 36 avenue Friedland. Recital of my songs with Doda chez Heugel in the rue Vivienne. Afterward, mob meal, including the imperious Marya Freund, chez Lipp. ...9 October, the 10 a.m. flight on Air France from Orly arrives in Casablanca at 5 p.m. That night in Fez Guy and I went to see *César.* With us was Jean-Claude who, since Shirley had quit France, was at loose ends, and had wandered far afield.

. . .

Back in Fez I immediately set to work again. The calendar notes on 26 October, "finished slow movement, piano concerto." By 20 December the entire three-movement affair was complete (except for the orchestration, which would be accomplished at leisure over the next six months). This concentration is surprising, given my state of health. Attacks of piles were increasing and painful. Perhaps the concerto was an antidote, composed, so to speak, through my tears. Yet the piece is living proof that what one endures in mind and body is not necessarily relayed to the page. It makes happy sounds.

Piano Concerto No. 2 (so-called because, as with String Quartet No. 2, there is a No. 1 which, though disavowed, must be counted) is a twenty-five-minute dessert in three Lisztian layers entirely confected around the quirks and virtues of Julius Katchen's pianism. (For various reasons the work waited over three years before its premiere, with Julius as soloist, under conductor Jean Giardino and the Orchèstre de la Radiodiffusion Française in Paris, May 1954. Julius would still have held out for a more auspicious unveiling had I not wearied of waiting. So Julius said okay, on the condition that I arrange for him to practice chez Marie-Laure each night for a week, from midnight to 6 a.m., since he was forbidden by his neighbors to use the piano during these hours. The performance itself, of which I retain an old 78 rpm, was of clattering grandeur, fast as hell, not unlike the playing today of Pollini with every note, in sprays of perhaps twenty-nine to the second, of equal value and equal clarity. This took place in the radio studio with no audience except the other composer who shared the program, Heitor Villa-Lobos. What a warm, unassuming, and physically short creature he was, for someone whose music was so glacial, aspiring, and physically problematic!)

The early autumn in Africa was passed, when not working, on reading (Lautréamont, Jarry, Maurice Sachs); on seeing movies (*Stromboli, Vulcano, Sarabande, Le cas Parradine*) with Jean-Claude and Guy and Lévesque; on attending lectures (Norbert Dufourq's presentation of Bach, after which we gave him a reception; Maurice Fombeure's "La vie à Saint-Germain-des-Prés); attending plays (at the Lux, *Huis clos* with Marie Déa, co-billed with *La putain respectueuse* starring Ginette Leclerc); and on arranging for Julius's December recital. On 23 October I turned twenty-seven, and took to bed with the flu.

In early November Julius sent me a long letter so heartfelt and soul-searching that my perception of him began to shift from one of mere passing affection to one of rich empathy. (His widow has denied permission for the letter to be reprinted here. Well, it might have injected a welcome change of voice.) In essence Julius confessed to more frequently occurring periods of depression, which I had never suspected; and said that he was taking stock of his social life which had turned lopsided and vacuous, of his flourishing career which left him lonely beyond bearing, and of a gnawing urge to settle down—all this garnished with a masochistic thankfulness for my having both brightened and darkened certain hitherto unknown corners of his subconscious. Over the years I received dozens of other letters from Julius, all wearing his heart on his sleeve, some grandly objective with musical insights that only an interpreter could think up, a few snidely witty but with a guileless honesty, and none reread by me until now. My reactions then would have been of embarrassment, discomfort (on being thought of as a figure of domination), and a bored noblesse oblige. Today I feel honored to have been so singled out by that busy friend.

The war in Korea dragged on. Possibilities of its expansion into China weighed heavily. The African autumn, garish in the crimson clarity of its drinkable air, seemed nonetheless polluted as the Dakota air must have seemed to Mother thirty-two years before when her brother was slain at Belleau Wood.

Michel Royer spent a fortnight at his sewing machine concocting a scarlet woolen monk's robe, complete with hood, for me to don on the ever-cooler evenings. More movies, more quiet nights, more Arab concerts, more tours of the *bled.* On 15 November we lit the first fire in the grate. A touring company of the Comédie-Française brought *Phèdre* and *Le malade imaginaire* after which were parties where Arab boys from Robert Lévesque's class recited Baudelaire.... More concerts. More work. More movies....

Julien Green's novel *Moira* was just published. This story of a dullish American redheaded boy who kills the thing he loves, transpiring in the small-town ambiance of the United States but recounted in the language of Lautréamont, had a timbre new to literature. Lévesque urged me to write Julien Green, whom, like Maurice Sachs, he had known through Gide in the thirties, and to enclose one of those snapshots taken at Moulay Idriss of myself with tan legs in white shorts.

On the 28th Yvonne Loriod arrived for her recital in the concert series, and stayed with me and with Guy, whom she always referred to as Le Bon Pasteur. Yvonne is an extraordinary performing musician. Just my age, old-maidish in appearance, she had until recently specialized in two-piano recitals with her sister. They were intensely solemn to behold while hunched over the keys with their steel-rimmed spec-

tacles. (Sauguet dubbed them "Les Soeurs Lissac," because their publicity photos resembled an ad for Les Frères Lissac, the well-known
manufacturers of glasses.) Now she was the mistress of Olivier Messiaen, France's greatest living composer (after Poulenc), whom she
would marry when Messiaen's wife eventually died, and of whom she
was the principal interpreter. Her extraordinariness lay in her memory. For example, when Messiaen presented her with the just-finished
manuscript of *Vingt regards sur l'enfant Jésu* (which Paul Jacobs translated as "Give My Regards to Jesus"), a two-hour suite for solo piano
in twenty movements of ferocious difficulty, she did not go immediately to the piano. She took the music to bed, studied it all night away
from the keyboard. Next morning she played it by heart without a
hitch. Similarly, when Guy learned that Yvonne's program in Fez
would contain no Beethoven, he pleaded with her to eliminate the
Schumann sonata and substitute the huge *Hammerklavier.* He would
lend her the music. "I don't need the music," said Yvonne. "I never
travel with the music for my programs—it's all in my head." Indeed,
the following winter, in a single week, she performed all twenty-seven
of Mozart's concertos, Boulez conducting, neither ever referring to
the score. (Yvonne's sister was said to have a similar knack with language. Not knowing a word of English, she took *Hamlet* to bed one
night, and next morning recited the whole play by heart—with a thick
accent.) None of which would have been particularly interesting were
Yvonne not a sublime artist. Regardless of how she learned a piece,
the result was consummate. Today she remains the most persuasive
performer of her late husband's music—so sensual and pristine, so
opulently holy—as she slaps the ivories with authoritative accuracy
without, seemingly, to move a muscle of her torso.

On the night of her arrival we took her, with Lévesque, to Gabriel
Marcel's play, *L'homme de dieu.* Next night, her performance, during
which I could hardly sit still with my piles. When she went away to
continue her tour, she gave me Cocteau's *Maalesh,* the diary of a
touring theatrical group in North Africa.

Days passed. Guy spent a weekend in Marrakech, to where he
would soon be transferred permanently. "Clattering piles," I noted in
the calendar on 5 December. "A dust storm, gloomy and interminable.
Rain." On the 6th, Mother had her fifty-fourth birthday back in Philadelphia. Then on the 7th, at the little Lux theater, during a lecture by
one Yves Tarlet on French humor which I attended with Lévesque, I
was stricken with an attack of trembling. Next morning I was examined
by Dr. Fauque of the Hôpital Cocard who scheduled me for an operation on the 9th at 6 a.m.

Have you ever had surgery for hemorrhoids in Morocco? It was an experience from which I've yet to recover. "Count backwards slowly from one hundred, in English if you prefer," advised Dr. Fauque, the procedure for showing, through an increasingly slurred voice, how rapidly the anesthetic was taking effect. Apparently I reached "nine" before the cutting could begin. Hours later, I came to, as though swimming up to the surface of a dark lagoon. The face of a young dark-skinned orderly smiled down at me, but when I reached out to stroke his cheek, I shrieked. Nurses arrived, and finally Guy, to whom I moaned simply, "Je veux mourir," words which Guy, in his impotence, said were the most hopeless he'd ever heard. The wise cannot imagine stupidity, the rich cannot imagine poverty, and the well cannot imagine sickness, despite Docteur Knock's hilarious observation: "Les bien-portants sont les malades qui s'ignorent."

A white-hot poker was in my rectum, but unlike the poker for King Edward II, it did not blessedly kill me. I remained in the hospital eight days. Regular visits from Guy. And from Lévesque who brought books —appropriately *La nausée* and *La peste*—and who flirted shamelessly in sign language with the orderly, named Abdullah, who spoke no French. I had a room to myself; the nurses called me *grand-père,* for the duffer who had died there last week. After five days I was given an emetic and told to move my bowels. The toilet was elsewhere. Thus I left the room for the first time, and was astonished to see the floor lined with silent Arab men and women and children, waiting, waiting for appointments, gazing unsmiling as I moved through them in the scarlet monk's robe toward the commode at the end of the hall. I closed the door, seated myself elaborately, pushed down, and fainted.

On 17 December I quit the clinic to convalesce chez Guy, reading the Camus and Sartre *récits* ("recitation" is not quite the translation for this uniquely French form), Cocteau's *Maalesh,* and swallowing doses of liquid paraffin to soften the stool. Constant rain.

It's hard to know to what extent I dramatized. Even as one cannot relive certain mental pangs (love affairs, for example, when we endow foolish mortals with godly gifts and feel that life had no meaning beyond them), so physical pain, once gone, cannot be reimagined.

Three days before Christmas I remained abed when Guy rose early to meet Julius's 5:30 plane at Casablanca. Which one of them told me later that, on the way back to Fez, they turned off into a field and, as the saying goes, "had sex"? The idea disgusted me. How could the two people who in this world most professed to love me, behave thus on such short notice? Indeed, how could anyone on earth, knowing I existed, be interested in anyone else?

I do remember, quite objectively, the sensation of the first ejaculation, induced masturbatorially I think, after the hemorrhoidectomy: violent anal contractions inciting simultaneous horror and ecstasy.

Young Docteur François Rémy and his wife, Hélène, very pregnant, were, along with Julius, now staying with us. François would inherit Guy's job when Guy moved to Marrakech, and would also occupy the house thereafter. Hélène was already stacking her artifacts in corners, ready to pounce when we decamped. We would have felt like squatters were not the Rémys so affable, cultivated, and handsome: she, a painter, would eventually design a cover for my little opera, *A Childhood Miracle;* he, a specialist in yellow fever of which, along with Guy, he would rid the land. (The Rémys eventually divorced amicably, and Hélène moved to New York where she maintains a modest but solid career.) In this makeshift household I was the ailing child ministered to by two specialists with more important tasks on their mind, and by Julius and Hélène who practiced and painted all day long while I orchestrated sitting on a pillow.

Rain. We went to one movie, *Dieu a besoin des hommes,* with my nether regions diapered. Julius explored the médina with a blasé fascination ("I have, after all, been around the world") and read Wilde and Gide for the first time. On the calendar for 27 December I wrote: "Oh, will there be a war? ... Continual depression." On the 28th the one word *Cafard!* which means blues—literally "cockroach."

On the 29th Julius gave his recital whereon my piece, listed as *Sonate Nº2 (dédiée à Guy Ferrand), Composée à Fes en 1949—Ière audition au Maroc,* was nestled among Schumann, Chopin, Beethoven, and Mendelssohn. I mailed the program, plus the hospital bill, to Father. Next day we piled into the Buick, me, Guy, Julius, Lévesque, and a mournful Islamic poet named Azéma, plus the mangy dog Xénia, and drove to Marrakech.

On the first of the year we lunched, the five of us, in nearby Asmi. Snow all about, laced with sunlight, and peacocks strutting amongst the tables. Conversation was lively. These faces and sounds of vital friends, all of them long dead, are retained in my still-living brain. Is it sentimental to ask if their voices have wafted or sped into the cosmos where they still fadingly resound, along with the voices of Maurice Ravel, Augustus Caesar, Moses, the sirens of the Mediterranean five millenniums ago, and the wails of a baby dinosaur sixty million years before that?

In the evening Guy took Julius to the notorious sauna of Marrakech where Julius found his element. Indeed, he would return on his own to this city in future years solely to patronize the lusty Turkish bath. I had been there once, strictly for medicinal purposes, suspecting little about the sexual bonuses of such establishments, and was startled to behold Michel Royer being systematically sodomized in the humid shadows by a series of Arab workmen. Despite my own promiscuity, I held to the prudish notion that there's a time and place for everything, and was annoyed (more probably envious) that the French Catholic and American Jew had no scruples about dispassionate semipublic demonstrations with paragons to whom I, in their place, would have wished to whisper, if only for the moment, "I love you."

It was agreed that I would now return to France with Julius, thence to accompany him on a brief tour of Holland where he would play my music, then two weeks later to London. On the calendar for 3 January 1951 is noted: "Dîner à Casa with family of Serge [who was Serge?]. Arrive in Paris."

The sadness cast over these weeks was no doubt partly accountable to my weakened physical condition which beclouded an ability to face the already fearsome world situation. Yet sadness has always lurked—still lurks—no matter how cheerful the weather and healthy the body. Like everyone, I am the sum of my contrasts. If, as an artist, I am a radical to conservatives by being a gay atheistic alcoholic pacifist, and a conservative to radicals by being an aristocratic believer that tonality is the core of all art, as a social creature I am a combination of my mother who was illogical, instinctive, emotionally unstable, a pessimist who all through life petitioned for equal rights, and who would die, as we all do, of a broken heart—and of my father who was logical, intelligent, emotionally stable, an optimist, who would also die of a broken heart.

30. Remembering Green

NR (front) *with Robert de Saint-Jean* (left) *and Julien Green, Théâtre des Champs-Elysées, February 1951.*

In September of 1972 I penned the following reminiscence of Julien Green in my journal. It seems as remote now as Green seemed in 1972, yet I still live where I lived then (on West Seventieth Street), and Julien continues to thrive across the ocean.

At Rizzoli's while searching for quite another book my hand fell upon Julien Green's latest *Journal* (1966–72) which I bought on the spot. Spent the whole afternoon reading it. Or *re*reading. The emphases, identical to those of past volumes, could have been composed in 1926.

Those perpetual obsessions with sin and the true way, with prayer and dream, with shop talk (Jesus talk) among clerical friends! If in this *Journal* Julien Green continues, through his specific belief in God, to miss more general points at every corner, in his fiction this very "miss" provides the Julienesque tonality, the singular Greenery. Surely if one-track-mindedness empties the spirit of humor, it does fill the mind with an explosive physicality which remains the sine qua non of virtually all large souls. (Humor is not physical but intellectual, and multiple-track-minded.)

Green's is a stance which no resident American, even a learned Italo-American Catholic, can comprehend; there is no room for comprehension, only for blind belief ripened for this convert who feels himself a nineteenth-century poet mislaid as a prosifier in the twentieth. Famous French dramas like Gide's *Saül* or Sartre's *Le diable et le bon Dieu,* Green's own plays or Mauriac's novels are bizarre for us because we are not involved with redemption, much less with going to hell. Emancipated Frenchmen (the surrealists, for instance) always deny God, whereas for even the most retarded of American literati God is not there to be denied. (Should one of them convert, he usually leaves the States.) That God is the same to all is as demonstrable a fallacy as that music is a universal language.

(Sincerity versus artistry. If you can locate a copy, read the Cocteau-Maritain correspondence of circa 1924. The poet's grief at Radiguet's death renders him vulnerable to the theologian who "leads him back to the sacraments." Maritain sees squarely ahead, Cocteau's glance veers skyward; Maritain labors for his trust in the Lord; Cocteau takes trust on faith and garnishes it with gargoyles. For Maritain religion is salvation, for Cocteau it is subject of rhapsodies. Maritain may plod toward heaven, yet Cocteau now dancing in hell wins hands down, for his imagination erupts from within while Maritain's appears superimposed from without—a label stamped by the Red Cross. The church never "took" for the inspired Jean; not for a minute do we Believe his Belief, but we believe it, since it is poetry. Still, the myth is ingrown in the French who take it for granted and are less stifled by Christ than we by Freud. The Vatican for centuries supplied a nest for a poetry grander than our Baptists and Mormons could dream of.)

I do believe in the belief in God when expressed believably by plebeian practitioners or revolutionaries, or fantastically by saints and artists. So here I sit absorbing fatuities that occasionally, when they pass the buck to God, seem unfeeling. Reiteration of faith is suspect to infidels: it never seems to go beyond itself, but proves itself only through the self-hypnosis of that very reiteration, not through good acts. A believer is narrow, an artist is wide. Julien Green, being both, becomes a magnet between, attracting the unwary.

•   •   •

If I demurred nearly two years after coming abroad in 1949 before reading the famous writer, it was because he was somehow confused in my mind with Elliott Paul. Then during the fall of 1950, while I was convalescing from the primitive hemorrhoidectomy, Robert Lévesque brought me *Moïra*. What an experience! to meet my double in a trance. Narrated in the compact Gallic language, the subject matter treated of American disorder: sexual guilt of, and murder by, a horny inarticulate red-haired youth in a southern university. New World puritan frustration described via the mother tongue of Mallarmé. Green speaks American in French, the opposite of, say, Janet Flanner, who speaks French in American.

A note received in November 1950 told me in effect:

> Very few letters have ever pleased me quite as much as yours and I do not want to wait to thank you for it. It is so direct, so friendly and so sincere. I think that only an American could write such a letter and I am only sorry that you did not write it sooner, but you had not read my book. . . .
>
> Now I shall look forward to seeing you in January. You have my address. I am always at home in the morning and at meal times. If I like your music as much as your letter you will have to count me as one of your fans! Many thanks too for the picture which I like very much although I wish it had been larger. My greetings to Robert Lévesque. It was nice of him to remember me.

(He signed Julian when writing in English, but I continue to call him Julien *à la française.*)

(Am I sincere? Sincerity, as opposed to honesty, is a minor virtue, no more than meets the eye, black and white, a bit right wing. . . . He can only be disappointed. Or sad. The wounds of unrequited love lie less in the broken heart than in the fact that one's judgment is contradicted.)

On the third day of the new year 1951, rectal region still swathed in cotton like an imported peach, I flew from Casablanca to Amsterdam with Julius Katchen who was including my Second Piano Sonata on his Dutch tour and wanted me along to take bows. (Incidentally, my agenda notes a meeting with Klemperer, and two dates with Mengelberg to go over scores, on 6 January and again on 10 January. These dates were doubtless arranged by Julius, a powerful star then in Holland; but despite my well-known total recall, I have no recollection of these men.)

Reestablished in Paris on the 12th, I made the acquaintance, in the Bar Montana, of the actor Jean Leuvrais who would for a while become my closest friend in France. He was then playing his first lead role, opposite Mademoiselle Jany Holt, in Mauriac's *Le feu sur la terre* which I saw next evening, a Saturday. Sunday I moved to the Hôtel du Bon La Fontaine, then dined chez Marie-Blanche de Polignac for the first time. On Monday I met Julien Green.

It rained viciously (like a pissing cow, as the French say) during the beautiful ten-minute walk at noon from rue des Saints-Pères to the three-story house in rue de Varenne which Julien Green occupied with his sister Anne (whom I never met during many a subsequent visit) and the debonair Robert de Saint-Jean. I recall the rain specifically as a blight to my appearance. Eyes looked down on me already as I crossed the courtyard like a wet rat, so there was no time to comb my hair before the front door opened.

At fifty-one, the age of wild oats, Julien's social pattern still centered, as it had for decades, round individual visitors received two or three afternoons weekly, one-shot interviews with thesis-writers or adapters of novels, or tête-à-têtes with regulars like the Père Couturier so in vogue then—and in *Vogue*—as official shepherd to recalcitrant celebrities, a sort of upper-class Billy Graham.

We had Cinzano (Julien never drank), went to lunch on the upper floor of the Maintenon, boulevard Saint-Germain, finished a bottle of Bordeaux, returned to rue de Varenne where Julien watched me drink more Cinzano, switching then to Cointreau, all the time speaking of mutual literary infatuations, mostly of the Old Testament which he was pleased to know I knew. The rain stopped. With my last liqueur a shaft of sunshine like a finger of the Lord entered the library, whereupon my host asked if I would don a djellaba which he brought out, a vast velvet apparel with red stone ornaments and a hood. Berobed thus, glass in hand, I sat sainted in a circle of light, while Julien's voice from the shadows, serene and nervous, questioned me. The sunshine gradually faded.

Something happened.

At five he canceled an appointment with Jouvet (*Sud* was being considered by l'Athénée), and we left instead to hear a run-through of my sonata five blocks away chez Julius Katchen. More apéritifs, rue Cognacq-Jay, where Jean Leuvrais also came to meet me before going to his theater. Instant mistrust of Jean by Julien. ("I can size up the French bourgeois perhaps more easily than you." But a few seasons later Leuvrais was to star in Green's play *L'ombre*. By such ironies do shadows lighten our small world!) . . . Next morning a gift was delivered to the desk of the Hôtel du Bon La Fontaine—"par un monsieur de bien en tenue sombre." A plaster cast of Chopin's hand.

He sent me a little book, "the story of a shy boy," with the admonition: "Don't read it now. Wait until you have plenty of time," adding that he had been thinking about me. "Will you remember your promise to call me up? I love and admire your music. There are many things I want to tell you."

The little book was a new edition of his 1930 memoir, *L'autre sommeil*. I read it in the waiting room at Marignane before boarding a plane for Casablanca in April. En route, I translated three extracts, and during the following week in Marrakech composed a baritone cycle on this English prose, calling it *Another Sleep*.

That early spring of 1951 Julien showed me Paris through his eyes. For one who virtually never writes about food, he had a passion for little sandwiches and cakes, English style, and we visited the hundred teahouses of Paris, the libraries and gardens, zoos and byways of the third arrondissement. His handsome stoical eyes could ferret out madness through a sunlit pane, yet much of what he found naughty was so innocent! For example, at his local bookstore he bought me an under-the-counter *Fanny Hill*. The clerk said: "I'll put it down as *Jane Eyre*.". . . Vicarious, he enjoyed my accounts of drunkenness and orgies (exaggerated), hoping nevertheless that I read the Bible each night. Each night in fact I would meet Jean Leuvrais at the Théâtre Hébertot.

I meanwhile forced him occasionally into *my* Paris despite his contention that anyone seen with me was automatically compromised: a musicale at Marie-Blanche's, a lunch with Marie-Louise Bousquet on Île Saint-Louis, the recital of Julius Katchen (*Paris-Match* pictured me in my silver necktie seated between Julien and Robert de Saint-Jean like proud parents), or my shoddy hotel room where he now saw Chopin's hand, broken, upright against the mirror with a cigarette between two fingers. I remember an afternoon chez Henri-Louis de la Grange with Menotti and Julien as sole audience to a concert of my songs by Nell Tangeman. And on another Tuesday (20 February), shaken from seeing Gide lying in state. And yet again the next afternoon. Indeed, my agenda indicates a meeting every few days until 10 March, a Saturday, when my involvement with Marie-Laure began.

In April I spent my first fortnight at Marie-Laure's little castle, Saint-Bernard in Hyères, which became the scene of my most productive years. Julien, in Monaco to receive an honor from Rainier, drove over with Charles de Noailles to pass a weekend with us. But we did not then, nor ever again, resume the unset pattern of our first rainy day. A cooling off began. Which is when I returned to Morocco until September.

In June he thanked me for the translation of *Another Sleep*, adding:

"I think it might be easier to sing the words if a few changes were made; perhaps we can go over it together. Of course I am dying to hear the music, which, I am sure, is very pretty. Has it occurred to you that we might leave the words in French? It seems to me that, had I written the book in English, I would have said something else, totally different perhaps."

The set of songs, *Another Sleep,* has been performed only twice: by Bernard Lefort in Salle Gaveau in 1954, and by Donald Gramm in Town Hall in 1956. The music is perhaps too "sensitive," but I remain fond of it. However, my translations are not good, nor are they really Green, nor yet me. The effect is bastardly. Still, I'd have liked to publish the cycle if I had received permission to use the words. What words? Correspondence about them was resolved by silence, and my hunch is that Julien did not want to be identified with the texts of my songs.

As to his suggestion that "we might leave the words in French," I can only reply that in French I would have composed "something else, totally different perhaps."

(In an essay, "The Poetry of Music," I have discussed the problem of multilingual composers. Frustration awaits the American impelled to write songs in French, for those songs will seldom be heard. The rare French recitalist who programs an American song will make an effort to learn one in English. Meanwhile, American singers find it more "legitimate" for their French group to be by Frenchmen. I am not the first to suffer from this irony. Yet the suffering is mild. Since few vocal concerts are given in any language by anyone anywhere anymore, little loss comes from indulging the unsalable challenges this precious medium provides. So I continue to write to whatever texts appeal to me.)

On the bus he sits across from a young redhead ("hair the same gold as the edge of his Bible"). When the boy gets off, he follows. When the boy walks faster, he likewise. When the boy finally stops in a doorway, he asks: Why do you let strangers chase you?

Cemeteries, which Julien finds unbearable, are for me always cheerfully tranquil. I feel protected, not by the past but by the casualness of the present. No effort is made there, not even by the gardener mowing the lawns, the gardener more beautiful than his roses. I, who so fear death, find nothing fatal about those lawns, just peace, while Julien quotes Maeterlinck: The dead would not exist if it weren't for cemeteries.

· · ·

He is concerned and cultured. Strangers who write him usually seem concerned and cultured. Strangers who write me are madmen. Disconcerting: the possibility that not opposites but similarities attract.

No denying that his oeuvre spills forth with obsessional folly, yet those who write to him identify with *him,* not with his characters, and he, though melancholy and visionary and godly, is not crazy.

I wrote him from Marrakech and in February 1952 he answered. "Your letter touched me almost as much as it surprised me. Not for one minute did I ever suspect you cared for me as you seem to now. Perhaps I lack intuition, but never mind: what remains in my mind is what you wrote and you may be sure that I will always think of you."

I have not seen Julien Green since the mid-1950s. Between then and the mid-1960s I've had four or five letters, all of them replies to professional inquiries. Occasionally when in Paris I telephone and he says he'll call back and doesn't, or a female voice explains that he is away. Meanwhile I keep in touch through his novels, his autobiography, and through his journals telling me about deaths, ever more frequent, of old friends or forgotten acquaintances. Among those pages my name remains invisible as by a determination to efface an identity that was ever conjoined to his own.

I had committed the unforgivable by nourishing his predecision of who and what I was, knowing the predecision to be untrue. For I was not always kind—though was the nourishment in fact so unkind? Yet even without nourishment, any predecision must become untrue, since the actual behavior of others cannot coincide with our fantasy about that behavior.

There's a distinction between the impression we think we give and the impression we do give, and neither relates necessarily to what we are. Julien writes continually of himself without revealing himself. The impression he would give, in words written and spoken, is of a magnanimity which strikes outsiders as old-maidish. If most people's character is revealed through their eyes, Julien's is revealed through his mouth which is thin, intelligent, withholding, and sly.

At the MacDowell Colony I once composed a brief piece for strings, *Pilgrims,* on a notion which had long been floating in my brain: an impression that through music the strangeness of Julien's first book, *Le voyageur sur la terre,* could be transmitted without words. The piece was later published with a cover of pale green on which, in deep green, the title, an epigraph, and appropriate credits are printed.

For his seventieth birthday in 1970 I mailed a copy of this music to Julien Green. But he never answered.

Though Green may be the most unusual author of our day, I've shown here not my reaction to his value, only his to mine, and none too well. I've not "seen" him but strived to show that he saw me. To acknowledge this in no way exonerates me, although the present sentence is a plea for indulgence.

Every artist, to be identified as such, does his unique number. Julien's number is honesty—an unflagging refusal to compromise. Now, every artist is honest, whether he tries or no, and for some the very act of compromise is artistry. (Julien might contend that compromise never tempted him, so why talk of "refusal"?)

My number is faking the shallow. But admitting to superficiality doesn't render one less superficial, only more self-serving. Can I prove I'm a fake? The admission, however, is far from my music, for there I'm too lazy for whoredom or gluttony; I compose only what I want to compose.

A fan letter today compliments me on my "Memoirs." Between diaries and memoirs lies the difference of years, the difference between now and then. I am incapable of the memoir as genre, as these diary pages on Julien Green precisely prove. Waste of retrospect. A retrogression. Failure. (Yet might not the seconds between these parentheses and that failure already place the failure in the past?)

31. 1951: The First Three Months

NR by Henri Cartier-Bresson, 4 February 1951.

That ambiguous nightmare, which rose and fell every few months since preadolescence, began to recur more frequently in 1951. The décor was the same—inert existence centered among gigantic enigmatic shapes revolving like sodden clouds—but the aftereffect was now more aural than tactile. Even as Messiaen's music contains no counterpoint properly speaking, unless it be mass against mass as distinct from line against line, so the nightmare imposed ponderous meaningless sounds which rolled deeply toward and away from me, in abstract sarcasm, without any actual contact. Depression on awakening.

Yet was there—*is* there (for the bad dream returns still, perhaps once a year)—an awakening, if what Pascal suggests is creditable: that our dreaming state is really our true life, from which we emerge into another sleep where we think we're awake? My sessions with Dr. Kraft had taught me, if nothing else, that Freud's interpretation of dreams was simply Freud's fantasy. Dreams are dreams, with their own integrity, not symbols designed to keep us asleep. Like music, whose sense and strength and very reason-for-being can never be explained by mere intelligence, the meaning of dreams forever evades us, not because that meaning is too vague for words but because it is too precise for words.

Which leaves one with the conundrum of the two opposing dream states, the waking and the sleeping that become finally interchangeable and from which we can never escape but are tossed continually between one and the other, until we enter a third state which, I suppose, is Death. Death just may be a new awareness; more likely there is no "life after death," which will infuriate those who think otherwise, after they kick the bucket.

These notions persisted until I reached menopause. If hangovers italicized morbidity, country air relieved it; and certainly while I was working—which was most of the time—I was neither down nor up, but out. Socially, though, the narcissism of gloom remained until my mid-forties when I threw in the sponge of self-indulgence and, not uncoincidentally, stopped drinking utterly, to become a good boy. Anyone can destroy himself, but only I can write my music.

We returned, Julius and I, from a cheerfully fructuous week in Amsterdam and the Hague on 11 January, and the rest of the month was passed in Paris. After a few nights at the sinister Hôtel Saint-Yves, I removed to the Hôtel du Bon La Fontaine, at 66 rue des Saints-Pères right next to José's, which would be home for the next many months. Room 14, directly above the entrance, looked across the street to a low building whereon shined a plaque commemorating Rémy de Gourmont. The premises were managed by Madame Morel, latterly of the Hôtel de l'Université now requisitioned by the American army. An overweight imperious peasant, Madame Morel had a clarinet-playing son with glasses and broad hands who tended the front desk from midnight to 8 a.m., and who witnessed my comings and goings with a benevolent eye. Room 14 could have been duplicated in any European hotel of the period: big brass bed, a table and chair, portable bidet, floor-to-ceiling windows protected outside by a lattice and inside by dusty drapes the drab hue of ox-blood. A blocked-off grate surmounted by a faux-marble mantle beneath a huge gold-framed mirror. Used rug, hall phone, hall toilet, no bath, in short, a student pad with little space to turn about, the corners being heaped with empty brandy

bottles. And with books too: Genet's *Quérelle de Brest* illustrated by
Cocteau. Cocteau's *Les parents terribles,* the movie version of which
was now revived. *Miss Lady Lou,* the French text for Mae West's *She
Done Him Wrong. Le grand Meaulnes* by Alain Fournier (donated
earnestly by Jean-Pierre Marty), and the novels of Giraudoux (donated
ecstatically by Yves Salgues), neither author of whom I ever quite got
the point, destined as they were for those of uniquely Gallic childhoods (Ravel had pondered making an opera of the Fournier), Cocteau's little mauve volume called *Théâtre de poche* (donated lovingly
by Jean Leuvrais) containing a series of monologues for Arletty, Piaf,
etc., all of which I memorized, and one of which, "Anna la bonne,"
designed for the Alsatian diseuse Marianne Oswald (whose spooky
recording of it Paul Bowles had played for me at 4 a.m. in 1943), I
would set to music in 1989. (Marianne Oswald, incidentally, was a
noonday regular at the Ministères restaurant, rue du Bac, where she
sat always alone, and where Kenneth Anger and I one day approached
her to star in a segment of the film he planned, with my music, on the
Chants de Maldoror. She agreed. Kenneth wrote the script, but back-
ing was never forthcoming.) All of these books, like the brandy bottles,
were procured for a song. There were then—there remain today—at
least one first-rate bookstore and liquor store on every block in Paris.

In this room of the Hôtel du Bon La Fontaine I began and solidified
a French life among the French, as distinct from a French life among
Americans.

In this room Jean Leuvrais spent nearly every night for months. We
had met late on 11 January in the Montana bar, where I for once was
sober, he high, and hit it off. Jean Leuvrais, who, one year earlier, had
graduated with honors as an actor from the Conservatoire, already
had the lead in François Mauriac's problematic and semireligious new
play *Le feu sur la terre,* which was something of a success at the
Théâtre Hébertot where Jean appeared nightly, twice on Sundays.
Rumor had it that Mauriac himself—an immense force in French intelligentsia with his well-plotted but painfully straitlaced novels, his daily
column called "Bloc Notes" (a sort of diary on Catholic matters
wherein he expressed dismay at the moral woes of his country and
conducted friendly feuds with his literary equals), and his son Claude
who also had a daily column, as movie critic, and who was vaguely
homophobic, albeit married to Proust's grand-niece, but who later
recanted when Cocteau died—was, at nearly seventy, in love with
Jean Leuvrais, a rumor that Jean pooh-poohed, though proudly. Jean
resembled a bourgeois boxer, broken nose, brutal hands, slightly
bowed legs. Like all unmarried sons in France he lived at home,
though independently, with his parents and his sister Colette, the

latter a perhaps Sapphic lass with a sweet soprano voice who studied with Noémie Perugia. Though as of now, since he spent the nights with me, he returned home in the late mornings to change clothes. I saw the play, found it didactic, and Jean a stiff interpreter. He was too intelligent to be a good actor, but knew his country's theater (and furniture and cooking and history and dress design and music) with the obsessive accuracy of an historian. If I have been married eleven times but never divorced, Jean must count as the fourth, though there was never the anguish or elation, much less the longevity, of his predecessors and replacements. He later told me, when I was involved with Number Six—or was it Seven?—that I was what he decided I was, his marionette, and that whatever my maneuver this was his choreography, I was locked in forever. . . . He came every night, after the show, to Saint-Germain-des-Prés where we would rendezvous in one of the cafés ("Je ne sais jamais dans quel état je vais te trouver," he once allowed without too much worry), finding me usually with a gang of friends. On Sundays I always went to Marie-Blanche de Polignac's who regularly arranged for tryouts of my works-in-progress. (On 21 January I showed up uninvited with Julien Green, to whom everyone was obsequious—he hadn't been seen in *le monde* for years.) Jean would meet me after these events, and we would, eventually, go back to the hotel.

In this room Henri Cartier-Bresson took his picture of me. I had been frequenting the "Thursdays" of Marie-Louise Bousquet, the French representative of *Harper's Bazaar,* who received weekly in her cramped sunny flat overlooking the place du Palais-Bourbon, and served diluted daiquiris to dozens of eminent visitors, mostly foreigners. On my first Thursday, on the arm of José who was launching me, Madame Bousquet took the bait. Unlike the English, who seldom introduce guests at parties, and never divulge the guest's profession for fear of invading their privacy, the French explain the raison d'être of everyone to everyone to put everyone at ease. Thus José to Madame Bousquet: "I bring you Ned Rorem, America's greatest young composer." Madame Bousquet, squat and stunted like an affable witch (or, in her own words, "like a vile old Semite"), had a canny flair along with her broad cultivation, as was the case back then with trendsetters in the French fashion world. She sized me up and answered: "*Justement,* we're planning an issue on 'Young Artists in Paris.' Would you," she squinted at me, "like to have your picture taken?"

I had never heard of Cartier-Bresson, but José assured me he was "Somebody."

When the great photographer phoned, a day or two later, we made a date for 4 February, the afternoon I would be returning from London. I was again in my green sweater—the one worn to Cocteau's—when he showed up at the dreary room with an American assistant, one Gail Vincent, and immediately set to rearranging the furniture, climbing onto the mantle and aiming his cameras down at me in trial poses, while Miss Vincent played with cords and sockets and promptly blew a fuse. Madame Morel and her clarinet-playing son accepted the inconvenience with comparative good humor (their hotel was to be immortalized) as they tended to the fuse box in the basement. Minutes later the hotel was again plunged in darkness. Madame Morel, irate now, would have evicted us all had not Cartier-Bresson, resorting to the *politesse* with which aristocrats calm their minions, offered her cash (duly accepted) for this dire incursion.

I never saw Cartier-Bresson again. But the portrait appeared, alongside portraits of Marcel Aymé, Roger Nimier, and Danielle Délorme, in the "Young Artists in Paris" issue of *Harper's Bazaar,* where I could not recognize myself. My traits look more generous, remote, gaunt, intelligent, and serious than I imagine myself. Exceptionally, I am not gazing into the lens—that is, at my alter ego—but focusing toward the floor. It grows clear that we are only what the photographer perceives; were there four photographers in that room, there would be four Neds. We cannot exist except in the eyes of others; sometimes those eyes freeze us for a time into an image on a page; we come to construe that image as us. Cartier-Bresson's image of Ned has been often reprinted. But that image was Ned for just a split second. Not even a split second, for even then Ned was his. And his, to be quickly forgotten.

The preceding week I took the Golden Arrow to London (first time since 1936) and settled with Julius Katchen at the Hyde Park Hotel whose nearby lanes gleamed thick with the still-classical waves of fog between which tuppeny-uprights materialized, uttered a seductive phrase, then vanished. Of this five-day sojourn I noted: Visit with Stephen Spender in the Saville Club at 69 Brook Street. Visit with old acquaintance, John Edmunds, the sole American composer—now, alas, unremembered—who cared about the fact of American Song. Visit with conductor Richard Austin, and with composer Lennox Berkeley (on the same page I noted *crabs!,* which were then as ubiquitous as bedbugs). Bar tour with someone called Angus. Reading: *Paul et Virginie*. These episodes are now lost in a London fog. Two others remain.

I took Julius to meet Sonia Orwell. She in turn brought along Lucian

Freud, and we convened in some expensive pub, later dined *à quatre* at some expensive restaurant suggested by our British friends, where Julius grudgingly footed the bill—he was, after all, the rich American. We were ill-assorted. Sonia and I liked to drink, Julius did not. Drinkers quickly inhabit a dimension that excludes abstainers. Lucian Freud, solemn, smart, and fetching of his person (was he queer? could one ever tell with the English?), cared no more about music than did Sonia, and neither seemed much taken with Julius who went off to practice at Steinway's factory, leaving the rest of us to drink until closing time, which was 11 p.m. Lucian, grandson of Sigmund Freud, seemed determined to impose his own identity. This he accomplished, over the years, with his meticulous pointilliste visual essays, mostly of other human beings, no less influenced by Francis Bacon than Bacon by him. Lucian interested me because of his unironic devotion to Marie-Laure de Noailles, whom—on learning I lived in Paris—he incorrectly assumed I knew. I assumed, meanwhile, that Marie-Laure, if she harbored this somber, thoughtful boy, might not be all froth. A year later, when I was living with Marie-Laure in the place des Etats-Unis, Lucian brought his fiancée for lunch. Lady Caroline Blackwood was heart-stoppingly beautiful, but vague. There she sat, in Marie-Laure's octagonal drawing room, on the edge of a sofa, legs crossed, one knee supporting an elbow extending into a smoking hand which flicked ash abstractedly onto the blue Persian rug. Caroline, very blond, with eyes the hue of the Persian rug and large as eagle eggs, uttered nary a word, neither approved nor disapproved, just smoked. Marie-Laure was leery of her, as of all attractive females. After Caroline divorced Lucian, she incongruously married the American composer Israel Citkowitz, with whom she lived on New York's Twelfth Street, across the way from me. From my second-story window I occasionally spotted her down there, still attractive and hazy in blue jeans, bargaining with the butcher. When Israel died, she married the poet Robert Lowell. She was—she remains—a savagely original novelist.

The other episode regards Stephen Spender, toward whom I had come to feel warmly. Since Julius was to give his recital on Saturday at three o'clock, since Stephen's wife, Natasha, was a pianist herself, and since neither of them had met Julius, why, Stephen wondered, couldn't we come to their house in Saint John's Wood for lunch at 12:30?

Natasha turned out to be an eager amateur. She had just mastered Sam Barber's big new sonata which she immediately played for us with tarnished splendor. The piece impressed me more than any other work of Sam's; its very scope (the sonata had been composed for

Horowitz who had premiered it in New York) was blinding, and made me apprehensive about my own more modest sonata which the Spenders would be hearing in a few hours. At lunch we chatted about Sam, who was their closest American musical friend, and about Chuck Turner, who had recently written a Barberesque orchestral poem, *Encounter,* so-named after Stephen's literary magazine, a magazine Spender would soon repudiate on learning it was subsidized by the CIA. Then we piled into a cab and made off for Wigmore Hall. After Julius's concert, at which his performance of my piece was, as usual, dazzling, the Spenders bade me a brusque good-bye—no other comment—and left.

Was their dismissal of my piece for its style or for its content? Not style, surely, since they were so pro-Barber who was more conservative than me. It must have been content. Stephen was never again congenial with me (yes, he was, at a Northwestern University picnic in 1966, but that was a nonmusical affair). Soon after, he pronounced Elliott Carter as America's only important composer (this, apropos of Elliott's admittedly powerful First String Quartet, performed in 1954 at Rome's CIA-sponsored festival of "Music of the Twentieth-Century"), and cooled off on Barber too.

Over the years I've kept track of Stephen mostly through his journal, from which extracts appear periodically here and there. In the mid-seventies I noted in my own journal that *his,* while holding the attention, made me dimly uneasy with its unflagging highmindedness. Is this because I feel that as he plows through life he surely must have fancies beyond (or beside) those of Grand Art and the need to be useful, or because my own diary seems so *déclassé*—so unnecessary —by comparison?

In his reflections on Venice, for instance, he observes what I never observe, finds continual connections between then and now, both personal and general, and has the discipline of history as voucher for opinions. Still it's a poet talking, and though one can't begrudge his urge for immortal utterance (since it takes one to know one, I spot his diarist's tricks in a trice—avoidance of dropping names by arranging to have his own name dropped, here by Peggy Guggenheim, there by total strangers in Harry's Bar), he's sometimes prosaically wrong. He hears like an author just as I see like a musician, but he commits the layman's fatal error of comparing the arts. Example: In an interestingly careless paragraph about Venetian painters he contends that "both allegorists and symbolists use visual imagery or symbolism as poets use them. . . . When Shelley saw eyes instead of nipples in his wife's breasts, he was merely projecting upon the external world the way in which images were juxtaposed in his poetry. A picture of breasts with nipples as eyes would seem surrealist, but not a line in poetry such as 'Thy paps are like eyes in thy breasts.' This use of associations springing from the unconscious is conventionally poetic. It is only when it is applied to painting that it seems surrealist." Let's overlook that what Spender says of Shelley ("saw eyes instead of nipples") and what Shelley may have actually said ("Thy paps are like eyes") is to confuse metaphor with simile. What Spender forgets is that language is itself symbolic, painting is not, which is why painting, like music, is not "translated." The word "bird" symbolizes (is a metaphor for) a bird. The painting of a bird signifies (is a representation of) a bird—or *ucello, oiseau, pájaro, Vogel*—and to a Chinese or Pole is a bird, whatever they name it. And however "abstracted," a bird is a bird is a *Vogel*. For painting is never metaphor. Since language is always metaphor, literary surrealism is always less startling than to the eye.

And music? Is music symbolic? Symbolic of what?

Reading further in Spender's diary, again the easy laugh. He may well lament the ornery ignorance of his Florida undergraduates, but when he notes that "the only modern poets they seem to have heard of are Bob Dylan and Rod McKuen (if I spell his name correctly)...," the parentheses, like a pair of tongs, distance Spender in our eyes from what he finds offensive. He does, in fact, spell McKuen's name correctly, and knows it, yet feigns the same indifference which is real in the students, and which he reproaches them for. How little we learn from the great unwashed, and how even less from our peers.

A day or two before London, José gave a lunch for just me and the Aurics. I hadn't seen Georges since that night in the Reine Blanche twenty months before when I hummed for him his various movie scores. Here he was again, the same homely, overweight, sexless, funny genius, as well versed (monolingually) in our world's books and pictures and politics as in music. Nora I had never met—though she was often pictured in the society pages—and was struck now by her delicately willful features. She was of that rare and lucky breed who, as they grow older, grow better-looking. On her prematurely white hair coiffed à la Jeanne d'Arc she wore a powder-blue satin pillbox like Eva Gauthier's. Her face, hard and clever, had a structure that could never deteriorate: high cheekbones, ivory brow, thin red mouth, sleek chic skin. In Dior clothes her body looked sensational, nude it looked its age, around forty-eight (as I would witness soon on the beaches of Hyères), fleshy, not stately.

Nora, of Russian-Jewish parentage, had married Georges in the late

1920s, and who knows what intimate rapports transpired between this stern beauty and that comic buddha. Perhaps none. No one ever knew much about Georges's sex life, while Nora from the start had lovers. Since long before I knew them, they had lived *à trois* with a younger Franco-American good-looking, amiable, dipsomaniacal fool, Guy de Lesseps, grandson of the Suez Canal builder. Now nominal chauffeur of the Aurics, Lesseps had a small room down the hall from the low-ceilinged fourth-floor apartment of his master and mistress in the place Beauvau. Georges called him always Monsieur de Lesseps, Nora did not go out with him in public; in public she and Georges were exemplary, worldly, knew everyone, treated Lesseps like hired help, though Nora shared his bed each night.

Nora Auric was a skilled painter of minor talent whose subjects were submarine fauna and human portraiture on small canvases. She referred to these canvases, mostly in pastel oils, as "songs." These "songs" were small potatoes, according to her, in the shade of her husband's masterpieces, for she was a good wife, faithful for all practical purposes, and protective of Georges's time and gifts and reputation.

Did Georges compose masterpieces? By 1945 he had become and would remain the premier composer of movie music in both France and England, having scored all the films of Cocteau, of René Clair, of Clouzot, and of classier Korda productions across the channel. Like each member of The Six he had in the 1920s composed ballets for Diaghilev, in the thirties for Lifar, and in the forties for Cuevas. But masterpieces? As the most intellectual member of The Six (he was breathtakingly well-read—when you and I were out carousing he was home with a book or a score and a bottle of whisky), he was also the most artistically repressed. His nearest friend in the art world was Poulenc whom—though they were exact contemporaries—he treated like a pupil. Every work of Poulenc, from his adolescence unto the present, was submitted to Georges's scrutiny. For if Georges had less natural a gift, he was more stylish a grammarian with a finer ear for shape than his more extroverted protégé. Did you know, for example, that the first version of Poulenc's 1919 cycle, *Le bestiare,* comprised twelve songs? Georges it was who whittled them down to six, corrected their awkward spelling, and switched their order. The cycle as it stands, less than ten minutes long, is, thanks to Auric's editorial hand, a chain of unflawed jewels as indispensable as any of Schubert's more bloated suites. But Auric himself could not have composed it. His own songs, though skilled, fell flat, with neither blood nor breath. Brains stifle instinct.

The Aurics as a couple were a witty contrast with enough power and charm to be accepted anywhere, creative bourgeois at ease in the post-Proustian milieu of crumbling nobility. Madame Verdurin herself was no less palpably opportunistic than the Aurics, about whom Marie-Laure once quoted Cocteau, "Ils ont l'âme chaussée par Raoul" ("their soul's decked out in second-rate goods"), which I never quite believed. Marie-Laure was always envious of Nora's lovelier face; and Cocteau was never unkind, whatever else he may have been.

Whatever the Aurics may have been, I was flattered to exist for them. So when Nora asked me to phone on my return from England, I felt glad.

During the seven weeks after the return from England I started and finished a ballet called *Mélos*. Since there was no piano at the hotel, Julius arranged for me to use the piano of his friend Michel Girard, a middle-aged art-loving businessman who owned a sumptuous *rez-de-chaussée* apartment with eighteen-foot-high ceilings and bottle-green sheer-velvet curtains, at 56 rue de Varenne, next door to Julien Green whom he used to know well but, astoundingly, had not seen for twenty years. Michel had already heard of me from Leda Fournier who said: "Ned is so insufferably pretty, you want to throw cyanide in his face."

Mélos was composed for a competition sponsored by Biarritz. Contestants were supplied with a scenario, commissioned from Marie-Laure de Noailles, who would also provide sets and costumes, and whose name presumably lent prestige. Her scenario would have been apt for any French ballet of a century earlier: Young Man wanders onto stage, communes with his Spirit, meets with figures of Architecture, of Science, of Drama, struggles individually with other Muses, ultimately settles for Music, represented by a soprano (Denise Duval in the ultimate production) who intones a parody of the aria from *Mignon*:

Connais-tu le pays
où fleurit l'adagio...?

as the assembly exits in a parade honoring the Seven Arts. All the composers in Paris—that is, Nadia's entire class, plus a few pupils from other professions—were busy writing their own *Mélos*. The winner would have his or her ballet mounted by the Cuevas Company in Biarritz that fall, while the two runners-up would receive a bit of cash. With hindsight the requirements seem excessive: when dozens of competitors compose and orchestrate a big ballet, what will the losers do with their leftover music, music which in principle is good for just one occasion?

I didn't, of course, know it yet, but Leo Préger, Nadia Boulanger's favorite protégé, would get first prize—and a production—while I got second. (Another Boulanger pet called Spivak won third.) By this time I was close to Marie-Laure, who was furious at the "mistrial of justice" which she credited to Boulanger's finagling, and refused for my sake to go to Biarritz. Still, we all got our pictures in *Paris-Match,* and I recycled my leftover music in other pieces. To be fair, Préger's work was better than mine.

I phoned the Aurics and during February visited them almost daily. Because Nora had decided to paint my portrait.

Isn't it funny how, when certain of our childhood pals grow up to be famous, we are proud and admiring, yet never quite take them seriously! They are, after all, just like us. (The richest man in the world may own a thousand living rooms, though he can't live in them all at the same time. The movie star may have her image exploded simultaneously on a thousand screens, while we know she's home brooding.)

But when we come to meet people whose glory precedes them, especially when they are of an earlier generation, we are intimidated. Indeed, these people are intimidated by each other, unless they grew up together. Even then, once we come really to know the gods, they all have feet of clay.

It seemed for the moment eerie that the mediocre student from Chicago's U-High should be exchanging anecdotes with these denizens of another place and time. Every morning I would show up at the Aurics', garbed in a black turtleneck and red scarf, and strike a pose in Nora's studio while Georges would orchestrate in the next room. Sometimes the three of us would carry on a yelling conversation, either on current gossip generated by Nora who was entertaining without intelligence, or on the state of music generated by Georges who was curious about the doings across the Atlantic where he had not yet been. Other times, if Nora were silent, biting her lip and squinting toward me while holding up a brush like a measuring rod, I might read aloud from a just-received book, cutting the pages as I turned them—from, for instance, Cocteau's illustrated memoir of Jean Marais. One of the Aurics might interject with a "Comme c'est vrai," or a "Yes, indeed, Jeannot [as Marais was called by those in the know] would become Jean's first healthy influence. Jeannot loathed Jean's use of drugs and alcohol, believed in Jean's immensity, and was forever apologetic about his own predominating fame in the cinema, for since he had no talent, he owed everything to Jean." Etcetera.

Still other times visitors stopped by to watch and chat as Nora and I maintained our stances, then stay for lunch. There came particularly

Georgette Chadourne, a blond photographer, who accordingly took some dramatic pictures of me. And André Dubois, the prefect of police in Metz who during the war, in conjunction with Gide, had effected the evacuation of hundreds of French Jews from the north into the Midi and beyond. Dubois was a seductive presence. Around fifty years old, he lived with his friend Lucien Sablé and their adopted son, Claude Romain, an actor (he played a featured role in Grémillon's *Pattes blanches)* whose feline eyes and stark crew cut were those of a Dostoyevski criminal, and with whom I had a brief, dispassionate liaison. Dubois would go on to direct the liberation of Morocco in 1956, making of that country an independent *département* rather than a colony of France. Ultimately as prefect of police in Paris, and thus a public figure as well as a member of the aristocratic *gratin,* he not only banned car-honking, he facilitated my *carte d'identité* so I wouldn't need to cross borders every three months to have my passport stamped. Dubois became known as The Prefect of Silence. He was in fact, though voluble, a font of taste and originality. So when he unaccountably married vulgar Carmen Tessier, the society columnist notorious as "The Gossip," Cocteau quipped: "Le Préfet du Silence épouse la Commère." In July of 1953 I composed a big song on a text of Marie-Laure, *Jack l'Eventreur,* for an extremely elastic voice, and dedicated it to André Dubois. He remained a comrade throughout my years abroad.

On 6 February, dined with Sam Barber and Chuck Turner, who were rooming luxuriantly chez Henri-Louis de la Grange, and we spoke about the Spenders. (Sam was bemused with the notion of Natasha playing his sonata.) It was at this time that Sam, prior to recording at his own expense a goodly chunk of his catalogue in Copenhagen, was practicing with Chuck his Violin Concerto. Pierre Boulez was the unlikely rehearsal pianist. Boulez sat there stonily when Sam, always the humorous atonalphobe, asked if the first four measures of Bizet's "Habañera" could qualify as a twelve-tone row.

On the 7th, dined with Gordon Sager. It was Gordon who complained: "The odds are against me: I'm Jewish, homosexual, alcoholic, and a Communist." To which Jane Bowles, extending her game leg, retorted: "I'm Jewish, homosexual, alcoholic, a Communist—*and I'm a cripple!"*

On the 8th, lunch with Chuck Turner. Tea with Julien Green. At seven o'clock, again with José, went to Marie-Louise Bousquet's "Thursday." Marie-Laure was there too, in royal blue wool, and sitting (everyone else was standing) on a sofa chain-smoking Gauloises. This was perhaps our third meeting, the only one at which we even slightly clicked. She appeared interested that I was at work on her scenario. That was that.

On the 9th, lunch with one Henri-Georges Tibaudin, 48 rue Lamarck, whom I had met a few evenings earlier at the Boeuf sur le Toit, an appealing roughneck, and the first mortal I had sex with (on his floor, after a cherry tart and coffee) since the hemorrhoidectomy.... Tea with Alfonso Ossorio at 4 rue Camille-Tahan, where he had now moved from MacDougal Alley. Dined at Michel Girard's.

On the 10th, lunch with José. At two o'clock, visit from Jean-Michel Damase, a composer who in succeeding years has been called my French counterpart, not least because we were both writing unapologetically delicious scores in defiance of Boulez's increasingly virulent Fascist takeover of France. At 4, pick up Cocteau drawing at framers. At 9:30, party chez H.-L. de la Grange.

On the 11th, a Sunday, Doda gave me a pair of shoes—heavy brown leather army stock—which I sorely needed. We then dined, rue Barbet-de-Jouy, at Marie-Blanche de Polignac's, with nine other guests. I thus within four days frequented Marie-Louise, Marie-Laure, and Marie-Blanche, known to upper-crust Paris as *Les trois Maries.* Always, after these sorties and minor infidelities, I would meet Jean Leuvrais around midnight at the Royale Saint-Germain, and recount my day, or as much as he needed to know. (During all those years in France the milieu I frequented, other than amours, was a generation older than I. Which is why today Paris represents not a college reunion but a graveyard.)

On the 12th, interview with *Match.*

On the 13th, lunch with Peter Watson, founder in London of *Horizon* magazine. In the evening, at the Théâtre des Champs-Elysées, Julius played the French premiere of my sonata, after which Nadia Boulanger reportedly said: "Quelle drôle de chose," and left. *Paris-Match* printed my picture, looking like a petulant brat, flanked by Green and Saint-Jean.

Following week, same pattern: visits to Nora for the portrait, visits to Michel Girard for work on the ballet, midday meals with Peter Watson, or Julius, or Doda, or José, and once a dinner at Nadia Boulanger's, another at the Azevedos'. The names of still other friends and vague lovers pepper the agenda, as does the frequent noun "cuite." For liquor seemed always an aim, a target, a climax, a dessert, a veritable *meaning;* its promise, its perspective, facilitated conversation, gave body to the soul of camaraderie, lent dimension to situations which, without it, would have seemed boring, if not intolerable, even gatherings in the homes of the justly celebrated.... There are visits to Henri et Isabelle Gouin, wealthy bourgeois melomanes who had well-planned soirées (Jacques Abram played there often, as did Leon Fleisher), and several dates with, simply, "the German," or sometimes "le boche" whom I seemed to have met at the Montana.

On the 20th Gide died. Julien gave me the news late in the afternoon, although thousands of mourners had already passed through the master's house in the rue Vaneau where he lay in state. Among these mourners, according to Julien as well as to next morning's paper, were Marie-Laure and Boris Kochno who, in an excess of zeal, wailed loudly while flinging bouquets on the body, then danced a sarabande accompanied by their own lamentations. Again I was unpleasantly impressed by this exhibition of a supposedly remarkable woman.

The following day at 1:30 I lunched at the Aurics who were careful in their criticism, Marie-Laure being one of their original sponsors as well as, in the summer months, their sort-of landlady (in the 1930s she had gifted them with a large cottage and garden on her property in Hyères, fifty yards downhill from the main house). That evening Nora took me to *Phèdre,* the latest collaboration of her husband with Jean Cocteau, as choreographed by Serge Lifar for the Ballets de l'Opéra.

An event! The adventure of French dance still lay in revamping of Greek classics even though Jerome Robbins had, in America, already irreversibly altered the aroma of ballet with *The Cage.* (True, Martha Graham had yet to proffer her version of Phaedra, not to mention Judith and Clytemnestra and other female monsters from the Graeco-Judaic past, but she did so on flat feet.) But if dance was blooming in New York as it faded in Paris—with the triteness of Petit and the pretension of Béjart—for the moment, like the storm before the calm, the slightly rotten apogee of the French agony lay in a work like *Phèdre.*

Cocteau had hoped for Greta Garbo to mime the main role. Garbo changed her mind. The happy substitute was Tamara Toumanova, that "baby ballerina" from the Ballets Russes of yore. Now thirty-three, she projected from the stage the same tragic eroticism that Garbo projected from the screen, just by being there, doing nothing.

From the blackness of the Salle Garnier a sudden spotlight blazes onto Cocteau's eighty-foot portrait of the barbarian queen, while a crunch from Auric's orchestra splits the opera house's brass, splaying the audience with audibly yellow splinters. The curtain rises. There stands Phaedra, arms extending fifteen feet in either direction by means of wands attached to her blood-red wings. Toumanova, solely by staring her public down with those haunted eyes, and by, every few minutes, shrugging imperceptibly so that the red wings shiver, evokes a horrible antiquity. Lifar, aptly effeminate and old enough to be at least her father, portrays her son Hippolytus, object of lewd cravings. Neither of them dances, they just move . . . that's all I recollect, but the recollection is indelible, as Nora swells with pride beside me.

It was the last important theater piece Georges Auric would compose. Within a year his professional image altered, as did his material status. *Moulin Rouge,* the hundredth movie for which Auric wrote the score, featured a little waltz sung by Zsa Zsa Gabor (as dubbed by Muriel Smith), known simply as "Song from *Moulin Rouge.*" The waltz quickly became number one on the charts; within months, as refashioned by Percy Faith into a foxtrot, it resounded from every jukebox across the world. Auric, who had sold the score outright to the film studio, sued for and won the rights to have the song extracted and represented as a discrete entity. He made millions in royalties, bought a mink for Nora, a Jaguar for Monsieur de Lesseps, and a house in Nogent where on Sundays they "received."

As when unsolved murders are committed, innocent eccentrics emerge from the woodwork and confess to the crime, so when successful pop tunes are penned, many a nobody rises up to affirm he penned it first. Each such affirmation must be legally heeded. Thus Auric first sailed to America, to answer a charge of plagiarism. (A like charge never occurs where "serious" music is concerned, only with money-making tunes.) And thus the definition of what constitutes musical plagiarism was defined by the lawyer—was it Nizer?—retained by ASCAP: If the first seven notes of two songs are not only tonally but rhythmically identical, the songs are the same, and the second one was filched from the first, *except* when the melodic outline stems from the basic overtone series—as in the horn-call opening of Beethoven's *Eroica,* or indeed, Auric's *Moulin Rouge*—when, the procedure being so ubiquitous, the first *twelve* notes must be identical in both, or in all, cases. (I'm of course paraphrasing a memory of this precedent, a paraphrase which now leaves me wondering about the unchallenged resemblance between the first seven notes of, say, Ellington's "In a Sentimental Mood" to Gershwin's "Someone to Watch Over Me.") In any case, Auric, having set a legal precedent, returned to France unconvicted and even richer.

But he grew crankier. He did not want money so much as praise for what he deemed his "true" work, like the work of colleagues who were poorer but whose fame was less flip. Auric's true music now turned gnarled, constipated, "meaningful," lest we forget he had not only outgrown the security of the movies but the charms of Poulenc, and was right up there with Pierre Boulez whose approval, though

Boulez was twenty-five years younger, Auric craved. He composed, for example, a partita for Fizdale & Gold which they claimed was so illegibly crabbed and minuscule they never could learn it.

If, during the approaching long seasons in Hyères, Georges became a continually refreshing neighbor, more relaxed than in Paris, coming up most afternoons at six, sometimes with Nora, when they had finished work, funny and exquisite, for them both, the exquisite fun was edged in rue. Georges, without admitting it, hated being loved for what he was, a creator of flawlessly synchronized and necessary film music, rather than for what he wasn't, a composer of unsettlingly profound noncollaborative masterpieces. Nora wanted to be admired for being a lady, whatever her notion of that could be, but in fact was an *arriviste* with a decorative gift, and no worse company than most.

Both smoked opium, a habit still not unusual at that late date in well-off artistic circles of their generation. They never discussed it, but their mood swings depended on the daily pipe. So far as I know they never, unlike Cocteau, underwent disintoxication, and Auric when in England was given special dispensation (i.e., was granted his regular dosage) by no less a person than King George VI. Apparently opium reliance does not increase with usage, once a norm is set.

Magnanimity was not among the many virtues of Nora and Georges. But once, when Auric had become the chief of the French Performing Rights Society, SACEM—the equivalent of our ASCAP—he did a favor for the son of Marie-Laure's gardener. This boy, Maxim, was a dwarf, grotesquely twisted, with giant hands and bulging eyes; worse, he had a younger brother who was handsome as an angel. Maxim fancied himself a composer, and showed some of his pitiful work to Georges and me. Georges spoke on Maxim's behalf to the board of examiners at SACEM, and the boy was duly accepted as a member. When the gardener and his family learned this great news they came en masse to kiss Auric's feet. Where, we all wondered, does Maxim go from here?

From here Georges himself went on to become head of the Paris Opéra, where his first gesture was to hire Boulez as guest conductor and grant him carte blanche for a production of *Wozzeck*. Nora gave up painting. In her role as "Madame Opéra" (Marie-Laure's caustic term) she grew ever more imperious, a great backstage hostess.

The Aurics remained affectionate during my various returns to France, until *The Paris Diary* appeared, when Nora—and by extension Georges—refused to acknowledge me. I stress "by extension," for Georges was growing vague. It was perhaps his strong intelligence that sapped him, or his long life of success at everything except what most counted. They both outlived Marie-Laure by many years (she died in 1970). But Nora, they say, behaved oddly. Like going to the bank at 4 a.m. in her nightgown. Guy de Lesseps died first. Then Nora. After which Georges married the housekeeper, a young girl from the Midi, to whom the family fortune fell when Georges himself passed on soon after. . . .

Oh well, it's only money. When Ravel, the most-played composer of the twentieth century, died, his estate went not to a museum of his artifacts but to his brother's chauffeur's wife's daughter by a second marriage.

That's enough about the Aurics.

People were reading Beckett. The novel *Molloy* appeared that spring, and a year hence *En attendant Godot* would be mounted (its sole décor a metal tree by Giacometti), taking the world by storm. I couldn't buy it: what did such language offer that wasn't equaled by the "experimental" dramas from Chicago's WPA theater in the 1930s, beginning with the sophomoric symbolism in the name Godot? Beckett was just another tiresome Irish wit. If life isn't worth living, or even worth dying, then how summon the energy or interest to write that life isn't worth dying, or even worth living? Silence is more eloquent than sound. But Beckett made of hopelessness something chic. And he surely wrote for posterity.

So the winter unrolled like a musky carpet or a dying cobra around the fetid fringes of the Tout Paris. One person led to another. The Neapolitan pianist Aldo Ciccolini was a constant presence at Michel Girard's. Aldo was the only virtuoso ever to specialize in slow music. At a party full of pianists upstaging each other with their Liszt and Chopin knucklebusters, he could coolly take over the keyboard with Ravel's *Pavane* or a Satie *Gymnopédie,* while gradually the rivals seemed to grow vain and empty in their non-Italianate overstatement.

Regular frequentation of the Comtesse Pastré, a papal countess (her late husband had bought the title in Rome), hence the lack of *la particule nobilaire*. Known to all as Lily, she was six-foot-two, homely, unkempt in her sheaths of baby-blue, sixty years old, and touchingly if indiscriminatingly devoted to the "better music." Her fortune came from the apéritif Noilly Prat. Regulars of her salon were Louise de Vilmorin (Poulenc's poet, money from grain, elegant with a congenital limp, nonstop talker, platonic mistress of Charles de Noailles), Boris Kochno (last *régisseur* of the original Ballets Russes, lover of Diaghilev

at whose Venetian funeral in 1929 he wrestled with Serge Lifar, hard
drinker, still electrically attractive with his crew-cut, Slavic accent, and
arrogant Tolstoyan affectations), Samson François (Cortot's prize student, another hard drinker, Debussy specialist, dead by 1970 at forty-
six), and Pierre Guérin (hanger-on, ungifted, useful, embarrassing).
Lily served a rich buffet, sang without talent accompanied by the wine-
filled greats, and owned a rambling mansion at Montredon near Marseilles, where fourteen years later I would complete most of *Miss
Julie*'s Act II. Meanwhile, it was here in her Paris garden that we all
were photographed on the occasion of my not winning first prize in
the Biarritz competition. And it was here that I met an American poet,
David Posner, with whom I immediately went to bed at the Hôtel du
Bon La Fontaine. David was a paragon of dusky beauty, muscular as
young King David, just my type. But the bed experience was not
repeated because: (1) he anathematically perfumed his anatomy, and
(2) his conversation, like the perfume, was a turn-off—he tried too
hard, and was socially masochistic. David, a gerontophile among other
things, had been beneficial to the aging Somerset Maugham, reading
to him, bathing him, and, when the occasion demanded, lying nude
upon the master and ejaculating by means of frottage. In 1959 David
was instrumental in my becoming composer-in-residence at Buffalo
University where he had become curator of the Lockwood Memorial
Library (in the john of which he would sometimes make passes at his
best friends, not realizing, because of his nearsightedness, that they
were his best friends), and where he received a doctorate for his
thesis on Julien Green. David eventually married. He died of AIDS at
the very start of the plague.

Carmel Snow, educated creature, not young and with a withered
right hand—an example of how style does not rely on beauty—was
my hostess on two occasions, she being the manager of *Harper's
Bazaar,* and hence the nominal boss of Madame Bousquet. . . . Dozens
of other names of humans sprinkle the calendar, as well as of theaters
and museums and parties and operas and movies and bars which may
have been mere reminders then, but which impress me now with
their inexhaustibility: all the regulars, plus Dean Witter (music student), Noël Lee (the most significant American pianist since Paul
Jacobs, and the most unjustly unsung song composer of our generation), Hélène Jourdan-Morhange, Themistocles, Ghislaine de Peyroux,
Marya Freund, Kathleen Ferrier, people from the embassy, etcetera.
. . . But I wanted to know Marie-Laure. Everyone else knew her.

Well, yes, a few weeks earlier as a concession to José, Marie-Laure
allowed him to bring me to her house postprandially, but this didn't
count. At ten we were ushered into the exquisite octagonal ground-

floor music room—one of the rooms where in future years I would work and play and live and love each day. We sat demurely, José and I, listening to the wine-edged laughter of the dinner guests in the small blue marble dining room across the teakwood hall. The laughter grew louder, and I more uneasy, as the dinner guests, eleven of them, and their hostess now entered our music room for coffee and brandy. All wore evening clothes. Among them tottered Sacheverell Sitwell, and also the Aurics. Nora, whom I was used to seeing in painter's togs, looked breathtaking in a deep red satin gown, a dark red lace stole, and pale red camellias in her short white hair. (Next morning, at our *séance de pose,* she said: "I was disappointed to see you there last night. That woman has no sense of your quality, she'll drag you down as she does everyone.") Marie-Laure flirted with me in her very English English—the kind rich Europeans learn at their nounou's knee —rather disdainfully, said I looked like Ginger Rogers dolled up in my new tan suit, introduced me to Mr. Sitwell (whom I asked to intercede on behalf of his distinguished sister about the rights to her poem, which he agreed to, but was surely too drunk to remember or care), then glided away and we said nothing more except good-bye.

A British acquaintance—or was he American?—called the gentle Charles Lovett, had a Norwegian boyfriend, Ferdinand Finn, who lived alone on his own island in the Oslofjorden, but was now vacationing in Paris. His robust aspect and reputation as a benign sadist were alluring. In the early evening of 8 March I found myself in Ferdinand's bed on the top floor of the Hôtel du Quai Voltaire overlooking—as all the beds there overlooked—the Seine. As we lay in postcoital ease, I asked:

"So what's the gentle Charles up to tonight?"

"He's out with that awful Noailles woman. They're going to see a play at the American Center."

I got up, dressed, waved farewell, rushed to the American Center, boulevard Raspail, and bought a ticket to Gertrude Stein's *Yes Is for a Very Young Man.* I liked Marie-Laure for being at such a play, she liked me for being at such a play. The gentle Charles Lovett invited us back to his place, rue Schoelcher. On Saturday afternoon Marie-Laure in turn invited me to a dress rehearsal of *La petite Lili,* a dreary vehicle starring Edith Piaf and her current beau, Eddie Constantine. She also suggested I go to the Midi with her the next Friday, along with Boris Kochno. Meanwhile, she began my portrait, for which I daily sat while talking of Satie's *Socrate.* I packed my little suitcase, and the briefcase full of manuscript paper (hoping to finish the copy and scoring of *Mélos* at Hyères), then socialized frenetically to say proud good-byes.

But when Friday morning came around, and Boris and I showed

up on her doorstep, Marie-Laure had already driven off, leaving no message with her concierge.

Anyone else would have crossed her off for good. But I was Rastignac. Since Nora and Georges were also planning to spend a month in Hyères, I asked Nora to ask Marie-Laure to ask me back. Meanwhile, two weeks were spent in sleeping mornings, working afternoons, and socializing nights with (let me check) Yves Vidal, Philippe Erlanger, Julius and Doda and Jean and José, Marie-Blanche, Boulanger, Boris Kochno, Elliott Stein (who was already busy on our libretto), Jacques Février, Lily Pastré, James Lord, the soprano Irene Joachim, Bernac, Fraigneau, Kanters, Seymour Barab who was passing through, and a host of other names I no longer recognize by either taste or smell. I would seem to be going in circles. Maybe we all were, maybe that's youth. But just as heartbreak and physical pain can be remembered but not reexperienced, so the prospects offered by a chance meeting or a new work of art can be reexperienced (since we now know the outcome) but no longer savored. I did get a lot of music written in this fortnight, and on Saturday, 24 March, I took a real bath in one of the *bains du quartier* (you rent a copper tub for half an hour, buy a cake of *savon de Marseille,* and scrub yourself silly), after which Jean Leuvrais said my skin was more satiny; all events before and after were dated according to Ned's Bath. We heard Prokofiev's new version of *War and Peace* and concluded: Shostakovich at his best is better than Prokofiev at his best, but Prokofiev at his worst is more fun than Shostakovich at his worst.

Then a telegram came from Marie-Laure advising me to take the night train for Toulon on Saturday, the 31st, at the Gare de Lyon. "Get a first-class ticket, Claude the concierge, place des Etats-Unis, will take care of it."

The hotel room, being paid up through April, I stored most of my stuff under the bed, locked the door, and left.

Ferdinand the benign sadist? He went back to his island in Norway. In the mid-1960s he phoned me in New York and came for tea. The gentle Charles Lovett? A year or two after *Yes Is for a Very Young Man* his life stopped oddly. At Hadrian's Villa one day he was taking a picture. He lowered his head into the camera, stepped back a few paces, and fell into a twelve-foot hole. He was killed instantly.

32. Marie-Laure in Hyères

What can be said of this unique monster, the most influential "older woman" besides Mother of my life? It's long ago. Neither the creature nor the land she dwelled in exist any longer. The aura, the verve, the smartness, the panache, have dimmed. The fact remains that if it weren't for Marie-Laure I would have returned to America years earlier.

Recently James Lord, whose early life was also long enhanced by—though not dependent on, as mine became—Marie-Laure, asked if I thought she were intelligent. It had never occurred to me that she was anything less. Perhaps, thinking back, she was not intelligent but had a flair for miming those who were. And her taste was good. Intelligence, of course, bears little relation to talent, and none at all to moral goodness. James Lord is intelligent. I am less so (nor am I more morally good than necessary). But we all three have talent, and we keep our eyes open. Intelligence means seeing relationships, while talent means *feeling* relationships and being capable of economically solidifying this feeling communicably on canvas or page or staff.

She was hardly beautiful, was frankly plain, though in youth had been an anorexically svelte tomboy, aware of posture, dressed to kill. She was, as the French say, *une belle laide,* like Lillian Hellman or Barbra Streisand: one not blessed with movie-star traits but who, through wit and guile, convinces you she's Lilith. By the time I knew her she had lost her figure and forsaken the high-fashion accoutrements of the rich. She lost her figure to a fibrous tumor in the belly which she refused to have excised and which made her look pregnant; she forsook high-fashion accoutrements of the rich during the Spanish Civil War when her right-thinking (that is, left-thinking) entourage considered her frivolous. With her thick stringy hair and spit curls she came to resemble Louis XIV in the same way Janet Flanner resembled George Washington—as a distaff incarnation of past political power, businesslike yet coy, no-nonsense yet ornate. In all the years with her I never saw Marie-Laure, while in the Midi, garbed in other than a voluminous peasant skirt, a peasant blouse on which she carelessly pinned a million-dollar brooch, and espadrilles which were the only seemly footwear for the grotesquely distorted toes which she loathed. In Paris, on high evening occasions, she did don a Rochas robe of royal blue, and by day wore real dresses and sheer stockings of bright red or green on her very good legs. Gone were the days of the shy spoiled brat in a new gown daily by Mainbocher. Yet she thought of herself as a *femme fatale,* batting her eyes, playing hard-to-get. (Henri Sauguet had once pointed me out from afar to Marie-Laure. "I don't think he's so good-looking," said she. And he: "Oh no? But he looks just like you.") Jean Cocteau had been an intimate of her childhood. Thirteen years his junior, she retained a crush on him from which she never quite revived. When in 1958 Cocteau suffered an attack and was expected to die, Marie-Laure told the press, "I was Jean's Lolita," which struck me then as drolly self-aggrandizing, as though the poet had simply devolved from her, but which now sounds plausible, if only because of the money that flowed between them.

Born Marie-Laure Bischoffsheim on Halloween in 1902, our mutual October birthdates, though twenty-one years apart, first endeared me to her, with her horoscopic obsession that Scorpios hurt everyone but each other—though I am a Scorpio only in France; Indiana with its four-thousand-mile eight-hour separation claims me on the cusp as Libra. Her father, a Jewish banker, died when she was an infant. Her mother, Marie-Thérèse, paternally descended from Lafayette, was the prim and proper offspring of the blazing Comtesse de Chevigné, one of the two models (the other was Madame Emile Straus, Bizet's widow, who survived the composer by half a century) for Proust's Oriane de Guermantes, and herself the last descendant of the Marquis de Sade, a fact of which Marie-Laure was boastful. Marie-Laure doted on the grandmother's memory, quoted her often, emulated the sparkle which had skipped a generation, wanted to *be* her. Marie-Laure, who adored what we today call "celebrities" and was in a position to meet anyone —or almost anyone—she wished, had in fact known Proust a bit, found him a *vieux raseur,* but by the time she was old enough to realize what she'd missed, the great man had died. She never, as a result, could allow that Proust had any interest whatsoever.

Marie-Thérèse remarried. Her new husband, Francis de Croisset, author and lyricist for, among others, Reynaldo Hahn, Proust's one-time lover, with whom he produced the delicious *Ciboulette,* was also, according to Marie-Laure, a child abuser. He had, she claimed, seduced her in her adolescence, a trauma which caused her later to pen a novella, *La chambre des écureuils,* privately printed and publicly distributed during the war years. When in 1954 Françoise Sagan's *Bonjour tristesse* came out (its title filched from a poem by Marie-Laure's dear friend Paul Eluard: "... adieu bonheur, bonjour tristesse"), better written but too close for comfort in incestuous shock value to *La chambre des écureuils,* Marie-Laure wanted to—but did not—sue. Croisset sired a son ten years younger than Marie-Laure, Philippe, who espoused an American heiress, Ethel Woodward. Widowed (Philippe died young in a car crash), Ethel thrives today in the rue Weber from where she, as a well-off music lover, promotes the well-being of Pierre Boulez, among others. (If facts are skewed, check with James Lord. Better yet, with Bernard Minoret. As a professional French historian of snobbery Bernard has a finer grasp on lineage than I as a befuddled Yankee.)

In 1922 Marie-Laure wedded by prearrangement the Vicomte Charles de Noailles, uniting the fortunes which contained, in real estate alone, half of Wall Street, and similar financial districts in Montreal and Geneva. The young couple dutifully produced two daughters, Laure and Natalie, after which they maybe never again slept together. Laure married Gaston de la Haye-Jousselin, an effete neutered type from a "good family," and she too, with her upper-crust accent, always seemed effete and neutral, taking after her tame grandmother as Marie-Laure had taken after her own wild grandmother. Their son, Egmont, about four or five in 1951, would, with his English nanny, inhabit an elaborate nursery directly above my room when I came to live in the place des Etats-Unis. Laure inherited her mother's three large Goyas which are still presumably lodged in the Haye-Jousselin chateau in Normandy. She herself perished in the mid-1980s from swallowing a chicken bone. Natalie married Sandro Perrone, director of the Roman daily *Il Messagiero,* and they had two sons—one of them, Mario, gravely autistic—before their divorce. Natalie, the only surviving Noailles now, lives in seclusion at Fontainebleau's Palais de Pompadour, bequeathed by her father. An accomplished equestrian, she fell violently from a thoroughbred at the time of her sister's death, and has not been the same since. Both daughters, though hardly pals, were of my generation, and staunch acquaintances.

Charles de Noailles, ten years his wife's senior, handsome, dapper, manly, a Gentleman to the bone, had manners whose perfection can only be called art, art which even then was all but past. He and Marie-Laure lived separately since the mid-thirties—since, that is, having provided the world with appropriate progeny and, as the most-envied young couple in their special society, provided their country with unique works of cinematic bravura via commissions and imposed tastes. It was when these works began provoking scandals with both church and state that the Noailles initiated their life of *chambres à part,* wherein Charles would pursue an existence of gentleman-gardener with his nominal mistresses in his own domains, and Marie-Laure, who thrived on scandal, would pursue as a rich bohemian her affairs of head and heart in the world of the arts, free to act promiscuously provided she did not besmirch the family name. The initiation was also surely impelled by Charles's discreet pederasty, he having been upset when rumors of an affair with his gymnast were bruited in the milieu. In all the years I knew her, Marie-Laure, who was otherwise outlandish, even slanderous in gossip and given to words like "enculer" and "godemichet" as the servants impassively passed the potatoes, never once, with me or with anyone I know, discussed the sexual proclivities or hints of indignity relating to her sacred mate.

She loved him, worshiped him, was a little in awe of him if only because, like all French husbands from every class, he legally controlled the purse strings. Her sole moments of intimidation came every three months when she was called to account for her expenditures. Though her allowance was unlimited, it *was* an allowance. Marie-Laure kept up a voluminous correspondence, including a daily letter to Charles when, as was usually the case, he was at his properties of Grasse or Fontainebleau or *en voyage,* or even in Paris when she too was there. The *hôtel* in Paris belonged to her by inheritance, but contained separate apartments for both daughters, and for Charles. Yes, even in Paris she would leave a letter under his door each night, which he each morning answered.

If Charles was more than a little queer, Marie-Laure was definitely straight. She never said "tu" to women except her daughters, never said "vous" to men except her husband. Once I asked the very American question: "Since you *vouvoyer* your husband, what do you say in bed?" (The question is American not just because we have no intimate form of address—can you even conjugate in English the second-person singular of any verb?—but because we have no sense of correct discourse among the well-brought-up.) Her answer: "We never talked in bed."

That answer, of course, betrayed an innocence beneath the bluff. Like many a notorious sophisticate, when you get down to brass tacks, Marie-Laure was sexually naïve. Had she really, beyond her husband, had more than, say, ten or twelve lovers in her life? To be fair, most of my straight women friends have not had more than around twenty lovers, including one-night stands, in their active premenopausal lives, as distinct from the hundreds, even thousands of partners enjoyed or abhorred by most gay males, myself included. (I classify my own libidinous encounters—steady lovers, passing affairs, one-night stands —as I do the authors I've set to music. Some, like Whitman and Goodman and Auden, I return to often; others, like Bishop and Ashbery and Roethke, remain recurring memories; still others, like Plath and Mew and Noailles herself, were one-shot deals.)

The first and most important of these extramarital and very public amourettes was Igor Markevich in the 1930s. Only twenty-one at the time, Markevich was an already famous enfant terrible as composer and protégé of both Boulanger's and Diaghilev's. Skinny, Slavic, charismatic rather than handsome, he would eventually marry Kyra Nijinsky, the dancer's daughter, then Topazia Caetani (offspring of one of Charles de Noailles's "mistresses," Cora Caetani, who traced her name back to the court of Nero) and evolve into a conductor of international stature. For now he was the caring and instructive partner of Marie-Laure who hitherto seemed to have been a poor little rich girl, educated to the teeth in every art except the art of love.

Three disruptive episodes transpired during their otherwise tranquil and lengthy liaison. In 1934, finding herself pregnant, it was decided, after "civilized" consultation with Igor and Charles, that, more or less against her desires, Marie-Laure would get an abortion in Switzerland. The procedure was botched, and told on her mind and body for the rest of her life. A year later, in the Alfa-Romeo she had impulsively bestowed upon Igor, the pair went over a cliff where the auto was caught by a protruding tree and hung in the balance. Igor, despite cracked ribs, emerged from the wreckage, but Marie-Laure remained trapped inside for hours before the car, by means of a derrick, was hoisted to safety. In what condition would Marie-Laure be found? She was quietly reading the poems of Hölderlin and appeared unhurt except for a broken cheekbone—broken in the very spot where Dali, in his 1929 portrait, had painted a perfect pink rose. A year later, while Igor was collaborating with Jean Cocteau on a sizable cantata, Marie-Laure accused them loudly, on no foundation except her jealousy, of a love that dare not speak its name. The accusation changed the weather: at a vernissage, Cocteau assailed her with a slap heard round the world, while Igor, fed up with unpredictable tantrums, imposed a decades-long estrangement. (By the time I knew Markevich he was married to the cheerful Topazia, and both were on the warmest terms with Marie-Laure.)

Though I am no longer one for ferreting out elective affinities, Freudian or otherwise, between past and present, cause and effect, it seemed immediately clear that her abortion was the decisive shock of the Vicomtesse's young life. As parent to Laure and Natalie, she went through the motions—which were more than mere motions—of irreproachable devotion. But she would have preferred a son, and was convinced that the embryo, flushed down the drain of the Swiss quack, would have emerged as the ideal boy. Sonless, she became, like many strong women (weak ones too, and some with sons), partial to homosexual men; indeed, nearly all of her lovers—though not Markevich—were, at the very least, what was then termed bisexual. Like many strong women (weak ones too) she imagined herself the unique being to convert these lovers into Ladies' Men, if only by transforming them into surrogate sons. The situation is ubiquitous in every class, more plaintive and hopeless for the women than for the men.

I have always despised the central quatrain of Cole Porter's "Anything Goes":

The world's gone mad today, and good's bad today,
And black's white today, and day's night today,
When those guys today that women prize today
Are just silly gigolos.

Today? It's been true since the Greeks. Silly? The "gigolos" are no sillier than the women who prize them. In Proust and Balzac, as in real life, how many of the males—females too—turn out to be AC–DC! So too with Marie-Laure's milieu, which Cole Porter skirted.

There is no solution. Though a woman speaks with the tongues of men and of angels, and has no penis, she is become as a tinkling cymbal in this Aristotelian comedy wherein two creatures love and need each other, but will never—by definition of their sex—unite.

More than once I have seen a woman in middle age wash her hands of the beautiful boys and set her cap for a homely heterosexual of her own age. That's what Libby Holman settled for, when I came to know her, with the husky abstract expressionist Louis Schanker, after a lifetime of impossible unions. Marie-Laure settled for it too, as we shall see, with the Spanish painter Oscar Dominguez, the ugliest man alive, and straight as a die in his crooked way.

Meanwhile, I would play on Marie-Laure's susceptibilities, as she would play on mine.

Fernand Bacchat, the chauffeur, greeted the Toulon train at 7:45 a.m. on Sunday, April Fool's Day, and together we drove the seventeen kilometers west to Hyères. Bacchat, not tall, very French, married, late thirties, great-looking with salty gray temples and a dashing smile, was rather dumb, overworked, and given to gossip. Of him I knew only this: he had an affair with Theodora Keogh contingent with Marie-Laure's affair with Theodora's husband, Tom. Theodora had instigated this upstairs-downstairs intrigue out of spite—she loathed Marie-Laure and the whole of the Tout Paris which fawned over Tom. (Not that Bacchat was anything to sneeze at, or that Tom's carnal rapports were very weighty—he was only heterosexual when sober, which was rare.) At this point I had never seen either of the Keoghs, although two weeks earlier, when Tom had attempted suicide with a razor in his room above the Montana bar and was rushed to emergency, Marie-Laure took me to the room to pick up his things, and we found it spattered in blood—the sheets, the windows, the ceiling. The Keoghs were an American couple living professionally in Paris. (Marie-Laure, I learned, knew few Americans, and those few she invoked, like Bernard Berenson or Glenway Wescott, never quite jibed with her clichéd notion of Americans—including the Keoghs and myself—as rustic cowboys.) Tom was an adroit craftsman to whom Christian Bérard, on his deathbed, bequeathed the mantle of Europe's sole Great Designer. He had designed sets and costumes for the movie *Kismet,* featuring the gilded body of Marlene Dietrich, whom he rather resembled with his pronounced cheekbones, lazy eyes, and cider-colored hair, and was now employed by the ballet companies of both Roland Petit and the marquis de Cuevas. Theodora, named for her grandfather Roosevelt, was a nimble novelist of prefeminist perceptions who had just published *Meg,* the tale of a young woman's sad self-discoveries, and was about to publish *The Double Door,* an acid portrait of the Cuevas milieu. (Why did she stop writing? Only last year I had a letter from her in a Virginia village dreaming of the old days.) Tom, after their divorce, returned to the States where he finally died. I covet the three watercolors he made for me: of a sleeping male nude, a green apple with two huge leaves, and a handsome clown in orange and black.

En route to Hyères Bacchat filled me in. Madame Keogh was past history. At Hyères I would find Madame la Vicomtesse with Monsieur Veyron-Lacroix and Monsieur Labisse. Monsieur Kochno was expected tomorrow. Chez les Aurics was a young American, a Monsieur Wilder Burnap. Bacchat himself would be dropping me at the front gate, since he must return to town immediately. His duties, in Hyères as in Paris, were to shop daily at the predawn market, wait nightly for his employer no matter how late, and to stay on call all through the day. In Hyères as in Paris the household personnel was comprised of fifteen souls, including the so-faithful Lithuanian maid, Emma, and a separate pastry cook on the kitchen staff in each city. For Marie-Laure, like me, had a sweet tooth (the quick fix of incipient dipsomaniacs) and served florid desserts—never cheese—thrice a day.

I was unprepared for the expansiveness of her property. Somehow I had pictured a house like anyone else's, comfortable yes, but not splendiferous. Hyères itself is a village on the southernmost tip of Provence, midway between Marseilles and Fréjus, five kilometers inland. Those five kilometers have kept this otherwise adorable enclave from becoming an overcrowded tourist trap, although in the 1890s and up until World War I it was a watering place for middle-class English. The population was perhaps seven thousand, of whom half lived in the *vieille ville,* a walled medieval labyrinth ascending a huge hill which was the start of the ever-larger mountain chain of Var which extends indefinitely northward.

At the top of the hill, approached by a twisting private winding road outside the wall, loomed Saint-Bernard, the chateau constructed in the 1920s by the young Noailles. Their architect, one Robert Mallet-Stevens, heretofore an interior decorator, had improvised according to fantasy like a child with blocks. The pleasant result, in the streamlined style of the period, sprawled every which way, with cellars and pools and fountains, corridors and porches and alcoves, ateliers and kitchenettes and cutting rooms, a separate servants' residence and a dozen guest rooms, each with its personal garden. The estate had in the thirties been a site for the Happy Few. Many a musical fête was heard, Sauguet and Koechlin and all of Les Six being recipients of Marie-Laure's and Charles's commissions, realized in their little theater or on the lawn by hired orchestras under the baton of, among others, Markevich or Desormière or the composers themselves. The scrapbook burst with snapshots of other voices, other rooms, a Dada costume ball, choreographed by Man Ray in that easier era, and occurring in the empty swimming pool where the guests donned horses heads and Roman togas. During the Second War the Germans had appropriated Saint-Bernard, as well as the paradisiacal knoll behind the chateau. Now the frivolously solid doings of yore were melancholy echoes, the swimming pool swathed in cobwebs, the cracked concrete of the dozen guest rooms home for crickets, and the paradisiacal knoll still strangled in barbed wire. That part of the house that had been re-reconverted was nonetheless vast, and fitted out in terms of convenient luxury—that is, while the walls featured Juan Gris and Giacometti and Fugita, while the waving drapes that discouraged insects at nightfall between terrace and parlor were of peach-hued chiffon, and while the remaining décor of the twenty-odd habitable rooms large and small was of that most aristocratic of furnishings—books by the thousands—the marbleized floor was yet unencumbered by rugs, barefoot living being the mode.

The house was surrounded by acres of walled gardens, one of which contained a lion's cage with two large lions—made of plaster. The walls were twelve feet high, pierced at intervals by ten-foot-square openings like animate paintings depicting scenes of Provence from various perspectives. Later that year Oscar Dominguez would construct, at the local blacksmith's, four huge steel designs which he arranged to have soldered to the top of the main wall (a dangerous proceeding above a sheer drop of sixty feet), and which he called "sky sculptures" because, between the metal filaments, the sunny-white ether successfully filtered down to us. The gardens in this season teemed with crocuses, their wee faces of violet and gold mirroring the rows of miniature blue pansies, each like an elf's plate with a poached hummingbird egg in the center.

So here she was, in her meridional shelter. Like the pet cat who is one thing in the city and another in the country, Marie-Laure became quite a novel person at Saint-Bernard. She shed her obligatory *mondanités* and, while remaining a hostess, disappeared into her own works for hours at a time. Since nothing is more contagious than work, her concentrated energy rubbed off on me. She was an organized artist. As a poet she was ornate, ladylike, macabre. As a prosifier her attraction was too close for comfort to the surrealists whose influence melted into watery affectation (and, being rich, she was unused to criticism). But as a painter she had to be taken seriously. Her language, in both style and substance, stemmed from that of Bérard.

I had known the work of Christian Bérard—referred to always as Bébé by those hundreds who adored him—from his many pictures on Virgil's walls at the Chelsea, and from Virgil's tales about this most talented of mortals. "I have witnessed," Virgil used to say, "the creative spirit at work only rarely. This spirit was most vitally active in Bébé." I never met the man. He died just months before I came to Paris, collapsing on stage during a rehearsal of Molière's *Les Fourberies de Scapin* for which he had provided the décor. Even as the French referred always to the "Occupation," never to the "War," which they evoked less with horror than with nostalgia for the solidarity it had created among themselves, so they evoked Bérard, *le cher Bébé,* as something wondrous and lost. Bearded in a time of no beards, and physically fat and filthy in a milieu of slim cleanliness, he was nonetheless quite swishy, living with Boris Kochno in the rue Casimir-Delavigne where the two smoked opium until the Occupation banned it, then switched to cognac which they imbibed during every waking hour. Bérard was the darling of society, partly because he played as hard as he worked, and partly because the work—portraits, stage sets, murals, interior decoration, wardrobe—was, all of it, flattering as well as first rate. Cocteau's palette owed its identity to Bérard's, and Marie-Laure's palette blended both. When Gertrude Stein died in July of 1946, Grace Cohen says that I said: "So she's dead. And she never knew me." Marie-Laure in 1951 repeatedly said: "To think that Bébé never knew you." Thus did my narcissism echo in the mouths of babes although Bérard's recent death was not "recent" to me, because it occurred before I was aware of his reality.

And thus did Marie-Laure in her studio concoct her luxuriantly sensual Bérards throughout the years while in my nearby studio where she had moved one of her two pianos—the green one—I composed my sensually luxuriant French music, which sounded French to everyone but them. More than anything, she respected work. Since I never stopped working, she never stopped respecting, though she might show the door to other vacationers who lolled too much around Saint-Bernard, eating her guinea hen and soiling her sheets. Admittedly, sometimes I worked beyond my energies precisely to keep her from "respecting" me too physically.

Of the three houseguests enumerated by the chauffeur, only Robert Veyron-Lacroix was known to me; we had met chez Marie-Blanche. Roro, as he was nicknamed, had become, already at twenty-seven, his country's preeminent player of the harpsichord, an instrument which he taught at the Conservatoire, which he recorded extensively (just out were the complete works of Rameau in a four-disc album boxed in gray satin), and which he made arrangements for. But it was as accompanist for flutist Jean-Pierre Rampal that he earned enough to buy a house in Majorca, and to pay the medical bills for fruitless tracings of a blood clot that roamed through his body, lodging intermittently in his brain, causing him to pass out unexpectedly on stage or at the table, and eventually killing him fairly young. He was an intimate of both Marie-Blanche and Marie-Laure, the latter being more fun if less musical. (Interestingly, though Marie-Laure's two main lovers hitherto, Markevich and Maurice Gendron, had both been great interpretive musicians, she herself was not musical. Indeed, her circle consisted mostly of visual artists, good ones, and she liked to think of herself as "one of them"—difficult, since she was rich, and the rich can never quite be "one of them." To her credit, quite literally, whenever in Paris we'd go out en masse to some restaurant, she always footed the bill, never demanding proof, like the American rich, that she was loved for herself alone. She knew that there is no "self alone," that money was part of what made her her.) Roro through the years became a platonic brother whom I admired no less for his performing ability—his rhythmic precision and digital accuracy were computer perfect, a trait inbred in the French—than for his Samaritan dependability when I was insufferably self-pitying.

Félix Labisse, a Belgian surrealist, though less adept on canvas than his nationalist contemporaries, Magritte and Delbos, created marvelous sets and worked in continual tandem with Jean-Louis Barrault. Were I to list the four most successfully evocative stage designs of my experience, they would be: Balthus's décor for Ugo Betti's *L'île des chèvres* for its aptly claustrophobic mystery which does not pall after two hours; Noguchi's pliably solid-gold Brancusi-like sculptures, in Martha Graham's study of Saint Joan, for their ability to transport the audience along with the dancers into a shining cruel paradise; Bill Ritman's huge room for Act II of Albee's *Tiny Alice* featuring the maquette of a castle with lighted windows that make us see Big and see Small simultaneously; and Labisse's portrayal, in Act I of Claudel's *Le partage de Midi,* of the deck of a lavish ocean liner where Barrault and Edwige Feuillère talk and talk and talk beneath the constantly rippling all-encompassing sails of snow-white satin shot with mauve. Félix himself, gray-haired and mischievous, with a wife named Jony who led her own life, was a self-portrait of seduction combined with sensible education.

Wilder Burnap, an American my age, bleached blond and highly excitable, had been a protégé of Roy Harris's pianist wife, Johana, but now fancied himself a baritone, and was a valuable fly-by-night. Six years hence he would commission from me five songs for five hundred dollars. These turned out to be settings of Whitman, and were first performed by him, with his small but expressive voice, self-accompanied on a miniature virginal placed on his knees in the front seat of his third-hand convertible Rolls-Royce on the sandy beach of Hyères.

Wilder was staying with the Aurics just down the hill from Saint-Bernard, in a house called Les Roches Fleuries which the Noailles had given them for a wedding present. Separated from Les Roches Fleuries by a sterile field of hydrangeas and lettuce (the soil of the Var is tragically dry) stood the house of the gardener, the one with the crippled son named Maxim who composed.

On a level some yards higher than these houses, about ninety yards west of Saint-Bernard but still on the Noailles property rose yet another house, three stories of tan granite called the Villa Saint-Pierre, inhabited by Tony Gandarillas. A generation older than Marie-Laure, Tony was cultural ambassador from Chile to England, now retired in France. *Mondain* without being snooty, Tony knew everyone and went everywhere, smoking opium with the best of them, continually dredging souvenirs from a special kind of past which still seeped uneasily into the present: memories of prerevolutionary *luxe* in Saint Petersburg, of Cole Porter's bagatelles with gondoliers, of George VI's dalliance with—but dare I name this still-living beauty? Tony himself, according to my hostess (or, as Michel Girard later named her, my landlady), dallied with his cockney chauffeur. Indeed, one afternoon through the large telescope permanently placed on the well-tended lawn, we vicariously focused on a session of flagellation that made us fear for Tony's old bones. With all Marie-Laure's belittling of her neighbor, with all her paradoxical meanness juxtaposed with kindness, arrogance, generosity, and indifference, it was to Tony's bedside that in 1970 she hied, sitting with him daily until he quit the world, and then, one week later, died herself, of emphysema aggravated by a four-pack-a-day dosage of Gauloises.

Among Tony's most valued guests was Nancy Mitford whose fortnightly visits every August I anticipated with salubrious glee. Nancy was somehow less neurotic than the others on our hill, as well as outdoorsy and anglophone. (Marie-Laure loathed the outdoors; she bought a swimsuit in our early days to impress me, but donned it only once. Bacchat later said he'd not seen her swim in twenty years.) Nora Auric was outdoorsy too; in fact it was with her that I made the regular trek to La Potinière for a vigorous swim each morning at ten. But Nora and Nancy were not close. Nora had painted a portrait called *Man with Glove* of the womanizing diplomat Gaston Palewski, with whom Nancy remained unrequitedly in love until her death. Nancy bought the portrait. But in order to make it fit the circular frame, she cut a foot off the canvas, including the glove of the title and Nora's signature. Nancy sketched in the signature, misspelt, and when Nora learned of this she was not amused. (For her gesture, Nancy did have a precedent in Misia, that arbiter of taste—taste that only money can buy. Misia commissioned a set of murals from Bonnard, then took shears to them so that they would fit her walls. Reproached for lack of respect, she replied: "I don't respect art, I love it.")

Nancy was good company, bitchy and keen, with complex stories of the current British upper class (was there any other?), and an occasional charitable corsage thrown toward the United States which she purported to disdain, except when I was around. We walked often together in the hills behind our hill, laced with untrodden paths extending indefinitely northward, with scarcely a sign of humanity except for a curl of purple smoke on the horizon twining toward the sky in early evening. This was a Garden of Eden, the Eden of Pagnol, with hardworking Eves and crusty-hot Adams descending into our village Saturday mornings to stock up and play pétanque. Their language— the *langue d'Oc* or Provençal—is, in inflection and accent and meter, the reverse of English as spoken in the southeastern United States. Our southern speech is somnolent, dropping final consonants while interpolating cooing vowels in an effort to beguile, in virtue as in vice, not only the Yankee philistine but the boy or girl next door. The speech of southern France is wide awake, takes its cue from northern Italy, is rapid, stressing the mute *e,* adding final vowels, eschewing the nasal Parisian twang, and grows incomprehensible to all but themselves.

One memorable promenade resulted from the decision to explore the fourth, and last, of the properties on our special hill. This was the Villa Sainte-Claire, another eighty yards off, which once belonged to Edith Wharton, but had stood empty for years. From the summit of the divinely lovely little knoll, where the Germans had raised a still-standing gallows only seven years before, one could look down upon our various roofs and plot a course. Marie-Laure had told us that she and Igor and Cocteau used to visit Berenson at Sainte-Claire; that in fact Cocteau once "created" a faux-Picasso and passed it off to Berenson, who assessed it as bona fide and gave it to Wharton, who adored Cocteau; that these people, like old Proust, were made for the scorn of adolescents, but now it was too late to atone; and that as far as she knew the nearby estate lay in ruins.

With the furtive insolence of foreigners Nancy and I gingerly tiptoed through the walled garden surrounding the mansion. The garden seemed the more hideous for having once been flawless, its concrete paths now cracked and slimy with snails, as were the leafless olive trees. (I remembered the India described by Jean Bertrand, where long-abandoned castles were inhabited by apes.) Here the snails were the sole remains of the day, animal or vegetable, to echo what may once have been laughter and greenery and strawberry shortcake. The house was easy of access: we simply stepped over the broken glass of a window sill. Like the phantom ship *Marie-Thérèse,* dozens of rooms retained signs of decrepit usefulness, wind blowing through tattered curtains and across unmade beds, as though no looter, no city inspector had set foot there since Mrs. Wharton vanished. In 1964, during a final stay in Hyères, I dined on the terrace of Sainte-Claire, now purchased by the township and become an expensive restaurant.

Another promenade a few years later: Nancy had just created an international stir with her tongue-only-half-in-cheek essay *Noblesse Oblige,* in which she launched the terms "U" (upper class) and "non-U," defining these categories according to speech patterns. It became a chic pastime in the better U homes to classify virtually anything according to Nancy's hilarious rules. (Non-U families, of course, didn't play the game: they couldn't, by definition, grasp the terms.) Except that Nancy didn't set the rules: the terms "U" and "non-U" were formulated by one Professor Alan Ross, a sociologist from whom Nancy filched the notion. One stifling July afternoon when the mistral wind, arid and sterile and unstoppable, was funneling down the Rhone Valley and driving everyone mad, Nancy and I were as usual staggering about the back hills. She suddenly stopped and said, in her high-pitched schoolmarm British U-voice: "Why lookie here! Ants!" Sure enough, an army of red ants, millions of them, was filing for perhaps twenty meters in one direction, while parallel in the opposite direction moved an army of black ants, two ribbons of squirming caviar. I observed Nancy, now on her knees, examining the motion with all the objective concentration of a Formicidae expert, and said to myself: God, how unlike my mother! What could Mother, the tragic egalitarian pacifist, make of this comedic snobbish foreigner? What did I myself make of the witty creature, the eldest (b. 1904) of six sisters, two at least of whom were Royalist-Fascist warmongers? I never thrilled as others did, to Nancy's famous wit, though in later years I came to admire Jessica Mitford's pithy examinations of California. The heat. The mistral. The clouds like tumors ready to burst, burst now, after a week of retaining their vomit, and the ants scurried, but *scurried slowly,* toward their respective hills, miniature versions of our own. What indeed did Nancy make of herself, rushing home in the rain with this wistfully ambitious Illinois composer, here in the landscape of Giono?

"How old is your mother?" she asked. "Is she one's age?"

English to the roots in her profundities, Nancy was French in her superficialities. She loved, for example, being up-to-date—being, as the French put it, *à la page*.

"How can you still be composing tonally," she would ask (who knew nothing of music), "when everyone else composes serially?" But to be up-to-date is to be quickly dated, since tomorrow is not today. And to be *à la page* for a fast reader is to turn the page so rapidly as to lose your place.

"I am of my time," said I, "by virtue of inhabiting that time. Thus whatever I do stems from my time."

Elsewhere her innocence was ever more pronounced.

"I fail to understand the nature of homosexuality," she wrote to her American counterpart, historian Robert Halsband, while struggling over a book on Frederick the Great. "I am excessively normal myself & have never had the slightest leaning in that direction even as a child." Was she unaware that Halsband was queer as a nine-dollar bill, as were most of her male friends?

On the other hand, Nancy was refreshingly level-headed. She realized that Marie-Laure was one-third insane, that in fact most of our friends, stupid and smart, are insane, but that we accommodate them as they accommodate us, until they cross the fatal border. She admired the Vicomtesse but wearied of her endless complications strewn in the paths of all and sundry. The level-headedness apparently prevailed through Nancy's final pain-filled days. We corresponded till the end, she writing either from stylish points on the Adriatic, or from her beautiful ground-floor apartment in Paris. She loved to bathe (in her old-maidish "swim-frock"), and to recall the gossip at our appropriately named beach at Hyères, La Potinière, where all the upper crust of the village united at noon, sans Marie-Laure who hated the sun but loved to hear about it at lunchtime.

Luna Hotel, Venice   26 June 57

Dearest Ned

Oh alas I'm here. I would have loved to lend my benighted ear to your melodies. I did lend it the other day—I was staying with Eddy Sackville West in Ireland & he put on a record saying this is by a very gifted American called Rorem. I was intensely gratified.

The beach here is like a *rather cleaner* Potinière. The fact is all beaches are alike. But oh I miss the Docteur, the Local Beauty, M. de Suez & You.

Give my love to Mary Laura

Love and Success from
Nancy

"M. de Suez" refers to Nora and her rapport with Guy de Lesseps, whose grandfather dug the canal into the Red Sea. Nancy refers to her own grandfather in another letter, this one to Salt Lake City where during 1966 I professed at the university. My first book, *The Paris Diary,* had just appeared.

7 Rue Monsieur VII   24 Ap 66

Dear Ned

Yes funnily enough I have heard of Utah—my grandfather went there, in a stove pipe no doubt, about 100 years ago. (But didn't join in the orgies —I spring from lawful wedlock on that side.)

Awfully pleased to have your news—the Diary will be fascinating & I long for it. I shall be in Ireland and England in May so I might be a little late in acknowledging it.

I saw Louise de V[ilmorin] yesterday—she is to sit on a film jury in Hyères. The organiser asked which hotel she would like—she said she would stay with M.-L.—the organiser said please don't "elle nous fait tant d'ennuis." So Louise is going to Tony instead. I thought this rather point-less tale would show you that things jog along here as per.

Yrs ever

Nancy

Back to that first day in Hyères.

On the calendar for Sunday is marked only: "The terrifying book of Dr. Magnus Hirshfield." . . . Even then it seemed dated.

Monday: "Walk with Nora at 5:00. Drunken arrival of Boris K.". . . Nora Auric was ever a ready companion for seaside or strolling. Marie-Laure disliked her but could not for my sake dismiss her, though did once consider refurbishing the swimming pool so I wouldn't need to leave each morning for the shore with Nora. Nora it was who introduced me to the books of Georges Simenon, Europe's greatest novelist of this mid-century, who was plotting a libretto for Auric. (Curtain rises on bridge spanning Canal Saint-Martin. Woman on bridge sings aria, then falls in water and drowns. The opera never got beyond this point because of the two men's schedules.) Since then I have read eighty books of Simenon, which miss the dimension of Proust or Zola only because they never touch on homosexuality. Boris Kochno's drinking would have been a bore were it not so grandiose, with a constant keening for his lost Bébé, the slurred insults for those around him followed by bear hugs *à la russe,* then brandy snifters smashed against the fireplace. His room was directly over mine in the little tower overlooking the front lawn. Boris paced all night, but never came down, as I vaguely hoped. Everyone talks of Boris's dissipation. Demurely I lower my eyes, a nearsighted nun, in hypocritical approval of their disapproval. Hadn't I, all last week, been too drunk to stand up?

Tuesday: "Saint-Tropez. Played *Mélos* for Boris. Evening of poetry reading.". . . Saint-Tropez was not yet—and certainly never in early April—the playground of movie stars. An hour's drive east from Hyères, it was the prettiest port on the Azure Coast with its little ships and little bistros and little rocky shoals. We had a lemonade at the Bateau Ivre, me and Roro and Burnap and Marie-Laure, then bought yellow shirts chez Vachon, and returned to Hyères via Cogolin where the ex-follies star Mistinguett owned a public farm from the front lawn of which she waved at us. (She made a comeback a few years later. Janet Flanner: "Mistinguett is an amazing sight; she still has her lovely, white, sharp-looking teeth, her handsome blue eyes are still empty of thought, and her voice still tintinnabulates on pitch, like a nice, weathered sheep bell"—a sentence which in 1965 I set to music for male unison chorus, saxophone, harmonium, percussion, and strings.) In playing for Boris the ballet score of *Mélos* based on Marie-Laure's scenario, I gratified the scenarist's anxiety as to whether I had a "sense of theater," a conclusion she hesitated to make for herself. But Boris, after all, should know a thing or two about such matters, or what's a Diaghilev for? "Dis-nous, Boris, est-ce qu'il a le sens du théâtre," she pleaded, as I plowed through the as-yet-unorchestrated score. Boris said he guessed I did. But if I did—or do—*Mélos* is no example. Of the poetry reading, I can not easily forget Kochno's keening of these sweeping strophes:

Un soir de demi-brume à Londres
Un voyou qui ressemblait à
Mon Amour . . .

then Marie-Laure echoing from another part of the parlor

. . . allez-y voir vous-même,
si vous ne voulez pas me croire

from the Lautréamont who foreshadowed the Apollinaire her surrealist mob so venerated. Apollinaire I knew already from Poulenc's songs, and from the jolly Sade-istic *récit* called *Les onze-mille verges,* but the larger poems were new territory. Lautréamont (b. 1809), Rimbaud's precursor, was so honestly shocking for his or any time, that my own attempts to shock in those high school verses were just that, attempts. Any attempt, by nature, fails.

Wednesday: "Roro's trial and departure. *L'héritage de la chair* with

M-L." . . . Roro had come south, interrupting his busy schedule at the Conservatoire, to stand trial in the department of Draguinan for the crime of having, the previous summer, bathed naked (and quite alone) on the beach of Saint-Tropez. This, in the land of logic! Auric, whose name carried clout, wrote a letter vouching for Roro's respectability. (A year later, Saint-Tropez became the first of many towns to legalize, in certain sections, nude bathing.) "*L'héritage de la chair* turned out to be *Pinky,* dubbed."

Thursday: "Bath. Read *The Cocktail Party* (T.S. Eliot)."

Friday: "Crisis of the dog Diego. Cannes with Burnap 2:00. *En panne—un cauchemar.*" . . . Diego, a bichon frisé, was old enough, Marie-Laure liked to point out, to have seen the rise and fall of Hitler. I never cared for him, but was undone this morning at seeing the animal writhe and stagger, fall limp and dead, then rise and leave the room unsteadily. He survived another year. Cannes, where we made no hotel reservations on the grounds that, as Charles Trenet used to sing, "There's always a crust of bread for a good-looking boy," turned out a fiasco. To be sure, there was the crust of bread, but Burnap and I lost sight of each other in our drunkenness, then the car broke down, then we called Saint-Bernard (2.91 à Hyères) to announce our return on Saturday, whereupon Labisse came to the phone, reporting that a Madame Morel from the Hôtel du Bon La Fontaine had called from Paris to say that my belongings had been stolen from room 14. This was not news to soothe a hangover. When Madame Morel tried to pass the buck to Jean Leuvrais, she being aware that I nurtured an unholy alliance with him, I was livid. She agreed to grant three months free rent, which I accepted. Though I was in no mood to return soon to Paris, and planned instead to return to Morocco for a month.

Saturday: "Reading *The Autobiography of Alice B. Toklas.*"

Sunday: "Reading Sartre's new play." (This must have been *Le diable et le bon Dieu,* for which Félix Labisse was designing the set.)

Monday: "Marie-Laure begins another portrait. I play *Socrate* for her, which she titles the portrait. 7:00 Tony Gandarillas."

Tuesday: "Reading *The Flower Beneath the Foot, The Marble Faun.* Lunch Tony Gandarillas, the Chilean, drunk."

Wednesday: "Gogol's *Le nez.*" The borders of each entry are cluttered with names of correspondents.

Thursday: "Pouchkine [Pushkin] *Un coup de pistolet.* Bath."

Friday: "Arrival of Charles de Noailles and of Julien Green." Knowing that Julien would be in Monte Carlo to receive a prize bestowed by Prince Rainier, and that Marie-Laure's venerable spouse, the Vicomte, whom I'd never met, would be coming from his estate in Grasse to pass the weekend at Saint-Bernard, I wondered if perhaps the Vicomte might not bring Julien along, knowing that Marie-Laure would consider this a feather in her cap. The Vicomte—"Appelez-moi donc Charles"—as always the essence of tact, of breeding, of old-world charm, passed most of his time discussing finances with Henri, the maître d'hôtel, and discussing the dreary floral output with the gardener. For Charles knew something about cultivation—spent most of his years commuting between the famous gardens of the Continent, and had a rose named for him. As for Julien, he seemed intimidated by Marie-Laure, inadvertently calling her Marie-Blanche (she: "Vous me blanchissez, cher ami"), and telling me in private that he'd come only for me, that wasn't I wasting precious time with these people? He was put in the room across from mine, and pleaded with me to visit that room during the night. I did not. (Do I sound like Harold Norse's memoir, *Bastard Angel,* which could be subtitled "Famous Men I Wouldn't Put Out For"?)

Saturday: "Départ Julien."

Sunday: "Fly from Marseilles to Casablanca."

So after my first two weeks in Hyères I returned to Guy Ferrand.

Enough is too much. But a little too much is just enough for me.

Notes on Her.

—Never apologize, never explain. That is her motto. Yet like a good little girl she tries to do better next time.

She is twenty-one years older than I, obviously her French is superior, and she has passed her life with the best conversationalists. When in an argument I might one-up her, she calls me Miss Sly. She pronounces it Meeze-Lye.

—She never stops reading, except while at the easel or asleep. The invaluable so-called New York Edition of Henry James, fifty volumes in discreet green leather on their own shelf at the entrance of the little bibliothèque, is not for show. She wends her way through these systematically, is already into *The Ambassadors,* nudges me constantly to follow suit.

At the moment she is devouring Ivy Compton-Burnett at Tom Keogh's say-so. And, because she loathes her body and face, allows herself to be photographed only from behind, like Henry Green.

A dozen signed books arrive on her doorstep each week. In Paris her daily sortie, other than to the coiffeur or to various vernissages (all squeezed into two hours), is to Galigniani's bookstore, rue de Rivoli, into which she shuffles in her espadrilles, rudely elbowing unsuspecting customers as her nose leads straight to *the* volume which she snatches from the shelf, calling out, "Je prends celui-ci. Mettez ça sur le compte du Vicomte," and leaves with her booty before the salesman can ring up the bill. Maurice Gendron's cruelly accurate imitation of this near-daily episode occasions my reluctantly uncontrolled laughter, and M-L's too. Reluctant, because I hate humor. I hate the sound of pseudo joy emerging from mediocre larynxes who have no other reaction. Even organized high-level drollery leaves me cold, like the black fairy at the gay party.

—She is as naïve as the suave Nancy Mitford on the subject of male homosexuality. Like many another normal female she feels that offering her rectum to be sodomized will solve the problem. But where does that leave the other half of the male population that wants to be sodomized, at least on Mondays, Wednesdays, and Fridays?

She belittles my pacifism as American puritanism, yet contradicts herself (the richest woman in France) as a victim of male chauvinism.

"All women are slaves of men," she contends. But I reply,

"All men, in turn, are slaves of the state. With no alternative but prison and ostracism, a billion boys are forced to serve their army, forced to fight for what they cannot believe, year after year. Forced to die. And in France they're not even paid for military service, where women go free."

"Miss Sly," says Marie-Laure.

—Nancy gives me a beautiful notebook in which to write stories. The cover, of dark-blue marbleized student-smelling cardboard, is embossed with tiny golden moles.

"The female mole," says Marie-Laure, "has a minuscule vagina and is penetrated only with great difficulty. Because Nancy is *une femme barrée* she gives people notebooks with moles on them. She waits on tiptoe for Palewski who never arrives, because he does not want *une femme barrée*. He wants a woman he can move around in. Like me."

"But," says Maurice Gendron, "no man wants a vagina he can move around in," leaving Marie-Laure without the last word.

—Because she is in love with me, she assumes the world also is. At the dinner table sit Arturo Lopez, Alexei de Rédé, Ghislaine de Polignac, and Christian Mégret, not intellects exactly (except for Christian), but not fools either, and worldly to a fault. Arturo, his South

American fortune in the magic hands of Alexei—Austrian and much younger—has the leisure to drink all day as the money rolls in. (He was also, twenty years earlier when Cocteau was looking for *figurants* for *Blood of a Poet,* one of those clapping in the loge, next to Barbette, when the poet kills himself.) Christian, a drama critic and mildly successful novelist, loves the idle and beauteous Ghislaine.

Everyone but Marie-Laure is full of wine—she doesn't touch wine —and nicely groggy. She holds an esoteric monologue comparing the use of dialogue in Diderot's novels with the same use in Henry James's fifteen plays. Noting Arturo's wealthy head drooping, she announces:

"Ned is America's gift to France. We all want to bugger Ned. Even Henri." She alludes to the maître d'hôtel who, pouring more blanc-des-blancs, interpolates without changing expression:

"It's an interesting notion, but I'm sure Monsieur Rorem would object. And I'm not made that way."

Though I shudder with discomfort, none of the others reacts, although Ghislaine, to be cordial, inquires:

"Is it true, Ned?" How can I affirm or deny? But Marie-Laure replies:

"Alas, I'm not made that way either," looking plaintively into her lap. Such an outburst at any time or place is not infrequent, and stems partly from the surrealist gang who still at this late date are out to shock, and partly from the need (still at this late date) to emancipate herself from the straitlaced Vicomte. Never in front of the Vicomte does she speak thus. When someone in front of the Vicomte refers to his wife's obstreperousness, neither he nor she feigns to notice.

—The surrealists, all male chauvinists, seem as naïve as she about homosexuality. Only two of them have been queer: Dali eventually withdrew, and Crevel committed suicide. If homosexuality is banned a priori, so too is music. But then, there *is* no surrealist music. Or rather: all music is surrealist.

—If, because she knows English, she has the edge on Auric, who is the other most literarily cultivated person on the hill, he obviously wins in musical culture. Her own musical culture is anecdotal only, and relies on quotes from Markevich or Gendron. But Markevich is history, and Gendron kids her. With Gendron, nevertheless, she shares another history: that of pining together in a concentration camp in northern Italy. This is hazy. Just as I have no idea how I would have behaved, or fared, during the Occupation, I'm always tentative about asking too many questions.

Am I, with all my ingrown Quaker magnanimity, at all anti-Semitic? I *am* a little bit anti-queer.

—Her menu twice a day is what other people serve once a year. Overabundant, fit for nobility. By 1970 how many thousand meals of lobster and Greek leaves and *figues à la creme* will I have enjoyed at her table? Still, after each meal I say thankyou.

She keeps a diary. (Because of that, I've resumed my own.) Drunk or sober she writes in it nightly, disappearing from a midnight fray in the parlor to tell the diary in the bedroom about the midnight fray in the parlor. Then, after a neat shot of *fine,* she returns.

—She has bought a donkey. Every year a roving theater group spreads its wares in the square in the front of the little cathedral of Hyères. The whole town shows up. Last summer it was André Gide's *Saül.* This year it is Alphonse Daudet's *L'arlesiènne* which could have unfolded in this very town a century ago. The noble Valentine Tessier, deaf now and missing lines, makes her entrance in a donkey-drawn cart.

"What becomes of that animal after tonight," asks Marie-Laure.

"To the abbatoir, Madame la Vicomtesse," answers the director.

"Let me buy him."

The animal is duly delivered. Named Alphonse, the donkey lives in the shed of the gardener who brings him every morning to graze on the lawn in front of the chateau. The gardener also brings a pair of sheep who wear bells, recalling Zeus and Hera in Vermont so long ago. The tinkling is my cue to get out of bed. The incongruous menagerie returns to the shed at sunset.

There is now an aviary too, with dozens of domesticated wrens and finches of those varieties I cultivated once, cobalt and tangerine, leading their own lives.

—She ignores her music library's value. It contains, among other treasures, scores Satie inscribed to Valentine Hugo, which Valentine was forced to sell. I still have two of these, *Parade* and *Socrate,* nor will I return them to Valentine.

—Regular guests from Nîmes include Jean Hugo (Victor's grandson), long divorced from Valentine, now married to a vigorous English woman, Loretta, as imposingly tall as himself. His oils, though, are cameo size. On a postage stamp—or almost—Jean Hugo (like Brion Gysin across the sea) paints Provençal landscapes replete with huts and humans and horses, expressive and characteristic as Van Gogh's.

Also from Nîmes, lured by a lunch of *brindade de morue* garnished with acid wit, comes Jean Godebski, now in his fifties and tall as Jean Hugo. It was for Godebski and his big sister, Mimi, that Ravel in 1908 composed the four-hand suite *Ma mère l'oye.* "We never really learned

it, or cared about the piano, which is why Ravel eventually orchestrated it," explains Godebski, without much interest. It was his Aunt
Misia who had set the deal in motion.

Young Jean Lafont too, a virile rustic with smiling eyes and hay-
colored hair smelling faintly of the bull pens of the Camargue. For he
is a *manadier,* a breeder of the great black mammals who fight to the
death in the corridas of Arles. Lafont is charm-filled and canny. He has
a boyfriend in the shape of a young apprentice at the *manade,* and
sometimes too he goes to Nice for the anonymity of the random
pickup or the rowdy bar. But he is also interested in the Noailles's
finances. Years from now, after I have quit France for good, he will
take over my rooms both here and in the place des Etats-Unis. Marie-
Laure will fall in love with him, run weeping through the streets at the
age of sixty-three, tearing her hair, as she runs now through the streets
at forty-nine and tears her hair for me, and did likewise for Raffaello
sometime back while he would pray to the Holy Madonna of Trieste
that the Vicomtesse would stay out of his bed. But Lafont is a decent
chap. He will negotiate a sizable personal subsidy from Charles de
Noailles. He speaks with a pronounced *accent du Midi,* irresistibly,
intelligently.

French is the tongue of homophones, not just for single words *(j'en-
vias janvier)* but for entire alexandrines, the most famous being Victor
Hugo's:

> Gall, amant de la reine, alla, tour magnanime
> Gallament, de l'arène à la Tour Magne, à Nîme.

Thus railway agents sigh each time they hear the awful pun on the
town of Sète: "Six billets pour Sète." ("Six tickets for seven.") And
thus, to the Gallic ear, Hyères is interchangeable with *hier*—or yesterday. "Demain je rentre à Hyères."
Tomorrow I'll return to yesterday.

Today I'll go back to Morocco.
Guy lived now in Marrakech. The new lodging, less "agreeable"
than the one in Fez, was a three-room flat, *premier étage,* on a nondescript European street leading to the red-light district. By day the
arcaded thoroughfare hummed with life: shops and hawkers vending
non-Arabic goods—sewing machines, French weeklies, canned goods,
gin. By night the silence was torn intermittently by légionnaires reel-
ing half-drunk, hands cupping their crotches, toward the *quartier réservé* where ornamental whores of every age, overly made up in red

chiffon and shaming the laws of purdah, waved the boys into a little *enceinte* from which came an aroma of spearmint tea.

On the plus side: the famed place Djemaa-el-Fnaâ, that twenty-four-hour ten-ring circus just two blocks away. Nothing there has altered since the Bible. Flanked by the green-tile Koutoubia minaret, Djemaa-el-Fnaâ is a gigantic market with fire-and-sword swallowers, cobra charmers, open-air barbers complete with their little tubs of leeches for healthy bloodletting, the ubiquitous smells of mint and cedar, unleavened bread and beef brochettes, storytellers, one veiled female to every fifty muscular-calfed men, and pile after pile of red and yellow peppers, raw camel meat, silver amulets shaped like scorpions, smoke everywhere, and the constant drone of prayer. Beyond was the Médina, merrier and brighter than Fez's, with, among the shops, cafés, liquorless nightclubs where overweight Phaedras do belly dances amid the fumes of kif.

In other words, an ideal ambiance on which to pull the shade and compose American music.

During the twenty-four-day stay I began and finished:

Another Sleep for voice and piano, the three melancholy recitations from Julien Green's book, with a hopeful dedication to Gérard Souzay who never sang them.

To a Young Girl, a cycle of six songs on poems of Yeats, which was already well underway in Hyères. These were dedicated to Doda Conrad who performed them at a League of Composers concert at the Museum of Modern Art the following year. Like *Another Sleep,* the cycle remains unpublished, except for the title song, printed two decades later, and dedicated to Sylvia Goldstein. And another movement, "O Do Not Love Too Long," I absorbed into an instrumental sextet in 1984 by eliminating the words, assigning the vocal part to a single line on the piano, and the accompaniment to a string quartet (rather than, as typecasting would have it, giving the vocal line to oboe or violin).

"Sweet Dancer," another Yeats song, about a girl in an asylum. Also unpublished and unsung (in fact, have I ever shown it to a singer?), it's one of many songs which must have struck me as, well, perfect, but without theatricality. For a song is no less a dramatic event than a miniature opera. Of the hundreds of true singers that I (used to) know, not one has admitted that, given the choice, he would rather perform opera than recitals. In a recital he is able—as they say—to communicate directly, without mask or costume, and to adopt twenty different egos, all in a row, moving from one three-minute impersonation to the next.

Mélos—the orchestration, which has also never been heard.

. . .

Were Guy and I still sleeping together? Did I, during this visit, have a brief fling with one of his colleagues, Jean La Forge, who taught French at the lycée? Yes. This took place during one of Guy's many excursions into the *bled*. When I told Guy, he entreated me not to *tutoyer* La Forge in front of him, else he'd be obliged to show anger, when in fact he liked La Forge. The brief fling ceased abruptly when the test records of my symphony arrived from Vienna. Together we listened to this fine performance of a piece I'd never heard, during which La Forge wanted to make love. Which seemed obtuse.

I also made love (if you called three minutes beneath the stairwell "love") with a young Arab who had followed me one night from Djemaa-el-Fnaâ into the front hall.

These were the only extramarital erotic episodes—almost—I ever had in Africa, until I returned a decade later.

From Marie-Laure I have retained a voluminous correspondence in a box with her books and pictures and other mementoes. Because she was a pack rat, she probably retained the same from me. (Nobody seems to know what's become of her writings, most importantly her diary which she coveted, but which Charles would have found a post-humous impropriety.) I do remember sending her a drawing from Morocco, on a sheet of 8½- by 11-inch paper, of a huge erect prick, surrounded with this message: *Mon amour pour toi est aussi dur et inébranable que cette bitte est dure et branlable.* Guy, peering over my shoulder, was aghast: "Are you really on such terms with the Vicomtesse?" It's difficult today to retrieve my motive, beyond opportunistic titillation, but Marie-Laure doted on that sort of thing.

Messaoud remained in Fez, and was replaced by Laoucine, an impersonal forty-year-old. He fixed meals, did the ménage, and that was it. Norris Embry, visiting Guy once when I was away, apparently made a pass at Laoucine, on the grounds that "all Arabs are available." The pass was unreciprocated, and Laoucine sulked at Guy for weeks.

Often we dined at the Mamounia Hotel, a venerable white elephant which Churchill had called home and which now was being edged out of the winter tourists' favor by the new Menara, which served a memorable *soufflé au Grand Marnier.* (I could still in those days indulge in a liqueur-drenched comestible without going off on a tear.) Outings to Mogador, picnics, swimming pools, movies thrice weekly, a concert series like the one in Fez, rain, public dances, reading (Genet, Malraux), visits from Lévesque, and socializing with a somber local poet named Azema. Mostly I just worked.

When people exclaimed at how inspiring I must find this wealth of exotica, I would feel mute contempt. Musicians don't compose scenery. Although I put total credence in the notion that a composer's nationality can be divined through his ineffable output according to the "phonetics" of that output (we are what we speak), I challenge anyone to situate the precise geography on which Bach or Tchaikovsky or Albéniz stood when they wrote *Saint Matthew* or *Francesca* or *Iberia*. There is nothing in my Moroccan catalogue (beyond what I've told you, in words, was borrowed and then aberrated from wisps of tunes overheard on the radio) that could indicate my whereabouts.

Finances? I must have been living still on what Father sent—a hundred dollars a month?—knowing that by the end of summer there would be regular supplementary checks (a hundred dollars a month?) from the Fulbright Foundation. Meanwhile rent had been unnecessary in Hyères and in Morocco, and would continue to be in Paris for the next three months. Until January of 1953 when I moved into her house(s), Marie-Laure paid hotel bills, bought all my clothes, and provided hundreds of meals. Were it not for her, would I have persisted? Not, certainly, in the same manner. Virgil once wrote: "Every composer's music reflects in its subject matter and in its style the source of the money the composer is living on while writing that music. This applies to introspective as well as to objective music." Well, Virgil might not still concur; nor might he ever have added that the *quality* was also dependent on the composer's income source.

Yet even today, if I am not regularly shown that, without having made concessions, I am appreciated (through regular performances, printed reviews—good or bad—and interviews, or my name in the crossword puzzle), I begin to doubt the rat race and want to throw in the sponge.

On 13 May I flew from Casablanca to Paris, arriving in time to dine with Marie-Laure and Oscar Dominguez.

In a current *TLS* one finds this quote from John Sturrock's just-published *The Language of Autobiography:* "Rousseau shows how facile it is to say, as we often hear it said, that an autobiographer 'relives' his past in the writing of it. The autobiographer alas knows differently: to narrate one's past is to be driven through it without stopping." To fall so fortuitously onto "without stopping," the title of Paul Bowles's autobiography and an echo of the book now in your hands, sounds like a warning.

"Rousseau presents two large and separate subjects to the reader: the self that was given to him by nature, and the self that he created for himself." Though of course the self we create for ourselves *is* the self given us by nature.

"... when he felt his career as an author was at an end, he reverted to his old aimless, cheerfully idle, natural self."

I've introduced a massive cast but haven't made them do anything, much less interact. Well, life has no plot. Yes, but a book isn't life. Still, I'm relieved at having made the decision to close these pages by the end of 1951. Meanwhile, like a horse which at evening, nearing the stable, gallops ever faster, I shall abridge increasingly.

Life is a book.

33. Marie-Laure in Paris

"You ain't no oil paintin', but you are a fascinatin' monster," declares Mae West at the close of *Klondike Annie,* pulling Victor McLaglen into her all-forgiving bosom. The description could fit Oscar Dominguez who was certainly a monster, if not quite fascinating, but in fact a sort of oil painting by nature. Elephantine of body, hydrocephalic of visage, semi-incomprehensible of speech, Oscar was an Hispanic artist completely in thrall (as were all Parisian artists) to his compatriot, Picasso. Because he was not Picasso, Oscar drank. Born ugly in Tenerife in 1906, he never accommodated to any beauties of our physical world and thus became a natural recruit for the surrealists as debunker of virtually all standards, high and low. He was proud of his Canary Islands origins, spoke fairly fluent French with a thick accent, flailed rather than walked, and was likable when sober. But his veneration of Picasso was abject, and Picasso, who doubtless felt warmly toward him in the good old days, was now wary of the woozy impromptu visits Oscar often paid. Oscar's own pictures and sculptures were not, except for an occasional foreshortened face with three eyes, especially Picassoesque; nor did they in any way resemble himself, as the work of a true artist somehow must. They were precise, geometrical, like a teacher's layout, with square or round spaces left for the pupil to fill in with primary colors. Marie-Laure's "rich-girl" pictures, with all their lack of discipline, vibrated with a more personal urgency than Oscar's, a fact which made her uncomfortable because males are better than females, and anyway her lover, by virtue of being her lover, is by definition a genius.

But Oscar and Marie-Laure were not yet lovers when I dined with them that May evening in the Bar d'Enfer on rue Campagne-Première, near Oscar's apartment in mid-Montparnasse. Oscar took an immediate shine to me, called me then and thereafter Dorian Gray or *mon fils,* loudly embracing me in public with the open-hearted extroversion of one safe in his heterosexuality. For the moment he was under control, attentive to Marie-Laure, filled with questions about me, answers about himself. His elephantiasis, for example, he credited to excessive masturbation in his youth. Did that happen too in Chicago?

She imagined herself a bohemian, mistress of a painter, benefactress to a composer, hostess to the needy. The "needy" were mainly well-known visual artists—Man Ray, Labisse, Leonor Fini, Giacometti, and especially Balthus and Dora Maar who were semiweekly lunch guests in her blue marble dining room, or dinner guests at the Catalan. Just as I recall Monsieur Vadot's Néocopie-Musicale, where I still went regularly for the duplication of scores, as a purposeful and thus an inspiring ambiance, I remember with the same pleasure four other Paris environments, icily purposeful in their nonsymbolic ability to aid in the birth of something more than themselves: the Desgobert lithograph parlor, where Marie-Laure took me to watch her etch on giant blocks in a vast space resembling Easter Island; Karinska's studio, also with M-L, another vast space with twelve seamstresses sitting amid numberless bolts of ecru satin stitching costumes; the Steinway factory where Julius Katchen was permitted to practice from midnight to dawn among dozens of grand pianos, and where, drunk in the obscurity, I played and sang *Socrate* for him and Heddy de Ré; and the Catalan restaurant near the rue Dauphine. The restaurant's tonality, being no more than four walls on a second floor, depended on its clientele, and this group, almost first-rate, gave off a thrilling smell not soon forgotten.

Man Ray, already sixty-one, was the eldest. For some reason I'd preimagined him as Parisian-born and was surprised to hear his broad Philadelphia accent refracted by his imperfect French. He had just returned from a wartime decade in California with his much younger wife, a dancer named Juliet, who resembled Ava Gardner. (Man Ray, in fact, had provided the cameo photo of Ava, emblem of the new film *Pandora,* using Juliet as model.) Though unafraid and decorative, Juliet, as a younger American, never quite fit into this nest of old buddies, relying on me as interpreter and as drinking partner. (Not that I fit in either.) Man Ray was a sober Oscar, in the sense that he never spoke without trying for effect; he spoke continually, and the effect was meant to be outrageous ("the holy-water fonts in Saint-Sulpice should be used as ashtrays"; "women are really men who have amounted to something"—that sort of thing) but not meant to offend. Like Sir Arthur Sullivan who thought his collaborations with Gilbert inferior to his now-vanished oratorios, Man Ray pooh-poohed his immeasurably special photography in favor of his comparatively mediocre oils and ready-mades. From our first meeting both he and Juliet talked always of how he had never used nonfemale models, and how I would be ideal to break the mold. After two years of this I said: Do it now. So, in a dark wool sweater, a bright red scarf, and Jerry Robbins's dirty white raincoat, I posed for Man Ray in 1953 at his wide, dark studio on the rue Férou. On one of the negatives, at his request, I calligraphed the opening bars of the waltz "Tout beau mon coeur," based on verses of Georges Hugnet, which I had dedicated to Man Ray and Juliet. (This song, never published, is recast as the "Bal Musette" in the 1983 suite *Picnic on the Marne* for saxophone and piano.)

Félix Labisse, like Man Ray, excelled more at what he belittled—in this case theater design—than in what he praised in himself: the somewhat embarrassing overrealistic nude women with blood in their hair. Like Man Ray he too was no slouch at repartee, but being francophone the words flowed more easily.

Leonor Fini, Argentinean raised in Italy, painted with a brush whose accuracy shamed Dali's, and used as her sole subject matter her own intimidatingly feline features portraying Death. Her technique, if not her imagination, surpassed Marie-Laure's, and she thrived in a world which may have found the Vicomtesse amateurish. Leonor, with that guttural stagy speech, those black muslin cloaks and turbans of green fur, and the intelligent self-assurance, scared me. Nor could one, everybody said, be friends with both her and Marie-Laure. She was not to be trifled with. Her lover, the willowy Stanislav Lépri, was the object of unrequited adoration by a certain duke. This duke asked Leonor to plead in his favor with Lépri. A week later the duke asked Leonor: "What did he say?" Leonor: "That you are garbage."

Alberto Giacometti's presence—*un beau laid,* he too—was so fa-miliar around the Saint-Germain quarter, with his sad face and care-less déshabille, that his appearance at Marie-Laure's table seemed incongruous. As for his work, I prefer his gray-and-pink portraits to the bottom-heavy elongated sculptures that brought him fame. He played on one note all his life, and that note is more fetching and dimensional in James Lord's reporting than in the work itself. I would never have predicted his posthumous glory any more than I'd have predicted Balthus's international canonization.

Balthus, single-named like Colette or Fernandel, was a count be-cause he said he was. Born in Poland, romantic to the teeth, emaciat-edly attractive, a self-pitying scold, and far more widely versed—including in music—than most painters who never read and so hang out in cafés all winter when night falls early (especially in northerly Paris) and it's too dark to paint, Balthus had a little-boy whine that counterbalanced his pedophilic paintings and an opportunistic way of denigrating Marie-Laure that got results (what's money for if not to nourish genius, etcetera). He longed to legitimize his bogus nobility by buying a castle. This he did, with a ramshackle fifty-room ruin somewhere above Nevers. We stopped there and took pictures en route to the Midi in 1952, and found only one habitable room. Below this room, weirdly, was the replica of—or was it the model for?—the cistern in which Alain Cuny is held prisoner in *L'île des chèvres.* As with Nancy Mitford, or for that matter with Giacometti, I was at first miffed at the fuss around Balthus's big-scale paintings, so overshad-owed was their style by their content. The content, like that of Alvin Ross who must have already known Balthus's work years before, was pubescent females, overweight with braids, being ogled by witches. The style was that of children's books. Marie-Laure, in fact, had on display in her octagonal parlor the original series of black-and-white illustrations for *Wuthering Heights* which seemed unexceptional. When Balthus noodled, the way they all did, with his black pencil on the white paper tablecloth of the Catalan, depicting what he called his Ancestors, Marie-Laure carefully clipped it and gave it to me saying: "Frame this." Only with the conditioning of time, and with the lectur-ing of those wiser than I, have I learned that Balthus is, yes, important.

Dora Maar: she of the limpid laughter, the long cigarette holder, the Mata Hari hair-bob, the acutely animated brain paradoxically wed-ded to a pathological lack of humor. Her position as Picasso's mistress and model for scores of his greatest portraits during the decade sur-rounding World War II stamped every aspect of her personality and conversation. But Dora was herself a portraitist of consequence: look at the rendition of her neighbor, Alice Toklas, in gray and black and brown, to realize how a spirit can be transferred to canvas and preserved indefinitely. Among my most chilling souvenirs is this: In 1956 she invited me to sit for her. During our *séances de pose* in her studio, rue de Savoie, I came to see another side to this nervous cool woman who at Marie-Laure's was on more formal behavior. She was ... not unhappy but somehow unrealized. How could she not be, having been abandoned by the pagan God in the shape of Don Pablo? After an analysis with the madman Lacan, she turned to the Christian God and would have liked me to turn there too. My portrait in oils (which I recall as orange, mostly), plus a little pointilliste pencil drawing, she gave to me. I in turn entrusted these to Claude Lebon to have photographed. Claude left them in a taxi. No amount of searching at a dozen lost-and-founds ever led to their retrieval. I never told Dora, and hope you won't tell her now.

Behold the dramatis personae of Marie-Laure's innings and outings. Put them all regularly at one table and hear them talk. Not one was born in France (Paris for a century was merely a crossroads), and all were heterosexual. Painters then as a rule were straight, while composers as a rule were gay—at least those crossing Marie-Laure's path like Poulenc and Sauguet and vaguely Auric and certainly me. Marie-Laure was, in a sense, akin to Frank O'Hara. Frank was a poet who had been a musician, but his social milieu, when he could choose, was that of painters, straight painters. He preferred, so to speak, the *nationality* of painters. At four in the morning, his magnetism and gin and patience paid off when he got to bed with them, straight though they were. Marie-Laure too, through patience and gin and charm and conversation, managed to get at least Oscar to bed.

Oscar in this social collection was ever more of a problem as the years rolled on. His peers found him a boring baby. Dora alone showed patience, curious always for any word of Picasso that Oscar might trade with her after one of his unwanted visits. But Marie-Laure thrived on his misbehavior; indeed, with the sadism typical of all masochists, she tacitly encouraged it. How many times at Hyères, late at night after some ghastly faux pas of Oscar's when she would chide him before guests and swear never to let him drink in her house again, would she, after the guests had left, sneak up to his room with a bottle! "You aren't nice to me," he would say, "always scolding." And to me, next day, the avowal that he could only screw Marie-Laure when he was drunk.

But they adored each other too, sported like adolescents, called each other Poochie when things were going well. "Dis-moi, Poochie," he would say, and she would answer, "Oui, Poochie," in a sort of circular craziness that echoed for me years later when observing roommates Bill Flanagan and Edward Albee, who called each other Mommy. (If Edward were not yet home when Bill and I decided, say, to go out to a bar, Bill would leave a note: "Dear Mommy, Ned & I are at the Old Colony, meet us there at midnight, Love Mommy.")

If Marie-Laure took him to a party in "her world" of the Tout Paris, Oscar, like as not, would disrobe completely and dance on the table, a spectacle unwelcome even in a young sexy man. A Parisian hostess's quandary lay in whether to invite Marie-Laure and risk getting the dreaded Oscar too, or not to invite Marie-Laure and risk having her party lack luster. (A like problem for party givers then was Jean Genet. Genet, a known thief, made a point, when accepting an invitation into the *grand monde,* of stealing bric-a-brac. It became chic for one hostess to tell another: "When he came to my house Genet stole a silver tray. What did he steal from you?") Oscar and Marie-Laure were both my confidants: she asking advice, but never following it, about his drinking; he confiding that his pride, not to mention his talent, was being devoured by the woman. I was the parent of these grotesques, twenty years older than me. Once when I appeared at a function with them, a newspaper reported: "Et puis, il y avait Marie-Laure de Noailles avec, comme d'habitude, la Belle et la Bête."

It had been exactly two years since I sailed from the USA. My countrymen again were everywhere, quickly spotted by their naïve demeanor and irrelevant paraphernalia. I felt removed, wishing maybe to play American for the French, but also to play French for Americans. Priorities are where you find them. (Tableau: Stravinsky and Picasso stand chatting in the Champs-du-Mars. Tourist with camera comes up and says: "Would you mind stepping aside while I get a shot of the Eiffel Tower.") The sun set ever later. May nights turned lubricious.

I would remain in Paris two months this time, seeing Marie-Laure every day, but leading my own life too, with my own drinking problems, or rather, compulsions, not discussable with her, not comparable to Oscar's. The vicious cycle was my own too, growing ever tighter around unhealthy booze followed by revivifying sex followed by unhealthy booze followed . . . Contrary to accepted patterns I never drank alone but did have sex alone, that is, namelessly. Recovering from a hangover, trapped in a shredded body, I memorized the topography of Paris by wandering from *pissotière* to *pissotière,* from Buttes-Chaumont to place Breteuil, brushing against strangers, sometimes going to their dingy mansardes, sometimes bringing them to the hotel. Or sitting on a bench interminably, in perhaps the Parc Monceau, beyond responsibility, beyond even time and space, heavy eyes fixed on a reeking urinal into which centipedes, strong ones and weak ones, enter and remain too long, while two yards away toddlers in pinafores were dandled on their nannies' knees. Occasionally there were the public baths, an ideal hell I would grow dependent on in the Manhattan of the sixties. A small one on rue Dauphine, another on rue de Penthièvre, were without private cubicles, but a fourth-dimensional fog afforded privacy. If alcohol, at least at the start, seems witty, gay baths are humorless by definition. A man can't sustain an erection while laughing.

When I first arrived in France I was still full of Freudianisms—"He's anal, she's oral," etcetera—until everybody yawned, contending that Freud had passed that way in the 1930s and was old-hat to the logical French. In fact, he had merely grazed the surface before invading the United States, and was now returning to Paris in the guise of Jacques Lacan, an expensive psychoanalyst who had sprung from an intellectualized surrealist milieu, and, from my vantage, seemed mad as Peter Sellers in *What's New, Pussycat?* He had treated Philippe Bemberg who later killed himself, and Dora Maar, and Raffaello de Banfield. (Raffaello had wanted to break with Lacan, but the doctor waited beneath Raffaello's stairway and threatened him with damnation.) Marie-Laure knew Lacan socially, so was an authority on psychiatry.

My extracurricular social life, during this hiatus in Paris, other than the *cuites* which were noted every third day in the calendar, revolved around a parade of old friends, just passing through: Gary and Naomi Graffman, composer Homer Keller, and Nell Tangeman, the latter whom I took to sing *Penny Arcade* at Marie-Blanche's where the two fell in love. (Nell fell in love too with Eleanor Steber, another landsman just passing through. They had never met, but broke the ice with room-service daiquiris, and remained holed up in Eleanor's hotel for three days. Of such is the kingdom of divas.) Fixed Parisian friends, always with Jean Leuvrais as official lover, until Guy visited for a week in early June: Souzay, Lily Pastré, Kochno, Julius, Julien, the Aurics, Madame Claude Alphand of the sauterne-hued locks and lavender voice for whom I wrote three folklike ditties on words of Marot, Doda, Jacques Bourgeois, Jennie Tourel very often, Barbara Hutton, and others documented in *The Paris Diary*. There was an enormous party given by Alexei de Rédé in his Palais Lambert on the Île Saint-Louis (the hôtel, formerly Chopin's, was Arturo's gift), to celebrate the ballet *Mélos*. Since I had won only second prize, the honor seemed dim. Boulanger accompanied the incomparable Denise Duval in Préger's —not my—setting of Marie-Laure's words (during which, in deference to me, Marie-Laure left the hall), followed by Poulenc joyfully accompanying Duval in "Envolez-vous, oiseau de ma détresse," followed by Javanese dancers miming some ponderous fairy tale during which Elsa Maxwell, sitting with her back to them, declared: "Aren't they lovely." Movies: *Sunset Boulevard, All About Eve.* Books: Mauriac's suffocatingly beautiful *Le sagouin,* and Sartre's *Saint Genet.* (I never met, or even saw, Sartre, but did once see Genet. I was sitting on the terrace of Le Rouquet, rue Saint-Guillaume, when Genet strolled by on the arm of Jean de Noël to whom he audibly said: "I can't even pick my nose in public anymore without someone saying 'That's from The Book, page 547.' " Beyond this gossip report came two events affecting my professional future:

The Consul, Gian Carlo Menotti's first full-length opera which the previous year had such success in New York, now took Paris by storm. Alternately in English, with Patricia Neway as Magda Sorel, and in French, with Ethel Semser, it was playing to SRO at the Théâtre des Champs-Elysées. If you remember, at the end the curtain falls on Magda as she puts her head in the oven. On opening night the chief stagehand went out for a drink. Pat Neway assumed her pose, the music stopped. But the curtain stayed up for five long minutes of breathless quiet before the stagehand could be found. In the bustle backstage Cocteau pronounced: "Quel coup de théâtre, cette fin! Quel silence vertigineux!" Neway became a star, a darling, a guest in demand. A dessert was named for her at Maxim's. Menotti likewise. During his fifteen minutes in the fickle French sun he could do no wrong, his image and interviews on every street corner. Likewise too, the very young conductor Thomas Schippers, Menotti's protégé, said by everyone to be more beautiful than the sky. One evening at the Montana bar I chanced upon Gian Carlo. He sat with Schippers, the latter all of twenty-one and sure of himself, was indeed beautiful, but too perfect, too slick. I was nonplussed. We chatted, I invited them for lunch at Marie-Laure's, they accepted, that was that. Tommy grew. Within a few years, emancipated but still faithful musically to Gian Carlo, Tommy had bloomed into a conductor of stature. Like all homosexual conductors of the period (except Mitropoulos), he married. His wife, heiress Elaine Phipps, provided the good life, and he worked hard. Tommy and I remained always wary of each other, even caustic; in an interview he once called me backward-looking, though he never, except for Menotti and Barber, conducted "forward-looking" pieces. His wife died of stomach cancer in Cincinnati where Tommy had been named head of the orchestra. His position in America, where only Europeans are permanent conductors of major orchestras, was singular, though his repertory stayed safe. I was thus astounded when in

1973 he commissioned me to write a large work for his symphony. The result was *Air Music,* a thirty-five-minute suite in ten movements, which won the Pulitzer Prize for 1976. A year later Schippers died, of cancer like his wife. Shortly after, the orchestra asked me to compose a double concerto, for cello and piano, in his memory. Named *Remembering Tommy,* the eighth of its ten movements, a nostalgic blues, is titled "One Minute in the Montana Bar."

On the afternoon of the Fourth of July Nell Tangeman sang the world premiere of *Six Irish Poems* in a live broadcast with the Orchès-tre de la Radiodiffusion Française conducted by Tony Aubin. This was the first of my symphonic music to be heard in France. Nell had never sounded more right. Each note, each series of notes, each molding of each series, and each contrasting movement containing the moldings, had been conceived for Nell's huskily silken and sensible mezzo-soprano, and she brought it off in a style which to French ears, geared to timbres at once tighter and more "Roman Catholic," showed a new dimension of Anglo-Saxon melancholy. That evening Marie-Laure threw a party, ostensibly in my honor, though most of the guests hadn't bothered to listen to the broadcast except the valiant Valentine Hugo who extraordinarily whistled much of the score to me, after one hearing.

The party finished badly. In street clothes and tieless, I was the only informal guest among the Tout Paris, and felt smug in my talent, my youth, and my champagne. Toward midnight, for no fathomable reason except exhibitionism and the knowledge that Cocteau had done the same seventeen years before, I slapped my hostess violently across the face and she fell to the floor. Picture the aghast faces of the servants who restrained me, and the abstracted smile of Marie-Laure as she was helped into a chair! This sort of misbehavior, I calculated, was what she adored. Guy and Nell rapidly escorted me back to Saint-Germain; but once we'd deposited Nell, I refused to go home, staying up all night at the Pergola, to the consternation of Guy who had never seen me thus.

The day before this demonstration Koussevitzky died, a fact which went unnoticed in the Parisian press but which would be reflected, in the ultimate ebb and flow of contemporary American music, as a kind of weaning from precocious adolescence into uncertain maturity. That same day, 3 July, Marie-Laure introduced me to Picasso, during a preview of Buñuel's *Los Olvidados.* Shortly thereafter she tried to introduce me again, this time at a vernissage of Masson, but I demurred.

"He won't remember," I mewled, scared stiff.

"Of course he'll remember, how could he not, *lui,* Picasso? He never forgets, you or anyone. With those photographic eyes—those black bullets—you're burned forever into his cerebellum."

Was it for this I hit her next day? To show that I too was someone, had black eyes, made my own rules?

The morning of 7 July, Marie-Laure and I motored to Hyères where I would remain until August.

Can the galloping horse cast a mere side glance as he speeds through the next twenty days? Come to think of it, the horse image is an obsession since childhood, the horse being the one creature to which I'm violently allergic. Because of an affection for this winged piano-shaped beast, and a proscription of contact, I depicted in *The Paris Diary* a boy—myself—who destroys a horse by piercing it with wooden spears. (I was bemused to learn that an English dramatist later wrote a play around the same obsession.)

Between 7 July and 1 August, 1951, Marie-Laure and I thought up a ballet scenario structured line for line on the three stanzas of Robert Browning's "Love in a Life." All that remains of this project is a vocal setting of the troubling poem wherein the poet, whenever he enters a room—"Room after room,/I hunt the house through/We inhabit together"—finds that "you" have just left. . . .

I composed, too, a suite of seven connected unaccompanied choruses, *From an Unknown Past,* so-called because the authors of the profane texts are mostly anonymous. The cycle, lasting less than ten minutes, I have never done better than.

And I finished the orchestration of the piano concerto, scribbling avidly like Penelope weaving her shroud, making the instrumentation maybe more ornate than required, since Marie-Laure in the evening stalked me from behind, moving ever closer, talking, talking, in her dark blue dressing-gown, yet not wanting to touch me for fear of smearing the ink. I dreaded our regular good-night kiss, wondering if my tact was dishonest, fearing her tongue, feeling I was using her while giving nothing in return.

Guests included Paul Eluard on whose long poem, *Figure humaine,* about the Résistance, Poulenc had composed his choral masterpiece. Nothing in Eluard's Grecian physiognomy hinted that he would be dead within a year, at fifty-seven. His tan skin, snowy hair, black turtle-neck sweater, cherry-colored mouth, deep kind eyes, and love of the fray indicated corporal immortality. Eluard and his third wife, a strong-limbed nurse named Dominique (his first wife, Nusch, had died; his second wife, Gala, had married Dali), were summering in Vallauris where the poet, with Picasso, was collaborating on artifacts. Eluard would improvise a poem by inscribing it literally upon or among the lines already limned by the painter, or Picasso would improvise a drawing by curlicuing charcoal lines among the already written words of the poet. (Even so would Frank O'Hara and Larry Rivers join talents in the next decade.) I noted at the time that Eluard quoted Picasso's famous remark: "Every artist is half man and half woman, and the woman is insufferable." The poet continued:

"Actually all creators are women in men's bodies [what, then, of female creators?—didn't the surrealists admit them?] and I myself have mainly feminine instincts. I feel like a penetrated woman. Normally an artist seeks to sleep with men, or with the various substitutes of men found in real women. Artists like me and Picasso who prefer women are abnormal: we're really just a pair of old dykes." And he downed his brandy. "It's better to be drunk than sober."

A firmly convinced Communist, emotionally and rationally, Eluard made me feel vaguely . . . well, American. Still, for him artists were the exception to any rule. This mishmash of surrealism, politics, and high art, plus the conflict and allure of different nationalities and generalities, repelled me, yet drew me to Eluard who always treated me gently, though he was clearly bored with Marie-Laure chanting my praises.

Claus von Bülow (without the "von" in those days) showed up, un-Eluardian, dapper, from London where he was learning law and speaking English almost perfectly for one born to Danish, excepting those little giveaways like "there" for "here," or "zed" for "zee." Georges Hugnet came by too, and the Markevitches with whom we drove to Aix to hear Nell sing her compramario roles. Schoenberg died on 16 May. David Herbert materialized with an entourage, during which, in another room, I phoned Philadelphia (the connection required thirty minutes) and spoke to Mother and Father for the first time in twenty-six months.

Scene:

Marie-Laure and Oscar and me, just the three of us, having lunch at Saint-Bernard. The sliding doors are wide open, aviary and sheep bells chirping and tinkling as background to a cordon-bleu meal and to a conversation of high culture between me and the hostess. Oscar at his worst, pie-eyed, not eating. He begins:

"Marie-Laure, you make awful noises when you eat. Get your jaws rewired. You won't sound so pretentious when you talk. I hate the sound of eating. I hate to fuck you with your fat twat and loud moaning. I want a young girl. Or boy. You disgust me."

"Oh, Poochie," says Marie-Laure. She can't bear others shushing Oscar. I am used to his ranting, so keep mum.

"Don't Poochie me, you capitalist bitch."

Finally, I pitch in: "Shut up, Oscar."

"As for you, you little fairy . . ."

Because he is attacking me and not her, I get up and, Quaker that I am, taking the water pitcher from the side table, empty it, cubes and all, over Oscar's head, then sit down and calmly resume eating. At which point Henri, the maître d'hôtel, enters, observes the mess, says nothing, and serves us dessert.

"You did right," says Marie-Laure to me. Oscar, nonplussed:

"Since everyone hates me in this house, I'm leaving." Off he goes to pack his bags. Henri later informs us that Bacchat has driven Monsieur Dominguez to the Toulon station, from whence he doubtless took a train to see Picasso. Perhaps I "did right," as Marie-Laure said, but she can't truly believe this. Any action taken by any person that might cause Oscar to disappear is a faulty action.

Marie-Laure often drank with him, just to goad him on. Sometimes this odd couple could look as touching as two adolescents on their first date. In Paris, Oscar generally spent the night, leaving at dawn before the concierge came on duty, for the rich are slaves to their servants. What the Vicomte felt privately about his wife's liaison is anyone's guess; no doubt he was relieved that Marie-Laure was occupied with something regular. Marie-Laure kept them apart, of course, though the few times they met Oscar said "vous" to Charles and never acted up. Marie-Laure, in turn, befriended Oscar's former wife, Maud, and his former mistress, Nadine Effront, a svelte Belgian sculptor; the three would meet regularly and shake their heads over their problem child.

But Oscar's behavior did not improve. Nor did Marie-Laure's tolerance waver. Indeed, Oscar grew ever more intractable, more convinced of the futility of persevering in a world where only Picasso could reign supreme. In 1959 he propped a canvas upon the easel of his studio, slit the veins of both wrists and ankles, and with the blood began a painting. But he expired before it was finished.

Marie-Laure never recovered, for this was the insulting close to an affair in which she had invested everything, patience and affection, the conviction that she was truly needed, and the hope that, with all its drawbacks, love will redeem us. (Auden: "Every farthing of the cost,/All the dreaded cards foretell, Shall by paid. . . .")

Marie-Laure survived Oscar by eleven years, but never drank another drop, and encouraged all others to abstain.

On 1 August, Bacchat drove me to Marseilles. There I visited for an hour with Yvonne de Casa Fuerte who had a little house in Mitre. We sat on her terrace and watched the pewter sky turn sick in the ceaseless mistral, talking of her daughter Flavy, whom she loved, and whom Virgil had musically portrayed in his *Tango Lullaby*. Then Yvonne drove me to the Marignane airport where I boarded the plane for Morocco.

During the next twenty-six days in Marrakech—my third African August—I wrote two songs, "The Nightingale" and "A Christmas Carol," both to anonymous texts, and, on record if not in spirit, duplicated previous visits, wincing from the heat, taking excursions, swimming some, and reading constantly (Giraudoux, Gide, Sartre's *Le mur,* and Peyrfitte).

Returned to Hyères at the end of the month. Whereupon Marie-Laure and I, with Christian Mégret, set out for Italy. Since Charles de Noailles never appeared with his wife in public, much less at social bagatelles, I would escort Marie-Laure to the Ball of the Century given by Mexican trillionaire Charles Bestigui in his Palazzo Labia with its Tiepolo ceilings. Coincidental with this international *mondanité* was the world premiere of the Stravinsky-Auden *Rake's Progress,* the cast of which contained three close friends, Cuénod and Tourel and Tangeman. These three scarcely paralleled in seriousness the guests of the ball, and the site itself was disconcerting, seeming everywhere to resound with the deaths of Wagner, of Diaghilev, of Aschenbach, or simply to echo with the sounds of quarreling. As a narcissist I felt somewhat de trop in this first trip to Venice, a city which perpetually reflects upon itself and has no eye for visitors. I romped at the core of a dying splendor. At the time, Bestigui's fête seemed like a moral indecency. With the fading of time, Stravinsky's opera seems even more grossly pretentious. I drank a lot; brought strangers back to the Danieli, where I shared a room with Marie-Laure, when I knew she was at the hairdresser; went to the film festival with Elliott Stein (we were quite taken with Vivien Leigh's *Streetcar*); went to museums with Arthur Weinstein, who told me in livid detail about a new Robbins ballet, *The Cage;* and generally behaved like the belle of the ball, while both Marie-Laure and Christian wept. Christian, using my names as anagram, penned this alexandrine: *Qu'il erre ou qu'il dorme, il orne le monde.*

After eleven days, Hyères again. Thence, since my Fulbright stipulated a course at the Ecole Normale with Honegger, to Paris. Of this voyage I have not forgotten the three-hour delay at the airport, during which Oscar primed himself at the bar. Once aloft, Oscar roamed the aisle like Frankenstein, bellowing: "We're going to crash. We're all going to die in profile!"—his surrealist contribution to the Liberty, Equality, and Fraternity of our terrified midair fellow travelers. Tom Keogh met us at Orly around midnight and we all repaired to Lipps for sauerkraut and ale. Tom had made a reservation for me at the Bisson, a delightful small hotel at 37 quai des Grands-Augustins overlooking the Seine. At 4 a.m., when I went to check in, as I stood on the pavement waiting for the night clerk to open the door, a Senegalese stranger approached me from behind, beat me to the ground, made off with my passport and all my money and cards.

Juliette Gréco too lived at the Bisson. We never spoke, but because I was in love with her, I enjoyed her presence like a fashionable ghost in the halls.

Jerry Robbins I had met twice in the States, but he only vaguely remembered. Here he was now on 2 October at the Boeuf on rue du Colisée, and we hit it off. I had seen two of his ballets. The carefree *Fancy Free* in 1944 had skyrocketed both him and Lenny Bernstein to fame. (One wonders at the fate of the world if Paul Bowles, the original choice, had composed the score and not Lenny.) The neurotic *Facsimile* in 1946, again with music by Bernstein, cemented the fame. Jerry danced in both of these madly American works, electrically sensuous with his swarthy complexion and thinning hair. The crescendoing score of *Facsimile* crackled like a hostile generator when, in a violent *pas de trois,* Robbins and another male dancer tossed the odd-looking Nora Kaye back and forth between them, until she screamed "Stop! Stop!" And they stopped. The three of them. The music too. And there was silence in the house.

Now Jerry talking, affable like the city, was informally stimulating. What was he doing in Paris, without a dance company, adrift but social? Was he biding his time before flying back home to face the McCarthy hearings, perhaps to name names, perhaps to be blackballed from gainful employment? The anti-Communist turmoil in America was not a fact of life to expatriates, at least not to me, and Jerry never rubbed this in, thinking me ingenuous on many a topic, especially painting and politics.

During this brief autumn, Jerry exhaled humor and innocence; it was a constant pleasure to behold the world through his choreographer's eyes, eyes as receptive as the enthralled eyes of those children in the Tuileries which Jerry found more engrossing than the Guignol that so bewitched them. Every situation which confronted him, Jerry saw as a prospective dance. For example, he was highly amused at the relation between Guy de Lesseps and Nora Auric, the handsome oaf and the domineering female.

"I must make a ballet," he announced, "called *Madame Auric's Lover.* Beautiful lady in leather, whip in hand, emerges onto long, slanted platform and summons her fool. . . ."

"What music might you use?"

(Pause) "A Liszt concerto."

Another time, at the Cirque d'Hiver, we witnessed an American trapeze artist, the black-eyed Rose Gould, whose silent style between demonstrations was as riveting as the leaps themselves. Motionless, she posed for a minute—two minutes, five minutes—on the fragile aerie in the highest curve of the tent, left hand gripping the trapeze bar, right arm stylishly behind her neck holding up the raven tresses until they flared, left leg rigid, right leg bent like the Venus di Milo's, waiting, waiting, as we too waited. Without warning she flung herself into space, with a drumroll of *ohs* and *ahs,* and alit somewhere miles off with self-congratulatory aplomb. Now she wriggled and bowed and blew kisses. "She is," said Jerry, "the Norma Desmond of the high wire, and I shall make a ballet on her."

Marie-Laure, who grew fond of Jerry, pronouncing his name "Jeddy," English-style, invited us for a weekend to her husband's estate, the Palais de Pompadour, in Fontainebleau (while the husband was abroad), and brought along Oscar too. Jerry both did and didn't take Marie-Laure seriously. If he was impressed by her luxury, he was appalled by Oscar. We played croquet. Also charades. He liked games, improvisations. Before the evening meal on Sunday Jerry came into my room, which adjoined his own, waving a piece of paper.

"Look what I found in the desk. Stationery marked Hôtel de Pompadour. She's rented a hotel for the weekend!"

I explained that the first definition of *hôtel* was mansion, or private town house. Still, Jerry wanted to play tricks.

"When we go down to the dining room let's say there was a lady moaning up here in the hall, dressed in white."

Later, in the dining room, Jerry said: "There was a lady moaning in the hall."

Marie-Laure, without missing a beat, asked: "Was she dressed in white? That must have been Charles's great aunt. She often shows up on Sundays."

We drove with Marie-Laure and Boris Kochno to Enghein where yet another ballet company spread its wares. Boris to Jerry:
"I'd love to commission a ballet from you, but I don't have any ideas at the moment." Jerry to Boris:
"Well, I've a few of my own."
He explained to me later that Boris dated from that Diaghilevian epoch where scenarios were provided to hirelings, as from the Ester-házys to Haydn.

Unreal yellow misty velvet weather.
We went Chez Geneviève in Montmartre and heard the *patronne* bleat Prévert to an accordion background. We went to Inez Cavan-augh's in the Latin Quarter and lent her money.
We went to visit a married pair called Tyne in the rue du Dragon where the very blond Shelley Winters, with her self-centered ear-splitting ungrammatical assertions, lent new meaning to the noun "vulgarity." Farley Granger, her recent partner in *Behave Yourself,* was there too, slow to react but very much the movie star in looks.
We went to hear Gieseking together.
At the Deux Magots Jerry introduced me to Ellen Adler, Stella's daughter, who had been living for some time with René Leibowitz. Ellen intimidated me, not only for her dizzying black-tiger beauty but because she seemed to know who she was, because she had the assurance of "popular girls," and because she and Jerry seemed to share something—something theatrical and Jewish—that excluded me. (A year later, when I met Stella in New York, I said I'd seen her daughter in Paris. "The beautiful one?" murmured Stella. I wondered if there were another ugly one.)
We conversed at length about collaborating on a ballet, to a point where in the following month I enthusiastically completed the piano score of a multimovement affair temporarily titled *Ballet for Jerry.* (Just as Copland had subtitled *Appalachian Spring,* "Ballet for Mar-tha.") He never used it; instead he took Debussy and made a dance called *Ballade.* I in turn stirred much of it, plus much of *Mélos,* into a third ballet written with Jean Marais early in 1952.

Jerry sadly flew home to face the music on the day of Saint Hilarion, 23 October, my twenty-eighth birthday.
"La vie est grave, l'art est gai," said Marie-Laure, quoting Schiller.

. . .

Our *entente* was *cordiale* during meetings thereafter, but never with the same ingenuous blush. When I lived again in New York we saw each other maybe once a year until 1965 when *The Paris Diary* came out. Since then, when we're in the same room together every five years or so, Jerry doesn't recognize me.

During this October, besides the *Ballet,* I composed a durable work called *Cycle of Holy Songs.* Where did I find the time?

Composers compose, twenty-four hours a day; that is their calling. Sonorous spores forever whirl in their semiconscious searching for a stable idea, a form, on which to regroup themselves and start to grow. For a composer of vocal music, the stable idea is a text that asks to be sung, and the spores are swatches of prose or poetry that can be glued together into an inevitable-sounding cycle.

If today, some hundreds of texts later, I have mixed feelings not just about the kinds of words that "ask to be sung" but about the very legitimacy of setting words at all, back then I felt that you can't go wrong with the Psalms of David; they were conceived for song and no other outlet will do. I selected four, bound the diverse tempos together with a recurring thematic chord, musicalized the effusions according to the one voice I knew best, Nell Tangeman's, and finished the ten-minute group in three weeks. Hugues Cuénod read them through for me one evening at the Gouin's, after which I sent them to Nell who gave the first public performance the following February, with Janet Fairbank's erstwhile accompanist, Henry Jackson, at the piano, in Washington's National Gallery.

Displaying these efforts at Honegger's class I felt both thrilled and gypped when he declared: "I've nothing to say. These songs are perfect." Wouldn't the other students resent me?

And Arthur Honegger himself?

He had the kindest face I've ever known, and an unaffected intelligence which served as both balm and kindling to his dozen pupils during his final years. Those years were nevertheless charged with both physical and moral torment which he dissimulated (at least with us) except for an occasional clenched fist or tired sigh. The quality of lucid restraint glimmered also through the surface fury of his art, and made him (thanks also to the somewhat sentimental and "visual" texts he often chose) the most accessible of so-called *modern* musicians for the general public.

In 1951 the French crowned Arthur Honegger (although he was

Swiss) their National Composer, voting his music as that most likely to survive the millennium. But a decade after his death in 1955, a curtain was pulled, not only on his life but on his work; nobody—not even the average Parisian to whom he was perhaps the one *known* composer—has talked much about him since. Those mid-fifties were already dominated by the traditional revolutions of the young even as Honegger and his friends had dictated the mid-twenties' tone, not so much in denigrating as in ignoring their elders. Nowadays the life span of new generations has shrunk to about five years, and musicians grow ever more quickly in and out of vogue. Unlike painters, death does not increase their market value. Except for Bartók (who was hardly cool in a debtor's grave before he was taken up internationally), no composer since the war has died with impunity—meaning with glory. Some, of course, like Griffes or Satie, are "discovered" by the intelligentsia a few decades late; others, like Ives or (to an extent) Poulenc, come in for revivals by the amateur. Neither category of listener seems yet inclined to disinter Honegger, although it had been his life's desire—and here maybe was his tragic flaw—to attract both the great mass and the elite through the same pieces.

Of those pieces, the one which most realized his desire, *Joan of Arc at the Stake,* seems now as frozen as a Griffith spectacular, featuring what Virgil once called "that least musical of instruments, the spoken voice." Yet Virgil cited *Pacific 231* as among the five most significant works of our first half century. That piece has not, however, remained noticeably in the concert repertory, while performances of a gem like *Pastorale d' été* are rare as hens' teeth. Certainly Honegger's String Symphony does not go unheard, and his oratorio, *King David,* is practically a staple in our more elegant Episcopal churches. Though all in all his music no longer fills a need for most audiences, particularly the young, and the young constitute the one public a maître most longs for.

This ostracism personally touched the gentle musician during his last years when (despite being such a vastly "appreciated" creator) he decided to publish some rather melancholy verbal reactions. These he modeled on Gide's *Corydon,* using as his duologistic foil Monsieur Bernard Gavoty who, under the pseudonym of Clarendon, was France's most redoubtable old-guard defender. Their conversations were published in 1967 with a resonance not unlike the music's: personal and poignant, bold and witty, a trifle old-fashioned.

The personal poignance lies in the composer's pessimism. "A few years hence the musical art as we conceive it will no longer exist," states Honegger, who goes on to deplore the performer's precedence over the composer: music now "comes nearer the domain of sport than of art." Not twice but twenty times he reiterates "that we are living in the last stages of our civilization; inevitably, these last moments are painful. They will be more and more so." He would advise young hopefuls against the profession of composer: "It is a mania—a harmless madness," a lifetime of dedication which will reap scant glory and even less money. The talks read like the laments of an unknown failure; indeed, the first five chapters are variations on the title *Complaints*. Not until the book's halfway point does a certain humor appear, albeit ironic.

His bold wit stems from this irony. Arthur Honegger was the most withdrawn—the least *mondain*—of Les Six who were promoted in the twenties as enfants terribles of a compound mentality, but who in reality soon went their six separate serious ways. Honegger's way was not like Poulenc's toward the salon and Roman ritual via Diaghilev and Latin liturgy, but toward mass culture and the Protestant ritual via professional pedagogy and vernacular Old Testament sagas. He did once collaborate, and gorgeously, with the stylish Cocteau, though his constant unqualified admiration was for the prose verse of the stuffier Claudel.

If his recollections seem a touch old-fashioned it is not so much in his wise bromides about matters professional; composers when they're not composing have always voiced pretty much the same complaints in different words. Rather it is in his assessment of the future, i.e., our present. Forty years ago he declared: "I strongly fear that the twelve-tone fad—we already see its decline—may initiate a reaction towards a too simplistic, too rudimentary music. The cure for having swallowed sulfuric acid will be to drink syrup." Certainly he had a blind spot—or was it a pang of jealousy?—about the newest Terrible Children. Still, greater than he have uttered worse, and anything, even a shopping list, is important if scribbled by a genius. Whether Honegger was or not remains to be seen.

Late in November I flew to Copenhagen for a weekend with Rosemary and her husband, John Marshall, who, as a biochemistical whiz, enjoyed a two-year fellowship for research paid for by Carlsburg beer. They had three children now, Christopher aged four, Mary, three, and the just-born Rachel. They called me Uncle Ned, gazing solemnly into my features through their glasses, eerie replicas of their grandparents. We went to Elsinore. How cold, how spartan, this Danish landscape after the giddy Catholic suavity of France! And handsome John, how boyish and paternal, sensible and stable!

Rosemary and I, these past years since our parents died, have grown nearer. As each other's closest kin, on the face of it we have little in common (she enjoys group work, and populist self-expression; I'm a hermetic snob), but beneath the surface we are seldom at a loss for conversation, enjoy each other's company, and are deferential to the individual paths.

Returning to the Hôtel Bisson from Denmark I went on another four-day binge of unprecedented darkness, during which I was robbed, and sent a suicide note to Jerry ("When you read this letter…"). Marie-Laure, shocked, urged me, when I reemerged into light, to forward a reassuring cable.

A few weeks later, same thing. On 19 December I smashed my forehead against the plumbing of the Pergola's john. Next evening I was to accompany Marie-Laure to the unveiling of Cocteau's *Bacchus*. She was dismayed, taped a bandage over the bulging sore which would not stay stanched. Thus garnished, in a black velvet suit, Marie-Laure in her bright blue gown, we arrived at the theater. During the second act, François Mauriac ostentatiously rose and fled the premises in a blaze of flashbulbs. Next day on the front page of *Le Figaro* he published a somewhat hypocritical diatribe against Cocteau's anticlerical pretensions, signed "Ton ennemi qui t'aime." (He too had tampered with the forbidden fruit.) A few days later Cocteau's rebuttal, a sort of "J'accuse" appeared on the front page of *Le Combat*. Despite the vitriol between old acquaintances, their public feud was still literary and coherently argued. Could one conceive of such behavior on the front page of American papers? It seemed reassuring to be living in France. I still retain the scar on my forehead. It's called "The Bacchus Mark" because, like the wound in the hand of *Blood of a Poet,* it cannot be rubbed out, and denotes my abiding faith in JC—that is, Jesus Christ and Joan Crawford.

Yet I felt myself sinking. Paris was too clever, too rich, too dangerous. I told this to Honegger, told him I craved the quiet of Morocco where settled work and love awaited. He had nothing more to give me really, and agreed that I should go away. He would sign my monthly Fulbright vouchers or whatever they were, would "cover" for me, would forward checks, and wished me a hopeful future.

We never saw each other again.

At the start of the new year I returned to Marrakech.

The racing horse slows to a trot as I gradually withdraw, sticking to the decision to cut this short on 31 December, a day celebrated calmly with Darius and Madeleine Milhaud, later frantically with Claus Bülow and Marie-Laure. Dare I dip a toe into 1952?

I would like to have talked about the ballet *Dorian Gray,* composed with Jean Marais on his houseboat in the Seine, and mounted in May in Barcelona where I spent an evening with Mompou, and learned to loathe Gaudi. (Every great art work is in some way a glorious mess. Gaudi is an inglorious mess—a mess of cowpads.)

I'd have liked to describe the breathless young woman, in navy-blue taffeta with ermine trim, whom Julius brought to Bousquet's salon one Thursday, and who became a determined chum for years. This was Jean Stein, and her immediate claim to fame lay in interviewing Faulkner for *The Paris Review.* (Am I alone in finding Faulkner stultifying? Every twelve years I try anew, and try anew in vain. He's the Bruckner of books. Their plodding matter! What they *do* with it!)

I'd have liked to enumerate the turmoil of lunches with Cocteau, where he arrived in black and yellow drag, to celebrate Poulenc's new *Stabat Mater.* Or where he claimed that "Only a fool believes that two plus two make four. For the banker two plus two make twenty-two, and for a poet, two plus two make five." Or his description of the leather-clad motorcyclists in *Orphée* as emissaries of Death whom they flank on either side: "O sacred cyclist, with your heart 'twixt your legs." (Auden: "I've often thought that I would like/To be the saddle of a bike.") Or his description of Marais: "Just as a camel will come to resemble a cloud, so Jean Marais now resembles a Cocteau drawing."

I'd have liked to commemorate Henri Fourtine more than in one little entry. We met in the shadows of the Observatoire, off the Boul Mich, on 22 April, fourteen years to the night after I lost my "virginity" with Perry O'Neil. He was among the eleven Great Loves. In early May I took the room next to his, 75 rue de Vaugirard, and we remained lovers for about eighteen months—he was my *beau idéal*—and friends thereafter.

I'd have liked to relate the sensation of revisiting New York in the autumn after twenty-eight months. Of, for instance, Jane Bowles's Halloween party, to which she asked anyone who hadn't been asked elsewhere, and where John Myers, after presenting Jane's puppet play, *A Quarreling Pair,* flung me into the arms of Tennessee Williams, which led, during the following years, to composing music for two of his plays—plays less fine than the finest of his stories. . . . Or of John Latouche's Christmas party where Frank O'Hara edged toward me on the floor and announced: "They say you're from Paris, don't you think

Boulez is divine?" which led, during the following years, to unique collaborations.... Or of the voice of Lenny, in the studio of his new apartment at the Osborne, intoning *Trouble in Tahiti* (premiered at Brandeis by Nell Tangeman earlier that summer) about an ill-fated marriage, composed on his recent honeymoon, and then Felicia entering the room to find us.... Other voices, other rooms.

Such occurrences are receding now, not looming. Many many many other crucial characters want to climb aboard, though I've grabbed a hatchet and begun to chop off their hands.

O, but what about that man who....

CHOP!

To stop a memoir midway is to sever a body with a buzz saw. Veins, arteries, intestines, threads of life hang limp, unattached, unresolved, plotless!

Yet where is midway? And are not all lives plotless, leading nowhere except to the unvarying inevitable? They may have themes—art, ambition, love, politics—but no satisfactory expositions, and never a recapitulation or a coda that make sense, least of all to the livers of the lives.

Epilogue

Encore un moment, Monsieur le bourreau . . .
—Madame DuBarry, on the scaffold

Encore un moment. J'étais au point de tout comprendre.
—Paul Valéry, when asked what his dying words
might be

"Can the jar be lovelier than the water?" asks Eluard. Can style survive content? Any self-portrait of the artist as a young person necessarily skirts the essential—the justification for the word "artist."

This book pathetically tries to revive a brash sad boy who is dead, to describe music which can only describe itself, to invoke the gods of craft through redundant incantation. Begun as an autobiography that would end as it starts, at my parents' deathbed, it became, when I realized how high it was growing, a mere memoir of my first twenty-seven years.

This book is all Content without Style, and Content is German while Style is French. Because autobiography is German while memoir is French, it poses as memoir while in fact it's autobiography. Speculation is fun, but tone of voice is a fingerprint. We don't change as we advance, we become more of what we always were. The Catholic priest is right: we're all pretty much "made" by age seven. So again the book reflects cantankerousness of age trying for spontaneity of youth.

Will it make people cry? Since I'm unable to write about what I think of others, only about what others think of me, it will not make people cry—people don't cry for Narcissus. Is Ned even what we call "a nice person"? Did he ever grow out of his didactic vanity, while becoming more of what he always was?

To write about your life while that life is still being lived, as in a diary, is to stand still on a merry-go-round. Viewpoint shifts hourly; past expands like a peacock's tail, while future shrinks like a decapitated head (or is it the reverse?). To write about your life in retrospect, as in a memoir, is to show how one thing leads to another (if you allow it to), and how finally, in medias res, you must call a halt. I could never today fall in love and move to Timbuktu, or arrange to be at the right place at the right time to meet someone who might be important to my career if I'm nervy enough to play the right cards.

None of it's true, or even fact. Dates may jibe with those on a parking ticket or concert program, but the sounds of a clock ticking between 4:55 and 5:00 on that warm special Friday are unrecapturable because they—solidly—never were. None of anything's true, there are no facts. Biography represents just one of seventeen simultaneous fugitive visions.

Truth or no truth, a whiff of melancholy does quicken the atmosphere as I recork the bottle after letting out so much air of an era gone, albeit plodding along chronologically, unironically. Whatever our bent, wherever the heart, we are all by definition spawned by our time. Poulenc's songs are more conservative than Mussorgsky's yet it is impossible to hear them as nineteenth century. Music does not *progress* in the sense of improving; it careens twixt harmonic and contrapuntal eras, back and forth, forever, never learning, but sometimes elating us poor listeners.

All is mudpies. World unrest now leaves me indifferent. It is hard to dote on the earth of today, the young with their loud blank stares, the old with their tireless warmongering. Or to believe even in song, my own or anyone's, or in the power of literature, or in man's goodness, or to behold other than unabatable enmity. Ninety percent of my hours are spent alone, not with the famous people used to flesh-out recollections. From such a vantage, how could I hope to snare a vanished perception? Gulps of experience, sweet and sour since 1951 (body collapsing, hair grizzling), with my music growing in and out of fashion, have inured me to trends of romance and sorrow. Or is this not true either?

Still, this book has been a friendly solace. It too, after its fifteen minutes in a pale sun, will sicken and turn to dust in a country library. But as I type these last few words, I feel unhappy at relinquishing it.

Unhappiness is not becoming after forty. Unhappiness is for the young. I'm seventy. Childhood ended forty-two years ago with the close of this book. Since 1970 I have had no alcohol, no tobacco. Nor have I ever suffered a venereal disease (except crabs, scabies, herpes simplex, and an oft-broken heart), and feel less "impelled" when I write music. I do ponder the paradox of the AIDS virus which has claimed so many friends, for it too wants to proliferate, but, being a parasite, must kill its host, and so itself die; and the paradox of inspiration without which one is free to write better music. Inspiration is a trammel, a smoke screen for amateurs. I feel ready to compose a perfect piece.

When he was eighty, Father declared, as man to man: "I never make love to your mother without her reaching a climax too." These words seemed uttered without boast, without pretense, but with a poignance (Mother already was growing vague), a generosity, even—dare I say it?—a puritanism that, though not eschewing nudity and lust, aspired to responsible fidelity, which scarcely jelled with my willy-nilly *mil e tre* mentality. I was deeply impressed that Father still proudly made love with Mother, the only creature, except for the distant Miss Ring, he had ever slept with, and that Rosemary and myself had once emerged from the vapors of those "climaxes."

More than sex or love, appreciation is what humans crave and seldom get. So I am lucky in having always known what I wanted to be, in being able to be it, and in being acknowledged for being it. If jealousy goes hand in hand with success, then no, that faraway Ned is not "a nice person."

It's not easy, in life as in art, to practice that most urgent virtue of knowing how to stop. But the Ned who was speaking has gone. The setting's the same, but new actors crowd the stage.

And that galloping horse? That literary conceit for my alter ego? He doesn't seem to be here in this stable where I'm about to cease writing. Indeed, some hours ago he veered off toward the horizon.

I've quite lost sight of him.

PICTURE CREDITS

Unless otherwise credited, all pictures are from the author's collection.

Pp. 4, 13:   Drawings by Jean Cocteau/collection of the author
P. 270:   Paul Parker Studio
P. 279:   © Herbert Kubly
P. 324:   © Hella Hammid
P. 357:   Victor Kraft
P. 381:   Fred Plaut
P. 441:   © Harold Halma
P. 508:   *Paris-Match*/d.r.
P. 516:   © Henri Cartier-Bresson/MAGNUM
P. 563:   Claude R. Michaelides

PHOTO SECTION:
1. Drawing by John Heliker
5. Courtesy of *Downbeat* magazine
6. Estate of Carl van Vechten, Joseph Solomon, executor
7. Naomi Siegler
13. © 1982 by Boosey & Hawkes, Inc. Reprinted by permission. "The Youth with the Red-Gold Hair" by Edith Sitwell from *The Collected Poems of Edith Sitwell,* © 1949. Copyright renewed; used by permission.
16. Patrick O'Higgens
19. Gianni Bates
22. Photo by Heka
23. © Harry Benson
25. © Andrew French

INDEX

(Page numbers in *italic* refer to illustrations.)